IFIP Advances in Information and Communication Technology 759

IFIP Advances in Information and Communication Technology

The IFIP AICT series publishes state-of-the-art results in the sciences and technologies of information and communication. The scope of the series includes: foundations of computer science; software theory and practice; education; computer applications in technology; communication systems; systems modeling and optimization; information systems; ICT and society; computer systems technology; security and protection in information processing systems; artificial intelligence; and human-computer interaction.

Edited volumes and proceedings of refereed international conferences in computer science and interdisciplinary fields are featured. These results often precede journal publication and represent the most current research.

The principal aim of the IFIP AICT series is to encourage education and the dissemination and exchange of information about all aspects of computing.

More information about this series at https://link.springer.com/bookseries/6102

Luis M. Camarinha-Matos · Filipa Ferrada
Editors

Technological Innovation for AI-Powered Cyber-Physical Systems

16th IFIP WG 5.5 / SOCOLNET
Advanced Doctoral Conference on Computing
Electrical and Industrial Systems, DoCEIS 2025
Caparica, Portugal, July 2–4, 2025
Proceedings

Springer

Editors
Luis M. Camarinha-Matos
School of Science and Technology
NOVA University Lisbon
Lisbon, Portugal

Filipa Ferrada
School of Science and Technology
NOVA University Lisbon
Lisbon, Portugal

ISSN 1868-4238 ISSN 1868-422X (electronic)
IFIP Advances in Information and Communication Technology
ISBN 978-3-031-97050-4 ISBN 978-3-031-97051-1 (eBook)
https://doi.org/10.1007/978-3-031-97051-1

This Springer imprint is published by the registered company Springer Nature Switzerland AG
The registered company address is: Gewerbestrasse 11, 6330 Cham, Switzerland

Preface

This proceedings book examines technological innovation in AI-driven cyber-physical systems (CPS), highlighting research conducted within engineering doctoral programs. The rapid evolution of digital technologies ignited the extensive use of complex and interconnected cyber-physical systems, where Artificial Intelligence (AI) has become a key enabler, extracting meaningful insights from CPS data and enhancing the efficiency, functionality, and market appeal of CPS solutions. Consequently, CPS technologies have become increasingly prevalent across diverse sectors such as industry, energy, healthcare, and services, demonstrating significant transformative potential.

This transformation is supported by a broad spectrum of technologies, including the Internet of Things, sensors, and human-machine interaction, together with application areas such as smart health systems, smart energy, smart manufacturing, and collaborative networks. These advancements have in turn accelerated the adoption and integration of machine learning, data analytics, cybersecurity, and computational intelligence. The conference seeks to advance the field of AI-powered CPS by promoting innovative responses to present-day challenges, with the ultimate goal of building a more efficient, sustainable society.

The 16th Advanced Doctoral Conference on Computing, Electrical, and Industrial Systems (DoCEIS 2025) served as a forum for doctoral students to present their ideas, hypotheses, and findings across a range of interconnected engineering disciplines. Its core mission was to foster multidisciplinary dialogue and facilitate collaborative opportunities among early-stage researchers, all within an environment focused on constructive peer engagement. Attendees were encouraged to look beyond their individual research topics and consider how their work aligns with and contributes to the central theme of technological innovation in AI-driven CPS.

Emerging research priorities increasingly emphasize the importance of multidisciplinary and interdisciplinary methodologies as catalysts for innovation. Conferences like DoCEIS, which promotes the participation of early-career researchers, have become especially relevant in light of growing expectations from funding agencies for integrated research strategies. While interdisciplinary collaboration holds immense promises for disruptive breakthroughs, it also presents organizational and conceptual challenges. Against this backdrop, DoCEIS plays a vital role in equipping young researchers with the critical skills and collaborative mindset needed for academic and professional success [1].

DoCEIS 2025, sponsored by SOCOLNET, IFIP, and IEEE IES, attracted 59 paper submissions from PhD students and their supervisors from 14 countries. The review process was double-blind, with submissions receiving an average of three reviews each. This book comprises 29 works selected by the International Program Committee for inclusion in the main program and covers a wide range of application domains. Research results and ongoing work are presented, illustrated, and discussed in areas such as:

- AI in Business Applications
- AI in Industry 4.0
- Smart Systems in Sustainable Development
- AI-Powered Healthcare
- AI in Systems, Decision & Control
- Intelligent Sensing & Transmission Systems
- Smart Power Systems
- Electronic Systems

We envisage that this compilation of papers will offer readers a captivating set of novel concepts and intellectually stimulating challenges crossing multiple disciplines. The diverse nature of the included findings is intended to spark and invigorate further research and development initiatives, encouraging a broader exploration of innovative multidisciplinary pathways.

We would like to express our sincere gratitude to all the authors for their valuable contributions to this publication. We also thank the PhD students involved in the organizing committee who were essential for the success of the conference. Additionally, we would like to extend our deepest appreciation to the dedicated members of the DoCEIS International Program Committee. Their assistance in the article selection process as well as their insightful comments immensely contributed to enhancing the overall quality of the papers.

May 2025

Luis M. Camarinha-Matos
Filipa Ferrada

Reference

1. L. M. Camarinha-Matos, J. Goes, L. Gomes, P. Pereira (2020). Soft and Transferable Skills Acquisition through Organizing a Doctoral Conference. *Education Sciences* 10(9), 235. https://doi.org/10.3390/educsci10090235

Organization

Conference and Program Committee Chair

Luis M. Camarinha-Matos	NOVA University of Lisbon, Portugal

Program Committee Co-chair

Filipa Ferrada	NOVA University of Lisbon, Portugal

Organizing Committee Co-chairs

Pedro Pereira	NOVA University of Lisbon, Portugal
Sanaz Nikghadam Hojjati	NOVA University of Lisbon, Portugal
Rodolfo Oliveira	NOVA University of Lisbon, Portugal
Luis Oliveira	NOVA University of Lisbon, Portugal

International Program Committee

António Abreu	Polytechnic Institute of Lisbon, Portugal
Valentina Emilia Balas	Aurel Vlaicu University of Arad, Romania
Anne-Marie Barthe-Delanoe	Toulouse University, France
Marko Beko	University of Lisbon, Portugal
Bachir Benhala	Sidi Mohamed Ben Abdellah University, Morroco
Luis Bernardo	NOVA University of Lisbon, Portugal
Xavier Boucher	École Nationale Superieure des Mines de Saint Etienne, France
Hadj Bourdoucen	Sultan Qaboos University, Oman
Luis M. Camarinha-Matos	NOVA University of Lisbon, Portugal
Wojciech Cellary	WSB University in Poznań, Poland
Noelia Correia	University of Algarve, Portugal
Filipa Ferrada	NOVA University of Lisbon, Portugal
Pedro Ferreira	Loughborough University, UK
Florin Filip	Romanian Academy of Sciences, Romania
Maria Fino	NOVA University of Lisbon, Portugal
Adrian Florea	'Lucian Blaga' University of Sibiu, Romania

José Fonseca	NOVA University of Lisbon, Portugal
Fabio Fruggiero	University of Basilicata, Italy
Sukhpal Singh Gill	Queen Mary University of London, UK
Luis Gomes	NOVA University of Lisbon, Portugal
Juanqiong Gou	Beijing Jiaotong University, China
Bruno J. N. Guerreiro	NOVA University of Lisbon, Portugal
Tomasz Janowski	UNU Unit on Policy-Driven Electronic Governance, Poland
Sachin Kumar	American University of Armenia, Armenia
Arianit Kurti	Linnaeus University, Sweden
Paulo Leitão	Polytechnic Institute of Bragança, Portugal
Paula Louro	Polytechnic Institute of Lisbon, Portugal
Marin Lujak	University Rey Juan Carlos, Spain
João Martins	NOVA University of Lisbon, Portugal
João Pedro Matos-Carvalho	Universidade Lusófona, Portugal
Paulo Miyagi	University of São Paulo, Brazil
Saraju Mohanty	University of North Texas, USA
Eric Monmasson	CY Cergy Paris Université, France
Filipe Moutinho	NOVA University of Lisbon, Portugal
Vincent Naessens	KU Leuven, Belgium
Phu Nguyen	SINTEF Digital, Norway
Sanaz Nikghadam	NOVA University of Lisbon, Portugal
Nnamdi Nwulu	University of Johannesburg, South Africa
Ana Inês Oliveira	NOVA University of Lisbon, Portugal
Luis Oliveira	NOVA University of Lisbon, Portugal
Rodolfo Oliveira	NOVA University of Lisbon, Portugal
Angel Ortiz	Universitat Politècnica de València, Spain
Reinaldo Palhares	Federal University of Minas Gerais, Brazil
Venkata Reddy Palleti	Indian Institute of Petroleum and Energy, India
Luís Brito Palma	NOVA University of Lisbon, Portugal
Nuno Paulino	NOVA University of Lisbon, Portugal
Pedro Pereira	NOVA University of Lisbon, Portugal
Armando Pires	Polytechnic Institute of Setubal, Portugal
Ricardo J. Rabelo	Federal University of Santa Catarina, Brazil
Luis Paulo Reis	Universidade do Porto, Portugal
Enrique Romero-Cadaval	University of Extremadura, Spain
Carlos Roncero-Clemente	University of Extremadura, Spain
Ioan Stefan Sacala	University POLITEHNICA of Bucharest, Romania
Claudio Sassanelli	Politecnico di Bari, Italy
Thilo Sauter	Danube University Krems, Austria
Thomas Schuster	Pforzheim University, Germany

Catarina Silva	Polytechnic Institute of Leiria, Portugal
Thomas Strasser	Austrian Institute of Technology, Austria
Slavisa Tomic	University of Lisbon, Portugal
Oleksandr Veligorskyi	Chernihiv National University of Technology, Ukraine
Manuela Vieira	Polytechnic Institute of Lisbon, Portugal
Ramon Vilanova	Universitat Autònoma de Barcelona, Spain

Local Organizing Committee (PhD Students)

Ali Sousaraei, Iran
Clarisse Feio, Portugal
Emanuel Mango, Angola
Eurico Clemente, Portugal
Fábio Gregório, Portugal
Francisco Silva, Portugal
Gelson Pembele, Angola
Hugo Matias, Portugal
Hugo Viana, Portugal
João Cabacinho, Portugal
José Calandula, Angola
José Luis, Angola
Rui Guerreiro, Portugal
Sérgio Sousa, Portugal
Tiago Reis, Portugal

Technical Sponsors

Society of Collaborative Networks

IFIP WG 5.5 COVE
Co-Operation infrastructure for Virtual Enterprises and electronic business

Organizational Sponsors

CTS – Center of Technology and Systems

Organized by:

PhD Program in Electrical and Computer Engineering

Contents

Intelligent Sensing and Communication Systems

Smart Power Systems

Electronic Systems

AI in Business Applications

A Collaborative Approach to Last-Mile Logistics

Dionisio Fama Noque(✉), Luis M. Camarinha-Matos, and Ana Inês Oliveira

School of Science and Technology, Uninova-CTS and LASI, NOVA University Lisbon, Campus de Caparica, 2829-516 Caparica, Portugal
dionisiofama@hotmail.com, {cam,aio}@uninova.pt

Abstract. Last-mile logistics faces significant challenges, such as operational inefficiencies, high costs, customer dissatisfaction, and environmental impacts. On the other hand, the rapid growth of e-commerce in recent years and the consequent proliferation of new stakeholders have further intensified these issues. In this context, by promoting resource sharing and operational optimization, collaborative networks appear as a promising solution to enhance the last-mile logistics by integrating ecosystem concepts and exploring emerging technologies. This work proposes the development of a collaborative logistics ecosystem, where various last-mile logistics actors share infrastructure and data to improve delivery efficiency and customer satisfaction, while also contributing to sustainability. The structure of this ecosystem is detailed, including its challenges, expected benefits, and initial implementation ideas. Ongoing research is focused on the development of a simulation model to evaluate different organizational structures and governance models in this sector. This proposal serves as a basis for implementing effective collaborative networks, promoting innovation and sustainability in last-mile logistics.

Keywords: Collaborative Networks · Last-Mile Logistics · Business Ecosystem · Sustainability

1 Introduction

In recent years, last-mile logistics is facing major challenges, driven by the exponential growth of e-commerce and urbanization. These challenges include operational inefficiencies, high costs, urban congestion, coordination failures among the different actors in the logistics chain, customer dissatisfaction and significant environmental impacts [1, 2]. The complexity of this phase is intensified by the fragmentation of deliveries, characterized by small-volume orders distributed across wide geographic areas, which further increases logistics complexity and costs [1, 3] Various estimates suggest that the global e-commerce market will grow at an annual rate of 14% until 2027, driving demand for more agile and sustainable logistics solutions [4]. A study by Juniper Research predicts that global investments in digital commerce will increase by 65% between 2024 and 2029, reaching 34 trillion dollars [5].

Published by Springer Nature Switzerland AG 2025
L. M. Camarinha-Matos and F. Ferrada (Eds.): DoCEIS 2025, IFIP AICT 759, pp. 3–25, 2025.
https://doi.org/10.1007/978-3-031-97051-1_1

Given this scenario, collaborative networks [6, 7] emerge as a promising approach for optimizing last-mile logistics. By enabling the sharing of infrastructure, vehicles and data among different actors – such as carriers, e-commerce platforms, distribution centers, micro-hubs and even consumers – collaboration can reduce costs, improve the use of available resources and enhance sustainability in the logistics operation process. However, although those potential benefits are widely recognized [8], implementing these networks requires new organizational models, efficient governance and advanced technological support, including Artificial Intelligence (AI), Internet of Things (IoT) and Blockchain [9].

Therefore, this work pursues a collaborative model for last-mile logistics, exploring how the integration of different actors in the sector can increase resilience, efficiency and sustainability. Through this framework, we seek to answer the following research question: "To what extent can a collaborative ecosystem improve the efficiency and resilience of last-mile logistics?".

Ongoing research aims to provide guidelines for establishing effective collaborative logistics ecosystems, promoting innovation, industry competitiveness and sustainability. The approach is based on a collaborative organizational model supported by technological enablers, along with a methodology based on Design Science and computational simulation to evaluate the benefits of logistics collaboration.

This paper is structured as follows: Sect. 2 presents a review of the evolution of modern logistics with a focus on the last mile; Sect. 3 describes the functioning of modern logistics systems and the role of collaborative networks in this context; Sect. 4 presents the proposed collaborative model, highlighting three fundamental dimensions: business model, organizational structure and sustainability. Section 5 describes the methodological approach based on Design Science, and future perspectives, while Sect. 6 concludes with contributions and subsequent steps.

2 Modern Logistics as an AI-Powered CPS

Modern logistics represents the evolution of traditional logistics processes, influenced by technological advances, changes in consumer expectations and the complexity of global markets. It integrates advanced technologies such as artificial intelligence (AI), internet of things (IoT), blockchain and automation to optimize and monitor logistics processes in real time. Furthermore, the analysis of large volumes of data enables more accurate predictions and agile decision-making [10, 11]. These innovations promote efficiency, reduce operational costs and improve customer experience, especially in the context of e-commerce, where speed and accuracy of deliveries are critical.

Digitalization and automation have driven the transformation of modern logistics, resulting in logistics systems capable of integrating the physical and digital worlds in an intelligent way. These systems use sensors, communication networks and artificial intelligence to improve the efficiency, resilience and flexibility of logistics operations [12]. Such cyber-physical systems (CPS) are characterized by aiming to improve Connectivity, Autonomy, Security, Resilience, Intelligence and Learning [13, 14].

Artificial Intelligence has played a fundamental role in the evolution of logistics as a CPS, enabling significant advances in several areas, such as: route optimization, demand forecasting, process automation, predictive analysis, inventory management and intelligent maintenance [15–18]. The adoption of AI-based CPS in modern logistics offers significant benefits, on the other hand, it faces major challenges as can be seen in Table 1.

The consolidation of CPS and AI-based logistics is likely to continue with the advancement of technologies such as cloud computing, blockchain, machine learning, drones and autonomous vehicles, and 6G. Complementarily, autonomous and decentralized logistics models are emerging, enabling greater collaboration among supply chain actors and promoting a more efficient and sustainable ecosystem [19].

Table 1. Benefits and challenges of AI-based CPS in logistics.

Benefits
• Reducing operational costs through route optimization and automated processes • Increasing operational efficiency through automation of warehouses and distribution centers • Minimizing waste of resources and reducing carbon emissions • Ability to adapt to unexpected changes, such as fluctuations in demand or disruptive events • Better predictability and reliability in deliveries • Improved customer experience through fast, personalized deliveries
Challenges
• Integration of different platforms and systems • High cost of implementing and maintaining advanced technologies • Significant investments in infrastructure at the time of implementation • Cybernetics vulnerabilities • Uncontrollable external factors and resistance to technology adoption • Need for investment in infrastructure due to the complexity of the logistics operation

3 Trends and Challenges in Modern Logistics

While Sect. 2 presented a historical and conceptual overview of logistics evolution, Sect. 3 aims to describe the current functioning of logistics systems, including their operational, technological and relational components. This distinction allows us to address in more depth the practices and technologies currently used in last-mile logistics.

3.1 Brief Overview and Evolution

Modern logistics faces growing challenges in ensuring fast, efficient, and sustainable deliveries. Figure 1 illustrates a logistics flow, covering both direct logistics (delivery of products to the end consumer) and reverse logistics (return and reuse of goods). This work focuses on last mile logistics, which represents one of the biggest challenges and opportunities for efficiency optimization.

The direct logistics flow begins at the manufacturer and may extend to long-distance transport, delivering products to international or national markets while passing through authorities and importers regulating entry of goods. After customs clearance, medium-distance transport moves the product to warehouses or distribution centers. Finally, they are distributed locally via short-distance transport, reaching retailers, physical stores, or customers directly. At this stage, last-mile logistics plays a crucial role, ensuring that products are delivered efficiently and with minimal environmental impact.

In addition to delivery to the consumer, Fig. 1 also highlights reverse logistics, which ensures proper handling of returned or recyclable products after their end of life. This flow begins with the consumer and moves through collection and reuse centers, where products are assessed to determine whether they are resold, recycled, or disposed of.

Integrating direct and reverse logistics in the last mile is crucial for minimizing costs and maximizing operational efficiency, ensuring a sustainable product circulation system.

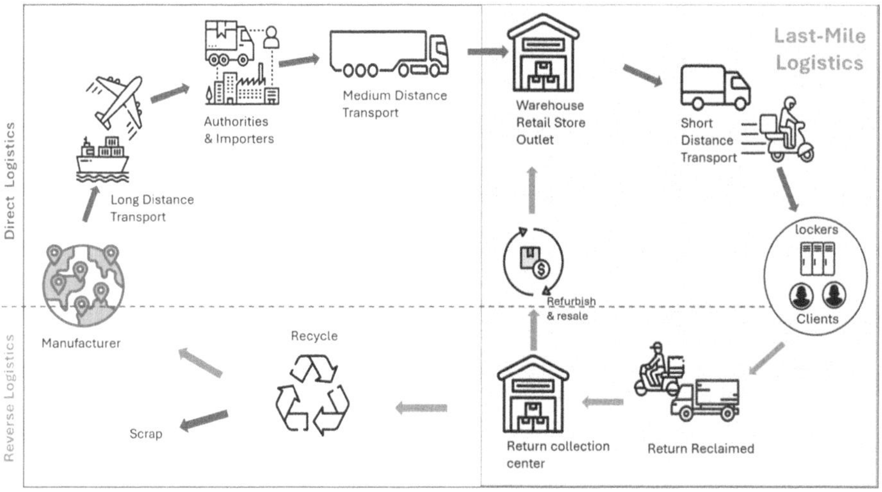

Fig. 1. Overview of the logistics process

Evolution of Last-mile Logistics. Last-mile logistics represents the most challenging stage, responsible for transporting products from distribution centers to the end consumers. The growth of B2C e-commerce and the increasing consumer expectations for fast and traceable deliveries drive the need for innovation in this sector [20].

To meet these demands, recent approaches aim to balance operational efficiency, sustainability, and cost reduction [21]. Table 2 summarizes some of the main advances identified in literature.

3.2 Platform and Technological Enablers

To address last-mile logistics challenges, several platforms and technological facilitators have been used and proposed to enhance efficiency, traceability, and optimization of the logistics operations. Key technologies include Artificial Intelligence, Internet of Things,

Table 2. Relevant topics in last-mile logistics.

Topic	Description	Limitations / Challenges	Ref
Growth of e-commerce and associated logistics challenges	- The growth of e-commerce has revolutionized last-mile logistics, significantly increasing the demand for fast and flexible deliveries. The rise in same-day delivery and expedited deliveries has forced logistic operators to offset their distribution strategies - The digitalization of logistics, including the use of AI, blockchain and IoT, has been essential to meet this growth	- Dependence on robust infrastructure for logistical support - High operational costs - Difficulty in standardizing operations across different platforms and delivery models - Urban congestion, consumer pressure for fast deliveries at low prices, seasonality, and fluctuations in demand are among the main challenges	[22–24]
Green Logistics and Sustainability	- Sustainable logistics seeks to minimize the environmental impact of urban distribution. Strategies such as the use of electric vehicles, cargo bikes and urban micro-hubs have been explored to reduce carbon emissions. Models such as crowd shipping and shared deliveries also emerge as solutions to minimize environmental impact - The Green Logistics concept involves cargo consolidation practices, route optimization and shared deliveries	- The main challenges are the high cost of initial investment in green technologies, companies' resistance to change, and lack of tax incentives and public policies for the adoption of sustainable practices - Difficulty in measuring the real impacts of sustainable practices in logistics - Resistance from companies and consumers to adopt sustainable models when this implies additional costs - Dependence on technological innovations for sustainable solutions to be truly viable and scalable	[20, 21, 25, 26]

(*continued*)

Table 2. (*continued*)

Topic	Description	Limitations / Challenges	Ref
Energy Consumption	- Energy consumption in last-mile logistics is directly related to the use of fossil fuels, route inefficiencies and the excess of vehicles circulating partially empty - Alternatives such as electric vehicle fleets and green hydrogen are seen as viable solutions	- Difficulty in integrating renewable energy sources into existing logistics infrastructure - Insufficient charging points for electric vehicles have delayed the transition process - Reliance on government regulations to promote the adoption of energy efficient practices - Lack of analysis of the impact of energy consumption on long-term logistics costs	[27, 28]
Role of the Consumer	- Consumers directly influence last-mile strategies, demanding transparency, real-time tracking and flexible delivery options. Often, consumers prioritize speed over environmental impact, which makes it difficult to reconcile convenience and sustainability - On-demand delivery models, smart lockers and crowd shipping are being explored as viable alternatives to offer greater convenience	- Difficulty in balancing consumer expectations with sustainable operational practices - Lack of integration between digital platforms and consumers to optimize the delivery process - Consumer resistance to new forms of delivery. The lack of consumer engagement in alternative logistics models, such as lockers and collection points, and the pressure for cheap and fast deliveries have been the main challenges in this topic	[27, 29, 30]

(*continued*)

Table 2. (*continued*)

Topic	Description	Limitations / Challenges	Ref
Limited Vehicle Capacity	- Limited vehicle capacity and transportation of small individual loads, often with low vehicle occupancy rates, results in wasted space and increased logistics costs - Load consolidation and vehicle sharing models have been studied as viable alternatives. Approaches such as Shared Truckload and crowd-shipping have been explored to maximize vehicle occupancy and reduce the number of trips. Technologies such as IoT and AI are also used to improve load planning and efficient use of vehicles	- Lack of integration between carriers and digital platforms to facilitate cargo sharing - Resistance to change by traditional carriers, which operate in isolation - Lack of standardized data on vehicle occupancy, making it difficult to develop efficient predictive and planning models	[29, 31, 32]
Distribution Strategies	- Last-mile distribution strategies have evolved significantly due to the rise of e-commerce and new logistics technologies. Models such as urban micro-hubs, smart lockers, environmental networks, and crowd-shipping have been explored as more efficient alternatives to the traditional home delivery model - Furthermore, strategies such as omnichannel logistics, where retailers integrate different sales and distribution channels, make it possible to reduce delivery times and optimize distribution of goods	- Low consumer adoption of shared collection points, as many still prefer home deliveries - Lack of integration between companies and logistics platforms to optimize collaborative distribution networks	[30, 33–35]

(*continued*)

Table 2. (*continued*)

Topic	Description	Limitations / Challenges	Ref
Optimization and Machine Learning Models	- The application of optimization and machine learning models in last-mile logistics has grown significantly. AI/ML are used to optimize routes, predict demand, reduce operational costs and improve inventory management and delivery efficiency - Techniques such as genetic algorithms, neural networks and deep learning are being tested to solve complex problems such as dynamic routing and predicting consumption patterns. Big data-based optimization allows for real-time adjustments, improving the ability to respond to unforeseen events	- Limited scalability of AI models, as many are developed for specific scenarios and do not work well on a large scale - Lack of transparency in machine learning models, making it difficult to interpret the decisions made by algorithms - Resistance of logistics operators to replace traditional processes by automated solutions - Lack of standardized and quality data, complexity in integrating AI with traditional logistics systems and costs of implementing advanced models	[36–38]

Blockchain, Drones, Autonomous Vehicles, Tracking Technologies and Smart Lockers stand [23, 37–39]. Briefly:

- Artificial Intelligence (AI). Allows transformation of logistics through process automation and predictive analytics. Among its main applications in the last mile, the following are highlighted: Routing Optimization, demand forecasting, and service automation [23, 34–36].
- Internet of Things (IoT). This technology enables monitoring and tracking of goods, ensuring real-time visibility across the supply chain.
- Smart Lockers. Innovative solutions for automatic collection of packages, reducing delivery failures and increasing consumer convenience [34]. They offer advantages such as cost reduction, greater safety, and sustainability (reduction of carbon emissions) [20, 30].
- Blockchain. Blockchain technology ensures transparency, traceability, security, and fraud prevention in last-mile logistics [21, 39, 40], ensuring trust among stakeholders, including suppliers, retailers, and consumers

- Drones and Autonomous Vehicles. The automation of logistics transport has advanced significantly, with drones and autonomous vehicles being tested for last-mile deliveries. These technologies have great potential, as they allow deliveries to remote areas, reduce carbon emissions, and reduce costs [38, 41]. However, challenges such as regulation, safety, and consumer accessibility continue to limit their large-scale implementation [32].
- Tracking technologies. Traceability is essential to increase consumer confidence and improve logistics efficiency. Among the most used solutions, the following stand out: Tracking by IoT and GPS; Geofencing and Smart Notifications, and Logistics Performance Analysis [23, 39].

Digitalization and the adoption of emerging technologies are transforming last-mile logistics, providing more efficiency, sustainability, and better consumer experience. AI, IoT, Blockchain, drones and smart tracking are increasingly integrated into logistics operations, enabling more flexible and resilient systems. The advancement of these technologies, combined with collaborative strategies, is expected to enhance last-mile efficiency and sustainability, reducing both costs and environmental impact.

3.3 Collaborative Networks in Logistics

The emerging notion of collaborative logistics is based on the idea that companies, suppliers, carriers, distributors, and even end consumers can work together to achieve common goals. It arises as a solution to the increasingly complex challenges faced by modern supply chains, promoting integration between different actors in the logistics ecosystem to optimize processes, reduce costs, and increase resilience [42].

Collaboration in logistics can take many forms, such as sharing information, infrastructure, transportation vehicles, and even inventory, creating synergies that benefit all parties involved. However, despite these benefits, collaborative logistics faces several challenges, the main ones being: (i) Identification of Operational, Technological and Environmental Impacts of Collaboration in Last-mile Logistics; (ii) Systems Interoperability; (iii) Dealing with an increasing number of stakeholders (including micro-operators); (iv) Trust among Participants; (v) Regulation and Public Policies; (vi) Inadequate Infrastructure; and (vii) Organizational Culture.

In fact, the need for collaboration in logistics is recognized by most operators, but there is still a lack of appropriate organizational and governance models [8].

4 A Collaborative Ecosystem Approach to Last-Mile Logistics

The growing complexity of last-mile logistics demands new organizational models that enhance operational efficiency, flexibility, and sustainability. Collaborative ecosystems emerge as an innovative solution by promoting interconnectivity and resource sharing among the various actors in the logistics chain [43].

This section proposes a collaborative ecosystem approach for last-mile logistics, describing its rationale, structure, benefits, and key technologies for its implementation. All analyses and proposals were developed with a specific focus on last-mile logistics, based on the operational and urban challenges characteristic of this phase of the logistics chain. The decentralized nature, direct contact with the consumer, and demand variability make the last mile the ideal environment for the application of the proposed collaborative model.

4.1 Justification for Collaboration

The fragmentation of logistics networks and the increasing consumer demand for faster, more sustainable deliveries have made collaboration essential. The main reasons for adopting a collaborative ecosystem approach are summarized in Table 3, which compares the limitations of traditional logistics with the benefits of a collaborative approach. This analysis considers three dimensions: business model, organizational structure, and sustainability.

The choice of the three dimensions is based on the interdependence between the critical elements that support effective collaborative networks. The business model defines the economic and operational incentives that enable collaboration; the organizational structure establishes the governance rules, the role of actors and decision-making mechanisms; and sustainability represents both the ecological viability and the resilience of the network over time. This triple approach allows for a holistic view that is aligned with the organizational design principles of collaborative networks [6].

Table 3. Limitations of Traditional Logistics and Required Collaborative Solutions

Focus	Aspects of traditional approaches	Required collaborative facets
Business Model	High operational costs	Resource sharing
	Underutilized transportation	Sharing of transport capacity between companies
	Fixed distribution model	Use of shared micro-hubs
	Warehouse dependency and capacity	Decentralization with collaborative warehouses on demand
	Low integration between different logistics players	Open platforms for data sharing
	Difficulty in scaling operations	Use of logistics marketplaces
	Fluctuating demand and seasonality	Crowd shipping and decentralized delivery
	High customer expectations for fast deliveries	Shared lockers and collection points
	The growth of e-commerce	Fulfillment model, collaborative tracking
Organizational Structure	Complexity due to multiplicity of small operators	Shared infrastructure
	Lack of urban infrastructure adapted for logistics	Collaborative lockers and collection point systems

(continued)

Table 3. (*continued*)

Focus	Aspects of traditional approaches	Required collaborative facets
	High rate of delivery failures	Strategic alliances between small carriers to gain scale
	Fragmentation in the sector and increase in small operations	Strategic alliances between small operators to gain scale
	Difficulty in accurately forecasting demand	Using big data, IoT and machine learning for collaborative demand forecasting
	Little flexibility in route planning	Dynamic routing based on collaborative transport networks
	Low route efficiency	Use of multiple modes for delivery
	Complexity in densely populated areas	Implementation of shared urban hubs
	Tracking accuracy	Using IoT and blockchain for decentralized tracking
	High environmental impact of transport	Use of electric bicycles, autonomous vehicles and shared drones
Sustainability	Lack of consolidation of deliveries	Grouping orders from multiple companies for consolidated deliveries
	Large generation of waste with disposable packaging	Collaborative programs for reuse and recycling packaging
	Lack of incentive for sustainable modes	Integration with public transport for sustainable deliveries
	Long distances between warehouses and customers	Expansion of shared urban hubs to reduce travel
	Low adoption of carbon offset policies	Joint emissions neutralization programs between companies in the sector
	Lack of regulations to encourage sustainable practices	Creation of public-private partnerships to drive green logistics policies
	Carbon emissions in high population density areas	Collaborative routing, integration of logistics with public transport
	Adaptation to climate change	Shared Infrastructure, Adaptive Transportation Solutions
	Lack of green infrastructure	Use of underutilized urban spaces

4.2 Early Examples

Various initiatives worldwide highlight the potential of collaborative ecosystems in logistics. Table 4 presents three examples of collaborative logistics solutions, emphasizing their strengths and limitations. These cases demonstrate how collaboration between companies, the adoption of emerging technologies, and shared infrastructure can drive innovation in logistics.

Table 4. Some early examples of collaborative logistics initiatives.

Name	Solution	Strengths	Limitations
Flexe (Flexible Warehousing Infrastructure) www.flexe.com	A collaborative on-demand storage platform that allows companies to rent space in shared warehouses without having to invest in fixed infrastructures. Its network connects more than 1,500 warehouses in the US and Canada, allowing companies to expand their logistics capacity flexibly and without long-term commitments. The platform also integrates services such as inventory management and rapid distribution	***Scalability and Flexibility*** - Companies can expand and reduce storage capacity as demand dictates ***Reduction of Fixed Costs*** - Companies do not need to invest in their own distribution centers ***Speed of Implementation*** - Logistics spaces can be activated and deactivated quickly without much bureaucracy	***Dependence on Local Partners*** - Service quality may vary between different partner warehouses ***Less Control over Operations*** - Companies do not have full control over processes within rented warehouses ***Geographic Availability*** - The warehouses network may not cover all strategic regions for some companies
Convoy Platform (Marketplace to match and execute freight) https://convoy.com/	A digital marketplace for road transport, connecting independent drivers and small transport companies with companies that need to transport cargo. The platform uses AI/ML to optimize routes, reduce empty mileage and minimize waste in transportation logistics	***Efficiency and Sustainability*** - Reducing empty trips improves fleet utilization and reduces carbon emissions ***Intelligent Automation*** - The platform allows load allocation and route optimization in real time ***Reduced Operating Costs*** - Companies save money by connecting directly to drivers without intermediaries	***Reliance on Independent Drivers*** - If the supply of truck drivers decreases, this could affect the availability of transportation ***Regional Coverage*** - Service quality may vary depending on the location and availability of partner truck drivers

(*continued*)

Table 4. *(continued)*

Name	Solution	Strengths	Limitations
Flock Freight (Shared truckload) www.flockfreight.com	This system optimizes road transportation through the Shared Truckload (STL) concept, allowing different loads to share the same truck without having to pass through multiple transshipment terminals. This reduces costs, transit time and damage to goods. Unlike traditional Less-than-Truckload (LTL), where loads are transferred multiple times before reaching their destination, STL directly connects shippers to final transportation	***Cost Reduction*** - Companies only pay for the space they use on the truck, without having to hire an entire vehicle ***Less Damage to Cargo*** - Eliminating intermediate transfers reduces the risk of damage ***Sustainability*** - Better use of load capacity reduces the number of empty trucks on the road ***Faster Delivery*** - Since there are no multiple transfers, delivery times are reduced	***Shared Demand Dependency*** - If there are not enough loads to fill a shared truck, there may be delays in consolidation ***Less Control Over Route Planning*** - Since the load is shared, shippers may have less flexibility in defining routes and schedules ***Limited Coverage*** - May not be viable in some regions with low density of compatible loads

These examples are not specifically focused on the last mile, but they illustrate the potential benefits of collaboration in logistics.

4.3 The Collaborative Logistics Ecosystem Notion

The effectiveness of last-mile logistics depends on its capacity to integrate, adapt, and remain resilient in response to internal and external factors. The logistics ecosystem proposed in this work seeks to create a collaborative and sustainable approach, where different actors operate in an interconnected manner, supported by emerging technologies while being influenced by external factors that shape operational dynamics. Figure 2 represents this ecosystem, which is composed of three main layers:

a) Core, which represents the key actors in the system.
b) Pillars, which provide the structural and technological basis for the efficient operation of the ecosystem.
c) External Factors, which directly influence the functioning and resilience of the system.

At the core of the ecosystem are the key players involved in last-mile logistics, each performing interdependent roles to ensure the efficiency, accessibility, and scalability of operations. Key elements of this core include:

- Distributors, which represent the distribution centers and retailers that store and ship products to customers.
- Transport, covering carriers, logistics operators, and independent delivery people responsible for moving goods.

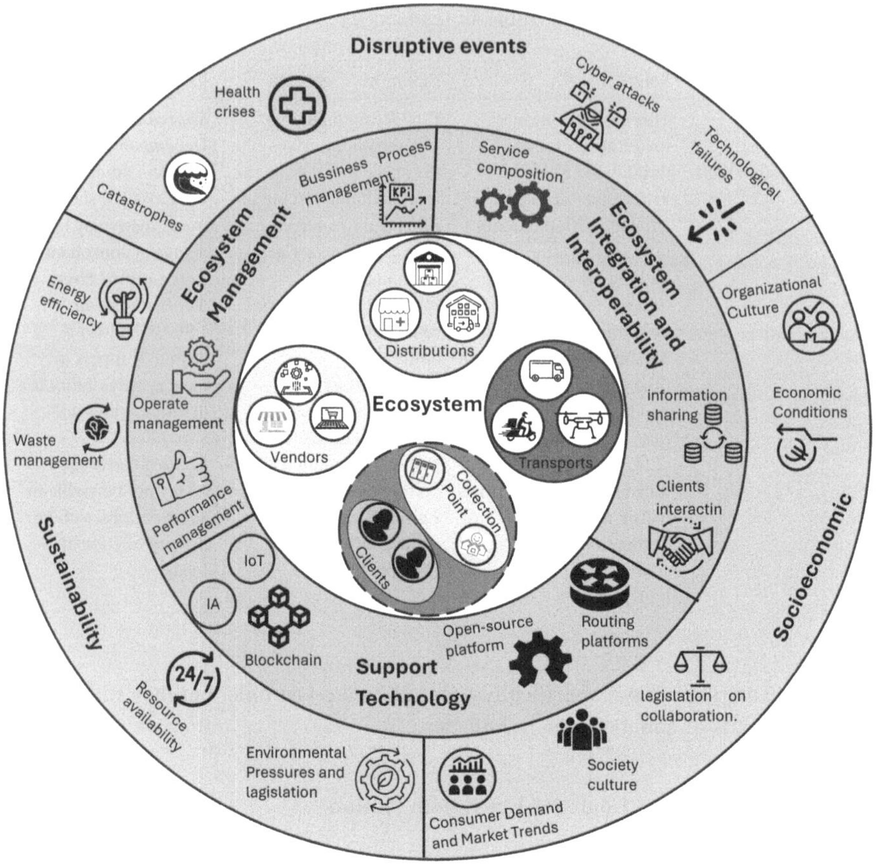

Fig. 2. Collaborative last-mile logistics ecosystem model

- Vendors, companies and suppliers that use the logistics network to market their products.

Furthermore, the core also includes:

- Collection points, which are strategic physical locations where customers can pick up their orders, thus reducing the need for home deliveries.
- Customers, the final link in the logistics chain which can play an active role in the collaborative model, being able to collect orders from lockers, participate in networks of neighbors, or even act as micro distributors.

The second layer of the model consists of the technological, operational, and collaborative pillars that support the ecosystem, ensuring its efficiency, interoperability, and resilience. These pillars establish a collaborative and technologically advanced environment, allowing the ecosystem to adapt to changes and challenges in a resilient and efficient way. Three subdimensions are considered:

- Ecosystem Management - which refers to the strategies and processes that ensure the efficient coordination of all ecosystem actors. The main aspects considered include operations management (monitoring and coordination of logistics activities), performance management (use of key performance indicators (KPIs) to ensure efficiency and quality), process management (automation and optimization of the stages of the logistics chain), and service composition (integration of different logistics services to offer flexible and scalable solutions).
- Ecosystem Integration and Interoperability - efficient collaboration depends on the ability to exchange information and ensure interoperability between systems and logistics agents. This layer includes Information sharing platforms, Customer interaction, and Intelligent Routing.
- Supporting Technologies - digitalization and automation of logistics are driven by emerging technologies, such as: (i) Open-Source Platforms that ensure interoperability and flexibility in systems integration, (ii) Blockchain that ensures traceability, transparency and security in logistics operations, and (iii) Artificial Intelligence and Internet of Things that facilitate process automation and improve real-time decision-making.

The last layer of the ecosystem represents the external factors that affect the resilience, efficiency, and sustainability of the ecosystem. These factors are divided into three main categories: Disruptive Events, Socioeconomic Factors, Sustainability, as summarized in Table 5.

Table 5. Examples of external factors

External Factors	Examples	Impact
Disruptive Events	Health Crises	Impact on the demand for deliveries and require rapid adaptations
	Natural Disasters	Can disrupt the supply chain and compromise logistics in certain regions
	Cyber Attacks and Technological Failures	Can compromise the digital infrastructure and impact critical operations
Socioeconomic Factors	Organizational Culture	Require adaptation of companies to the collaborative and digital model
	Economic Conditions	Impact consumption and investments in logistics infrastructure
	Market Trends and Consumer Demand	Push industry to adopt faster, more convenient deliveries

(*continued*)

Table 5. (*continued*)

External Factors	Examples	Impact
Sustainability	Waste Management and Energy Efficiency	Require reducing the environmental impact of logistics operations
	Resource Availability	Impacts the ability to maintain sustainable operations over the long term
	Environmental Pressures & Regulations	Demand the development of greener logistics models

These external factors present both challenges and opportunities, making it essential that the logistics ecosystem is flexible and adaptable to ensure resilience and operational continuity. The proposed model presents a comprehensive collaborative ecosystem for last-mile logistics, however, it is important to recognize that in practice, collaboration can coexist with competition. In markets where multiple operators offer similar logistics services, challenges related to competition arise [44, 45]. Companies that share micro-hubs, lockers, demand data and technology platforms may, at the same time, compete for contracts, routes and end customers. This duality requires clear mechanisms of governance, conflict management and mutual trust, so that collaboration is not undermined by economic rivalry [45].

4.4 Expected Benefits

The implementation of collaborative logistics models, including sharing resources between different operators and optimizing delivery routes, can bring a series of benefits for both logistic operators and society and consumers [7, 8, 46]. Some of these benefits are presented below:

- Benefits for operators:
  a) Reduction of Operating Costs: (i) Sharing of resources, such as vehicles and warehouses, among multiple stakeholders. (ii) Consolidation of loads to minimize empty trips and optimize vehicle utilization. (iii) Reduction in fuel consumption and delivery times through efficient routing.
  b) Empowerment of Small Operators: Facilitation of access to shared resources and collaborative networks, enhancing competitiveness and operational efficiency.
- Benefits for society:
  a) Support for Sustainability: Promotion of environmentally friendly transportation modes, such as electric and low-emission vehicles.
  b) Route Optimization: Decrease in carbon emissions due to fewer vehicles on the road.
- Benefits for consumers:

Improvement in Customer Experience: (i) Faster deliveries are enabled by optimized operations and real-time tracking systems. (ii) Greater reliability and transparency in delivery processes.

5 Research Approach

Research on collaborative networks in last-mile logistics requires a structured methodological approach, combining concepts from design science, computational simulation and artificial intelligence. The objective is to develop an experimental model that allows evaluating the impact of collaboration on last-mile logistics efficiency, operational costs and sustainability.

The research was structured in sequential stages, beginning with a systematic literature review to identify gaps and challenges in last-mile logistics. Subsequently, the proposed collaborative ecosystem was conceptually modeled, guided by requirements identified in prior studies and the practical needs of the sector. Based on these inputs, the model was designed for simulation and subsequent performance evaluation.

The validation of the organizational model will be conducted through a combination of computer simulations and qualitative analysis. The primary objective of the validation process is to assess the robustness, practical feasibility, and scalability of the proposed ecosystem. Furthermore, the validation aims to confirm whether the model aligns with the principles of operational efficiency, resilience, sustainability, and adaptability required in modern last-mile logistics environments.

In this section, we detail the adopted methodology, the simulation approaches, the integration between AI and collaborative networks (CNs), as well as the main activities underway in the development of the proposed model.

5.1 Design Science Steps

Design Science Research (DSR) is a methodological approach that seeks to solve complex problems through the development and evaluation of innovative artefacts [47]. In the context of last-mile logistics, DSR facilitates the construction of a collaborative model, aiming at optimizing operations, reducing costs, and increasing logistical resilience.

The Design Science process is structured around three main elements: the Application Domain, the Design Science Research process, and the Knowledge Base. These elements are interconnected by three cycles: relevance, rigor, and design, which ensure the connection between theory and practice [48]. Figure 3 represents this structure and its respective steps.

5.2 Simulation Approaches

The complexity of last-mile logistics demands advanced modeling and simulation approaches to test and validate new solutions. Simulation allows you to analyze different scenarios, identify operational bottlenecks and measure the impact of collaboration between logistics agents. To validate the proposed collaborative model, three complementary simulation approaches are used: Agent-Based Modeling (ABM), System Dynamics (SD), and Discrete Event Simulation (DES). Each of these approaches

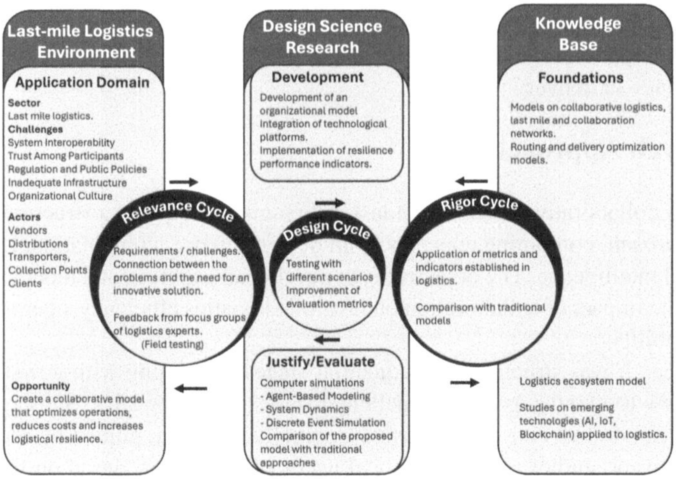

Fig. 3. Design Science Steps for the collaborative last-mile logistics ecosystem.

offers a unique contribution to understanding and optimizing the proposed ecosystem. The choice of these methods reflects the dynamic and interdependent nature of last-mile logistics.

Agent-based modeling is a simulation technique used to test the impact of different levels of collaboration between logistics network participants. This approach enables the simulation of the individual behavior of each agent (transports, vendors, distributors, collection points and clients) and their interactions over time. ABM is particularly useful for evaluating the impacts of collaboration between transport companies on operational efficiency, testing different resource sharing strategies and their effects on logistics resilience, and simulating consumer behavior in response to new delivery methods, such as lockers and crowd shipping.

System dynamics is used to analyze the cause-and-effect relationships within the collaborative network. This approach allows for modeling the evolution of the logistics system over time, considering variables such as consumer demand, transport capacity, and the influence of public policies. By using this simulation, it becomes possible to assess the impact of variations in demand and seasonality on logistics capacity and test the effect of digitalization and automation on the performance of the logistics network.

Discrete event simulation is used to optimize logistics operations and resource allocation by modeling individual events that occur over time, such as deliveries, waiting times, and infrastructure usage. This approach enables optimization of the delivery routes considering urban traffic and response times. Additionally, it allows for the simulation of micro-hubs and collection points, analyzing their impact on logistics efficiency and evaluating the performance of collaborative fleets.

For prototype development, the AnyLogic platform is used.

5.3 Ongoing Activities

The simulation approach is being implemented through three main activities, which focus on developing, testing, and validating the proposed collaborative model:

1. Development of the Organizational and Structural Model. At this stage, the conceptual and operational model of the collaborative network is developed, detailing the actors involved, their interactions and the rules that govern the system. This model serves as a basis for simulations, enabling the testing of different scenarios.
2. Testing and Defining Performance Metrics. To assess the effectiveness of the model, key performance indicators (KPIs) are being defined, including: Vehicle occupancy rate to measure efficiency in the use of transport capacity; Average delivery time to assess the impact of collaborative strategies; Reduction of CO2 emissions as a sustainability metric; and Operating cost per delivery, allowing comparison with traditional models.
3. Validation with Focus Groups. After the simulations are implemented, the results will be validated by groups of logistics experts. This validation will allow adjusting the model parameters, ensuring that the proposed solutions are applicable in the real-world context.

5.4 Future Developments: AI-Powered Logistics

Artificial Intelligence (AI) has emerged as an essential element to improve decision-making and maximize the potential of collaborative logistic ecosystems. By integrating AI into collaborative logistics, it is possible to predict demand more accurately, identify more efficient collaboration patterns, optimize routes and coordinate multiple logistics operators in an intelligent and automated way [49].

In several previous works, AI already plays a fundamental role in the automation and optimization of logistics processes, enabling more efficient use of available resources. Through techniques such as machine learning and optimization algorithms, AI can process large volumes of data in real time, extracting insights that facilitate strategic decision-making within collaborative networks [50, 51]. Through a combination with other technologies such as the Internet of Things, Blockchain and Big Data, AI can improve the visibility and traceability of the logistics chain, reducing failures and increasing the reliability of operations [52].

One of the biggest challenges in last-mile logistics is dealing with variations in demand caused by factors such as seasonality, consumer trends, and disruptive events. In this context, the implementation of AI-based demand forecasting enables collaborative networks to act in a more agile and resilient way, avoiding operational bottlenecks and optimizing delivery flows [53]. AI also plays a crucial role in identifying more efficient collaboration patterns between different actors in last-mile logistics, and using advanced network analysis and machine learning techniques, AI can detect opportunities for optimization in logistics collaboration. As such, collaborative ecosystems can evolve into a dynamic and adaptable model, where participants continuously adjust their operations to maximize logistical performance [29].

Route optimization is one of the main challenges in last-mile logistics, as factors such as traffic, urban restrictions and tight delivery windows directly affect the efficiency of operations. AI can draw on real-time traffic data, weather forecasts, and historical delivery patterns to calculate faster, more efficient routes [1, 38]. However, the fragmentation of logistics operators represents one of the main barriers to the efficiency of collaborative logistics, as companies operate with different systems and non-standardized processes, making it difficult to progress and optimize available resources [54]. AI can act as an intelligent matcher, facilitating integration between platforms, fleets and service providers. Additionally, it can transform collaborative logistics, by enabling companies to share infrastructure, optimize resources and increase the efficiency of the logistics system.

The combination of AI with Collaborative Networks in last-mile logistics is likely to offer major advances in operational efficiency, sustainability and system flexibility. As such, our future work intends to explore the integration of AI and emerging technologies in the proposed collaborative last-mile logistics ecosystem.

6 Conclusions

The increasing complexity of last-mile logistics, driven by the growth of e-commerce and the demand for more sustainable and efficient solutions, reinforces the importance of collaborative approaches in addressing the identified challenges. This paper proposes a collaborative ecosystem for last-mile logistics, highlighting the role of collaboration among different actors, the integration of emerging technologies, and the adoption of more flexible and adaptable organizational models. Based on the literature review and conducted analyses, collaboration among companies, carriers, technology platforms, distribution centers, and end consumers can significantly enhance operational efficiency, reduce costs, and minimize environmental impacts.

The integration of various logistics agents through open platforms enables better use of available infrastructure, greater precision in tracking deliveries, and increased flexibility in managing demand fluctuations. Furthermore, the adoption of sustainable vehicles, urban micro-hubs and smart lockers has proven to be a viable solution for reducing congestion and carbon emissions in densely populated areas.

However, several challenges remain, including the need for greater standardization in system communication, the establishment of clear governance rules for collaborative networks, and overcoming cultural and operational barriers to adopting new sharing-based business models. Furthermore, consumer acceptance of these solutions and the economic viability for small and medium-sized businesses need to be better evaluated.

As a next step, the research proposes validating the collaborative model through simulation and experiments in real environments. Furthermore, future studies can deepen the analysis of the economic impact of collaboration in the logistics sector, as well as explore new approaches to encourage the adoption of collaborative practices by companies and governments.

Acknowledgments. This work is supported in part by the Portuguese Foundation for Science and Technology through the projects CTS/00066.

References

1. Savelsbergh, M., Woensel, T.V.: City logistics: challenges and opportunities. Transp. Sci. **50**(2), 579–590 (2016). https://doi.org/10.1287/trsc.2016.0675
2. World Economic Forum. The Future of the Last-Mile Ecosystem: Sustainability and Efficiency. www.weforum.org (2020)
3. Saito, R., Monteiro, L.C., Gomes, R.: Last mile distribution logistics: the challenges in choosing logistics operators. In: Proceedings of the Symposium on Production Engineering (2006). https://submissao.singep.org.br/11singep/proceedings/arquivos/71.pdf
4. Statista 2023.: Global E-Commerce Market Growth Forecast, www.statista.com
5. Juniper Research, https://www.juniperresearch.com/press/pressreleasesdigital-commerce-spend-to-hit-34tn-by-2029/
6. Camarinha-Matos, L.M., Afsarmanesh, H.: Collaborative networks: a new scientific discipline. J. Intell. Manuf. **16**, 439–452 (2005). https://doi.org/10.1007/s10845-005-1656-3
7. Camarinha-Matos, L.M., Fornasiero, R., Ramezani, J., Ferrada, F.: Collaborative networks: a pillar of digital transformation. Appl. Sci. **9**(24), 5431 (2019). https://doi.org/10.3390/app9245431
8. Ko, S.Y., Sari, R.P., Makhmudov, M., Ko, C.S.: Collaborative model for service clustering in last-mile delivery. Sustainability **12**, 5844 (2020). https://doi.org/10.3390/su12145844
9. Idrissi, Z.K., Lachgar, M., Hrimech, H.: Blockchain, IoT and AI in logistics and transportation: a systematic review. Transport Econ. Manage. **2**, 275–285 (2024). https://doi.org/10.1016/j.team.2024.09.002
10. Christopher, M.: Logistics and Supply Chain Management, 5th edn. Pearson, London (2016)
11. Didast, F.Z., Nassih, R., Elbachir, I.: Artificial Intelligence and Logistics: Recent Trends and Development. Preprints v1.2141 (2024). https://doi.org/10.20944/preprints202410.2141.v1
12. Lee, J., Bagheri, B., Kao, H.-A.: A cyber-physical systems architecture for industry 4.0-based manufacturing systems. Manuf. Lett. **3**, 18–23 (2015). https://doi.org/10.1016/j.mfglet.2014.12.001
13. Monostori, L.: Cyber-physical production systems: roots, expectations and R&D challenges. Procedia CIRP **17**, 9–13 (2014). https://doi.org/10.1016/j.procir.2014.03.115
14. Rani, S., Kataria, A., Kumar, S., Karar, V.: A new generation cyber-physical system: a comprehensive review from security perspective. Comput. Secur. **148**, 104095 (2025). https://doi.org/10.1016/j.cose.2024.104095
15. Bertsimas, D., Kallus, N.: From predictive to prescriptive analytics. Manage. Sci. **66**(3), 1025–1044 (2020). https://doi.org/10.1287/mnsc.2018.3253
16. Sodiya, E.O., Umoga, U.J., Amoo, O.O., Atadoga, A.: AI-driven warehouse automation: a comprehensive review of systems. GSC Adv. Res. Rev. **18**(2), 272–282 (2024). https://doi.org/10.30574/gscarr.2024.18.2.0063
17. Lee, J., Davari, H., Singh, J., Pandhare, V.: Industrial Artificial Intelligence for industry 4.0-based manufacturing systems. Manuf. Lett. **18**, 20–23 (2018). https://doi.org/10.1016/j.mfglet.2018.09.002
18. Tao, F., Qi, Q., Wang, L., Nee, A.Y.C.: Digital twins and cyber–physical systems toward smart manufacturing and industry 4.0: correlation and comparison. Engineering **5**(4), 653–661 (2019). https://doi.org/10.1016/j.eng.2019.01.014
19. Pournader, M., Ghaderi, H., Hassanzadegan, A., Fahimnia, B.: Artificial intelligence applications in supply chain management. Int. J. Product. Econ. **241**, 108250 (2021). https://doi.org/10.1016/j.ijpe.2021.108250
20. Buldeo Rai, H., Verlinde, S., Merckx, J., Macharis, C.: Crowd logistics: an opportunity for more sustainable urban freight transport? Eur. Transp. Res. Rev. **9**(3), 1–13 (2017). https://doi.org/10.1007/s12544-017-0256-6

21. Andreoli, D., Goodchild, A., Vitasek, K.: The rise of mega distribution centers and the impact on logistical uncertainty. Transport. Lett. **2**(2), 75–88 (2010). https://doi.org/10.3328/TL.2010.02.02.75-88
22. Mangano, G., Zenezini, G.: The Value Proposition of innovative Last-Mile delivery services from the perspective of local retailers. IFAC-PapersOnLine **52**(13), 2590–2595 (2019). https://doi.org/10.1016/j.ifacol.2019.11.597
23. Boysen, N., Fedtke, S., Schwerdfeger, S.: Last-mile delivery concepts: a survey from an operational research perspective. OR Spectrum **43**(1), 1–58 (2021). https://doi.org/10.1007/s00291-020-00607-8
24. Akdogan, K., Özceylan, E.: Applications of artificial intelligence in last mile delivery operations: a literature review. In: Proceedings of 11th International Symposium on Intelligent Manufacturing and Service Systems, Sakarya/Turkey , 27–29 May 2021
25. Demir, E., Syntetos, A., van Woensel, T.: Last mile logistics: research trends and needs. IMA J. Manage. Math. **33**(4), 549–561 (2022). https://doi.org/10.1093/imaman/dpac006
26. Arnold, F., Cardenas, I., Sörensen, K., Dewulf, W.: Simulation of B2C e-commerce distribution in Antwerp using cargo bikes and delivery points. European Transport Res. Rev. **10**(1), 1–13 (2017). https://doi.org/10.1007/s12544-017-0272-6
27. Halldórsson, A., Wehner, J.: Last-mile logistics fulfilment: a framework for energy efficiency. Res. Transp. Bus. Manag. **37**, 2210–5395 (2020). https://doi.org/10.1016/j.rtbm.2020.100481
28. Juan, A.A., Mendez, C.A., Faulin, J., De Armas, J., Grasman, S.E.: Electric vehicles in logistics and transportation: a survey on emerging environmental, strategic, and operational challenges. Energies **9**(2), 86 (2016). https://doi.org/10.3390/en9020086
29. Perboli, G., Brotcorne, L., Bruni, M.E., Rosano, M.: A new model for last-mile delivery and satellite depots management: the impact of the on-demand economy. Transport. Res. Part E: Logist. Transport. Rev. **145**, 102184 (2021). https://doi.org/10.1016/j.tre.2020.102184
30. Ranieri, L., Digiesi, S., Silvestri, B., Roccotelli, M.: A review of last mile logistics innovations in an externalities cost reduction vision. Sustainability **10**(3), 782 (2018). https://doi.org/10.3390/su10030782
31. Kim, J., Kweon, S.J., Hwang, S.W., Lee, S.: Crowdsourcing integration on the last mile delivery platform considering floating population data. Expert Syst. Appl. **248**, 123312 (2024). https://doi.org/10.1016/j.eswa.2024.123312
32. Kahr, M.: Determining locations and layouts for parcel lockers to support supply chain viability at the last mile. Omega **113**, 102721 (2022). https://doi.org/10.1016/j.omega.2022.102721
33. Janjevic, M., Winkenbach, M.: Characterizing urban last-mile distribution strategies in mature and emerging e-commerce markets. Transport. Res. Part A: Policy Pract. **133**, 164–196 (2020). https://doi.org/10.1016/j.tra.2020.01.003
34. Olsson, J., Hellström, D., Pålsson, H.: Framework of last mile logistics research: a systematic review of the literature. Sustainability **11**(24), 7131 (2019). https://doi.org/10.3390/su11247131
35. Hagen, T., Scheel-Kopeinig, S.: Would customers be willing to use an alternative (chargeable) delivery concept for the last mile? Res. Transport. Busi. Manage. **39**, 100626 (2021). https://doi.org/10.1016/j.rtbm.2021.100626
36. Giuffrida, N., Fajardo-Calderin, J., Masegosa, A.D., Werner, F., Steudter, M., Pilla, F.: Optimization and machine learning applied to last-mile logistics: a review. Sustainability **14**(9), 5329 (2022). https://doi.org/10.3390/su14095329
37. Silva, P., Barwaldt, R., Santos, H.S., Lucca, G.: A systematic review on the use of machine learning in last mile delivery vehicle routing problems. Int. J. Dev. Res. **13**, 63290–63295 (2023). https://doi.org/10.37118/ijdr.26940.07.2023

38. Goodchild, A., Toy, J.: Delivery by drone: an evaluation of unmanned aerial vehicle technology in reducing CO2 emissions in the delivery service industry. Transp. Res. Part D: Transp. Environ. (2017). https://doi.org/10.1016/j.trd.2017.02.017
39. Marcucci, E., Le Pira, M., Gatta, V., Inturri, G., Ignaccolo, M., Pluchino, A.: Simulating participatory urban freight transport policy-making: accounting for heterogeneous stakeholders preferences and interaction effects. Transport. Res. Part E: Logist. Transport. Rev. **103**, 69–86 (2017). https://doi.org/10.1016/j.tre.2017.04.006
40. Cherrett, T., Allen, J., Mcleod, F., Maynard, S., Hickford, A., Browne, M.: Understanding urban freight activity – key issues for freight planning. J. Transp. Geogr. **24**, 22–32 (2012). https://doi.org/10.1016/j.jtrangeo.2012.05.008
41. Murray, C.C., Chu, A.G.: The flying sidekick traveling salesman problem: Optimization of drone-assisted parcel delivery. Transport. Res. Part C: Emerg. Technol. **54**, 86–109 (2015). https://doi.org/10.1016/j.trc.2015.03.005
42. Nguyen, L., Duong, K., Chong, J.: Supply chain collaboration in the presence of disruptions: a literature review. Int. J. Product. Res. **58**(11), 3488–3507 (2020). https://doi.org/10.1080/00207543.2020.1712491
43. Graça, P., Camarinha-Matos, L.M.: Performance indicators for collaborative business ecosystems – literature review and trends. Technol. Forecast. Soc. Chang. **116**, 237–255 (2017). https://doi.org/10.1016/j.techfore.2016.10.012
44. Roketskiy, N.: Competition and networks of collaboration. Theoret. Econ. **13**(3), 1077–1110 (2018). https://doi.org/10.3982/TE2492
45. Bergendahl, M., Magnusson, M.: Combining collaboration and competition: a key to improved idea management? Eur. J. Internat. Manage. **8**(5), 528 (2014). https://doi.org/10.1504/EJIM.2014.064603
46. Aktas, E., Bourlakis, M., Zissis, D.: Collaboration in the last mile: evidence from grocery deliveries. Int. J. Log. Res. Appl. **24**(3), 227–241 (2020). https://doi.org/10.1080/13675567.2020.1740660
47. Hevner, A.R., March, S.T., Park, J., Ram, S.: Design science in information systems research. MIS Q. **28**(1), 75–105 (2004)
48. Hevner, A.R.: A three cycle view of design science research. Scandinavian J. Inform. Syst. **19**(2) (2007) https://aisel.aisnet.org/cgi/viewcontent.cgi?article=1017&context=sjis
49. Gonzalez-Feliu, J., Salanova, J.M.: Defining and evaluating collaborative urban freight transportation systems. Procedia. Soc. Behav. Sci. **39**, 172–183 (2012). https://doi.org/10.1016/j.sbspro.2012.03.099
50. de Oliveira Rustice, L.A., de Carvalho, J.S., Barcelos, A.F.V., Santana, V.B.: Aplicação de técnicas de inteligência artificial na otimização de processos logísticos. Observatório de la Economía Latinoamericana **22**(5), e4460 (2024). https://doi.org/10.55905/oelv22n5-015
51. Ferigato, E., Finom: Intelligent logistics: advances, challenges and future perspectives, Humanidades Tecnol. 41, 192–213 (2023). https://doi.org/10.5281/zenodo.8225572
52. Montoya-Torres, J.R., Muñoz-Villamizar, A., Mejía Argueta, C.: Mapping research in logistics and supply chain management during COVID-19 pandemic. Int. J. Log. Res. Appl. **26**, 1–21 (2021). https://doi.org/10.1080/13675567.2021.1958768
53. Tordecilla, R.D., Juan, A.A., Montoya-Torres, J.R., Quintero-Araujo, C.L., Panadero, J.: Simulation-optimization methods for designing and assessing resilient supply chain networks under uncertainty scenarios: a review. Simul. Model. Pract. Theory **106**, 102166 (2021). https://doi.org/10.1016/j.simpat.2020.102166
54. Taniguchi, E.: Concepts of city logistics for sustainable and liveable cities. Procedia. Soc. Behav. Sci. **151**, 310–317 (2014). https://doi.org/10.1016/j.sbspro.2014.10.029

Processes Classification Tool Development Based on BERT for Logistics Laboratory

Rene Maas[1,2](✉), Eduard Shevtshenko[1,2], Hendrik Laanemets[1,2], and Tatjana Karaulova[2]

[1] University of Tartu, Ülikooli 18, 50090 Tartu, Estonia
Rene.Maas@ut.ee
[2] TTK UAS Pärnu Mnt 62A, 10135 Tallinn, Estonia
{Eduard.Sevtsenko,Hendrik.Laanemets,Tatjana.Karaulova}@tktk.ee

Abstract. While companies have adopted AI and automated work processes, a key unresolved issue remains-how to test new digital solutions for process automation-both from an environmental and economic perspective, quickly and cost-effectively. Companies have not always mapped their processes, so using plain text process descriptions to get process maps is challenging. Our research aims to understand how AI could be used in the context of process extraction from company text documents to simulate reference process models in a logistics laboratory. We propose a workflow and tools for adapting AI in process extraction in a laboratory context. Extracted and classified processes are paired with reference processes model, SCOR model KPIs, and software dedicated to logistics, enabling us to build up the simulator quickly and cost-effectively. For classification, we use the EstBERT (Estonian Bidirectional Encoder Representations from Transformers) language model, which is explicitly devoted to Estonian words and fine-tuned for the definition of logistics process classes based on textual processes descriptions extracted from bachelor's thesis and project data. The trained model showed an accuracy of 80% in classifying the processes. We validate our method by applying logistics company examples, using their process descriptions and showing how we could integrate our method into logistics laboratory work. A successful case study demonstration extends the current process mining approach by broadening the scope of valid input formats. It suggests that natural language-based representations of processes can be directly converted to corresponding reference process models.

Keywords: Artificial Intelligence · Supply Chain Laboratory · BERT · SCOR · Process Extraction

1 Introduction

Despite AI adoption and automation, companies struggle to test new digital solutions for process automation efficiently and cost-effectively. Research highlights AI's (Artificial Intelligence) potential to enhance competitiveness [1] and its underexplored role in sustainability [2]. To stay competitive, companies must embrace digitalisation and AI-driven advancements.

Published by Springer Nature Switzerland AG 2025
L. M. Camarinha-Matos and F. Ferrada (Eds.): DoCEIS 2025, IFIP AICT 759, pp. 26–38, 2025.
https://doi.org/10.1007/978-3-031-97051-1_2

A key challenge is to propose the supply chain process test centre, where companies can evaluate business processes enhancing software solutions' impact on sustainability and measure expected results by predefined KPIs (Key Performance Indicators) in a risk-free environment. Such a centre would assess ICT (Information Communication Technology) implementation impacts, ensuring solutions align with company goals and are compatible with business processes. Recently, AI has gained research attention in process extraction, mining, classification [3], and logistics [4].

Uncertainty in technology adoption underscores the need for an educational component in testing centres. Success depends on a company's ability to learn and adapt to develop the required capabilities [5]. This study aims to create company-based process data for test centres, eliminating manual data preprocessing. We propose an AI-driven method using EstBERT to extract process categories from company process documents, enabling faster test setup and optimisation.

Testing centres also foster collaborative reference process mapping, with companies contributing to a shared knowledge base of best practices [6, 7]. Our solution leverages a fine-tuned EstBERT model to identify generic processes and KPIs in logistics laboratories, addressing two research questions:

RQ1: How does the AI tool speed up process mapping for the logistics laboratory?
RQ2: Are generic process category definitions sufficient for company business processes describing and mapping to corresponding SCOR (Supply Chain Operations Reference) processes and KPIs?

The paper is structured as follows: Sect. 1 reviews existing literature, Sect. 2 describes the data collection from logistics companies and theses, Sect. 3 defines reference processes and maps them to SCOR processes and metrics, and Sect. 4 validates the concept with a case study, demonstrating process extraction, mapping, and visualisation.

2 Relation to the Conference Topic

AI-powered cyber-physical systems drive automation, adaptability, and data-driven decision-making. Enterprise data often holds valuable insights into processes, performance, and inefficiencies, typically unstructured and scattered across databases. Since businesses prioritise performing core activities over structured data collection, process mapping remains challenging, with little perceived value in extensive documentation.

AI can analyse vast amounts of unstructured process data, uncover patterns, and structure workflows with minimal human effort. AI-driven text classification enables machine-readable process descriptions, supporting simulations that test modifications before real-world implementation. Once structured, this data integrates into workflow optimisation and validation simulation tools.

In this study, AI-enhanced cyber-physical systems create a unified database systematically converting textual descriptions of enterprise workflows into reference process models. This database bridges physical and digital systems, improving efficiency, reducing risk, and enhancing competitiveness. The proposed AI-driven tool for logistics laboratories transforms unstructured data into actionable insights, enabling businesses to optimise operations and make informed strategic decisions.

3 Related Literature

Two general classifications have emerged in the development of logistics laboratories: physical equipment and IT (Information Technology) solutions. Authors divide IT solutions into general-purpose and industry-specific applications [8].

At the TTK UAS test centre, companies can simulate process characteristics based on their data. A controlled environment enables the replication of predefined conditions [9]. The advantage of logistics test centres lies in their ability to operate within a controlled environment.

Beyond educational use, research organisations utilise logistics laboratories for business collaboration and service provision [10]. The continuous advancement of the industry has also driven the evolution of logistics laboratories, where AI, IoT, blockchain, and similar technologies have been implemented [11]. Integrating various virtual elements within a networked system creates a realistic research environment [12]. The TTK logistics laboratory applies AI for efficient and rapid textual process description data processing.

A key aspect extracted from the literature review is that the primary focus is on developing and researching laboratory components and stakeholders. While the TTK logistics laboratory has the prerequisites for future software applications, the test centre lacks a structured methodology for business process creation (in terms of data formats) that would facilitate process simulation. This study focuses on logistics processes, employing an innovative approach to process discovery that eliminates the need for extensive manual data generation.

BPM (Business Process Management) provides a framework for managing organisational processes, integrating various solutions for efficient process handling [13]. BPM utilises multiple data collection methods, including evidence-based, interview-based, and workshop-based discovery [14]. Digital discovery techniques include process mining and process extraction [14, 15].

Process mining is a method for analysing and gathering business process information based on input event logs from enterprise information systems [14]. Although automated process discovery lets one analyse or collect data, it contains multiple challenges. M. Dumas et al. pointed out that log data extraction challenges like correlation, timestamping, longevity, and granularity make it difficult for organisations to use this method [14].

On the other hand, process information extraction is defined as setting up an algorithm function that could identify and transform text-based process descriptions into a desired structure [15]. Compared to process mining, this could identify processes from organisational textual documents without needing information systems-based log data gathering. Automated process discovery, a process mining method, generates process models from software log data but requires structured and accurate organisational data [14]. As a result, research emphasises information gathering.

NLP (Natural Language Processing) techniques have been applied in BPM to generate process models and handle textual process descriptions [16].

BERT is an advanced AI model that enhances a computer's understanding of human language. It generates high-quality text representations for various NLP tasks and outperforms other models in multiple benchmarks [17–19]. BERT, pre-trained in over 100 languages, includes EstBERT, a transformer-based model specialised in the Estonian language [20].

Researchers have successfully applied BERT to classify business descriptions into industries because it captures nuanced domain-specific information [21, 22]. Ito et al. [23] explored BERT-based company representations using annual reports.

The current study uses EstBERT as a reference process model to classify logistics operations efficiently. By leveraging its pre-trained capabilities, we aim to develop a Transformer-based solution for identifying generic processes and KPIs within the logistics laboratory database.

Efficient coordination of logistics processes enhances supply chain performance [24]. The SCOR model provides a structured framework for aligning process architecture with business objectives [25, 26] and is a standardised tool for seamless communication and performance optimisation.

To assess supply chain performance, the SCOR model focuses on key performance attributes and collections of metrics guiding strategic decisions [27]. It divides the KPIs into economic, such as reliability (RL), responsiveness (RS), agility (AG), costs (CO), asset management (AM) and sustainability, such as environmental (EV) and social (SC) (Supply Chain Council). Achieving supply chain excellence depends on selecting and implementing relevant KPIs [28]. Enterprises define strategic process goals, enabling the establishment and evaluation of KPIs [29–31], with this study applying the SCOR standard for analysis.

Research on logistics laboratory focuses mainly on physical labs (infrastructure) and IT-based labs. Technological advancements have been in the direction of AI, IoT, blockchain and virtual systems (software).

Traditional process mining has been done by analysing the event logs from information systems, but it has limitations like data granularity and the existence of logs. Information extraction, on the other hand, uses algorithms to extract processes from text, removing reliance on system logs.

Two main generations of approaches have been applied in process extraction. The first generation primarily focused on rule-based solutions, where predefined linguistic or structural rules were used to extract process elements from texts [32]. In contrast, the second generation has increasingly shifted towards machine learning-based solutions, leveraging models that learn extraction patterns automatically from data [33].

4 Research Contribution and Innovation

4.1 Logistics Laboratory

We chose to adopt a case study approach to analyse supply chain processes at the operational level and present the results. This approach allowed us to test and apply our methodology, which we intended to integrate into daily operations in the logistics laboratory of Tallinn University of Applied Sciences. The laboratory operates within an applied higher education institution and has recently been established with dedicated laboratory engineers. Therefore, the primary focus of this study was to explore the feasibility of offering new services to companies in the logistics sector, particularly for small and medium enterprises with fewer investments in process mapping. Having such a market in Estonia, we found that a tool for process extraction is essential and paves the way for future services like analytics, strategy alignment, etc., in the laboratory.

In addition, students will use the laboratory throughout their logistics studies. Future workers should have future tools and knowledge; thus, we would like to add logistics analytics and process extraction to the curriculum. These factors underscore the importance of the practical applicability of our approach. Consequently, the input data used for training the AI model must be based on real-world examples provided by companies.

4.2 AI Tool Development Framework

This study explicitly classifies business processes based on company-documented tasks that traditionally demand significant human effort. By leveraging AI, we aim to accelerate and enhance data processing while unlocking new possibilities for in-depth analysis and simulation of operational processes (Fig. 1).

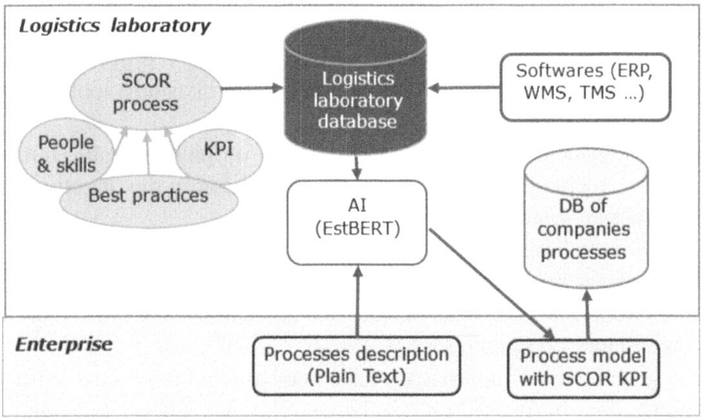

Fig. 1. Research framework visualization.

4.3 Taxonomy

We developed a process taxonomy framework to address the challenge of extracting process categories from textual descriptions; based on process categories, we introduce to the user the reference process models, define and allocate KPIs, and their relationships with supported software solutions from company documents (Fig. 2).

This taxonomy is a structured framework for organising and classifying various business processes, defining their key metrics, and linking them to specific software solutions. The systematic approach enables process mapping and optimisation within the laboratory environment, making processes more manageable and automation-ready.

The core element of the developed taxonomy is the process category (Table 1), which represents a high-level classification of business processes. The authors have mapped

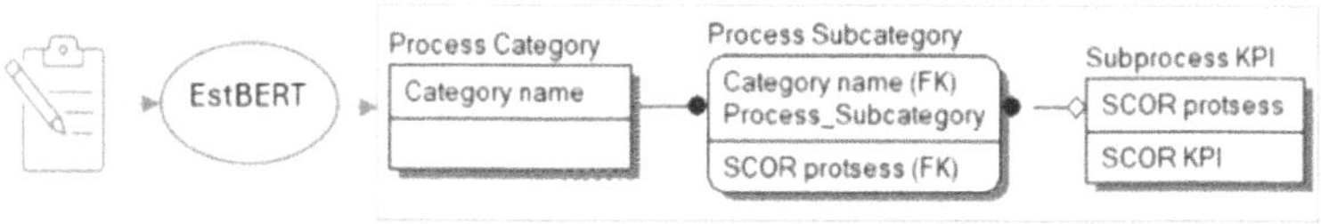

Fig. 2. Logistics laboratory database structure.

each subcategory within the taxonomy to reference processes defined by logistics institute experts, specifically aligned with the SCOR model and corresponding subprocess KPIs. When extracted from company documents, this mapping ensures that the identified process categories are linked to measurable performance indicators, enabling the simulation of automation-driven process changes.

However, the current development phase does not yet support automated KPI identification in the laboratory, and the authors perform this step manually.

Table 1. Process categories related to ID and suggested software for automation. ERP- Enterprise Resource Planning, PMS- Procurement Management System, WMS- Warehouse Management System, IMS- Information Management System, TMS- Transport Management System, FMS- Financial Management System.

Category ID	Logistics Operation Categories	Software
0	Purchase planning	ERP, PMS
1	Perform Procurement, Negotiate Contracts and Terms	PMS
2	Receiving goods in the warehouse	WMS, ERP
3	Organising the storage of goods	WMS, ERP
4	Inventory Tracking and Control	ERP, IMS
5	Assembling and packaging cargo for shipment	WMS
6	Selection of vehicles and routes	TMS, FMS
7	Organising transportation	TMS, FMS
8	Monitoring and controlling the movement of goods	TMS, FMS

A software classification framework was introduced alongside the process taxonomy to enhance process classification. The taxonomy is dynamic and evolves as more data is collected. The more companies engage with the logistics laboratory, the more new text-based business process descriptions will be gathered, capturing real-world variations in operational workflows. This continuous data acquisition process enhances the accuracy and adaptability of AI, enabling it to classify and recommend processes with increasing precision.

4.4 Choosing and Training AI Model

The choice of AI model was driven by the requirement for efficient training with limited data availability, ensuring that fine-tuning would be sufficient rather than requiring an extensive dataset [19]. Using a language model capable of effectively processing Estonian text was also crucial. We adopted EstBERT (Fig. 3), a model trained on an Estonian language corpus, for the classification task. EstBERT has been pre-trained on 1.2 billion Estonian words [20], making it well-suited for handling Estonian-language business process descriptions.

Furthermore, BERT-based models have been proven to outperform other classification models in both speed and accuracy [34]. EstBERT's architecture allows for fine-tuning with a relatively small dataset, which is a key advantage for rapid deployment in the logistics laboratory. Additionally, the model's adaptability ensures that new training data, such as business process descriptions from company visits or student research projects, can be continuously incorporated to enhance classification accuracy.

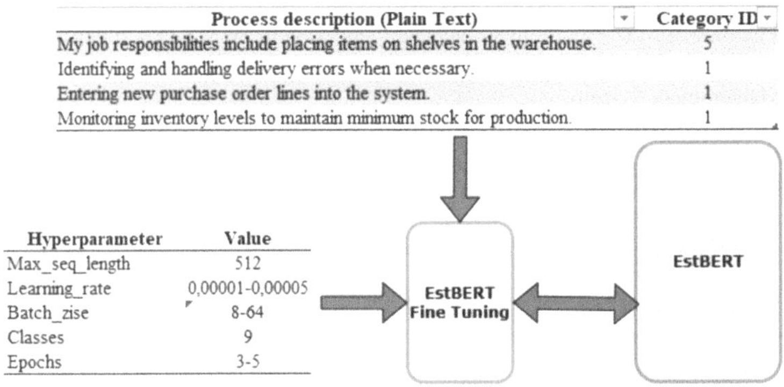

Fig. 3. EstBERT training parameters and training data example.

In the training phase, we compiled natural language examples from business process descriptions in company textual documents and logistics bachelor's theses. The Dspace repository [35] of the Logistics Institute contains 451 bachelor's theses, of which 430 were publicly available. Using search terms such as "case study of a company" and "processes", we identified 289 bachelor's theses, from which 500 representative sentences describing business processes were manually labelled with process categories.

Additionally, we utilised business documents from three industrial projects, process descriptions, and data were extracted. As with the bachelor's thesis, authors have manually extracted relevant text excerpts and sentences, describing specific process characteristics. Since manual sentence extraction from these theses and memos was time-intensive, we implemented data augmentation techniques to optimise the process. This technique included paraphrasing, rewording, translation, and synonym replacement, effectively expanding our dataset while maintaining semantic consistency.

In total, the authors have generated 1,246 labelled training sentences. Although this dataset is considered micro-sized, the BERT architecture, particularly its fine-tuning approach that trains only the last layer, is well-suited for handling smaller datasets [36]. The dataset was split 90/10, as the limited data made allocating a larger portion for validation impractical.

Logistics experts from the logistics institute subjectively defined process categories. The primary focus was identifying key sentence structures and their relationship to process categories rather than merely training the model to recognise a broad range of sentences. This definition ensured that the AI model remained highly relevant to logistics process classification and analysis.

5 Discussion of Results

5.1 AI Training Results

During the training phase, we interpreted the results and evaluated hyperparameter suitability against model accuracy. The model's accuracy initially declined after the first epoch, indicating that the learning rate was too high, leading to suboptimal convergence. We achieved a more stable optimisation process and improved accuracy by reducing the learning rate. The initial learning rate likely prevented the model from finding the optimal function parameters.

The initial validation loss was 0.80. Initial normalised matrix analysis indicated that categories 6 and 7 lacked sufficient distinction, leading to classification errors (Fig. 4). We reviewed and refined category definitions to address this, introducing more clearly defined sentence examples. After implementing these improvements, the validation loss decreased to 0.65, and the F1 score improved to 0.8.

The final model achieved an 80% classification accuracy, sufficient for the logistics laboratory's process categorisation needs. These results confirm that the model can effectively classify and support logistics process automation, making it a valuable tool for business process extraction within the test centre environment. However, evaluation results revealed that category three still exhibited low validation accuracy, suggesting the need for further refinement.

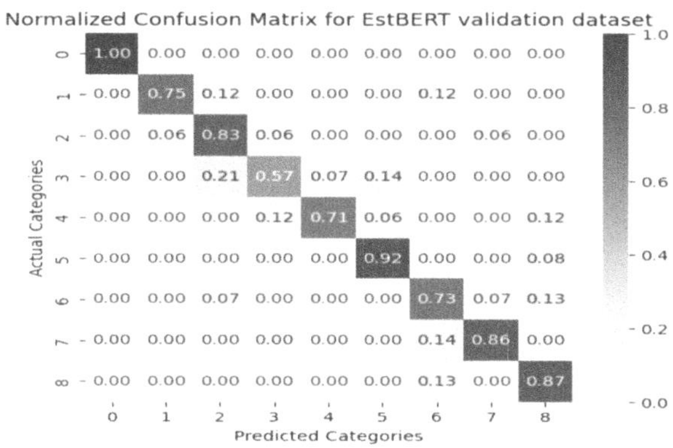

Fig. 4. EstBERT validation dataset (124 labels). A diagonal indicates good predictions.

To enhance classification precision, companies can contribute by providing additional process descriptions, particularly for category 3, thereby improving dataset quality.

Despite the model's improvements, it remains insufficient for broader generalisations due to the limited availability of training data. Expanding the dataset through logistics institute theses and process descriptions from companies participating in the test centre will be crucial for refining classification accuracy.

5.2 Case Study

The case study-based validation was chosen to demonstrate and prove both the concept of the test centre and the associated approach for classifying process categories, identifying reference process maps and KPIs, and linking them to software classes. The case study also became important because the testing centre and laboratory will serve companies providing real-life cases and datasets to refine training data.

The case study company is a logistics service provider in the transportation sector. It is a small to medium-sized enterprise employing 195 people. First, we demonstrate how we identified process categories from the company's textual documents using the previously trained EstBERT model. Then, we determine which reference process maps the company's operations should be linked to. KPIs were defined alongside the SCOR

Text: *The warehouse worker receives the goods and performs an inspection. Based on the inspection, confirmation is obtained regarding the quality of the goods, determining whether it is packaging or a product. ...*

Category ID	0	1	2	3	4	5	6	7	8
Probability	0.11	0.30	0.96	0.88	0.14	0.86	0.03	0.06	0.78

Category name	Process Subcategory (Reference model)	SCOR process
Receiving goods in the warehouse	The delivered goods are received and checked for compliance with the shipping documents.	sS1.2 - Receive Product
	Quantity and quality control ensure that only products meeting the requirements enter the warehouse.	sS1.3 - Verify Product
	The goods are entered into the warehouse software or ERP system.	sS1.2 - Receive Product

SCOR process	SCOR KPI
sS1.2 - Receive Product	RL.3.18% Orders/ Lines Processed Complete
	RL.3.20% Orders/ Lines Received On-Time to Demand Requirement
	RL.3.22 % Orders/ lines received with correct packaging
	RL.3.23% Orders/ Lines Received with Correct Shipping Documents
	RS.3.113 Receiving Product Cycle Time
sS1.3 - Verify Product	RL.3.19 % Orders/ Lines Received Defect Free
	RL.3.21 % Orders/ lines received with the correct content
	RL.3.24 % Orders/lines received damage free
	RS.3.140 Verify Product Cycle Time

Fig. 5. Case study example of classification into the most probable category with identification of reference processes, SCOR processes, and KPIs.

processes, and we identified which software classes could be used to automate these processes.

5.2.1 Case Study Results

We demonstrate how the entire chain is carried out using a company example, starting with predicting the process category based on text, followed by identifying the subcategory (reference process model). The processes must be linked to SCOR processes, after which it becomes possible to assess SCOR KPIs (Fig. 5).

The authors previously evaluated the selected text as belonging to the warehousing category, specifically in the subcategory of goods receiving. The highest-ranking category was "receiving goods in the warehouse," which is the correct classification to describe the process of receiving goods in the warehouse. The outcome of the process extraction is the basis for building a process testing model in the test centre, consisting of needed processes and KPIs. Taxonomy suggests WMS and ERP for digitalization.

6 Practical and Theoretical Contribution

This work contributes to the theoretical foundations of process mining by expanding the scope of valid input formats. It demonstrates that process descriptions articulated in natural language can be systematically interpreted as reference process models, enabling the integration of unstructured textual data into formal process analysis.

Prior studies highlight BERT's domain-specific capabilities [21, 22], and our results confirm its 80% accuracy in predicting logistics-specific process categories.

To our knowledge, AI has not been used before to set up testing centres or extract and modify processes from company texts. In contrast, process mining aims for accuracy [13], but incorrect results require reruns or adjustments. Previous research process mining has focused on data preprocessing, emphasising data processing challenges [37].

For practical contribution, our approach enables organisations to extract and analyse processes without needing dedicated process mapping efforts or generating event logs. This approach offers a more efficient and accessible alternative for organisations seeking insights into their operational workflows.

We also addressed our research questions:

RQ1: How does the AI tool speed up process mapping for the logistics laboratory?

Using EstBERT for process categorisation yields results aligned with real-world practices supported by a database of reference process models. Unlike process mining, which extracts processes from logs, our method identifies relevant processes from minimal textual descriptions, offering a significant time advantage.

From the perspective of cyber-physical systems, AI presents an opportunity to integrate the acceleration of process automation with the later physical modification of processes in a secure environment- the test centre.

RQ2: Are generic process category definitions sufficient for company business processes describing and mapping to corresponding SCOR processes and KPIs?

Although the tool developed in this study can classify groups of processes based on textual input reflecting an organisation's core operations, it also presents certain limitations. To identify SCOR KPIs, reference process models must first be mapped to SCOR processes, as only then can they be effectively linked to corresponding KPIs. One of the key challenges we foresee is the automated alignment of reference processes with SCOR processes and KPIs, which would help reduce subjectivity in the analysis. This mapping was performed manually in this study, making the task time-consuming and labour-intensive.

7 Conclusions and Future Work

This study aimed to enable faster setup of a logistics laboratory testing centre by extracting process categories from company textual documents. A key challenge is that companies often lack documented processes, requiring prior data collection before implementing a model. Traditional process extraction and mining methods are ineffective without sufficient logs, and process mining may yield incorrect results, making it unreliable.

Work has limitations, including insufficient training data, as indicated by high validation loss. Future improvements should involve extracting more process descriptions from the thesis and adopting unsupervised training to replace time-consuming manual labelling.

The study focuses on a single company, limiting its generalisability, but the introduced approach can be expanded to other domains. While this research targets logistics processes, the methodology could also apply to manufacturing, where AI-driven process categorisation would aid process description extraction.

Companies bringing textual process descriptions to the testing centre can experiment with process changes and automation. Strong reference process models are essential, especially for companies that have not mapped their processes.

Future Work. Our solution is an EstBERT-trained tool for identifying process categories, reference models, SCOR processes, and KPIs. The study revealed the need for automated linking between reference and SCOR processes. While our tool effectively classifies process groups, linking them to SCOR KPIs requires prior mapping of reference processes to SCOR models. Automating this process remains a key future challenge, as the current manual approach is time-consuming, especially for KPI selection.

References

1. Esper, T.L., Fugate, B.S., Davis-Sramek, B.: Logistics learning capability: sustaining the competitive advantage gained through logistics leverage. J. Bus. Logist. **28**, 57–82 (2007). https://doi.org/10.1002/j.2158-1592.2007.tb00058.x
2. Akbari, M., Do, T.N.A.: A systematic review of machine learning in logistics and supply chain management: current trends and future directions. Benchmark.: An Int. J. **28**(10), 2977–3005 (2021). https://doi.org/10.1108/BIJ-10-2020-0514
3. Lin, W., Liu, D.: Status and analysis of process mining algorithm classification. IEEE Inform. Technol. Netw. Electron. Autom. Control Conf. **2021**, 322–328 (2021). https://doi.org/10.1109/ITNEC52019.2021.9587033

4. Becker, T., Intoyoad, W.: Context aware process mining in logistics. Procedia CIRP **63**, 557–562 (2017). https://doi.org/10.1016/j.procir.2017.03.149
5. Ellinger, A.E., Ellinger, A.D., Keller, S.: Logistics managers' learning environments and firm performance. J, Bus. Logist. **23**(1), 19–37 (2011). https://doi.org/10.1002/j.2158-1592.2002.tb00014.x
6. Bakalo, A., Bogale, M.: Trust and collaboration in practices of supply chain management: systematic review. Am. J. Manage. Sci. Eng. **9**(3), 64–74 (2024). https://doi.org/10.11648/j.ajmse.20240903.12
7. Ho, T., Kumar, A., Shiwakoti, N.: Supply chain collaboration and performance: an empirical study of maturity model. SN Appl. Sci. (2020). https://doi.org/10.1007/s42452-020-2468-y
8. Jedliński, M., Malinowska, M., Rzeczycki, A.: The laboratory of logistics research and analysis "loglab" as an environment for modeling the professional competencies in logistics. zeszyty naukowe uniwersytetu gdańskiego. Ekonomika Transportu i Logistyka. **71**, 49–64 (2017). https://doi.org/10.5604/01.3001.0010.5723
9. Deck, C., Smith, V.: Using laboratory experiments in logistics and supply chain research. J. Bus. Logist. **34**(1), 6–14 (2013). https://doi.org/10.1111/jbl.12006
10. Tamás, P., et al.: Development possibilities of the high-tech logistics laboratory established at the institute of logistics of the university of Miskolc. J. Eng. Res. Reports (2020). https://doi.org/10.9734/jerr/2020/v13i317127
11. Zeng, Q.: Research on the necessity of building intelligent logistics laboratory in digital times. Academic J. Sci. Technol. **2**(3), 78–80 (2022). https://doi.org/10.54097/ajst.v2i3.1500
12. Uckelmann, D.: The role of logistics labs in research and higher education, pp. 1–12 (2012).. https://doi.org/10.1007/978-3-642-28816-61
13. vom Brocke, J., Jans, M., Mendling, J., Reijers, H.A.: A five-level framework for research on process mining. Bus. Inf. Syst. Eng. **63**(5), 483–490 (2021). https://doi.org/10.1007/s12599-021-00718-8
14. Dumas, M., la Rosa, M., Mendling, J., Reijers, H.A.: Fundamentals of Business Process Management. Springer Berlin Heidelberg (2018). https://doi.org/10.1007/978-3-662-56509-4
15. Bellan, P., Dragoni, M., Ghidini, C.: Extracting business process entities and relations from text using pre-trained language models and in-context learning. In: Almeida, J.P.A., Karastoyanova, D., Marco Montali, G.G., Maggi, F.M., Fonseca, C.M. (eds.) Enterprise Design, Operations, and Computing: 26th International Conference, EDOC 2022, Bozen-Bolzano, Italy, October 3–7, 2022, Proceedings, pp. 182–199. Springer International Publishing, Cham (2022). https://doi.org/10.1007/978-3-031-17604-3_11
16. Licardo, J.T., Tanković, N., Etinger, D.: A method for extracting bpmn models from textual descriptions using natural language processing. Procedia Comput. Sci. **239**, 483–490 (2024). https://doi.org/10.1016/j.procs.2024.06.196
17. Yang, B., Zhang, B., Cutsforth, K., Yu, S., Yu, X.: Emerging industry classification based on BERT model. Inform. Syst. 128, (2025). https://doi.org/10.1016/j.is.2024.102484
18. Ruder, S.: A Review of the Neural History of Natural Language Processing (2018). http://ruder.io/a-review-of-the-recent-history-of-nlp/
19. Devlin, J., Chang, M.-W., Lee, K., Google, K. T., Language, A.I.: BERT: Pre-training of Deep Bidirectional Transformers for Language Understanding (n.d.). https://github.com/tensorflow/tensor2tensor
20. Tanvir, H., Kittask, C., Eiche, S., Sirts, K.: EstBERT: a pretrained language-specific BERT for Estonian. In: Proceedings of the 23rd Nordic Conference on Computational Linguistics (NoDaLiDa), pp. 11–19. Linköping University Electronic Press, Sweden, Reykjavik, Iceland (2021)
21. Jagrič, T., Herman, A.: AI model for industry classification based on website data. Information **15**(2), 89 (2024). https://doi.org/10.3390/info15020089

22. Slavov, S., Tagarev, A., Tulechki, N., Boytcheva, S.: Company industry classification with neural and attention-based learning models. In: 2019 Big Data, Knowledge and Control Systems Engineering (BdKCSE), pp. 1–7. Sofia, Bulgaria (2019). https://doi.org/10.1109/BdKCSE48644.2019.9010667
23. Ito, T., Camacho, J., Collados, H., Sakaji, S.: Schockaert Learning company embeddings from annual reports for fine-grained industry characterization. In: Proceedings of the Second Workshop on Financial Technology and Natural Language Processing (IJCAI) (2021)
24. Ayyildiz, E., Gumus, A.T.: Interval-valued Pythagorean fuzzy AHP method-based supply chain performance evaluation by a new extension of SCOR model: SCOR 4.0. Complex Intell. Syst. **7**(1), 559–576 (2021). https://doi.org/10.1007/s40747-020-00221-9
25. Taghizadeh, H., Hafezi, E.: The investigation of supply chain's reliability measure: a case study. J. Indust. Eng. Int. **8**, 22. https://doi.org/10.1186/2251-712X-8-22
26. APICS, Supply Chain Operations Reference Model SCOR, Version 12.0, 2017 APICS
27. Jothimani, D., Sarmah, S.P.: Supply chain performance measurement for third party logistics. Benchmark.: An Int. J. **21**(6), 944–963 (2014). https://doi.org/10.1108/BIJ-09-2012-0064
28. Chae, B.: Developing key performance indicators for supply chain: an industry perspective. Supply Chain Manage.: An Int. J. **14**(6), 422–428 (2009). https://doi.org/10.1108/13598540910995192
29. Shevtshenko, E., Mahmood, K., Karaulova, T.: Enhancing the partner selection process in a sustainable partner network. IFAC-PapersOnLine **52**(13), 2425–2430 (2019). https://doi.org/10.1016/j.ifacol.2019.11.570
30. Maas, R., Karaulova, T., Shevtshenko, E., Popell, J., Raji, I.O.: Development of SCOR database for digitalisation of supply chain customer feedback analysis. Eng. Econ. **34**(4), 439–455 (2023). https://doi.org/10.5755/j01.ee.34.4.31618
31. Shevtshenko, E., Maas, R., Murumaa, L., Karaulova, T., Raji, I.O., Popell, J.: Digitalisation of supply chain management system for customer quality service improvement. J. Mach. Eng. **22**(3), 78–90 (2022)
32. Ackermann, L., Neuberger, J., Jablonski, S.: Data-Driven annotation of textual process descriptions based on formal meaning representations. In: La Rosa, M., Sadiq, S., Teniente, E. (eds.) Advanced Information Systems Engineering: 33rd International Conference, CAiSE 2021, Melbourne, VIC, Australia, 28 June–2 July 2021, Proceedings, pp. 75–90. Springer International Publishing, Cham (2021). https://doi.org/10.1007/978-3-030-79382-1_5
33. Qian, C., Wen, L., Kumar, A., Lin, L., Lin, L., Zong, Z., Li, S., Wang, J.: An approach for process model extraction by Multi-Grained text classification. In: Dustdar, S., Yu, E., Salinesi, C., Rieu, D., Pant, V. (eds.) CAiSE 2020. LNCS, vol. 12127, pp. 268–282. Springer, Cham (2020). https://doi.org/10.1007/978-3-030-49435-3_17
34. Garrido-Merchan, E.C., Gozalo-Brizuela, R., Gonzalez-Carvajal, S.: Comparing BERT against traditional machine learning models in text classification. J. Comput. Cognit. Eng. **2**(4), 352–356 (2023). https://doi.org/10.47852/bonviewJCCE3202838
35. Dspace of TTK, University of applied sciences. https://dspace.tktk.ee/collections/79b0b910-afcf-47b3-97b4-0fe04aa9bf71. Accessed 04 Jan 2025
36. Zhou, C., et al.: A comprehensive survey on pretrained foundation models: a history from BERT to ChatGPT. Int. J. Mach. Learn. Cybern. (2024). https://doi.org/10.1007/s13042-024-02443-6
37. Jokonowo, B., Rochimah, S., Claes, J., Sarno, R.: Process mining in supply chains: a systematic literature review. Int. J. Electr. Comput. Eng. (2018). https://doi.org/10.11591/ijece.v8i6.pp4626-4636

An Access Control Method Against Unauthorized and Noncompliant Behaviors Leveraging Large Language Models

Nastaran Farhadighalati(✉), Sepideh Kalateh, Luis A. Estrada-Jimenez, Sanaz Nikghadam-Hojjati, and José Barata

NOVA School of Science and Technology, Center of Technology and Systems (UNINOVA-CTS) and Associated Lab of Intelligent Systems (LASI), NOVA University Lisbon, 2829-516 Lisbon, Portugal

{nastaran.farhadi,sepideh.kalateh,lestrada,sanaznik, jab}@uninova.pt

Abstract. In today's digital world, protecting sensitive data is crucial for organizations. Traditional access control systems, which rely on fixed roles and attributes, often fail to adapt to evolving security threats. Behavior-Based Access Control (BBAC) addresses the shortcomings of conventional methods by dynamically adjusting user permissions in real time based on observed actions. To enhance BBAC, Large Language Models (LLMs) are incorporated, leveraging advanced language processing to interpret access policies, analyzing behavior patterns, and making context-aware decisions. Integrating Large Language Models (LLMs) enables the system to detect suspicious activities, such as unauthorized actions or policy violations, with greater accuracy. Consequently, BBAC systems achieve flexible and intelligent access control, balancing security with workflow efficiency. Early experiments using synthetic data confirm the model's effectiveness. The experimental results demonstrate that the model is efficient, accurate, and shows potential in detecting abnormal behaviors among authorized users.

Keywords: Behavior-Based Access Control Model · Privacy Protection · Data · Large Language Model

1 Introduction

Keeping data secure is one of organization's most important priorities in the current era of digital transformation. However, the rapid growth in data volume, increasingly sophisticated cyber threats, and the widespread adoption of remote work have exposed the limitations of traditional security approaches [1]. Balancing strong security with user-friendly workflows is essential to prevent unauthorized access while maintaining efficiency.

"Access control (AC)" is a core mechanism for protecting data and systems. It is defined as "the prevention of unauthorized use of a resource, including the prevention

Published by Springer Nature Switzerland AG 2025
L. M. Camarinha-Matos and F. Ferrada (Eds.): DoCEIS 2025, IFIP AICT 759, pp. 39–50, 2025.
https://doi.org/10.1007/978-3-031-97051-1_3

of its use in an unauthorized manner" [2]. Without effective AC, sensitive data can be compromised, leading to privacy violations, financial losses, and reputational harm. For example, in 2023, UniCredit S.p.A. faced a €2.8 million fine due to poor data security practices, underscoring the risks of weak access control [3].

Over the years, AC research has evolved to address challenges in securing distributed systems. Traditional models like Mandatory Access Control (MAC) (access determined by system policies and labels), Role-Based Access Control (RBAC) (access granted based on role), and Attribute-Based Access Control (ABAC) (access granted based on attributes) remain widely used. Recent advancements, such as machine learning (ML) and blockchain, have further improved these systems [4].

Despite progress, traditional AC models struggle in dynamic fields like healthcare and finance, where real-time adaptability is crucial. Even ML-enhanced systems rely on rigid policies and historical data, limiting their ability to respond to emerging threats.

To overcome these challenges, we propose a new approach: Behavior-Based Access Control (BBAC) enhanced by Large Language Models (LLMs). Unlike static models, BBAC dynamically evaluates user behavior, context, and historical patterns to continuously adapt access decisions. This approach enables continuous assessment of how users interact with the system, providing a more adaptive and secure access control mechanism. Integrating LLMs into BBAC offers key advantages:

- **Simplified policy management:** LLMs interpret natural language policies and convert them into actionable rules.
- **Real-time decision-making:** LLMs analyze live data to make flexible access decisions.
- **Quick adaptation to changes:** LLMs adjust to new threats and behavioral changes without full retraining.
- **Consistent enforcement:** LLMs automatically apply policies across systems, reducing errors and ensuring reliability.

To demonstrate the practicality of our framework, we provide an opensource implementation of BBAC with LLM integration on GitHub (https://github.com/nastaran-farhadi/LLM-BBAC). This repository includes code, synthetic datasets, and documentation to support replication and future extensions.

The paper is organized as follows: Section 2 describes the main contributions and explains their relevance to the conference. Section 3 reviews previous work in the field. Section 4 introduces our proposed behavior-based access control model. Section 5 outlines the implementation setup. Section 6 presents a case study and evaluation of the model. Finally, Section 7 concludes the paper with a summary.

2 Contribution to Technological Innovation for AI-Powered Cyber-Physical Systems

DoCEIS 2025 highlights the critical role of Artificial Intelligence (AI) in advancing Cyber-Physical Systems (CPS), particularly in enhancing autonomy, adaptability, and decision-making for complex environments. However, securing resource access in interconnected AI-driven CPS remains a major challenge. Traditional access control models, designed for static systems, struggle to address the dynamic and evolving nature of modern CPS, necessitating innovative AI-powered solutions that prioritize context-aware security.

To bridge this gap, we propose a Behavior-Based Access Control (BBAC) framework enhanced by Large Language Models (LLMs). Our model strengthens CPS security through three core mechanisms:

- **Continuous behavior monitoring:** Dynamically tracks user actions to identify deviations from normal patterns.
- **Real-time policy adaptation:** Adjusts access permissions instantly based on contextual data (e.g., location, time, role).
- **Unauthorized action detection:** Flags suspicious activities, such as policy violations or unusual resource access attempts.

By integrating LLMs, our approach enables smarter decision-making, reduces risks from emerging threats, and aligns with the adaptive requirements of next-generation AI-driven CPS.

3 Background and Related Work

Based on the studies summarized in Table. 1, existing Behavior-Based Access Control models have notable limitations. Trust evaluation methods depend on predefined metrics, making them rigid and unable to adapt to evolving behavioral patterns [5]. Real-time behavior monitoring is effective in dynamic environments but often overlooks the deeper intent behind user actions, reducing accuracy. Machine learning classifiers improve decision-making but struggle with unstructured data, such as natural language queries, limiting their applicability [6]. Semantic analysis enhances privacy in AC but cannot generate policies dynamically based on real-time user intent [7]. Additionally, basic NLP techniques used in AC rely on simple keyword matching, which fails to capture the full meaning of user interactions [8].

Our proposed approach, which integrates LLMs into BBAC, addresses these limitations. Unlike static trust evaluation, real-time adaptability is achieved through continuous learning from diverse data sources. Additionally, semantic analysis is enhanced, enabling more effective policy generation based on contextual awareness. Overall, a more intelligent, flexible, and context-aware access control system is ensured compared to the existing methods outlined in the table.

4 Proposed Approach

This section introduces the Behavior-Based Access Control (BBAC) model. First, the key features of BBAC are discussed, emphasizing its adaptability to user behavior and dynamic environments. A step-by-step pipeline for integrating BBAC with Large Language Models (LLMs) is then outlined, detailing the implementation process.

Table 1. Overview of reviewed Access Control models.

Ref	Main focus	Mechanism	Limitation
[9] 2023	Dynamically adjust access based on trust scores derived from user behavior in ABAC.	Trust evaluation using behavior metrics	- Relies on predefined trust metrics. - Lacks adaptability to context-aware or semantic scenarios.
[10] 2022	Adapt access policies in IoT ecosystems applied RuBAC updated via real-time behavior monitoring.	Real-time behavior monitoring	- Ignores semantic intent of user actions - Limited to structured IoT data.
[6] 2021	Integrate behavioral attributes into ABAC using ML classifiers trained on structured behavioral data.	Machine Learning classifiers	- Limited to structured data - Cannot process unstructured text (e.g., queries, documents).
[7] 2020	Preserve privacy in RBAC using semantic analysis of data sensitivity with role-based access.	Semantic analysis	- Policies lack dynamic generation based on user intent.
[5] 2017	Assess user trustworthiness in RBAC using behavioral patterns.	Trust evaluation	- Static thresholds limit adaptability to complex or evolving behavioral patterns.
[8] 2016	Combine text and behavior analysis in ABAC using basic NLP for keyword extraction paired with behavior logs.	NLP	- Relies on simple NLP (e.g., keyword matching) - Lacks advanced semantic understanding.

4.1 Behavior-Based Access Control Model

"Behavior-Based Access Control" (BBAC) is a security framework that governs resource access by dynamically evaluating users' real-time actions and contextual behaviors. Unlike traditional models relying on static roles or predefined attributes, BBAC continuously monitors user activities to enforce adaptive access decisions, enhancing security through continuous adaptation to current behavior patterns.

BBAC offers significant advantages over conventional access control systems. First, its real-time analysis of user behavior enables proactive risk mitigation, reducing the likelihood of unauthorized access and security breaches. Secondly, the framework's adaptability ensures a flexible, context-aware approach by dynamically responding to evolving environmental conditions. Additionally, BBAC simplifies regulatory compliance by aligning access controls with real-time security demands, ensuring that policies automatically adjust to meet current standards. The concept of user behavior can be used in different ways to make access control decisions. In this paper, BBAC leverages user behavior through two complementary approaches: daily behavior and historical behavior. Here is a brief explanation of each concept:

- **Daily behavior:** Daily behavior focuses on short-term actions within a 24-hour period, such as login/logout times, accessed resources, and interaction frequency. For instance, if an HR manager typically reviews employee records between 10:00 AM and 3:00 PM but suddenly logs in after midnight to repeatedly access confidential salary data, BBAC flags this anomaly and enforces multi-factor authentication.
- **Historical behavior:** Historical behavior, conversely, analyzes long-term pat-terns over weeks or months, including access frequency trends and recurring resource usage. For example, if the same HR manager - who usually accesses payroll data once a month - starts accessing it daily for weeks, BBAC detects this deviation from established norms and escalates the activity for auditing.

4.2 A Pipeline for Secure Behavior-Based Access Control Framework

The Behavior-Based Access Control (BBAC) framework is designed to leverage Large Language Models (LLMs) and Retrieval-Augmented Generation (RAG) for granting or denying access based on user behavior and contextual attributes. As illustrated in Fig. 1, the system's operation is structured into four key phases: (1) User request initiation, (2) Vector database creation & indexing, (3) Query & access control, and (4) RAG-based policy generation. A detailed description of each phase is provided in the following sections.

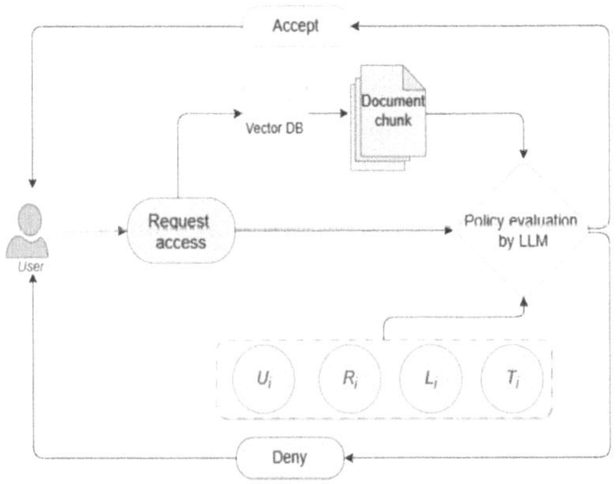

Fig. 1. Behavior-Based Access Control framework leveraging LLM.

Step 1. User request initiation: The process begins when a user submits an access request, defined by four parameters, (U_i, R_i, L_i, T_i), where:

- Identity verification (U_i): A unique identifier (e.g., username or employee ID).
- Role identification (R_i): The user's organizational role (e.g., HR Manager).
- Location tracking (L_i): Geographic/IP-based location data.

- Timestamping (T_i): The time at which the request is made, useful for temporal pattern analysis.

  These parameters enable anomaly detection; for example, if an HR Manager (R_i) attempts to access sensitive data from an unfamiliar location (L_i), the system flags the request for further review.

Step 2. Vector database creation & indexing: To organize and access information efficiently, the system converts document chunks into numerical embeddings and stores them in a vector database. This process involves two key steps:

1. *Embedding generation:* Document chunks are converted into numerical vectors (embeddings) using an LLM (e.g., gemini-2.0-pro-exp). These embeddings capture the semantic meaning of the text, enabling effective information retrieval. Formally, let

$$D = \{d_1, d_2, \ldots, d_n\} \quad (1)$$

   Denote the set of document chunks, where each chunk d_i is converted into an embedding e_i using a function f:

$$e_i = f(d_i). \quad (2)$$

   The resulting collection of embeddings is represented as

$$E = \{e_1, e_2, \ldots, e_n\}. \quad (3)$$

2. *Vector storage:* The generated embeddings are stored in a specialized vector database optimized for high-dimensional data. This database facilitates efficient similarity searches, enabling rapid retrieval of semantically related information during query processing.

Step 3. Query & access control: This phase ensures that user requests are processed with established security policies and comprises three critical steps:

1. *Contextual retrieval:* The system gathers relevant user information to understand the context of the request, including:

   - User history: Analysis of past interactions to identify usage patterns.
   - Permissions: Assessment of the user's authorized access levels.
   - Current context: Evaluation of situational factors such as location (L_i), time (T_i), and role (R_i).

     These elements are combined into a contextual vector:

$$C_i = \{U_i, R_i, L_i, T_i\}. \quad (4)$$

2. *Similarity search:* The system computes a relevance score, $S(q, e_i)$, between the user's query q and each document embedding e_i in the vector database. This score quantifies the semantic similarity between the query and the document, thereby facilitating the retrieval of information that aligns with the user's request.

3. *Initial filtering:* Access control policies are applied to the retrieved information based on the user's permissions and predefined behavior rules. This filtering ensures that only data the user is authorized to access is presented, maintaining security and compliance standards.

Step 4. Retrieval-Augmented Generation (RAG)-based policy generation: In this phase, the system leverages a RAG framework to dynamically produce access control policies that are tailored to the user's context. This approach integrates external knowledge and internal repositories with an LLM to generate precise, context-aware policies. The process involves three sequential stages:

1. *Policy retrieval:* The system retrieves relevant policy fragments or templates from external knowledge bases or internal repositories. Let

$$P = \{p_1, p_2, \ldots, p_m\} \tag{5}$$

denote the set of all available policy fragments. Given a query context

$$q = (U_i, R_i, L_i, T_i), \tag{6}$$

the retrieval process identifies a subset

$$P_q = \{p \in P : \mathrm{sim}(q, p) \geq \theta\}, \tag{7}$$

where $\mathrm{sim}(q, p)$ is a similarity function comparing the context q to each policy fragment p, and θ is a predetermined threshold.
2. *Policy generation:* The system synthesizes a complete, tailored access control policy by combining the retrieved fragments with the user's current context. This is achieved by constructing a composite prompt that integrates both the retrieved policy fragments P_q and the query context q. Formally, let $\mathrm{prompt}(P_q, q)$ denote the combined input. This prompt is then provided to an LLM to generate a new policy p^*:

$$p^* = \mathrm{LLMprompt}\big(P_q, q\big). \tag{8}$$

3. *Policy application:* The generated policy p^* is then applied to determine the user's access rights. The system evaluates the conditions specified in p^* against the user's current attributes. Define the evaluation function as

$$\text{Decision} = \begin{cases} \text{Permit, if } p^*(q) = \textit{true}, \\ \text{Deny, } \quad \text{otherwise.} \end{cases} \tag{9}$$

Here, $p^*(q)$ denotes the Boolean outcome when the generated policy p^* is applied to the query context q. This final decision governs whether the requested information is accessible to the user.

5 Implementation and Evaluation Setup

This section outlines the implementation specifics, detailing the dataset employed, the LLM model utilized, and the evaluation metrics applied in this study.

5.1 Data Preparation

The method described in Section 4.1 was applied to evaluate synthetic data. Although using actual organizational policies would have been ideal, no publicly available policies were found. Therefore, sample policies were developed to mimic those in relevant application areas, even though they were not directly taken from real-world examples.

- **Synthetic dataset generation:** To evaluate the BBAC system, we generated synthetic employee data to protect privacy. The dataset was created using the "Faker" library, which produces realistic but fake data. We began by simulating an organizational chart and then randomly generated user and resource attributes. The dataset includes details such as Name, Employee ID, Address, Phone number, and Salary.
- **Synthetic policy behavior generation:** User behavior patterns were simulated to develop the BBAC system's access control rules. In this process, policies associating user actions with permission based on their roles and behavior were created. Additionally, attributes were synthesized to model access behavior, including:

  - *Role:* Job titles (e.g., HR manager, IT support).
  - *Action:* Activities performed (e.g., Read, Write, Execute, Troubleshoot).
  - *Information type:* Categories of accessed data (e.g., user accounts, logs, financial records, HR data).
  - *Daily behavior:* Time of access and location.
  - *Historical behavior:* Frequency of past access to specific resources.

5.2 Advantages of Integrating RAG with LLM

Large Language Models (LLMs) improve our query-based access control system by better understanding user requests. In our study, the "gemini-2.0-pro-exp" model from DeepMind at Google - released in February 2025 - was used to handle various types of data such as text, images, audio, video, and code [11]. This model interprets queries like "What is John Doe's salary?" by identifying the needed information and linking it to the correct roles and permissions.

The model was integrated using the "LangChain" framework, which employs tools like "ChatGoogleGenerativeAI" [12] and "GoogleGenerativeAIEmbeddings" classes [13] to process inputs smoothly and generate context-aware responses.

Moreover, combining Retrieval-Augmented Generation (RAG) with LLMs offers many benefits. Traditional models can be costly when applied to specific areas because they are trained in general data. RAG makes these models more cost-effective and accessible by blending data retrieval with response generation to deliver accurate and relevant results. Our experiments confirm that this approach not only enhances security but also provides reliable and timely information.

5.3 Evaluation Metrics

To evaluate the effectiveness of each method, various metrics are employed, including accuracy, precision, recall, and F1-score [14].

- *Confusion matrix:* To evaluate the performance of a detection model, the first step is to create a confusion matrix. This matrix helps quantify two types of classification errors: False Positives (FP), where human-generated content is incorrectly flagged, and False Negatives (FN), where bot-generated content remains undetected, True Positives (TP), where the model correctly identifies botgenerated content as bots and True Negatives (TN) where the model correctly identifies human-generated content as humans.
- *Accuracy:* Accuracy represents the proportion of correctly classified instances in relation to the total dataset. It is a commonly used metric to determine the overall effectiveness of a classifier:

$$\text{Accuracy} = \frac{TP + TN}{TP + TN + FP + FN}. \tag{10}$$

- *Precision:* Precision measures the proportion of correctly identified positive instances among all instances predicted as positive:

$$\text{Precision} = \frac{TP}{TP + FP}. \tag{11}$$

- *Recall:* Recall indicates how many actual positive instances were correctly identified by the model:

$$\text{Recall} = \frac{TP}{TP + FN}. \tag{12}$$

- *F1-Score:* The F1-Score balances precision and recall by computing their harmonic meaning. This metric provides a single measure that accounts for both aspects:

$$\text{F1 - Score} = 2 \cdot \frac{\text{Precision} \cdot Recall}{\text{Precision} + \text{Recall}}. \tag{13}$$

These formulas ensure that the model achieves an optimal balance between protecting sensitive information and delivering accurate responses.

6 Experimental Result

6.1 Result of Sample Query

To evaluate the effectiveness of our framework, we conducted experiments using two datasets (10 and 20 policies) (Table 2) and a database of 100 employee records (including names, roles, salaries, and access logs).

Queries were executed under varying user contexts (role, time, location) to test access control decisions. For example:

!python query data.py "John Doe" "What is Tony Clark's salary?" "Working Hours" "In the Department"

When a query is issued by a user with Time and Location privileges, the system correctly returns the Salary value. In contrast, the sensitive salary information is appropriately concealed if the same query is performed by a user with Developer permissions. The result in Fig. 2 demonstrates that our framework effectively enforces context-aware, behavior-based access control, ensuring that access to sensitive information is granted only to authorized users.

Table 2. Policies sample.

Policy	Person Name	Role	Permissions	Information Access	Daily Behavior	Historical Behavior
P1	Emily Davi	Compliance Officer	Read, Monitor	Audit Logs, Access Logs, Compliance Reports: Access to audit reports for regulatory compliance, and user behavior monitoring logs.	Working Hours	Home
P2	Jane Smi	IT Support	Read, Execute, Troubleshoot	System Logs, User Accounts: Diagnostic data, system performance reports, user technical support data, but no access to confidential HR or financial in- formation.	Night Shift	Home
P3	John Doe	Administer	Read, Write, Execute, Manage Users	All Information: Access to all systems, configuration data, user accounts, logs, financial records, HR data, and authority to modify security policies, roles, and access rules.	Working Hours	In Dept.
P4	Sop Mill	Develop	Read, Write Code, Access Development Tools	Source Code, Technical Documentation, Development Data: Access to code repositories, project documentation, product blueprints, but no access to financial or employee personal data.	Night Shift	Home

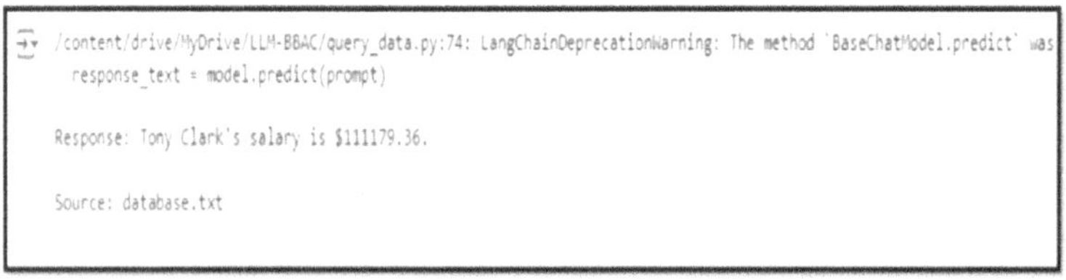

Fig. 2. Example query output demonstrating BBAC framework.

6.2 Accuracy and F1-Score Result

A confusion matrix is essential for accurately assessing the performance of a detection model. Fig. 3 provides a visual representation of a confusion matrix and its components in the context of the two policies.

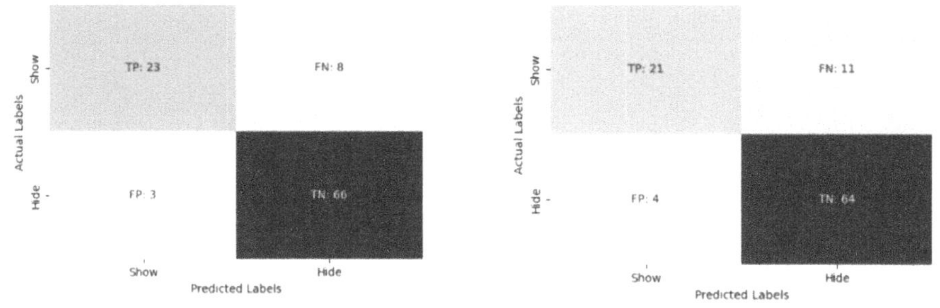

(a) (b)

Fig. 3. Confusion matrix values: (a) 10 policies and (b) 20 policies.

The system's performance was primarily evaluated using the F1-score. Unlike traditional accuracy metrics, the F1-score provides a more comprehensive understanding of a model's ability to correctly classify both positive and negative instances. Table 3 presents the results of the experiments leveraging LLM on two datasets.

Table 3. Performance of BBAC in the platform leveraging LLM.

Test Description	Accuracy	F1-score
Dataset with 10 policies	0.8891	0.8036
Dataset with 20 policies	0.8521	0.7390

7 Conclusion and Further Work

In this paper, we demonstrated the effectiveness of integrating Large Language Models (LLMs) into Behavior-Based Access Control (BBAC) systems to address modern security challenges. Our system adapts user behavior, interprets complex access policies, and enhances both security and workflow efficiency. Experimental results, including a high F-score on a semantic dataset, validate the system's reliability and its ability to overcome limitations of traditional access control methods. The system's context-aware decision-making and adaptability to evolving threats significantly reduce the risk of unauthorized access, offering a foundation for more intelligent and robust security frameworks.

Future research directions include integrating multi-modal data sources, enabling real-time learning for continuous improvement, evaluating scalability in large-scale environments, and addressing ethical and privacy concerns. These advancements will further strengthen the system's adaptability and usability in real-world applications, ensuring its relevance in dynamic digital landscapes.

Acknowledgements. This research was partly supported by EU Funded project CAIOC with Grant Agreement ID: 101190339, the Portuguese FCT program, Centre of Technology and Systems (CTS) CTS/00066, and Nova University Lisbon's PhD program of Department of Electronics and Computer Engineering.

References

1. Jain, P., Gyanchandani, M., Khare, N.: Big data privacy: a technological perspective and review. J. Big Data **3**, 1–25 (2016)
2. Mohamed, A.K.Y.S., Auer, D., Hofer, D., K u¨ng, J.: A systematic literature review for authorization and access control: definitions, strategies and models. Int. J. web Inform. Syst. **18**(2/3), 156–180 (2022)
3. IAPP: Garante fines bank for data breach, https://iapp.org/news/b/garante-fines-bank-for-data-breach
4. Farhadighalati, N., Estrada-Jimenez, L.A., Nikghadam-Hojjati, S., Barata, J.: A systematic review of access control models: Background, existing research, and challenges. IEEE Access (2025)
5. Jing, X., Liu, Z., Li, S., Qiao, B., Tan, G.: A cloud-user behavior assessment based dynamic access control model. Int. J. Syst. Assur. Eng. Manage. **8**, 1966–1975 (2017)
6. Afshar, M., Samet, S., Usefi, H.: Incorporating behavior in attribute based access control model using machine learning. In: 2021 IEEE International Systems Conference (SysCon), pp. 1–8. IEEE (2021)
7. Chen, A., Lu, G., Xing, H., Xie, Y., Yuan, S.: Dynamic and semantic-aware access-control model for privacy preservation in multiple data center environments. Int. J. Distribut. Sensor Netw. **16**(5), 1550147720921778 (2020)
8. Lu, Z., Sagduyu, Y.: Risk assessment based access control with text and behavior analysis for document management. In: MILCOM 2016-2016 IEEE Military Communications Conference, pp. 37–42. IEEE (2016)
9. Zhang, H., Wen, G., Liu, D., Dong, G.: A dynamic access control method based on user behavior trust evaluation in edge cloud environment. In: Proceedings of the 2023 3rd Guangdong-Hong Kong-Macao Greater Bay Area Artificial Intelligence and Big Data Forum, pp. 92–97 (2023)
10. Zhang, X.: Dynamic access control model based on user access behavior in the internet of things environment. In: 2022 4th International Conference on Frontiers Technology of Information and Computer (ICFTIC), pp. 1020–1023. IEEE (2022)
11. Kavukcuoglu, K.: Gemini 2.0 is now available to everyone, https://blog.google/technology/google-deepmind/gemini-model-updates-february-2025/
12. LangChain, I.: Chatgooglegenerativeai, https://python.langchain.com/docs/integrations/chat/google_generative_ai/?utm_source=chatgpt.com
13. LangChain, I.: Google generative ai embeddings, https://python.langchain.com/docs/integrations/text_embedding/google_generative_ai/?utm_source=chatgpt.com
14. Ouyang, L., et al.: Training language models to follow instructions with human feedback. Adv. Neural Inform. Process. Syst. **35**, 27730–27744 (2022)

A Pattern-Based Approach to Data Privacy in Business Processes

Lukas Waidelich(✉) and Thomas Schuster

Pforzheim University, Tiefenbronner Str. 65, 75175 Pforzheim, Germany
{Lukas.Waidelich,Thomas.Schuster}@hs-pforzheim.de

Abstract. Privacy protection is a fundamental right in the EU, codified in regulations such as the GDPR, and a key prerequisite for developing compliant AI-powered Cyber-Physical Systems. However, its complexity poses major implementation challenges for organizations. Privacy Patterns (PP) offer best practices for addressing privacy concerns, but critical gaps remain: missing legal links, fragmented knowledge, limited centralized access, and insufficient guidance for selection and application. This research introduces the early-stage conceptual framework, the Data & Process Privacy Pattern Model (DPPPM), to bridge these gaps by linking PP to GDPR requirements, while illustrating best practices through privacy workflows. The DPPPM is embedded within a PP Toolkit, featuring a centralized online catalog with context-sensitive selection capabilities. Initial evaluations indicate that privacy workflows based on this framework support privacy-by-design, connecting legal obligations with operational processes and enhancing data protection in business processes and information systems.

Keywords: Data Privacy · Privacy Patterns · Privacy Workflows · Data & Process Privacy Pattern Model · EU GDPR

1 Introduction to Data Privacy

The information age has unleashed a surge in digital data processing, powering new business models and disruptive technologies. Yet as data analytics drive innovation, they also heighten risks like surveillance, identity theft, and data loss. Strong privacy protection is essential [1], pushing organizations to embed robust safeguards into their information systems (IS) and business processes. Since the EU GDPR [2] came into force, the demand for effective data protection has soared. Today, privacy is not just a legal obligation — it is a catalyst for innovation, user trust, and technology adoption. Especially for AI-powered Cyber-Physical Systems (CPS), privacy forms the foundation for compliance, resilience, and public acceptance. However, the data-driven nature of AI intensifies the pressure on organizations to overcome the challenge of turning complex regulations into actionable, compliant solutions.

We consider Privacy Patterns (PP) as a key approach to embedding privacy into business processes, IS and as an underlying prerequisite for enabling compliant AI-powered CPS. PP provide best practices to support core privacy principles like data

Published by Springer Nature Switzerland AG 2025
L. M. Camarinha-Matos and F. Ferrada (Eds.): DoCEIS 2025, IFIP AICT 759, pp. 51–62, 2025.
https://doi.org/10.1007/978-3-031-97051-1_4

minimization, purpose limitation, and storage limitation, in line with GDPR Article 25 on privacy by design [2]. As digital technologies advance, the role of PP will become even more critical, requiring continuous adaptation by developers, legal experts, and organizations. In our view, PP offer an effective means to bridge the gap between privacy legislation and the practical implementation of processes and systems.

Our analysis [3–7] shows that existing PP face key weaknesses limiting their broader application. Hundreds of PP exist, varying widely in structure, goals, detail, and scope. Major challenges include weak links to legal requirements (e.g., GDPR), lack of procedural guidance and curated online catalogs, no systematic support for selecting relevant PP, and few concrete implementations in business processes and IS. The doctoral research addresses these challenges, summarized in the following research question (RQ):

- RQ1: How can a structured framework for Privacy Patterns support the GDPR-compliant design of business processes?

This work is structured as follows: First, it explores how data privacy enables compliant AI-powered CPS. It then reviews PP research, identifying key insights and gaps. The core contribution introduces the early-stage Data & Process Privacy Pattern Model (DPPPM) for embedding privacy into business processes and IS. The final section outlines current progress, emphasizing that substantial development and practical evaluation are still ahead.

2 Data Privacy in AI-Powered Cyber-Physical System

CPS underpin modern industrial and technological applications, integrating software with mechanical components for real-time data exchange and system control. These systems include mobile installations, devices, machinery, embedded systems, and interconnected objects. However, traditional CPS lack autonomous intelligence, limiting their ability to adapt dynamically in complex environments. This constraint reduces their effectiveness in scenarios requiring real-time decision-making and process optimization [8, 9]. Advances in AI, particularly transformer-based architectures, have significantly enhanced CPS capabilities. Originally developed for natural language processing, transformer models demonstrate scalability and adaptability across various domains. Their self-attention mechanism enables efficient analysis of complex patterns, making them valuable for predictive maintenance, anomaly detection, and autonomous decision-making in CPS. AI Agents, powered by transformers, go beyond data processing by generating and executing adaptive strategies based on contextual understanding. This enables CPS to operate more efficiently and autonomously, optimizing processes in industries such as manufacturing, logistics, and infrastructure management [10]. Despite these benefits, AI-powered CPS introduce challenges related to data privacy, security, and regulatory compliance. AI models depend on vast training datasets, making them susceptible to intellectual property concerns, biases, and privacy breaches. Problematic data inputs can propagate systemic risks, necessitating robust oversight and governance. The complexity of retraining AI models further complicates risk mitigation, requiring comprehensive data management strategies and ethical frameworks. Regulatory frameworks such as the EU GDPR and the EU AI Act provide essential guidelines for responsible AI deployment. These regulations translate legal principles into actionable requirements, promoting transparency, fairness, and accountability in AI systems. Rather than hindering innovation, strong data protection measures support sustainable AI-driven CPS by fostering societal trust and compliance. Integrating AI into CPS must balance technological advancement with legal obligations. Embedding privacy-centric methodologies and regulatory compliance into AI-driven CPS fosters resilient and responsible ecosystems. The convergence of transformer-based AI agents and CPS signals a new era of industrial automation, where intelligent, adaptive systems optimize processes while upholding societal values and legal standards [1, 10].

3 Current State of Privacy Patterns Research on...

A pattern can be defined as a structured blueprint offering a generalized strategy for solving recurring problems within a specific context. Originating in architecture [11, 12] the concept was later adopted in software development by the Gang of Four, who applied it to object-oriented design, providing structured solutions to recurring challenges in information systems [13]. Patterns are commonly organized into catalogs that group them thematically to support their application in relevant domains [14]. In this context, Pattern Language and Pattern System describe structured relationships between patterns: a Pattern System [13] denotes a set of interrelated patterns within a domain, while a Pattern Language [11] offers a systematic framework for their combination and application. Terminology usage varies depending on the discipline and author.

PP and their approaches are part of a broader discourse, explored further in the next sections. The insights presented build on the external systematic literature review by Lenhard et al.[15], and our own more comprehensive review [6].

3.1 Pattern Taxonomy

Taxonomies are crucial for structuring and categorizing concepts based on defined criteria. In PP research, they enable the systematic classification of PP, promoting a shared understanding and facilitating their application across different contexts. Two key contributions to PP taxonomy are *Privacy Design Strategies* [16] and *A Critical Analysis of Privacy Design Strategies* [17]], which introduce Privacy Design Strategies (PDS) and Privacy Design Tactics (PDT) as recognized frameworks for classifying PP.

PDS represent high-level architectural principles that integrate privacy into system design, aligning with the *Privacy by Design* concept, while PDT offer practical, lower-level measures to implement these strategies. PP can be classified into both levels: PDS define overarching principles, and PDT specify actionable steps supporting them. The literature identifies eight PDS and 25 PDT, systematically categorized in Table 1.

For example, tactics such as *exclude*, *select*, *strip*, and *destroy* align with the *Minimize* strategy, aiming to reduce data exposure. Specifically, the *Minimize* strategy seeks to limit personal data usage by excluding, selecting, removing, or destroying unnecessary data, while *Exclude* refers to refraining from processing an individual's personal data through mechanisms like blacklisting or opt-outs.

Table 1. Privacy Design Strategies (bold) by Privacy Design Tactics (italic) [17].

Minimize	Hide	Separate	Abstract (Aggregate)
Exclude Select Strip Destroy	Restrict Mix Obfuscate Dissociate	Distribute Isolate	Summarize Group
Inform	Control	Enforce	Demonstrate
Supply Notify Explain	Consent Choose Update Retract	Create Maintain Uphold	Log Audit Report

Refinements of privacy taxonomies include Caiza et al. [18], who analyze PP relationships within a structured system. Colesky et al. [19] map 155 GDPR-based forces to existing PP, enhancing legal applicability. Al-Momani et al. [20] add classification criteria based on privacy objectives and scope. Colesky [21] consolidates and integrates taxonomies, contributing to a standardized PP framework.

3.2 Privacy Patterns

We define PP as structured blueprints offering generalized, reusable solutions to protect individuals' privacy rights. Research in this field is largely driven by regulatory mandates and societal concerns over digital privacy. External and own Literature reviews [6, 15] identify over 300 existing PP, though the research remains fragmented and lacks contextual integration, limiting its practical impact. Nevertheless, these works have the potential to form a cohesive pattern system or language, supporting a more systematic approach to privacy protection.

Literature categorizes PP into four types: Conventional Patterns, Anti-Patterns, Dark Patterns, and Threat Patterns, each offering a distinct perspective on privacy. Details are provided in Table 2. While all patterns focus on privacy, Dark Patterns and Threat Patterns highlight undesirable behaviors, helping to identify risks and strengthen privacy strategies.

Table 2. Overview of Privacy Pattern Types.

Pattern Type	Description/Example/Sources
Pattern	Patterns define a problem within a specific context and provide a reusable solution [11]. For instance, the 'Storage Limitation' pattern enforces data retention limits, ensuring irreversible deletion or anonymization through technical measures like a data lifecycle model. [22]

(continued)

Table 2. (*continued*)

Pattern Type	Description/Example/Sources
Anti Pattern	An Anti Pattern includes ineffective practices to avoid, suggesting alternative solutions. For example, the 'Privacy Policy' Anti Pattern shows how users rarely read policies due to impracticality, while their presence may falsely imply trust in an organization's data practices. [23–25]
Dark Pattern	A Dark Pattern manipulates users through misleading experiences, often compromising privacy. For example, 'Privacy Zuckering' involves complex or confusing privacy settings, causing frustration or unintended user actions.[26, 27]
Threat Pattern	A Threat Pattern identifies privacy vulnerabilities and suggests countermeasures. For example, 'Vulnerable Data in Motion' highlights risks in NoSQL databases distributing data globally, emphasizing the need for secure data transfer to prevent exposure. [28, 29]

3.3 Privacy Patterns

PP are rarely considered individually; they are typically organized into catalogs to foster structured classification and practical use. Repositories like www.privacypatterns.org, offer curated collections, partially drawing on the taxonomy outlined in Section 3.1 (e.g., PDS, but not PDT). While such catalogs improve accessibility and consistency, they usually present a limited selection and differ in thematic focus, such as standardization [30], IoT applications [31], or dark patterns [26, 32].

3.4 Privacy Pattern System

PP systems define structured interrelationships and dependencies among individual PP, offering a comprehensive framework for addressing privacy challenges. Extensive systems have been developed by Colesky et al. [33] and Boesch and Papoutsakis [34], focusing particularly on the PDS of inform and control [21]. While these works provide valuable theoretical insights, they lack practical validation, such as external evaluation in business processes and IS.

3.5 Modeling and Notation

The modeling of PP within business processes is discussed in the literature, covering conceptual ideas [35], methodological approaches [36] and evaluated implementations [37], often leveraging standardized modeling frameworks like BPMN to structure workflows and interactions. Some approaches extend beyond software development [38] to process-oriented applications, including Workflow PP [39].

3.6 Current Challenges

A review of secondary literature and independent research [4, 6, 15] reveals that, despite numerous foundational works on PP, several challenges persist. PP are intended to offer practical benefits by enabling effective data protection in IS and business processes, thus meeting legal requirements. However, many PP remain largely theoretical and are not easily accessible to key stakeholders such as software developers, data protection officers, and system users. This issue can be analyzed from three perspectives:

1. Provision (Where): Although valuable preliminary work on PP exists, these patterns are rarely made accessible. Online catalogs, such as www.privacypatterns.org, offer only about 70 patterns—merely a fraction of the existing body of work—and are primarily academic in nature, requiring prior domain knowledge to be effectively utilized by neutral users.
2. Selection (What): Even when PP are available, users face the critical challenge of determining which PP are relevant to their specific problems to obtain a good-practice solution. Our research did not identify any systematic selection criteria for PP. While some platforms allow filtering by PDS and display interdependencies, they fall short of providing problem-specific guidance.
3. Application (How): There is a clear need to bridge the gap between legal frameworks—such as the GDPR—and their integration into business processes and IS (a top-down approach) and identifying PP that address specific legal requirements within existing business processes or IS (a bottom-up approach). In other words, starting with a given process or system, it is essential to determine which PP can be applied to meet relevant legal obligations. Our research did not reveal a coherent framework that effectively connects PP with specific legislation and practical application.

These challenges underscore the necessity for further work to integrate, systematize, and validate PP, to support compliance with regulatory requirements.

4 Data and Process Privacy Pattern Model: From Legislation to Application

To address these outlined challenges, we propose developing a comprehensive PP Toolkit, centered on the DPPPM and made accessible through an PP online catalog. The toolkit supports three key aspects: Provision—ensuring broad access to PP; Selection—using context-sensitive approach to identify relevant PP; and Application—showcasing best practice workflows and linking legal requirements to practical use. The DPPPM forms the theoretical foundation of this research and constitutes a novel contribution (A brief overview of the PP Toolkit, its components, and architecture will be provided in the Outlook section.):

Figure 1 introduces the DPPPM and its six elements, arranged in a hierarchical structure that progresses top-down from abstract to concrete. At the highest level, Laws and Guidelines (see 4.1) defines the overarching legal context, subject to ongoing change. Below are Principles (see 4.2), which function as broad maxims. Strategies (see 4.3) follow, aligning with legislation and guiding principles to pursue overarching privacy goals. These strategies are further operationalized by Tactics (see 4.4), translating them into concrete actions. PP (see 4.5) act as privacy blueprints, each addressing at least one strategy and one or more tactics. Standardized business processes, represented as concrete

Workflows (see 4.6), can integrate multiple PP as best practices, thereby fulfilling tactics and strategies, adhering to guiding principles, and meeting legislative requirements. This hierarchy directly addresses the Application challenge.

The six elements are detailed in the following sections and illustrated through a specific privacy workflow in Fig. 2. By linking legislation, principles, strategies, tactics, PP, and workflows, this research provides a comprehensive model that addresses challenges and enhances privacy protection in business processes and IS.

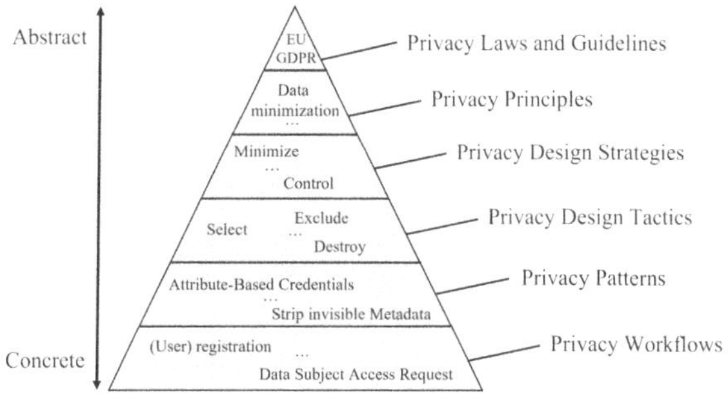

Fig. 1. Conceptual Presentation of the Data & Process Privacy Pattern Model.

4.1 Privacy Laws and Guidelines

The EU GDPR [2] applies to all EU member states and to any organization processing personal data. Since its adoption in 2016, the GDPR has established a uniform and high standard of data protection across the European Union, standardizing requirements and strengthening the rights of data subjects. It is built on fundamental principles such as transparency, purpose limitation, data minimization, and the integrity and confidentiality of personal data. Due to its comprehensive scope, the GDPR serves as the primary legal framework for privacy law and guidelines within the DPPPM.

4.2 Privacy Laws and Guidelines

Several authoritative works define key privacy principles relevant to the DPPPM. The ISO/IEC 29100 Privacy Framework [40] provides a high-level model outlining concepts such as consent, collection limitation, and data integrity, serving as a blueprint for implementing privacy controls in IS. The OECD Guidelines [41] articulate internationally recognized principles—like collection limitation, purpose specification, use limitation, and accountability—that have shaped national and international regulations. The seven Privacy by Design principles [42] propose a proactive approach to embedding privacy into system architecture from the outset, emphasizing default privacy settings, end-to-end security throughout the data lifecycle, and transparency to ensure that privacy is integral to system design and operation.

4.3 Privacy Design Strategies

The DPPPM includes the eight PDS (introduced in the 3.1 Pattern Taxonomy). Four of these strategies—Minimize, Hide, Separate, Abstract/Aggregate—are oriented towards the data level (Focus on IS), emphasizing technical measures for privacy protection. In contrast, the remaining four—Inform, Control, Enforce, Demonstrate—operate at the process level (Focus on business processes), focusing primarily on organizational measures. These eight PDS facilitate the classification of overarching privacy principles as well as relevant laws and guidelines, thereby serving as directional indicators for the effectiveness of PP [16].

4.4 Privacy Design Strategies

The DPPPM draws on the 25 PDT (presented in 3.1 Pattern Taxonomy). These tactics further refine the PDS, enabling a more granular classification of PP. In complex domains such as privacy, tactics provide an effective means to differentiate and analyze the specific mechanisms and objectives of PP [17]. However, the categorization and delineation of individual PP within the PDT framework is not always clear-cut, with some tactics exhibiting fluid boundaries between PDT categories.

4.5 Privacy Design Strategies

At the core of the DPPPM are over 300 identified and analyzed PP (classified into PDS and PDT) [6, 7] from our systematic literature review [6], which must be further assigned into Privacy Laws and Guidelines, and Principles. Each PP will be systematically evaluated for clarity, practicality, and relevance; those meeting the criteria will be included in the DPPPM. The interrelationships among PP will also be analyzed to construct a PP system, with gaps addressed through the development of new patterns. This approach aims to provide a comprehensive suite of privacy solutions.

4.6 Privacy Design Strategies

The implementation of PP in business processes and IS is operationalized through standardized privacy workflows. The central idea is to model recurring processes—such as user registration, data subject access requests, or account deletion—and strategically integrate relevant PP at critical decision or interaction points. This approach builds upon the work of Russell et al. [43], who introduced the concept of workflow patterns as a method for structuring business activities. An initial demonstration of this concept is presented in Fig. 2, which illustrates a user registration process modeled using BPMN. Within the workflow, the decision step Consent to Privacy Policy (indicated by a black circle) references the PP Appropriate Privacy Feedback, which is aligned with Article 7 of the GDPR. Additional relevant PP are depicted by dark gray circles, exemplifying how multiple PP can be systematically embedded into a structured business process to enhance privacy compliance.

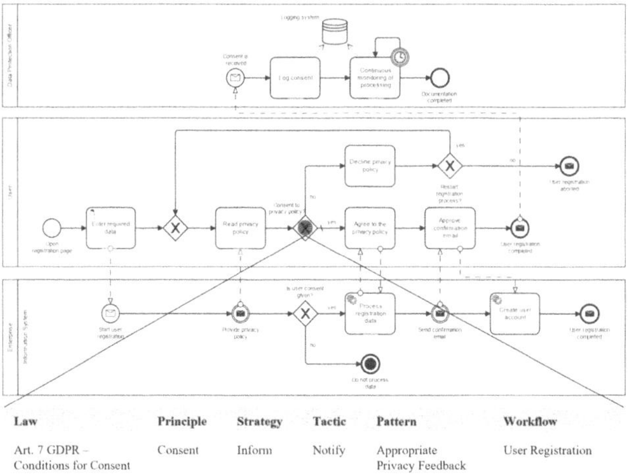

Fig. 2. Exemplary PP Use Case in a GDPR-Compliant User Registration Workflow.

5 Conclusions and Further Work

This contribution details the current state of the research and doctoral project. Through a systematic review, over 300 PP were identified, analyzed, and partly classified within PDS and PDT, as outlined in Section 4. The DPPPM was introduced as a framework organizing PP across six hierarchical levels, with further work needed on Guidelines, Principles, and Workflow elements. An evaluation framework is also being developed to assess the suitability of the identified PP, as not all patterns are expected to provide added value [4]. The concrete example offers a first glimpse of how PP can later be visualized and applied within business process workflows.

Further, we plan to develop the PP Toolkit: Once the theoretical foundations are established, they will undergo practical evaluation through testing and validation and be made publicly accessible via an online PP catalog. This catalog may initially be published through our tech blog (https://futurelab.hs-pforzheim.de/), which runs on WordPress, or alternatively as a cross-platform tool to allow greater context-sensitivity and flexibility. That will not only provide access to DPPPM but also serve as an interactive framework, offering a context-sensitive, question-driven selection approach to enhance usability. In addition, as online catalog representation, the PP Toolkit is intended for integration into BPMN software, serving as both a blueprint for designing privacy-aware processes and an explanatory tool guiding the systematic application of privacy. While significant work remains, this approach addresses the major challenges identified: Provision (where to access PP), Selection (which PP to use), and Application (how to implement them). By this, the project aims to integrate PP into operational business processes and IS, enhancing GDPR compliance (answering RQ1). Ultimately, this will strengthen data protection and enable privacy-aware AI-driven CPS.

References

1. Fayayola, O.A., Olorunfemi, O.L., Shoetan, P.O.: Data privacy and security in it: a review of techniques and challenges. Comput. sci. IT res. j. **5**, 606–615 (2024). https://doi.org/10.51594/csitrj.v5i3.909
2. Regulation (EU) 2016/679 of the European Parliament and of the Council of 27 April 2016 on the protection of natural persons with regard to the processing of personal data and on the free movement of such data, and repealing Directive 95/46/EC (General Data Protection Regulation). Regulation (EU) 2016/679 (2016)
3. Waidelich, L., Schuster, T.: Exploring the Maturity of Privacy Patterns:. A Case Study. In: AMCIS 2024 Proceedings, vol. (2024)
4. Waidelich, L., Lambert, M., Schuster, T.: Evaluating privacy patterns within collaborative frameworks for AI ecosystem development. In: Camarinha-Matos, L.M., Ortiz, A., Boucher, X., Barthe-Delanoë, A.-M. (eds.) Navigating Unpredictability: Collaborative Networks in Non-linear Worlds: 25th IFIP WG 5.5 Working Conference on Virtual Enterprises, PRO-VE 2024, Albi, France, October 28–30, 2024, Proceedings, Part I, pp. 189–206. Springer Nature Switzerland, Cham (2024). https://doi.org/10.1007/978-3-031-71739-0_13
5. Waidelich, L., Schuster, T.: Privacy pattern catalog approach for GDPR compliant appliance: from legal requirements to technology design. In: Maślankowski, J., Marcinkowski, B., da Cunha, P.R. (eds.) Digital Transformation: 15th PLAIS EuroSymposium on Digital Transformation, PLAIS EuroSymposium 2023, Sopot, Poland, September 28, 2023, Proceedings, pp. 88–102. Springer Nature Switzerland, Cham (2023). https://doi.org/10.1007/978-3-031-43590-4_6
6. Waidelich, L., Schuster, T.: Literature Review on Privacy Patterns: Insights, Challenges and Future Directions. In: ACIS 2023 Proceeding, vol. 37 (2023)
7. Waidelich, L., Schuster, T.: Privacy patterns analysis: a classification by types, strategies and tactics of existing patterns. In: AMCIS 2024 Proceedings, vol. (2024)
8. Kim, H., Ben-Othman, J.: Toward integrated virtual emotion system with AI applicability for secure CPS-enabled smart cities: ai-based research challenges and security issues. IEEE Netw. **34**, 30–36 (2020). https://doi.org/10.1109/MNET.011.1900299
9. Fulton, N., Platzer, A.: Safe AI for CPS (Invited Paper). In: 2018 IEEE International Test Conference (ITC), pp. 1–7. IEEE (2018). https://doi.org/10.1109/TEST.2018.8624774
10. Yang, E., Beil, C.: Ensuring data privacy in AI/ML implementation. New. Drctns Hghr. Edu. **2024**, 63–78 (2024). https://doi.org/10.1002/he.20509
11. Alexander, C., Ishikawa, S., Silverstein, M., Jacobson, M., King, I.F., Angel, S.: A Pattern Language – Towns Buildings Construction. Oxford University Press, Oxford (1977)
12. Alexander, C., Ishikawa, S., Silverstein, M., Czech, M., Jacobson, M., King, I.F.: Eine Muster-Sprache. Städte, Gebäude. Konstruktion, Wien (1995)
13. Gamma, E., Helm, R., Johnson, R., Vlissides, J.: Design patterns: elements of reusable object-oriented software. Pearson Deutschland GmbH (1995)
14. Huth, D.: A Pattern Catalog for GDPR Compliant Data Protection. PoEM Doctoral Consortium, vol. 34–40 (2017)
15. Lenhard, J., Fritsch, L., Herold, S.: A literature study on privacy patterns research. In: 2017 43rd Euromicro Conference on Software Engineering and Advanced Applications (SEAA), pp. 194–201. IEEE (2017). https://doi.org/10.1109/SEAA.2017.28
16. Hoepman, J.-H.: Privacy design strategies. In: Cuppens-Boulahia, N., Cuppens, F., Jajodia, S., El Kalam, A.A., Sans, T. (eds.) ICT Systems Security and Privacy Protection, pp. 446–459. Springer Berlin Heidelberg, Berlin, Heidelberg (2014). https://doi.org/10.1007/978-3-642-55415-5_38

17. Colesky, M., Hoepman, J.-H., Hillen, C.: A Critical Analysis of Privacy Design Strate-gies. In: 2016 IEEE Security and Privacy Workshops (SPW), pp. 33–40. IEEE (2016). https://doi.org/10.1109/SPW.2016.23
18. Caiza, J.C., Martín, Y.-S., Del Alamo, J.M., Guamán, D.S.: Organizing design patterns for privacy. In: Proceedings of the 22nd European Conference on Pattern Languages of Programs, pp. 1–11. ACM, New York, NY, USA (2017). https://doi.org/10.1145/3147704.3147739
19. Colesky, M., Demetzou, K., Fritsch, L., Herold, S.: Helping software architects familiarize with the general data protection regulation. In: 2019 IEEE International Conference on Software Architecture Companion (ICSA-C), pp. 226–229. IEEE (2019). https://doi.org/10.1109/ICSA-C.2019.00046
20. Al-Momani, A., Wuyts, K., Sion, L., Kargl, F., Joosen, W., Erb, B., Bösch, C.: Land of the lost: privacy patterns' forgotten properties. In: Hung, C.-C., Hong, J., Bechini, A., Song, E. (eds.) Proceedings of the 36th Annual ACM Symposium on Applied Computing, pp. 1217–1225. ACM, New York, NY, USA (2021). https://doi.org/10.1145/3412841.3441996
21. Colesky, M.: Patterns for Privacy. Data Subject Right Blueprints for Privacy Engineers. Nijmegen, Netherlands (2021)
22. Colesky, M., Caiza, J.C., Del Álamo, J.M., Hoepman, J.-H., Martín, Y.-S.: A system of privacy patterns for user control. In: Haddad, H.M., Wainwright, R.L., Chbeir, R. (eds.) Proceedings of the 33rd Annual ACM Symposium on Applied Computing, pp. 1150–1156. ACM, New York, NY, USA (2018). https://doi.org/10.1145/3167132.3167257
23. Doty, N., Gupta, M.: Privacy Design Patterns and Anti-Patterns. Patterns Misapplied and Unintended Consequences. A Turn for the Worse: Trustbusters for User Interfaces Workshop, vol. 1–5 (2013)
24. Shastri, S., Wasserman, M., Chidambaram, V.: GDPR Anti-Patterns: How Design and Operation of Modern Cloud-scale Systems Conflict with GDPR. arXiv (2019)
25. Gabel, A., Schiering, I.: Privacy patterns for pseudonymity. In: Kosta, E., Pierson, J., Slamanig, D., Fischer-Hübner, S., Krenn, S. (eds.) Privacy and Identity Management. Fairness, Accountability, and Transparency in the Age of Big Data: 13th IFIP WG 9.2, 9.6/11.7, 11.6/SIG 9.2.2 International Summer School, Vienna, Austria, August 20-24, 2018, Revised Selected Papers, pp. 155–172. Springer International Publishing, Cham (2019). https://doi.org/10.1007/978-3-030-16744-8_11
26. Bösch, C., Erb, B., Kargl, F., Kopp, H., Pfattheicher, S.: Tales from the dark side: privacy dark strategies and privacy dark patterns. Proc. Privacy Enhanc. Technol. **2016**, 237–254 (2016). https://doi.org/10.1515/popets-2016-0038
27. Fritsch, L.: Privacy dark patterns in identity management. In: Fritsch, L., Roßnagel, H., Hühnlein, D., Gesellschaft für Informatik e. V. Bonn, G.f.I.e.V. (eds.) GI Edition Proceedings Band 277 "Open Identity Summit 2017". 5.-6. October 2017 Karlstad, Sweden. GI-Edition. Proceedings. Köllen, Bonn (2017)
28. Goel, K., ter Hofstede, A.H.M.: Privacy-breaching patterns in NoSQL databases. IEEE Access **9**, 35229–35239 (2021). https://doi.org/10.1109/ACCESS.2021.3062034
29. Deng, M., Wuyts, K., Scandariato, R., Preneel, B., Joosen, W.: A privacy threat analysis framework: supporting the elicitation and fulfillment of privacy requirements. Requirements Eng **16**, 3–32 (2011). https://doi.org/10.1007/s00766-010-0115-7
30. Drozd, O.: Privacy pattern catalogue: a tool for integrating privacy principles of ISO/IEC 29100 into the software development process. In: Aspinall, D., Camenisch, J., Hansen, M., Si Fischer-Hübner, C., Raab, (eds.) Privacy and Identity Management. Time for a Revolution?: 10th IFIP WG 9.2, 9.5, 9.6/11.7, 11.4, 11.6/SIG 9.2.2 International Summer School, Edinburgh, UK, August 16-21, 2015, Revised Selected Papers, pp. 129–140. Springer International Publishing, Cham (2016). https://doi.org/10.1007/978-3-319-41763-9_9

31. Fernandez, E.B., Washizaki, H., Yoshioka, N., Okubo, T.: The design of secure IoT applications using patterns: State of the art and directions for research. Internet of Things **15**, 100408 (2021). https://doi.org/10.1016/j.iot.2021.100408
32. Boesch, C., Erb, B., Kargl, F., Kopp, H., Pfattheicher, S.: Dark .privacy patterns.eu (2016), https://dark.privacypatterns.eu/
33. Colesky, M., et al.: Patterns (2018), https://privacypatterns.org/patterns/
34. Papoutsakis, M., Fysarakis, K., Spanoudakis, G., Ioannidis, S., Koloutsou, K.: Towards a collection of security and privacy patterns. Appl. Sci. **11**, 1396 (2021). https://doi.org/10.3390/app11041396
35. Buchmann, E., Anke, J.: Privacy Patterns in Business Processes. INFORMATIK 2017, pp. 793–798 (2017). https://doi.org/10.18420/in2017_79
36. Diamantopoulou, V., Argyropoulos, N., Kalloniatis, C., Gritzalis, S.: Supporting the design of privacy-aware business processes via privacy process patterns. In: 2017 11th International Conference on Research Challenges in Information Science (RCIS), pp. 187–198. IEEE (2017). https://doi.org/10.1109/RCIS.2017.7956536
37. Barati, M., Rana, O.: Design and verification of privacy patterns for business process models. In: Patnaik, S., Wang, T.-S., Shen, T., Kumar Panigrahi, S. (eds.) Blockchain Technology and Innovations in Business Processes, pp. 125–139. Springer Singapore, Singapore (2021). https://doi.org/10.1007/978-981-33-6470-7_8
38. Fernandez, E.B., Yoshioka, N., Washizaki, H.: Patterns for security and privacy in cloud ecosystems. In: 2015 IEEE 2nd Workshop on Evolving Security and Privacy Requirements Engineering (ESPRE), pp. 13–18. IEEE (2015). https://doi.org/10.1109/ESPRE.2015.7330162
39. Robak, M., Buchmann, E.: Deriving workflow privacy patterns from legal documents. In: Proceedings of the 2019 Federated Conference on Computer Science and Information Systems. Annals of Computer Science and Information Systems, pp. 555–563. IEEE (2019). https://doi.org/10.15439/2019F275
40. ISO: ISO/IEC 29100:2024 Information technology – Security techniques – Privacy framework. https://www.iso.org/standard/85938.html (2024)
41. OECD: Recommendation of the Council concerning Guidelines Governing the Protection of Privacy and Transborder Flows of Personal Data (2013)
42. Cavoukian, A.: Privacy by design: The 7 Foundational Principles, vol. 5, 12. Information and Privacy Commissioner of Ontario, Canada (2009)
43. Russell, N., van der Aalst, W., ter Hofstede, A.: Workflow patterns. The definitive guide. The MIT Press, Cambridge, Massachusetts, London, England (2016)

AI in Industry 4.0

Large Language Models to Support Altruistic Collaborative Healing in Smart Manufacturing

Luis A. Estrada-Jimenez[1,2](✉), Nastaran Farhadighalati[1,2], Sepideh Kalateh[1,2], Sanaz Nikghadam-Hojjati[1,2], and José Barata[1,2]

[1] UNINOVA - Centre of Technology and Systems (CTS), and Associated Lab of Intelligent, Systems (LASI), FCT Campus, 2829-516 Lisbon, Portugal
{lestrada,nastaran.farhadi,sepideh.kalateh,sanaznik, jab}@uninova.pt

[2] Department of Electrical Engineering, NOVA School of Science and Technology, Nova, University Lisbon, 2829-516 Lisbon, Portugal

Abstract. The growing complexity of manufacturing systems calls for innovative approaches like biologicalisation (application of biological principles to industrial process design). In this context and building on our previous work on altruistic collaborative healing, where manufacturing elements ("Donors") share resources with those in need ("Recipients"), this paper addresses key research challenges by integrating Large Language Models (LLMs). By enabling natural language communication between altruistic and recipient resources, LLMs enhance reasoning, coordination, and adaptability in dynamic manufacturing environments. To demonstrate this concept, we propose an LLM-driven framework for decision-making and resource allocation, validated through a peer-to-peer energy-sharing scenario involving Automated Guided Vehicles (AGVs). Using the gpt-4o-mini model in simulation, the results show improved system adaptability and 80% reliability. The paper concludes by discussing the implications, limitations, and future directions of this approach, emphasizing the potential of LLMs in smart manufacturing.

Keywords: Biologicalisation · Self-organization · Smart Manufacturing · Self-healing · Artificial Intelligence · Altruism · Collective Behaviour

1 Introduction

In recent years, globalization, shifting customer preferences, and the demand for personalized products have pushed companies to adopt innovative control strategies. These strategies tackle the growing complexity of manufacturing design by using advanced methods like multi-agent systems and nature-inspired approaches [1], which offer greater adaptability, resilience, and robustness compared to traditional approaches.

Following this field, our research group has been exploring the concept of altruism applied to cooperative systems in smart manufacturing [2–4].

Published by Springer Nature Switzerland AG 2025
L. M. Camarinha-Matos and F. Ferrada (Eds.): DoCEIS 2025, IFIP AICT 759, pp. 65–76, 2025.
https://doi.org/10.1007/978-3-031-97051-1_5

We believe that applying this principle offers significant advantages, particularly in healing and maintenance operations, by enabling entities that under specific conditions can "repair" or support others while continuing their own tasks.

A key challenge in designing bio-inspired, self-organized, and altruistic cooperative manufacturing systems lies in developing and applying artificial intelligence mechanisms to enhance communication, reasoning, and autonomous behavior [4], while also addressing the engineering design requirements to implement these principles effectively.

Large Language Models (LLMs) offer interesting principles that can be used in this context. LLMs are defined as advanced artificial intelligence systems designed to understand, generate, and manipulate human-like text based on vast amounts of training data [5].

LLMs were popularized around 2020-2021, with the release of GPT-3 by OpenAI in mid-2020 being a major milestone. The widespread adoption of LLMs accelerated with the launch of ChatGPT, which made AI-powered natural language processing accessible to the general public [6].

LLMs are increasingly being applied across diverse fields, such as industrial robotics [7], multi-robot systems [8], Human Robot Collaboration [9], and, more recently, to enable Multi-agent Manufacturing Systems [10]. Their versatility and advanced capabilities are driving innovation in these areas.

Thus, the primary focus of this paper is to explore the intersection of altruistic healing in smart manufacturing, enhanced by the capabilities of Large Language Models (LLMs) (See Fig. 1).

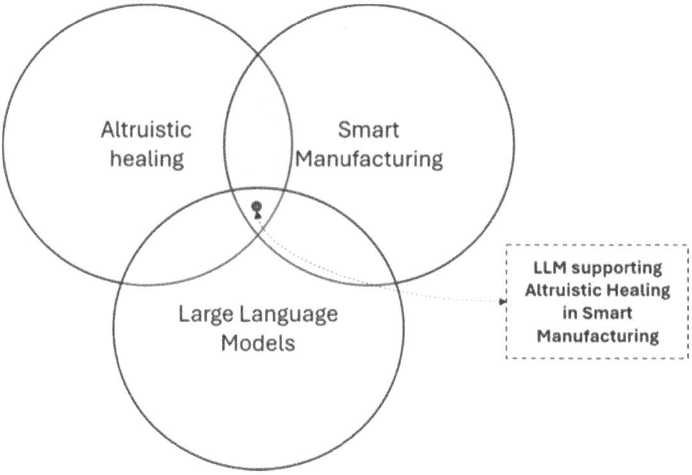

Fig. 1. LLM supporting altruistic healing in smart manufacturing.

We believe that combining these three areas can yield valuable and innovative results. The next sections of this paper are driven by the following research question (RQ) and hypothesis (H).

RQ: How can a manufacturing framework for altruistic healing operations be implemented while denoting autonomous and collaborative behavior?

H: A framework with preceding characteristics can be implemented if the decision-making behavior of the altruistic/non-altruistic resources is modeled using Large Language Models (LLMs) so that they can reason and act through natural language.

The remainder of this paper is structured as follows: Sect. 2 explores the paper's connection to AI-powered Cyber-Physical Systems (CPS). Section 3 introduces the main framework and key concepts. Section 4 details the validation process, and finally, Sect. 5 presents the conclusions and outlines directions for future work.

2 Relation to AI-Powered Cyber-Physical Systems

This paper aligns with AI-powered Cyber-Physical Systems (CPS) by integrating conversational agents into smart manufacturing. It explores how Large Language Models (LLMs) can enhance CPS by enabling altruistic collaboration among manufacturing resources, optimizing resource use in real time.

Furthermore, the proposed framework leverages LLM-driven reasoning to support autonomous decision-making within CPS, where mobile robots assess energy availability and generate control actions dynamically. This contributes to self-organizing manufacturing systems, allowing CPS to reconfigure operations efficiently in response

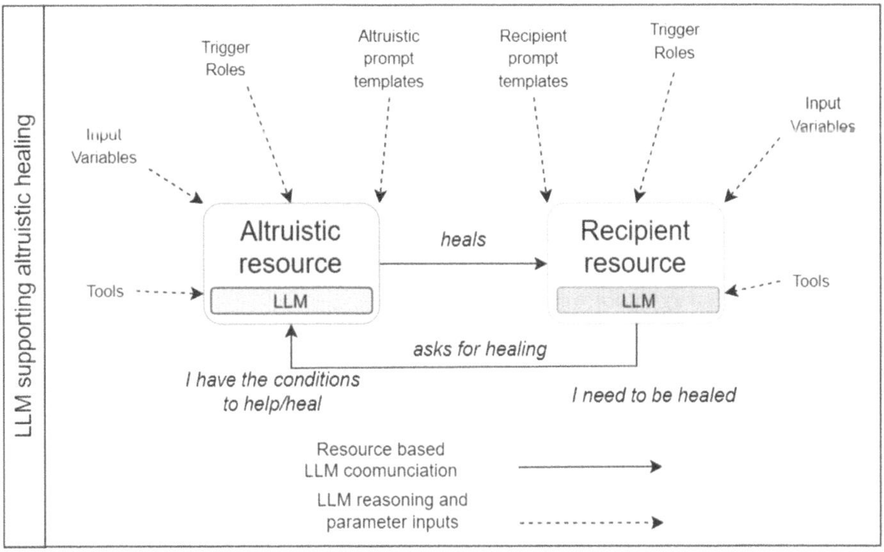

Fig. 2. LLM and altruistic collaborative healing framework.

to real-time constraints. By demonstrating peer-to-peer energy sharing through AI-powered interactions, this research advances CPS toward more decentralized, scalable, and intelligent manufacturing ecosystems.

3 Framework

The proposed framework is built upon intelligent resources capable of autonomy, reasoning, communication, and adaptability [3, 4]. These capabilities are enhanced by Large Language Models (LLMs), which enable human-like interactions between altruistic and non-altruistic resources, fostering coordination and cooperation within a self-healing system. The framework proposed for this work is shown in Fig. 2.

3.1 Main Components

The main elements that describe the framework are shown below:

- ***LLM base Recipient Resource:*** Resources that, under current conditions, have detected anomalies in their operation and require assistance or repair, rely on decision-making and autonomy powered by large language models.
- ***LLM base Altruistic Resource:*** Resources that, in their current state, have received healing requests. They can assist, repair, or provide a cure by sacrificing a portion of their fitness while simultaneously completing their own tasks. Their decision-making and autonomy are powered by Large Language Models (LLMs).

- ***Resource-based LLM Communication:*** Refers to the communication exchange between resources, which may involve APIs, sockets, shared knowledge, and multi-agent frameworks.
- ***Altruistic and Recipient prompt templates:*** predefined prompt structures designed to facilitate interactions where one entity (altruistic) offers support or resources, and another (recipient) benefits from that assistance. These templates formulate responses that align with an altruistic collaborative framework. These prompts will guide specific conditions of collaboration.
- ***Trigger roles:*** Refers to the threshold value of a specific operational manufacturing variable that activates either the Recipient role or the capacity to act as an Altruist, e.g., available energy, tool wear, etc.
- ***Input variables:*** Operational variables associated with the manufacturing resource that impact decision-making within the altruistic process.
- ***Tools:*** External functions, APIs, or modules that the LLM can call to extend its capabilities beyond text generation, e.g., Sensor Data Query Tool, Action tools.

3.2 Execution Diagram

The execution of the framework involves multiple key steps. Under normal op- operating conditions, an anomaly or failure is detected when a specific variable falls behind a predefined threshold, triggering a corresponding role (Recipient or Altruistic) in the available resources.

Subsequently, the values of the active variables are used as inputs for the recipient/altruistic templates. The process begins with the Recipient Resource initiating the prompt, followed by a response from the altruistic resource. This "conversation" continues until both resources reach a mutual agreement on a possible solution.

If a specific action is required, a library of specialized "tools" will be deployed to extend the LLM's capabilities. These tools may include functionalities such as code generation or interfacing with a robotic system. Once the appropriate tool has been activated and the necessary action executed, the altruistic operation concludes.

If multiple Altruistic Resources are available, one approach is to broadcast a request and select the first resource that responds. This ensures a swift allocation while minimizing delays in the altruistic operation.

Additionally, advanced decision-making methods can be integrated into the framework to enhance efficiency and optimize resource selection. These methods can prioritize responses based on factors such as availability, proximity, or capability, ensuring optimal allocation. Figure 3 presents the activity diagram of the proposed framework.

4 Validation: Peer-to-Peer Altruistic Energy Sharing by Conversational Manufacturing Resources

4.1 Scenario Description

In a shop floor with flexible transportation, mobile robots perform different tasks, leading to varying levels of residual energy. The availability of energy is also influenced by the number and placement of charging stations. In critical situations, such as rush orders, an energy shortage could result in production delays or bottlenecks. Motivated by this challenge and following a similar evaluation methodology as the one presented in [11], the current work tests the benefits of the framework considering a scenario with the following characteristics:

- The scenario involves two mobile robots performing a transport task, with one nearing a critical energy threshold that may impact task completion.
- Key parameters, including current energy levels, energy required for the next task, and robot positions are defined as variables in a Python script.
- Predefined prompts, integrated into Python scripts, are detailed in Fig. 4.
- For demonstration purposes, a simplified predefined tool is used, as illustrated in Fig. 4. This tool facilitates control code generation, enabling the robots to navigate to specified positions.

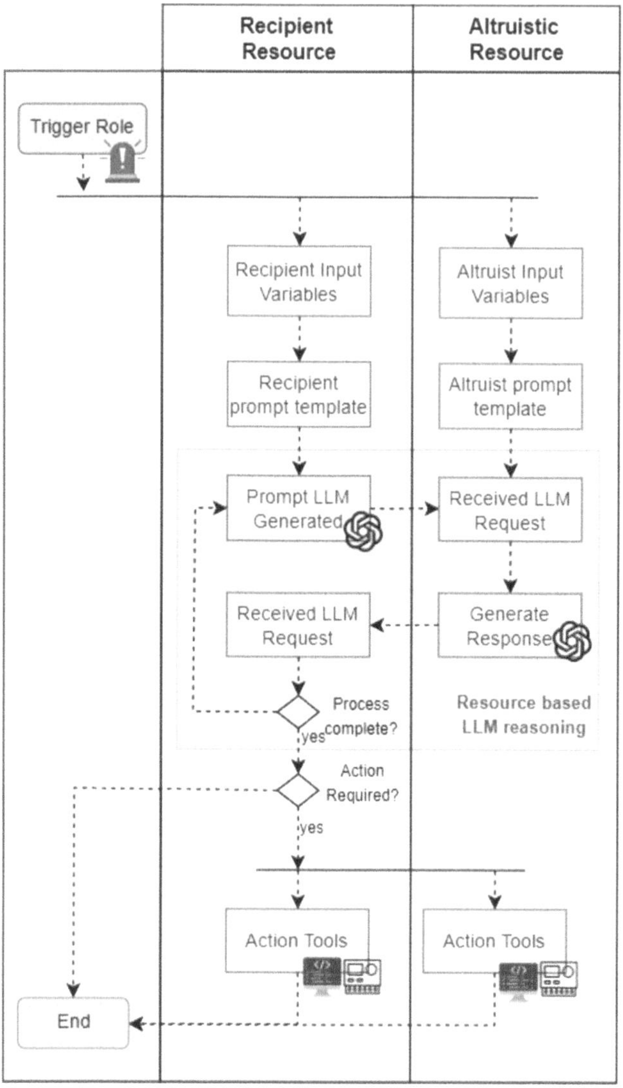

Fig. 3. Activity diagram of the framework.

4.2 Tests and Reliability Measurement

The validation tests utilize the ChatGPT API [6], specifically the gpt-4o-mini model, to evaluate the reliability of the generated solution. The assessment focuses on verifying whether the reasoning within the resource interaction leads to a logical conclusion, both in terms of altruistic decision-making and the development of the necessary control code for robot movement and altruistic actions. These tests were conducted by randomly assigning input variables to both altruistic and recipient resources, repeating the experiment ten times, and manually verifying the logical consistency of the solution.

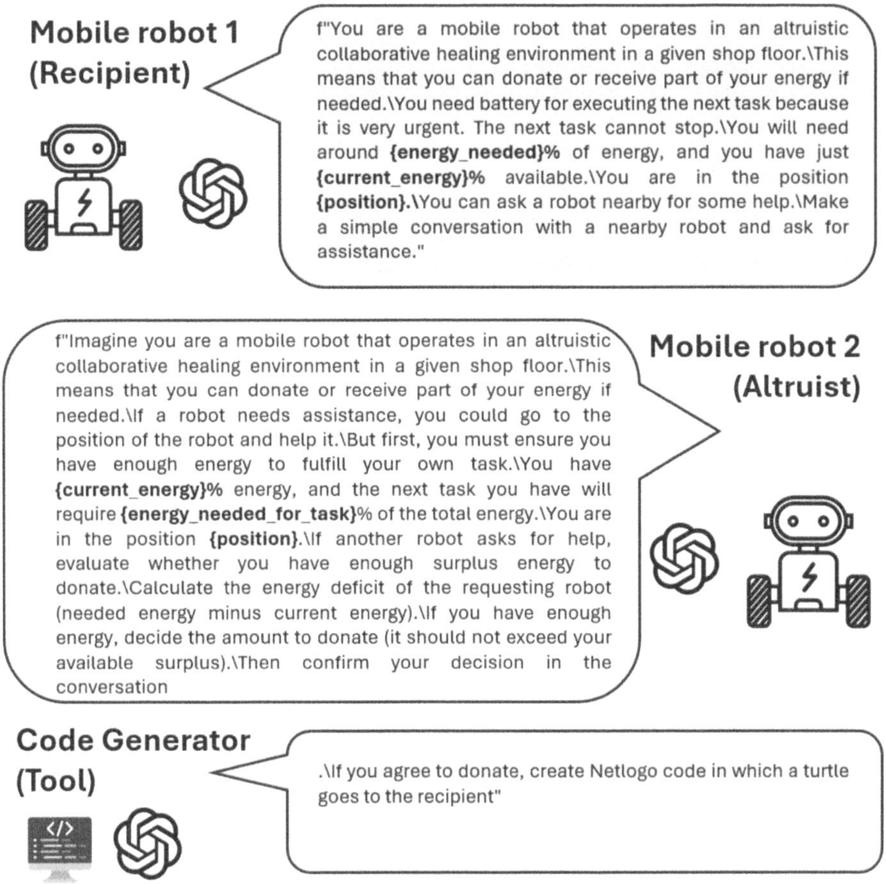

Fig. 4. Designed prompts for the recipient robot, altruist robot and tool associated to generate a specific code.

Initial results, presented in Figs. 5 and 6, illustrate the logical structure of the conversational process during altruistic interactions and a portion of the generated code for simulated movement within the NetLogo framework (NetLogo, widely used for studying complex behaviors in multi-agent systems, was chosen for its simplicity and ease of logic verification). It is important to emphasize the sequential logic process used to reach a conclusion regarding the altruistic activity, beginning with an assessment of energy availability based on the mobile robot's own requirements.

The results of these tests are presented in Table 1. The table displays the position (XY), current energy (CE), and energy required (EN) for both mobile robots, along with the outcomes measured in terms of decision time (DT), decision accuracy (AD), and the accuracy of the generated control code (CG).

We use a reliability metric to measure the accuracy of the solution, as defined in (1):

$$Reliability = \frac{AccurateDecisions}{TotalSamples} \cdot 100, \tag{1}$$

where:

- *Reliability*: Reliability of the LLM system;
- *AccurateDecisions*: Decisions that correspond to the expected logic.

Table 2 presents the results of Reliability of the solution, the reliability of the code and the average computing time.

From these experiments, the following remarks should be considered.

- Some of the NOK results in the logic reasoning were due to incorrect calculations.
- Some of the incorrect results in the code generation reasoning were caused by misassigning coordinates.
- In cases like samples 19 and 20, no altruistic need existed (as the mobile robot had enough energy to complete its task). However, the reasoning concluded that an altruistic strategy was necessary. In contrast, sample 4 correctly concluded that sharing was not required.

```
Mobile Robot1:
Hi there

Mobile Robot2:
Hi

Mobile Robot1:
I'm in need of some assistance. I'm currently at position
(1,2) and require an additional 15% energy to complete my
next urgent task, but I only have 10% available. If you'r
e nearby and can spare some energy, I'd greatly appreciat
e it!

Mobile Robot2:
Let's evaluate the situation step-by-step:

1. **Current Energy Status**:
   - Your energy: 80%
   - Energy required for your next task: 10%
   - Your remaining energy after the next task: 80% - 10%
= **70%**

2. **Requesting Robot's Energy Status**:
   - Required energy: 15%
   - Current energy: 10%
   - Energy deficit: 15% - 10% = **5%** (this is how much
the requesting robot needs)

3. **Available Surplus Energy**:
   - You initially have 80%, and you will need 10% for yo
ur next task, leaving you with 70%.
   - Therefore, your surplus energy available is:
   - Initial energy - Energy needed = 80% - 10% = 70%

Since you have **70% energy left**, which is more than th
e **5%** energy deficit of the requesting robot, you can
help.

4. **Decision on Donation**:
   - You can donate the full **5%** needed by the request
ing robot.
```

Fig. 5. Part of the conversation generated between the Altruistic and Resource mobile robots.

– In cases such as sample 3, both robots were in the same position, yet the generated code still attempted to move one robot from one position to another.

````
to setup
  clear-all
  ; Setting up the turtles
  create-turtles 2 [
    set color blue
    setxy random-xcor random-ycor
  ]
  ; Initializing energies
  ask turtle 1 [ set energy 80 ] ; your energy
  ask turtle 2 [ set energy 10 ] ; requester's energy
  setxy 9 8 ; place yourself at (9,8)
  setxy 1 2 ; place requested at (1,2)
end
```
````

Fig. 6. Part of the code generated for the Altruistic robot to be implemented in Netlogo.

Table 1. Validation Results: Labels. XY: Simulated coordinates of the mobile robots; CE: Current Energy (%); EN: Energy needed for next task; DT: Decision time; AD: Accurate Decision; CG: Accurate Code Generated; Value (-), represents partially OK results for the CG category.

	Mobile Robot 1			Mobile Robot 2			Results		
	XY	CE	EN	XY	CE	EN	DT	AD	CG
1	(1,2)	10	15	9,8	80	10	20,1	OK	-
2	(3,3)	5	20	(0,0)	90	20	21,5	OK	OK
3	(0,5)	18	25	(0,5)	70	15	30	OK	-
4	(1,9)	20	10	(4,4)	49	20	17,6	OK	-
5	(0,0)	12	30	(3,3)	80	17	13,6	NOK	-
6	(8,4)	6	30	(1,5)	70	20	18,78	OK	-
7	(10,10)	19	20	(10,10)	90	15	14	OK	NOK
8	(3,3)	5	15	(2,3)	80	20	22,1	OK	OK
9	(6,9)	14	20	(4,7)	85	10	13,9	OK	-
10	(0,0)	30	40	(1,5)	75	15	19,82	OK	NOK
11	(1,2)	5	15	(9,8)	60	50	30	OK	-
12	(3,3)	15	10	(0,0)	70	30	19,3	OK	NOK
13	(0,5)	10	20	(0,5)	50	20	37,1	OK	NOK
14	(1,9)	7	20	(4,4)	79	14	57	OK	OK

(continued)
````

Table 1. (*continued*)

	Mobile Robot 1			Mobile Robot 2			Results		
	XY	CE	EN	XY	CE	EN	DT	AD	CG
15	(0,0)	8	15	(3,3)	85	40	43	OK	-
16	(8,4)	5	12	(1,5)	100	30	17	OK	-
17	(10,10)	20	4	(10,10)	100	90	42	NOK	NOK
18	(3,3)	4	4	(2,3)	67	80	13	OK	OK
19	(6,9)	5	4	(4,7)	85	40	13,5	NOK	-
20	(0,0)	15	3	(1,5)	100	20	31	NOK	-

Table 2. Reliability results.

Results	Value
Reliability of decision	80%
	20% (OK)
Reliability of the code	55% (-)
	25% (NOK)
Average computing time	24.73 secs

5 Conclusion

The key takeaways of this paper are:

- Introduces a novel approach that integrates large language models with biologisation to enable collaborative healing in smart manufacturing.
- Proposes a framework that conceptualizes this idea, featuring an LLM-powered altruistic and recipient resource, supported by tools, input variables, and altruistic templates as core components.
- Demonstrates preliminary results using the gpt-4o-mini model in a simulated peer-to-peer energy-sharing scenario.

Future research directions include developing a communication strategy for multiple resources using an LLM-based platform or a multi-agent structure to enhance scalability. Additionally, integrating the solution into real-world scenarios with physical hardware will allow for evaluating potential delays and performance constraints. Further refinement of the framework, including the development of additional tools and the incorporation of more variables, will improve its realism and applicability. Exploring alternative applications, such as load sharing or tool sharing, can further demonstrate its versatility. Moreover, fine-tuning the prompt engineering process is essential to mitigate NOK results (80%) and incorrect conclusions, ensuring more reliable decision-making in complex and context-dependent machine control scenarios. Integrating this framework with conversational models for operators could be highly valuable, aligning with the vision of a more human-centric manufacturing industry. It is important to test the framework with hardware to understand the implications and possible software-related delays. This is of high importance as running GPT-4o-mini in a real-time, industrial setting could introduce latency and high computational overhead. Other variables that could be potentially measured to enhance the reliability of this work are: latency, accuracy, and operational impact. Also, LLMs were tested in isolation, but they need to be compared (bench-marked) to existing AI and optimization techniques like: Reinforcement Learning (RL) (for dynamic resource allocation), Graph-based heuristics (e.g., shortest-path al- algorithms for AGV routing), Neural Networks (trained on past data for better predictive power) to understand the potential advantages.

These advancements will contribute to the broader adoption of AI-driven collaborative manufacturing, fostering more efficient, adaptive, and resilient production systems.

Acknowledgements. This research was partly supported by the Portuguese FCT program, Centre of Technology and Systems (CTS) CTS/00066 and Nova University Lisbon's PhD program of Department of Electronics and Computer Engineering. L. Estrada-Jimenez acknowledges the Fundação para a Ciência e Tecnologia for the Ph.D. Grant 2023.03106.BD.

References

1. Wegener, K., et al.: Biologicalisation in manufacturing–current state and future trends. CIRP Ann. **72**(2), 781–807 (2023)
2. Estrada-Jimenez, L.A., Pulikottil, T., Nikghadam-Hojjati, S., Barata, J.: Self-organization in smart manufacturing - background, systematic review, challenges and outlook. IEEE Access **11**, 10107–10136 (2023)
3. Estrada-Jimenez, L.A., Kalateh, S., Nikghadam-Hojjati, S., Barata, J.: An altruistic-based framework to support collaborative healing of manufacturing resources in a self-organized shop-floor. IEEE Access (2024)
4. Estrada-Jimenez, L.A., Macuacua, J.S., Nikghadam-Hojjati, S., Barata, J.: Towards implementing altruistic collaborative healing: Context, simulation and analysis. IEEE Access (2025)
5. Zhao, W.X., et al.: A survey of large language models. arXiv preprint arXiv:2303.18223 **1**(2) (2023)
6. OpenAI: Chatgpt: Language model (2023). https://openai.com/chatgpt, accessed: 4 March 2025
7. Fan, H., Liu, X., Fuh, J.Y.H., Lu, W.F., Li, B.: Embodied intelligence in manufacturing: leveraging large language models for autonomous industrial robotics. Journal of Intelligent Manufacturing, pp. 1–17 (2024)
8. Li, P., An, Z., Abrar, S., Zhou, L.: Large language models for multi-robot systems: A survey. arXiv preprint arXiv:2502.03814 (2025)
9. Gao, F., Xia, L., Zhang, J., Liu, S., Wang, L., Gao, R.X.: Integrating large language model for natural language-based instruction toward robust human-robot collaboration. Procedia CIRP **130**, 313–318 (2024)

10. Lim, J., Vogel-Heuser, B., Kovalenko, I.: Large language model-enabled multi-agent manufacturing systems. In: 2024 IEEE 20th International Conference on Automation Science and Engineering (CASE), pp. 3940–3946. IEEE (2024)
11. Estrada-Jimenez, L.A., Kalateh, S., Hojjati, S.N., Barata, J.: A bio-inspired and altruistic-based framework to support collaborative healing in a smart manufacturing shop-floor. In: Doctoral Conference on Computing, Electrical and Industrial Systems, pp. 111–121. Springer (2023)

Data Pre-processing of Hard Disk Drive Data for Failure Prediction in the Context of Industry 4.0

Kazeem Balogun(✉) and Lai Xu

Faculty of Science and Technology, Bournemouth University, Poole, Dorset, UK
{kbalogun,lxu}@bournemouth.ac.uk

Abstract. Hard disk drive failure prediction is one of the crucial application domains of predictive maintenance in Industry 4.0. While a vast amount of hard disk drive (HDD) monitoring data from SMART attributes and sensors is available, effective pre-processing techniques to pre-process these data for failure prediction are still lagging in the context of Industry 4.0, where data originates from diverse and multiple sources. Traditionally, HDD data preprocessing focuses on a single data source and uses a static predefined approach which is unsuitable in the Industry 4.0 context. This paper addresses this research gap by developing a unique and iterative data pre-processing framework that is specifically designed to cater to varying hard disk drive data from different data sources in the context of service-oriented or component-based systems. Our research objectives include identifying the unique challenges of HDD data pre-processing in industrial settings, developing a unified and adaptive data pre-processing workflow, and creating a framework that supports future automation through automated AI. Methodologically, we adopt the FIWARE smart architecture to harness HDD failure prediction capabilities in the Industry 4.0 settings. Our framework implements a specialized technique to handle SMART data problems such as missing values, feature dependencies, class imbalance, and SMART attributes inconsistencies, which are intrinsic to Industrial HDD operations. We validate the effectiveness of the framework via a series of experiments with machine learning models such as Gradient-Boosted Decision Trees (GDBT) and Decision Trees (DT), achieving over 90% Failure Detection Rate (FDR) across several performance metrics. The key contributions of this study include a validated and iterative data pre-processing pipeline that is adaptable to service-oriented industrial systems, and implementation strategies for hard disk drive predictive maintenance in the Industry 4.0 ecosystem. It also contributes to the theoretical understanding and practical application of HDD failure prediction in modern manufacturing environments.

Keywords: Industry 4.0 · Data pre-processing · Machine learning · Feature selection

L. M. Camarinha-Matos and F. Ferrada (Eds.): DoCEIS 2025, IFIP AICT 759, pp. 77–100, 2025.
https://doi.org/10.1007/978-3-031-97051-1_6

1 Introduction

Industry 4.0 is rapidly transforming industrialization. By integrating the Internet of Things (IoT), machine learning, and artificial intelligence, the industry is embracing new technologies and concepts in the production process and increasing sustainability in manufacturing [1]. This advanced technological infusion enables real-time data exchange and automation that foster greater efficiency, while also generating a huge amount of data. The data accessibility enhances the overall machine and equipment operation performance which leads to improvement in the quality of production [2].

In the context of Industry 4.0, predictive maintenance (PdM) can cover different areas such as machines, machine components, single machines, multiple machines, and related components within the product line, and hard disk drive failure prediction to mention a few. This is because the networking of machines, related machines, equipment, and other factory devices in the production line enables production, and the data acquired are used to make statements concerning the quality of production and machine condition [3]. Predictive maintenance is at the core of Industry 4.0 which leverages acquired data to predict looming failure among interconnected machines within the product line [4]. To effectively implement any of the predictive maintenance solutions within Industry 4.0 requires quality data streams to build effective models. This is of utmost importance as the model performance depends on the integrity and quality of data available for development.

In traditional predictive maintenance, most of the developed models are implemented on a single data stream which is considered stationary [5]. However, this concept does not fit into the Industry 4.0 context as the model developed in such a scenario becomes obsolete over a short period due to data drift. Data drift can be defined as periodic changes in the data stream or distribution of data over time [6]. In the industrial context, data pre-processing is still based on experts' knowledge, usually adopted as the company's own process for analysis. While we recognize that there is no one-for-all all-data pre-processing method in the context of Industry 4.0, this research gap forms the motivation for the development of the hard disk drive data pre-processing method for failure prediction in Industry 4.0.

Over the years, reasonable effort has been geared towards data pre-processing for industrial-based models. However, there is less consideration of dynamic data pre-processing framework that caters to multiple data streams and varying characteristics as such in the Industry 4.0 environment. One research area that offers complex and dynamic data pre-processing as such that is needed in the Industry 4.0 settings is hard disk drive data pre-processing.

Hard disk drive manufacturers use self-monitoring and reporting technology (SMART) to monitor and report impending failures in operational disks. The SMART collects operational metrics in the form of attributes that monitor and report using a set threshold for an impending failure of the disk components. However, the implementation of the SMART attributes varies from one manufacturer to the other, model to model, and even from models of the same manufacturer to the other. The never-ending differences create varying types of hard disk drive datasets, and the complexities and dynamism in the characteristics of hard disk drive datasets require a robust and dynamic data pre-processing framework as such that aligns with the Industry 4.0 settings [7].

With a focus on pre-processing hard disk drive data streams for Industry 4.0 predictive maintenance, this paper integrates hard disk drive failure prediction into the Industry 4.0 ecosystem using FIWARE smart architecture and presents hard disk drive data pre-processing framework that could serve as templates for analyzing other matching data streams. The varying nature of hard disk drive datasets in terms of dimensionality of feature attributes, size, heterogeneity, and homogeneity offers dynamic methods of data pre-processing that could be automated to cater to matching datasets in Industrial settings. This could serve as a foundation for automation using agentic AI.

1.1 Structure of the Paper

The structure of this paper is arranged as follows: the remaining part of Sect. 1 highlights the research questions and hypothesis. Section 2 discussed hard disk drive data pre-processing in AI-powered cyber-physical systems. In Sect. 3 the design science research method is explained to show that the architectural framework adapts to Industry 4.0. Section 4 presents the research context with varying forms of data pre-processing approaches for failure prediction in the literature. Section 5 discussed Industry 4.0 and hard disk drive data. Section 5.1 presents the Hard Disk Drive Data Pre-processing Pipeline. Section 6 presents the experiments. Section 7 the discussion and Sect. 8 discusses the conclusion and future work.

1.2 Research Question and Hypothesis

Primary Research Question: How can hard disk drive data be effectively pre-processed for hard disk drive failure prediction in the Industry 4.0 context?

Sub-question 1: what data pre-processing strategies are necessary to analyze varying and diverse HDD data in the Industry 4.0 ecosystem?

Sub-question 2: how can the data pre-processing technique address the challenges of class imbalance, feature dimensionality, and variances in data size in HDD datasets?

Sub-question 3: How can we develop a unified data pre-processing pipeline that supports AI-powered predictive maintenance and caters to HDD data from multiple sources?

Research Hypothesis: a robust and iterative hard disk drive data pre-processing pipeline that incorporates necessary data pre-processing strategies such as missing value treatment, feature scaling, sampling, and advanced feature extraction techniques will not only cater to diverse HDD datasets from multiple sources but also significantly enhance the efficiency of the developed model within the Industry 4.0 cyber-physical system (CPS) compared to the traditional pre-processing method.

2 Hard Disk Drive Data Pre-processing in AI-Powered Cyber-Physical Systems

In Industry 4.0 settings, AI-powered cyber-physical systems (CPS) represent the integration of computing intelligence with physical infrastructures to create an autonomous and smart monitoring industrial system [8]. Hard disk drives serve as a crucial component within this system storing the operational data [9]. The quality of the data pre-processing has a significant impact on the reliability and efficiency of AI-powered cyber-physical systems. While modern cyber-physical systems include several subsystems with multiple and varying data formats, the hard disk drive data pre-processing framework will offer robust and dynamic data pre-processing workflow with a unified data representation for implementing effective failure prediction in the industrial ecosystem. The hard disk drive data pre-processing methodologies within the AI-powered cyber-systems remained a significant advancement in the implementation of not just HDD failure prediction but also other PdM solutions within Industrial settings. Also, by addressing the data pre-processing problem within Industrial environments, an effective and robust data pre-processing framework ensures the reliability of HDD which is the core storage component thereby promoting efficiency in manufacturing systems [10].

3 Methodology

From the Industrial context, Design Science Research (DSR) is one of the well-known methodologies and is very crucial in real-world applications as it provides guidelines in the implementation of large-scale systems as such in Industry 4.0 [11]. However, our evaluation is tailored around HDD data that is made available by Backblaze [12]. We centered our analysis around the 4th quarter of 2022 and the 1st quarter of 2023. Model development is in Python programming within the Jupyter Notebook environment and underpinned by the CRISP-DM at the Design and development phase of the DSR methodology. The six phases of DSR are discussed in detail and how we harnessed both methodologies to guide this project work.

- **Problem Identification and Motivation:** This research commences by addressing the crucial problem of predicting hard disk drive failure in the Industry 4.0 environment and is motivated by the limitations of and the challenges in pre-processing varying HDD data streams towards the implementation of hard disk drive failure prediction in the context of Industry 4.0. This research identified the need for proactive maintenance strategies within the Industry 4.0 environment and the significant impact of hard disk drive data pre-processing towards the enablement and implementation of other predictive maintenance solutions within the ecosystem
- **Objectives of the solution:** From the industrial context, an artifact in the form of a hard disk drive predictive maintenance solution is created and integrated using the FIWARE smart reference architecture. The developed artifact provides a scalable and adaptable solution that supports the implementation of hard disk drive failure prediction in Industry 4.0. The provision of advanced and effective data pre-processing techniques for varying HDD data streams from different manufacturers is also presented in the form of an artifact that can be offered as a service within the Industry 4.0 settings. This is expected to create a robust hard disk drive data analytic module where varying and different methods of HDD data analytics offer readily available templates for analyzing other related data with matching characteristics within industrial settings.

- **Design and Development:** This phase involves the architectural design of the components using FIWARE and the data-driven model of the hard disk drive predictive maintenance system. The creation of the model is done through the development of advanced and robust data pre-processing techniques that cater to varying hard disk drive data streams in terms of datatypes, size, characteristics, year of release, dimensionalities, etc. To achieve the design and development, the SMART data and other required sensor data are collected to develop a hard disk drive predictive model using machine learning. This is done through the implementation of various components like the machine learning building blocks and other pre-processing strategies. The machine learning is chosen based on the model requirements that best fit the task with the HDD data characteristics. Specifically, the development process of the predictive model artifact will follow an iterative loop procedure which is guided by CRISP-DM methodology at this stage of the DSR to ensure standardization of the technical implementation of the hard disk drive data pre-processing in the Industry 4.0 ecosystem. The Cross Industry Standard Process for Data Mining (CRISP-DM) is an open standard process model that guides the data mining process, and it consists of six stages such as business understanding, data understanding, data preparation, modeling, evaluation, and development. These stages are processed iteratively at this stage of the project to understand the data and identify the key components in terms of attributes and factors influencing HDD failure in the Industry 4.0 ecosystem, prepare the data, identify the right machine learning algorithms for developments, and evaluate the developed model before deployment.
- **Demonstration:** This phase involves demonstrating the effectiveness of the proposed approach while validating the predictive maintenance solution using hard disk drive data in industrial settings. Hard disk drive data obtained from operational data centers is used to build a data-driven predictive model while demonstrating the effectiveness of the data analytic framework and the developed model towards hard disk drive failure prediction in Industry 4.0 settings. This phase also showcases the predictive accuracy of the developed models while proving the effectiveness of the integration capabilities towards the implementation of HDD predictive maintenance solutions in Industry 4.0 settings. The capabilities of the required components are also demonstrated by proof-of-concept implementation of the hard disk drive data pre-processing using the mix-match approach to map the influx data streams to required data pre-processing strategies for analysis and model development.
- **Evaluation**: Evaluation is to be performed through a series of experiments using the Backblaze HDD dataset in Sect. 6. The built models from the series of experiments are evaluated through performance analysis using different metric evaluation that conforms with the Industry 4.0 standards. Section 6.1 will report the performance output of the series of experiments and compare it with other approaches to check the validity, and scalability of our proposed approach. The outcome of the evaluation of the hard disk drive predictive model for Industry 4.0 using machine learning approaches will demonstrate the effectiveness and the applicability of the solution to solving the problem of hard disk drive failure prediction in the Industry 4.0 settings.

- **Communication:** this phase shall present the acquired knowledge through the necessary medium to stakeholders in the field of predictive maintenance in Industry 4.0 and cloud engineering sectors, manufacturing sectors, industrialists, and most importantly, the researchers. Different communication channels will be explored, such as academic conferences, scientific publications, and presentations at exhibitions.

4 Research Context

In this section, we reviewed some of the previous works on HDD data pre-processing. For ease of review, we have divided these into sub-sections with different approaches such as data pre-processing, feature extraction, sampling, and model selection methods.

Previous studies such as [13] and [14] have considered data pre-processing and data cleaning of hard disk drive data respectively for disk failure prediction and supervised learning. However, there is a need to address hard disk drive data pre-processing in the context of Industry 4.0 while considering the characteristics of the datasets and the performance output of the adopted learning model. The reason for this is that every dataset is unique and the approach towards its analysis will determine the model performance and the predictive accuracy of HDD in the Industry 4.0 environment.

In other studies, by [15–17], the focus was on feature selection towards improving model performances and detecting a failure in hard disk drives. Other pre-processing strategies such as missing value treatment, sampling, and feature scaling were done within the cross-validation without considering the context of Industry 4.0. This is somewhat a snippet of the general process of pre-processing and analyzing hard disk data. While the studies present good performance with models of Random Forest, GDBT, and SVM with FDRtest of over 80%, the studies do not consider varying data streams and Industry 4.0 concepts in their work.

Most studies about hard disk drive failure placed focus on improving the models towards HDD failure prediction with less focus on integrating hard disk drive failure prediction into the Industry 4.0 settings and how to effectively pre-process and analyze HDD data for PdM in the context of Industry 4.0. The majority only present a summary brief of the HDDs data analysis or rather reference to previous works on the adopted approach e.g., [18].

Prior works like [19–21] have also considered hard disk drive data pre-processing in their work with a focus on model selection and performance comparison. Unfortunately, these prior works do not focus their study on the methods of pre-processing HDD data. They did not address the challenges of constantly relegating the pre-processing approach due to data drift. They also failed to consider the impact and viability of the data pre-processing approach on the selected model and how it affects the model performance in a multi-faceted Industry 4.0 environment.

Other authors such as [22, 23] have also addressed HDD failure prediction using real-life datasets with primitive methods of data pre-processing for HDD data analysis. However, these studies do not consider the impact of the characteristics and size of the datasets in their study. Subsequent studies by [24, 25] the impact of data size but with a focus on a single model of hard disk which is contrary to the real-life situation in an industrial environment. A few studies that considered the effect of data size, metrics sets, and feature selection techniques are focused on software failure prediction and not hard disk drive failure prediction. Our view on this is that there is a need for a more comprehensive study such as the one we present that looked at HDD data pre-processing strategies towards HDD PdM and integrated it into the Industry 4.0 ecosystem for other predictive maintenance solutions. This would allow analysts to draw a valid conclusion on the suitable approach and technologies that best work when analyzing specific HDD data and for implementing other predictive maintenance solutions in Industry 4.0 settings. Also, the robustness of the proposed data pre-processing approach addresses the challenges in the cited previous studies by harnessing all necessary pre-processing strategies in an iterative way that align with the Industry 4.0 settings.

5 Industry 4.0 and Hard Disk Drive Data

The emergence of Industry 4.0 depicts a major shift in manufacturing via the integration of cyber-physical systems, advanced analytics, machine learning, and the Internet of Things (IoT) [26]. With data centers emerging as a critical component of digital transformation, hard disk drive data, machine data, and other machine-related data pre-processing also become crucial in the realization of effective production in Industry 4.0. To address the problem of HDD data processing in Industry 4.0, FIWARE smart architecture offers an open-source framework to integrate and address the problem of HDD data pre-processing in the Industrial ecosystem through the availability of different interfaces and components.

FIWARE provides a robust framework that aligns with the standards and principles of Industry 4.0. It conforms to the principles of interoperability, openness, and scalability which is a core characteristic of implementing solutions in the Industry 4.0 ecosystem. FIWARE is also a well-known architecture that demonstrates enormous technical features and assets for presenting Industry 4.0 concepts in literature. It consists of four different layers the data layer, the IoT or connectivity layer, the data analytic layer, and the application layer. Adopting FIWARE for the implementation of predictive maintenance avails researchers and developers of the open-source nature that promotes innovation and enables the development of new predictive maintenance solutions e.g. single machine predictive maintenance, HDD predictive maintenance, related machines predictive maintenance, etc.

In this paper, we proposed an adaptive FIWARE architectural framework. We have designed the proposed framework with an iterative and robust data pre-processing module to integrate hard disk drive failure prediction into the Industry 4.0 environment. In this section below, we explained in detail each layer and the building block in each of the layers as presented in the architectural framework. We first harnessed hard disk drive failure prediction into the Industry 4.0 ecosystem and then discussed in detail the data pre-processing approach for pre-processing the hard disk drive dataset in the ecosystem.

The hard disk drive SMART data are fed as an input into the adaptive FIWARE smart architecture framework in layer 1 (from bottom up). Layer 2 offers IoT adapters for connectivity and transfer of data. While the SMART data does not necessarily need an IoT adapter for data transfer, FIWARE offers varying forms of IoT adapters to facilitate seamless transportation of different datasets for pre-processing in the Industrial ecosystem. Layer 3 is the data analytic layer which is the core of the architectural framework.

The infused data are pre-processed and analyzed using different machine learning building blocks and evaluated for better performance before deployment. The platforms offer an iterative process that enables a continuous loop in a vicious cycle until performance proves satisfactory before implementation (Fig. 1).

Each valid process is deployed as a template for datasets of similar characteristics for analysis. Layer 4 is the application layer for expert and maintenance engineers to monitor alerts, make decisions, and schedule maintenance appropriately. Figure 2 below depicts an overview of the research concept with a detailed explanation below.

Figure 2 details the adaptive reference architecture of our research in this paper, and it is built upon the FIWARE Smart Industry Reference Architecture [27]. To adapt HDD failure prediction into the reference architecture in the context of Industry 4.0, the data layer is adapted to the hard disk drive data sources. The second layer is also modified to include the IoT adapters relevant to hard disk drive data and the third layer with data pre-processing module and several building blocks for HDD failure prediction. The fourth layer includes varying applications for solution deployment.

The first layer (from the bottom up) depicts the data layer with the physical hard disk drive and data from different data centers like Backblaze, Google, Microsoft, Baidu, Alibaba, etc., This is the foundational layer that provides raw and essential data needed for the implementation of HDD predictive maintenance. The raw data from this layer is passed through the connectivity or IoT layer for further processing.

The second layer (from the bottom up) is the connectivity layer with different IoT agents and standard protocols for data transmission between the layers. For hard disk drive failure prediction in Industry 4.0, the IoT layer can facilitate the ingestion and process of sensor data from hard disk drives such as the temperature, humidity, read/write error, etc. The IoT adapters such as the Message Queuing Telemetry Transport (MQTT), and HTTP which are standards-based messaging protocols used for machine-to-machine communication, can be used to integrate hard disk drive data into the FIWARE ecosystem from the existing storage system in the first layer. It is worthy of note that, unlike machine data, datasets such as SMART data can be infused directly without an IoT adapter into the predictive maintenance module level for analysis. However, HDD predictive maintenance may involve IoT sensors to monitor factors such as the temperature, and humidity of HDD in data centers, hence the inclusion of the second layer in our reference architecture.

The third layer (from the bottom up) is the data analytic layer. It comprises of data pre-processing module with different building blocks of machine learning algorithms to analyze HDD data either directly from the first layer or through the IoT agents. Data is derived from either HDD data alone or from the combination of HDD data and other IoT data sensors that are deployed for data collection. This layer processes influx data using different processing engines such as Spark, Hadoop, etc. Machine learning, deep learning, etc. can be implemented to analyze data and derive insight for smart decisions.

It is pertinent to state that this work only focused on the pre-processing of hard disk drive data streams and machine learning building blocks to develop an HDD predictive model within industrial settings. However, other building blocks such as Deep learning, and neural networks are included as they can also be used for HDD failure prediction in the Industry 4.0 context.

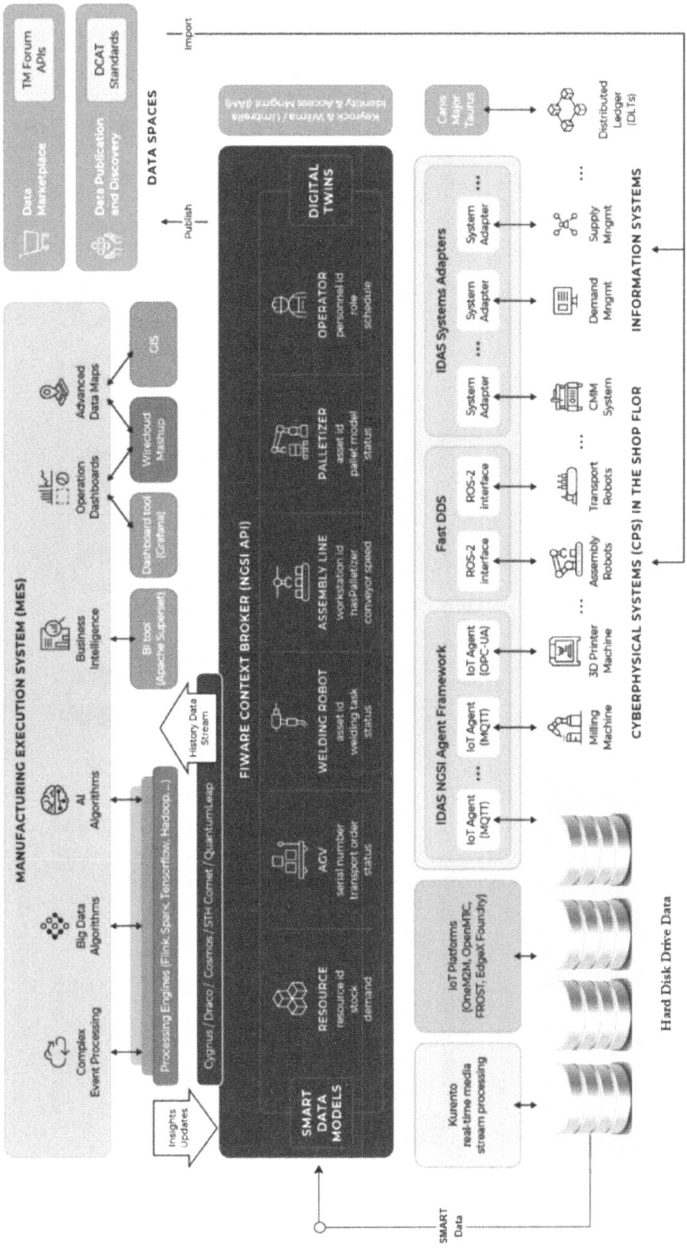

Fig. 1. FIWARE Smart Industry Reference Architecture [27].

The fourth layer (from the bottom up) is the application layer. It offers an interactive interface for end-users such as the maintenance teams and engineers to interact with the systems. This can include the dashboard and alert system for monitoring and scheduling

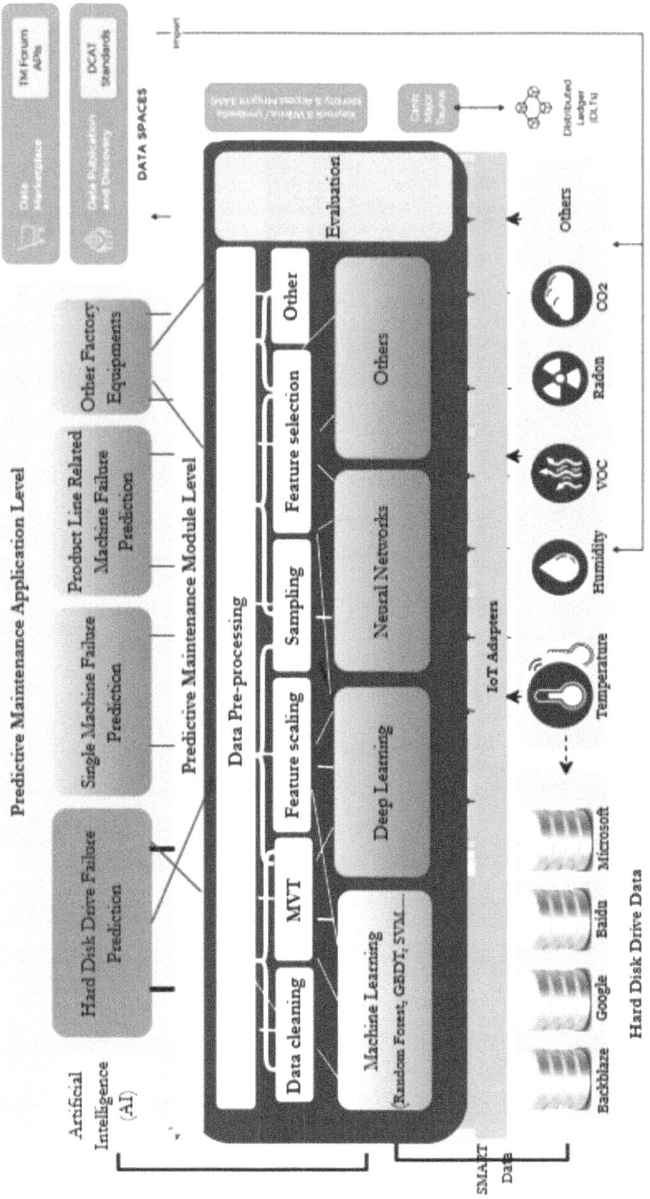

Fig. 2. Adaptive FIWARE smart architecture framework.

maintenance. It supports the deployment of different predictive maintenance solutions such as hard disk drive PdM, single machine PdM, product line-related machines PdM, and other factory equipment. As depicted in Fig. 2, it is pertinent to state that pre-processing HDD data for hard disk drive failure prediction is the focus of this paper, however, other predictive maintenance applications such as single machine PdM, related machines PdM, etc. are depicted in our architectural diagram as they are major components in manufacturing and could be included in the context of Industry 4.0 for future research.

5.1 Hard Disk Drive Data Pre-processing for Failure Prediction in Industry 4.0

Various forms of data pre-processing methods and analytical strategies have been proposed in the literature for analyzing HDD data for failure prediction [28]. After reviewing the hard disk drive failure prediction literature, our observation revealed that previous studies failed to acknowledge the analysis of HDD data in the context of Industry 4.0. This paper looked at hard disk drive data pre-processing in terms of the characteristics of the dataset i.e. data type (single model and multi-model), feature dimensionality, varying sample size, and machine learning performance in analyzing HDD dataset towards effective PdM in an industrial environment. While we recognize the influx of varying datasets in the Industry 4.0 ecosystem, we established an iterative pathway to pre-process the hard disk drive dataset that can serve as a template for other datasets within the ecosystem for effective data pre-processing. The proposed method named the Hard Disk Drive Data Pre-processing Pipeline (HDD-DPP) is kept generic and can be used to analyze a broad range of hard disk drive data and other related machine data with matching characteristics in the industrial settings.

In the HDD-DPP approach, the pre-processing strategies such as data cleaning, missing value treatment (MVT), feature scaling, sampling, and feature selection are all carried out within the cross-validation before partitioning the dataset into training and validation sets. The training and validation sets offer an effective step to select sample size before data pre-processing, allowing for data reduction in the training set to be used for analysis. This, in turn, helps optimize the predictive model. Subsequently, we can evaluate the hyperparameters of the selected machine learning using the validation results with metrics of FDRcv and FDRtest as adopted by [17]. Cross-validation by exempting some sets of data samples and holding certain sample sets for testing also offers great potential in evaluating the data pre-processing methodologies in hard disk drive data analysis. In such a scenario, if the predictive model built with the pre-processed data lacks bias and produces high generalization with both single-model and multi-model HDD datasets, then we can deduce that the cross-validation methodology for data pre-processing has a high generalization capability. However, to the best of our knowledge, there have been no previous studies with the application of cross-validation in the pre-processing stage of HDD data analysis as such that we have introduced in the Industrial settings. It is pertinent to state that cross-validation is an important tool for HDD data pre-processing in the industrial environment (Fig. 3).

In this sub-section, we adopt the adaptive FIWARE smart architectural framework presented in Fig. 2 to align the hard disk drive data pre-processing to the Industry 4.0 environment. We used a process model to present an iterative workflow for the hard disk drive data pre-processing across the four layers of the architecture. The process model offers an explicit representation of the proposed data pre-processing framework as a

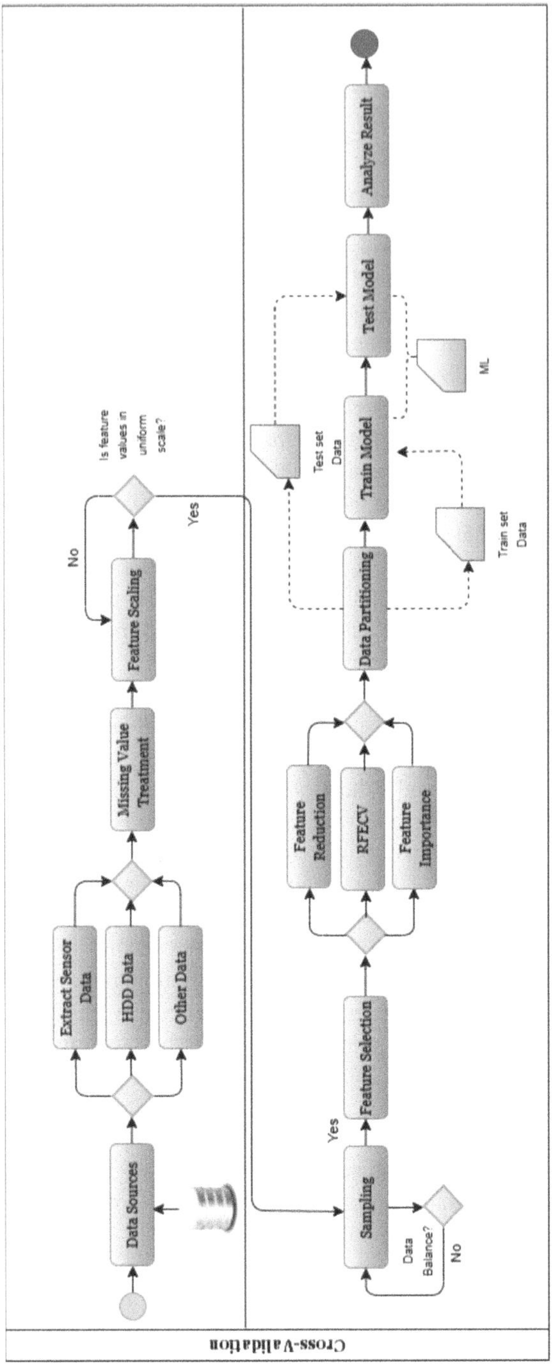

Fig. 3. Hard Disk Drive Data Pre-processing Pipeline for Pre-processing hard disk drive data in Industry 4.0.

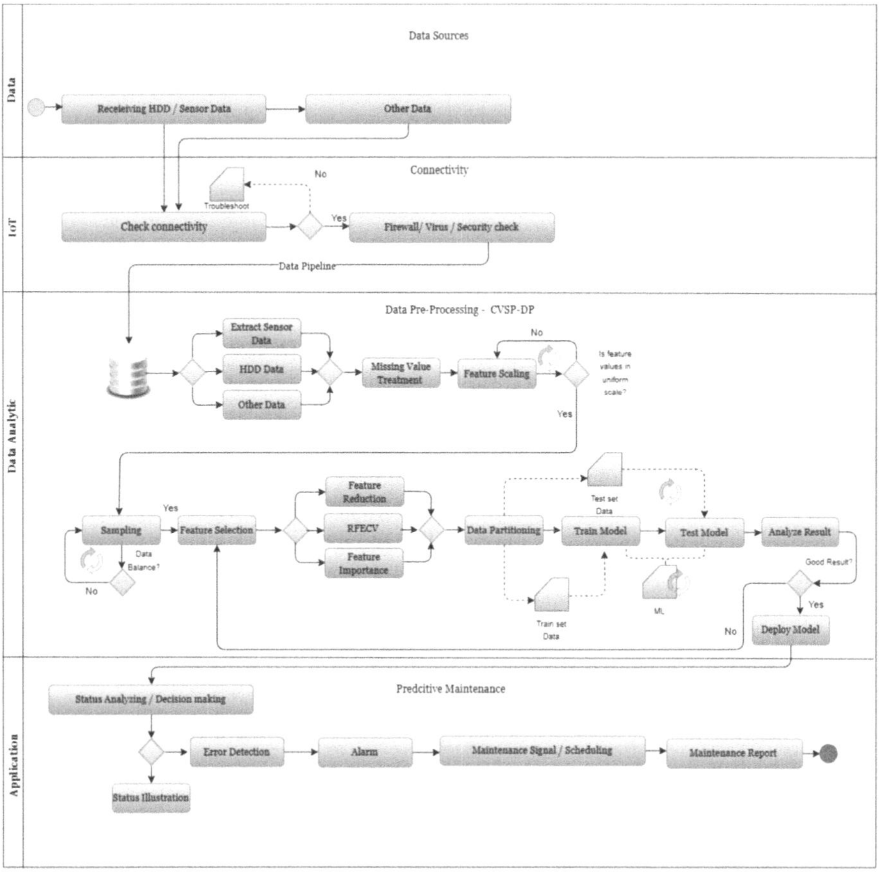

Fig. 4. Adaptive Process Model of HDD Data Pre-processing for Failure Prediction in Industry 4.0.

module within the architectural framework. Figure 4 presented below presents an adaptive process model for hard disk drive data pre-processing towards the implementation of HDD predictive maintenance in Industry 4.0.

The Data layer illustrates the data sources where varying hard disk drive data and other datasets are infused into the ecosystem. The IoT layer allows for data transfers from physical devices and components using different IoT adapters. The credibility of the dataset is checked via firewall and other data protection technologies to delay or remove corrupt data and viruses that could disrupt operations in the Industry 4.0 environment. The data analytic layer is the core of HDD predictive maintenance, and it embodies the data pre-preprocessing strategies, and the machine learning building block used for model development. Varying forms of datasets ranging from the SMART data, sensor data, etc. can be infused and pre-processed at this layer. Each data pre-processing strategy at this layer operates an iterative/loop procedure that allows for continuous execution of the process until the analysis result proves satisfactory for model deployment. For every developed model, the analytic procedure is also deployed as a template at this layer. This could be automated using agentic AI to detect and map matching datasets for analysis in future work. The application layer is an illustration and presentation stage that presents maintenance engineers and experts with analytic results, alarms, and detailed information needed for decision-making, planning, and adequate maintenance scheduling.

6 Experiments

6.1 Experiment

Motivation: to validate our proposed approach (HDD-DPP) using different datasets with variance in size, and imbalance ratio (IR). This is to ensure the capability and stability of our proposed approach to produce effective predictive performance irrespective of the input data size using traditional learning algorithms in Industrial settings.

Rationale: Experiment 1 will validate the viability of our proposed approach. Experiment 2 is to check the consistency and versatility of our approach. Using the same model of hard disk drive Seagate model ST10000NM0086 from the 4th quarter of 2022 and 1st quarter of 2023, we check the effect of data drift, imbalance ratio, and size on the HDD Seagate model dataset. We reduced the disk size with a difference in imbalance ratio in experiment 2 to compare to experiment 1. We aim to observe the performance of the selected models to determine if a larger dataset of the same model can produce similar results with a smaller dataset from the same model using the same analytical approach in industrial settings.

6.1.1 Data Description and Pre-processing

The dataset for this experiment was collected from Backblaze (Q4) 2022 and (Q1) 2023. The reason for choosing this quarter was to check the viability and consistency of our approach on different batches of datasets using 4th Quarter 2022 and 1st Quarter 2023 specifically. The dataset consists of total disks of 107,973 and 5,855 of the same model of Seagate ST10000NM0086 with 107955 healthy disks and only 18 failures for the last quarter of the year 2022 and a total of 14 failures in the first quarter of 2023 with an imbalanced ratio (IR) of $\approx$ 419.21. We observed consistency in the number of SMART features with 174 SMART (Raw and Normalized) excluding date, serial_number, model, capacity_bytes, and failure in the 1st Quarter of 2023.

Using the HDD-DPP, we used the same pre-processing approach in experiments 1 and 2. SMART features with zero nullity in their entirety were dropped and feature values with zero variances were also removed as such features are bound to be neglected by learning algorithms [17, 29]. A total of 124 SMART features (Raw and Normalized) recorded null values and 17 SMART features were observed with zero variances in the feature values. We treated missing values for the remaining 33 SMART features by filling all missing columns with zeros (0). Table 1 displays snippets of the datasets in a dataframe after missing value treatment.

Table 1. Dataframe containing Seagate model ST10000NM0086 datasets for 2022 (Q4).

1	model	failure	smart_1_r	smart_1_r	smart_3_r	smart_4_r	smart_5_r	smart_5_r	smart_7_r	smart_7_ra	smart_9_r	smart_9_r	smart_12_	smart_187	smart_187	smart_188	smart_189	smart_189	smart_190	smart_190
2	ST10000NM0086	0	80	95645500	92	12	100	0	85	336368091	81	16770	11	100	0	0	93	7	62	38
3	ST10000NM0086	0	79	76709580	92	13	100	32	90	952800976	49	44682	13	100	0	0	83	17	77	23
4	ST10000NM0086	0	76	40344348	94	6	100	0	96	4.182E+09	49	44686	6	100	0	0	73	27	79	21
5	ST10000NM0086	0	76	40746480	91	40	100	0	96	4.226E+09	49	44685	40	100	0	0	96	4	79	21
6	ST10000NM0086	0	79	71097224	92	10	100	104	70	9271390	49	44688	10	100	0	0	47	53	79	21
7	ST10000NM0086	0	77	48922488	91	20	100	0	96	4.143E+09	49	44680	20	100	0	0	27	73	75	25
8	ST10000NM0086	0	79	76839176	91	16	100	8	96	4.108E+09	50	44049	16	100	0	1	79	21	77	23
9	ST10000NM0086	0	82	1.7E+08	93	17	100	8	96	4.22E+09	49	44686	15	100	0	0	78	22	80	20
10	ST10000NM0086	0	81	1.19E+08	92	14	100	8	96	4.286E+09	49	44689	14	100	0	0	83	17	79	21
11	ST10000NM0086	0	72	15817344	91	15	100	40	96	4.235E+09	49	44693	15	100	0	0	98	2	77	23
12	ST10000NM0086	0	80	1.02E+08	91	11	100	0	96	4.256E+09	49	44688	11	100	0	0	89	11	78	22
13	ST10000NM0086	0	83	1.87E+08	91	10	100	0	78	61537557	49	44688	10	100	0	0	76	24	76	24
14	ST10000NM0086	0	83	1.87E+08	92	11	100	0	83	211993708	70	26340	10	100	0	0	82	18	76	24
15	ST10000NM0086	0	75	32280380	91	8	100	40	96	4.192E+09	49	44683	8	100	0	0	94	6	74	26

6.1.2 Feature Scaling for Backblaze Hard Disk Drive Dataset

From Table 1, we can see the differences in the range of feature values across the SMART features. Also, compared to the 1st quarter 2023 dataset, where the normalized feature values tend to remain static and similar across the SMART features, we observe differences in the feature values for not only the raw values but also for the normalized values in the 4th quarter 2022 dataset.

We implemented the MinMax method of feature scaling from Sklearn while setting feature_range = (0,1) to transform and fit the feature values in ranges to improve the performance of the learning algorithms. We can see from Figs. 5 and 6 that both the normalized and the raw feature attributes present fall in a uniform range after the feature scaling technique is implemented on the datasets. While we consider the same approach in experiments 1 and 2, both the raw and normalized feature values are adopted for analysis as in studies such [17, 25, 30]. Using Seaborn, we displayed the result of MinMax Scaler where the feature values are set in a range of 0 to 1 after scaling.

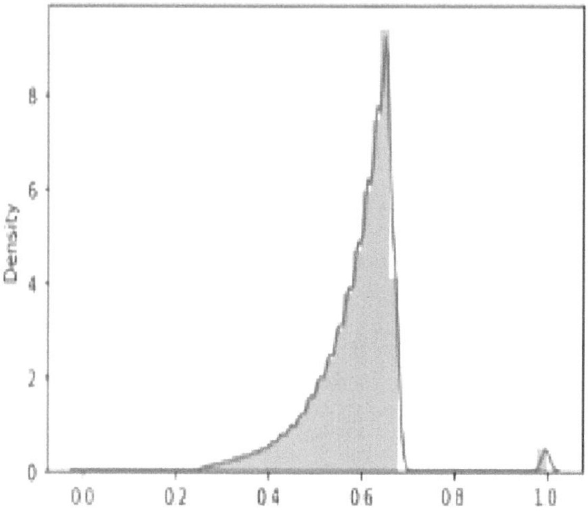

Fig. 5. Smart_3_normalized.

6.1.3 Data Sampling

It is pertinent to note that imbalanced learning problems consist of several factors that usually lead to uneven distribution among classes. This could be the number of HDD models deployed, disk quality, and weather conditions amongst several other factors [31]. For instance, in hard disk drive data, the data samples for failed disks are usually very rare compared to healthy disks. Therefore, the ratio of the minority class (failed disks) to the majority class (healthy disks) can be significant e.g., 1:1000 or more. However, to accurately predict HDD failure considering the high-class imbalance in the HDD dataset and the performance of the learning algorithms, it is essential to resolve the class imbalance to allow for better predictive performance. In this study, we adopted the use of the ADASYN sampling approach to remedy the class imbalance. The reason for choosing ADASYN is based on the performance output from our experiments 1 and 2. Our analytical observation using several learning algorithms and different HDD datasets in varying sizes has also shown better performance across 5 evaluation metrics (FDR, G-mean, AUROC, Accuracy, and Recall).

In experiments 1 and 2, we adopted the same model of the HDD model of Seagate ST1000NM0086 from Backblaze. For both datasets, we implemented ADASYN using

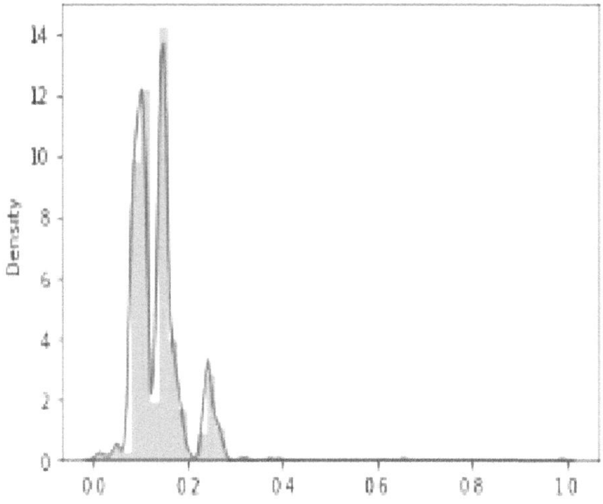

Fig. 6. Smart_4_raw.

the Imblearn library in a Jupyter Notebook environment to generate more synthetic data for the minority (1) class which is harder to learn compared to the majority class (0).

6.1.4 Feature Selection Scaling for Backblaze Hard Disk Drive Data

Based on previous works and the performance output in Yang et al., 2021 using a single model HDD dataset, we implemented the Recursive Feature Selection Cross-Validation (RFECV) algorithm to select the relevant features from both datasets. This approach has been used in several studies such as [32, 33] to improve HDD failure prediction accuracy. We envisage that the major issue with this approach is dealing with overfitting while improving accuracy and not removing relevant records. At the earlier stage, we applied pre-processing methods that will aid and support better performance. This is because RFECV works better with wrapped learning algorithms to extract relevant features from the dataset. Four learning algorithms were used in this experiment (Random Forest, Logistic regression, Gradient Boosting Decision Trees, and Decision Trees). We also achieve better results by setting cv = 5 in experiments 1 and 2. Please see below the number of features selected using RFECV and four wrapped learning algorithms.

From Table 2, experiment 1, RF-RFECV selected 5 features with an FDR score of 0.9642 while DT-RFECV selected only 2 features with an FDR score of 0.9414. Both Logistic Regression and Gradient Boosted Decision Trees with RFECV selected 30 and 27 features respectively. Training our model with such a high number of features (27 and 30 features) will foster high dimensionality in our dataset and increase computing time in Industrial settings.

In experiment 2, Random Forest and Decision Tree both selected two features each while Logistic Regression selected 25 features. GBDT selected only 10 features. Even though both RF and DT show better FDR, the performance output is poor using other metrics of evaluation. On the other hand, the number of selected features by LR-RFECV will increase the computing time and storage. We have selected the 5 features selected

Table 2. Learning models and RFECV with maximum FDR of **0.9851**.

Models	Feature selection	Scaling Method	Experiment 1 (Q4, 2022)		Experiment 2 (Q1, 2023)	
			n_features	FDR	n_features	FDR
Random Forest	RFECV	MinMax (0,1)	5	0.9642	2	0.9312
Logistic Regression			30	0.9458	25	0.7266
Gradient Boosted Decision Trees			27	0.9817	10	0.9564
Decision Trees			2	0.9414	2	0.8947

by Random Forest for experiment 1 and 10 features selected by GBDT-RFECV to train our model in experiment 2 respectively (Figs. 7 and 8).

Diagram Index – the highest point in the graph depicts the number of selected features marked ■. While the tail mark ■ indicates the FDR score point of the selected features.

For comparison purposes, we first used the metrics of FDRtest and FDRcv to evaluate the performances of the four learning algorithms using the 5 and 10 selected features for experiments 1 and 2. This is to allow us to measure the performances of the models relative to other work such as [17] where the same metrics are adopted for evaluation. We then present in Table 4 the performance result across other metrics.

Table 4 presents the performance results of the selected models across other metrics. We evaluate the effectiveness of our approach in exp #1 and #2 while considering variances such as the size and dimensionality, and overall characteristics of the dataset. By investigating the Model performances in exp #1 and in comparison, with exp #2, Logistic Regression shows the lowest performance across all metrics while GBDT shows better performance across all metrics. Based on G-mean and AUROC, GBDT remains consistence and still shows higher performance compared to other models. The consistencies in GBDT performance can be seen not only across the metrics in Table 4 but also with FDRtest and FDRcv in Table 3, where GBDT shows a maximum FDRtest of 0.9688.

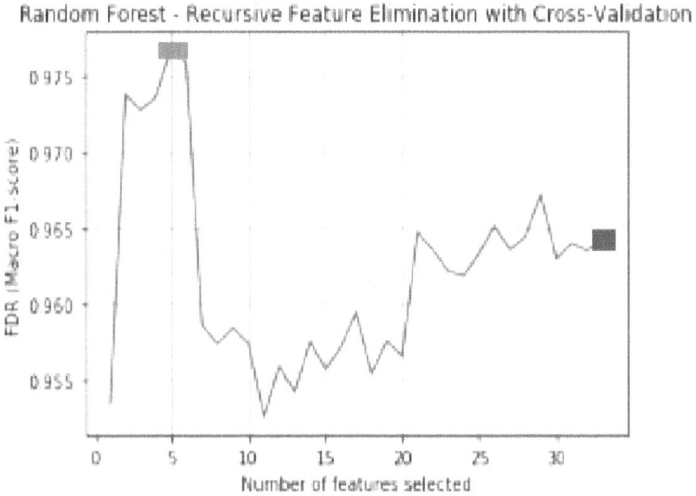

Fig. 7. Random Forest – RFECV (Experiment 1).

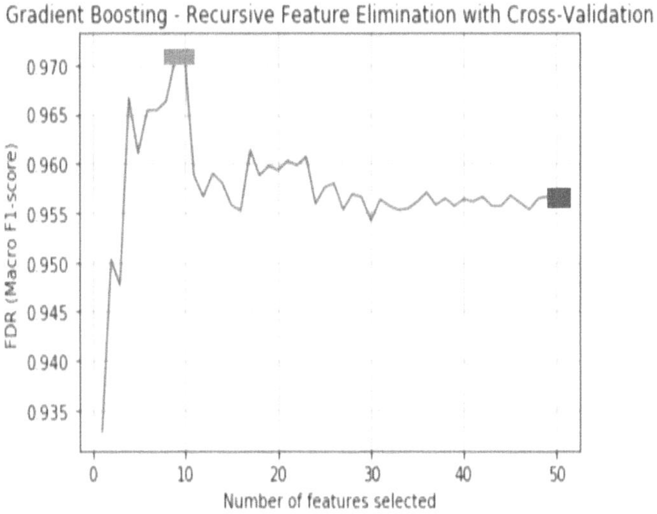

Fig. 8. GBDT – RFECV (Experiment 2).

Failure Detection Rate (FDR) measures the proportion of the correctly predicted failures while FDRtesting is a corresponding FDR in the testing stage which is deemed suitable for all the combinations of feature selection methods and anomaly detection algorithms [17]. While experiments 1 and 2 share the same analytical approach, the two experiments vary in terms of data size and IR. Hence, a need to acknowledge the versatility and consistency of GDBT in this study. However, there is a need for further experiments using other dataset models (Figs. 9 and 10).

Table 3. Performance Evaluation on Model ST10000NM0086 with the maximum FDR of Testing = 0.9688.

Experiment 1									
STAGE	Feature selection	Yang Approach				HDD-DPP Approach			
		RF	LR	GBDT	DT	RF	LR	GBDT	DT
CV	RFECV	0.7778	0.7778	0.6944	-	0.9761	0.8863	0.9851	0.9692
Testing	RFECV	0.8000	0.8800	**0.8800**	-	0.9778	0.8863	**0.9851**	0.9598
Experiment 2									
CV	RFECV	0.7778	0.7778	0.6944	-	0.9370	0.7031	0.9687	0.9361
Testing	RFECV	0.8000	0.8800	**0.8800**	-	0.9435	0.7031	**0.9688**	0.9306

Table 4. Performance Evaluation across other metrics for the HDD-DPP approach.

	Experiment 1			
Metrics	RF	LR	GBDT	DT
FDR	0.9642	0.9458	**0.9817**	0.9414
G-mean	0.9784	0.8926	0.9855	0.9633
AUROC	1.0000	0.9752	0.9997	0.9997
Accuracy	0.9998	0.9034	0.9972	0.9997
Recall	0.9998	0.8473	0.9999	0.9995
	Experiment 2			
FDR	0.9312	0.7266	**0.9565**	0.8948
G-mean	0.9467	0.7131	0.9703	0.9377
AUROC	0.9999	0.8235	0.9999	0.9963
Accuracy	0.9986	0.7501	0.9963	0.9954
Recall	0.9983	0.7523	0.9989	0.9949

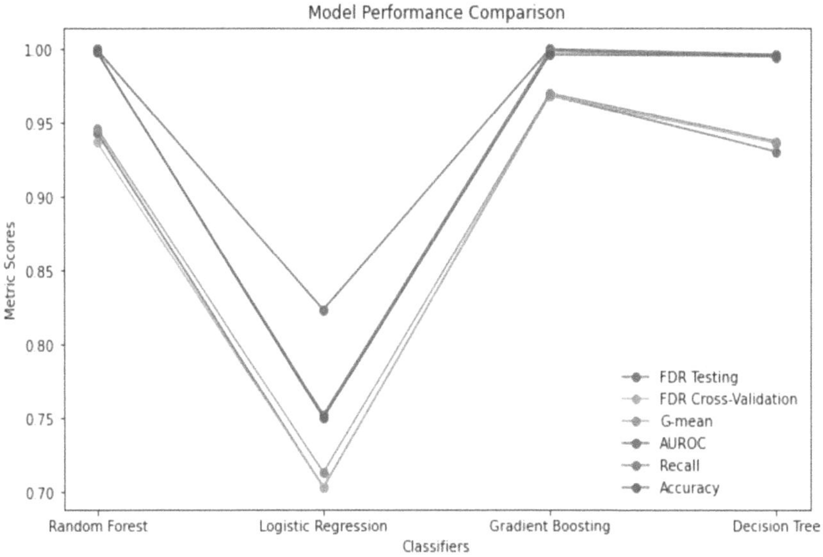

Fig. 9. Model Comparison for Experiment 1.

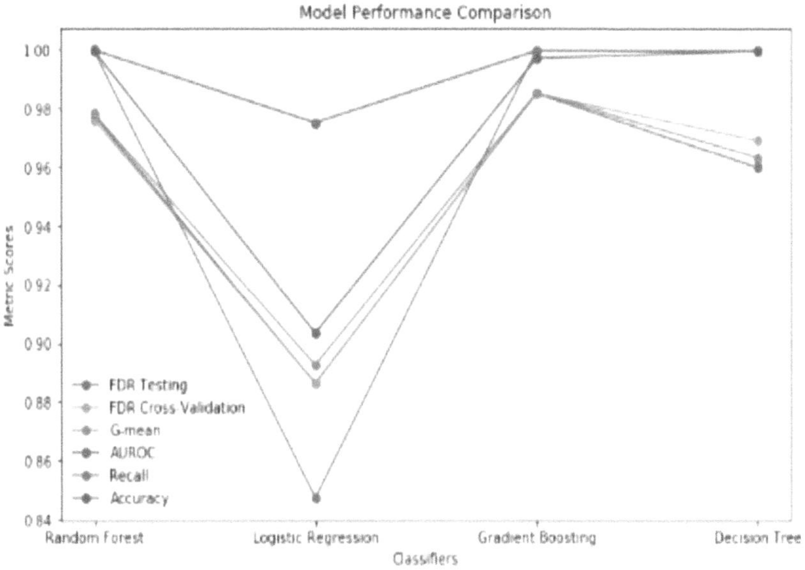

Fig. 10. Model Comparison for Experiment 2.

7 Discussions

The need for storage systems continues to grow with the rapid development in the manufacturing environment. Hard disk drives are the core of storage systems and are generally considered the most replaced components in Industrial data centers. Traditional hard drive failure prediction is usually based on SMART machine learning approach using an expert or company's own data pre-processing approach that is not consistent with the ever-changing nature of SMART attributes and Industry 4.0 settings. This approach is considered not suitable for hard disk drive failure prediction in the Industry 4.0 context due to the following: (1) the consistency of the SMART attributes cannot be guaranteed and it is challenging that the data integrity may not meet up with the I4.0 standard (2) that the heterogeneity nature of HDD data, the size, the data type (single-model and multi-model), years, time window, multiple-sources requires a dynamic and robust analytic method of analysis and there is currently no provision for this context. This work used a specialized data pre-processing and machine learning model. The experiment results show the viability of the data pre-processing approach and the selected machine learning methods to overcome the difficulty of variances in the SMART differences, data size, and year using a single model of the Backblaze dataset.

There is still much work to be done in terms of the scalability of the model and the data types. Other machine learning models are yet to be experimented with, which may show better results and stability across different datasets. In terms of the dataset, we adopted a single model of the Seagate ST10000NM0086 dataset from Backblaze across different years. In the future, we will adopt datasets from other HDD vendors and data centers. We will analyze other HDD model datasets to verify the effectiveness of our approach. To support the analysis of other disk models, we will look at the impact of varying data size, year and time of release, and the quality of data on the selected machine learning model. We will also consider other feature selection methods in combination with the selected machine learning model. Finally, other advanced sampling methods will be explored in combination with the machine learning algorithm and feature selection method.

8 Conclusion and Future Work

This paper presents the data pre-processing of hard disk drive data in the context of Industry 4.0. This is done by first integrating hard disk drive failure prediction into the Industry 4.0 ecosystem while focusing on the HDD pre-processing within the framework. The cross-validation standard process data pre-processing (CVSP-DP) method proposed in this work offers a dynamic and varying data pre-processing method for not only the HDD dataset but also for other matching datasets. This paper exploits the technological features of the FIWARE smart architecture to create an adaptive solution for the implementation of HDD data pre-processing which is a sub-process of HDD failure prediction in Industry 4.0.

The challenges of harmonizing and pre-processing different forms of HDD datasets for the implementation of HDD predictive maintenance in Industry 4.0 has been a problem in the industrial environment and this study proffers a solution to the problem. The data pre-processing approach utilizes supervised machine learning such as GDBT,

Random Forest, Decision Trees, and Logistics regression. The approach also handles crucial issues such as high dimensionality and class imbalance to ensure data quality and integrity for HDD datasets within the Industrial ecosystem. The consistence performance of the model of GDBT and Decision across the varying datasets shows the viability of our approach to handle data drift within the Industrial settings. Future work is required in terms of verification using other forms of HDD datasets using different use cases via experiments to further check the viability and consistency of the approach. Further research on automating the data pre-processing framework using agentic AI should also be considered.

References

1. Zonta, T., et al.: Predictive maintenance in the Industry 4.0: A systematic literature review. Comput. Ind. Eng. **150**, 106889 (2020). https://doi.org/10.1016/J.CIE.2020.106889
2. Czwick, C., Anderl, R.: Data Pre-Processing Method for Industrie 4.0 Applications. Procedia Comput. Sci. **200**, 327–336 (2022). https://doi.org/10.1016/J.PROCS.2022.01.231
3. Lee, E.A.: Cyber physical systems: design challenges. In: 2008 11th IEEE International Symposium on Object and Component-Oriented Real-Time Distributed Computing (ISORC), pp. 363–369 (2008). https://doi.org/10.1109/ISORC.2008.25
4. Sankhye, S., Hu, G.: Machine learning methods for quality prediction in production. Logistics **4** (2020). https://doi.org/10.3390/logistics4040035
5. Krawczyk, B., Minku, L.L., Gama, J., Stefanowski, J., Woźniak, M.: Ensemble learning for data stream analysis: a survey. Information Fusion. **37**, 132–156 (2017). https://doi.org/10.1016/J.INFFUS.2017.02.004
6. Gama, J., Žliobaitundefined, I., Bifet, A., Pechenizkiy, M., Bouchachia, A.: A survey on concept drift adaptation. ACM Comput. Surv. **46** (2014). https://doi.org/10.1145/2523813
7. Yuan, S., Wu, P., Chen, Y. and Li, Q.: A Survey of Methods for Handling Disk Data Imbalance. arXiv preprint arXiv. (2023)
8. Sony, M., Naik, S.: Key ingredients for evaluating Industry 4.0 readiness for organizations: a literature review. Benchmarking: An International J. **27**, 2213–2232 (2020). https://doi.org/10.1108/BIJ-09-2018-0284
9. Su, C.J., Jorge, A.Q.Y.: Big Data preventive Maintenance for Hard Disk Failure Detection. Int. J. Info. Educ. Technol. **8** (2018)
10. Miller, Z., Medaiyese, O., Ravi, M., Beatty, A., Lin, F.: Hard disk drive failure analysis and prediction: an industry view. In: 2023 53rd Annual IEEE/IFIP International Conference on Dependable Systems and Networks - Supplemental Volume (DSN-S), pp. 21–27 (2023). https://doi.org/10.1109/DSN-S58398.2023.00020
11. Peffers, K., Tuunanen, T., Rothenberger, M.A., Chatterjee, S.: A design science research methodology for information systems research. J. Manag. Inf. Syst. **24**, 45–77 (2007). https://doi.org/10.2753/MIS0742-1222240302
12. Backblaze, https://www.backblaze.com/
13. Kotsiantis, S.B., Kanellopoulos, D., Pintelas, P.E.: Data preprocessing for supervised leaning. Int. J. Comp. Sci. **1**, 111–117 (2006)
14. Kumar, V., Khosla, C.: Data cleaning-a thorough analysis and survey on unstructured data. In: 2018 8th International Conference on Cloud Computing, Data Science & Engineering (Confluence), pp. 305–309 (2018). https://doi.org/10.1109/CONFLUENCE.2018.8442950
15. Ahmad, W., Khan, S.A., Kim, C.H., Kim, J.-M.: Feature selection for improving failure detection in hard disk drives using a genetic algorithm and significance scores. Applied Sciences **10** (2020). https://doi.org/10.3390/app10093200

16. Cai, J., Luo, J., Wang, S., Yang, S.: Feature selection in machine learning: a new perspective. Neurocomputing **300**, 70–79 (2018). https://doi.org/10.1016/J.NEUCOM.2017.11.077
17. Yang, Q., Jia, X., Li, X., Feng, J., Li, W., Lee, J.: Evaluating feature selection and anomaly detection methods of hard drive failure prediction. IEEE Trans. Reliab. **70**, 749–760 (2021). https://doi.org/10.1109/TR.2020.2995724
18. Aussel, N., et al.: Predictive models of hard drive failures based on operational data. In: 2017 16th IEEE International Conference on Machine Learning and Applications (ICMLA), pp. 619–625 (2017). https://doi.org/10.1109/ICMLA.2017.00-92
19. Ding, J., Tarokh, V., Yang, Y.: Model selection techniques: an overview. IEEE Signal Process. Mag. **35**, 16–34 (2018). https://doi.org/10.1109/MSP.2018.2867638
20. Pitakrat, T., van Hoorn, A., Grunske, L.: A comparison of machine learning algorithms for proactive hard disk drive failure detection. In: Proceedings of the 4th International ACM Sigsoft Symposium on Architecting Critical Systems, pp. 1–10. Association for Computing Machinery, New York, NY, USA (2013). https://doi.org/10.1145/2465470.2465473
21. Shreemali, J., et al.: WITHDRAWN: Comparing performance of multiple classifiers for regression and classification machine learning problems using structured datasets. Mater Today Proc. (2021). https://doi.org/10.1016/J.MATPR.2020.12.480
22. Rincón, C.A., P.J.F., V.R., C.A.M., L.D.D.: Disk failure prediction in heterogeneous environments. International Symposium on Performance Evaluation of Computer and Telecommunication Systems (SPECTS), pp. 1–7 (2016)
23. Shen, J., Wan, J., Lim, S.-J., Yu, L.: Random-forest-based failure prediction for hard disk drives. Int. J. Distrib. Sens. Netw. **14**, 1550147718806480 (2018). https://doi.org/10.1177/1550147718806480
24. Anantharaman, P., Qiao, M., Jadav, D.: Large scale predictive analytics for hard disk remaining useful life estimation. In: 2018 IEEE International Congress on Big Data (BigData Congress), pp. 251–254 (2018). https://doi.org/10.1109/BigDataCongress.2018.00044
25. Amram, M., Dunn, J., Toledano, J.J., Zhuo, Y.D.: Interpretable predictive maintenance for hard drives. Machine Learning with Applications. **5**, 100042 (2021). https://doi.org/10.1016/J.MLWA.2021.100042
26. Achouch, M., et al.: On Predictive Maintenance in Industry 4.0: Overview, Models, and Challenges. Applied Sciences. **12** (2022). https://doi.org/10.3390/app12168081
27. Adolph, R.: FIWARE Smart Industry Reference Architecture, https://www.fiware.org/about-us/smart-industry/
28. Bhardwaj, S., Saxena, A.A.N.: Exploratory data analysis on hard drive failure statistics and prediction. Int. J. Adv. Res. Comp. Sci. Manage. Stud. **6** (2018)
29. Tomer, V., Sharma, V., Gupta, S., Singh, D.P.: Hard disk drive failure prediction using SMART attribute. Mater Today Proc. **46**, 11258–11262 (2021). https://doi.org/10.1016/J.MATPR.2021.03.229
30. Botezatu, M.M., Giurgiu, I., Bogojeska, J., Wiesmann, D.: Predicting disk replacement towards reliable data centers. In: Proceedings of the 22nd ACM SIGKDD International Conference on Knowledge Discovery and Data Mining, pp. 39–48. Association for Computing Machinery, New York, NY, USA (2016). https://doi.org/10.1145/2939672.2939699
31. Ahmed, J., Green, R.C., II.: Predicting severely imbalanced data disk drive failures with machine learning models. Machine Learning with Applications. **9**, 100361 (2022). https://doi.org/10.1016/J.MLWA.2022.100361
32. Queiroz, L.P., et al.: A fault detection method for hard disk drives based on mixture of gaussians and nonparametric statistics. IEEE Trans. Industr. Inform. **13**, 542–550 (2017). https://doi.org/10.1109/TII.2016.2619180
33. Chaves, I.C., et al.: BaNHFaP: a bayesian network based failure prediction approach for hard disk drives. In: 2016 5th Brazilian Conference on Intelligent Systems (BRACIS), pp. 427–432 (2016). https://doi.org/10.1109/BRACIS.2016.083

Forecasting Power Demand in Complex Buildings Using Machine Learning: A Shopping Center Case Study

Bruno Palley[1](✉), Hermano Bernardo[1], João Poças Martins[2], and Rosaldo Rossetti[3]

[1] INESC TEC - Institute for Systems and Computer Engineering, Technology and Science, Faculty of Engineering (FEUP), University of Porto, Porto, Portugal
{bruno.palley,hermano.bernardo}@inesctec.pt

[2] CONSTRUCT - Gequaltec, Faculty of Engineering (FEUP), University of Porto, Porto, Portugal
jppm@fe.up.pt

[3] LIACC - Artificial Intelligence and Computer Science Laboratory), Faculty of Engineering (FEUP), Department of Informatics Engineering, University of Porto, Porto, Portugal
rossetti@fe.up.pt

Abstract. Recent studies have focused on forecasting power demand in buildings to enhance energy management. However, the literature still lacks comparative analyses of power demand forecasting algorithms. In addition, more case studies involving different building typologies are needed, as each building exhibits distinct behavior and load profiles. This paper aims to develop machine learning models to forecast the power demand of a large shopping center in the northern region of Portugal. The main objective is to compare the performance of several machine learning models. The results are promising, demonstrating adequate performance even during most holidays.

Keywords: Machine Learning · Energy Demand Forecasting · Linear Regression · Random Forest · Artificial Neural Network · XGBoost · Support Vector Regression

1 Introduction

Climate transition and the need for more sustainable resource management are highly relevant topics today. At the same time, urban populations continue to grow steadily each year [1–4]. In this context, buildings are a major contributor to both energy consumption and carbon emissions [5–8]. The ability to forecast power demand accurately is increasingly important, as effective energy management and resource optimization become more feasible when all elements of the system are well understood. For example, in energy optimization models for buildings—where variables such as PV generation, energy storage systems, electric vehicle (EV) demand must be considered—accurate demand forecasting becomes even more critical. Among these variables, power demand forecasting plays a key role in enabling efficient optimization and, consequently, improving energy management in buildings.

Published by Springer Nature Switzerland AG 2025
L. M. Camarinha-Matos and F. Ferrada (Eds.): DoCEIS 2025, IFIP AICT 759, pp. 101–112, 2025.
https://doi.org/10.1007/978-3-031-97051-1_7

At the same time, the Fourth Industrial Revolution—also known as Industry 4.0—has introduced several technologies with applications across various fields. One of these is artificial intelligence (AI), a topic that is becoming increasingly popular, with rising demand and a broad range of applications. Within the field of AI, machine learning refers to the process of identifying patterns in data, generating predictions, and supporting decision-making. This trend is further reinforced by the growing availability of data, largely driven by the expansion of Internet of Things (IoT) devices [9]. In this context, the presence of smart meters in buildings, combined with the use of machine learning, represents a promising approach to improving energy management and accurately forecasting demand.

There has been a growing number of studies applying machine learning to forecast power demand in buildings [10–12]. Nevertheless, further efforts are needed to compare the performance of different algorithms for short-term power demand forecasting [10]. This paper applies machine learning models to measured data from a case study to forecast power demand. The main objective is to compare several algorithms and assess their performance under real-world conditions, highlighting the practical challenges associated with forecasting in such environments. This contribution aims to enrich the existing body of knowledge by presenting a detailed case study with its unique characteristics. Accordingly, this study addresses the following research questions:

- How can machine learning be used to forecast energy consumption in complex buildings?
- What is the load profile behavior of complex buildings, such as shopping centers?
- What are the main challenges in forecasting power demand in complex buildings, such as shopping centers?

The remainder of this paper is organized as follows. Section 2 presents a background review of the literature and discusses the paper's relevance to technological innovation in AI-Powered Cyber-Physical Systems. Section 3 describes the materials and methods used in this study. Section 4 presents the results, relevant charts, and a discussion. Finally, Sect. 5 outlines the main conclusions and suggests directions for future work.

2 Background and Technological Innovation in AI-Powered Cyber-Physical Systems

Cyber-Physical Systems (CPS) are closely related to the integration of the physical and digital worlds [13–15]. A typical CPS comprises two main components: a physical element—such as a device, machine, or building—and a digital counterpart, which includes data, software, and communication networks [16]. CPS play a crucial role in enabling continuous feedback loops between the physical and digital layers [13], thereby enhancing information flow, process monitoring, and overall system efficiency and control.

This real-time information mechanism, enabled by the CPS, creates significant potential for analyzing what is happening in the physical domain. Indeed, many building systems already collect real-time data through sophisticated sensors and smart devices [16]. However, this data flow becomes even more relevant when combined with AI techniques.

In this context, CPS integrated with machine learning models can play a crucial role in improving real-time decision-making.

Recent research has demonstrated that machine learning models are effective tools for forecasting energy usage [17, 18]. Several review articles on the application of machine learning models in building energy demand estimation underscore the growing prevalence of studies in this domain [10, 17, 19, 20]. Likewise, Corticos and Duarte [11] reported a significant increase in publications related to "AI," "Energy Efficiency," and "Buildings" since 2018. Accordingly, de Wilde [12] identified a sharp rise in research on machine learning and Building Performance Simulation after 2015. Collectively, these studies highlight the expanding role of machine learning in energy management, driven by the growing demand for sustainable and efficient energy use.

Notwithstanding the progress in machine learning applications for energy forecasting, further research is needed to compare algorithms for predicting energy usage in buildings [10, 21]. In this context, the present study focuses on developing machine learning models to estimate short-term energy demand in complex buildings. The primary objective is to assess the performance of Linear Regression, Random Forest, Artificial Neural Network (ANN), Extreme Gradient Boost (XGBoost), and Support Vector Regression (SVR) in forecasting short-term energy use. The findings aim to deepen the understanding of machine learning applications in energy management and provide practical insights for building managers.

3 Materials and Methods

The overall methodology adopted for developing and evaluating the machine learning models is summarized in Fig. 1, outlining the key stages from data collection to performance evaluation.

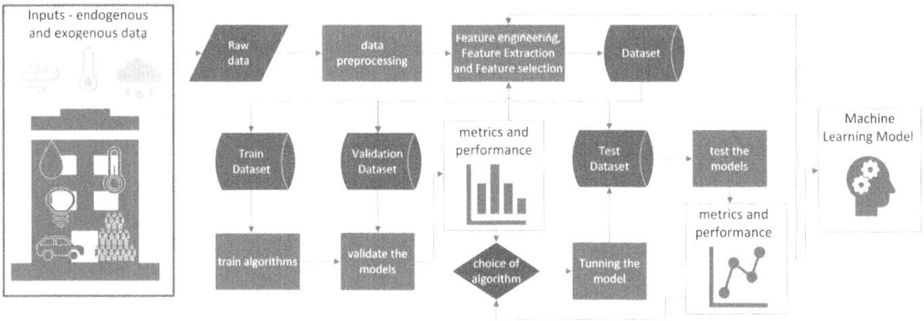

Fig. 1. Process diagram for machine learning-based power demand forecasting in the building.

The process begins with data collection and verification, using data either directly from the building or from external sources, in search of both endogenous and exogenous variables. The raw data is then preprocessed to address issues such as missing values and outliers, and to ensure a uniform time resolution across all variables. Feature engineering can be valuable in time-series forecasting, especially for incorporating historical data insights. Furthermore, feature selection is essential for identifying the most relevant combinations of variables.

The red lines in the diagram show that the process is iterative and recursive, allowing modifications in earlier phases to improve outcomes in the validation or testing stages. The overall goal is to identify the optimal combination of elements (algorithms, hyperparameters, features, and others) to develop the most robust and reliable machine learning models.

3.1 Case Study and Dataset

The case study selected is a large shopping center located in the Northern Region of Portugal. This type of building presents specific characteristics in terms of energy consumption behavior, making it a valuable subject for analysis.

The building is equipped with smart meters installed on the electrical panels, which record energy data, such as the power demand—the target variable of this study. In addition, data on occupancy rates for both people and vehicles are available. The building also includes sensors that monitor indoor environmental quality. For external weather conditions, open-source data from Open-Meteo, was used [22].

The first step in Fig. 1 involves the integration of all data sources into a single raw dataset. The available period spans 21 June 2022 to 31 December 2023. The raw data was preprocessed to identify and correct inconsistencies, outliers, missing values, and other anomalies. For example, to handle daylight saving time transitions, interpolation was applied during the shift to summer time (to fill missing values), while duplicated records during the return to winter time were averaged.

To ensure consistency in model training, the data were normalized so that all features shared a common scale. Techniques such as the Min-Max scaler and MaxAbsScaler are sensitive to outliers, whereas the Standard Scaler—based on the mean and standard deviation—is less so but can still be affected by extreme values. Therefore, the Robust Scaler was selected, as it uses statistics that are less sensitive to outliers. Specifically, the Interquartile Range (IQR)—defined as the range between the 25th and 75th percentiles—was used for scaling [23].

Since some features were recorded at a 10-min or 15-min interval, all data were resampled to an hourly resolution by computing average values.

Feature engineering plays a vital role in developing accurate machine learning models, particularly for time-series forecasting, where capturing historical patterns is essential. For example, including the power demand of the previous day helps establish temporal dependencies.

An initial set of potentially relevant features was created. However, adding more features does not necessarily improve model performance. Therefore, feature selection was performed using the XGBoost algorithm [24], which ranked feature importance both before and after hyperparameter tuning. Features that consistently ranked lowest—such as rain data and indoor environmental quality parameters (e.g., indoor temperature and relative humidity)—were excluded.

Once feature engineering and selection were completed, the dataset was finalized for model training. A summary of the resulting dataset is presented in Table 1.

Table 1. Dataset summary: selected features and target variable.

Name	Type	Unit	Description
Power Demand	Float	kW	Power demand (target)
People	Integer	units	People occupancy rate in the building
Cars	Integer	units	Car occupancy rate in the parking lot
temperature_2m	Float	°C	Outdoor air temperature (Open-Meteo)
month	Integer	1 to 12	Month
day	Integer	1 to 31	Day of the month
hour	Integer	0 to 23	Hour of the day
day_of_week	Integer	0 to 6	Day of the week
is_closed_holiday	Integer	binary	Closed-building holiday
is_open_holiday	Integer	binary	Open-building holiday
hour_sin	Float	-	Cyclic variable to capture periodicity
hour_cos	Float	-	Cyclic variable to capture periodicity
day_sin	Float	-	Cyclic variable to capture periodicity
Lag_1,…,Lag_48	Float	kW	Features regarding historical Power Demand for the last 48 h

3.2 Machine Learning Algorithms and Error Metrics

Several well-known Machine Learning algorithms were tested, including Linear Regression, Random Forest, ANN, XGBoost, and SVR. The selection was based on incorporating a variety of modelling strategies, combining both linear and nonlinear approaches. The primary objective was to compare the performance and behavior of these algorithms.

For the ANN model, the MLPRegressor from Scikit-learn [23] was used due to its clarity and interpretability. Scikit-learn [23] served as the primary library for implementing the models, with additional packages used in Python [25].

The performance of each model was evaluated using multiple error metrics: Root Mean Squared Error (RMSE), Mean Squared Error (MSE), Mean Absolute Error (MAE), Mean Absolute Percentage Error (MAPE), and the Coefficient of Determination (R2) [26]. While no single metric is universally superior, using a combination provides a more comprehensive assessment.

MAE provides a simple interpretation of average error magnitude. RMSE, expressed in the same units as the target variable, highlights the influence of larger errors. MSE also penalizes larger deviations by squaring the errors, making it useful for identifying models with occasional large prediction errors. R2 indicates how well the model captures variance in the data, with higher values representing better performance. Finally, MAPE provides insight into the relative size of errors, which is especially useful when comparing predictions across varying magnitudes.

3.3 Hyperparameter Tuning

The goal of the hyperparameter tuning was to identify optimal hyperparameters for each algorithm across multiple training data splits. Tuning was performed using Optuna [27], an open-source framework for automated hyperparameter optimization, in combination with TimeSeriesSplit from Scikit-learn [23]. Optuna was configured to minimize the average RMSE across five data splits and was set to run 100 optimization trials.

This approach reduces the risk of overfitting and improves the models' ability to generalize to unseen data.

4 Results and Discussion

A summary of the error metrics and performance results for all evaluated models is shown in Table 2.

Table 2. Performance and error metrics summary.

Error Metric	Model				
	Linear Regression	Random Forest	ANN	XGBoost	SVR
RMSE [kW]	125.34	140.35	150.29	129.00	129.11
MSE [kW^2]	15,710.90	19,697.53	22,587.51	16,641.49	16,669.74
MAE [kW]	80.35	82.48	115.48	78.34	74.95
MAPE [%]	0.14	0.14	0.29	0.13	0.11
R^2 [%]	0.93	0.91	0.91	0.93	0.93
Processing times					
Training time[s]	0.01	63.09	29.15	4.04	5.04
Prediction time[s]	<0.01	0.02	0.01	0.02	0.46

It is important to highlight the processing time differences of the models. On the one hand, the SVR demands more time to make predictions. On the other hand, Random Forest demands more time to train the models.

XGBoost stands out for its balanced performance, achieving strong error metrics while maintaining relatively low training and prediction times. It achieved the best results in terms of R2 and MAPE, and ranked second-best for RMSE, MSE, MAE, as well as training and prediction time.

In contrast, the ANN demonstrated the weakest performance across all error metrics. These results suggest the potential benefit of more complex neural networks in future work.

4.1 Scatter Dispersion Plots

Figure 2 presents the scatter dispersion plots and corresponding R2 values for each model. These plots are essential for analyzing the overall behavior of the models by comparing actual versus predicted values.

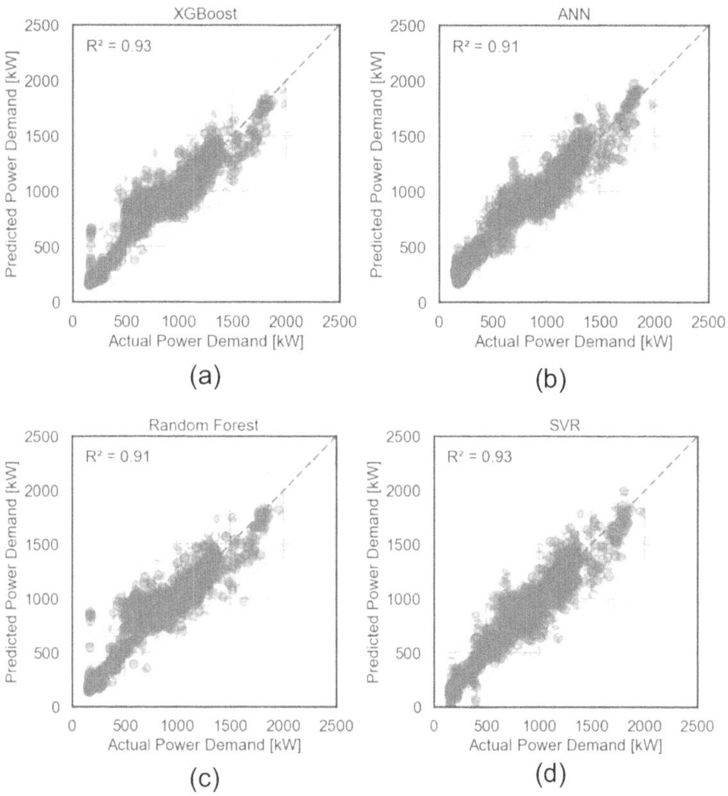

Fig. 2. Scatter plots: XGBoost (a), ANN (b), Randon Forest (c), and SVR (d).

The results indicate that the models generally provide accurate predictions; however, in some cases, they fail to fully capture the trends present in the actual values. Load profiling plots are particularly useful for analyzing specific periods and identifying critical days where model performance may degrade.

4.2 Load Profiling

Figure 3 illustrates the overall strong performance of all the developed models. Furthermore, it highlights November 6th as a representative example of the ANN model's poorest performance relative to the other models.

Since XGBoost presented the best overall performance, the following plots will focus on the behavior of this model. Figure 4 demonstrates that the predicted trend closely follows the actual values for the XGBoost model.

Moreover, as shown in Fig. 5, the model remains accurate even on atypical days such as the holiday on November 1st, successfully forecasting the increase in power demand.

Nevertheless, the models face challenges in prediction on holidays when the building is closed. In this case, the building is closed only on Christmas Day (December 25th)

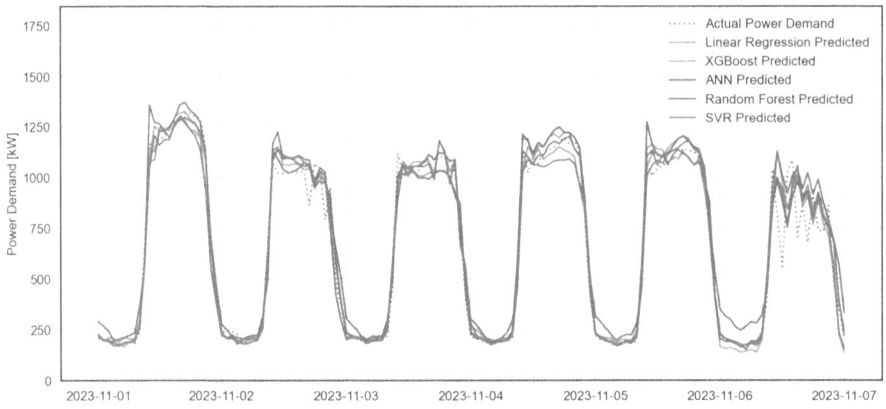

Fig. 3. Predictions of load profiling.

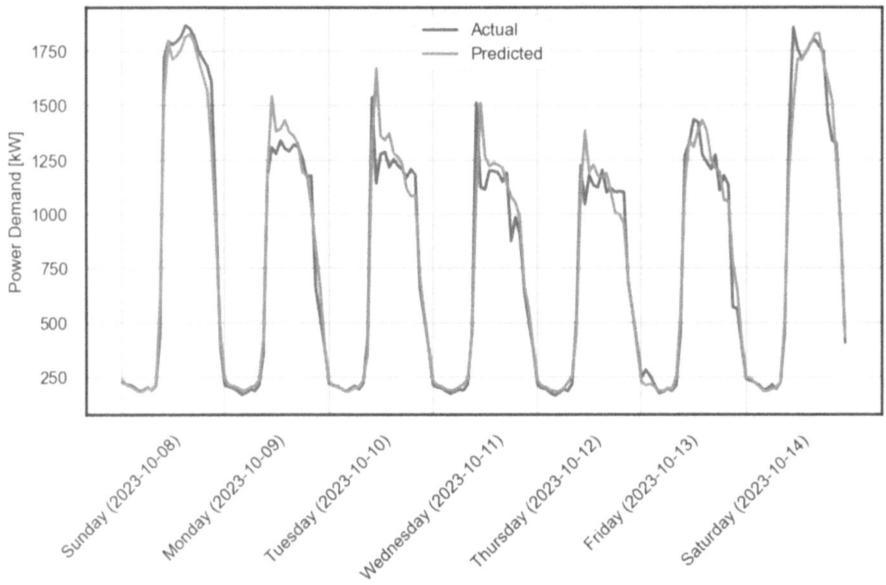

Fig. 4. Predictions of load profiling using XGBoost

and New Year's Day (January 1st). Figure 6 shows this behavior for the XGBoost model on December 25th.

Notably, this forecasting challenge on Christmas Day is observed across all the models, not just XGboost. Firstly, the model did not anticipate the building closure and consequently failed in its prediction. Secondly, shopping centers often experience higher occupancy in the days leading up to Christmas, resulting in increased power demand on unexpected days. These factors, combined with the limited availability of historical data for similar closure periods, contribute to the reduced prediction accuracy.

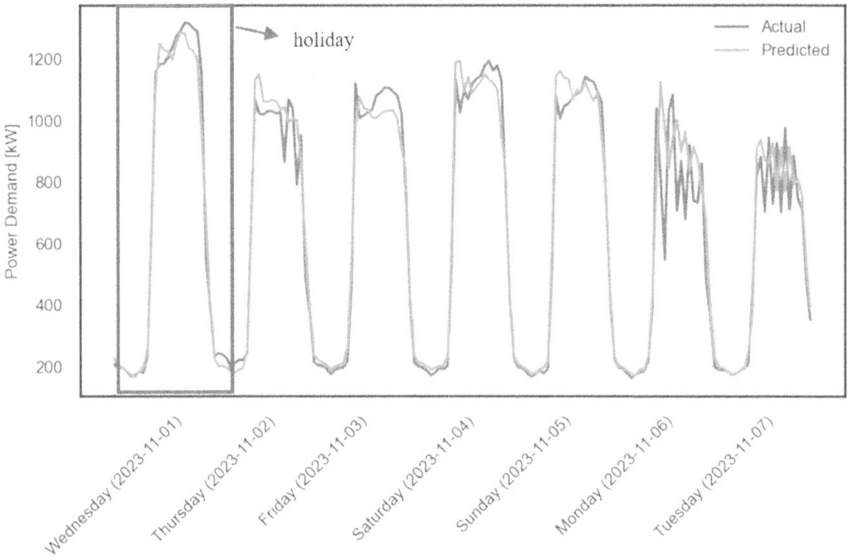

Fig. 5. Predictions of load profiling on a holiday using XGBoost.

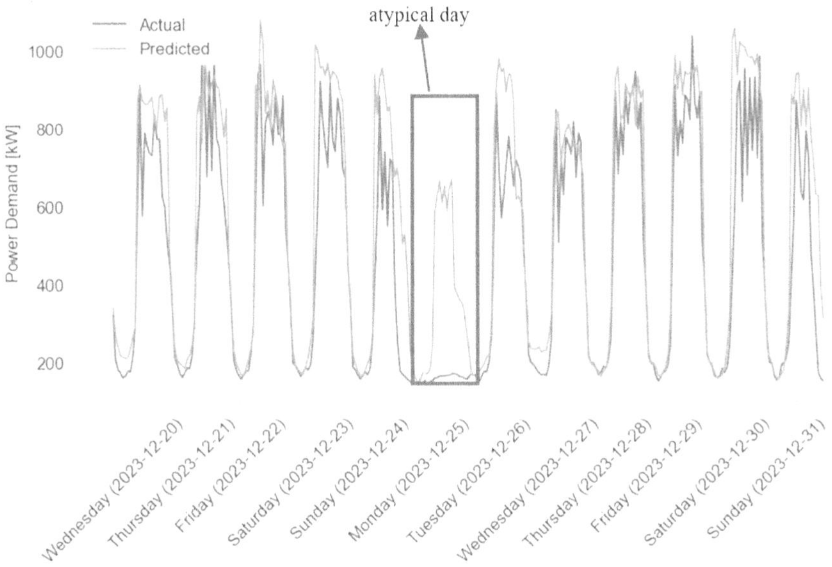

Fig. 6. Predictions of load profiling using XGBoost during the Christmas season.

5 Conclusions and Future Work

This paper presented a case study on forecasting the power demand of a shopping center, highlighting the unique characteristics of this building typology. Five machine learning models were tested and generally demonstrated strong performance, supported by careful data preprocessing, feature engineering, feature selection, and hyperparameter tuning. The results were promising, even on holidays when the building remained in operation, suggesting that well-designed feature engineering can effectively handle atypical days. However, the models struggled to produce accurate predictions when the building was closed.

This study contributes to the literature by providing a detailed case study focused on a specific and underrepresented building typology. It illustrates the diversity of load profiles and consumption behaviors that a single building can exhibit. Furthermore, the study offers valuable insights into the tailored approaches required to model the energy demand using machine learning, depending on the characteristics of the time series.

This paper makes a scientifically relevant contribution by analyzing shopping centers, a complex and underrepresented building typology in existing research. It addresses the challenges of applying machine learning to buildings with diverse usage patterns and compares several algorithms to identify the most suitable approach. By highlighting peculiarities of complex buildings, particularly the models' differing responses to holidays when the shopping center is open versus closed, this work helps fill a gap in the literature on intelligent pattern recognition and real-world energy demand forecasting.

Future work could explore new techniques to improve model performance on atypical days such as Christmas and New Year. For instance, gathering additional historical data from multiple years could help the models better capture the patterns of these irregular periods. Another promising direction is the use of more advanced ANN architectures, including deep learning models, to evaluate potential gains in accuracy and computational efficiency.

Acknowledgments. This work was funded by Component 5–Capitalization and Business Innovation, integrated into the Resilience Dimension of the Recovery and Resilience Plan under the Recovery and Resilience Mechanism (RRM) of the European Union (EU), framed in Next Generation EU, for the period 2021-2026, within the scope of the Alliance for Energy Transition project, with reference 56.

References

1. Caragliu, A., Del Bo, C., Nijkamp, P.: Smart Cities in Europe. J. Urban Technol. **18**, 65–82 (2011)
2. Pärn, E.A., de Soto, B.G.: Cyber threats and actors confronting the Construction 4.0. Construction 4.0 441–459 (2020)
3. Odeh, K., de Wilde, P.: Exploring the potential of digital twins at the district scale: a framework for investigation. In: Building Simulation Conference Proceedings, pp. 516–523 (Year)
4. O'Dwyer, E., Pan, I., Charlesworth, R., Butler, S., Shah, N.: Integration of an energy management tool and digital twin for coordination and control of multi-vector smart energy systems. Sustain. Cities Soc. **62**, 102412 (2020)

5. Jiao, Z., et al.: Sustainable operation and maintenance modeling and application of building infrastructures combined with digital twin framework. Sensors **23** (2023)
6. Ni, Z., Zhang, C., Karlsson, M., Gong, S.: A study of deep learning-based multi-horizon building energy forecasting. Energy and Buildings **303** (2024)
7. Pan, Y., et al.: Building energy simulation and its application for building performance optimization: a review of methods, tools, and case studies. Advances in Applied Energy **10** (2023)
8. Zhou, Y., Zheng, S.: A co-simulated material-component-system-district framework for climate-adaption and sustainability transition. Renewable and Sustainable Energy Reviews **192** (2024)
9. Abella, A., Ortiz-de-Urbina-Criado, M., De-Pablos-Heredero, C.: A model for the analysis of data-driven innovation and value generation in smart cities' ecosystems. Cities **64**, 47–53 (2017)
10. Arowoiya, V.A., Moehler, R.C., Fang, Y.: Digital twin technology for thermal comfort and energy efficiency in buildings: a state-of-the-art and future directions. Energy and Built Environment **5**, 641–656 (2024)
11. Corticos, N.D., Duarte, C.C.: Artificial Inteligence Impact on Buildings Energy Efficiency. In: Proceedings - 2023 7th International Conference on Computer, Software and Modeling, ICCSM 2023, pp. 56–61 (Year)
12. de Wilde, P.: Building performance simulation in the brave new world of artificial intelligence and digital twins: a systematic review. Energy and Buildings **292** (2023)
13. Lee, E.A.: Cyber physical systems: design challenges. In: 2008 11th IEEE International Symposium on Object and Component-Oriented Real-Time Distributed Computing (ISORC), pp. 363–369 (Year)
14. Sawhney, A., Riley, M., Irizarry, J.: Construction 4.0 an innovation platform for the built environment. pp. E-book [526 p.]-E-book [526 p.]. Routledge, London (2020)
15. Griffor, E.R., Greer, C., Wollman, D.A., Burns, M.J.: Framework for cyber-physical systems: Volume 2, working group reports. (2017)
16. Pishdad-Bozorgi, P., Gao, X., Shelden, D.R.: Introduction to cyber-physical systems in the built environment. Construction 4.0, pp. 23–41. Routledge (2020)
17. Amasyali, K., El-Gohary, N.M.: A review of data-driven building energy consumption prediction studies. Renew. Sustain. Energy Rev. **81**, 1192–1205 (2018)
18. Bourhnane, S., Abid, M.R., Lghoul, R., Zine-Dine, K., Elkamoun, N., Benhaddou, D.: Machine learning for energy consumption prediction and scheduling in smart buildings. SN Applied Sciences **2**, 297 (2020)
19. Wei, Y., et al.: A review of data-driven approaches for prediction and classification of building energy consumption. Renew. Sustain. Energy Rev. **82**, 1027–1047 (2018)
20. Bourdeau, M., Zhai, X.q., Nefzaoui, E., Guo, X., Chatellier, P.: Modeling and forecasting building energy consumption: A review of data-driven techniques. Sustainable Cities and Society **48**, 101533 (2019)
21. Seyedzadeh, S., Rahimian, F.P., Glesk, I., Roper, M.: Machine learning for estimation of building energy consumption and performance: a review. Visualization in Engineering **6**, 1–20 (2018)
22. Zenodo, https://doi.org/10.5281/zenodo.7973572
23. Pedregosa, F., et al.: Scikit-learn: Machine learning in Python. The Journal of Machine Learning Research **12**, 2825–2830 (2011)
24. Chen, T., Guestrin, C.: XGBoost: A scalable tree boosting system. Proceedings of the 22nd ACM SIGKDD International Conference on Knowledge Discovery and Data Mining, pp. 785–794. Association for Computing Machinery, San Francisco, California, USA (2016)
25. Van Rossum, G., Drake, F.L.: Python reference manual. Centrum voor Wiskunde en Informatica Amsterdam (1995)

26. Naser, M.Z., Alavi, A.H.: Error metrics and performance fitness indicators for artificial intelligence and machine learning in engineering and sciences. Architecture, Structures and Construction **3**, 499–517 (2023)
27. Akiba, T., Sano, S., Yanase, T., Ohta, T., Koyama, M.: Optuna: A Next-generation Hyperparameter Optimization Framework. Proceedings of the 25th ACM SIGKDD International Conference on Knowledge Discovery & Data Mining, pp. 2623–2631. Association for Computing Machinery, Anchorage, AK, USA (2019)

Smart Systems in Sustainable Development

Ensemble Deep Learning Model for AI-Powered Cyber-Physical Systems in Precision Agriculture

Laura Cosma(✉), Ștefan Vasile Oniga, and Ovidiu Cosma

Technical University of Cluj Napoca, North University Center of Baia Mare, Baia Mare, Romania

{Laura.Cosma,Stefan.ONIGA,Ovidiu.COSMA}@mi.utcluj.ro.ro

Abstract. The integration of Artificial Intelligence into Cyber-Physical Systems (CPS) is transforming precision agriculture by enabling automated, real-time plant health monitoring. AI-driven models enable the early detection of nutrient deficiencies, infections, and pests, allowing for timely intervention with effective treatments. This paper presents an ensemble deep learning model for image-based plant health monitoring, optimized for mobile agricultural equipment and autonomous systems. Preliminary results show significant improvements over existing plant monitoring solutions. Future research will focus on integrating this model into an AI-powered CPS, such as a drone or ground vehicle, for systematic field scanning, and crop health reporting. Unlike conventional CPS with multiple sensors, the final system will rely solely on computer vision, demonstrating that a high-resolution camera can serve as a powerful data acquisition tool in an AI-driven CPS.

Keywords: AI-Powered Cyber-Physical Systems · Precision Agriculture · Plant Health Monitoring · Ensemble Learning · Computer Vision · Autonomous Crop Surveillance

1 Introduction

The integration of cyber-physical systems (CPS) into agriculture has led to a shift from traditional crop monitoring to autonomous, AI-powered approaches. In precision farming, sensors installed on mobile or stationary equipment gather real-time data on plant health and environmental conditions. This reduces manual work and supports faster, more informed decisions. However, deploying such systems often involves high initial costs due to the number of sensors and the complexity of setup.

This research starts from the idea of creating a fully autonomous crop monitoring system equipped with only a single camera. The present study contributes to this goal by developing its core component: an image-based model for detecting plant diseases, pests, and nutrient deficiencies.

According to existing studies, the performance of image classification models can be improved by integrating them into ensemble networks that allow multiple models to work together efficiently. In this context, we aim to assess the effectiveness of such models in plant disease detection by addressing the following research questions:

Published by Springer Nature Switzerland AG 2025
L. M. Camarinha-Matos and F. Ferrada (Eds.): DoCEIS 2025, IFIP AICT 759, pp. 115–127, 2025.
https://doi.org/10.1007/978-3-031-97051-1_8

- Is it possible to create a highly effective ensemble classifier composed solely of weak classifiers?
- Can the performance of a strong classifier be enhanced by combining it only with weak classifiers in an ensemble network?

These research questions, though technical, stem from a practical goal: detecting multiple co-occurring plant conditions from a single RGB image in real agricultural settings. By combining lightweight, specialized classifiers in an ensemble, we address the challenges of multi-label classification under limited computational resources, while capturing the visual diversity of fungal, viral, nutrient, and pest-related symptoms. This strategy directly supports the development of a camera-based autonomous CPS for crop monitoring.

The motivation behind this research is to build a multi-label classification model that is lightweight and fast enough for mobile platforms such as field robots, yet accurate enough to minimize false positives, which lead to unnecessary treatments, and false negatives, which allow problems to spread undetected.

1.1 Link to AI-Powered CPS

The main theme of the DoCEIS 2025 conference emphasizes the synergy between cyber-physical systems (CPS), artificial intelligence (AI), and their applications across various fields, including Embedded Intelligence and Smart Biotechnology. Autonomous crop health monitoring is a concrete example of smart biotechnology, where AI and CPS technologies enhance yields and prevent losses.

This paper aligns with this theme by proposing a plant disease classification model that can be integrated into a simplified CPS (based on a single camera) for automated crop monitoring. Our research highlights the role of technological innovation in precision agriculture and presents the advantages of a robust and autonomous cyber-physical system.

By reducing the sensor infrastructure to a single camera, the costs are minimized, and installation and maintenance are simplified, making the technology accessible to a broader range of users. The proposed solution can be integrated into an autonomous robot, a mobile device, or a drone, contributing to Embedded Intelligence by enabling real-time execution of the proposed model directly on the device, without relying on Internet connectivity or external servers for processing.

Consequently, this research makes a relevant contribution to the development and implementation of cyber-physical systems in agriculture, addressing the challenges and objectives set by DoCEIS 2025.

2 Literature Review

The integration of artificial intelligence (AI) and deep learning in plant health monitoring has gained significant attention in recent years. To enhance accuracy and robustness in disease detection, several studies have investigated ensemble learning approaches, which have proven effective for plant disease classification.

In [1], an ensemble of convolutional neural networks (CNNs) detected paddy leaf diseases with 95.54% accuracy. Similar approaches reached even higher accuracy: [4] achieved 99.22% using a stacked CNN ensemble with transfer learning for bean leaf disease, [10] obtained 98.86% with a transfer learning-based ensemble for potato leaf disease, and [13] reported 99.48% using pre-trained CNNs for cotton leaf disease. Likewise, a majority-voting ensemble of six CNN models in [9] attained 97.56% accuracy for plant disease and pest detection, while deep ensemble learning in [12] resulted in an ROC AUC of 99% for palm disease detection. Other studies report near-perfect results, such as 99.91% accuracy in [3] using a CNN ensemble optimized with genetic algorithms, 99.75–100% accuracy in [7] through stacked hybrid learning, and 99.58% in [14] with a hybrid ensemble model.

Alternative ensemble strategies incorporate preprocessing techniques. In [2], deep feature extraction was combined with SVM classification, reaching 98% accuracy. Image preprocessing was used in [5] before applying a deep ensemble for grain plant disease detection, achieving 99.56% accuracy, and improved image segmentation in [6] helped achieve 94% accuracy. A stacking ensemble with SVM and random forest classifiers in [8] reached 96.82% accuracy, while a two-stage segmentation-plus-ensemble scheme in [11] enhanced leaf abnormality detection.

Specialized CNN models trained with data augmentation have shown strong performance in tomato plant pathology. In [16], a CNN trained on the PlantVillage and TomatoVillage datasets achieved 99.31% accuracy in identifying 11 tomato diseases and pests, outperforming earlier models and proving suitable for mobile deployment. Similarly, the model in [17] reached 98.2% accuracy, exceeding previous state-of-the-art results by 4–17%. These results emphasize the impact of dataset augmentation and tailored CNN architectures.

Overall, these studies highlight the value of ensemble deep learning in plant disease detection. When integrated into cyber-physical systems, such models enable accurate, real-time health monitoring with minimal sensor requirements, offering significant potential for advancing precision agriculture. Building on this progress, our research proposes an ensemble deep learning model tailored for autonomous agricultural equipment, aiming to improve scalability and efficiency in crop monitoring.

3 Proposed Multi-label Plant Disease Classification Model (Tiny Plant Net – TPN)

To address the research questions, we developed a lightweight deep neural network for multi-label classification of tomato plant diseases, named Tiny Plant Net (TPN). This architecture was later refined in the second part of the research by incorporating it into a meta-model built as an ensemble of classifiers for plant disease detection.

3.1 Building the Dataset

To train our model, we used a combined dataset created from two public sources: PlantVillage [19] and Tomato-Village [18]. PlantVillage, widely cited in the literature, contains tomato leaf images taken under controlled conditions, covereing both healthy plants and cases of isolated fungal or viral infections. However, it lacks samples of nutrient deficiencies and pest damage.

To address this, we incorporated Tomato-Village, which includes both lab and real-field images, representing plants with pest infestations, nutrient deficiencies, and multi-symptom cases. We manually reviewed this dataset to remove duplicates and correct mislabeled images, ensuring consistency.

The final merged dataset includes 12 classes, categorized as follows:

- Single-label classes: Healthy (He), Early Blight (EB), Late Blight (LB), Spotted Wilt Virus (SWV), Leaf Miner (LM), and Magnesium Deficiency (MD).
- Multi-label classes: EB + LM, LB + LM, SWV + LM, MD + LM, SWV + MD, SWV + LM + MD.

These classes comprehensively cover the main conditions affecting tomato plants: fungal, viral, nutritional, and pest-related issues. Figure 1 presents representative images for both single and multi-label categories.

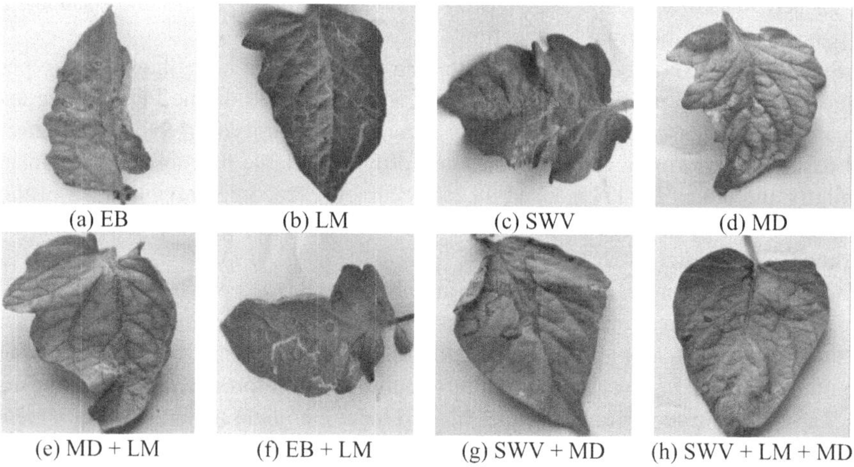

Fig. 1. Sample tomato leaf images from the dataset.

3.2 Tiny Plant Net (TPN) Architecture

The proposed Tiny Plant Net (TPN) is a compact deep neural network tailored for multi-label classification of plant leaf diseases. It offers high accuracy while remaining efficient enough for deployment on mobile or embedded devices, making it suitable for real-time crop monitoring. TPN is based on a modern convolutional architecture (illustrated in Fig. 2) that balances model complexity and performance, being specifically optimized for this task.

Initial layers: The network begins with an input layer configured for color images, followed by two convolutional layers with 30 and 60 filters (kernel size 3). Each convolutional layer is followed by a Swish activation and a MaxPooling2D layer for downsampling. We chose the Swish activation function instead of the more common ReLU to mitigate the "dying neurons" problem, thus improving learning stability and performance.

Residual blocks: After the initial Conv2D layers, TPN includes three residual blocks with filter sizes of 120, 240, and 480, respectively. The architecture of a residual block is shown in Fig. 4.

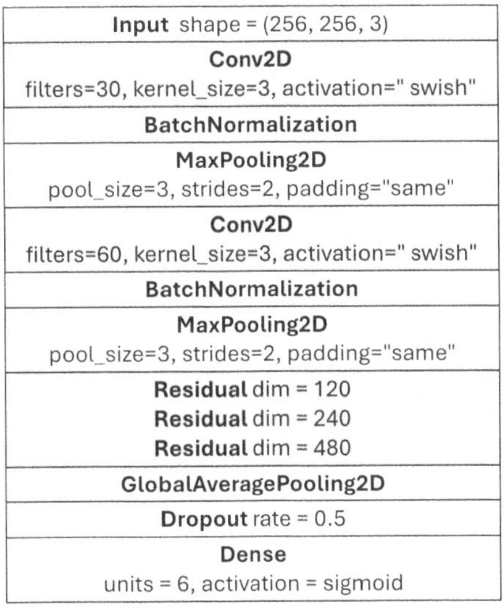

Fig. 2. Schematic diagram of the TPN architecture.

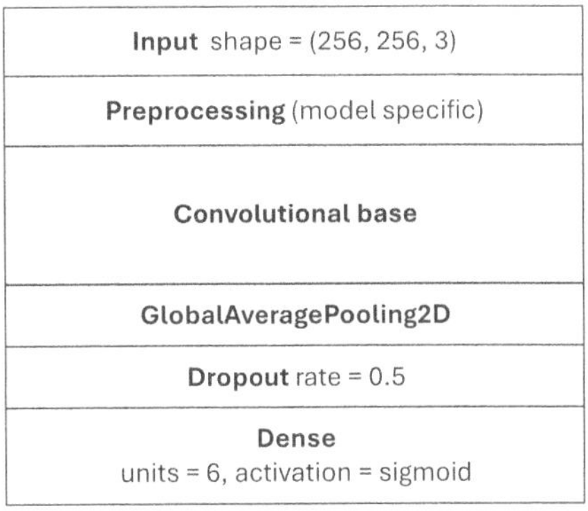

Fig. 3. Transfer learning architecture for adapting pre-trained CNN models to the tomato leaf multi-label classification task.

Each residual block contains three SeparableConv2D layers, which greatly reduce the number of parameters (and hence the model's size), followed by a MaxPooling2D layer to reduce the spatial dimensions of the feature maps. Each block also has a residual shortcut connection implemented via a 1×1 Conv2D layer with stride 2, which downsamples the input so it can be added to the output after the block's max pooling. All convolutional layers within the residual blocks use the Swish activation for the mentioned advantages.

Final layers: Following the residual blocks, a GlobalAveragePooling2D layer is applied. This layer replaces the traditional Flatten step to convert feature maps into a single vector, significantly reducing the number of parameters and preventing over-fitting. Next, a Dropout layer (with 50% drop rate) is used to randomly deactivate half of the neurons during training, which helps avoid overtraining and improves generalization. Finally, the network outputs through a Dense layer with six output neurons (corresponding to the six labels in our dataset) and a Sigmoid activation function. The Sigmoid activation allows each of the six outputs to be activated independently, making it appropriate for multi-label classification (where multiple disease labels can be present simultaneously).

The TPN model was trained using the following experimental setup: The dataset was split into 70% training, 15% validation, and 15% test sets. The model was compiled with the binary cross-entropy loss function and optimized using the Adam optimizer with an initial learning rate of 0.0002. Training was conducted for up to 200 epochs with a batch size of 32. These hyperparameters were fine-tuned empirically based on validation performance. To prevent overfitting, early stopping was applied based on validation loss.

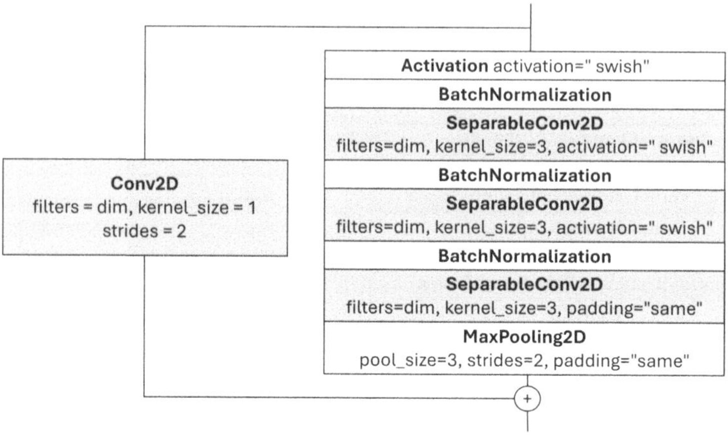

Fig. 4. Internal structure of the residual block used in the TPN architecture.

3.3 Performance Comparison with Baseline Models

To evaluate the effectiveness of TPN, we compared its performance against several well-known deep convolutional neural network models used as baseline classifiers. We selected a range of state-of-the-art architectures of varying sizes and capacities, specifically: DenseNet121 (DN_121), DenseNet169 (DN_169), DenseNet201 (DN_201), EfficientNetB0 (EN_B0), InceptionV3 (Inc_v3), MobileNetV2 (MobN_v2), ResNet50V2 (RN_50_v2), ResNet152V2 (RN_152_v2), and Xception (Xcept). Each of these models was first initialized with weights pre-trained on ImageNet and then adapted to our tomato disease dataset through transfer learning and fine-tuning. The general transfer learning adaptation setup for these models is illustrated in Fig. 3.

In our adaptation, we added the required preprocessing layers specific to each model after the input, and the TPN final classification layers after the convolutional base.

We trained each modified model on our tomato leaf dataset using the same experimental settings applied to TPN. In the first stage, we trained only the final classifier layers for up to 100 epochs. In the final stage of training, we fine-tuned the deeper layers by selectively unfreezing the convolutional base just enough to include the last three Conv2D layers. These unfrozen layers were then trained jointly with the final classifier for additional 100 epochs, using a lower learning rate of 1e-5, to refine the feature representations and improve overall performance on the plant disease classification task.

All baseline models were trained and evaluated using the same dataset splits, batch size, optimizer, and early stopping criteria as the proposed TPN model. A common data augmentation layer was applied across all models.

The classification results for TPN and all baseline models are summarized in Table We report a comprehensive set of multi-label evaluation metrics for each model: macro-averaged Precision, Recall, and F1-score; micro-averaged Precision, Recall, and F1-score; as well as Subset Accuracy (S_A), Hamming Accuracy (H_A), and Hamming Loss (H_L) (Table 1).

Table 1. Multi-label classification performance of the proposed TPN versus various transfer-learning baseline models.

Model	Macro			Micro			S_A	H_A	H_L
	Prec	Rec	F1	Prec	Rec	F1			
TPN	99.35	99.54	99.45	99.27	99.47	99.37	98.29	99.67	0.33
EN_B0	92.02	85.54	88.05	89.23	85.23	87.18	68.29	93.39	6.61
DN_201	91.41	83.46	86.89	88.51	82.19	85.23	64.72	92.48	7.52
RN_50_v2	89.49	83.33	85.72	86.56	83.04	84.76	64.12	92.12	7.88
RN_152_v2	90.03	82.65	85.56	86.43	82.34	84.34	63.38	91.93	8.07
DN_169	92.08	80.57	84.93	89.17	79.24	83.91	62.41	91.98	8.02
MobN_v2	89.95	80.96	84.60	86.56	80.03	83.17	60.97	91.45	8.55
DN_121	89.43	78.46	82.68	86.24	77.13	81.43	57.64	90.72	9.28
Xcept	88.71	77.90	82.03	84.92	77.54	81.06	57.59	90.44	9.56
Inc_v3	86.13	77.60	80.96	83.47	76.90	80.05	55.32	89.88	10.12

Additionally, Fig. 5 provides a graphical comparison of two representative metrics for all models: part (a) shows the macro F1-score and part (b) shows the Hamming Loss achieved by each model.

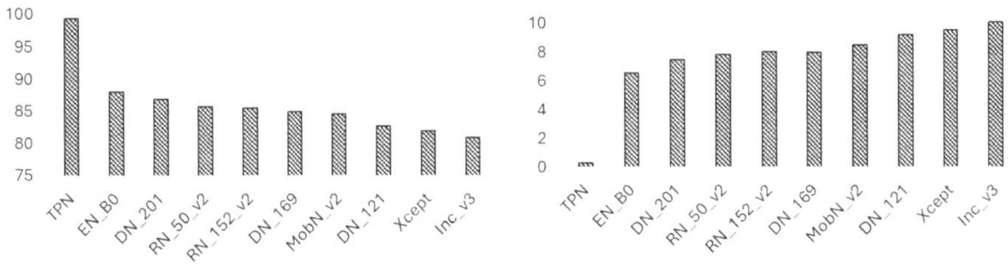

(a) macro-averaged F1-score (b) Hamming Loss

Fig. 5. Performance comparison of TPN and baseline models.

The results clearly demonstrate that TPN outperforms all baseline models by a substantial margin. TPN achieves a nearly perfect macro F1-score of 99.45%, whereas the best-performing baseline (EfficientNetB0) reaches only 88.05%, and most other models are in the 80–86% range. Similarly, TPN obtains a micro F1-score of 99.37% and an exceptionally low Hamming Loss of 0.33%, while the baselines have Hamming Loss values around 6.6–10.1%. Notably, TPN's Subset Accuracy is 98.29%, meaning it correctly predicts all labels for 98.29% of test samples – in contrast, the next best model achieves only 68.29% subset accuracy. Hamming Accuracy (which measures label-wise accuracy) is also highest for TPN (99.67%, versus ~ 90–93% for the baselines). These metrics underscore the effectiveness of our specialized model compared to pretrained CNN architectures that were only fine-tuned for this task.

We also compared the model sizes of TPN and the baselines, as shown in Table 2. TPN's model size is only about 11,372 kB. This is significantly smaller than most of the pre-trained models; for example, DenseNet201 is ~ 74,133 kB and ResNet152V2 is ~ 229,930 kB. The only model more compact than TPN is MobileNetV2 at ~ 9,491 kB, but MobileNetV2's accuracy is much lower (macro F1 around 84.6%). Figure 6 visualizes these model sizes, highlighting that TPN offers an excellent trade-off between accuracy and efficiency – it is nearly as small as the most lightweight model, yet far more accurate than all others.

Table 2. Model file sizes.

Model	Size [kB]
TPN	11,372
EN_B0	16,738
DN_201	74,133
RN_50_v2	92,864
RN_152_v2	229,930
DN_169	51,544
MobN_v2	9,491
DN_121	29,040
Xcept	82,137
Inc_v3	86,386

The strong performance of TPN is largely due to its design and training strategy. Unlike the other models, TPN was built and trained from scratch on our tomato disease dataset, enabling it to learn domain-specific features effectively. In contrast, the benchmark models were pre-trained on ImageNet, a generic dataset that does not include plant disease images and were only later adapted to our task. Their higher complexity, combined with the limited size of our dataset, also increased the risk of overfitting, which reduced their accuracy. TPN's compact architecture helped avoid this issue, leading to better generalization.

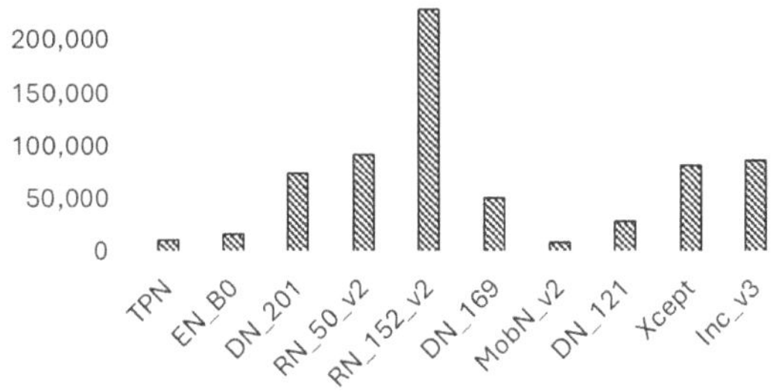

Fig. 6. Model file size comparison.

This stage of the research successfully delivered a high-performance model for tomato plant disease classification (TPN), along with several weaker models obtained through fine-tuning pre-trained architectures. These results set the stage for the next phase, which focuses on ensemble learning. In Sect. 4, we explore how combining multiple classifiers can improve overall performance, both by aggregating weak models and by enhancing the output of an already strong classifier.

4 Proposed Ensemble Classification Network Architecture

In this section, we present the development and performance evaluation of an ensemble classification model constructed using the base classifiers described in the previous section.

4.1 Ensemble Model Architecture

The architecture of the ensemble classifier is illustrated in Fig. 7. The first level of this network consists of multiple image classification models operating as input classifiers. The output predictions from these classifiers are fed into a second-level multi-layer perceptron (MLP) that produces the final multi-label prediction. The MLP is composed of three fully-connected layers with 128, 64, and 6 units, respectively. We use ReLU activation for the first two dense layers and a sigmoid activation for the final output layer. Additionally, batch normalization and dropout layers are applied after the first two dense layers to improve stability and prevent overfitting.

The second-level MLP was trained using the predictions made by the base models on the validation set. A validation split of 0.05 was applied during training. The model was trained for up to 200 epochs using the Adam optimizer (learning rate = 0.0002) and a batch size of 32.

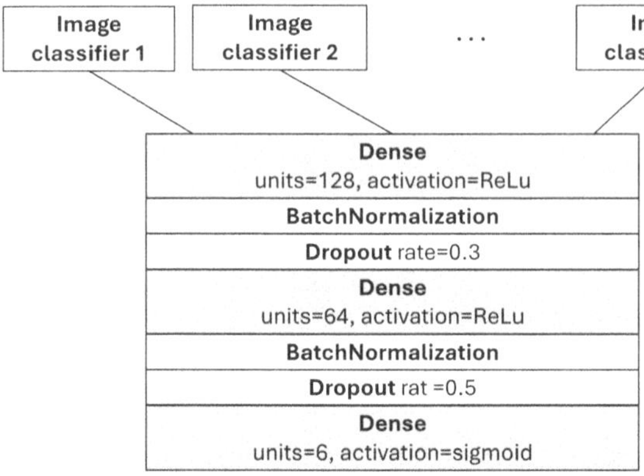

Fig. 7. Architecture of the proposed ensemble classification network.

4.2 Experimental Results and Discussion

To evaluate the effectiveness of this ensemble design, we experimented with multiple configurations by varying the set of input classifiers. In total, we constructed eight different ensemble models, divided into two groups based on their composition: four ensembles (denoted EN1_1 through EN1_4) consisting solely of relatively "weak" baseline classifiers, and four ensembles (EN2_1 through EN2_4) that include one "strong" classifier (the TPN model) combined with several weak classifiers.

The EN1 series was designed to test whether an ensemble of only weaker models can achieve high accuracy for the plant disease classification task. The EN2 series was designed to test whether incorporating a strong model into an ensemble with other weak classifiers can further improve upon the strong model's performance.

The input classification models used in each ensemble are as follows:

- EN1_1: 3 base classifiers (EN_B0, DN_201, RN_152_v2)
- EN1_2: 4 base classifiers (EN_B0, DN_201, RN_50_v2, MobN_v2)
- EN1_3: 4 base classifiers (EN_B0, DN_169, RN_50_v2, DN_121)
- EN1_4: 6 base classifiers (EN_B0, DN_201, RN_50_v2, MobN_v2, Xcept,Inc_v3)
- EN2_1: 4 base classifiers (TPN, EN_B0, DN_201, RN_50_v2)
- EN2_2: 4 base classifiers (TPN, EN_B0, MobN_v2, DN_121)
- EN2_3: 6 base classifiers (TPN, EN_B0, DN_201, RN_152_v2, DN_169, Xcept)
- EN2_4: 4 base classifiers (TPN, EN_B0, DN_201, RN_152_v2)

The multi-label classification results for all these ensemble models are presented in Table 3, and a visual comparison is provided in Figs. 8 and 9. Figure 8 plots the performance metrics of the EN1_x ensembles, and Fig. 9 shows the performance of the EN2_x ensembles.

The results in Table 3 show a clear difference between the two groups of ensembles. All EN2 ensembles (which include TPN) achieve near-perfect performance, with macro F1 scores around 99.5% and very low Hamming losses (~0.3%). All EN1 models (with only weak classifiers) offer results that are significantly better than any single baseline model, with macro F1 scores around 93% and Hamming losses of about 4–5%. The best

Table 3. Multi-label classification performance of the eight ensemble configurations

Model	Macro			Micro			S_A	H_A	H_L
	Prec	Rec	F1	Prec	Rec	F1			
EN1_1	92.59	92.72	92.65	90.78	91.26	91.02	77.04	95.25	4.75
EN1_2	92.82	92.54	92.66	90.89	91.35	91.12	76.90	95.30	4.70
EN1_3	92.69	93.27	92.95	90.42	91.93	91.17	76.99	95.30	4.70
EN1_4	93.20	92.97	93.07	91.46	91.75	91.61	78.10	95.56	4.44
EN2_1	99.38	99.59	99.48	99.36	99.50	99.43	98.52	99.70	0.30
EN2_2	99.30	99.65	99.48	99.30	99.56	99.43	98.47	99.70	0.30
EN2_3	99.44	99.70	99.57	99.33	99.59	99.46	98.52	99.71	0.29
EN2_4	99.47	99.68	99.58	99.39	99.56	99.47	98.56	99.72	0.28

weak-classifier ensemble, EN1_4, reached a macro F1 score of 93.07%. Furthermore, every ensemble that includes TPN delivers better performance than TPN by itself, raising the macro F1 to as high as 99.58% and reducing the Hamming loss to as low as 0.28%.

We also observe that increasing the number of classifiers in an ensemble does not significantly improve the results. Within the EN1 group, adding more base models led to only slight improvements. For example, EN1_1 (3 models) achieved 92.65% macro F1 vs. EN1_4 (6 models) which achieved 93.07%, a gain of about 0.4 percentage points – and the Hamming Loss decreased modestly from 4.75% to 4.44%. In the EN2 group, all four configurations performed nearly equivalently (macro F1 ranging only from 99.48% to 99.58%), indicating that once a strong model is included, the ensemble's performance is almost saturated, and additional models do not worsen its performance, but they provide limited benefit.

In summary, our experiments indicate that (1) an ensemble of weak classifiers can indeed function as a much stronger classifier (substantially surpassing the individual models' accuracies), and (2) incorporating a strong classifier into an ensemble with weaker models can further improve the strong classifier's performance (albeit marginally, given TPN's already high accuracy).

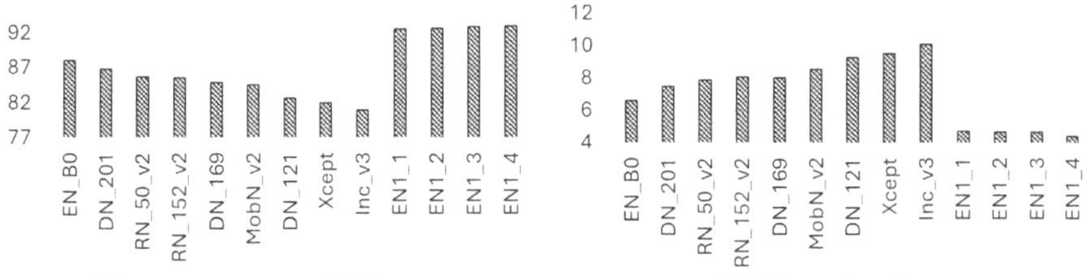

(a) macro-averaged F1-score (b) Hamming Loss

Fig. 8. Performance of weak classifier ensembles.

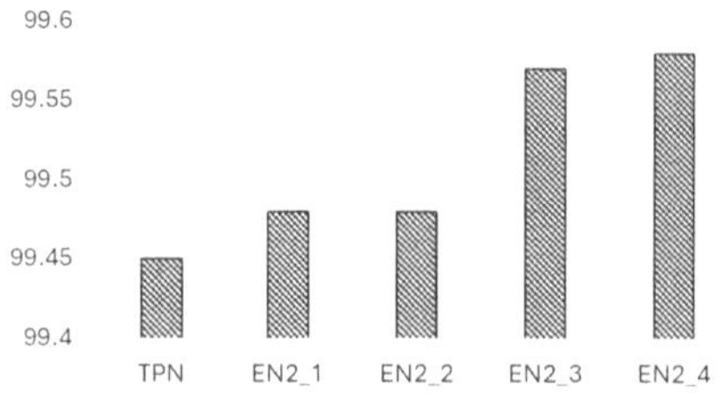

(a) macro-averaged F1-score

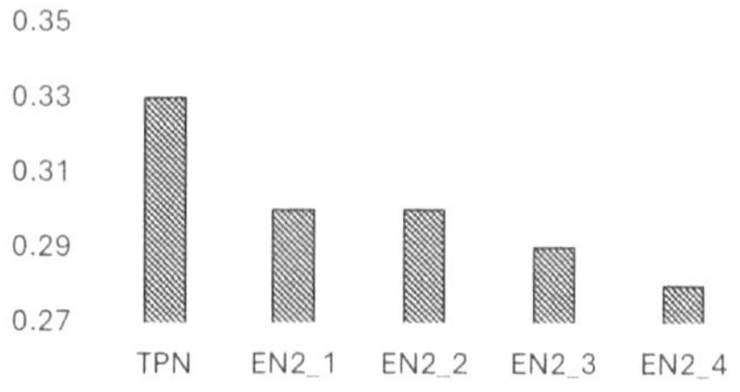

(b) Hamming Loss

Fig. 9. Performance of ensembles including the strong TPN classifier.

5 Conclusions

In this work, we introduced Tiny Plant Net (TPN), a compact yet highly effective model for multi-label classification of plant diseases. TPN consistently outperforms well-known architectures like EfficientNetB0, DenseNet, and ResNet across all major evaluation metrics, confirming its strong performance and suitability for deployment on resource-limited platforms. Unlike conventional CNN-based classifiers, TPN is specifically designed to combine high accuracy with low computational cost. It uses SeparableConv2D layers to reduce the number of trainable parameters and residual connections to improve gradient flow and training stability. This design enables efficient detection of diverse crop conditions in multi-label scenarios, making TPN suitable for real-time use on mobile devices and in cyber-physical systems with limited hardware capabilities.

Furthermore, ensemble learning is used to increase prediction stability and boost generalization. These architectural choices collectively distinguish our model from existing plant disease detection approaches and ensure its practical applicability in field scenarios.

As part of future work, we plan to extend the model to support other crop species and to evaluate its performance on more diverse, real-world multi-label datasets.

Acknowledgements. This work was partially supported by the project "Collaborative Framework for Smart Agriculture" – COSA that received funding from Romania's National Recovery and Resilience Plan PNRR-III-C9-2022-I8, under grant agreement 760070.

References

1. Acharya, A., Muvvala, A., Gawali, S., Dhopavkar, R., Kadam, R., Harsola, A.: Plant disease detection for paddy crop using ensemble of CNNs. IEEE Int. Conf. Innov. Technol. (INOCON). **2020**, 1–6 (2020)
2. Sharma, P., Sharma, D.P., Bansal, S.: Optimum RBM Encoded SVM Model with Ensemble Feature Extractor-Based Plant Disease Prediction. Chemom. Intell. Lab. Syst. **258**, 105319 (2025)
3. Hussain, W., Mushtaq, M.F., et al.: Ensemble Genetic and CNN Model-Based Image Classification by Enhancing Hyperparameter Tuning. Sci. Rep. **15**, 1003 (2025)
4. Ghannam, N.E., El Zein, O.M., Fathy, D.R., Mancy, H.: Enhanced detection of bean leaf diseases using a stacked CNN ensemble with transfer learning. Int. J. Intel. Eng. Sys. **18**(1), 304–322 (2025)

5. Goyal, P., Verma, D.K., Kumar, S.: Detection and monitoring for enhanced prevention of grain plant disease using classification-based deep ensemble neural networks in smart agriculture. International Journal of Remote Sensing. 1–31 (2025)
6. Kumar, P.S., Kalaivani, K., et al.: Enhanced segmentation and ensemble classification for accurate plant disease detection. J. Phytopathol. **172**(6), e13426 (2024)
7. Sheneamer, A.: Early detection of plant leaf diseases using stacking hybrid learning. PLOS One. 1–15 (2024)
8. Vishnoi, V.K., Kumar, K., Kumar, B., Bhutiani, R.: A stacking ensemble machine learning-based approach for classification of plant diseases through leaf images. Environ. Conserv. J. **25**(3), 767–778 (2024)
9. Turkoglu, M., et al.: PlantDiseaseNet: convolutional neural network ensemble for plant disease and pest detection. SIViP **16**(2), 301–309 (2022)
10. Jha, P., Dembla, D., Dubey, W.: Deep learning models for enhancing potato leaf disease prediction: implementation of transfer learning-based stacking ensemble model. Multimedia Tools and Applications. **83**(13), 37839–37858 (2024)
11. Buakum, B., et al.: Two-stage ensemble deep learning model for precise leaf abnormality detection in Centella Asiatica. Agri. Eng. **6**(1), 620–644 (2024)
12. Savaş, S.: Application of deep ensemble learning for palm disease detection in smart agriculture. Heliyon. **10**(17), e37141 (2024)
13. Rai, C.K., Pahuja, R.: An ensemble transfer learning-based deep convolution neural network for the detection and classification of diseased cotton leaves and plants. Multimedia Tools and Applications. **83**(36), 83991–84024 (2024)
14. Sriprateep, K., Khonjun, S., Pitakaso, R., et al.: Hybrid adaptive multiple intelligence system (HybridAMIS) for classifying cannabis leaf diseases using deep learning ensembles. Smart Agricultural Technol. **9**, 100535 (2024)
15. Waheed, Z., Gui, J., Amjad, K., Waheed, I., Asif, S.: An ensemble approach of deep CNN models with beta normalization aggregation for gastrointestinal disease detection. Biomed. Signal Process. Control **105**, 107567 (2025)
16. Cosma, O., Cosma, L.: TPC_Net: An Efficient CNN architecture for tomato plant disease and pest classification. The 19th International Conference on Soft Computing Models in Industrial and Environmental Applications SOCO 2024, pp. 188–198 (2025)
17. Cosma, O., Cosma, L.: A novel CNN approach for accurate tomato disease classification. IEEE Int. Conf. on Engineering, Technology, and Innovation. 1–7 (2024)
18. Gehlot, M., Saxena, R.K., et al.: Tomato-village: a dataset for end-to-end tomato disease detection in a real-world environment. Multimedia Syst. **29**, 3305–3328 (2023)
19. Hughes, D.P., Salathe, M.: An open access repository of images on plant health to enable the development of mobile disease diagnostics. arXiv. 1511.08060 (2015)

An Integrated Framework for the Development of a Multi-sensor Node to Support Wildfire Management

Miguel Lourenço[1,2(✉)], Luis B. Oliveira[1,2], and Henrique Oliveira[3,4]

[1] NOVA School of Science and Technology, Caparica, Portugal
mag.lourenco@campus.fct.unl.pt, l.oliveira@fct.unl.pt
[2] Center of Technology and Systems, UNINOVA, Caparica, Portugal
[3] Instituto de Telecomunicações, Aveiro, Portugal
hjmo@lx.it.pt
[4] Instituto Politécnico de Beja, Beja, Portugal

Abstract. Wildfires are complex and destructive events with widespread impacts across several domains. Advances in sensor technology have led to more accurate tools for wildfire management. Existing solutions use airborne and ground-based platforms to monitor wildfire spread, environmental parameters, pollutant concentrations and firefighter health. Post-wildfire research focuses on mapping burned areas and detecting hotspots. This paper proposes the design of an integrated framework for developing a multi-sensor node (MSN), featuring an Alarm Module (AM) and a Thermal Mapping Module (TMM). The AM monitors weather parameters, firefighting assets, and firefighter health, while the TMM detects hotspots, identifying potential reignition zones. The MSN connects to nearby smartphones via Bluetooth Low Energy (BLE) and uses them to transmit sensor data to the Internet, simplifying hardware design and reducing costs. Results demonstrate that the smartphone successfully receives sensor data from the MSN via BLE and transmits it to the Internet.

Keywords: Wildfires · Multi-Sensor Node · Firefighting · Sensors

1 Introduction

Innovative sensor technology has the potential to significantly impact wildfire management by enabling real-time monitoring during active wildfires. The rapid and dynamic nature of wildfires, characterised by localized and often unpredictable behaviour, requires monitoring systems capable of capturing real-time data directly from the field. Monitoring environmental conditions on a broader scale may prove ineffective for wildfire management, as it may overlook critical fluctuations within small distances to a wildfire outbreak location. These localized differences in parameters may influence the accuracy in predicting wildfire spread and guiding wildfire suppression tactics. The miniaturization and increased affordability of new sensors make these technologies more affordable and widely available [1].

Published by Springer Nature Switzerland AG 2025
L. M. Camarinha-Matos and F. Ferrada (Eds.): DoCEIS 2025, IFIP AICT 759, pp. 128–142, 2025.
https://doi.org/10.1007/978-3-031-97051-1_9

Airborne platforms offer valuable support in monitoring wildfires. Satellites are the primary Remote Sensing (RS) platform for wildfire monitoring, offering broad spatial coverage but with limited resolution. Several research works have employed satellite imagery for wildfire-related applications [2, 3]. Unmanned Aerial Vehicles (UAVs) are a widely adopted tool for wildfire monitoring using RS. Their high maneuverability and flexibility enable rapid deployment across diverse terrains without being restricted by the landscape. They have been extensively utilized in wildfire-related research [4, 5]. High-altitude balloons serve as a complementary airborne platform for wildfire monitoring, bridging the gap between UAVs and satellites by balancing resolution and spatial coverage. These systems range from high-cost platforms that carry large payloads [6] to more affordable, disposable latex balloons with limited payload capacity [7]. Ground sensors can be useful in wildfire monitoring by providing precise and localized data in real-time. In contrast to airborne systems, they can capture detailed data directly from the wildfire's surroundings [8]. Deploying a Wireless Sensor Network (WSN) for wildfire monitoring has several challenges, namely: the complexity and cost of installing and maintaining a WSN across large areas; the high energy consumption of sensor nodes, that can be challenging in remote locations; ensure wide geographic coverage for proper functioning of the WSN; and the risk of sensor nodes being damaged or destroyed by wildfires [9]. Given the highly localized nature of wildfire conditions, a more practical approach is to deploy sensors directly at wildfire outbreak locations [10]. Beyond environmental monitoring, ground sensors also provide the capability to monitor the status of firefighting assets and track firefighters' health [11, 12].

Assessing whether a wildfire has been fully extinguished in its aftermath is essential for effective management and preventing potential reignitions. Even when a wildfire appears to be fully extinguished, residual thermal activity (or 'hotspots') may persist within the affected area [13]. Real-time sensor data enables the detection of subtle temperature changes across the wildfire-burned area, helping to identify hotspots that may lead to potential reignitions. Ground crews with thermal cameras can perform close-up inspections, while UAVs offer an aerial perspective that allows for rapid scanning of large areas with sufficient resolution to identify hotspots [14]. Using UAVs to detect hotspots in the aftermath of wildfires offers several advantages. They can cover vast areas quickly, allowing for rapid assessment of the affected landscape. Equipped with advanced thermal cameras, UAVs provide a high-altitude perspective that can detect heat signatures across large, potentially inaccessible or hazardous terrains. UAVs have become the platform of choice for detecting hotspots, with numerous studies highlighting their effectiveness and application in post-wildfire monitoring [13, 15]. Equipping ground crews with thermal cameras to detect hotspots in the aftermath of a wildfire offers several advantages over relying solely on UAVs. While UAVs provide a broad aerial view and can cover larger areas, ground-based thermal cameras allow for closer inspection and detect more minor, less visible hotspots that may be missed from higher altitudes. Using ground crews for wildfire hotspot detection has primarily been integrated with other technologies, such as UAVs, to ensure comprehensive coverage of affected areas [16, 17]. Studies centered on portable handheld devices often rely on standalone cameras that are not integrated into systems where their data can be utilized for other applications [1]. In recent years, advancements in sensor technology have significantly improved their performance and reduced their costs, making these tools more accessible. Therefore, the integration of these new sensors with proprietary software would be highly beneficial, as it could facilitate adoption and increase the effectiveness of these tools. Table 1 provides a comparative overview of different platforms used for wildfire monitoring, evaluated across several metrics.

Table 1. Comparison of various platforms used for wildfire monitoring based on different evaluation metrics. Symbols indicate the performance in each metric (↑↑ Great performance, ↑ Positive performance, ↓ Negative performance, – Not relevant) [18].

Metrics	Satellite	UAV	High-altitude balloon	Ground sensors
Spatial/ temporal resolution	↓	↑↑	↑	↑↑
Controllability	–	↑↑	↓	↑
Autonomy	↑↑	↓	↑	↑
Payload capacity	↑↑	↓	↑	↑
Customization	↓	↑↑	↑	↑↑
Coverage	↑↑	↓	↑	↓↓
Cost	↑↑	↓	↑	↑

Based on the available solutions in the literature, the following research question was stated, along with its research hypothesis:

- Research Question: How can sensor data be transmitted from the wildfire outbreak location to the Internet?
- Research Hypothesis: A device called the Multi-Sensor Node (MSN) will be created, containing atmospheric and infrared data, as well as data on the status of firefighting assets. This device will transmit its sensor data via Bluetooth Low Energy (BLE) to a nearby smartphone, which will relay the data to the Internet for further analysis and monitoring.

2 Relationship to Computational and Perceptional Systems

The rapid advancement in computational power, along with the miniaturization and decreasing costs of technological equipment, has enabled the development of new tools and the conceptualization of integrated frameworks that combine multiple technologies to achieve higher performing results. These frameworks must be designed with flexibility, allowing for the seamless incorporation of new tools and sensors to fully capitalize on ongoing technological advancements. In wildfire management, this technological evolution has facilitated the integration of computational and perceptional systems, enhancing real-time monitoring, decision-making, and wildfire response.

Computational systems process, analyze, and transmit data, while perceptional systems collect and interpret sensory data from the environment. The increase in processing capabilities has enabled more sensor data to be processed locally, allowing only the transmission of relevant information with added value that can be further interpreted by other systems. This paper proposes a framework that integrates these two domains by utilizing a MSN that gathers diverse environmental and operational data, processes it locally, and transmits relevant information for further analysis. Furthermore, the framework's adaptability aligns with the rapid pace of technological innovation, allowing for the integration of other sensors with enhanced processing capabilities over time.

3 Proposed Approach

A multi-sensor node designed for wildfire monitoring and post-wildfire assessment is discussed, focusing on its design, development, and testing. It comprises two main modules tailored to each task, as represented in Fig. 1:

- Alarm Module (AM) - is designed to transmit atmospheric sensor data that can be visualized or utilized to enhance fire spread predictions by providing more accurate and localized atmospheric data;
- Thermal Mapping Module (TMM) - is a handheld device equipped with a thermal sensor intended for use in the wildfire aftermath to detect hotspots effectively.

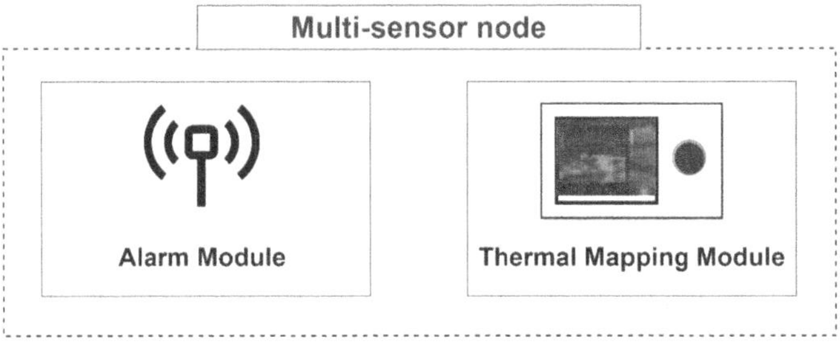

Fig. 1. Diagram of the proposed multi-sensor node, consisting of a 'Thermal Mapping Module' and an 'Alarm Module'.

The multi-sensor node was designed without a built-in network interface for direct internet connectivity, as it is intended for local use near firefighters. It connects to a smartphone via a BLE connection, with the smartphone acting as an intermediary to transmit its sensor data to the Internet. A custom smartphone application serves as an interface to the underlying system. Figure 2 illustrates a diagram showing how the multi-sensor node transmits its data to the Internet.

It gathers data during wildfires through its 'Alarm Module' (AM) and during the aftermath phase through its 'Thermal Mapping Module' (TMM). The AM transmits atmospheric data directly, while the TMM processes thermal sensor data locally, transmitting only the processed results. All data is transmitted via BLE to a smartphone running a custom-designed application and stored locally in a database to ensure availability without an internet connection. Once internet access is restored, it is transmitted to the Internet. The sensor data from the AM can be visualized on the smartphone, while the data from the TMM is displayed on an onboard LCD integrated into that module.

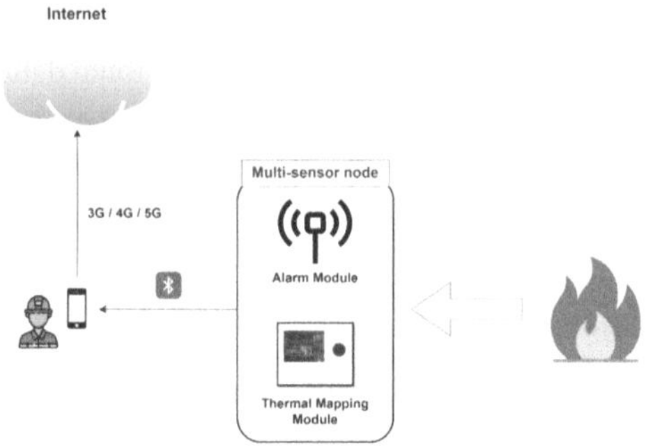

Fig. 2. Diagram illustrating how the multi-sensor node works to transmit its data to the Internet.

3.1 Implementation of the Alarm Module

The AM has several atmospheric sensors that measure key environmental parameters essential for wildfire monitoring. These sensors collect localized data on weather conditions near the wildfire, offering valuable insights for assessing the current state of the wildfire and predicting its potential behaviour. Figure 3 shows the schematic of the developed AM with its sensors.

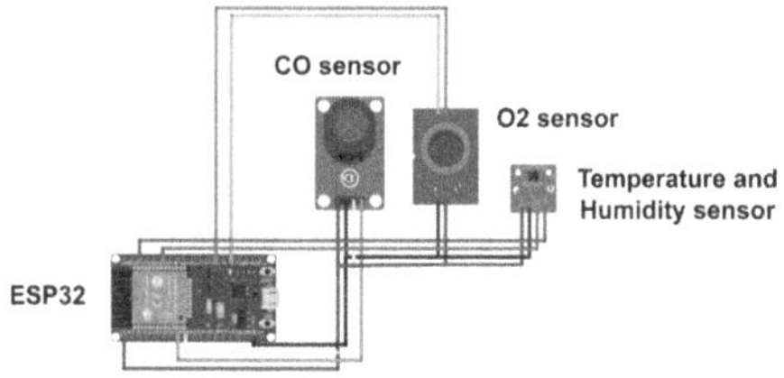

Fig. 3. Schematic representation of the 'Alarm Module' design, showcasing its current sensors: a CO sensor, an O2 sensor, and a temperature and humidity sensor.

To assess air quality for firefighting personnel, the current design of the AM incorporates an MQ-9 sensor to measure CO concentrations and an MQ-2 sensor to measure O2 concentrations. Additionally, it includes an HTU21D sensor to measure the temperature and humidity of the air at the wildfire outbreak location. These sensors are connected to an ESP32 development board responsible for data collection and transmission. Sensor data is transmitted via BLE to a smartphone running a custom-designed application. No calibration or optimisation was performed on the sensor data for this device. Instead, the focus was placed on creating a robust data collection and transmission framework that is agnostic to specific sensor technologies.

Communication between the AM and the smartphone is achieved using BLE [19], enabling the smartphone to act as a bridge between the AM and the Internet, maintaining its Internet connection while receiving real-time sensor data from the AM via BLE.

Sensor data in the AM (BLE server) follows a Generic Attributes Profile (GATT) structure, containing a Service with four BLE Characteristics – for temperature, humidity, CO, and O_2 concentrations—each assigned a unique Universally Unique Identifier

(UUID) and accessible by the smartphone (BLE client). Within its respective BLE Characteristics, the actual sensor data is stored in the Value field. Each BLE Characteristics has the 'Notify' Property that notifies the client whenever the sensor values change. The specific Descriptor used was BLE2902 [19, 20] which allows clients to enable or disable notifications for real-time updates from the AM.

Once connected, the smartphone signals the 'Notify' Property for continuous and automatic updates of new sensor data. The received sensor values are locally stored in a database on the smartphone. Periodically, and whenever internet access is available, the smartphone transmits the locally stored data to the Internet. Figure 4 exemplifies the interaction between the smartphone (BLE client) and the AM (BLE server).

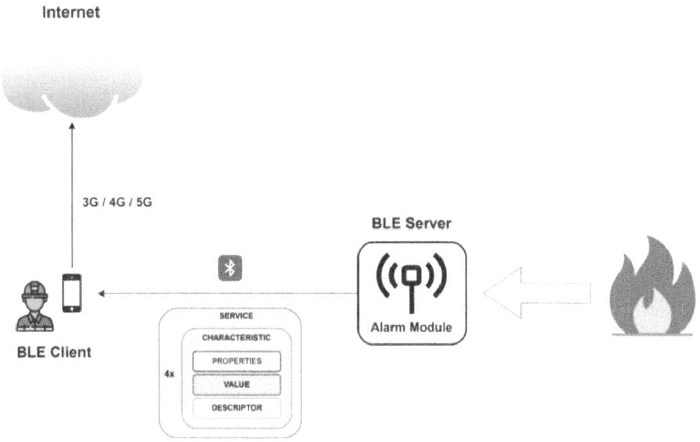

Fig. 4. Diagram illustrating the interaction between the smartphone (BLE client) and the 'Alarm Module' (BLE server).

3.2 Implementation of the Thermal Mapping Module

The TMM utilizes infrared scanning to detect hotspots or smouldering fires in the aftermath of a wildfire. This device enhances the efficiency of post-wildfire patrols by quickly identifying high-risk areas, thus reducing the time required for individual measurements while ensuring that potential sources of reignition are promptly identified and addressed. Sensor data from the TMM is transmitted via BLE to a client application running on a smartphone. This communication protocol enables the smartphone to maintain simultaneous connections to the TMM and the Internet, facilitating the seamless transmission of data to a server where it can be accessed by other peers.

The current design of the TMM, as illustrated in Fig. 5, is equipped with an MLX90640 IR sensor featuring a 31×24 array of thermopile sensors [21], functioning as a low-resolution thermal imaging camera. Additionally, an ILI9341 2.8″ TFT display is integrated to allow the device operator to visually interpret the thermal data generated by the sensor. A button is included in the design to initiate data transmission via BLE

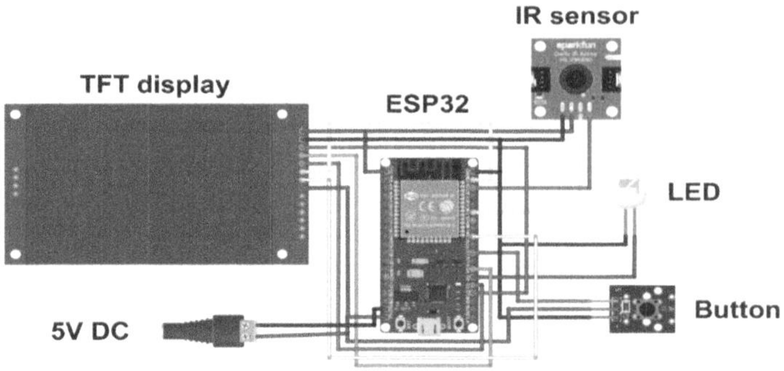

Fig. 5. Schematic of the 'Thermal Mapping Module', showcasing its MLX90640 IR sensor, a TFT display, an LED indicator, and a button for user interaction.

to a smartphone, and an LED indicator to provide visual confirmation of the transmission process. The TMM firmware was programmed using Arduino IDE software that contains a 'setup' function for variable and settings initialization and a "loop" function where the MLX90640 sensor is continuously read.

Hotspot detection leverages the principles of the Normal distribution, specifically the empirical rule, which states that approximately 99.7% of the values in a normally distributed dataset lie within three standard deviations of the mean – that is, within the range of −3 times the standard deviation to +3 times the standard deviation [22]. This indicates that most of the observations in a Normal distribution are clustered around the mean, with fewer observations occurring as the values deviate further from it. Temperature values exceeding this range are identified as outliers. To implement this approach, the mean temperature is first calculated, followed by the computation of the standard deviation. Under normal conditions without hotspots, temperature values exhibit minimal variation from the mean, resulting in a low standard deviation. On the other hand, a significantly high standard deviation indicates considerable dispersion in temperature values, which might be indicative of the presence of a hotspot. The detection algorithm outputs a binary value, where '1' indicates the presence of a hotspot and '0' corresponds to its absence.

On the other hand, the structure implemented in the TMM consists of one Service containing one BLE Characteristic, designed to indicate the presence or absence of a hotspot, each identified with a unique UUID. This BLE Characteristic holds a Value of either '1' or '0,' corresponding to whether a hotspot has been detected or not, respectively. Each BLE Characteristic has the 'Notify' Property, which will notify the client whenever the Value changes. To manage these notifications, the BLE2902 Descriptor [19, 20] is utilized, allowing the client to enable or disable notifications as needed for real-time updates. A connection is established between the smartphone (BLE client) and the TMM (BLE server), which organizes its data using a GATT structure and provides a single BLE Characteristic that indicates the presence or absence of a detected hotspot. Upon establishing the connection, the smartphone enables the 'Notify' Property to receive continuous and automatic updates whenever the value of the BLE Characteristic changes. The transmitted sensor value, representing the detection status (presence or absence of a hotspot), is locally stored in a database on the smartphone to ensure data retention even when internet connectivity is unavailable. Periodically, and whenever internet access is restored, the smartphone transmits the stored data to the Internet. Figure 6 illustrates the interaction between the smartphone (BLE client) and the TMM (BLE server).

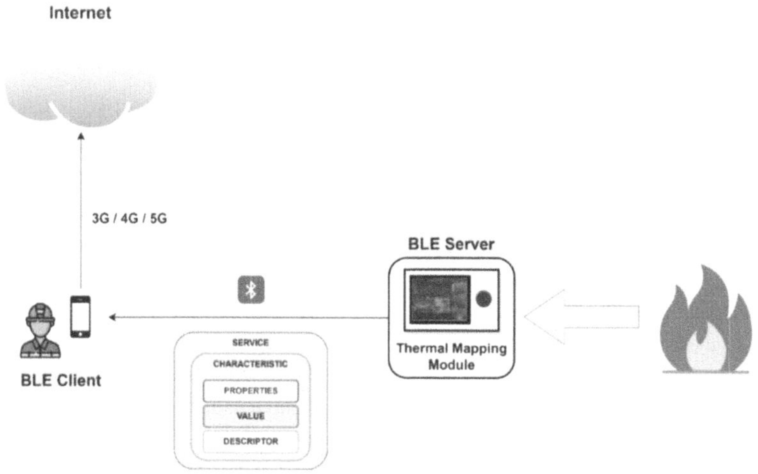

Fig. 6. Diagram illustrating the interaction between the smartphone (BLE client) and the 'Thermal Mapping Module' (BLE server).

4 Discussion of Results

4.1 Discussion on the Alarm Module

The evaluation phase of the system was conducted in two distinct stages to ensure the reliability of the AM for data collection and its integration with other tools for transmitting its sensor data. The first phase tested the connection between the AM and the smartphone. This involved validating the creation of a stable BLE connection, the transmission of sensor data from the AM to the smartphone, and the smartphone's storing the received data locally in a database. The second phase addressed the connection between the smartphone and the Internet. This phase evaluated the successful transmission of the locally stored data from the smartphone to the Internet whenever connectivity was available.

The first phase of the evaluation process demonstrated successful results, validating the reliable data collection and its transmission from the AM to the connected smartphone through BLE. No processing or calibration was performed on the sensor data during this phase, as the primary aim was to evaluate the reliability of data transmission. A BLE server was implemented on the ESP32 development board inside the AM, with one Service created to host all BLE Characteristics containing the sensor data. Four BLE Characteristics were defined, each assigned a unique UUID to identify the corresponding sensor data within the smartphone application that processes the received data.

The 'nRF Connect' mobile application [23] validated the BLE data transmission. After establishing a Bluetooth connection between the smartphone and the AM, notifications for all four BLE Characteristics were enabled, allowing the automatic reception of new sensor readings. Their UUIDs are the following:

- 2c359568-a423-454d-b218-ad802f4dd37e - UUID for the Temperature BLE Characteristic.
- 8d3b4d0d-f4a0-4a07-9bfb-76a2776aed3f - UUID for the Humidity BLE Characteristic.
- c12a67df-e318-4127-b2b1-e890ef3fddb1 - UUID for the CO level BLE Characteristic.
- 90749b8b-94f8-47ec-bd9f-1dd3d4595658 - UUID for the O2 level BLE Characteristic.

The second phase of the evaluation process demonstrated reliable communication between the smartphone and the Internet. An ArcGIS Online (AGOL) Feature Service was developed to host the sensor data transmitted from the AM, enabling seamless visualization and manipulation within AGOL and other ArcGIS ecosystem applications. This proprietary platform was selected due to its recognized robustness and wide-spread acceptance among authorities. Leveraging a familiar and trusted platform ensures greater ease of integration and reduces hesitancy among end-users when adopting new tools.

4.2 Discussion on the Alarm Module

The evaluation process had 3 phases: (1) determining the distance at which a more realistic flame would be reliably detected (and how an environment with high thermal "noise" would affect the TMM performance); (2) assessing the reliability of the hotspot detection algorithm; (3) validating the data transmission between the TMM and the smartphone (client). The initial phase of testing was conducted exclusively using wood as the fuel source. Further evaluations were carried out at distances ranging from 20 to 50 m. Additional tests were conducted at a 20-m distance from a location approximately 5 m below the flames, with a partially obstructed line of sight.

- Phase 1 of the Evaluation Process: An initial set of control tests was conducted on a partly cloudy day, starting at a distance of 1,5 meters followed by additional measurements made from a lower elevation at a 20-meter distance. Results from the 20-metre measurements indicated a few pixels with significantly higher temperatures than their surroundings. Although satisfactory, these results suggested the need to assess whether a high ambient temperature could diminish the performance of the TMM, thus a second set of tests was conducted. These control tests were performed under clear, sunny weather with elevated air temperatures and sandy terrain. Measurements were taken at distances between 26 and 50 meters. After this first control check, the flame was ignited for a second control test, in which the sensor captured temperatures close to its maximum range of 300ºC, at which point the measurements became unreliable. However, the detection of very high temperatures is far more important than the precision of the temperature measurements.

  Following these control measurements, long-distance tests began at 30 meters. The first test scenario is depicted in Figure 7a, where the target flame, marked by a red circle, is located in the upper center of the image (see Figure 7b). Results demonstrated that the TMM consistently identified the flames. Further tests were conducted at 50 meters, where the thermal signature of the flame was barely noticeable on the TMM screen. As a result, 30 meters was determined as the maximum operational distance for this device. The second test scenario was conducted at a distance of 26 meters to assess whether the presence of vegetation (see Figure 7c) would obstruct hotspots and interfere with the TMM's ability to detect them. As shown in Figure 7d, the target flame, partially concealed by vegetation, remained identifiable on the thermal display. The results were positive, demonstrating that the TMM successfully detected the hotspot despite partial occlusion.

Fig. 7. (a) First test scenario in an open field with the target flame marked by a red circle, (b) with the flame detected and shown in the screen. (c) Second test scenario in a covered field with the target flame marked by a red circle, (d) with the flame detected and shown in the screen (Color figure online).

- Phase 2 of the Evaluation Process: Phase 2 of the evaluation process was meant to test the reliability of the hotspot detection algorithm. The detection of temperature outliers (hotspots) uses the empirical rule of the Normal distribution, where approximately 99.7% of the values in a normally distributed dataset lie within three standard deviations of the mean (meaning within the range of -3 times the standard deviation to $+3$ times the standard deviation) [22]. Every data point outside this range is considered an outlier. The results are summarized in Table 2.

Table 2 highlights the exponential decrease in standard deviation as the distance from the heat source increases. This trend demonstrates the expected decline in temperature variability as distance increases, resulting in a more uniform thermal profile at greater ranges. Hotspots were successfully detected at distances up to 23 m. However, beyond

Table 2. Test results outside (*minimum standard deviation reduced to 2.5).

Distance (m)	Hotspot	Standard deviation (m)	Mean temperature (° C)	Max temperature (°C)	Min temperature (°C)
0 m	DETECTED	60.3	57.8	301.0	19.9
5 m	DETECTED	11.9	15.9	208.7	9.9
10 m	DETECTED	5.9	11.5	141.4	1.3
15 m	DETECTED	4.3	11.4	84.1	0.1
20 m	DETECTED	4.3	10.6	57.7	−3.7
22 m	DETECTED*	2.6	11.7	62.4	3.6
± 23 m	DETECTED*	2.7	12.7	57.7	3.2
> 23 m	NOT DETECTED	1.9	12.6	26.0	5.4

this range the algorithm was unable to detect any hotspot, indicating the system's limitations under the tested conditions. These results demonstrate the algorithm's effectiveness for this sensor within a limited operational range.
Phase 3 of the Evaluation Process: Lastly, phase 3 of the evaluation process aimed to validate the data transmission between the TMM (BLE server) and the smartphone (BLE client). The 'nRF Connect' mobile application [23] was utilized to monitor the BLE data transmission. Following the establishment of a Bluetooth connection between the smartphone and the TMM, notifications for the hotspot data BLE Characteristic were enabled, facilitating the automatic reception of new sensor readings. Its UUID is the following:
4ac8a682-9736-4e5d-932b-e9b31405049c - UUID for the BLE Characteristic indicating the presence ('1') or absence ('0') of a hotspot.

The evaluation process, divided into three phases, provided insights into the performance and limitations of the TMM under various conditions. Phase 1 focused on two aspects: (1) determining the maximum distance for reliable flame detection, and (2) assessing the impact of high thermal noise on TMM performance. Phase 2 evaluated the reliability of the hotspot detection algorithm, and Phase 3 validated data transmission between the TMM and a smartphone to ensure seamless communication and integration with the remaining system.

Phase 1 of the evaluation process assessed the performance of the TMM, including the influence of environmental factors on hotspot detection and the occlusion of hotspots by vegetation. It was determined that hotspots could be reliably detected at a distance of 20 m in a sandy field on a partly cloudy day. Additional tests were performed at distances between 26 m and 50 m, where hotspots were successfully detected even on clear sunny days, despite the increased background temperature. However, it was verified that 30 meters is the maximum operational distance for this device, beyond which the detection temperature of the hotspot becomes barely discernible from the surrounding temperatures. The final set of tests demonstrated the TMM's capability to detect hotspots at 26 m, even when partially occluded by vegetation. Phase 2 results, as summarized in Table 2, show that hotspots were detected up to a maximum distance of approximately 23 m. Beyond this range, the standard deviation in pixel temperature measurements captured by the MLX90640 sensor was too small, rendering the developed algorithm unable to identify hotspots reliably. Lastly, Phase 3 validated the seamless transmission of hotspot detection results via BLE to a connected smartphone.

Overall, the evaluation process demonstrated that the TMM becomes ineffective at calculating real temperatures as the distance increases, with the primary impact of this limitation affecting the performance of the hotspot detection algorithm. As the distance increases, the sensor's ability to detect temperature values significantly higher than the surrounding environment diminishes. This reduction leads to a decreased standard deviation, ultimately preventing the distinction of these values from those of adjacent pixels. This method is only effective within a certain range, beyond which the MLX90640 sensor is unable to measure sufficiently high temperatures for hotspot detection. Therefore, it was found that the MLX90640 sensor has a limited performance for detecting hotspots at distances beyond those tested (ranging from 20 to 50 m). Additionally, the ILI9341 display's low refresh rate of 16 Hz poses a challenge for operators attempting to verify temperature readings in real-time.

5 Conclusions

This paper detailed the design, development, and evaluation of MSN, a device intended to provide critical data during wildfire monitoring and in the wildfire aftermath stage. The system consists of two primary components: the AM, which transmits atmospheric sensor data for visualization or for integrating into fire spread simulators; and the TMM, a handheld device equipped with a thermal sensor for detecting hotspots in the aftermath of wildfires. To ensure field suitability near firefighters, the MSN lacks a built-in network interface for direct internet access. Instead, it connects via BLE to a smartphone, which serves as an intermediary for data transmission. A custom smartphone application, developed using proprietary software, facilitates this process by enabling data transmission to the Internet and providing an interface for data visualization.

The AM is part of the MSN and is equipped with multiple atmospheric sensors that measure localized environmental gas concentrations near wildfires. The evaluation process validated its reliable operation for data collection and seamless integration with both the smartphone and the Internet. Communication between the AM and the smartphone via BLE was successful, with the transmitted data displayed in a custom Android application. An AGOL Feature Service was created to host the collected sensor data, and validation using AGOL Map Viewer confirmed the accurate reception of data in the test Feature Service. By leveraging a platform already familiar to authorities, the system benefits from the robustness and widespread adoption of this technology. Rather than assessing individual sensor performance, this research focused on developing a versatile framework for collecting and transmitting data from a broad range of arbitrary sensors.

The TMM is the other component of the MSN, utilizing IR scanning to detect hotspots or smouldering fires in the aftermath of a wildfire. Sensor data from the TMM is transmitted via BLE to a client application running on a smartphone. This communication protocol enables the smartphone to maintain simultaneous connections with both the TMM and the Internet, ensuring seamless data transmission to a server where other users can access it. Evaluation results demonstrated the TMM's potential as a reliable tool for hotspot detection in environments characterized by thermal noise and partial obstructions up to a distance of 23 m. It also indicated that processing thermal data onboard the TMM and transmitting only the binary hotspot detection output via BLE is a more efficient approach than sending the full thermal data. Additionally, introducing a button in the TMM design could allow users to decide whether to use the hotspot detection algorithm or manually evaluate the thermal data displayed on the screen. The TMM's value lies in its data collection and transmission framework, which uses a smartphone as an intermediary and can be replicated with other hardware.

The proposed system provides a cost-effective and versatile solution to support wildfire management operations. The AM can deliver critical atmospheric sensor data directly from wildfire locations, improving fire spread simulations by accounting for local microclimate conditions created by the wildfire [24]. It can also enhance firefighter safety by generating local alerts based on hazardous atmospheric conditions, such as low O_2 or high CO concentrations and can be adapted to monitor the operational status of firefighting assets like fuel or hydrant levels. In parallel, the TMM enables the detection of small sources of residual thermal activity (hotspots) that may not be visible to the naked eye but can reignite wildfires if left unnoticed. By fully integrating these modules and relying on smartphones for network connectivity, the system eliminates the need for dedicated network hardware, providing a practical, low-cost, and easily deployable solution that can be seamlessly incorporated into wildfire monitoring and management workflows.

Acknowledgements. This work was financially supported by FCT (National Foundation of Science and Technology) within the Research Unit CTS – Centre of Technology and Systems, under the PhD Grant 2021.06054.BD Ref. CRM:0033101.

References

1. Allison, R.S., Johnston, J.M., Craig, G., Jennings, S.: Airborne optical and thermal remote sensing for wildfire detection and monitoring. Sensors **16**(8) (2016). https://doi.org/10.3390/s16081310
2. Ban, Y., Zhang, P., Nascetti, A., Bevington, A.R., Wulder, M.A.: Near Real-Time Wildfire Progression Monitoring with Sentinel-1 SAR Time Series and Deep Learning. Sci. Rep. **10**(1), 1322 (2020). https://doi.org/10.1038/s41598-019-56967-x
3. Xu, G., Zhong, X.: Real-time wildfire detection and tracking in Australia using geostationary satellite: Himawari-8. Remote Sensing Letters **8**(11), 1052–1061 (2017). https://doi.org/10.1080/2150704X.2017.1350303
4. Bailon-Ruiz, R., Bit-Monnot, A., Lacroix, S.: Real-time wildfire monitoring with a fleet of UAVs. Robot. Auton. Syst. **152**, 104071 (2022). https://doi.org/10.1016/j.robot.2022.104071
5. Ribeiro, R., et al.: Towards the automation of wildfire monitoring with aerial vehicles: The FIREFRONT Project. In: Rousseau, J.-J., Kapralos, B. (eds.), Pattern recognition, computer vision, and image processing. ICPR 2022 international workshops and challenges. Lecture notes in computer science, Vol. 13644, pp. 183–193. Springer (2023). https://doi.org/10.1007/978-3-031-37742-6_15

6. Gonzalo, J., López, D., Domínguez, D., García, A., Escapa, A.: On the capabilities and limitations of high altitude pseudo-satellites. Prog. Aerosp. Sci. **98**, 37–56 (2018). https://doi.org/10.1016/j.paerosci.2018.03.006
7. Sharma, S., et al.: BEAVIS: balloon enabled aerial vehicle for IoT and sensing. Proceedings of the 29th Annual International Conference on Mobile Computing and Networking (2023). https://doi.org/10.1145/3570361.3592498
8. Linn, R., Winterkamp, J., Edminster, C., Colman, J.J., Smith, W.S.: Coupled influences of topography and wind on wildland fire behaviour. Int. J. Wildland Fire **16**(2), 183–195 (2007). https://doi.org/10.1071/WF06078
9. Salaria, A., Singh, A., Sharma, K.K.: Wireless sensor networks for forest fire monitoring: Issues and Challenges. J. Phys: Conf. Ser. **2327**(1), 12030 (2022). https://doi.org/10.1088/1742-6596/2327/1/012030
10. Tan, Y.K., Panda, S.K.: Self-autonomous wireless sensor nodes with wind energy harvesting for remote sensing of wind-driven wildfire spread. IEEE Trans. Instrum. Meas. **60**(4), 1367–1377 (2011). https://doi.org/10.1109/TIM.2010.2101311
11. Parker, R., Vitalis, A., Walker, R., Riley, D., Pearce, H.G.: Measuring wildland fire fighter performance with wearable technology. Appl. Ergon. **59**, 34–44 (2017). https://doi.org/10.1016/j.apergo.2016.08.018
12. Liolíopoulos, P., Oikonomou, P., Boulougaris, G., Kolomvatsos, K.: Integrated portable and stationary health impact-monitoring system for firefighters. Sensors **24**(7) (2024). https://doi.org/10.3390/s24072273
13. Viseras, A., Marchal, J., Schaab, M., Pages, J., Estivill, L.: Wildfire monitoring and hotspots detection with aerial robots: measurement campaign and first results. 2019 IEEE International Symposium on Safety, Security, and Rescue Robotics (SSRR), pp. 102–103 (2019). https://doi.org/10.1109/SSRR.2019.8848961
14. Pasini, D., Jiang, C., Jolly, M.-P.: UAV and UGV Autonomous cooperation for wildfire hotspot surveillance. IEEE MIT Undergraduate Research Technology Conference (URTC) **2022**, 1–5 (2022). https://doi.org/10.1109/URTC56832.2022.10002208
15. Lin, Z., Bohdanov, D., Liu, H.H.T., Wotton, M.: Autonomous wildfire hotspot detection using a fixed wing UAV. Int. J. Aerosp. Sys. Sci. Eng. **1**(1), 68–84 (2021). https://doi.org/10.1504/IJASSE.2021.114121
16. Burnett, J.D., Wing, M.G.: A low-cost near-infrared digital camera for fire detection and monitoring. Int. J. Remote Sens. **39**(3), 741–753 (2017). https://doi.org/10.1080/01431161.2017.1385109
17. Syaufina, L., et al.: Development of hotspots ground check module in the mobile application for forest and land fires prevention patrol. 2022 International Conference on Electrical and Information Technology (IEIT), pp. 333–337 (2022). https://doi.org/10.1109/IEIT56384.2022.9967891
18. Moutinho, A., Henriques, D., Ferreira, N., Silva, D., Almeida, M.: Using high-altitude balloons for decision-support in emergency scenarios — a proof of concept on wildfire detection and monitoring. 2023 6th Experiment@ International Conference (Exp.at'23), pp. 266–270 (2023). https://doi.org/10.1109/exp.at2358782.2023.10545826
19. Bluetooth SIG. (n.d.). Learn about Bluetooth: Bluetooth technology overview. Retrieved November 23, 2024, from https://www.bluetooth.com/learn-about-bluetooth/tech-overview/
20. Kolban, N.: BLE2902.h [Library file]. In: Espressif (ed.), Arduino-ESP32 repository. GitHub (2017). Retrieved November 26, 2024, from https://github.com/espressif/arduino-esp32/blob/master/libraries/BLE/src/BLE2902.h
21. Melexis: MLX90640 32x24 IR array (2018). Retrieved from https://cdn.sparkfun.com/assets/3/1/c/6/f/MLX90640-Datasheet.pdf
22. George, D., Mallery, P.: Descriptive statistics. In: IBM SPSS Statistics 25 Step by Step, pp. 126–134. Routledge (2018)

23. Nordic Semiconductor: nRF Connect for Mobile (2024). Retrieved from https://www.nordicsemi.com/Products/Development-tools/nRF-Connect-for-mobile
24. Kiefer, M.T., Zhong, S., Heilman, W.E., Charney, J.J., Bian, X.: A numerical study of atmospheric perturbations induced by heat from a wildland fire: Sensitivity to vertical canopy structure and heat source strength. J. Geophy. Res. Atmosp. **123**(5), 2555–2572 (2018). https://doi.org/10.1002/2017JD027904

Detection and Characterization of Plume-Dominated Wildfires

Afonso Oliveira[1](✉), Nuno Fachada[1,2], and João P. Matos-Carvalho[2,3]

[1] Lusófona University, Campo Grande 376, 1749-024 Lisbon, Portugal
{afonso.oliveira,nuno.fachada}@ulusofona.pt
[2] Center of Technology and Systems (UNINOVA-CTS) and LASI, 2829-516 Caparica, Portugal
[3] LASIGE, Departamento de Informática, Faculdade de Ciências, Universidade de Lisboa, 1749-016 Lisboa, Portugal
jpecarvalho@ciencias.ulisboa.pt

Abstract. Extreme wildfires are increasingly hazardous, particularly plume-dominated fires, which exhibit unpredictable behavior due to their self-sustaining convective columns. Despite their significance, these fires remain poorly understood, hindered by limited observational data and fragmented remote sensing approaches. This paper proposes an Artificial Intelligence-based method adaptive framework for real-time detection and characterization of plume-dominated wildfires using satellite and aerial imagery. The framework focuses on three critical aspects: fire intensity, vertical plume development, and rotational motion. Leveraging satellite data, alongside aerial datasets, the methodology dynamically adapts to available data to ensure accurate assessments. The final output is a risk-graded map identifying zones of active or potential plume-dominated activity, and a deeper characterization of the plume internal mechanisms. The proposed framework has significant potential for improving wildfire prediction, management, and mitigation strategies, contributing to improved safety and resource allocation in wildfire-prone regions.

Keywords: fires · risk assessment · remote sensing · multispectral imagery · geoscience

1 Introduction

Extreme wildfires are increasingly intensified by climate [1] and land-use trends [2, 3]. Understanding their mechanisms is crucial for effective mitigation. Wildfires are influenced by topography, fuel, and weather—the wildfire triangle [4].

Weather, particularly wind, significantly impacts fire spread, intensity, and longevity [5, 6]. Rothermel [7] identifies two distinct mechanisms through which wind influences wildfire behavior: wind-driven and plume-dominated fires. A transverse view of these two fire types is illustrated in Fig. 1.

In wind-driven fires, strong ambient winds push the fire front forward, driving rapid and directional spread. These fires typically exhibit predictable behavior, with the rate of spread largely determined through wind speed, fuel type, and topography.

Published by Springer Nature Switzerland AG 2025
L. M. Camarinha-Matos and F. Ferrada (Eds.): DoCEIS 2025, IFIP AICT 759, pp. 143–153, 2025.
https://doi.org/10.1007/978-3-031-97051-1_10

Plume-dominated fires, on the other hand, generate self-sustaining convective columns, creating localized wind systems that override external winds. These fires, often extreme, exhibit unpredictable behavior, including fire whirls and rapid growth. Collapse of the convective column can cause erratic, multidirectional fire spread via embers.

Fig. 1. Transverse representation (a) wind-driven and (b) plume-dominated wildfires. Adapted from [7].

Despite being the most hazardous, plume-dominated fires are also the least understood, to the extent that reliably and accurately predicting them remains unfeasible. Although it is widely accepted that the associated self-sustaining wind events exist and heavily influence fire behavior, the finer details regarding how and when this process initiates and is maintained remain poorly understood, hindering validation efforts for novel modeling, simulation, and prediction solutions. Furthermore, remote sensing solutions specifically for plume-dominated fire assessment are limited, often focusing on singular aspects of these fires [8].

This project aims to: (1) identify components of plume-dominated fires using satellite/aerial imagery; (2) assess and delineate zones of active/potential plume-dominated dynamics; and (3) achieve (2) in real or near-real time. The paper is structured as follows. Section 2 elaborates on the significance of this research within the broader landscape of innovation in AI-powered Cyber-Physical Systems. Section 3 reviews literature on real/near-real-time identification of plume-dominated wildfires. Section 4 outlines the proposed methodology. Section 5 analyzes risks and contingency strategies during the framework's development. Finally, Sect. 6 discusses the potential contributions and implications of the proposed framework.

2 This Research Within the Context of Technological Innovation for AI-Powered Cyber-Physical Systems

This research leverages advanced remote sensing, computational methods, and Artificial Intelligence (AI) to develop a cyber-physical system for real-time wildfire monitoring and analysis. Integrating satellite and aerial imagery with AI-driven data processing, the framework bridges physical environmental phenomena and digital intelligence, improving decision-making and response strategies. An innovation is the use of AI to dynamically adapt methodologies based on data characteristics, addressing the variability and unpredictability of wildfires.

3 Literature Review

The earliest works recognized that large wildfires could create intense vertical air currents, or plumes, due to the heat generated through combustion [9], which could transport heat and particulates high into the atmosphere [10]. It was also understood that under hot and dry conditions, the massive release of smoke into the atmosphere could give rise to pyroconvective clouds [11]—heat-driven clouds formed above intense heat sources—which have the potential to form fire-induced thunderstorms [12, 13].

Subsequent studies revealed that, upon reaching a critical intensity, these fires could exert significant influence over their local wind systems [14]. The intense convection generated has the capacity to disrupt and modify local wind patterns, which, in turn, can accelerate the spread of fires [15]. This feedback mechanism became a foundation for the development of fire behavior modeling in simulations under plume-dominated conditions [16, 17]. Nevertheless, despite these advances, predicting whether or when a fire becomes plume-dominated remains challenging, limiting the accuracy of real-world fire simulations [18].

Lareau et al. [18] highlight three fundamental characteristics of plume-dominated wildfires: high fire intensity, vertical plume development—i.e., the emergence of fire-induced updrafts and associated fire clouds—and rotational motion of the plume, discussed in the following subsections.

3.1 Fire Intensity

Wildfires are sustained through a process of combustion, where fuel reacts with oxygen in the atmosphere, releasing energy in the form of heat and light. The rate at which energy is released—fire intensity [9, 19]—directly affects heat output and is closely related with the type and amount of fuel spent [20]. Consequently, the rate of spread [21] and the quantity and type of fuel burning [22, 23] can serve as indirect estimators of fire intensity.

Thermal Infrared Remote Sensing (TIR) imaging is the most widely accessible method for measuring fire intensity, with satellite-based sensors—such as the Moderate Resolution Imaging Spectroradiometer (MODIS) [24] and the Visible Infrared Imaging Radiometer Suite (VIIRS) [25]—being the most employed tools in the literature for this purpose [26–28]. Airborne platforms equipped with thermal sensors can also be used effectively to achieve accurate results [29, 30]. Fire Radiative Power (FRP) [31], which quantifies the rate of radiative energy released by a fire, is the primary metric derived from TIR imagery to estimate fire intensity and is mathematically expressed through the Stefan-Boltzmann law:

$$\mathrm{FRP} = \sigma \cdot \epsilon \cdot \mathrm{A} \cdot \mathrm{T4} \tag{1}$$

where σ represents the Stefan-Boltzmann constant (5.67×10^{-8} W m^{-2} K^{-4}), ϵ denotes the emissivity of the fire (typically between 0.85 to 1.0), A corresponds to the fire-affected area in square meters, and T is the absolute temperature of the fire in Kelvin.

3.2 Vertical Plume Development

Remote sensing solutions for studying the vertical development of wildfire plumes primarily focus on two areas: measuring plume injection height and detecting fire clouds. There are far fewer methods available for analyzing fire-induced updraft dynamics, and the existing approaches are mostly observational in nature. The limited research on detecting fire-induced updrafts relies on technologies such as infrared [32], radar [33], and Light Detection and Ranging (LiDAR) [34]. Although studies in this area are scarce, there is general agreement that these updrafts are extremely powerful and develop quickly as wildfires grow in intensity.

Accurate estimations of plume injection height have been achieved using active remote sensing technologies [35], such as radar [36] and LiDAR [37], which provide high-resolution vertical profiles of plume height. Satellite-based methods have also proven highly effective, particularly through satellite multispectral stereoscopic imaging. This technique uses the parallax effect—the apparent shift in the position of an object when viewed from different angles—between two or more sensor views of the same plume to estimate height. Studies employing this approach have demonstrated its ability to deliver spatially extensive plume height data [38, 39]. Additionally, TIR imagery, such as that from the MODIS satellite, can be used for this purpose [40].

Satellite-based observations, such as those from MODIS and Geostationary Operational Environmental Satellite (GOES) [41], have been widely used to detect and analyze fire clouds. Studies have utilized multispectral and TIR imagery to characterize their development [42, 43] and distinguish them from other cloud types based on their unique spectral signatures [44, 45]. Additionally, radar and LiDAR-based techniques have proven effective in capturing the vertical structure and dynamics of fire clouds [37, 46, 47]. Advances in machine learning and automated algorithms have further improved the ability to classify these phenomena [48].

3.3 Data Collection and Preprocessing

The literature suggests various relatively limited methods for studying the motion of wildfire plumes. However, most of these methods focus on general turbulence detection and localized flow mapping [49, 50], failing to assess whole-plume rotation.

Several authors demonstrated the use of LiDAR to study vorticity (local rotation) and turbulence in wildfire plumes, providing high-resolution air velocity data [17, 49]. LiDAR is advantageous for its ability to operate up to several kilometers, but it requires clear atmospheric conditions and can be limited by signal attenuation. Radar-based techniques have also been used to measure rotational motion in fire plumes [51], offering the benefit of operating in adverse weather conditions, though with a potentially lower spatial resolution.

Infrared thermography has been employed to infer flow patterns and rotational motion in fire plumes. In [50], the authors used infrared thermography to study plume dynamics, including the development of vortical structures. This method is non-intrusive and provides simultaneous temperature and flow data, but it is limited by its indirect measurement of velocity and the need for calibration.

Satellite-based remote sensing offers a wide perspective for studying largescale fire plumes. Techniques such as multispectral and hyperspectral imaging can detect rotational motion by analyzing plume morphology and temperature gradients [52]. However, while satellite remote sensing provides global coverage, its spatial and temporal resolution may be insufficient for detailed studies of rotational motion if care is not taken when choosing the instrument and its specifications.

4 Methodology

This project aims to assess plume-dominated wildfire behaviors using satellite imagery and aerial imagery. It builds on the framework of Laureau et al. [18], which identifies three prime characteristics of plume-dominated wildfires: high fire intensity, vertical plume development and rotational motion of the plume. Figure 2 summarizes the project's architecture, including the planned data sources, supported methodologies, data fusion steps, and mapping of results.

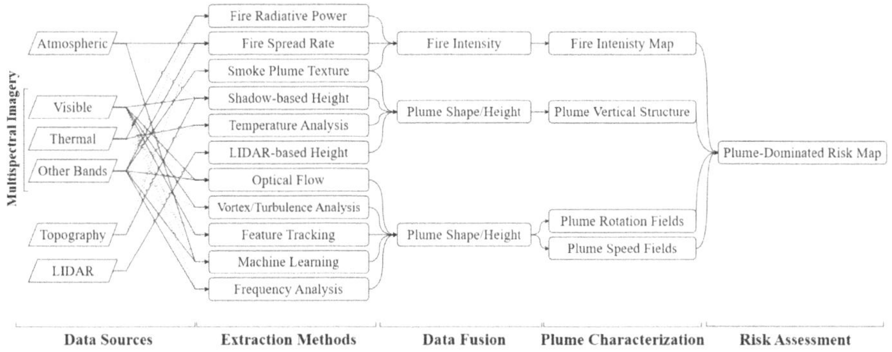

Fig. 2. High-level architecture of the proposed methodology. In the Data Sources section, solid lines indicate primary sources, while dashed lines represent secondary (optional) sources. Other Bands include Near Infra-Red, Infra-Red and Red Edge.

4.1 Rotational Motion

A selection of data sources was curated, covering both real-world and simulated datasets. The objective of using real-world data is to analyze actual patterns and behaviors in real environments, ensuring authenticity and relevance for decision-making. It reflects real-world complexities, though it may be noisy, biased, or incomplete due to limitations in data collection and privacy concerns. In contrast, simulated data is used to test hypotheses, model behavior under controlled conditions, and explore scenarios where real-world data is unavailable or difficult to obtain.

Real-world data sources are categorized into satellite and aerial imagery. To enhance feature tracking, priority is given to satellite imagery with the highest available temporal resolution. Specifically, data from the GOES and Himawari9 [53] will be utilized, offering temporal resolutions of 5 and 10 min, respectively. If necessary—should the data be of poor quality or insufficient for accurate feature tracking—supplementary imagery may be acquired from the VIIRS [25], Sentinel-3 [54], and the MODIS, albeit with lower temporal resolutions. In addition to satellite data, precompiled aerial datasets will be incorporated, including the FLAME dataset [55], the WIT-UAS dataset [56], and the UAVs-FFDB dataset [57]. Furthermore, the authors are developing their own dataset that will include multispectral imagery with fire and smoke masks, as illustrated in Fig. 3.

(a) (b)

Fig. 3. Typical fire image sample in dataset under development: a) RGB image; and, b) the accompanying fire/smoke mask. In the mask, the background is represented in black, fire in white, and smoke in grey.

Simulated datasets are also considered, as their structured nature allows for controlled experimental conditions. Relevant sources include WildfireDB [58] and PyroVision [59]. Additionally, the Fire Dynamics Simulator (FDS) [60] will be employed to generate high-precision datasets for analysis.

To ensure accuracy and consistency, all imagery will undergo several preprocessing steps. First, radiometric and atmospheric corrections will be applied to mitigate atmospheric interference. Next, cloud masking will be performed to remove pixels obscured by clouds, ensuring clear visibility of fire plumes. Finally, all data layers, including imagery, weather data, and topography, will be georeferenced to a common coordinate system to facilitate spatial alignment and analysis. All image processing tasks will be implemented using Python, using libraries such as Raster Forge [61], Rasterio [62], PyProj [63] for data handling and transformation.

4.2 Plume Detection and Characterization

As discussed in Sect. 3, the proposed methodology builds on the observations of Laureau et al. [18]. The primary philosophy underpinning the design of this architecture is to maximize adaptability. Specifically, the system is designed to dynamically adjust its methodologies based on the available data for a given region of interest using AI, with the goal of extracting the most accurate assessment possible. This approach inherently involves a data fusion step, where results from multiple methods are integrated to provide a unified evaluation of the same characteristic. This process not only enhances the robustness of the output but also offers a unique opportunity to evaluate the performance of individual methods within the context of specific regions of interest.

Given a dataset, the system will employ a AI-driven approach—e.g., random forests or gradient boosting machines—to identify and apply the most appropriate methodologies based on the inherent characteristics of the data (type, resolution, format, etc.), which aims to optimize efficiency and usability. Following the application of these techniques, the results are integrated, after which a preliminary statistical evaluation of results is conducted. Spatial representations of the three main attributes are subsequently derived, enabling a detailed assessment of plume-dominated activity. This analysis facilitates the identification of areas with the highest likelihood of exhibiting or developing extreme fire behavior dynamics. The final output is presented as a risk-graded map, which spatially delineates zones according to their probability of plume-dominated wildfire activity.

4.3 Validation

To ensure the robustness of the results, this study will employ multiple validation techniques. The limited observational data available on plume-dominated wildfire events will serve as a foundational basis for validation. Additionally, specific isolated characteristics of the phenomena will be validated using established tools and datasets. For instance, plume height estimates will be cross-validated using data from the Cloud-Aerosol LiDAR and Infrared Pathfinder Satellite Observations (CALIPSO) [64] instrument, which provides independent measurements of aerosol vertical distribution. This multi-faceted validation approach ensures the reliability of the findings and enhances the credibility of the analytical outcomes.

5 Contingencies

In any research study, anticipating challenges and developing mitigation strategies is crucial. One primary risk is the unavailability or poor quality of satellite and aerial imagery, which could hinder the analysis of plume-dominated wildfire behaviors. This risk, with a moderate to high probability depending on the region, will be mitigated by relying on multiple data sources for redundancy.

Another potential risk is computational limitations, as processing high-resolution imagery and large datasets may overwhelm available resources, leading to delays. This risk has a moderate probability of occurring and can be mitigated by processing only a subset of the data while ensuring the viability of the proposed framework is maintained. Furthermore, in the event of local computational failure, cloud computing can serve as a viable solution to safeguard processing capabilities.

Methodological limitations, with a low to moderate probability, may arise if plume detection and characterization methods perform inconsistently across regions or datasets. To address this, the methodology will undergo rigorous testing and validation in diverse environments to ensure its generalizability. In cases of under-performance, alternative or complementary techniques will be explored to enhance the robustness and accuracy of the extraction methodology. Additionally, the framework will be designed for seamless integration of alternative data sources and methods, which will not only help mitigate this risk but also improve the general usability of the framework.

Finally, unforeseen external factors like changes in satellite missions or geopolitical issues, though with low but increasing probability, could disrupt data access. To address this, the study will maintain flexible data sourcing and periodically update contingency plans to adapt to changing circumstances.

6 Conclusions

This research project aims to make several significant contributions to the field of wildfire research and remote sensing through a novel methodology for assessing plume-dominated wildfire behaviors.

The study will introduce a framework for analyzing plume-dominated wildfires, focusing on three critical aspects: thermal assessment, vertical development, and rotation of the plume. In addressing these dimensions simultaneously, the proposed methodology aims to provide a more comprehensive assessment of plume dynamics than previous studies, which often focus on isolated aspects.

The four primary potential contributions of this study are as follows. First, it advances the understanding of plume-dominated wildfires, addressing the current gap in knowledge by providing a structured, data-driven approach to analyze their complex dynamics. Second, the adaptive nature of the framework ensures its applicability across diverse regions and datasets, making it a versatile tool for global wildfire monitoring. Third, the risk-graded maps generated by the framework offer actionable insights for emergency responders and land managers, facilitating more effective resource allocation and mitigation strategies. Finally, the study's emphasis on real-time or near-real-time assessment addresses a critical gap in current wildfire monitoring capabilities, paving the way for improved early warning systems and predictive modeling.

By bridging the gap between remote sensing technology and plume-dominated fire understanding, this study has the potential to significantly boost our ability to monitor, predict, and manage plume-dominated wildfires, contributing to reduced risks and improved safety in wildfire-prone regions.

Acknowledgements. This research was partially funded by: Fundação para a Ciência e a Tecnologia (FCT, https://ror.org/00snfqn58) under Grants Copelabs ref. UIDB/04111/2020, Centro de Tecnologias e Sistemas (CTS) ref. UIDB/00066/2020, LASIGE Research Unit ref. UIDB/00408/2025, and COFAC ref. CEECINST/00002/2021/CP2788/CT0001; Instituto Lusófono de Investigação e Desenvolvimento (ILIND, Portugal) under Project COFAC/ILIND/COPELABS/1/2024.

References

1. Abatzoglou, J.T., Park Williams, A.: Impact of anthropogenic climate change on wildfire across western us forests. Proc. Natl. Acad. Sci. U.S.A. **113**(42), 11770–11775 (2016)
2. Pausas, J.G., Keeley, J.E.: Abrupt climate-independent fire regime changes. Ecosyst. **17**(6), 1109–1120 (2014)
3. Balch, J.K., Bradley, B.A., Abatzoglou, J.T., Nagy, R.C., Fusco, E.J., Mahood A.L.: Human-started wildfires expand the fire niche across the united states. Proc. Nat. Academy Sci. **114**(11):2946– 2951 (2017)

4. Barrows, J.S.: Fire behavior in northern rocky mountain forests. Station Paper No. 29. Missoula, MT: US Department of Agriculture, Forest Service, Northern Rocky Mountain Forest and Range Experiment Station. 103 p., 1951
5. Rothermel, R.C.: A Mathematical Model for Predicting Fire Spread in Wildland Fuels, volume 115. Intermountain Forest & Range Experiment Station, Forest Service, US (1972)
6. Cruz, M.G., et al.: Anatomy of a catastrophic wildfire: the black saturday kilmore east fire in victoria, australia. For. Ecol. Manage. **284**, 269–285 (2012)
7. Rothermel, R.C.: Predicting behavior and size of crown fires in the Northern Rocky Mountains, volume 438. US Department of Agriculture, Forest Service, Intermountain Research Station (1991)
8. Artés, T., Castellnou, M., Durrant, T.H., San-Miguel, J.: Wildfire–atmosphere interaction index for extreme-fire behaviour. Natural Hazards Earth Syst. Sci. **22**(2), 509–522 (2022)
9. Byram, G.M.: Combustion of forest fuels. Forest fire: Control and Use, pp. 61–89 (1959)
10. Haines, D.A.: Horizontal roll vortices and crown fires. J. Appl. Meteorol. Climatol. **21**(6), 751–763 (1982)
11. Dowdy, A.J., Pepler, A.: Pyroconvection risk in australia: climatological changes in atmospheric stability and surface fire weather conditions. Geophys. Res. Lett. **45**(4), 2005–2013 (2018). https://doi.org/10.1002/2017GL076654
12. Latham, D.: Lightning flashes from a prescribed fire-induced cloud. J. Geophys. Res.: Atmos. **96**(D9), 17151–17157 (1991)
13. Peterson, D.A, et al.: Wildfire-driven thunderstorms cause a volcano-like stratospheric injection of smoke. NPJ Climate Atmos, Sci, **1**(1), 30 (2018)
14. Countryman, C.M.: The Fire Environment Concept. Pacific Southwest Forest and Range Experiment Station (1972)
15. Clark, T.L, Jenkins, M.A., Coen, J., Packham, D.: A coupled atmosphere–fire model: convective feedback on fire-line dynamics. J. Appl. Meteorol. Climatol. **35**(6):875–901, 1996
16. Filippi, J.B., et al.: Coupled atmosphere-wildland fire modelling. J. Adv. Model. Earth Syst. **1**(4) (2009)
17. Lareau, N.P., Clements, C.B.: The mean and turbulent properties of a wildfire convective plume. J. Appl. Meteorol. Climatol. **56**(8), 2289–2299 (2017)
18. Lareau, N.P., et al.: Observations of a rotating pyroconvective plume. Int.. J. Wildland Fire **33**(3), 2024
19. Keeley, J.E.: Fire intensity, fire severity and burn severity: a brief review and suggested usage. Int. J. Wildland Fire **18**(1), 116–126, 2009.
20. Manzello, S.L.: Encyclopedia of Wildfires and Wildland-Urban Interface (WUI) fires. Springer (2020)
21. Cheney, N.P., Gould, J.S., Catchpole, W.R.: The influence of fuel, weather and fire shape variables on fire-spread in grasslands. Int. J. Wildland Fire **3**(1), 31–44 (1993)
22. Alexander, M.E., Cruz, M.G.: Interdependencies between flame length and fireline intensity in predicting crown fire initiation and crown scorch height. Int. J. Wildland Fire **21**(2), 95 (2012). https://doi.org/10.1071/WF11001
23. Heward, H., et al.: Is burn severity related to fire intensity? observations from landscape scale remote sensing. Int. J. Wildland Fire **22**(7), 910–918 (2013)
24. NASA. Moderate resolution imaging spectroradiometer (modis), 2024. Spatial resolution: 0.25–1 km, Temporal resolution: 24–48 hours
25. NASA. Visible infrared imaging radiometer suite (viirs), 2024. Spatial resolution: 0.375–0.750 km, Temporal resolution: 12 hours
26. Mupfiga, U.N., Mutanga, O., Dube, T., Kowe, P.: Spatial clustering of vegetation fire intensity using modis satellite data. Atmosphere **13**(12), 1972 (2022). https://doi.org/10.3390/atmos13121972

27. Loupian, E.A., Lozin, D.V., Bartalev, S.A., IV., Balashov, FV Stytsenko.: Assessment of damage to russian forests by fires in the xxi century based on analysis of fire intensity using modis instrument. Assessment **21**(6), 233–249 (2024)
28. Aditi, K., Pandey, A., Banerjee, T.: Forest fire emission estimates over south asia using suomi-npp viirs-based thermal anomalies and emission inventory. Environ. Pollut. **366**, 125441 (2025)
29. Yuan, C., Liu, Z., Zhang, Y.: Fire detection using infrared images for UAV-based forest fire surveillance. In: 2017 International Conference on Unmanned Aircraft Systems (ICUAS), pp. 567–572. IEEE (2017)
30. Sherstjuk, V.. Zharikova, M.: Evaluation of fire intensity based on neural networks in a forest-fire monitoring system. In: 2019 IEEE 39th International Conference on Electronics and Nanotechnology (ELNANO), pp. 802–807. IEEE (2019)
31. Kaufman, Y.J., et al.: Potential global fire monitoring from EOS-MODIS. J. Geophys. Res.: Atmospheres **103**(D24), 32215–32238 (1998). https://doi.org/10.1029/98JD01644
32. Coen, J., Mahalingam, S., Daily, J.: Infrared imagery of crown-fire dynamics during frostfire. J. Appl. Meteorol. **43**(9), 1241–1259 (2004)
33. Rodriguez, B., Lareau, N.P., Kingsmill, D.E., Clements, C.B.: Extreme pyroconvective updrafts during a megafire. Geophys. Res. Lett. **47**(18), e2020GL089001 (2020
34. Banta, R.M., et al.: Smoke-column observations from two forest fires using doppler lidar and doppler radar. J. Appl. Meteorol. Climatol. **31**(11), 1328–1349 (1992)
35. Krishna, M., Saide, P.E., Ye, X., Turney, F.A., Hair, J.W., Fenn, M., Shingler, T.: Evaluation of wildfire plume injection heights estimated from operational weather radar observations using airborne lidar retrievals. J. Geophys. Res.: Atmosph. **129**(9), e2023JD039926 (2024)
36. Haruzi, P , Schmäck, J , Zhou, Z , van der Kruk, J., Vereecken, H., Vanderborght, J., Klotzsche, A : Detection of tracer plumes using full-waveform inversion of time-lapse ground penetrating radar data: A numerical study in a high-resolution aquifer model. Water Resour. Res. **58**(5), e2021WR030110 (2022)
37. Winker, D.M., et al.: Overview of the calipso mission and caliop data processing algorithms. J. Atmospheric Oceanic Technol. **26**(11),:2310–2323 (2009)
38. Kahn, R.A., et al.: Wildfire smoke injection heights: Two perspectives from space. Geophys. Res. Lett. **35**(4), (2008)
39. Sofiev, M., et al.: An operational system for the assimilation of the satellite information on wild-land fires for the needs of air quality modelling and forecasting. Atmos. Chem. Phys. **9**(18), 6833–6847 (2009)
40. Lyapustin, A., Wang, Y., Korkin, S., Kahn, R., Winker, D.: Maiac thermal technique for smoke injection height from modis. IEEE Geosci. Remote Sens. Lett. **17**(5), 730–734 (2019)
41. NOAA: Geostationary operational environmental satellites (goes), 2024. Spatial resolution: 2 km, Temporal resolution: 0.08 hours
42. Fromm, M., et al.: Pyro-cumulonimbus injection of smoke to the stratosphere: Observations and impact of a super blowup in northwestern Canada on 3–4 Aug 1998. J. Geophysi. Res. Atmosph. **110**(D8) (2005)
43. Peterson, D.A., Hyer, E.J., Campbell, J.R., Solbrig, J.E., Fromm, M.D.: A conceptual model for development of intense pyrocumulonimbus in western north america. Monthly Weather Rev. **145**(6), 2235–2255 (2017)
44. Prins, E.M., Menzel, W.P.: Trends in south American biomass burning detected with the goes visible infrared spin scan radiometer atmospheric sounder from 1983 to 1991. J. Geophys. Res.: Atmosph. **99**(D8), 16719– 16735 (1994)
45. Chu, D.A., Kaufman, Y.J., Remer, L.A., Holben, B.N.: Remote sensing of smoke from modis airborne simulator during the scar-b experiment. J. Geophys. Res.: Atmosph. **103**(D24), 31979–31987 (1998)

46. McCarthy, N., Guyot, A., Dowdy, A., McGowan, H.: Wildfire and weather radar: a review. J. Geophys. Res.: Atmosph. **124**(1), 266–286 (2019)
47. Liu, Y., Scott, L.G., Gary, L.A., Ken, F., David, C.: Smoke plume height measurement of prescribed burns in the south-eastern united states. Int. J. Wildland Fire **22**(2), 130–147 (2012)
48. Randerson, J.T., et al.: Machine learning and artificial intelligence for wildfire prediction. Technical report, Univ. of California, Irvine, CA (United States); Univ. of California, Los (2021)
49. Charland, A.M., Clements, C.B.: Kinematic structure of a wildland fire plume observed by doppler lidar. J. Geophys. Res.: Atmosph. **118**(8), 3200–3212 (2013)
50. Švantner, M., Vacíková, P., Honner, M.: IR thermography heat flux measurement in fire safety applications. Infrared Phys. Technol. **55**(4), 292–298 (2012)
51. Zrnic, D., Zhang, P., Melnikov, V., Mirkovic, D.: Of fire and smoke plumes, polarimetric radar characteristics. Atmosphere **11**(4), 363 (2020)
52. Nakata, M., Sano, I., Mukai, S., Kokhanovsky, A.: Characterization of wildfire smoke over complex terrain using satellite observations, ground-based observations, and meteorological models. Remote Sens. **14**(10), 2344 (2022)
53. JMA. Himawari-9 satellite data, 2024. Spatial resolution: 0.5–2 km, Temporal resolution: 0.16 hours
54. ESA. Sentinel-3 satellite data, 2024. Spatial resolution: 0.3 km, Temporal resolution: 24–48 hours
55. Shamsoshoara, A., et al.: Aerial imagery pile burn detection using deep learning: the flame dataset. Computer Netw. **193**, 108001 (2021)
56. Jong, A., et al.: Wit-uas: A wildland-fire infrared thermal dataset to detect crew assets from aerial views. In: 2023 IEEE/RSJ International Conference on Intelligent Robots and Systems (IROS), pp. 11464–11471 (2023)
57. Mowla, Md.N., Asadi, D., Tekeoglu, K.N., Masum, S., Rabie, K.: Uavs-ffdb: A high-resolution dataset for advancing forest fire detection and monitoring using unmanned aerial vehicles (uavs). Data in Brief **55**, 110706 (2024)
58. Singla, S., et al.: Wildfiredb: An open-source dataset connecting wildfire occurrence with relevant determinants. In: NeurIPS Thirty-fifth Annual Conference on Neural Information Processing Systems (2021)
59. Pyronear Contributors. Pyrovision: wildfire early detection (2019). https://github.com/pyronear/pyro-vision
60. McGrattan, K., Hostikka, S., McDermott, R., Floyd, J., Weinschenk, C., Overholt, K.: Fire dynamics simulator user's guide. NIST Spec. Publ. **1019**(6), 1–339 (2013)
61. Oliveira, A., Fachada, N., Matos-Carvalho, J.P.: Raster forge: Interactive raster manipulation library and gui for python. Softw. Impacts **20**, 100657 (2024)
62. Gillies, S., et al.: Rasterio: Geospatial raster i/o for Python programmers (2013)
63. Snow, A.D., et al.: pyproj4/pyproj: 3.7.1 release (2025)
64. Winker, D.M, Pelon, J.R., McCormick, M.P.: Calipso mission: spaceborne lidar for observation of aerosols and clouds. In: Lidar remote sensing for industry and environment monitoring III, vol. 4893, pp. 1–11. SPIE (2003)

AI-Powered Healthcare

Device Prototype for Kinematic and Electromyographic Analysis of the Upper Limb

Patrícia Santos[1,2,4](✉), Filipa Marquês[3], Carla Quintão[1,2,3], and Cláudia Quaresma[1,2,3]

[1] LIBPhys, NOVA School of Science and Technology, NOVA University of Lisbon, 2829-516 Caparica, Portugal
par.santos@campus.fct.unl.pt

[2] Associated Laboratory in Translation and Innovation Towards Global Health (REAL), 2829-516 Caparica, Portugal

[3] Physics Department, NOVA School of Science and Technology, NOVA University of Lisbon, 2829-516 Caparica, Portugal

[4] Health Department, Superior School of Health, Polytechnic Institute of Beja, 7800-111 Beja, Portugal

Abstract. Neuromotor diseases are leading causes of performance limitations in Activities of Daily Living (ADLs), with the evaluation of upper limb (UL) movement patterns being essential for patient rehabilitation. Evaluation methods often rely on subjective assessments, and existing biosignal equipment lacks a combination of essential features such as portability, synchronized muscle contraction monitoring, and range of motion. To bridge this gap, a prototype of a portable, low-cost device was developed to assess biomechanical and electrophysiological parameters, integrating electromyography (EMG) sensors and an inertial measurement unit (IMU). A pilot study with twelve individuals was conducted to monitor contraction patterns and range of motion in both ULs using the developed device. The objective of this article is to present the results of applying this device to characterize neuromotor patterns during a bilateral ADLs performed in healthy subjects, to understand human movement patterns.

Keywords: Technology · Electromyography · Inertial Measurement Units · Upper Limb · Activities of Daily Living · Biomechanics

1 Introduction

The upper limbs (ULs) are directly correlated with performance in Activities of Daily Living (ADLs) making them fundamental for their execution [1]. However, this performance can be highly compromised by limitations in the functionality of the ULs, particularly in neurological disorders [2].

Within neurological disorders, Stroke is a major contributor to neuromotor dysfunction in the ULs, affecting 50–70% of survivors in the acute phase and significantly

Published by Springer Nature Switzerland AG 2025
L. M. Camarinha-Matos and F. Ferrada (Eds.): DoCEIS 2025, IFIP AICT 759, pp. 157–169, 2025.
https://doi.org/10.1007/978-3-031-97051-1_11

impairing their ability to perform ADLs [3]. Stroke patients may develop compensatory movements based on altered movement patterns through the contraction of other muscles that would not normally be expected to contract during a specific movement but compensate for reduced strength, altered tone, among other factors [4]. These compensatory movement patterns disrupting normal ULs movement, leading to functional impairments in the arm, forearm, and hand. These alterations may increase the risk of repetitive strain injuries, further aggravating post-stroke deficits [5].

To prevent this, it´s necessary to objectively analyze the neuromotor pattern of the ULs [6] in a more detailed and precise manner using quantitative data. This approach provides a more accurate assessment than traditional clinical evaluations, which rely on scales for muscle contraction and ULs functionality, as well as imprecise joint range of motion instruments with high measurement variability, like a manual goniometer.

This limitation has driven the increasing use of sensor fusion technologies such as electromyography (EMG) sensors to measure the amplitude of muscle [7] and inertial measurement unit (IMU) to measure kinematic variables of movement, that allows the movement to be characterized and complement other assessments.

Although some devices can simultaneously use EMG and [8] their use has limitations related to portability for patients' daily life contexts, as they are mostly used in laboratories. Other challenges include ease of use for healthcare professionals, application to small muscles and segments without restricting patients' movements during ADLs, and synchronization of signals obtained from a single device.

1.1 EMG and IMU Technology Integrated in Motion Analysis

The integration of IMU and EMG sensors for ULs analysis offers advantages in the rehabilitation, allowing the correlation of kinematic data and biosignals [9].

Regarding EMG, it measures the electrical activity signal associated with muscle activity meaning that the more motor units are recruited, the greater the signal amplitude and the stronger contraction [10]. The EMG signal allows for the acquisition of data on muscle contraction and relaxation, indicating when a muscle is actively participating in a movement. This data enables a better understanding of muscle contraction and the identification of possible muscle compensations during ADLs [11].

Regarding IMU sensors, these are composed of an accelerometer, a gyroscope and a magnetometer in a single module, which correspond to the measurement of acceleration, angular rotation, as well as spatial orientation. Additionally, its internal processing allows the calculation of Euler angles (roll, pitch, and yaw), offering a comprehensive assessment of movement dynamics and the system's spatial orientation. [12]. IMU are often used to measure variables in the joints of the extremities of the body, such arm, forearm and hand, providing data that correspond to position, velocity, range of motion of a joint of up to 9 degrees of freedom [9]. The use of IMU sensors in portable devices integrated with EMG becomes an asset since the measuring joint movement angles during an activity allows a more precise characterization of the movement.

The integration of IMU and EMG sensors facilitates the identification of muscle imbalances, which are common in patients with stroke sequelae [13]. This technology allows healthcare professionals to obtain objective and precise data, enabling them to establish a more reliable relationship between the movement performed and the activation of muscle groups (agonists, antagonists, synergists, and stabilizers). This relationship is crucial for understanding changes in muscle synergies and compensatory movements, preventing the establishment of improper movement patterns [4].

Although some studies have analyzed the motor pattern of the ULs during ADLs, they focus solely on the use of EMG in a single upper limb (UL) [14, 15], only on the use of IMU [16], or consider only functional activities rather than ADLs performance [17]. As a result, there is limited scientific evidence in this field and a scarcity of studies that utilize the synchronized integration of both EMG and IMU technologies.

1.2 Technological Innovation and Improve Life

The analysis of the neuromotor pattern through a prototype of a portable, low-cost device integrating EMG and IMU, allowing the evaluation in any context, being essential for the rehabilitation process. Only by this integrated data it's possible to know the neuromotor pattern, analyzing the activation amplitude of a specific muscle group, synchronized with the degrees of movement performed by the respective segment.

It will also allow, through the establishment of a normative neuromotor pattern in healthy subjects, a better understanding of the alterations present in neurological patients, such as stroke patients. The functional changes in the neuromotor pattern [18] observed in stroke patients require attention, particularly in the shoulder during ADLs, due to the frequent development of compensatory movements [4]. The prolonged establishment of this type of inadequate neuromotor pattern negatively impacts joint alignment, contributing to contractures, muscle weakness, inflammation of surrounding tissues, and the recurrent presence of pain [19, 20], hindering the rehabilitation process.

The aim of this study is to explore the bilateral neuromotor pattern of the shoulder (muscle activation amplitude pattern and triaxial joint movement pattern) using a portable, low-cost and user-friendly developed device with integrated EMG and IMU sensors, during one of the ADLs most prone to compensatory movements (cutting food) [21]. To achieve this, the main shoulder muscles [22] were analyzed: Pectoralis Major (PM), Anterior Deltoid (AD), Middle Deltoid (MD), Posterior Deltoid (PD), Upper Trapezius (UT), and Lower Trapezius (LT), as well as the triaxial movements of the arm segment occurring through the shoulder joint: Flexion (F), Extension (E), Medial Rotation (MR), Lateral Rotation (LR), Abduction (ABD), and Adduction (ADD).

The research question of this study is to explore the applicability of this device for characterizing the bilateral neuromotor pattern of the UL.

Subsequently, the validation of this device will be carried out using gold-standard technology (Qualisys® Motion Capture System for validating the joint range of motion acquired by the IMU sensors and BiosignalsPlux® for validating the muscle activation amplitude acquired by the EMG sensors) in a larger sample of healthy adult subjects, to address a research question related to the doctoral project: what are the characteristics of the neuromotor pattern of the main shoulder muscles during ADLs in stroke patients.

2 AI-Powered Cyber-Physical Systems

This study presents a prototype of a wearable and portable system designed for the simultaneous acquisition and analysis of kinematic and electromyographic (EMG) data, enabling comprehensive assessment of the relationship between muscle activation and joint mobility during Activities of Daily Living (ADLs). Positioned within the domain of Cyber-Physical Systems (CPS), the solution bridges physical sensing components with computational intelligence. The sensor data are digitized and prepared for advanced analytical processing, offering the potential for future integration of Artificial Intelligence (AI) techniques – particularly machine learning algorithms – to build personalized predictive models. These models may be capable of detecting normative versus pathological motor patterns, predicting rehabilitation progress, and informing clinical decisions based on objective, data-driven insights.

Beyond a proof-of-concept, this prototype establishes a foundational platform for AI-enhanced rehabilitation, enabling scalable and adaptive assessment tools for upper limb (UL) functional analysis in both research and clinical contexts.

3 Materials and Methods

3.1 Device Prototype

This study developed a portable and cost-effective data acquisition system tailored for biomechanical and electrophysiological analysis. The hardware, designed by WallySci (Neuriot Technologies LLP, India), consists of two Data Communication and Processing Units (DCPUs). Each unit incorporates an ESP32-WROOM-32D microcontroller powered by a battery and integrated on a board featuring 10 GPIO pins, 6 12-bit analog inputs, and 2 8-bit analog outputs. The DCPUs interface with six integrated EMG sensors and one 9DoF IMU sensor via the I2C communication protocol. Data transmission to the graphical interface is facilitated via Bluetooth connectivity, ensuring seamless wireless communication. The two microcontrollers, designated as master and slave, were programmed using the Arduino IDE. Bluetooth communication was established between the master, slave, and graphical interface using the BluetoothSerial library, ensuring synchronized data transfer. The SparkFun_BNO080_Arduino_Library was used to read data from the IMU sensor, while the Wire.h library facilitated I2C communication.

Upon communication with the interface, the master microcontroller receives the command 1 from the interface. In response, the master sends a synchronization pulse through a designated synchronization pin (syncPin), configured as an output, to the slave's syncPin, configured as an input. Upon receiving the pulse, the slave synchronizes it´s data acquisition with the master and collecting data from sensors.

EMG signals were sampled at a rate of 1000 Hz using analog pins 36, 39, 32, 34, 35, and 33, while IMU data were sampled at 100 Hz. The I2C bus was initialized using the Wire.begin() function, and the IMU sensor was configured with the imu.begin() function. Following initialization, the microcontrollers entered a continuous loop to monitor sensor data availability. When data were available, the imu.dataAvailable() function retrieved orientation quaternions from the IMU. These quaternions were subsequently converted into Euler angles (yaw, pitch, and roll).

3.2 Interface

A Python-based interface was developed to facilitate seamless interaction between the portable device and a computer, with a primary focus on real-time data visualization. The interface includes a user-friendly button for establishing a connection with the microcontroller and a feedback mechanism to confirm connection success.

Additionally, it offers functionalities for initiating and terminating data acquisition, along with customizable options for selecting specific channels for visualization. Users can choose to display data from individual muscles or IMU sensors of each limb.

The interface includes a section for entering patient information and displays the acquired data through graphical representations. Each graph is color-coded for clarity, with units explicitly indicated.

The parameters visualized include muscular activity from six muscles and the rotational angles (roll, pitch, and yaw) of each limb. This tool was designed to optimize usability and enhance data accessibility and interpretability, thereby supporting more effective analysis and decision-making by users.

3.3 Study Participants

The study initially included 12 participants, 3 were excluded due to Bluetooth connectivity issues between the device and the computer, resulting in a sample of 9 individuals (5 females and 4 males; 9 right-handed; age 23,5 ± 5.2 years; height 170 ± 5 cm). Exclusion criteria included neuromotor, musculoskeletal, cognitive, language deficits and changes in visual acuity not compensated [23].

Ethical approval was obtained from NOVA's Faculty of Science and Technology Ethics Board (CE_FCT_002_2022), and the study occurs in institution's Physics Department. All participants written informed consent, and anonymity was ensured.

3.4 Experimental Setup and Protocol

A protocol was adapted from previous studies [14, 15] and the subjects were sitting in the same position them previous studies. A plate with a small cake to cut was positioned (3 cm from the edge of the table and aligned with the subjects' midline), a fork (non-dominant side) and a knife (dominant side) next to the plate.

The activity was first performed at a comfortable speed [24]. Five attempts were repeated with a 5-s rest to minimize fatigue. Two cameras with a resolution of 30 frames/s (coronal and sagittal plane) were used to establish the ADLs phases (Table 1).

The collection of EMG and IMU data were acquired by the prototype, connected via Bluetooth to the software on the computer. The EMG sensors were placed in muscles, both ULs, using the bipolar method, defined by SENIAM. The 2 IMU, placed above the lateral epicondyle, and the reference electrode on the olecranon [25].

Table 1. Phases of bilateral ADLs cutting food. Abbreviation: P1 (Phase 1, Starting position to reaching); P2 (Phase 2, Grasping); P3 (Phase 3, Manipulating); P4 (Phase 4, Transporting to the mouth); P5 (Phase 5, Introduced in the mouth); P6 (Phase 6, Return to the table); P7 (Phase 7, Return to initial position).

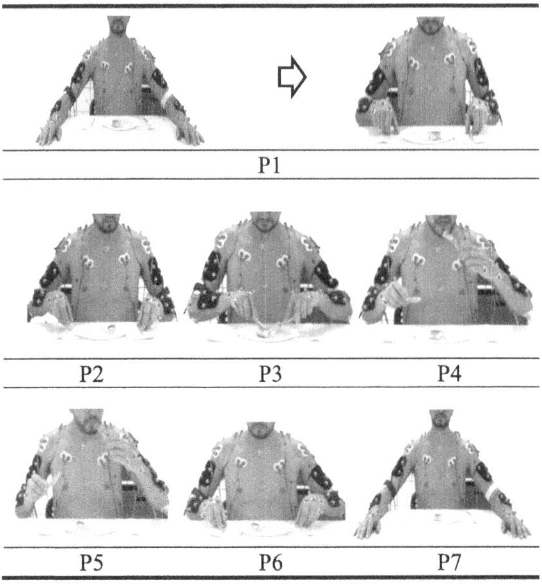

3.5 Data Analysis: Phases, EMG and IMU

For the ADLs phases, videos captured with the cameras were analyzed. The analysis of.avi video files was performed using Matlab® by processing each frame. A function was implemented to record the start and end times of each phase in an Excel file. The time (in seconds) was extracted from the frames, considering the camera's frame rate, and the mean and standard deviation (SD) of the phase durations were calculated.

To obtain the EMG data, the.csv files extracted from the interface of each subject were first imported into Matlab®. From the loaded data, rows containing valid values were filtered, retaining only the columns of interest, namely the time and EMG signals from the various channels. The data were then cropped according to the time limits provided for each subject, with the time adjusted to zero within the defined interval. Following this, the EMG values, initially recorded in bits, were converted to millivolts (mV) using the ADC parameters (12-bit resolution and a 1.6 V range).

A moving average filter was applied to smooth the EMG signals, using a window size of 1000 samples, corresponding to one second of data based on a 1000 Hz sampling rate. This process ensured that the data were adjusted to one-second sampling intervals, helping to reduce noise and unwanted fluctuations in the signals. Then the EMG data were cropped based on the time intervals specified in the DurationCycle_cut.xlsx file, which delineate the start and end times of each phase. Each cycle was then extracted and stored in separate variables, with the pause intervals between cycles also isolated.

The extracted EMG cycles and intervals were resampled to ensure uniformity across signals. Resampling was performed using the interp1 function, which interpolated the original time data onto a new time vector, yielding 16,000 points per cycle and 4,000 points per interval, this leads a more consistent comparison of signals across subjects and cycles. The cycles and intervals were averaged, and the EMG signal amplitudes normalized to a range between 0 and 1. Finally, the normalized signals from muscles were concatenated, with empty data discarded, and averages made for each muscle.

To the IMU, data were extracted from.csv files. The signal was then trimmed based on predefined start and end times, and the time values were adjusted so that the start of each signal was set to 0 s, according to the time limits defined for each subject. A moving average was applied to the Roll, Pitch, and Yaw signals with a window size of 100 points, to smooth out fluctuations in the data. This technique reduce noise and provides a clearer representation of the signals. The data were subsequently segmented into movement cycles based on predefined time intervals (movement phases) and cut according to the cycle length. Each cycle was then shifted to start at zero, with reference to the first second of each cycle, and the results were stored for subsequent analysis. For each cycle, 16000 points were resampled, as done with the EMG signals, and the average values for Roll, Pitch, and Yaw were calculated across all subjects.

4 Results

The average phase durations of cutting food are presented in Table 2.

Table 2. Mean time interval of each movement phase (%) and phase duration (%).

Phases	Interval of mean time (%)	Mean duration ± SD%)
P1	[0, 13.23]	13.23 ± 2.35
P2	] 13.23, 18.75]	5.52 ± 1.31
P3	] 18.75, 50.34]	31.59 ± 6.92
P4	] 50.34, 59.15]	8.81 ± 2.13
P5	] 59.15, 66.50]	7.35 ± 1.68
P6	] 66.50, 80.40]	13.90 ± 2.75
P7	] 80.40, 100,00]	19.60 ± 4.71

Figures 1a and b show the mean muscle activation amplitude of the AD, PD, MD, PM, UT, and LT during the food cutting activity in both ULs. Across all analyzed muscles in ULs, muscle activation progressively increases, reaching peak amplitude in phase 3(P3). As shown in Table 3, the maximum peaks of the muscles of the dominant UL (UT 0.66 mV at 36.58%, MD 0.74 mV at 34.36%, AD 0,74 mV at 35.40%, PD 0.73 mV at 36.83%, LT 0.69 mV at 36.76% and PM 0.66 mV at 36.79%) and non-dominant UL (UT 0.79 mV at 38.98%, MD 0.77 mV at 37.27%, AD 0.76 mV at 34.15%, LT 0.70 mV at 38.53%, PD 0.69 mV at 38,59%, and PM 0.68 at 38.63%), occur between the range to the duration of P3, between 18.75% and 50.34% (Table 1).

A subsequent decline in activation occurs until phase 5(P5) in all muscles of the dominant UL. In the non-dominant UL, PD and MD exhibit a decrease until P5, while PM, LT, and AD show a reduction in phase 6 (P6). UT is an exception, displaying a stabilization rather than a distinct inflection between P5 and P7. Then an inflection peak occurs with a new increase in the amplitude of muscle activation that culminates in all muscles of the dominant UL in the middle of P7 and in the muscles of the non-dominant UL in P6 (PM) and P7 (PD, LT, MD and AD), followed by a decrease in contraction until the resting phase. The UT of the non-dominant UL is an exception, as it does not show a pattern of variation in these phases, remaining with few variations until the end of P7, from which the activation amplitude decreases (Table 3).

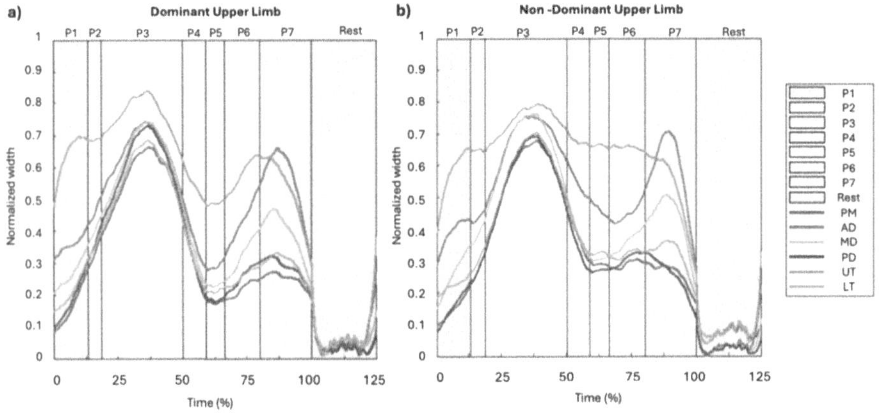

Fig. 1. Pattern of bilateral muscles activation amplitude in the dominant and non-dominant UL.

Regarding the average of the joint range in dominant UL (Fig. 2a), in P3 (18.75% and 50.34% of Table 1) there is an increase in E (peak maximum range of 1,11° at 36.91%) and MR (with a maximum amplitude peak of – 10.46° at 45.34%). Although the amplitude of the ADD increases in P3, its maximum peak is reached in P5, ADD (1.65° at 88.80%). After these, reverse movements begin. After 45.34% the LR begins and increases until the end of the activity where it reaches its maximum peak (1.46º at 100.00%). After 36.91%, F begins, which reaches its maximum in P6 (between 66.50% and 80.40%) from – 8.25° at 73.28%, followed by the E until the end. In the non-dominant UL (Fig. 2b), during P3 (18.75% and 50.34% of Table 1), there is an increase in the range of movement, with all movements reaching their peak maximum, F (−6.23° at 40.79%), LR (−4.86° to 31.49%) and ABD (−4.90° at 43.49%). After, the reverse movements begin. After 31.49% the MR begins and increases until the end where it reaches its maximum peak (1.25° at 100.00%). After 40.79%, E begins and reaches its maximum in P6 (between 66.50% and 80.40%, Table 1), from 1.25° at 73.28%, followed by the E until the end (Table 4).

Table 3. Mean time (%) of maximum normalized peaks by muscle.

Muscle	Mean time of amplitude peak (%)	Mean amplitude contraction peak (mV)
Dominant limb		
PM	36.79	0.66
AD	35.40	0.74
MD	34.36	0.74
PD	36.83	0.73
UT	36.58	0.84
LT	36.76	0.69
Non-dominant limb		
PM	38.63	0.68
AD	34.15	0.76
MD	37.27	0.77
PD	38,59	0.69
UT	38.98	0.79
LT	38.53	0.70

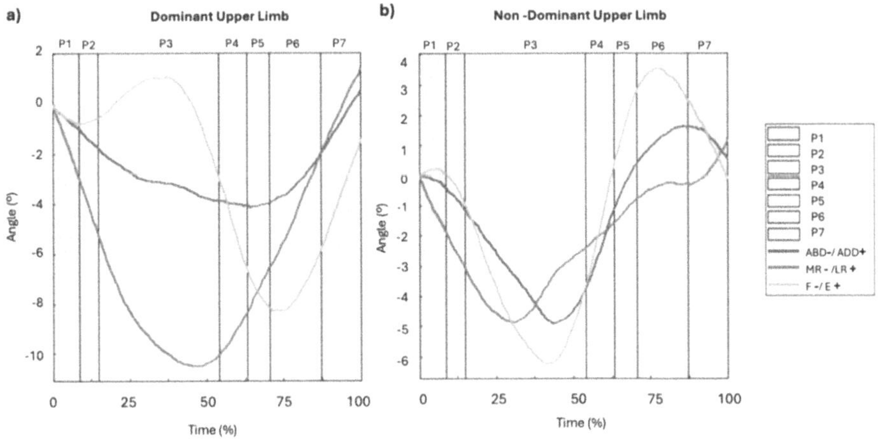

Fig. 2. Joint range of motion of the arm in the dominant and non-dominant UL.

Table 4. Mean time (%) of maximum normalized peaks of joint range of motion (°) of the arm.

Motion	Mean time of amplitude peak (%)	Average Arm Joint Range of Motion (°)
Dominant limb		
F	73.28	– 8.25
E	36.91	1.11
MR	45.34	–10,46
LR	100,00	1.46
ABD	64.24	– 4.13
ADD	100.00	0.53
Non-dominant limb		
F	40.79	– 6.23
E	78.05	3.57
MR	100,00	1.25
LR	31.49	– 4.86
ABD	43.49	– 4.90
ADD	88.80	1.65

5 Discussion of Results

Given that this study employed two integrated technologies within the same device, the results will also be analysed in an integrated manner, aiming to verify the synergies between joint range of motion, measured using the IMU, and muscle activation, through EMG. To our knowledge, no previous studies have conducted a comprehensive joint analysis of bilateral ADLs of the ULs using integrated EMG and IMU. Therefore, these findings have significant implications for rehabilitation. Understanding the synergy between joint range of motion and muscle activation in bilateral ADLs allows clinicians to design more targeted interventions for restoring motor control and independence.

In the dominant UL, it appears that until halfway through P3 (Fig. 2a) there is an increase in the joint range of E, which is accompanied by the activation of the PD (Fig. 1a). The same occurs between MR and AD, and ADD and PM. This corroborates the relationship between agonists, Fig. 1a, and movements, Fig. 2a. It is aline with the movements required for the arm to go from P1 to P2, and P3, needing E, ADD and MR.

Then there is a change in the movement from E to F, from MR to LR and a stabilization of ADD, and consequently there is a decrease in the agonists of E, MR and ADD. Although F is verified, the transition from the position of slight E (when manipulating the knife during cutting), to the more static position in which the knife is in the hand, while the fork in the other limb takes the food to the mouth, is carried out through the effect of the force of gravity and does not require activation of agonists. Therefore, there is no activation of F agonists, that is, AD. These findings highlight the importance of assessing compensatory movement patterns. In clinical, deviations from these normative patterns may indicate deficits in motor planning or muscle recruitment, guiding rehabilitation programs. This reliance on passive movement due to gravity could be relevant in clinical assessments of neuromuscular disorders, where reduced voluntary muscle activation may lead to inefficient or compensatory movement patterns. Identifying these adaptations help therapists tailor interventions for improving controlled voluntary activation.

In the final phases (P5, P6 and P7), there is a marked increase in the range of joint LR, E and ABD, with an increase also in the range of muscle activation of the respective agonists (AD, PD and MD). The activation of the other muscles can be explained by the symbiotic relationship between agonists and antagonists, because to maintain the position of the arm, both muscle groups adjust the number of muscle fibers that contract, remaining active for this reason. These phases correspond to the movements of placing the knife next to the plate and returning to the initial position, justifies a several movements that activate all muscles. Understanding how agonist-antagonist coactivation stabilizes movement could help develop motor retraining exercises.

In relation to the non-dominant UL, it appears that the pattern of muscle activation (Fig. 1b) and the range of joint (Fig. 2b) present a more defined pattern. In the first phases (P1, P2 and P3) there are well-defined amplitudes in the movement of ABD, LR and F accompanied by the activation of MD, PD and AD, which are agonists of ABD, LR, F, together the PM can also be synergy of F and UT being activated to elevate the scapula when fixing the food with the fork, so that the other limb can process the cut with the knife. These findings reinforce the importance of bilateral coordination. Training interventions could focus on restoring symmetrical activation patterns and improving sensorimotor integration in ADLs. After this phase, there is a period of transition of movements in which the arm begins movements opposite to the previous ones, that is, E, MR and ABD, with a new phase of activation of their agonist muscles, AD (in addition to being agonist). The MR is also F, which is why it stands out from the others, and the MD is an ABD agonist. The remaining muscles are activated due to the synergies between agonists and antagonists necessary for a harmonious movement.

6 Conclusion

This study reveals the added value of developing an integrated system with two essential technologies for understanding human movement. In addition to enabling the measurement of kinematic variables and biosignals in a single portable device, it is easy to operate. It allowed us to verify the relationship between the muscle activation pattern and the range of joint during ADLs and which represents a great challenge for patients.

This study identified a common movement and muscle activation pattern in the UL, characterized by four phases with synchronized motion and activation amplitudes. These findings not only enhance the understanding of neuromotor coordination during ADLs, but also hold significant relevance for stroke recovery, neuromuscular disorders (such as multiple sclerosis, muscular dystrophies, and others), and functional motor training. Future studies should expand the sample size and include a broader age range, particularly with stroke and multiple sclerosis patients. The quantitative data obtained (activation patterns, joint range of motion, and ADLs phase transitions) may serve as a valuable foundation for the development of predictive analytical models to identify recovery trajectories, classify compensatory versus functional movements, and predict individual rehabilitation outcomes. This opens the door to personalized, data-driven therapeutic plans tailored to each patient's neuromotor profile.

Acknowledgements. This work was supported by national funds from FCT – Foundation for Science and Technology, I.P. through the UIDB/FIS/04559/2020 (LIBPhys-UNL) and LA/P/0117/2020 (REAL).

References

1. Proietti, T., Bandini, A.: Wearable technologies for monitoring upper extremity functions during ADL in neurologically impaired individuals. IEEE Trans. Neural Syst. Rehab. Eng. **32**, 2737–2748 (2024)
2. Okita, S., Lucena, D., Reinkensmeyer, D.: Movement diversity and complexity increase as arm impairment decreases after stroke: quality of movement experience as a possible target for wearable feedback. IEEE Trans. on Neural Syst. Rehab. Eng. **32**, 2961–2970 (2024)
3. Foley, E.L., Nicholas, M.L., Baum, C.M., Connor, L.T.: Influence of environmental factors on social participation post-stroke. Behav. Neurol. **2019**, 1–8 (2019). https://doi.org/10.1155/2019/2606039
4. Ellis, M., Holubar, B., Acosta, A., Beer, R., Dewald, J.: Modifiability of abnormal isometric elbow and shoulder joint torque coupling after stroke. Muscle Nerve **32**, 170–178 (2005)
5. Levin, M.F., Kleim, J.A., Wolf, S.L.: What do motor "recovery" and "compensation" mean in patients following stroke? Neurorehabil. Neural Repair **23**, 313–319 (2009)
6. Gulde, P., Hermsdörfer, J.: Both hands at work: the effect of aging on upper-limb kinematics in a multi-step activity of daily living. Exp. Brain Res. **235**(5), 1337–1348 (2017)
7. Cotton, R.J., Rogers, J.: Wearable Monitoring of joint angle and muscle activity. In: IEEE International Conference on Rehabiliation Robot, pp. 258–263. IEEE Press, Toronto (2019)
8. Šlajpah, S., Čebašek, E., Munih, M., Mihelj, M.: Time-based and path-based analysis of upper-limb movements during activities of daily living. Sensors **23**(3), 1289 (2023). https://doi.org/10.3390/s23031289
9. Wang, Q., Markopoulos, P., Yu, B., et al.: Interactive wearable systems for upper body rehabilitation: a systematic review. J. NeuroEng. Rehabil. **14**, 20 (2017)
10. Abas, N., Bukhari, W., Abas, M., Tokhi, O.: Electromyography assessment of forearm muscles: towards the control of exoskeleton hand. In: 5th International Conference Control, Decision and Information Technologies, pp. 822–828. IEEE Press, Thessaloniki (2018)
11. Sethi, A., Ting, J., Allen, M., Clark, W., Weber, D.: Advances in motion and EMG based wearable technology for upper extremity function rehabilitation. J. Hand Ther. **33**, 180–187 (2020)
12. Crowd Supply. Wallysci E3k biosensing platform (2024)
13. Repnik, E., Puh, U., Goljar, N., Munih, M., Mihelj, M.: Using IMU and electromyography to quantify movement during action research arm test execution. Sensors **18**, 2767 (2018)
14. Santos, P., Quaresma, C., Garcia, I., Quintão, C.: Neuromotor evaluation of the UL During activities of daily living: a pilot study. In: Camarinha-Matos, L.M. (eds.) Technological Innovation for Digitalization and Virtualization. DoCEIS 2022. IFIP Advances in Information and Communication Technology, vol. 649. Springer, Cham (2022)
15. Santos, P., Garcia, I., Quaresma, C., Quintão, C.: Analysis of UL contraction pattern using electromyographic signal during activities of daily living: a pilot study. In: HEALTHINFO 2022 Editors (Eds.), The Seventh International Conference on Informatics and Assistive Technologies for Health-Care, Medical Support and Wellbeing (2022)

16. Held, J., et al.: Inertial sensor measurements of upper-limb kinematics in stroke patients in clinic and home environment. Front. Bioeng. Biotechnol. **12**, 6–27 (2018)
17. Blaszczyszyn, M., Szczesna, A., Opara, J., Konieczny, M., Pakosz, P., Balko, S.: Functional differences in upper limb movement after early and chronic stroke based on kinematic motion indicators. Biomed. Pap. **162**(4), 294–303 (2018). https://doi.org/10.5507/bp.2018.061
18. Dipietro, L., et al.: Changing motor synergies in chronic stroke. J. Neurophysiol. **98**(2), 757–768 (2007)
19. Ludewig, P., Cook, T.: Alterations in shoulder kinematics and associated muscle activity in people with symptoms of shoulder impingement. Phys. Ther. **80**(3), 276–291 (2005)
20. Kerr, L., Cheng, S., Jones, T.: Experience-dependent neural plasticity in the adult damaged brain. J. Commun. Disord. **44**(5), 538–548 (2011)
21. Oosterwijk, A., Nieuwenhuis, M., Schans, P., Mouton, L.: Shoulder and elbow range of motion for the performance of activities of daily living: a systematic review. Phys. Theory Pract. (2018)
22. Esperança Pina, J.: Anatomia da Locomoção (5ª edição). Lidel, Lisboa (2017)
23. Alt Murphy, M., Sunnerhagen, K., Johnels, B., Willén, C.: Three-dimensional kinematic motion analysis of a daily activity drinking from a glass: a pilot study. J. Neur. Rehab. **3**, 18 (2006)
24. Alt Murphy, M., Willén, C., Sunnerhagen, K.S.: Kinematic variables quantifying upper-extremity performance after stroke during reaching and drinking from a glass. Neurorehabil. Neural Repair **25**, 71–80 (2011)
25. Freivalds, A.: Biomechanics of the ULs: Mechanics, Modeling and Musculoskeletal Injuries. CRC Press (2011)

Explainable Normative Modeling: Subcortical Changes in Frontotemporal Dementia Subtypes

Helena Rico Pereira[1,2](✉), José Manuel Fonseca[1], and Hugo Alexandre Ferreira[2,3]

[1] NOVA School of Science and Technology, Uninova CTS and LASI, NOVA University of Lisbon, Campus de Caparica, 2829-516 Caparica, Portugal
hri.pereira@campus.fct.unl.pt, jmf@uninova.pt

[2] Institute of Biophysics and Biomedical Engineering, Faculty of Sciences, University of Lisbon, 1749-016 Lisbon, Portugal
hhferreira@fc.ul.pt

[3] Instituto de Fisiologia, Faculdade de Medicina da Universidade de Lisboa, 1649-028 Lisbon, Portugal

Abstract. Normative modeling is a valuable tool for analyzing brain morphometry in patients. We used the isolation forest algorithm, trained on 93 Cognitively Normal (CN) subjects, to detect subcortical volume deviations from the norm in Frontotemporal (FTD) dementia subtypes (122 subjects). The SHapley Additive exPlanations (SHAP) method was used to interpret the models' output. In the test set, our left and right subcortical models correctly identified 90.9% of the CN subjects as Control-like (20 out of 22), and 73.3% (left)/65.5% (right) of the FTD patients as Anomalous: 31-left, 34-right out of 52 behavioral variant FTD (bvFTD); 22-left, 16-right of out 33 progressive non-fluent aphasia (PNFA); 35-left, 28-right out of 35 semantic-variant (SV). FTD patients classified as Control-like showed lower subcortical atrophy than Anomalous. SHAP analysis highlighted distinct features relevant for each subtype, with the inferior lateral ventricle being the most significant. These findings suggest the models' potential to detect different stages of FTD subtypes.

Keywords: normative-modeling · dementia · isolation-forest · SHAP · model-explainability · frontotemporal-dementia

1 Introduction

1.1 Research Question and Motivation

The heterogeneity of brain changes found in psychiatric and neurodegenerative disorders created the need to quantify individual-level deviations from healthy aging [1]. Given that, researchers have been developing methods aiming to modulate normal brain aging (normative modeling). With these models, it is possible to characterize each lifespan at the individual level and to monitor the progression and the effects of a brain disease [1–3]. Normal aging is already associated with decreased brain volumes. Nonetheless, in dementia, this volume reduction is even more pronounced [4].

Published by Springer Nature Switzerland AG 2025
L. M. Camarinha-Matos and F. Ferrada (Eds.): DoCEIS 2025, IFIP AICT 759, pp. 170–182, 2025.
https://doi.org/10.1007/978-3-031-97051-1_12

Frontotemporal dementia (FTD) covers a group of neurodegenerative diseases that mainly affect the frontal and temporal areas, causing behavior and language issues [5]. At early stages and during disease courses, these diseases can overlap in symptoms, hindering an accurate diagnosis [6]. For these diseases, normative modeling could be a helpful tool to individually map brain changes in each patient and promote better treatments. Although promising, current methods for normative modeling still have a few drawbacks: they only measure a single brain feature or, in a multi-feature scenario with more complex models, they lack explainability. However, most models have been mainly applied to Alzheimer's disease or psychiatric disorders, lacking application in FTD.

For small sample sizes, anomaly detection methods, namely one-class support vector machine (One-class SVM), have shown the ability to identify deviations from the norm in psychiatric and neurodegenerative diseases [7, 8]. In contrast to One-class SVM) [9], isolation forest has the advantage of having few hyperparameters and being fast, efficient and scalable [10].

Considering the above-mentioned, we aimed to assess this method's potential to identify brain anomalies in FTD patients, which was not yet reported in the literature, by answering the following question: "Can integrating the isolation forest algorithm with explainability methods modulate healthy brain aging at the subcortical level and identify abnormal brain volumes in FDT patients?".

To address this research question, we proposed a machine-learning (ML)-based methodology for identifying subjects with anomalous brain subcortical volumes. Then, we used an explainability method to understand our models' output scores and find the most relevant features associated with each FTD subtype. Finally, we compared the subcortical brain volumes of the patients classified as Control-like or Anomalous using statistical methods.

1.2 Relationship to Technological Innovation for AI-Powered Cyber-Physical Systems

In healthcare, medical cyber-physical systems (MCPS) interconnect equipment (embedded software in medical devices), network capabilities and patient physiology [11, 12]. MCPS is structured into 3 or 4 layers covering the following components: data acquisition, pre-processing, storage (e.g. in the cloud) and the action or application layers. The latter layer is responsible for data processing and mining, aiding in decision-making, treatment, diagnosis, and remote monitoring of the patients [13, 14].

Considering this, our study perfectly inserts into this layer as it aims to be a valuable tool to aid in patients' diagnosis or monitorization and, thus, be incorporated into any MCPS. AI-powered MCPS has shown its potential in cyber security and privacy – detect bio-modality and bio-identifiable spoofing [9, 11] – and in smart hospital enhancement. For instance, Zhang et al. [15] proposed a framework where integrating real-time patient data and medical records enables the prediction of disease progression. Although we created our methodology using retrospective data, our model could be enhanced to receive the patient's data after the immediate MRI exam if integrated into such systems.

Characterized by providing transparent outputs, our model could be an asset for facilitating the decision-making that physicians and doctors must deal with daily. Indeed, interpretability and transparency should be equally important to the model's performance [16]. Being aware of the model's potential and limitations increases confidence. Therefore, adding a transparent and interpretable ML model to the MCPS potentiates ethical decision-making and enables regulatory compliance [17]. Besides, it also promotes an understanding of the clinical rationale behind the system's behavior and output [17].

2 State-of-the-Art

Normative modeling of brain morphometry is one of the most used approaches to characterize dementia subtypes. Regression models are the preferred method to assess how much individuals deviate from the norm [18, 19]. Most studies focused on Alzheimer's disease [4, 20–22], and only a few have explored its potential in FTD subtypes. Using three regression models (linear, quadratic and cubic), Planche et al. [23] were able to individually characterize each FTD subtype in progression stages and identify the order of the affected brain regions (subcortical and cortical regions). Similarly, Vernooij et al. [24] used the Lambda Mu and Sigma methods for creating the growth curves (norm reference curves) and Vector Generalized Linear and Additive Models to create the respective percentile. In that study, they focused only on the total brain, lobar brain, hippocampal, and white matter lesion volumes to quantify FTD, Alzheimer's disease (AD), and mild cognitive impairment (MCI) subjects. Those above-mentioned approaches are promising tools towards a more precise diagnosis [18, 19]. Nonetheless, these models can only handle one brain feature (usually vs. age). Thus, they are usually time-consuming and computationally costly, as it is necessary to get one model per brain region [3]. A more recent alternative for normative modeling emerged with the evolution of autoencoders. By using the same rationale as the above-mentioned methods, autoencoders can be trained on healthy subjects, but with the advantage of handling multiple data and thus providing a global brain measure of the deviation from the form. Besides, it is also possible to obtain the contribution of each brain region in the global measure. Given this, Pinaya et al. [25] proposed an autoencoder model trained on CN data to estimate how much AD and MCI subjects differ from the norm and identify which brain regions contributed the most to this deviation. They obtained the same performance as the traditional classifiers in classifying these patients' groups. Nonetheless, these models are also resource and memory-intensive as they require a large sample for training (at least 11000 observations). Moreover, these types of models are known for their lack of transparency. In clinical practice, health professionals should at least identify clinically meaningful insights from the model's output [26].

3 Research Contribution and Innovation

3.1 Study Data

This study used prospectively acquired data from the Frontotemporal Lobar Degeneration Neuroimaging Initiative (NIFD), a publicly available dataset. We selected 105 cognitively normal (CN) and 122 FTD patients with a high-resolution 3D T1-weighted MRI acquired at baseline. From the 122 FTD subjects, we had the following subtypes: 52 behavioral-variant frontotemporal dementia (bvFTD), 33 progressive non-fluent aphasia (PNFA) and 35 semantic-variant (SV) patients.

3.2 Image Processing and Morphometric Feature Extraction

MRI images from NIFD were acquired using a magnetization-prepared rapid gradient echo (MPRAGE) sequence (field strength = 3.0T, 160 slices, voxel size = 1 × 1 × 1 mm, scanner = Siemens TrioTim). We used the standard Freesurfer 7.1.1. Processing stream [27] to pre-process our MRI images. Details about each Freesufer step are reported elsewhere [28]. Then, for the subcortical regions, we used the Sequence Adaptive Multimodal SEGmentation (SAMSEG) of Freesurfer with the intensity normalized MRI as input [29]. To better characterize the FTD subtypes, we focused only on the left and right subcortical brain regions commonly affected by these diseases [23]: hippocampus, amygdala, inferior-lateral ventricle, putamen and thalamus. All volumes were normalized to the estimated intracranial volume.

3.3 Normative Modeling and Anomaly Detection

We divided the morphometric features into two groups: left-subcortical and right-subcortical. Then, we randomly split our CN data into training (80%) and test (20%) sets. To guarantee the same proportion of age and sex data (balanced sets), we ensured that no statistically significant differences were found between them (Mann-Whitney U test for age and Chi-squared test for sex). All FTD patients were left to test our models. Our models were created using the Isolation Forest algorithm [30]. This algorithm is an unsupervised anomaly detection method that identifies outliers through an ensemble of binary decision trees. The final output is a score ranging from -1 to 1, with -1 being the highest distance value of anomaly and 1 being the highest control-like value (zero is the value that splits both classes). To train our models, we used the training set only (parameters: n_estimators = 100, contamination = 0.1), and we ended up with two models (left and right). During the training set, we used the bootstrapping option that internally optimizes the parameters of the binary decision trees (available in the sklearn package) to avoid model leaking. Since brain regions have inherently different volumes, we standardized morphometric features using the StandardScaler method in training and test sets, ensuring that all features contribute equally to the model. Age was also added to the model as it showed statistically significant differences in train vs. test sets (please see Sect. 4.1, Table 1).

3.4 Model Evaluation and Explainability

After testing the models, we applied the SHapley Additive exPlanations (SHAP) [31] method to interpret their output. SHAP uses a game theoretic approach that measures the features' importance and contribution (SHAP values) to the model's output values. It also provides information about interactions between features and how they affect the model's predictions. We evaluated the models' performance using the F1-score, precision and recall (sensitivity). Then, we also computed the z-scores of features in the test set relative to the training set to provide additional clinical interpretable information about the model's predictions: Control-like vs Anomalous. Additionally, we statistically compared the z-scores from the Control-like vs. Anomalous in each diagnosis group using the Student's T-test (significance level = False Discovery Rate (FDR) adjusted p-value of 0.05). Models and SHAP were implemented using Python 3.10.9 (sklearn and SHAP packages).

4 Results

4.1 Study Data and Models Performance

The demographic and clinical characteristics of each CN and FTD subjects are shown in Table 1. Only the PNFA subjects showed statistically significant differences in age with the subjects from the training set ($U = 897$, $p < 0.001$, effect size = 0.415- medium effect]). Table 2 shows the output of the test set's left and right subcortical models. Of the CN subjects, 20 had both right and left subcortical regions correctly identified as Control-like, while two were identified as anomalous. The bvFTD group presented 23 subjects as left-right abnormal, 10 as left-right control-like, 8 abnormal left-only and 11 as abnormal right-only. The PNFA had 13 identified as left-right abnormal, 8 as left-right control-like, 9 as abnormal left-only and 3 as abnormal right-only. The SV group had 28 identified as left-right abnormal and 7 as abnormal left-only. The left-subcortical model identified more pathological subjects as abnormal (90 of 142) than the right-subcortical model (80 of 142).

Table 1. Baseline demographic and clinical data of the subjects

Set	Diagnosis	Age	Sex (Male/Female)
Training (n = 93)	CN	62 ± 8	40/53
Test (n = 142)	bvFTD	61 ± 7	33/19
	PNFA	68 ± 8*	16/17
	SV	63 ± 6	21/14
	CN	66 ± 7	9/13

bvFTD: behavioral variant frontotemporal dementia; CN: cognitively normal; PNFA: progressive non-fluent aphasia, SV: semantic variant.
*Differ significantly from the training set ($p < 0.001$).

For the left subcortical regions, the model showed higher performance in SV vs. CN (F1-score = 97.2%; precision = 94.6% and recall = 100.0%), followed by PNFA vs. CN (F1-score = 77.3%; precision = 91.7% and recall = 66.7%) and bvFTD vs. CN (F1-score = 72.9%; precision = 93.9% and recall = 59.6%). For the right subcortical regions the model showed higher performance in SV vs. CN (F1-score = 86.1%; precision = 93.3% and recall = 90.9%), followed by bvFTD vs. CN (F1-score = 77.3%; precision = 94.4% and recall = 65.4%), and PNFA vs. CN (F1-score = 62.6%; precision = 88.9% and recall = 48.5%).

Figure 1 illustrates the output score of each subject (per diagnosis) given by the two subcortical models. Overall, the CN group presented higher scores, and the SV the lowest scores.

Table 2. Output of the left and right subcortical models in the test set

	Left subcortical model		Right subcortical model	
Diagnosis	Anomalous	Control-like	Anomalous	Control-like
CN (n = 22)	2	20	2	20
bvFTD (n = 52)	31	21	34	18
PNFA (n = 33)	22	11	16	17
SV (n = 35)	35	0	28	7
Total	90	52	80	62

bvFTD: behavioral variant frontotemporal dementia; CN: cognitively normal; PNFA: progressive non-fluent aphasia, SV: semantic variant.

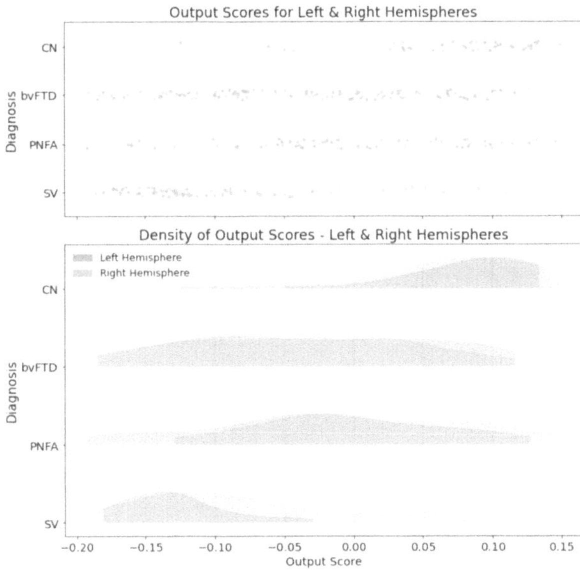

Fig. 1. Output scores (and respective density plot) of left and right subcortical models. In red: results from the model using the left cortical features. In blue: the results from the model using the right cortical features (color figure online).

4.2 Models Explainability and Interpretability

The feature relevance for identifying abnormal subjects in each FTD subtype is shown in Fig. 2 for the left subcortical features (data not shown for the right subcortical regions to avoid repetitions). Age was the most relevant feature in all FTD subtypes but not in the left-subcortical model of SV. By showing positive SHAP values, age positively contributed to the models, i.e., age values push the final score closer to Control-like. In contrast, the SHAP values of the right and left inferior lateral ventricle (second most

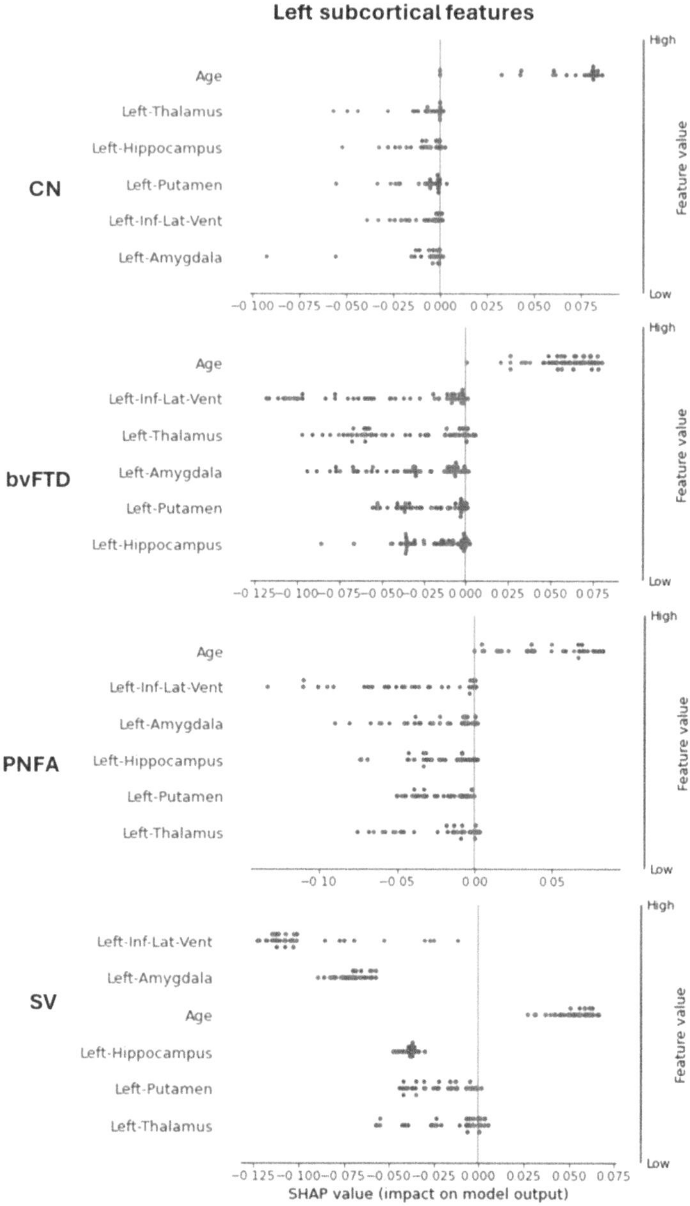

Fig. 2. Feature importance and their impact on the model output based on SHAP values. Negative SHAP values indicate that those features contribute negatively to the model output (i.e., lower scores – closer to anomalous). Positive SHAP values that those features contribute positively to the model output (i.e., higher scores – closer to Control-like).

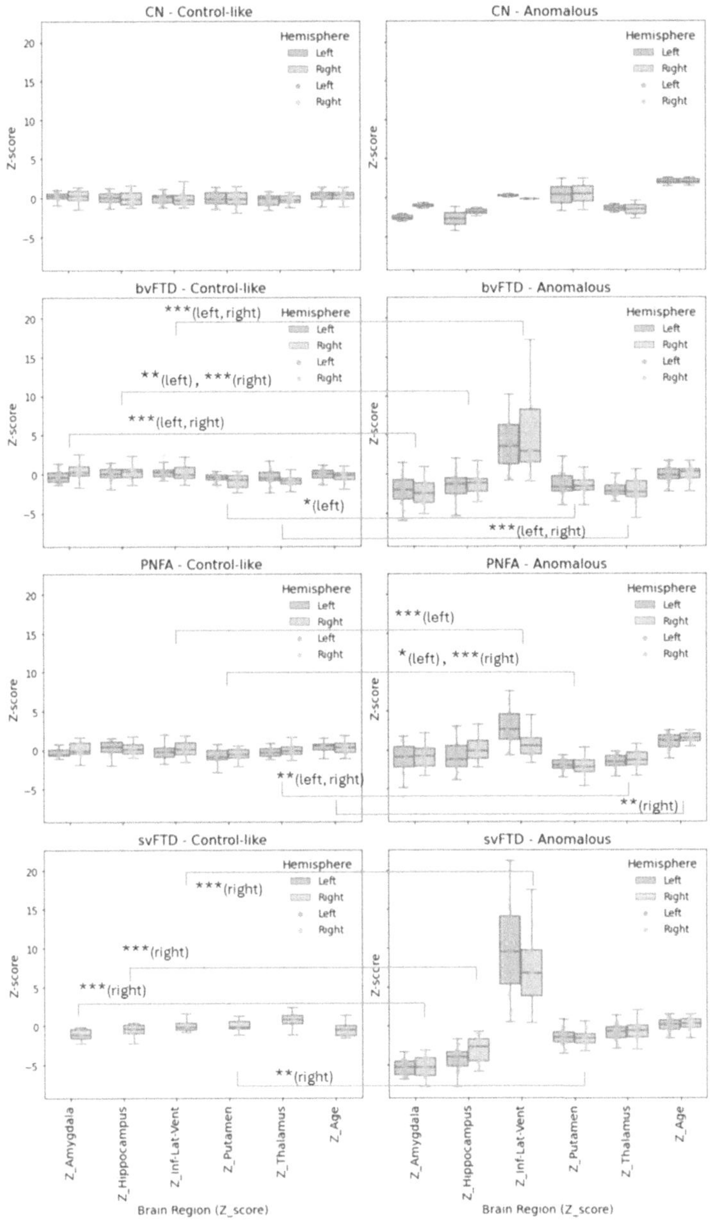

Fig. 3. Boxplots of the z-scores of the left and right subcortical features used in each subcortical model with the models' output: Control-like and Anomalous. bvFTD: behavioral variant frontotemporal dementia; CN: cognitively normal; PNFA: progressive non-fluent aphasia, SV: semantic variant. *Differ significantly from the training set ($p < 0.05$); **Differ significantly from the training set ($p < 0.01$); ***Differ significantly from the training set ($p < 0.001$). (left, right) – both right and left subcortical regions; (left) – left subcortical regions only; (right) – right subcortical regions only.

relevant feature in all) pushed the final scores to Anomalous: the higher this feature volume, the lower the SHAP value. The order of the features' relevance in the classification differed between FTD subtypes. The amygdala (lower volume, lower SHAP value) was the third most important feature for the PNFA and SV but not for the bvFTD. In bvFTD, the hippocampus was the less important subcortical region.

The z-scores from the right and left subcortical features from the FTD subtypes are shown in Fig. 3. Subjects identified as Anomalous by the models show higher z-scores (above $\pm$ 2 standard deviation) than the patients identified as Control-like (the results from statistical analysis are depicted in Appendix I).

5 Discussion

Accurate diagnosis of dementia subtypes has substantial effects on patient's monitorization [32]. We implemented two models using left and right subcortical volumes to identify deviations from normative brain aging. By using SHAP, we were able to clinically interpret the output from the models and identify the order of feature importance in each FTD subtype. By dividing the models into left and right features, we also observed the hemisphere laterally characteristic of the FDT subtypes. Finally, we were able to justify the anomalous and Control-like classifications of the models using a statistical analysis of the features' z-scores.

Previous studies mainly use a large dataset of CN subjects to train their normative models [33]. Unfortunately, we cannot directly compare this with other studies because this is the first study that used a normative model to predict anomalies in FTD patients at right and left subcortical levels. Most studies are focused on classification, while ours also provides an anomaly score, which is more relevant for clinical practice to staging FTD. In CN vs bvFTD, Meyer et al. [34] obtained a recall of 77.3% using temporal morphometric features, which is higher than our methods (left features: 59.6%; right features: 65.4%). Nonethless, our study contrasts with the previous method because we tried to separate the disease by the hemisphere using a different dataset. Also, in a previous study, SV vs. bvFTD (82.0 to 83.0% recall) was easier to discriminate than SV + PNFA vs. bvFTD (74% to 79% recall) [35], as we also observed with SV subjects. In fact, we observed that SV showed a higher number of correctly identified anomalous subjects than PNFA and bvFTD, indicating that the latter groups shared similar morphometric characteristics at the subcortical level between themselves.

Even with a limited CN sample size, our models correctly classified 91% of CN subjects (20 out of 22) in the test set, indicating a good fit for both models. As expected, most FTD subjects diverged from the norm, which aligns with the literature [32]. In the left subcortical model, this divergence was more evident for the PNFA and SV, with more subjects being classified as anomalous than in the right subcortical model (PNFA: 22 left vs. 17 right; SV: 35 left vs. 27 right). Moreover, even among patients with left and right atrophy, the left score was mainly lower (more negative) than the right one.

We also observed 11 bvFTD subjects with right atrophy only, a group that was reported to be clinically misdiagnosed with bvFTD, SV or Alzheimer's disease. Nonetheless, these patients were reported to have a unique clinical presentation [36]. In fact, combining neuroimaging data with negative amyloid status seems to lead to 100% sensitivity in discrimination against other dementias. Therefore, our models could be useful for characterizing these clinically similar groups.

According to the SHAP method, age contributed positively to all demented subtypes, meaning that our models are not using age to define the brain as pathological. This finding is relevant because age is a risk factor that promotes brain volume reduction [4]. Followed by age, the inferior lateral ventricle was the most important subcortical region (in both left and right models) to differentiate dementia subtypes from the CN. Then, the diseases start to show different profiles. We confirmed the bilateral thalamus, amygdalar and striatal atrophy (by this importance order) found in bvFTD [23]. However, not all bvFTD patients showed this atrophy pattern. Both SV and PNFA also showed amygdalar atrophy, with SV presenting lower SV volumes. In contrast to bvFTD, the putamen and thalamus were the least important for SV and PNFA. Besides, the hippocampus was the least relevant for the bvFTD compared to SV and PNFA, as previously observed [23].

This study also has some limitations. Firstly, only a small size group of FTP subtyping data were available to build and test the models, which could have impacted on the model performance. Therefore, testing the model with other FTD datasets will confirm its accuracy, robustness and generalizability. Lastly, we did not consider disease severity and age at disease onset, which may justify why we observed heterogeneity between patients within each disease. In fact, the asymmetry can be reduced over time as both left and right subcortical regions start to get equally affected [32]. However, when analyzing the z-scores, we found statistically significant differences between the Control-like and anomalous patients, showing the robustness of the models. Therefore, this methodology demonstrated its clinical potential by providing an anomaly score of the subcortical regions affected by each disease, allowing for more personalized monitoring of the disease progression.

6 Conclusion and Future Work

Our study demonstrates the potential of explainable normative modeling to identify subcortical deviations in FTD subtypes. By employing left and right hemisphere models and SHAP analysis, we highlighted key subcortical regions contributing to disease classification and confirmed known atrophy patterns. Despite a small control sample, our models correctly classified 91% of cognitively normal subjects, suggesting robustness. The observed hemispheric asymmetries, particularly in PNFA and SV, align with existing literature, while bvFTD cases with higher right atrophy than left reinforce the need for refined diagnostic approaches. Limitations such as sample size and lack of disease severity data should be addressed in future studies. Nonetheless, our findings support the use of normative modeling as a valuable tool for characterizing FTD subtypes and distinguishing them from each other.

Acknowledgements. This research was partly supported by the Portuguese FCT program, Centre of Technology and Systems (CTS) CTS/00066.

Appendix I. Statistical Results from the Student's T-Test

Diagnosis	Hemisphere	Feature	T-Statistic	P-Value	P-Value Adjusted (FDR)	Effect Size (Cohen's d) (large effect)
bvFTD	Left	Z_Amygdala	4.714	0.000	0.000	1.250
	Left	Z_Hippocampus	3.421	0.001	0.003	0.924
	Left	Z_Inf-Lat-Vent	−4.421	0.000	0.000	−1.133
	Left	Z_Putamen	2.875	0.006	0.014	0.771
	Left	Z_Thalamus	5.134	0.000	0.000	1.449
	Right	Z_Amygdala	7.206	0.000	0.000	1.977
	Right	Z_Hippocampus	5.030	0.000	0.000	1.409
	Right	Z_Inf-Lat-Vent	−5.054	0.000	0.000	−1.249
PNFA	Right	Z_Thalamus	3.808	0.000	0.001	1.064
	Left	Z_Inf-Lat-Vent	−4.239	0.000	0.001	−1.362
	Left	Z_Putamen	2.810	0.012	0.026	1.066
	Left	Z_Thalamus	4.293	0.000	0.001	1.505
	Right	Z_Putamen	4.588	0.000	0.000	1.607
	Right	Z_Thalamus	3.776	0.001	0.002	1.320
	Right	Z_Age	-3.564	0.001	0.003	−1.243
SV	Right	Z_Amygdala	9.376	0.000	0.000	3.186
	Right	Z_Hippocampus	5.316	0.000	0.000	1.847
	Right	Z_Inf-Lat-Vent	−7.392	0.000	0.000	−2.060
	Right	Z_Putamen	3.847	0.002	0.005	1.424

bvFTD: behavioral variant frontotemporal dementia; PNFA: progressive non-fluent aphasia, SV: semantic variant.

References

1. Rutherford, S., et al.: Evidence for embracing normative modeling. Elife **12**, 1–24 (2023). https://doi.org/10.7554/elife.85082
2. ENIGMA Clinical High Risk for Psychosis Working Group, et al.: Normative modeling of brain morphometry in clinical high risk for psychosis. JAMA Psychiat. 81(1), 77–88 (2024). https://doi.org/10.1001/jamapsychiatry.2023.3850
3. Oliveira-Saraiva, D., Ferreira, H.A.: Normative model detects abnormal functional connectivity in psychiatric disorders. Front. Psychiat. (2023). https://doi.org/10.3389/fpsyt.2023.1068397
4. Bethlehem, R.A.I., et al.: Brain charts for the human lifespan. Nature **604**(7906), 525–533 (2022). https://doi.org/10.1038/s41586-022-04554-y
5. Bang, J., Spina, S., Miller, B.L.: Frontotemporal dementia. Lancet **386**(10004), 1672–1682 (2015). https://doi.org/10.1016/S0140-6736(15)00461-4
6. Boeve, B.F., Boxer, A.L., Kumfor, F., Pijnenburg, Y., Rohrer, J.D.: Advances and controversies in frontotemporal dementia: diagnosis, biomarkers, and therapeutic considerations. The Lancet Neurol. **21**(3), 258–272 (2022). https://doi.org/10.1016/S1474-4422(21)00341-0
7. Mourão-Miranda, J., et al.: Patient classification as an outlier detection problem: an application of the one-class support vector machine. Neuroimage **58**(3), 793–804 (2011). https://doi.org/10.1016/j.neuroimage.2011.06.042

8. de Oliveira, A.A., et al.: Defining multivariate normative rules for healthy aging using neuroimaging and machine learning: An application to Alzheimer's disease. J. Alzheimer's Diseas. **43**(1), 201–212 (2014). https://doi.org/10.3233/JAD-140189
9. Sato, J.R., Rondina, J.M., Mourão-Miranda, J.: Measuring abnormal brains: building normative rules in neuroimaging using one-class support vector machines. Front. Neurosci. **6**(December), 1–6 (2012). https://doi.org/10.3389/fnins.2012.00178
10. Togbe, M.U., et al.: Anomaly detection for data streams based on isolation forest using scikit-multiflow. In: Gervasi, O., et al. (eds.) Computational Science and Its Applications – ICCSA 2020: 20th International Conference, Cagliari, Italy, July 1–4, 2020, Proceedings, Part IV, pp. 15–30. Springer International Publishing, Cham (2020). https://doi.org/10.1007/978-3-030-58811-3_2
11. Sokolsky, O.: Medical cyber-physical systems. In: 2011 18th IEEE International Conference and Workshops on Engineering of Computer-Based Systems, p. 2 (2011). https://doi.org/10.1109/ECBS.2011.40
12. Chen, F., et al.: Medical cyber-physical systems: a solution to smart health and the state of the art. IEEE Trans. Comput. Soc. Syst. **9**(5), 1359–1386 (2022). https://doi.org/10.1109/TCSS.2021.3122807
13. Mowla, N.I., Doh, I., Chae, K.: On-device ai-based cognitive detection of bio-modality spoofing in medical cyber physical system. IEEE Access **7**, 2126–2137 (2019). https://doi.org/10.1109/ACCESS.2018.2887095
14. Babar, M., Rahman, A., Arif, F., Jeon, G.: Energy-harvesting based on internet of things and big data analytics for smart health monitoring. Sustain. Comput. Inform. Syst. **20**, 155–164 (2018). https://doi.org/10.1016/j.suscom.2017.10.009
15. Zhang, L., Yang, G., Li, J., Liang, J.: A novel medical cyber-physical systems based on digital twin-driven platform. Int. J. Hi. Spe. Ele. Syst. (2024). https://doi.org/10.1142/S0129156425401299
16. Alimonda, N., Guidotto, L., Malandri, L., Mercorio, F., Mezzanzanica, M., Tosi, G.: A Survey on XAI for cyber physical systems in medicine. In: 2022 IEEE International Conference on Metrology for Extended Reality, Artificial Intelligence and Neural Engineering (MetroXRAINE), pp. 265–270 (2022). https://doi.org/10.1109/MetroXRAINE54828.2022.9967673
17. Hoenig, A., Roy, K., Acquaah, Y.T., Yi, S., Desai, S.S.: Explainable AI for cyber-physical systems: issues and challenges. IEEE Access **12**, 73113–73140 (2024). https://doi.org/10.1109/ACCESS.2024.3395444
18. Verdi, S., Marquand, A.F., Schott, J.M., Cole, J.H.: Beyond the average patient: how neuroimaging models can address heterogeneity in dementia. Brain **144**(10), 2946–2953 (2021). https://doi.org/10.1093/brain/awab165
19. Marquand, A.F., Kia, S.M., Zabihi, M., Wolfers, T., Buitelaar, J.K., Beckmann, C.F.: Conceptualizing mental disorders as deviations from normative functioning. Mol. Psychiatry **24**(10), 1415–1424 (2019). https://doi.org/10.1038/s41380-019-0441-1
20. de Oliveira, A.A., et al.: Defining multivariate normative rules for healthy aging using neuroimaging and machine learning: An application to Alzheimer's disease. J. Alzheimer's Diseas. **43**(1), 201–212 (2014). https://doi.org/10.3233/JAD-140189
21. Coupé, P., Manjón, J.V., Mansencal, B., Tourdias, T., Catheline, G., Planche, V.: Hippocampal-amygdalo-ventricular atrophy score: Alzheimer disease detection using normative and pathological lifespan models. Hum. Brain Mapp. **43**(10), 3270–3282 (2022). https://doi.org/10.1002/hbm.25850
22. Verdi, S., et al.: Personalizing progressive changes to brain structure in Alzheimer's disease using normative modeling. Alzheimer's Dement. **20**(10), 6998–7012 (2024). https://doi.org/10.1002/alz.14174

23. Planche, V., et al.: Anatomical MRI staging of frontotemporal dementia variants. Alzheimer's Dement. **19**(8), 3283–3294 (2023). https://doi.org/10.1002/alz.12975
24. Vernooij, M.W., et al.: Automatic normative quantification of brain tissue volume to support the diagnosis of dementia: a clinical evaluation of diagnostic accuracy. NeuroImage. Clin. **20**, 374–379 (2018). https://doi.org/10.1016/j.nicl.2018.08.004
25. Pinaya, W.H.L., et al.: Using normative modelling to detect disease progression in mild cognitive impairment and Alzheimer's disease in a cross-sectional multi-cohort study. Sci. Rep. **11**(1), 15746 (2021). https://doi.org/10.1038/s41598-021-95098-0
26. Payrovnaziri, S.N., et al.: Explainable artificial intelligence models using real-world electronic health record data: a systematic scoping review. J. Am. Med. Inform. Assoc. **27**(7), 1173–1185 (2020). https://doi.org/10.1093/jamia/ocaa053
27. Fischl, B., et al.: Whole brain segmentation: automated labeling of neuroanatomical structures in the human brain. Neuron **33**(3), 341–355 (2002). https://doi.org/10.1016/S0896-6273(02)00569-X
28. Fischl, B.: Automatically parcellating the human cerebral cortex. Cereb. Cortex **14**(1), 11–22 (2004). https://doi.org/10.1093/cercor/bhg087
29. Puonti, O., Iglesias, J.E., Leemput, K.V.: Fast and sequence-adaptive whole-brain segmentation using parametric Bayesian modeling. Neuroimage **143**, 235–249 (2016). https://doi.org/10.1016/j.neuroimage.2016.09.011
30. Liu, F.T., Ting, K.M., Zhou, Z.-H.: Isolation-based anomaly detection. ACM Trans. Knowl. Discov. Data **6**(1), 1–39 (2012). https://doi.org/10.1145/2133360.2133363
31. Lundberg, S.M., Lee, S.-I.: A unified approach to interpreting model predictions. In: Advances in Neural Information Processing Systems, vol. 30 (2017). https://proceedings.neurips.cc/paper_files/paper/2017/file/8a20a8621978632d76c43dfd28b67767-Paper.pdf
32. Harper, L., Barkhof, F., Scheltens, P., Schott, J.M., Fox, N.C.: An algorithmic approach to structural imaging in dementia. J. Neurol. Neurosurg. Psychiatry **85**(6), 692–698 (2014). https://doi.org/10.1136/jnnp-2013-306285
33. Pinaya, W.H.L., et al.: Using normative modelling to detect disease progression in mild cognitive impairment and Alzheimer's disease in a cross-sectional multi-cohort study. Sci. Rep. (2021). https://doi.org/10.1038/s41598-021-95098-0
34. Meyer, S., et al.: Predicting behavioral variant frontotemporal dementia with pattern classification in multi-center structural MRI data. NeuroImage Clin. **14**, 656–662 (2017). https://doi.org/10.1016/j.nicl.2017.02.001
35. Bruun, M., et al.: Detecting frontotemporal dementia syndromes using MRI biomarkers. NeuroImage: Clin. **22**, 101711 (2019). https://doi.org/10.1016/j.nicl.2019.101711
36. Ulugut Erkoyun, H., et al.: A clinical-radiological framework of the right temporal variant of frontotemporal dementia. Brain **143**(9), 2831–2843 (2020). https://doi.org/10.1093/brain/awaa225

User-Centered and Technical Requirements for Myoelectric Pediatric Arm Prosthesis Design: A Preliminary Study

Ana Oliveira[1,2,3(✉)], Ana Londral[3,4,5], Ana Giordano[3], Bruno Soares[1,2], and Cláudia Quaresma[5,6]

[1] Department of Mechanical and Industrial Engineering (DEMI), NOVA School of Science and Technolgy, NOVA University Lisbon, 2892-516 Caparica, Portugal
amg.oliveira@campus.fct.unl.pt

[2] NOVA Research and Development Unit for Mechanical and Industrial Engineering (UNIDEMI), NOVA School of Science and Technolgy, NOVA University Lisbon, 2892-516 Caparica, Portugal

[3] Value for Health CoLAB (VOH CoLAB), 1050-115 Lisbon, Portugal

[4] Department of Physics (DF), NOVA School of Science and Technolgy, NOVA University Lisbon, 2892-516 Caparica, Portugal

[5] Associated Laboratory in Translation and Innovation Towards Global Health (REAL), 2829-516 Caparica, Portugal

[6] Laboratory of Instrumentation, Biomedical Engineering and Radiation Physics (LIBPhys-UNL), Nova School of Science and Technology, Nova University Lisbon, 2892-516 Caparica, Portugal

Abstract. Developing pediatric prostheses that are seamlessly accepted by children with upper-limb malformations remains a challenge, with no existing solutions fully meeting their needs. Understanding their daily routines and perspectives is essential for defining user-driven technical requirements to enhance prosthetic adoption and usability. This study applied semi-structured interviews, following Thematic Analysis and principles of Interpretative Phenomenological Analysis, with congenital arm amputees (n = 6), caregivers (n = 7), and healthcare professionals (n = 5) to identify key prosthetic requirements. Comfort, functionality, and movement versatility were identified as key priorities, with essential activities including eating with cutlery, tying shoelaces, cycling, and object manipulation. Findings highlight the importance of involving stakeholders in the development of human-machine systems like myoelectric prostheses.

Keywords: user needs · technical requirements · pediatric myoelectric prostheses

Published by Springer Nature Switzerland AG 2025
L. M. Camarinha-Matos and F. Ferrada (Eds.): DoCEIS 2025, IFIP AICT 759, pp. 183–197, 2025.
https://doi.org/10.1007/978-3-031-97051-1_13

1 Introduction

Prosthetic devices play a crucial role in the developmental trajectory of children with upper limb malformations. Early prosthetic introduction promotes psycho-motor development, prehension and crawling, body symmetry and self-body awareness, while also promoting future acceptance of more advanced devices [1]. Despite their significance in child development, pediatric upper limb prostheses, especially myoelectric models, remain scarce [2]. Moreover, the existing solutions fail to meet most user needs, leading to high rejection rates due to high weight, limited function, reduced sensation, poor aesthetics, discomfort, large size, and high costs [3–5]. Therefore, it is essential to understand the factors contributing to prosthesis abandonment and to establish technical specifications and priorities, in order to design more appealing prostheses for children with upper limb deficiencies.

Several studies applying a qualitative approach have been made to find out which are the main requirements for developing upper limb prostheses. In 2017, T. Sims [4] investigated the perspectives of children with upper limb deficiency, their parents and therapists using the BRIDGE methodology. Their feedback relied on the necessity of more easily operated prosthesis, versatility, appearance, and safety of these devices. N. Kerver [6] tried to identify the factors that would influence upper limb amputees' prosthesis choice. Key factors in choosing a prosthesis included lesion-related aspects, psychological and social factors, rehabilitation services and costs, prosthetic features, and task performance. However, these factors vary significantly among users. AK. Einfeldt et al. [7] conducted a similar study on myoelectric prosthesis requirements, considering user and healthcare professional perspectives. The main mentioned features were weight, battery capacity, socket design, robustness, safety, cleanliness, aesthetics, grip force and speed, and fine and gross movement capability.

Although several studies have been made, none of them define the requirements priority or explore the activities made with or without a prosthesis. Therefore, addressing these gaps is crucial to identify user-centered technical requirements for improving pediatric prosthetic design, ensuring long-term acceptance. Thus, to assess these user and technical requirements, four research questions were identified:

- What are the key requirements for children's prostheses?
- What is the priority order of the user's needs?
- What are the activities that should be accomplished with a prosthetic arm?
- What type of sensory feedback is desired by prosthetic users?

Qualitative research has shown the value of stakeholders in product development. In T. Sims [4] study is a fitting example of how users, families and healthcare professionals can play a key role in the development of new prostheses that truly fulfil their needs. By using BRIDGE methodology, children were equally involved in the development of their aiding devices. Besides, parents also experience what it is "to live without a limb" and they can provide valuable insights [8]. As such, this study consists of qualitative research, from a co-creation perspective, involving both primary stakeholders, children with congenital upper limb deficiencies and their families, and secondary stakeholders, such as experienced healthcare professionals in the field. The aim is to define the technical requirements for designing a myoelectric prosthesis.

Relationship with User-Centered and Technical Requirements for Myoelectric Pediatric Arm Prosthesis and Technological Innovation for AI-Powered Cyber-Physical Systems. This study defines key requirements for pediatric myoelectric prostheses, aiming to guide the development of a modular, user-centered system that, by leveraging digital technologies, enhances patient customization, while also addressing current limitations. Beyond informing physical design, the findings pave the way for integrating Artificial Intelligence (AI) into prosthetic Cyber-Physical Systems (CPS), enabling systems that personalize control strategies, predict user intentions, and adapt to each child's evolving needs. By learning from daily interactions, AI-powered prostheses can enhance autonomy, usability, and user experience. Additionally, this user-centered methodology can be broadly applied to the development of AI-powered CPS, emphasizing the importance of understanding systems purpose and user needs to advance effective, intelligent human-machine interaction.

2 Materials and Methods

2.1 Study Design

Thematic Analysis (TA), using principles of Interpretative Phenomenological Analysis (IPA), was applied in order to understand the stakeholders' perspectives and translated them into different themes that would lead to user and technical requirements. While TA allowed for an exploration of broader patterns and themes across participants, IPA offered deeper insights into the specific, lived experiences of individuals, enriching the overall analysis [9].

Three semi-structured interviews guides were developed using a consistent topic structure, with tailored approaches for children, caregivers, and healthcare professionals to capture diverse perspectives. Both the children's and caregivers' interview guides were adapted based on whether the child was a regular prosthesis user, ensuring the relevance of different lived experiences. Table 1 presents the topics addressed for the different participants. As this article presents the preliminary study, aspects related to training resilience, medical follow-up and market research were not included in the analysis.

2.2 Participants

The study group was identified through purpose sampling. The total sample size was eighteen participants, including six children with upper limb deficiencies, along with seven caregivers, and five healthcare professionals with experience in the prosthetic field from two different hospitals. Inclusion criteria for children were isolated unilateral transverse malformation of the upper limb, ages between 6 and 10 years.

Lesions with preservation of less than two thirds of the forearm were excluded as well as the presence of phalanxes or complete fingers. Healthcare professionals had to have at least five years of experience in pediatric prosthetic care.

All the participants signed their informed consent form. For the children, this document was signed by the legal guardian. Severe medical or psychological conditions that could significantly interfere with the course of protocol or lack of communication ability

Table 1. Interviews addressed topics. Depending on the participants, different topics were covered.

Topics	Child uses prosthesis		Child doesn't use prosthesis		Healthcare professionals
	Child	Caregiver	Child	Caregiver	
Children reaction to prostheses					×
Prosthetic adhesion					×
Prosthesis/defected arm interaction in daily activities	×	×	×	×	
Desire and contact with prostheses			×	×	
Common prostheses issues					×
Prostheses market research		×			
Dream prosthesis	×	×	×	×	×
Training resilience and medical follow-up	×	×	×	×	×
Additional requirements and stimuli		×	×	×	×
Requirements priority order	×	×	×	×	×
Impact of the project					×

to participate in the interview (due to language barriers and/or severe cognitive impairments) were also considered as exclusion criteria. This sample was chosen to provide a comprehensive yet manageable dataset, ensuring the triangulation of perspectives while allowing in-depth qualitative analysis. Table 2 presents the study group characteristics.

2.3 Procedures

Participants were informed about the project scope and interview procedures, with permission requested before recording. Interviews were conducted individually, except for a pair of parents who both wished to participate. Personal data was collected with participant consent, and caregivers and healthcare professionals provided details about their roles and experience.

Caregivers were interviewed first, followed by the children, to help them become familiar with the types of questions that would be asked. During the children's interviews, caregivers were present but instructed not to interfere unless the child expressed a need

Table 2. Characteristics of the study group.

Children						
Gender		Lesion Level			Lesion Side	
Male	Female	Transmetacarpal	Transradial	Transhumeral	Left	Right
4	2	3	2	1	2	4
Prosthetic use					Age (years)	
Daily	Occasionally	Previously used	Never used		8±1	
1	1	2	2			
Caregivers						
Gender		Degree of kinship			Age (years)	
Male	Female	1st degree	2nd degree		52±8	
2	5	6	1			
Healthcare Professionals						
Gender		Area of Specialization		Experience (years)	Age (years)	
Male	Female	Physiatrist	Occupation Therapist	27±6	52 ± 7	
0	5	1	4			

for help or support. Whenever possible, children were not present during the caregivers' interviews to avoid influencing their future answers.

Throughout all the interviews, in addition to open-ended questions, visual cards were used for two main purposes. For children, cards illustrating different daily activities were presented to help them recall their daily routines and explain how they would use their affected arm or prosthesis. Depending on the participant group, a different set of cards was used, reflecting known user needs [3–7] to help establish a priority order for the requirements. For each question, participants were encouraged to elaborate on their responses. All silences and answers such as "I don't know" were respected, especially with pediatric participants. Table 3 presents the cards presented for each group, along with the description presented to participants for each card.

The needs and requirements were adapted for each stakeholder, with healthcare professionals receiving the full list. Children were shown appearance, comfort, and functionality, and the caregivers received the same list with the price added. Both groups rank their preferences using adjectives (e.g., 'Pretty,' 'Affordable'), as if they were purchasing a prosthesis. Comparisons helped children understand some of the concepts, like likening comfort to favorite sneakers.

Table 3. Description of the known user needs and technical requirements presented to participants in cards for priority definitions.

Requirement	Description
Appearance	The prosthesis looks like a human hand
Comfort	The prosthesis doesn't hurt or bother the user while wearing it
Functionality	The prosthesis allows the user to perform daily life activities
Modularity	The prosthesis is composed of different parts for easy assembly, cleaning, and replacement
Price	The prosthesis is affordable for families
Size	Proportion between child's body parts and the prosthesis' dimension
Weight	Sensation of lightness or heaviness promoted by the prosthesis
Force	Force applied to objects when grabbed
Movements variety	The prosthesis presents different anatomical movements
Velocity	Response speed between muscle contraction and prosthesis activation

2.4 Qualitative Data Management and Analysis

All personal data was stored in a password-protected Excel document and pseudonymized. Recording file names were coded with unique identifiers ('U' for children, 'C' for caregivers, and 'P' for healthcare professionals) upon upload to the main investigator's password-protected computer.

Transcriptions were generated using Microsoft Notepad with the Windows 11 Dictation tool and manually revised for accuracy while listening to recordings. Identifiable information was removed, and important notes, such as gestures or emphasized quotes, were documented. A final review ensured all errors were corrected for rigorous data handling.

Following Braun and Clarke's [10] Thematic Analysis guidelines, transcripts were read multiple times for familiarization. Initial codes were assigned to relevant data, and preliminary themes were identified. Using Taguette software, codes were refined and merged into final themes. Yes-or-no responses and requirement priorities were compiled in Excel. Priority order was analyzed using a weighted scoring method, where higher-ranked requirements received higher scores. Total scores were summed to reflect overall preferences.

All initial tasks, including interview organization, file naming and coding, transcription and transcript review, as well as the collection of quantitative data such as yes-or-no responses and the prioritization of requirements, were carried out by the main researcher, given the quantitative nature and sensitivity of the data. Although the initial coding was primarily conducted by the main researcher, the thematic coding process was subsequently discussed with a second researcher. While Braun and Clarke [11] note that high-quality coding does not necessarily depend on multiple coders, collaborative review was employed in this study to minimize bias and avoid misalignment. Accordingly, the initial codes and themes were discussed and refined jointly by the main and second researchers.

Based on the information obtained from the TA and the priority order definition, some design recommendations were explored.

3 Results

The results are divided into four sections, focusing on key research questions. The first section discusses the priority of user needs and technical requirements. The second describes key activities and environments where prostheses are used. The third addresses the role of sensory feedback. The fourth presents additional insights, such as robustness, customization, and factors influencing prosthesis' adoption. Participant quotes are included throughout to illustrate key points. Each section incorporates direct participant quotes to illustrate the identified themes.

3.1 User Needs, Technical Requirements and Preference Order

Comfort and functionality were the top priorities for all three participant groups. Regarding specific requirements for myoelectric prostheses, all healthcare professionals ranked them in the same order, except for one, who considered velocity the most important requirement. Table 4 presents the results of the priority orders for both previously known user and technical requirements. In addition to these predefined categories, new themes emerged from the interviews, shedding light on various aspects of prosthesis adoption, that will be briefly explored in this current paper. The following sections present these requirements in detail, incorporating user descriptions to illustrate their significance.

Comfort. According to participants, a prosthesis must prioritize comfort to ensure consistent use, otherwise it will be rejected. Comfort was referred to be deeply related to the stump-prosthesis interface, which should provide patients well-being with a proper fit, without causing any pain. These interfaces were reported to increase stump temperature, which can cause skin irritation and unpleasant odors.

> "*If we have a pebble in our shoe and walk two kilometers, it's over. (...) The same applies to a prosthesis... If the socket isn't good, (...) if the fit isn't properly adjusted, snug... So, comfort is primordial.*" (P005).

Functionality. Functionality was considered a critical factor in prosthesis acceptance, often leading to rejection when lacking. It was primarily associated with finger movement and the ability to grasp objects, facilitating the performance of daily living activities. To be effective, a prosthesis must offer reliable performance while remaining intuitive, practical, and easy to use and placed correctly in the limb.

> "*It would be a prosthesis that (...) he could use by himself, put on by himself... It would need to have some functionality, even if it was just to grasp certain types of objects.*" (C005).

Table 4. Priority order of already known user needs and requirements for pediatric myoelectric prostheses. For each group of participants, requirements are sorted from the most important one to the less important, from top to bottom line.

Type of requirements	Children	Caregivers	Healthcare professionals
User needs	Comfortable	Comfortable	Comfort
	Easy to use	Functional	Functionality
	Pretty	Affordable	Weight
		Realistic	Size
			Appearance
			Modularity
			Price
Technical requirements			Variety of movements
			Force
			Velocity

Weight. Prostheses were referred to be often too heavy, which leads to rejection. Excessive weight makes them uncomfortable, requiring significant postural control and hindering their use. As a result, external assistance is frequently needed to handle them.

"*And then, of course, the weight as well, because if it's something heavy... It demands better trunk control, we have to think about staying aligned because there's extra weight on the other side.*" (P004).

Size. Size was considered a requirement with minimal impact. When discussed, it was generally assumed that the prosthesis would naturally correspond to the child's Size.

"*Well, the size (...) usually it's according to the person's size.*" (P004).

Appearance. Although considered a relevant criterion for users, leading to prosthesis rejection, its interpretation varied among different stakeholders, depending on the age group. For some caregivers, it is crucial that the device resembles a human arm, while others deem this feature irrelevant. On the other hand, for some children, especially female, color and the ability to personalize the device are key factors in its acceptance.

"*Change the colour that we want... blue, yellow. (...) With glitter!*" (U001).

"*Personally, I don't really care if it's realistic. Realism isn't important to me; in fact, I think I prefer the artificial, super bionic, futuristic look... nothing real!*" (C002).

Modularity. This requirement was associated with the possibility of having different terminal devices for each task. It was once referred to as a possible leading factor in prosthesis complexity.

"For me, modularity is what it will be: one thing for each task. And that's what will make the difference. (…) But for me, this is the future! It's a rough base, and it's the tips that matter!" (P001).

Price. Prostheses were considered expensive, with price being a key factor in their acquisition. Despite some financial support, many families lack the means to afford them, making price crucial. Once families can afford it, price becomes irrelevant.

"Affordable, because, well, no one wins the lottery! And the truth is, there really isn't much support for this. Even though there is some support, it doesn't always match the prices of these mechanisms and gadgets." (C002).

Variety of Movements. Motion was highly valued, as it enables the performance of activities of daily living that would otherwise be impossible. However, the addition of a lot of different movements with different triggers (e.g., buttons) was considered disadvantageous.

"A prosthesis that performs all the movements we need, right? Flexion, hand grip, wrist flexion-extension, pronation-supination, and sometimes the elbow, right? If we go further up… Damn, that's a lot, isn't it?" (P001).

Force. Not much was said about prostheses grasping force, only that it should be adjustable depending on the object that is being manipulated. Depending on how the prosthesis is integrated with the user, they may not be aware of the force they are exerting, which could lead to damage.

"The grip strength as well (…) it should be adjustable, so that one can pick up a plastic cup filled with water or a heavier shopping bag." (P004).

Velocity. Velocity was emphasized as crucial for safety and reaction times, but also as a key factor in engaging and motivating children, since quick actions resulting from muscular activation help maintain their interest while using the prosthesis.

"Speed is important because children are very impatient. And, therefore, if they don't see immediate success… They won't understand." (P005).

3.2 Activities and Places

The most frequently mentioned locations were the school, both the playground and the classroom, and home environment. Key activities included tying shoelaces, using cutlery, cycling, and bimanual object manipulation. Other tasks mentioned were writing, playing sports (e.g., football, volleyball, or gymnastics), engaging in handicrafts, playing instruments (e.g., piano and guitar), and performing bimanual tasks, like putting on socks, holding a backpack while closing the zipper or pulling up pants.

"I put the ball here (points to antecubital fossa), *I have a ball at school, and then I throw it."* (U001).

"But there are still some things he finds difficult. For example, putting on socks, if needed… Pull or tie shoelaces, it's also harder. For instance, during meals, eating with a fork and knife, he can't do it at the same time." (C002).

3.3 Sensory Feedback

Regarding sensory feedback, the lack of sensation in common prostheses was highlighted. However, therapists noted that this feedback can influence prosthetic acceptance in older children and should accurately correspond to the stimuli detected by the prosthesis, aiding in the neurological representation of the limb. Thus, sensory feedback can provide additional information, enhancing the user's perception of their surroundings and requiring less attention for tasks and allowing for more natural task execution without constant checking of the prosthesis' actions.

> "*Any kind of stimulus, whatever it may be, is beneficial so that… they don't have a 'dead hand,' so to speak, right? Because, in reality, it helps them have a more integrated limb. (…) They often have to look at what they need to do and sometimes even use their other hand to check if something is hard or soft.*" (P004).

Sensory Feedback Integration. Several suggestions for sensory feedback, including stronger stimuli for delicate tasks and temperature as a mechanism to cope with potential dangers (e.g., proximity to hot objects) were made. Sound feedback was seen as a solution and a problem, while one therapist found it inappropriate due to the noise in daily life, while another considered it useful as an alarm.

> "*And it could even vary in intensity… reversing the force. For example, if holding an egg, the feedback would have to be very strong to ensure extra caution.*" (P005).

3.4 Other Insights

Robustness. According to participants, the prosthesis should be robust enough to avoid damaging while using it.

> "*A prosthesis made of a comfortable material, lightweight, yet at the same time robust enough to not come apart, break, or get damaged, right?*" (P004).

Physical Impact. Participants referred that these children's conditions already have a series of physical consequences, and for that reason, prostheses should have the least physical impact possible.

> "*So, it would be a prosthesis that (…) physically, wouldn't have a significant impact; (…) because (…) we know what his condition (…) will do to their body, how it will affect them in terms of tendonitis, strain, imbalances. (…) Therefore, the ideal prosthesis would likely be one that has a low impact on their musculature.*" (C002).

Customization. Therapists believe that Additive Manufacturing with the support of biomedical engineers and orthotic-prosthetic specialists, can help develop devices that adapt to a child's growth and allow for prosthetic customization.

> "*This laboratory process seems to represent what I would consider the ideal change: producing a prosthesis tailored to that person (…) as customized as possible to their needs, interests, and preferences.*" (P003).

Prosthetic Adoption. Several external factors were referred to influence prosthetic adoption, including the child, families, prior exposure to prosthetic devices, and the nature of limb loss. Due to well-established compensatory mechanisms, children must perceive a tangible benefit from using the prosthesis, even if limited to a single task.

> "*He needs to understand that it truly helps him being faster; it helps him grasp things easily, without having to compensate. (…) So, he needs to be able to hold things properly and quickly.*" (C004).

Myoelectric Prostheses Valorization. Regardless of prosthesis usage, all interviewed patients showed interest in prosthetic devices. One child, despite regularly using a cosmetic prosthesis, expressed a strong preference for a robotic prosthesis, indicating a demand for enhanced functionality, a sentiment also shared by his mother. Although therapists had no prior experience with such devices, they unanimously supported the project, recognizing the potential value of a myoelectric prosthesis with sensory feedback in improving rehabilitation and user integration.

> "*It's a field that, unfortunately, or perhaps fortunately, we don't have much experience with here in (…), but it's amazing.*" (P005).

4 Discussion

Prosthetic rehabilitation is crucial for the development of children with upper limb congenital malformations. However, ensuring these children actively use prosthetic devices requires careful consideration of their specific needs in prosthetic design [4].

Literature already supports myoelectric prostheses with sensory feedback represent a significant advancement in prosthetic technology and can improve patients life quality [12, 13], but this was further reinforced by therapists and caregivers in this study. Their insights confirm that such can enhance user experience, ultimately increasing acceptance and long-term use while demanding less attention when using such devices.

TA revealed strong interdependencies among requirements, highlighting the need for integrated design approaches. For instance, comfort, though prioritized over functionality, was deemed impractical without functionality and vice versa. Size and weight were linked to comfort, with larger prostheses being heavier and less comfortable. Size also affects appearance, as disproportionate prostheses impact aesthetics. Appearance and cost were subjective factors, leading to lower prioritization.

Although modularity ranked lower in the requirements, it was closely linked to functionality. Initially presented as the ability to easily clean and replace parts, modularity was understood as the capacity to change terminal devices and increase the range of possible tasks. However, increased modularity could add complexity, potentially reducing functionality.

Understanding the activities and environments where children need a prosthesis is crucial to translating these into prosthetic movements and technical requirements, as prostheses must support daily activities to promote independence. Tying shoelaces, using cutlery, cycling, and object manipulation such as balls, pencils, backpacks, scissors or clothes while dressing, were identified as keys tasks aligning with the existing in literature [4, 14]. Designing prostheses that support these tasks can motivate children to use them, as these are common challenges. However, too many movements could increase complexity, but gradually introducing movements during training can help children adapt to the prostheses.

Technical aspects of myoelectric prostheses revealed a strong connection between force control and sensory feedback. As already pointed in In Emily L. Graczyk et al. study [13], users must be able to gauge the force they exert while gripping objects, emphasizing the importance of effective sensory integration. Additionally, temperature and sound were identified as potential feedback mechanisms, though both have been addressed in previous studies [7, 15].

Additional insights from the interviews, including robustness, particularly important in the context of 3D-printed prosthetic devices, customization, and the physical impact of prostheses, emerged as key considerations that should be further explored in future work to ensure durable, tailored, and physiologically safe prosthetic designs.

These findings suggest that myoelectric prostheses (or others) should be designed with comfort and functionality as priorities. Developers must balance size, weight, modularity, and movement variety, using robust yet lightweight and comfortable materials. Complexity should be avoided, and ultimately the prosthesis should enable to perform otherwise impossible tasks. Although little was mentioned about the preferred sensations, sensory feedback must be a main requirement.

As with any research, this study has its limitations, particularly regarding sample size. While a larger number of participants could have strengthened the results, the specific context of the target population makes the current sample size more justifiable. According to the most recent Portuguese National Report on Congenital Abnormalities (RENAC), covering the years 2018 and 2019 [16], only 36 children were born with upper limb reduction malformations, corresponding to 2.07 cases per 10,000 births. In the preceding two years, this figure was slightly higher at 2.99 per 10,000 births. Based on these statistics and considering that not all these children would meet the inclusion criteria, a sample of six children (adding their caregivers and healthcare professionals specialized in the field) can be considered significant for this highly specific population. Furthermore, after analyzing several interviews, thematic saturation appeared to emerge, suggesting that increasing the sample size would likely not have yielded substantially different findings.

Regarding future work, although several themes have emerged in this preliminary study, the extensive dataset requires further analysis. Topics such as training resilience, medical follow-up, and other identified aspects have yet to be fully explored. These topics were addressed during the interviews not only because they were highlighted in previous studies [17], but also because understanding how children respond to training and medical consultations can directly influence the development of testing protocols. Designing any system, especially those involving human-machine interaction, requires multiple iterations of testing with stakeholders. In this study, since the primary stakeholders are children, not only the prosthesis design must be appealing to them but also the testing protocols should be structured to foster and sustain their interest in using the device. Therefore, understanding training methodologies, children's resilience, and the role of medical consultations in monitoring both malformations and prosthetic devices is essential for the successful design and implementation of the prosthesis. Furthermore, for the purpose of this paper, the coding analysis was conducted aiming to define technical requirements for designing a pediatric myoelectric prosthesis. While this initial analysis provides a solid foundation for a preliminary approach, a more in-depth exploration is essential, as contextual and behavioral factors may significantly influence prosthesis adoption and in turn the design requirements.

Therefore, future work will involve a deeper analysis of the collected data, applying resulting insights for sensor technology selection, motor control, material selection, and prosthetic design. Key stakeholders such as biomedical engineers, roboticists, and prosthetists will be crucial in this phase. However, the current findings already offer valuable contributions, particularly in establishing a prioritized list of requirements, with significant implications for clinical rehabilitation. Further pediatric prosthetic designs should then consider the following questions:

- How can comfort and functionality be ensured at the same time?
- How can the prosthesis be modular without compromising simplicity?
- What can the designed prosthesis offer to the user that motivate them?
- Which materials ensure comfort, robustness and lightness at the same time?
- How can the prosthesis be customizable?
- What anatomical movements can best translate the identified desired daily activities?
- How can temperature and force feedback be addressed?
- How can this all be done without compromising size and appearance?

Finally, it is important to highlight how this methodology can be applied in the development of AI-driven CPS. When designing a system intended for end-users, it is critical to understand both the purpose of the system and how it can better support those who will use it. Whether developing a prosthesis or any other system, identifying and addressing user needs is essential for improving human-machine interaction and ultimately advancing the development of effective and user-centered AI-powered CPS.

5 Conclusion

This study consisted of qualitative research on user needs and requirements for developing a myoelectric prosthesis with sensory feedback. Key priorities identified in this study were comfort, functionality, and movement versatility, with using cutlery, tying shoelaces, cycling, and object manipulation emerging as critical tasks. Despite limited feedback on preferred sensory modalities, sensory integration remains a crucial factor in prosthetic usability and long-term acceptance.

Despite its limitations, this research highlights the importance of different stakeholders through rich qualitative methods like TA and IPA. These approaches provided a deep understanding of the lived experiences of prosthetic users, offering valuable insights into users' lived experiences, guiding prosthetic design to increase acceptance rates. Additionally, this study significantly contributed to defining both user and technical requirements for pediatric prostheses, particularly by establishing a clear order of priorities. Furthermore, this methodology can be applied to the development of other solutions involving human-machine interaction.

Acknowledgements. Author acknowledge Fundação para a Ciência e Tecnologia, I.P., for its financial support via 2023.0593.BDANA (PhD scholarship), UIDB/00667/2020, UIDP/00667/2020 (UNIDEMI projects), UI/BD/151321/2021 (LIBPhys-UNL) and LA/P/0117/2020 (REAL).

References

1. Peterson, J.K., Prigge, P.: Early upper-limb prosthetic fitting and brain development: considerations for success. JPO J. Prosthet. Orthot. **32**, 229–235 (2020). https://doi.org/10.1097/JPO.0000000000000320
2. Mohammadi, A., Lavranos, J., Tan, Y., Choong, P., Oetomo, D.: A Paediatric 3D-Printed Soft Robotic Hand Prosthesis for Children with Upper Limb Loss. In: 2020 42nd Annual International Conference of the IEEE Engineering in Medicine & Biology Society (EMBC). pp. 3310–3313. IEEE, Montreal, QC, Canada (2020). https://doi.org/10.1109/EMBC44109.2020.9176848
3. Smail, L.C., Neal, C., Wilkins, C., Packham, T.L.: Comfort and function remain key factors in upper limb prosthetic abandonment: findings of a scoping review. Disabil. Rehabil. Assist. Technol. **16**, 821–830 (2021). https://doi.org/10.1080/17483107.2020.1738567
4. Sims, T., Cranny, A., Metcalf, C., Chappell, P., Donovan-Hall, M.: Participatory design of pediatric upper limb prostheses: qualitative methods and prototyping. Int. J. Technol. Assess. Health Care **33**, 629–637 (2017). https://doi.org/10.1017/S0266462317000836
5. James, M.A., Bagley, A.M., Brasington, K., Lutz, C., McConnell, S., Molitor, F.: Impact of prostheses on function and quality of life for children with unilateral congenital below-the-elbow deficiency. J. Bone Jt. Surg. **88**, 2356–2365 (2006). https://doi.org/10.2106/JBJS.E.01146
6. Kerver, N., Van Twillert, S., Maas, B., Van Der Sluis, C.K.: User-relevant factors determining prosthesis choice in persons with major unilateral upper limb defects: A meta-synthesis of qualitative literature and focus group results. PLoS ONE **15**, e0234342 (2020). https://doi.org/10.1371/journal.pone.0234342
7. Einfeldt, A.-K., et al.: What do users and their aiding professionals want from future devices in upper limb prosthetics? A focus group study. PLOS ONE. **18**, e0295516 (2023). https://doi.org/10.1371/journal.pone.0295516
8. Sims, T., Donovan-Hall, M., Metcalf, C.: Parental perspective: the role of prostheses and prosthetics services in adjusting to a child's upper limb difference. Technol. Disabil. **33**, 45–51 (2021). https://doi.org/10.3233/TAD-200300
9. Spiers, J., Riley, R.: Analysing one dataset with two qualitative methods: The distress of general practitioners, a thematic and interpretative phenomenological analysis. Qual. Res. Psychol. **16**, 276–290 (2019). https://doi.org/10.1080/14780887.2018.1543099
10. Braun, V., Clarke, V.: Using thematic analysis in psychology. Qual. Res. Psychol. **3**, 77–101 (2006). https://doi.org/10.1191/1478088706qp063oa
11. Braun, V., Clarke, V.: Conceptual and design thinking for thematic analysis. Qual. Psychol. **9**, 3–26 (2022). https://doi.org/10.1037/qup0000196
12. Kaluf, B., Gart, M.S., Loeffler, B.J., Gaston, G.: Evaluating the ability of congenital upper extremity amputees to control a multi-degree of freedom myoelectric prosthesis. J. Hand Surg. **47**(1019), e1-1019.e9 (2022). https://doi.org/10.1016/j.jhsa.2021.08.011
13. Graczyk, E.L., Gill, A., Tyler, D.J., Resnik, L.J.: The benefits of sensation on the experience of a hand: a qualitative case series. PLoS ONE **14**, e0211469 (2019). https://doi.org/10.1371/journal.pone.0211469
14. Cordella, F., et al.: Literature review on needs of upper limb prosthesis users. Front. Neurosci. (2016). https://doi.org/10.3389/fnins.2016.00209

15. Ccorimanya, L., Watanabe, R., Hassan, M., Hada, Y., Suzuki, K.: Design of a myoelectric 3D-printed prosthesis for a child with upper limb congenital amputation. In: 2019 41st Annual International Conference of the IEEE Engineering in Medicine and Biology Society (EMBC). pp. 5394–5398. IEEE, Berlin, Germany (2019). https://doi.org/10.1109/EMBC.2019.8857899
16. Braz, P., Machado, A., Roquette, R., Dias, C.M.: Registo Nacional de Anomalias Congénitas: relatório 2018–2019. Instituto Nacional de Saúde Doutor Ricardo Jorge, Lisboa (2021)
17. Egermann, M., Kasten, P., Thomsen, M.: Myoelectric hand prostheses in very young children. Int. Orthop. **33**, 1101–1105 (2009). https://doi.org/10.1007/s00264-008-0615-y

Embedding Predecessor Information in Optimization of Genetic Algorithm (GA) Based Blind Image Restoration

Chaudhary Muhammad Shahbaz Anjum and Aftab Khan(✉)

Department of Computer Science (DCS), Allama Iqbal Open University (AIOU), Islamabad, Pakistan
aftab.khan@aiou.edu.pk

Abstract. Blind image restoration is performed by a history based Genetic Algorithm (GA) approach which is presented in this research. The motivation of the proposed method is that GA has evolutionary process: it will pair the chromosomes to create the optimized children preserve the best restoration quality. Fewer effective solutions are discarded and only the most optimized values make it to the subsequent processing. This iterative refinement goes on and on in multiple generations in order to improve the quality of an image progressively. Due to the lack of prior knowledge about the Point Spread Function (PSF), blind image deblurring is a key challenge, which makes the restoration process highly complex. This challenge is effectively addressed by the proposed algorithm, which successively refines optimized values by iteratively selecting optimized values, and achieves better deblurring result. An approach is developed and successfully implemented and verified to restore degraded images through the automatic detection and application of appropriate corrections and to extract accurate information from such images.

Keywords: Genetic Algorithm (GA) · Point Spread Function (PSF) · Blind Image Deblurring (BID) · Digital Image Restoration

1 Introduction

In today's world, imaging data such as phones, satellite, CCTV footage and other means of capturing such data including handheld or smartphone camera can now be effortlessly captured with rapid technological advancements. Nevertheless, the imaging data tend to suffer from various kinds of degradation due to imperfections in acquisition and processing; the resultant images are corrupted or blurred, degrading the images' discriminability or critical information.

There is a wide range of optimization techniques used in the context of computational problems, with one problem being the time required to converge. Of these techniques, the Genetic Algorithm (GA) has been extensively used for solving complex computational problems in a number of fields ranging from image processing, to the Internet of Things

Published by Springer Nature Switzerland AG 2025
L. M. Camarinha-Matos and F. Ferrada (Eds.): DoCEIS 2025, IFIP AICT 759, pp. 198–209, 2025.
https://doi.org/10.1007/978-3-031-97051-1_14

(IoT), to computer arithmetic. The architecture of GA has been particularly effective such that we have obtained more compact and efficient circuit design solutions, with an approximate throughput [1]. To that end, in computational arithmetic, optimization of such problems can be interpreted as a circuit minimization problem, or equivalently, a minimization of the number of logic gates required for a computation, without exceeding a certain limit in the accuracy.

In addition, the atmospheric disturbances in satellite or aerial photography, as well as the lens defocusing and optical imperfections, may direct to image degradation. However, in the case of practical scenarios, the captured image because of digital device, the scene is not accessible any longer, only with acquired data available. As shown in [2], the presence of real-world blur in images has a significant impact in retrieving accurate information (Fig. 1).

Fig. 1. Blurred images in practical scenario [2].

In this case, there is no prior knowledge of the Point Spread Function (PSF) or the impulse response of the captured imaging data. As a result, the degraded image must be restored without any predefined information about the impulse response, a process known as Blind Deconvolution [3]. Restoring imaging data under such conditions is highly challenging, as it requires recovering essential details without any reference to the original image properties.

To enhance the quality of low-resolution images, various restoration algorithms have been developed, including the Wiener filter, Richardson-Lucy algorithm, and Total Variation methods. However, these techniques are not well-suited for high-quality image restoration.

GA has been widely utilized in image processing tasks, particularly for image restoration. In cases of non-uniform motion blur, conventional deconvolution techniques cannot directly determine the blur kernel, making restoration more complex. This study aims to leverage history-based GA to recover and restore a single distorted image. The challenge of blind deblurring with a single input image is significant, yet our approach demonstrates that GA can effectively tackle this problem. The deployment of GA in this context proved successful, highlighting its potential for blind image deblurring applications.

2 Relation to AI-Powered Cyber-Physical Systems

Cyber-Physical Systems function by connecting computer algorithms to physical operational components. The research adds value to this area by developing automatic technology that restores deteriorated visual information to enable smarter visual perception. The integration of history-based GAs operating with AI logic defines a cyber element to process faulty visual content which shapes the central cycle of CPS.

The proposed solution finds use in self-driving systems, security operations and aerial data collection because it provides strong recovery capabilities for noisy visual data. The proposed system implements autonomous learning and adaptation capabilities which correspond with self-adjusting functionality found in CPS frameworks.

The combination of Artificial Intelligence with Cyber-Physical Systems allows digital and physical operations to merge through their new framework of intelligent choices and instantaneous processing and flexible design. The research project based on blind image restoration through history-based Genetic Algorithm (HGA) maintains complete compatibility with these fundamental principles. Multiple CPS systems including autonomous vehicles along with surveillance systems robotic industries and satellite imaging encounter performance reductions due to environmental disturbances which impede their ability to perform real-time decision-making based on visual inputs. The algorithm provides a solution to restore degraded images without requiring any knowledge about degradation mechanisms so CPS systems can restore effective operation capabilities.

The GA receives an enhancement using optimization historical data which simulates adaptive learning capabilities that are essential for AI systems in CPS. The integration of this method results in essential traits such as self-correction and autonomy as well as resilience for systems working within unpredictable environments. Our research develops CPS by implementing robust evolutionary AI-powered visual restoration capabilities which improves the perception modules reliability within AI-powered CPS systems.

The research investigates whether incorporating previous optimization data into Genetic Algorithms improves blind image restoration results when blur knowledge is lacking by asking "Does precursor information processing enhance Genetic Algorithm optimization for restoration tasks?" The research hypothesis states that adding previous optimization records into Genetic Algorithm evolutionary processes brings about improved convergence while producing better image blur restorations. A history-based GA goes through development and evaluation testing for multiple datasets as researchers validate its performance against standard restoration techniques.

3 Related Works

The field of digital image restoration focuses on recovering imaging data from degraded or corrupted sources. To address this challenging problem, numerous techniques have been proposed and implemented to enhance image quality. The primary objective of image restoration methods is to reconstruct an approximation of the original image that has been degraded due to various factors, thereby making it more informative and usable [4, 5].

The applications of image restoration extend across multiple domains, including satellite and biomedical imaging [6, 7], as well as images and videos captured by handheld devices such as modern cameras and smartphones [8–10]. Additionally, image restoration techniques play a crucial role in remote sensing [11, 12] and even in audio signal processing [13]. Various methods have been developed to mitigate image degradation, as outlined in [14–17], to restore and enhance the quality of imaging data.

Several approaches have been explored in the literature for image restoration. For instance, the work presented in [18] utilizes Discrete Wavelet Transform (DWT) combined with Particle Swarm Optimization (PSO) to restore cracked imaging data, with the results illustrated in Fig. 2.

Fig. 2. Input image and the resultant restoration with IPSO-DWT and PSO-DWT.

Imaging data used in vision-based navigation must be clear and informative to ensure accurate interpretation and decision-making. Various deblurring techniques have been employed to enhance image quality, as demonstrated in Fig. 3. The figure illustrates the restoration of images using the proposed method in comparison with other conventional restoration techniques, such as the Wiener filter, Lucy-Richardson algorithm, and Regularized filter.

Figure 3 clearly presents the original image, followed by restored or deblurred versions produced using different techniques. The final image (f) showcases the results obtained with the proposed method, highlighting its effectiveness in comparison to existing approaches.

Fig. 3. (a) Original Image (b) Blind deconvolution (c) Image restored with Wiener filter (d) Image restored with Lucy-Richardson (e) Image restored with Regularized filter (f) Image restored with Proposed method

4 Proposed History-Based Genetic Algorithm (HGA)

We propose a History-based Genetic Algorithm (HGA) technique that selects parent chromosomes based on their optimal values to generate improved offspring. As a result of pairing these chromosomes, several offspring exhibit enhanced optimization compared to their parents, and only the best-performing offspring are selected for further

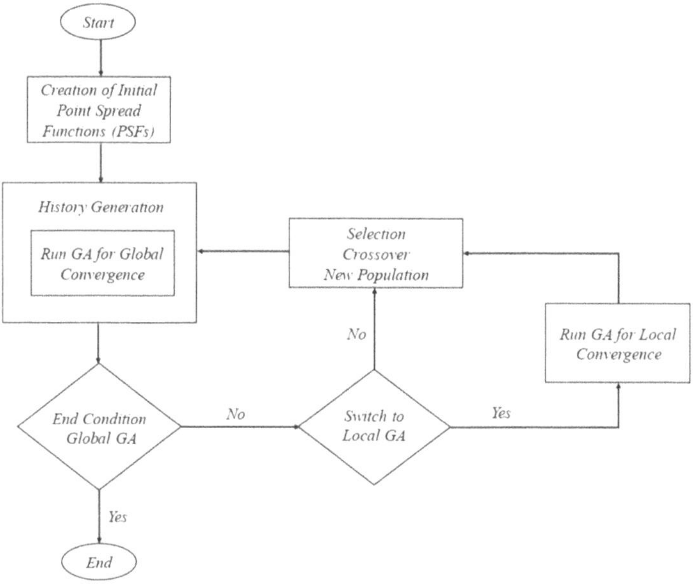

Fig. 4. Methodology of the proposed algorithm

processing. By consistently choosing offspring with the most optimized values, the algorithm progressively refines the solution to the problem.

Offspring with superior optimization are further paired to produce even better results. Utilizing historical optimization data, the proposed algorithm effectively identifies and selects improved values, ensuring continuous enhancement in subsequent generations. This iterative process leads to the generation of offspring with increasingly optimized outcomes. The proposed technique is illustrated in Fig. 4. In this work, the term pairing is used interchangeably with the standard Genetic Algorithm term crossover.

The definition aligns the research terminology with mainstream Genetic Algorithm terminology. The main originality of this work exists in using historical predecessor data for optimization purposes during blind image restoration. All experiments adopted these GA parameters: Population size of 100, Number of generations (iterations) of 200, Crossover rate of 0.85, Mutation rate of 0.05 and Tournament selection method. Empirical tests determined these parameters to achieve convergence when also preventing premature stagnation.

5 Results and Discussion

The experiments were conducted using the Waterloo BragZone grayscale image dataset [19]. Additionally, the study was extended to real-life blurred images captured by the authors using a digital camera. These real-world images exhibited a certain degree of noise, which influenced the effectiveness of the deblurring process.

The HGA was employed for search optimization. The proposed scheme was efficiently implemented using MATLAB's GA optimization toolbox [20] and executed in a parallel computing environment on a multi-core system to enhance performance and processing speed.

The proposed method's outcomes were evaluated in experimental tests comparing the results with Wiener filter and Lucy-Richardson deconvolution and Regularized filter traditional restoration methods. Various objective quality metrics were used for performance evaluation as shown across Table 2. The proposed HGA showed better performance than baseline approaches for BRISQUE, NIQE and custom IQM indices which demonstrated its enhanced ability in restoring images (Fig. 8).

The proposed algorithm exhibits effective performance according to the recorded results. HGA delivers superior results without needing any previous information about blur models which traditional approaches need. The HGA method demonstrates enhanced solution space exploration capabilities which leads to improved results in multiple benchmarks. Statistical analysis through SSIM and PSNR metrics supports that improved image visual quality derives from measurable enhancements suitable for industrial applications of CPS systems that encounter unpredictable environmental deterioration (Fig. 9).

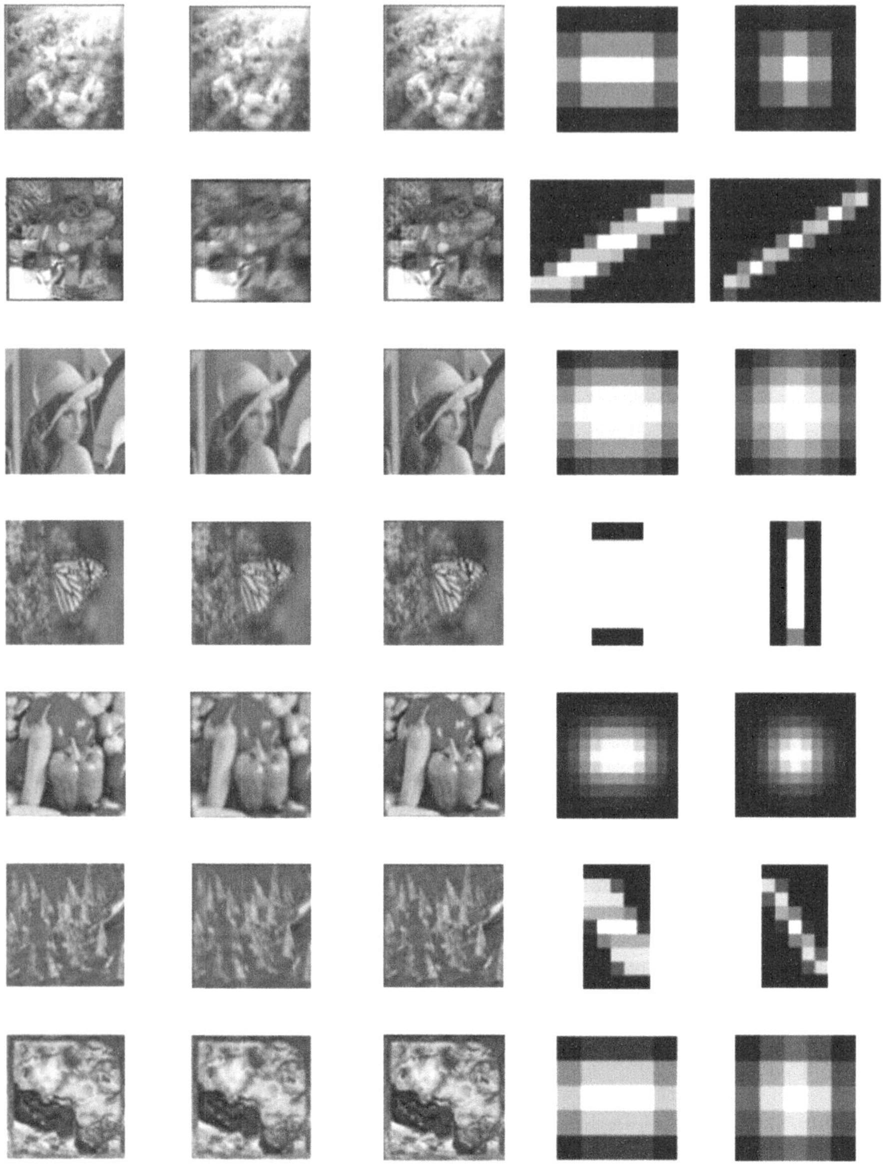

Fig. 5. Results of deblurring an 100 x 100-pixel image with a Wiener filter (Column-1) Original Image (Column-2) Blurred Image (Column-3) Deblurred Image (Column-4) Blurring PSF (column-5) Estimated PSF (Figs. 6 and 7 and Table 1).

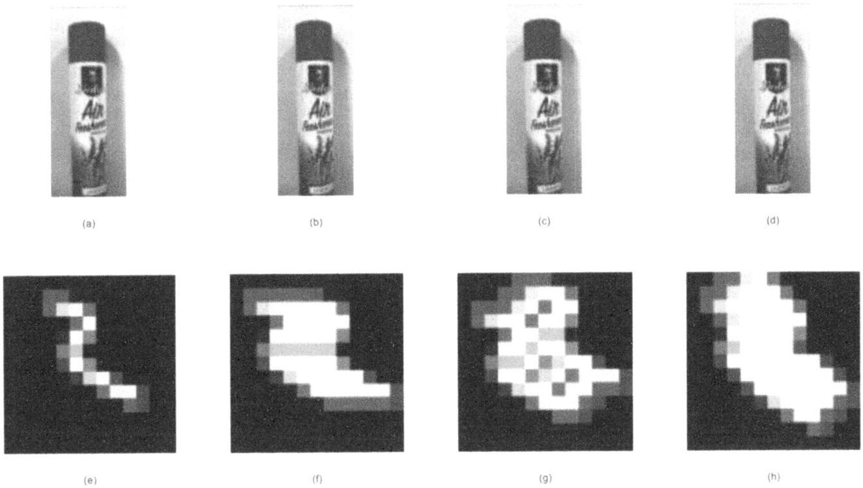

Fig. 6. The restoration of air freshener image.

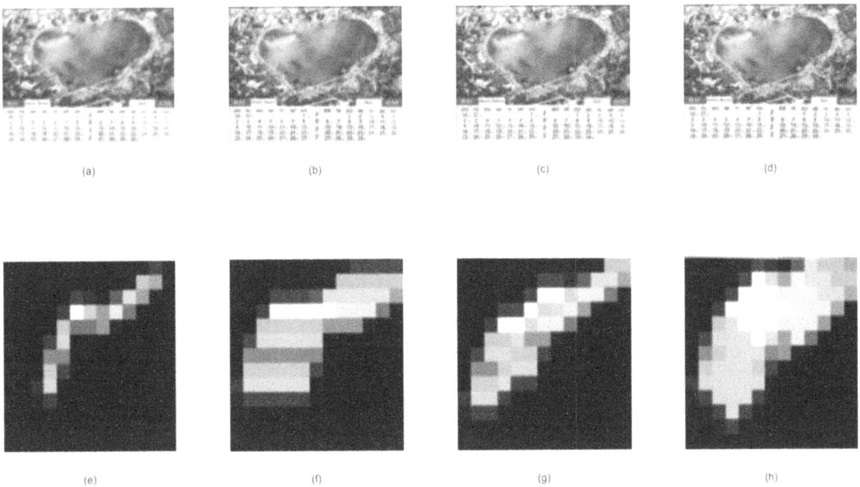

Fig. 7. Calendar image restoration.

Table 1. Restoration results for the images in Fig. 5. BRISQUE and NIQE image quality measures were used.

Figure	*Filter*	*Size (pixels)*	*Parameter Values*
WB1	Gaussian	5×5	Var = 1
WB2	Motion	9×13	Length = 13, Angle = 33
WB3	Gaussian	7×7	Var = 3
WB4	Motion	7×3	Length = 6, Angle = 91
WB5	Gaussian	11×11	Var = 2
WB6	Motion	9×5	Length = 8, Angle = 121
WB7	Motion	5×5	Length = 5, Angle = 2
Figure	*BRISQUE (Original)*	*BRISQUE (Corrupted)*	*BRISQUE (Restored)*
WB1	5.18	33.63	45.24
WB2	7.72	15.97	50.42
WB3	48.04	28.37	62
WB4	12.58	13.74	37.58
WB5	12.79	16.58	34.81
WB6	13.91	20.25	48.52
WB7	47.68	29.28	40.83
Figure	*NIQE (Original)*	*NIQE (Corrupted)*	*NIQE (Restored)*
WB1	3.59	4.29	6.44
WB2	4.56	3.25	6.75
WB3	3.57	5.19	8.54
WB4	3.3	2.98	6.63
WB5	4.37	5.27	6.47
WB6	3.96	4.16	4.95
WB7	6.26	8.3	6.91

Table 2. IQM values of our scheme and the various benchmarks used. Benchmarks are represented by B.

Method	Avg. PSNR (dB)	Correlation Coefficient
Proposed Scheme	**31.24**	**0.87**
Blind Deconvolution	27.9	0.55
Wiener Filter	26.5	0.43
Lucy–Richardson Algorithm	28.1	0.6
Regularized Filter	29	0.68
Inverse Filter	25.8	0.35
Total Variation (TV) Filter	29.7	0.7

Fig. 8. Vase image restoration.

(a)

(b)

(c)

Fig. 9. Cropped results of vase image for better visualization.

6 Conclusions and Future Work

Blind image restoration has been effectively addressed using the proposed history-based Genetic Algorithm (GA) technique. This approach has been successfully applied to blind image restoration, tackling the challenge of image blurring and ensuring the retrieval of accurate information.

One of the primary challenges in blind image deblurring is the absence of prior knowledge about the Point Spread Function (PSF). The proposed algorithm effectively mitigates this issue by iteratively refining optimized values, leading to improved restoration results. The implementation was carried out on a multi-core system in a parallel computing environment to enhance efficiency and computational performance.

Future work envisions the integration of faster convergence algorithms for local search optimization to further enhance the restoration process.

References

1. Katoch, S., Chauhan, S.S., Kumar, V.: A review on genetic algorithm: past, present, and future. Multimedia Tools and Applications **80**(5), 8091–8126 (2021)

2. Khan: Efficient Methodologies for Single-Image Blind Deconvolution and Deblurring, Ph.D. dissertation, School of Electrical and Electronic Engineering. The University of Manchester (2014)
3. Ge, X., et al.: Blind image deconvolution via salient edge selection and mean curvature regularization. Signal Process. **190**, 108336 (2022)
4. Prince, Kumar, A.: Enhancement of camera blur image using optimization techniques. In: 2021 International Conference on Forensics, Analytics, Big Data, Security (FABS) (2021)
5. Dan, M., Liu, M., Gao, F.: Motion deblurring for single-pixel spatial frequency domain imaging. Appl. Sci. **12**(15), 7402 (2022)
6. Janghel, R.R., et al.: Satellite image enhancement and restoration using RLS adaptive filter. In: International Conference on Innovative Computing and Communications. Springer (2022)
7. Peng, L., et al.: Blind image restoration enhances digital autoradiographic imaging of radiopharmaceutical tissue distribution. J. Nucl. Med. **63**(4), 591–597 (2022)
8. Dudhane, et al.: Burst image restoration and enhancement, in Proceedings of the IEEE/CVF Conference on Computer Vision and Pattern Recognition (2022)
9. Mehta, N., Murala, S.: Con-Net: a consolidated light-weight image restoration network. IEEE Transactions on Broadcasting (2022)
10. Achddou, R., Gousseau, Y., Ladjal, S.: Fully synthetic training for image restoration tasks. SSRN Journal, no. 4176695 (2022)
11. Kong, X., et al.: Hyperspectral image restoration via spatial-spectral residual total variation regularized low-rank tensor decomposition. Remote Sensing **14**(3), 511 (2022)
12. Wang, Y., et al.: Application of improved RBF neural network in remote sensing image restoration. In: Proceedings of the 7th China High Resolution Earth Observation Conference (CHREOC 2020) Springer (2022)
13. Derebssa, et al.: Detection and restoration of click degraded audio based on high-order sparse linear prediction. Zede Journal **40**(1), 99–116 (2022)
14. Forsgren, E., et al.: High-throughput widefield fluorescence imaging of 3D samples using deep learning for 2D projection image restoration. PLoS ONE **17**(5), e0264241 (2022)
15. Wang, et al.: Iterative learning for distorted image restoration. In: ICASSP 2022–2022 IEEE International Conference on Acoustics, Speech and Signal Processing (ICASSP). IEEE (2022)
16. Zhu, F., et al.: Blind face restoration via integrating face shape and generative priors. In: Proceedings of the IEEE/CVF Conference on Computer Vision and Pattern Recognition (2022)
17. Suin, M., Purohit, K., Rajagopalan, A.: Image Restoration using Feature-guidance, arXiv preprint, no. 00187 (2022)
18. Rizwan, S., Muhammad, B.Q., Muhammad, M.J.: Deconvolution and De-Noising of SAR-based GPS images using Hybrid Particle Swarm Optimization. Chin. J. Electron. **32**(1), 1–11 (2023)
19. Kominek, J.: Waterloo BragZone and Fractals Repository. University of Waterloo, Ontario, Canada. https://links.uwaterloo.ca/oldwebsite/bragzone.base.html
20. The MathWorks, Inc., MATLAB Optimization Toolbox, 1994–2022

AI in Systems, Decision and Control

Deep Learning Models for GNSS-Denied Target Navigation

Ricardo Serras Santos[1,2](✉), João P. Matos-Carvalho[2,3], Carlos T. Calafate[4], Sérgio D. Correira[2,5], Slavisa Tomic[1,2], Marko Beko[1,2,6], and Pietro Manzoni[4]

[1] COPELABS, ECATI, Lusófona University, Campo Grande 376, 1749-024 Lisbon, Portugal
{ricardo.santos,slavisa.tomic}@ulusofona.pt

[2] UNINOVA-CTS - Center of Technology and Systems, NOVA School of Science and Technology, 2829-516 Caparica, Portugal

[3] LASIGE, Faculdade de Ciências, Universidade de Lisboa, 1749-016 Lisboa, Portugal
jpecarvalho@ciencias.ulisboa.pt

[4] Department of Computer Engineering (DISCA), Universitat Politècnica de València, Camino de Vera, 46022 Valencia, S/N, Spain
{calafate,pmanzoni}@disca.upv.es

[5] VALORIZA, Instituto Politécnico de Portalegre, Campus Politécnico N. 10, 7300-555 Portalegre, Portugal
scorreia@ipportalegre.pt

[6] Instituto de Telecomunicações, Instituto Superior Técnico, Universidade de Lisboa, 1049-001 Lisbon, Portugal
marko.beko@tecnico.ulisboa.pt

Abstract. This work tackles the problem of target navigation in Global Navigation Satellite Systems (GNSS)-denied scenarios by adapting two Deep Learning (DL)-based approaches: the Temporal Fusion Transformer (TFT) and the Neural Hierarchical Interpolation for Time Series (NHITS). These methods are trained on custom created datasets from which the methods learn, after which they are able to make their own predictions. Obtained numerical results via simulations and real testbed reveal that, on the one hand, the proposed methods improve navigation accuracy and are less vulnerable to noise when compared to existing Machine Learning (ML) approaches. On the other hand, the results also exhibit a reduction in training time. The superior performance of the proposed solutions is primarily attributable to the enhanced network architecture they are based on, which facilitates more efficient learning, which consequently leads to more accurate predictions, when compared to Long-Short Term Memory (LSTM) approach. In this way, the proposed methods allow navigation in GNSS-denied scenarios without relying on expensive hardware (*e.g.*, LiDARs or cameras).

Keywords: Artificial Intelligence (AI) · Deep Learning (DL) · Temporal Fusion Transformer (TFT) · Neural Hierarchical Interpolation for Time Series (NHITS) · Navigation Indoor

Published by Springer Nature Switzerland AG 2025
L. M. Camarinha-Matos and F. Ferrada (Eds.): DoCEIS 2025, IFIP AICT 759, pp. 213–225, 2025.
https://doi.org/10.1007/978-3-031-97051-1_15

1 Introduction

Target navigation in Global Navigation Satellite Systems (GNSS)-denied environments is one of the key challenges in future autonomous robots, vehicles and Unmanned Aerial Vehicles (UAVs). Solving this problem allows future developments in the automatization of tasks such as infrastructure inspection [1], surveillance [2], real-time stock monitoring [3], and many more. Generally, these vehicles use GNSS signals to estimate their location and still require certain amount of human control to navigate themselves, especially in complex environments (tunnels, confined indoor spaces, *etc.*). Moreover, these signals do not penetrate buildings with sufficient quality; thus, alternative means of localization are required.

Considering the fact that there is no uniquely accepted solution to navigate targets in the considered environment, the motivation for this work started with the following research question: "*How can one exploit Deep Learning (DL) tools to semi-autonomously navigate a target in GNSS-denied scenarios?*". To address the research question, this work is based on the following hypothesis: "*Autonomous target navigation can be achieved through a conjunction of data-driven DL models with statistical estimation methods, where DL models are trained by using predictions of the statistical estimation method to learn and make their own predictions.*" More specifically, the current work employs Temporal Fusion Transformer (TFT) [4] and Neural Hierarchical Interpolation for Time Series (NHITS) [5] models, whose training is accomplished based on a General Trusted Region Sub-Problem (GTRS) estimator, and are then able to make their own predictions, making navigation possible.

The remainder of this work is organized as follows. Firstly, Sect. 2 states the contributions of the current work to AI-driven Cyber-Physical Systems. Secondly, the related work is presented, followed by problem formulation in Sects. 3 and 4, respectively. Then, the proposed solutions are presented and tested in Sects. 5 and 6. Finally, the conclusions and future research directions are described in Sect. 7.

2 Contribution to AI-Driven Cyber-Physical Systems

The system considered in this work fits perfectly in what is considered an AI-driven Cyber-Physical System (AI-CPS), *i.e.*, an intelligent system that integrates cyber (computational) and physical (UAV, robot) components, enhanced by AI. The proposed system operates in real-time, processes data from the physical world (acquired radio measurements) to gain awareness about the location of the target, and makes intelligent decisions to optimize performance, enhance autonomy, and ensure reliability. The work demonstrates how AI models can be adapted to target navigation problems, making tasks such as real-time warehouse stock monitoring and counting, infrastructure (pipelines, bridges) inspection, and autonomous transportation of tools, supplies and organs possible. Moreover, the proposed solutions can easily be installed on the edge (for instance in a robot, vehicle or UAV, with the required hardware resources), allowing real-time data processing and decision-making, thus contributing to the embedded AI-CPS field.

3 Related Work

The usage of artificial intelligence and machine learning algorithms for target navigation has attracted significant attention in the research community in recent years. In [6], the authors proposed a deep neural network formed by a Convolution Neural Network (CNN) that retrieves local spatial features from measurements, and afterwards a deep LSTM module that deals with temporal features. In [7] computer vision and DL are used. More specifically, resorting to images captured via an onboard camera and a CNN it is possible to predict the location and orientation of the target. The usage of CNNs is also proposed in [8], where a deep-CNN is used to analyze objects and compute the trajectory with this information. In [9], a double deep Q-network was proposed. By discretizing the 3D space into grids, that serve as an input to the neural network and resorting to a continual reward function the target is navigated. An LSTM combined with Ultra-Wide Band (UWB) data is proposed in [10] to estimate the location and navigate the target. Afterwards, an Extended Kalman Filter is used to combine the prediction with other onboard sensors to compute the final estimations. A similar approach is presented in [11], but this time the LSTM is trained using predictions from existing algorithms. With the training stage, the LSTM is able to learn and make its own location predictions. A similar logic is presented in [12]; however, this time, the authors resort to two LSTMs trained using different algorithms. The final location estimation is performed by averaging the two LSTMs. Other techniques that do not resort to AI but rely on radio measurements are also widely available, for instance, in [13], the authors proposed novel inertial measurement system based on measurements from ultra-wide band reference points.

In contrast with the described solutions, on the one hand the proposed models do not resort to expensive hardware like cameras and other sensors, achieving low-cost solution and allowing better agility. On the other hand, the more advanced architecture of the TFT and NHITS models enables a better feature extraction from the training data when compared to the LSTM and CNN, resulting in increased accuracy.

4 Problem Formulation

Considering a 2-dimensional (2D) scenario containing a mobile target (for instance, a UAV, robot, vehicle, *etc.*, with sufficient computational power to process small AI models) and N stationary reference points, where their positions are denoted by $\boldsymbol{x}^{(t)} \in \mathbb{R}^2$ and $\boldsymbol{a}_i \in \mathbb{R}^2$, respectively, for a given time instant t. This work seeks accomplishing navigation of the target throughout a given scenario, by resorting to intermediate points deployed at predefined locations and range measurements acquired from wireless communication with the reference points. The work considers a nearly constant velocity model, where the target changes its direction of movement according to:

$$\left[\left(\boldsymbol{x}^{(t+1)}\right)^T, \left(\boldsymbol{v}^{(t+1)}\right)^T\right]^T = \boldsymbol{S}\left[\left(\boldsymbol{x}^{(t)}\right)^T, \left(\boldsymbol{v}^{(t)}\right)^T\right]^T, \quad (1)$$

where $\boldsymbol{S}$ is a state transition matrix represented as:

$$\boldsymbol{S} = \begin{bmatrix} 1 & 0 & \Delta & 0 \\ 0 & 1 & 0 & \Delta \\ 0 & 0 & 1 & 0 \\ 0 & 0 & 0 & 1 \end{bmatrix}$$

with Δ being the sampling interval between two consecutive time steps, and:

$$\boldsymbol{v}^{(t)} = \boldsymbol{v}^{(t)} \begin{bmatrix} cos\left(\varphi^{(t)}\right) \\ sin\left(\varphi^{(t)}\right) \end{bmatrix} \in \mathbb{R}^2, \tag{2}$$

is the velocity vector of the target, $\varphi^{(t)}$ represents the azimuth angle between the current target's location and destination, and $\boldsymbol{v}^{(t)}$ is the target's speed, a parameter used to smooth out the arrival at the (intermediate) destination point. This is accomplished by introducing a threshold distance, τ, to control the target's speed with respect to its vicinity to the (intermediate) destination. Thus, on the one hand if $\tau > 4$, $\boldsymbol{v}^{(t)}$ is computed via:

$$\boldsymbol{v}^{(t)} = \boldsymbol{\omega}^{(t)} \cdot P_{vmax}, \tag{3}$$

being P_{vmax} the maximum speed allowed. On the other hand, when $\tau \le 4$, $\boldsymbol{v}^{(t)}$ is computed via:

$$\boldsymbol{v}^{(t)} = \boldsymbol{\eta}^{(t)} \cdot \left(\frac{\boldsymbol{\lambda}^{(t)}}{\tau}\right)^{\gamma}, \tag{4}$$

where γ is a smoothing factor and $\boldsymbol{\eta}^{(t)} = \boldsymbol{x}_{\text{dest}} - \hat{\boldsymbol{x}}^{(t)}$, $\boldsymbol{\lambda}^{(t)} = \|\boldsymbol{\eta}^{(t)}\|$ is the distance between the current target location estimate and the desired destination.

To estimate the location of the target, terrestrial radio measurements (for instance, by employing UWB, Wireless Fidelity (Wi-Fi), Bluetooth or Zigbee technologies) are exploited by extracting distance (range) measurements from the received signal. This can be accomplished via different techniques such as Time-Of-Flight (TOF) [14, 15] or RSS [16, 17]. Note that the choice between which technique to employ (*e.g.*, TOF or RSS) can have major influence on localization accuracy, but it is ultimately determined by the user's resources. Thus, the k-th distance sample ($1 \le k \le K$) between the target at time t and a reference point i is defined as:

$$d_{i,k}^{(t)} = \left\|\boldsymbol{x}^{(t)} - \boldsymbol{a}_i\right\| + \delta_{i,k}^{(t)} + n_{i,k}^{(t)}, \ i = 1, ..., N, \ k = 1, ..., K, \tag{5}$$

where the Euclidean norm is denoted as ||•||, the non-line of sight bias introduced by possible obstacles is denoted as $\delta_{i,k}^{(t)} \ge 0$ and $n_{i,k}^{(t)}$ stands for the measurement noise, modeled as a zero-mean Gaussian random variable with standard deviation $\sigma_{i,k}^{(t)}$, *i.e.*, $n_{i,k}^{(t)} \sim \mathcal{N}\left(0, \sigma_{i,k}^{(t)}\right)$. With the goal of adding robustness against outliers, and for the sake of simplicity, the median of the K distance samples, $d_i^{(t)}$, is used in the following derivations. In this way, resorting to the maximum likelihood (ML) criteria [18] and from (**5**), the target's location at time t can be estimated as:

$$\left(\hat{\boldsymbol{x}}^{(t)}, \hat{\delta}_i^{(t)}\right), = \underset{\boldsymbol{x}^{(t)}, \delta_i^{(t)}}{\arg min} \sum_{i=1}^{N} \frac{1}{2\left(\sigma_i^{(t)}\right)^2} \left(d_i^{(t)} - ||\boldsymbol{x}^{(t)} - \boldsymbol{a}_i|| - \delta_i^{(t)}\right)^2. \tag{6}$$

However, since (**6**) is highly non-convex and under-determined, it is difficult to solve the ML estimator directly.

5 The Proposed Methodologies

This section describes how to adapt TFT and NHITS models for target navigation. A brief description on how the models make their predictions, and how they are trained, is described in the following subsections.

5.1 Proposed Models for Target Navigation

In this work, two existing DL models are customized to predict the location and navigate the target. The first one is the TFT proposed in [4] and the second one is the NHITS proposed in [5]. First, a dataset is created using the predictions of the GTRS algorithm for a fixed $\sigma = 3$ m. Afterwards, this dataset is split into train and validation parts and fed to each model (TFT, NHITS and the LSTM in [11] is used as a benchmark) so that they can be trained. After the training, various performance metrics can be extracted (*e.g.*, Root Mean Squared Error (RMSE), Loss and training time). These steps are visually represented in Fig. 1 for better comprehension.

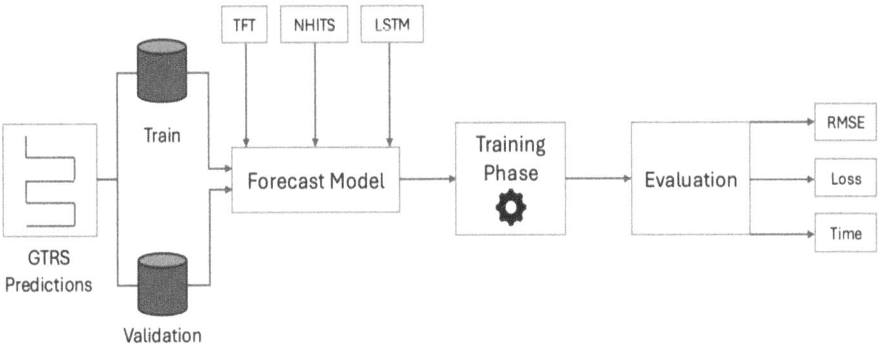

Fig. 1. Visual representation of the system model.

5.2 Training of the Models

The TFT and NHITS models require the dataset to be formatted into 4 columns as follows: "*unique_id; ds; y; trend*", where *unique_id* is an identifier, *ds* is an index, *y* is the location estimation (X- or Y-axes) and *trend* is an auxiliary feature used to train the model. In this way, for demonstration purposes, predictions from the GTRS algorithm proposed in [19] were chosen to populate the dataset (namely, the '*y*' column). Thus, the dataset used in the training phase of the models was created by letting the GTRS algorithm predict the target's position from the initial position to the desired destination.

This algorithm circumvents the ML problem in (**6**) by transforming it into a GTRS framework as follows. First, weights are introduced with the purpose of assigning more trust to *closer* reference points as:

$$w_i^{(t)} = \frac{\left(d_i^{(t)}\right)^{-1}}{\sum_{i=1}^{N}\left(d_i^{(t)}\right)^{-1}}. \tag{7}$$

Afterwards, a squared-range approach is applied, and a vector form of the problem is achieved as:

$$\begin{aligned} &\underset{z^{(t)}}{\text{minimize}}\ ||\boldsymbol{A}^{(t)}\boldsymbol{z}^{(t)} - \boldsymbol{b}^{(t)}||^2 \\ &\textit{subject to}: \\ &\left(\boldsymbol{z}^{(t)}\right)^T \boldsymbol{D}\boldsymbol{z}^{(t)} + 2\boldsymbol{f}^T\boldsymbol{z}^{(t)} = 0, \end{aligned} \tag{8}$$

with $\boldsymbol{z}^{(t)} = \left[\left(\boldsymbol{x}^{(t)}\right)^T, ||\boldsymbol{x}^{(t)}||^2\right]^T \in \mathbb{R}^3$,

$$\boldsymbol{A}^{(t)} = \begin{bmatrix} \left[\sqrt{w_1^{(t)}}2\boldsymbol{a}_1^T, \boldsymbol{0}_{1\times 2}\right] & -\sqrt{w_1^{(t)}} \\ \vdots & \vdots \\ \left[\sqrt{w_N^{(t)}}2\boldsymbol{a}_N^T, \boldsymbol{0}_{1\times 2}\right] & -\sqrt{w_N^{(t)}} \\ \left(\hat{\boldsymbol{P}}^{(t|t-1)}\right)^{-1/2} & \boldsymbol{0}_{4\times 1} \end{bmatrix} \in \mathbb{R}^{(N+4)\times 5},$$

$$\boldsymbol{b}^{(t)} = \begin{bmatrix} \sqrt{w_1^{(t)}}\left(||\boldsymbol{a}_1||^2 - \left(d_1^{(t)}\right)^2\right) \\ \vdots \\ \sqrt{w_N^{(t)}}\left(||\boldsymbol{a}_N||^2 - \left(d_N^{(t)}\right)^2\right) \\ \left(\hat{\boldsymbol{P}}^{(t|t-1)}\right)^{-\frac{1}{2}}\hat{\boldsymbol{\theta}}^{(t|t-1)} \end{bmatrix} \in \mathbb{R}^{N+4},$$

$$\boldsymbol{D} = \begin{bmatrix} \boldsymbol{I}_2 & 0_{2\times 1} \\ 0_{1\times 2} & 0 \end{bmatrix} \in \mathbb{R}^{4\times 4}, \boldsymbol{f} = \begin{bmatrix} 0_{2\times 1} \\ -1/2 \end{bmatrix} \in \mathbb{R}^3,$$

being $\hat{\boldsymbol{\theta}}^{(t|t-1)}$ and $\hat{\boldsymbol{P}}^{(t|t-1)}$, respectively, the mean and the covariance of the one-step predicted state, while $\boldsymbol{I}_G$ and $\boldsymbol{0}_{p\times q}$ represent the identity matrix of size G and the matrix of all-zero entries of size $p \times q$.

The solution for the GTRS problem is found resorting to the bisection procedure [20] applied in an interval where the problem is a monotonically decreasing function. For more details, the reader is referred to [19].

6 Performance Analysis

This section evaluates the performance of the proposed methods resorting to computer simulations performed on a machine equipped with an Intel Core® i9-9880H CPU running at 2.3 GHz, 16 GB of RAM, and MacOS 15.2. The software versions used were MATLAB® R2024b and Python 3.12. In all simulations, a scenario with a width of 100 (m) and a length of 150 (m) was used. In addition, obstacles were added to simulate a warehouse scenario containing several shelves that introduce attenuations [21]. In the simulations, this effect is obtained resorting to a uniform distribution as $\tilde{\delta}_{i,k}^{(t)} \sim U[0.5, 1.5]$ (m) and $\delta_{i,k}^{(t)} = \mathrm{N}_{\mathrm{obst,i}}^{(t)} \times \tilde{\delta}_{i,k}^{(t)}$, with $N_{obst,i}^{(t)}$ denoting the number of obstacles within the i-th reference point at instant t. In addition, no inertial parameters were considered in the motion of the target.

To test the proposed methods, a dataset with size *look_back* is created at each waypoint and is fed to the model. As an example, considering the initial position of the target $[10, 5]^{\mathrm{T}}$ and the next waypoint $[75, 5]^{T}$, the following dataset is created for the X- and Y-axes: $testX = [10, 11, 12, 13, 14]$, $testY = [5, 5, 5, 5, 5]$. Note that, the *testY* dataset is constant since, considering the second waypoint, one desires to move horizontally only. The model then uses these datasets to make its own predictions. Each prediction is added to the dataset, making it dynamic. A visual representation of this behavior can be seen in Fig. 2.

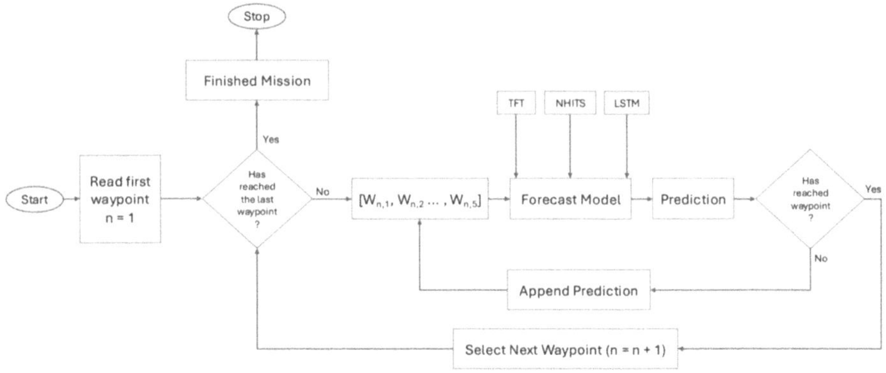

Fig. 2. Visual representation of how the system makes predictions until it reaches the final destination.

The remaining simulation parameters were defined as follows: $N = 6$, $\sigma = 3$, $\tau = 1$, $look\_back = 5$ and the number of times the model iterates throughout the dataset, $Epochs = 300$. The model configurations were set as follows: $input\_size = 5$, $hidden\_size = 20$, $learning\_rate = 0.005$, $early\_stop\_patience\_steps = 10$ and the loss function used was *StudentT*.

To assess the learning of the models, the last 10 positions of the dataset were used as test and the RMSE between the estimation and the test dataset was computed. These results, together with the average training time (*i.e.*, the average time it took for each model to finish the training stage) and the average prediction time for the models (*i.e.*, the average time each model takes to compute the next position after it is trained) of all models are summarized in Table 1.

Table 1. RMSE, average training time (using CPU) and average prediction time (using CPU) comparison for the three models.

Model	RMSE X (m)	RMSE Y (m)	Training Time (s)	Avg. Prediction Time (s)
TFT	0.63	1.22	24.4	0.71
NHITS	0.72	3.06	11.2	0.72
LSTM	0.72	7.07	186.1	0.12

Table 1 reveals that the most accurate model in terms of learning is TFT, followed by NHITS and LSTM. Regarding the training time, the fastest is NHITS, followed by TFT. In both cases they are roughly 7x faster than the LSTM, making them more suitable for dynamic scenarios where the retraining of the models is required. The reduction in training time is owed to the more advanced architectures of TFT and NHITS models, which allows them to learn more efficiently when compared to LSTM, consequently finishing the training faster than LSTM.

The mean trajectory taken by the target and its deviation from the mean trajectory is illustrated in Fig. 3 for each of the considered models. Figure 3a. Shows the results for the TFT model, and one can see that it achieved a nearly perfect trajectory even when the training data is noisy. Next, the NHITS model was tested, and the achieved results can be seen in Fig. 3b. This figure reveals that when compared with TFT, the predictions are not as accurate, thus indicating more vulnerability to noise present in the training data. Nonetheless, the overall trajectory still closely resembles the desired one. To further validate both models, a comparison with the existing LSTM model [10] was also performed. The trajectory predicted by the LSTM can be seen in Fig. 3c. From this figure it is visible that the LSTM exhibits an overall less smooth trajectory, presenting in some cases, high fluctuations, for instance after the target has changed direction.

To conclude this section, real experimental tests were also conducted. These tests were performed using MakerFabs DW3000 ESP32 UWB micro-controllers that implement both the target and the reference points. The micro-controllers were programmed so that the target is able to compute the distance to each anchor by exchanging messages and measuring the time it takes to send and receive them back. In these experimental tests, an office with a width of 4.53 (m) and a length of 3.26 (m) was used, which can be seen in Fig. 3 (d)-(f) alongside the obtained results. In this scenario, instead of shelves, steel cabinets visible in Fig. 4, were used as objects and the attenuation was defined by measurement calibration. The movement of the target was created using a fixed size step along the trajectory. In addition, no inertial parameters were included in the motion of the target. The parameters remain the same apart from N, which is now 7. Given the

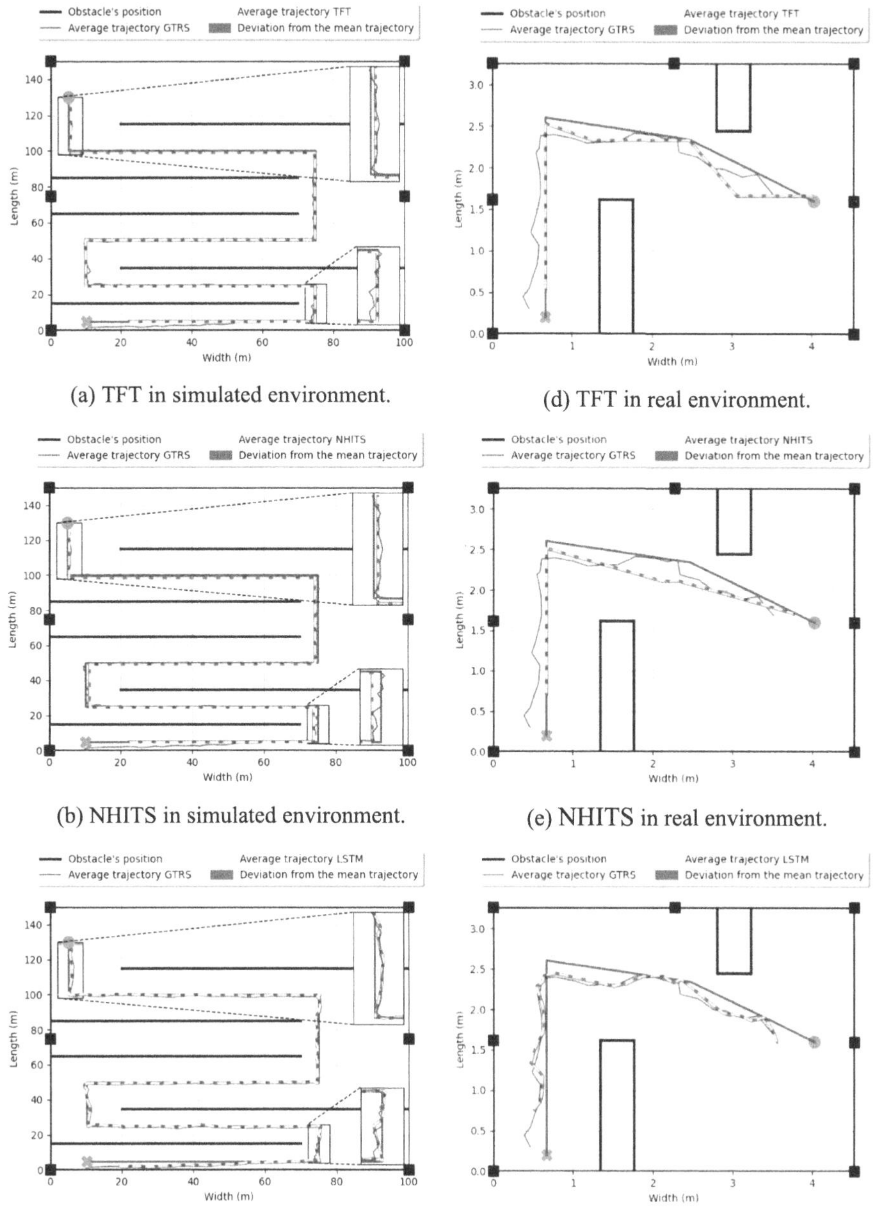

(a) TFT in simulated environment.

(d) TFT in real environment.

(b) NHITS in simulated environment.

(e) NHITS in real environment.

(c) LSTM in simulated environment.

(f) LSTM in real environment.

Fig. 3. Navigation performance in simulated/experimental environment: the solid blue line denotes the ideal trajectory (*i.e.*, the trajectory that the target would ideally follow, since it is the most efficient and the safest one), the blue cross represents the initial position, and the blue circle represents the final destination.

reduced size of the scenario, the size of the acquired dataset was 27 samples. As this is not sufficient to run the models, extrapolation was performed by computing the average between two subsequent positions to obtain a new one. This strategy doubled the size of the data set. From Fig. 3 (d)-(f), one can see that, on the one hand, the TFT and NHITS models minimize the distance towards the desired trajectory, despite some deviations in the latter part. On the other hand, the LSTM closely matches the GTRS predictions, and consequently presents higher fluctuations overall, especially in the initial part of the trajectory. Overall, considering the size of the dataset, and the error introduced by the GTRS used in the training stage, all models achieve relatively good results, being that TFT and NHITS require significantly reduced training time and navigation steps, and still introduce minimal errors in terms of trajectory when compared to the ideal case.

(a) (b) (c)

Fig. 4. The real scenario environment: a) Setup used in the tests, where the reference points are placed on the walls and the tag is placed on a chair connected to a computer; b) The metallic cabinets used as obstacles; c) MakerFabs DW3000 ESP32 UWB.

To summarize, and given that the models produce different numbers of estimates, one way to quantify the results was to make orthogonal projections of the estimates onto the line depicted by the desired trajectory and calculate the average distance between the points and the lines as the error, *i.e.*, the Average Root Mean Squared Error (ARMSE) was calculated according to:

$$ARMSE = \sqrt{\sum_{i=1}^{MC}\sum_{t=1}^{T}\frac{\left\|\boldsymbol{x}_i^{(t)} - \hat{\boldsymbol{x}}_i^{(t)}\right\|^2}{T \times MC}} \tag{9}$$

where T is the number of iterations the model took to reach the final destination, MC is the number of Monte Carlo (MC) runs, $\boldsymbol{x}_i^{(t)}$ is the point of projection of the estimation, $\hat{\boldsymbol{x}}_i^{(t)}$, onto the desired trajectory in the t-th iteration. The obtained results can be seen in Table 2.

Table 2 reveals that, in the simulations, the TFT model achieves the lowest ARMSE, but the LSTM reaches closer to the final destination. In contrast with the simulations, in the real testbed, the NHITS model achieves the lowest ARMSE and the TFT achieves a closer distance to the final destination. In both experiments, the new models require a lower number of iterations to conclude the respective scenarios, which not only reduces their running time, but also preserves energy resources due to lower number of computations. Overall the new models outperform the LSTM both in terms of RMSE, distance to the destination and number of iterations required to complete the scenario.

Table 2. ARMSE for the trajectory, distance from the destination comparison $||\boldsymbol{x}_{dest} - \hat{\boldsymbol{x}}_{final}||$ and average number of iterations required to complete the scenario.

Model	ARMSE (m)	$\|\|\boldsymbol{x}_{dest} - \hat{\boldsymbol{x}}_{final}\|\|$(m)	Iterations
TFT Simulation	0.55	0.84	148
NHITS Simulation	0.86	1.07	189
LSTM Simulation	0.80	0.37	222
TFT Real Testbed	0.10	0.06	37
NHITS Real Testbed	0.09	0.29	16
LSTM Real Testbed	0.11	0.48	53

7 Conclusions and Future Work

This work proposed adapting two DL methods to solve the problem of target navigation in GNSS-denied environments. By training the models using existing data, they were able to make their own predictions afterwards. The obtained simulation and real testbed results corroborate that the proposed methods reveal less vulnerability to noise and an accurate overall trajectory estimation when compared to the existing LSTM, while reducing training time and the number of iterations to reach the desired destination.

Future research will focus on integrating obstacle avoidance strategies, as well as eliminating the need for the intermediate destination points to enhance and expand upon the current work.

Acknowledgments. This research was partially funded by the European Union's Horizon Europe Research and Innovation Programme under the Marie Skłodowska-Curie grant agreement No. 101086387 and Fundação para a Ciência e a Tecnologia under Projects UIDB/04111/2020, UIDB/50008/2020, 2021.04180.CEECIND, and LASIGE Research Unit, ref. UID/000408/2025, as well as Instituto Lusófono de Investigação e Desenvolvimento (ILIND) under Project COFAC/ILIND/COPELABS/4/2023 and COFAC/ILIND/COPELABS/1/2024.

References

1. Zhang, X., et al.: Inspection and classification system of photovoltaic module defects based on uav and thermal imaging. In: 2022 7th International Conference on Power and Renewable Energy (ICPRE), pp. 905–909 (2022)
2. Wu, C., Tu, S., Tu, S., Wang, L., Chen, W.: Realization of remote monitoring and navigation system for multiple uav swarm missions: Using 4g/wifi-mesh communications and rtk gps positioning technology. In: 2022 International Automatic Control Conference (CACS), pp. 1–6 (2022)
3. Chong, Z.H., et al.: An innovative robotics stowing strategy for inventory replenishment in automated storage and retrieval system. In: 2018 15th International Conference on Control, Automation, Robotics and Vision (ICARCV), pp. 305–310 (2018)
4. Lim, B., Arık, S.O., Loeff, N., Pfister, T.: Temporal fusion transformers for interpretable multi-horizon time series forecasting. Int. J. Forecast. **37**(4), 1748–1764 (2021)
5. Challu, C., et al.: Nhits: Neural hierarchical interpolation for time series forecasting. Proceedings of the AAAI Conference on Artificial Intelligence **37**, 6989–6997 (2023)
6. Yang, B., Li, J., Shao, Z., Zhang, H.: Robust uwb indoor localization for nlos scenes via learning spatial-temporal features. IEEE Sens. J. **22**(8), 7990–8000 (2022)
7. Akremi, M.S., Neji, N., Tabia, H.: Visual navigation of uavs in indoor corridor environments using deep learning. In: 2023 Integrated Communication, Navigation and Surveillance Conference (ICNS), pp. 1–6 (2023)
8. Arshad, M.A., et al.: Drone navigation using region and edge exploitation-based deep cnn. IEEE Access **10**, 95441–95450 (2022)
9. Ma, Y., Xu, Y.: A ddqn-based path planning method for multi-uavs in a 3d indoor environment. In: 2022 4th International Conference on Control and Robotics (ICCR), pp. 476–480 (2022)
10. Zhang, Y., Qi, J., Wu, C., Liu, Y., Pu, J.: Indoor uav formation system based on uwb positioning. In: 2023 42nd Chinese Control Conference (CCC), pp. 8545–8550 (2023)
11. Serras Santos, R., Matos-Carvalho, J.P., Tomic, S., Beko, M., Correia, S.D.: Applying deep neural networks to improve uav navigation in satellite-less environments. In: 2022 International Young Engineers Forum (YEF-ECE), pp. 63–68 (2022)
12. Serras Santos, R., Matos-Carvalho, J.P., Tomic, S., Beko, M., Correia, S.D.: A hybrid lstm-based neural network for satellite-less uav navigation. In: 2023 6th Conference on Cloud and Internet of Things (CIoT), pp. 91–97 (2023)
13. Fernando, E., De Silva, O., Mann, G.K.I., Gosine, R.: Toward developing an indoor localization system for mavs using two or three rf range anchors: An observability based approach. IEEE Sens. J. **22**(6), 5173–5187 (2022)
14. Comuniello, A., Angelis, A., Moschitta, A., Carbone, P.: Using bluetooth low energy technology to perform tof-based positioning. Electronics **11**, 111 (2021)
15. Hashem, O., Khaled, A., Harras, M.Y.: Accurate indoor positioning using ieee 802.11mc round trip time. Pervasive and Mobile Computing **75**, 101416 (2021)
16. Rappaport, T.: Wireless communications - principles and practice. Prentice Hall (1996)
17. Tomic, S., Beko, M., Dinis, R.: Rss-based localization in wireless sensor networks using convex relaxation: Noncooperative and cooperative schemes. Vehicular Technology, IEEE Transactions on **64**, 2037–2050 (2015)
18. Kay, S.: Fundamentals of Statistical Signal Processing: Estimation Theory, 1st ed. Prentice Hall Upper Saddle River, NJ, USA (1993)
19. Matos-Carvalho, J., Santos, R., Tomic, S., Beko, M.: GTRS-based algorithm for UAV navigation in indoor environments employing range measurements and odometry. IEEE Access **9**, 89120–89132 (2021)

20. Tomic, S., Beko, M., Dinis, R.: 3-D target localization in wireless sensor network using RSS and AoA measurement. IEEE Trans. Vehic. Technol. **66**(4), 3197–3210 (2017)
21. Golubeva, T., Zaitsev, Y., Konshin, S., Duisenbek, I.: A study on the wi-fi radio signal attenuation in various construction materials (obstacles). In: 2018 Tenth International Conference on Ubiquitous and Future Networks (ICUFN), pp. 718–723 (2018)

Coarse-Grained Reconfigurable Arrays for High-Performance Low-Power Deep Neural Networks on Embedded Devices

João D. Lopes(✉), Horácio C. Neto, and José T. Sousa

INESC INOV/IST/UL, Rua Alves Redol, 9, 1000-029 Lisboa, Portugal
{joao.d.lopes,horacio.neto,jose.t.de.sousa}@tecnico.ulisboa.pt

Abstract. Reconfigurable hardware architectures offer an effective platform for AI-powered Cyber-Physical Systems (CPS) by enabling efficient local computation, energy efficiency, and adaptability. This work presents a novel hardware architecture for executing Deep Neural Networks (DNNs) on resource-constrained edge devices. The architecture is organized as a Coarse-Grained Reconfigurable Array (CGRA) featuring flexible arithmetic units that support Precision Trade-off Floats (PT-Floats) II, customizable floating-point formats. By dynamically adjusting the precision of computations based on the sensitivity of different neural network layers, the proposed architecture achieves significant improvements in energy efficiency and memory footprint. Experimental results show 73% and 65% gains in die area and power consumption, respectively, to the cost of 0.02% in accuracy, compared with the standard IEEE-754. They evidence substantial performance gains in Convolutional Neural Network (CNN)-based image classification tasks while operating within the stringent power and resource constraints of edge devices.

Keywords: Variable-Precision Floating-Points · Coarse-Grained Reconfigurable Array · Deep Neural Network · Low-Power Edge Devices

1 Introduction

Since the latter decades of the 20th century [1–3], Machine Learning (ML) and Artificial Intelligence (AI) have been instrumental in automating complex tasks such as natural language processing, object detection, and speech recognition. These advancements have revolutionized diverse domains, including medicine, computer vision, and finance. The computational demands of these tasks, often reliant on Deep Neural Networks (DNNs), have driven the development of specialized hardware architectures, particularly to enable efficient deployment on low-power, battery-powered edge devices.

Reconfigurable computing architectures can improve the DNN execution performance of specific applications by several orders of magnitude, compared to General-Purpose Processors (GPPs) [4], and save about one order of magnitude in energy, compared to Graphics Processing Units (GPUs) [5]. Field-Programmable Gate Arrays

Published by Springer Nature Switzerland AG 2025
L. M. Camarinha-Matos and F. Ferrada (Eds.): DoCEIS 2025, IFIP AICT 759, pp. 226–237, 2025.
https://doi.org/10.1007/978-3-031-97051-1_16

(FPGAs) are widely used for implementing DNN hardware accelerators [6] due to their high hardware flexibility and good energy efficiencies. However, being fine-grained reconfigurable architectures, FPGAs need extra silicon area for the reconfiguration process and require significant amounts of time for reconfiguration. On the other end, Application-Specific Integrated Circuits (ASICs) achieve minimum size and maximum power efficiency [7] but require much time and effort to develop, and upgrades and bug fixes cannot be done since they are not programmable.

A Coarse-Grained Reconfigurable Array (CGRA) is a matrix of arithmetic units, also called Processing Elements (PEs), and memories, with reconfigurable interconnects between them. Being reconfigurable, the communication network allows the user to change the datapath post-fabric. Thus, CGRA platforms are programmable at the word-level, unlike FPGAs, which are programmed at the bit-level. This feature significantly reduces the reconfiguration time and silicon area. So, CGRAs provide a middle ground between ASICs and FPGAs.

The proposed hardware architecture is organized as a CGRA and is based on efficient Floating-Point Units (FPUs) that effectively trade-off the required precision and dynamic range, using the new proposed Precision Trade-off Float (PT-Float)-II family of formats. Although most common CGRAs use integer arithmetic units only, many real number algorithms, such as DNNs require floating-point arithmetic to achieve accuracy requirements.

In summary, this work introduces a high-performance hardware architecture for executing real number algorithms on low-power edge devices using the new PT-Float-II formats. The FPUs that implement such formats have been integrated into the Deep Versat CGRA [8], which is included in the IOb-SoC [9, 10] System-on-Chip (SoC) template.

The remaining sections are organized as follows. Section 2 relates this work with the conference theme. Section 3 summarizes the existing CGRA architectures, and the issues of the more common formats used to represent real numbers. Section 4 describes the proposed CGRA which integrates the new FPU. Section 5 details the new family of formats, PT-Float-II, implemented in the FPU, while Sect. 6 illustrates the FPU architecture, including ASIC implementation results. Section 7 shows accuracy results on running a simple Neural Network (NN) for image classification using PT-Float-II data, and compare them with results on running the same algorithm using the standard IEEE-754. Finally, Sect. 8 presents conclusions and future work.

2 Relation to AI-Powered CPS

Cyber-Physical Systems (CPS) are rapidly becoming ubiquitous in our interconnected world, blending physical processes with sophisticated computational intelligence. The integration of AI into these systems enables unprecedented levels of autonomy, real-time adaptability, and intelligent decision-making. From smart grids and autonomous vehicles to industrial automation and healthcare, AI-powered CPS are driving innovation and addressing critical challenges across diverse domains. Future success requires the development of robust and efficient solutions that effectively combine AI with physical systems.

The increasing complexity of AI models, particularly DNNs, poses a significant challenge for their deployment in resource-constrained edge-based CPS. The computational demands of DNNs often exceed the capabilities of traditional embedded hardware, leading to performance bottlenecks and excessive energy consumption. To fully realize the potential of AI-powered CPS, there is a pressing need for specialized hardware architectures that can deliver high performance while adhering to strict power and resource limitations.

This paper addresses this challenge by proposing a novel reconfigurable hardware architecture specifically designed for executing DNNs on resource-constrained edge devices. Reconfigurable hardware, such as CGRAs, offers a promising avenue for achieving the necessary balance between performance, energy efficiency, and adaptability. Our proposed architecture leverages the inherent flexibility of CGRAs, coupled with customizable floating-point formats, to dynamically adjust computational precision based on the sensitivity of different neural network layers. This approach enables significant reductions in energy consumption and memory footprint without compromising accuracy. By optimizing the hardware for the specific characteristics of DNNs, we aim to unlock the full potential of AI-powered CPS at the edge, paving the way for more intelligent, efficient, and responsive applications. This work contributes to the growing body of research focused on developing innovative hardware solutions that empower the next generation of AI-driven cyber-physical systems.

3 Background

The hardware architecture developed builds upon the Versat CGRA [11]. Versat is a highly parameterizable CGRA architecture designed to have a small area footprint while achieving low-power consumption. It is partially reconfigurable, considerably reducing the reconfiguration time compared to other CGRA architectures that only support full reconfiguration. Versat has a C + + Application Programming Interface (API), used by a host CPU program, to ease the CGRA's integration in a SoC.

Although CGRAs have been researched for over three decades [12], most architectures target media applications [13–15] that have very tight requirements regarding execution time, silicon area and energy consumption. Therefore, most common CGRAs are low-power and have integer PEs only. Although they have not been widely used, some of these architectures ended up in the industry [16–18]. CGRA architectures for deep learning have been investigated [19–21]. However, these architectures also only use integer arithmetic units, penalizing results' accuracy in order to increase performance and reduce chip size and energy consumption.

CGRAs may have both integer units and FPUs. A few CGRA architectures use 32-bit FPUs implementing IEEE-754 formats [22–24]. One recent CGRA architecture was designed to support three floating-point IEEE-type formats [25] with 32, 16 and 8 bits data widths. By supporting three alternative precisions in the floating-point calculations, the precision can be reduced whenever possible, thus achieving higher performance while saving energy consumption.

FPUs occupy a considerable amount of silicon area and consume significantly more energy than integer units, which is a problem on edge computing devices. Therefore, the FPUs need to be optimized to support variable (and smaller) precisions to efficiently adjust to the accuracy requirements of the DNN models to be implemented. Furthermore, the commonly used IEEE-754 standard has several issues reported [26–28], which limit its efficiency for this type of algorithms:

- Overflows/underflows: representable values abruptly turn into $+/- \infty$ or $+/- 0$, which results in an infinite relative error;
- Fixed-precision: precision is constant along the whole dynamic range, then suddenly collapses;
- Waste in binary combinations: redundant Not-a-Number (NaN) representations can be replaced for representable numbers;
- Most exponent values use too many bits.

Variable-precision formats, such as Posits [29], have higher precision on represented numbers with an exponent equal to zero (numbers next to 1) and go to overflow/underflow more gracefully, compared with the IEEE-754. Additionally, they eliminate the NaN and $\pm$ infinite combinations, using them to represent more real numbers. Moreover, Posits implement only one binary combination (Not-a-Real - NaR) to represent NaNs and $\pm$ infinite and have a unique representation of 0 rather than two, as the IEEE standard. However, the Posit formats have some limitations which should be improved upon.

In general, implementing applications with variable-precision has many advantages, such as performance, memory storage and bandwidth [30]. Therefore, we have proposed the PT-Float-II family of formats due to its improved flexibility. PT-Float-II solves the above-mentioned limitations of the standard IEEE-754 and efficiently implements tapered precision (originally proposed by R. Morris [31]), significantly improving the family of formats Posit and the previously proposed PT-Float-I [32].

4 Deep Versat CGRA

The Deep Versat CGRA [8] is an improved version of the Versat CGRA [11]. Deep Versat is composed of several cores linked in a linear and circular array, as shown in Fig. 1. Each core has a Configuration Module and a Data Engine. The host CPU directly accesses the configuration registers from each Versat core and configures the CGRA configurations through a C + + API. The communications to the host CPU and the external memory use the AXI-4 Lite and Full interface protocols [33], respectively.

The Data Engine is an array of PEs. Each PE can select as input any of the PE's outputs from that core plus the ones from the previous core in a fully connected graph topology so that the data can flow from one core to the next, eliminating the need for complex routing algorithms. To avoid the high cost of the communication network that interconnects the PEs, as explained in [11], each Data Engine can have no more than 10 PEs. Thus, in the worst-case scenario, each PE can select an input from 1 to 20 PE's outputs, which does not impact the frequency of operation as studied. This fact allows Deep Versat to have an unlimited number of PEs in its architecture, allowing the CGRA to expand until the application's needs are fulfilled. The PEs are heterogeneous, i.e., there are several types of PEs and each one implements different functions. The number of cores and PEs of each type per core is configurable at compile time.

The Configuration Module holds the current configuration, which runs on the Data Engine, while the next one is being built. It is organized as a register file with asymmetric registers, allowing the host CPU to configure the Data Engine with minimal configuration bit changes (for instance, select input A, input B, and/or function of the PE_N in the $Core_M$). This partial reconfigurability feature is used to speed up the reconfiguration time by taking advantage of the similarity between sequential configurations.

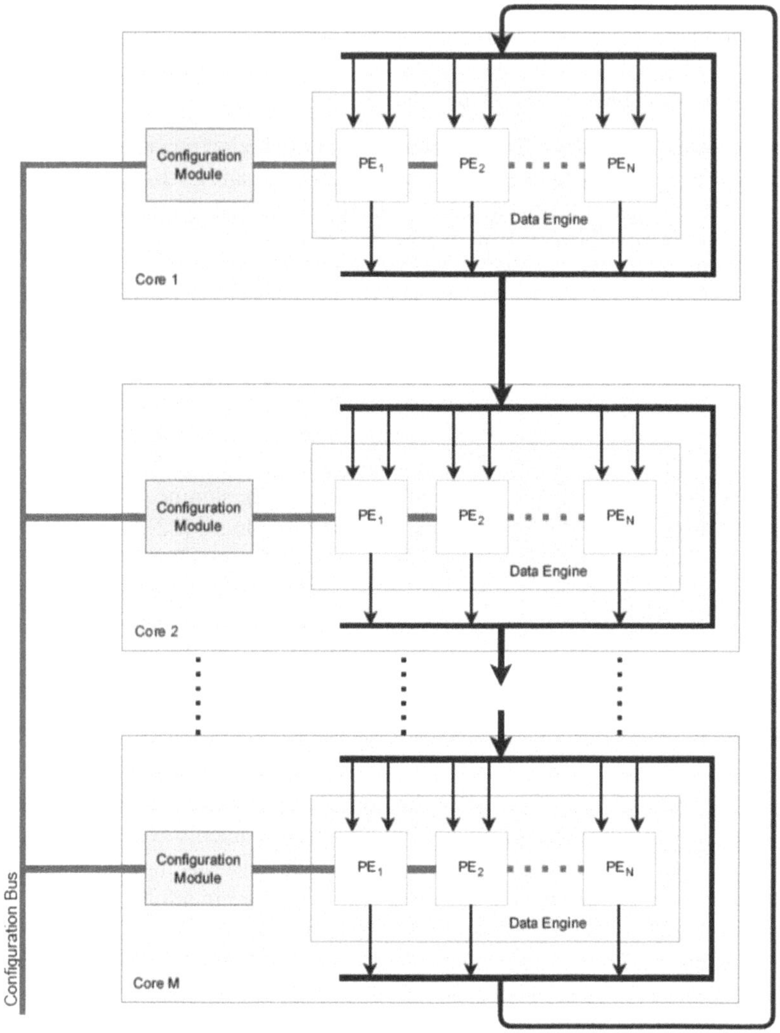

Fig. 1. Deep Versat CGRA architecture.

5 The PT-Float-II Floating-Point Generic Format

The *Precision Trade-off Float (PT-Float) II* is an enhanced version of the formerly presented PT-Float-I [32]. In this version, the numbers representation is monotonic (the binary word treated as a signed integer maps monotonically to the signed reals) and the zero and Not-a-Real (NaR) are unique (the real number zero is represented with all bits set to 0 and the NaR is represented with the first bit set to 1 and all the others set to 0). Figure 2 illustrates the generic PT-Float-II representation format.

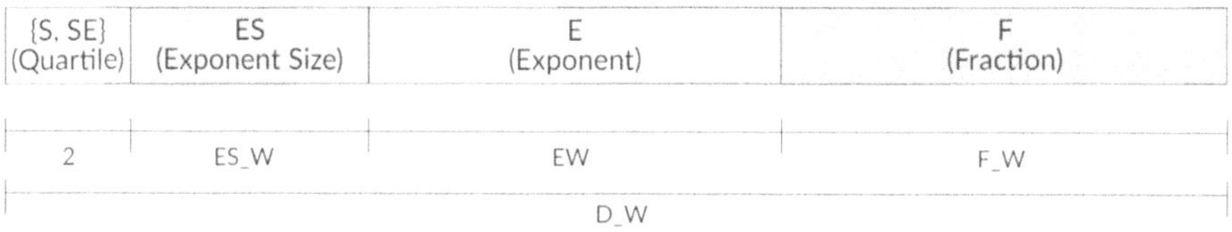

Fig. 2. Generic PT-Float-II representation format.

The PT-Float-II has two parameters: the data width (D_W) and the exponent size width (ES_W). Each pair of these parameters defines a format $< \text{D\_W}, \text{ES\_W} >$. The format incorporates four fields: the Quartile, the Exponent Size, the Exponent, and the Fraction. The fraction width (F_W) is given by Eq. 1:

$$\text{F\_W} = \text{D\_W} - \text{ES\_W} - \text{EW} - 2. \quad (1)$$

The leftmost bit S defines the sign of the number. Negative numbers are represented as the 2's complement of the positive ones. The SE field encodes the exponent sign inverted, i.e., if SE is set to 1, the exponent is positive; otherwise, it is negative.

The ES field defines the variable exponent size. Whenever the exponent is negative, the bitwise NOT operation is performed to the ES value. The EW field represents the explicit bits of the exponent (excluding the exponent hidden bit). The number of explicit bits in EW is therefore ($\text{EW} = \text{ES} - 1$ if $\text{ES} > 0$, otherwise $\text{EW} = 0$).

The significand is an unsigned integer with a hidden bit, always set to 1, plus the remaining bits (if any). As a result of this normalization, the significand is in the interval [1; 2[, as in the standard IEEE-754.

Table 1 shows some numerical examples to better illustrate the PT-Float-II. The first column presents PT-Float-II numbers encoded in the $< 8, 2 >$ format. Next, the bits of the encoded values are sorted by field (S, SE, ES, E and F). Then, the extracted values are presented: sign, exponent, significand and value. The last column presents comments.

The table only shows examples for positive numbers, since negative numbers are their 2's complement, plus the special case NaR. As shown, the maximum (max) value is 224.0 (the minimum is the symmetric –224.0) and the minimum positive (minp) value is $0.0048828125 = 1.25 \times 2^{-8}$.

Table 1. PT-Float-II $< 8, 2 >$ numerical examples.

Binary	Fields					Extracted Values			
	S	SE	ES	E	F	sign	exponent	significand	value
01111111	0	1	11	11	11	+	0(1)11 = 7	(1).11 = 1.75	224.0
01100011	0	1	10	0	011	+	0(1)0 = 2	(1).011 = 1.375	5.5
01011001	0	1	01	–	1001	+	0(1) = 1	(1).1001 = 1.5625	3.125
01000000	0	1	00	–	0000	+	0 = 0	(1).0000 = 1.0	1.0
00100011	0	0	10	–	0011	+	1(0) = −2	(1).0011 = 1.1875	0.296875
00000001	0	0	00	00	01	+	1(0)00 = −8	(1).01 = 1.25	0.0048828125
00000000	0	0	00	00	00	+	1(0)00 = −8	(0).00 = 0.0	0.0
10000000	1	0	00	00	00	-	1(0)00 = −8	(0).00 = 0.0	NaR

6 PT-Float-II FPU

The PT-Float-II FPU implements the four basic operations: addition, subtraction, multiplication and division. The arithmetic units are fully pipelined except for the divider, which implements the iterative restoring division algorithm to reduce the hardware circuit area since divisions are less common. Table 2 outlines arithmetic units' features.

Table 2. PT-Float-II functional units.

Operation	Latency (cycles)	Pipelined	#Stages	Throughput (op/cycle)
unpack	1	yes	1	1
add/sub	4	yes	6	1
mult	3	yes	4	1
div	$5 + 2 \times$ SIG_W	no	1	1/latency
pack	2	yes	3	1

The arithmetic operations require three steps: decode, operation and encode. In the decode step, operands' sign, exponent and significand are extracted in the Unpack unit. The arithmetic operations occur in the operation step in the respective unit: Addition/Subtraction, Multiplication, and Division. Finally, the result's sign, exponent and fraction are encoded in the Pack unit.

The Unpack unit uses an adder to 2's complement the negative numbers. Then, it uses a right shifter, with some extra logic gates, to extract the number's exponent and significand.

Figure 3 shows the Addition/Subtraction and Multiplication block diagram units. The Addition/Subtraction unit initially subtracts the exponents of the operands to determine if a swap among them is needed. Next, the absolute value of the exponent's difference is used to align the significand of the smallest operand. On subtractions, the significand of the biggest operand is 1's complemented. Then, in the actual significands' adder, the carry-in is set to 1 to complete the 2's complementation. The 1's complemented step is performed over Significand A in parallel with the Significand B alignment to avoid impacting the critical path. The result is normalized. The final rounding is performed in the Pack unit.

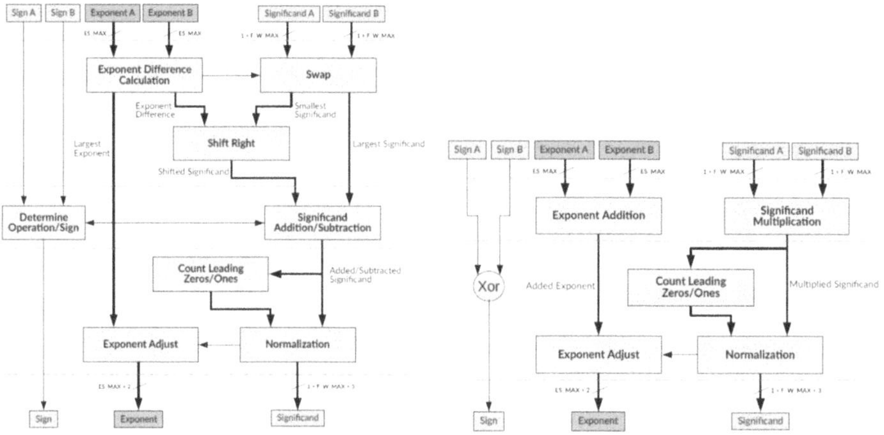

Fig. 3. PT-Float-II Addition/Subtraction (left) and (right) units' block diagram.

The Multiplication unit multiplies the significands while the exponents are added (the multiplication does not require alignment). Note that the integer multiplier's output has double the operands' bit-width. The final result is normalized, as in the Addition/Subtraction unit.

The Division unit uses minimal hardware to compute the significands' divisions using the restoring division algorithm. This implementation saves circuit area at the cost of execution time, since divisions are much less common than additions, subtractions, and multiplications. In parallel with the significands division, the sign is computed and the exponents are subtracted. As soon as serial division ends, the result is also normalized.

The Pack unit uses three additional bits for rounding: Guard, Round and Sticky. These bits determine if the result is truncated or needs to be rounded. As the format has a variable-precision, the round must be performed in a bit selected according to the exponent size. After rounding, the Pack unit encodes the result as explained in Sect. 5. Finally, negative numbers are 2's complemented.

Table 3 summarizes FPU ASIC implementation results in the UMC 130 nm technology node for a set of PT-Float-II formats for comparison with the standard IEEE-754 in terms of: die area, power consumption and frequency of operation. For a better comparison of the formats, the dynamic range (DR) and the precision bits for each format are also present on the table.

Table 3. FPU ASIC implementation results for 130 nm technology node.

Format's Family	Data Width	ExpSize Width	DR ($\log_{10}$)	Precision	Area (mm^2)	Power (mW)	Frequency (MHz)
PT-Float-II	32	4	19731.61	13 to 27	0.073	9.62	200
	16	3	78.25	6 to 12	0.030	4.19	200
	8	2	4.99	3 to 5	0.013	1.90	200
IEEE-754	64	–	83.39	53	0.141	9.04	200
	32	–	631.56	24	0.049	5.42	200

Table 3 shows that, for the same bit-width, a PT-Float-II FPU uses more silicon area. Nonetheless, PT-Float-II formats have a much higher dynamic range [34], and therefore smaller data width formats can match a wider standard IEEE-754 in specific applications. For instance, the PT-Float-II $< 32, 4 >$ format has a dynamic range much higher than the IEEE-754 double-precision one, which is a result of the maximum precision bits decrease. Section 7 presents an example which consists in running a simple NN for image classification, using a small PT-Float-II data width, without compromising the final results.

To validate the proposed architecture, we implemented a software library written in C, with a C++ API which allows the user to easily evaluate the new PT-Float-II data types in a regular C program. The library provides a set of functions which perform the four basic arithmetic operations plus the Multiply-ACcumulate (MAC) and accumulation, while the API interfaces those functions by means of overloading operators.

7 Simple Neural Network with Small Floating-Point

For a better understanding of the PT-Float-II family of formats, we evaluate the use of the small PT-Float-II $< 8, 2 >$ format to execute a simple neural network for image classification, resorting to the software library and its API.

The input images use RGB colors with 96×96 resolution. The neural network consists of 3 hidden layers (one convolutional layer with 16 $3 \times 3 \times 3$ filters, one max-pooling layer and one fully-connected layer) and one final softmax layer. The NN has a total of 353,898 parameters and the total number of MAC operations is 4,170,592 (3,817,152 + 353,440). The NN structure is shown in Fig. 4.

The NN was trained using PyTorch, with IEEE-754 single-precision, on the STL-10 dataset [35, 36]. The dataset has 10 classes: airplane, bird, car, cat, deer, dog, horse, monkey, ship, truck, and is organized with 5000 training images and 8000 test images.

```
  layer     filters     size                    input                 output
0 input                                                            96 x 96 x 3
1 conv         16     3 x 3 / 1            96 x 96 x 3   ->  94 x 94 x 16
2 max-pool            2 x 2 / 2            94 x 94 x 16  ->  47 x 47 x 16
3 fc                             35,344 = 47 x 47 x 16  ->  10
4 softmax                                                          10
```

Fig. 4. Neural Network structure.

Results were obtained by running inference on the 8000 images test dataset. The neural network model was directly converted from the original 32-bit IEEE floating-point format to the reduced bit-width representation, without any retraining and without any complex post-training quantization algorithm. Results obtained with the IEEE 32-bit format and with the PT-Float-II < 8, 2 > format are compared in Table 4.

Table 4. NN's accuracy for the IEEE-754 32-bit and PT-Float-II < 8, 2 > formats.

Format	Accuracy (top-1)
IEEE-754 32-bit	99.97% (7998/8000)
PT-Float-II < 8, 2 >	99.95% (7996/8000)

Results show that NN's accuracy using PT-Float-II < 8, 2 > drops only 0.02% compared to IEEE-754 32-bit, while saving about 73% of circuit area and 65% of power consumption. Table 4 indicates that a small PT-Float-II format as the < 8, 2 > can replace the standard IEEE-754 32-bit for computing Convolutional Neural Networks (CNNs) applications on very constrained-resources devices.

8 Conclusions

This paper introduces a novel hardware architecture for executing DNNs applications targeting low-power devices. The architecture is organized as a CGRA featuring flexible arithmetic units that support customizable PT-Float-II formats to improve the architecture's accuracy/area/performance trade-off.

Experimental results show substantial performance gains on running a specific low-complexity CNN application, with a minimal reduction of 0.02% in accuracy compared to the IEEE-754 32-bit standard, while achieving a 73% reduction of circuit area and 65% of power consumption. This highlights the potential of the proposed architecture to substitute the standard IEEE-754, enabling efficient computation, energy efficiency, and adaptability for AI-powered CPS.

For future work, we will implement a wider set of benchmarks. Moreover, we will implement applications using several PT-Float-II formats mixed. Furthermore, we will evaluate the new floating-point formats for training DNNs.

Acknowledgments. João D. Lopes acknowledges FCT, Fundação para a Ciência e a Tecnologia, for the support through grant 2021.05020.BD.

References

1. Dietterich, T.G.: Machine learning. Annual Review of Computer Science **4**(1), 255–306 (1990)
2. Mitchell, T.M., Mitchell, T.M.: Machine learning, vol. 1. McGraw-Hill New York (1997)
3. Winston, P.H.: Artificial intelligence. Addison-Wesley Longman Publishing Co., Inc (1984)
4. Todman, T.J., Constantinides, G.A., Wilton, S.J.E., Mencer, O., Luk, W., Cheung, P.Y.K.: Reconfigurable computing: architectures and design methods. IEE Proceedings-Computers and Digital Techniques **152**(2), 193–207 (2005)
5. Betkaoui, B., Thomas, D.B., Luk, W.: Comparing performance and energy efficiency of FPGAs and GPUs for high productivity computing. 2010 International Conference on Field-Programmable Technology, pp. 94–101 (2010). https://doi.org/10.1109/fpt.2010.5681761
6. Guo, K., Zeng, S., Yu, J., Wang, Y., Yang, H.: A survey of FPGA-based neural network inference accelerators. ACM Transactions on Reconfigurable Technology and Systems **12**(1), 1–26 (2019). https://doi.org/10.1145/3289185 National Center for Biotechnology Information. http://www.ncbi.nlm.nih.gov
7. Machupalli, R., Hossain, M., Mandal, M.: Review of ASIC accelerators for deep neural network. Microprocessors and Microsystems **89**, 104441 (2022). https://doi.org/10.1016/j.micpro.2022.104418
8. Mário, V., Lopes, J.D., Véstias, M., de Sousa, J.T.: Implementing CNNs using a Linear Array of Full Mesh CGRAs. 16th International Symposium on Applied Reconfigurable Computing (2020)
9. IOb-SoC – A Computing Machines using a RISC-V architecture. https://github.com/IObundle/iob-soc (2019). Accessed: 23 April 2025
10. Merendeira, A., et al.: IOb-SoC - An Open-source RISC-V System-on-Chip (2021). https://doi.org/10.5281/zenodo.5791412
11. Lopes, J.D., Véstias, M.P., Duarte, R.P., Neto, H.C., de Sousa, J.T.: Coarse- grained reconfigurable computing with the versat architecture. Electronics **10**(6), 669 (2021)
12. Podobas, A., Sano, K., Matsuoka, S.: A Survey on Coarse-Grained Reconfigurable Architectures from a Performance Perspective. arXiv preprint arXiv:2004.04509 (2020)
13. Singh, H., Lee, M.H., Lu, G., Kurdahi, F.J., Bagherzadeh, N., Chaves Filho, E.M.: MorphoSys: an integrated reconfigurable system for data-parallel and computation-intensive applications. IEEE Trans. Comput. **49**(5), 465–481 (2000)
14. Ye, Z.A., Moshovos, A., Hauck, S., Banerjee, P.: CHIMAERA: a high-performance architecture with a tightly-coupled reconfigurable functional unit. ACM SIGARCH Computer Architecture News **28**(2), 225–235 (2000)
15. Chalamalasetti, S.R., Purohit, S., Margala, M., Vanderbauwhede, W.: MORA – an architecture and programming model for a resource efficient coarse grained reconfigurable processor. In: 2009 NASA/ESA Conference on Adaptive Hardware and Systems, pp. 389–396. IEEE (2009)
16. Salefski, B., Caglar, L.: Re-Configurable Computing in Wireless. In: Proceedings of the 38th Design Automation Conference (IEEE Cat. No. 01CH37232), pp. 178–183. IEEE (2001)
17. Kyo, S., Okazaki, S.: IMAPCAR: A 100 GOPS In-Vehicle Vision Processor Based on 128 Ring Connected Four-Way VLIW Processing Elements. Journal of Signal Processing Systems **62**(1), 5–16 (2011)
18. Kim, C., et al.: ULP-SRP: ultra low power samsung reconfigurable processor for biomedical applications. In: 2012 International Conference on Field-Programmable Technology, pp. 329–334. IEEE (2012)
19. Fan, X., Wu, D., Cao, W., Luk, W., Wang, L.: Stream processing dual-track CGRA for object inference. IEEE Transactions on Very Large Scale Integration (VLSI) Systems **26**(6), 1098–1111 (2018)

20. Parashar, A., et al.: SCNN: an accelerator for compressed- sparse convolutional neural networks. ACM SIGARCH Computer Architecture News **45**(2), 27–40 (2017)
21. Chen, Y.H., Yang, T.J., Emer, J., Sze, V.: Eyeriss v2: a flexible accelerator for emerging deep neural networks on mobile devices. IEEE Journal on Emerging and Selected Topics in Circuits and Systems **9**(2), 292–308 (2019)
22. Käsgen, P.S., Weinhardt, M., Hochberger, C.: A coarse-grained reconfigurable array for high-performance computing applications. 2018 International Conference on ReConFigurable Computing and FPGAs (ReConFig), pp. 1–4. IEEE (2018)
23. Prabhakar, R., et al.: Plasticine: A Reconfigurable Architecture for Parallel Patterns. In: 2017 ACM/IEEE 44th Annual International Symposium on Computer Architecture (ISCA), pp. 389–402. IEEE (2017)
24. Lee, D., Jo, M., Han, K., Choi, K.: FloRA: coarse-grained reconfigurable architecture with floating-point operation capability. In: 2009 International conference on field-programmable technology, pp. 376–379. IEEE (2009)
25. Mach, S., Rossi, D., Tagliavini, G., Marongiu, A., Benini, L.: A transprecision floating-point architecture for energy-efficient embedded computing. 2018 IEEE International Symposium on Circuits and Systems (ISCAS), pp. 1–5. IEEE (2018)
26. Gustafson, J.L.: The end of error: Unum computing. CRC Press (2015)
27. Kahan, W., Darcy, J.: How Java's floating-point hurts everyone everywhere. Workshop on Java, pp. 1–81 (1998). https://people.eecs.berkeley.edu/~wkahan/JAVAhurt.pdf
28. Ternovoy, E., Popov, M.G., Kaleev, D.V., Savchenko, Y.V., Pereverzev, A.L.: Comparative Analysis of Floating-point Accuracy of IEEE 754 and Posit Standards. 2020 IEEE Conference of Russian Young Researchers in Electrical and Electronic Engineering (EIConRus), pp. 1883–186 (2020). https://doi.org/10.1109/EIConRus49466.2020.9039521
29. Gustafson, J.L., Yonemoto, I.T.: Beating floating point at its own game: Posit arithmetic. Supercomputing Frontiers and Innovations **4**(2), 71–86 (2017)
30. Judd, P., et al.: Proteus: exploiting precision variability in deep neural networks. Parallel Comput. **73**, 40–51 (2018)
31. Morris, R.: Tapered floating point: a new floating-point representation. IEEE Transactions on Computers C-20(12), 1578–1579 (1971). https://doi.org/10.1109/T-C.1971.223174
32. Sousa, J.T.d., Lopes, J.D., Serôdio, M., Neto, H.C., Véstias, M.P.: PT-float: a floating-point unit with dynamically varying exponent and fraction sizes. 2024 IEEE 31st Symposium on Computer Arithmetic (ARITH) **00**, 139–146 (2024). https://doi.org/10.1109/arith61463.2024.00031
33. ARM.: AMBA AXI and ACE Protocol Specification: AXI3, AXI4, and AXI4-Lite, ACE and ACE-Lite (February 2013), document ID: ID033013
34. Lopes, J.D.: Precision Trade-off Floating-Point Units for Coarse-Grained Reconfigurable Arrays. PhD thesis, Instituto Superior Técnico (2025)
35. STL-10 Dataset. http://cs.stanford.edu/~acoates/stl10, accessed: 2025–04–23
36. Coates, A., Ng, A., Lee, H.: An analysis of single-layer networks in unsupervised feature learning. In: Proceedings of the fourteenth international conference on artificial intelligence and statistics, pp. 215–223. JMLR Workshop and Conference Proceedings (2011)

Autonomous Vehicle Decision Making Through Multi-grid Markov Decision Processes

Tiago Caldeira[1](✉), Majid Khonji[2], Jorge Dias[2], and Pedro U. Lima[1]

[1] Instituto Superior, Técnico University of Lisbon, Lisboa, Portugal
{tiago.caldeira,pedro.lima}@tecnico.ulisboa.pt
[2] Khalifa University, Abu Dhabi, United Arab Emirates
{majid.khonji,jorge.dias}@ku.ac.ae

Abstract. As the automotive industry advances toward higher levels of autonomy, decision-making frameworks must evolve to address increasingly complex and dynamic environments. This paper presents a novel approach called Multi-Grid Markov Decision Processes (mg-MDP), designed to enhance scalability, robustness, and efficiency in autonomous vehicle decision-making. Building on the foundations of traditional Markov Decision Processes (MDPs), mg-MDP utilize a hierarchical multi-layer grid structure to better represent distinct aspects of the environment. Through extensive simulations, we show that mg-MDP incrementally adjusts decision-making across multiple grid- based layers, efficiently handling dynamic traffic scenarios such as intersections, lane merging, and obstacle avoidance. This approach intends to reduce the computational effort while improving decision accuracy. This paper also discusses how mg-MDP can be applied in Cyber-Physical Systems for better real-world modeling that will leverage intelligent transportation.

Keywords: Multi-Grid Markov Decision Processes · Autonomous Vehicles · Hierarchical Planning · Urban Navigation · Decision-Making · Computational Efficiency

1 Introduction

The prospect of fully autonomous vehicles has galvanized both academia and industry, promising safer, more efficient mobility solutions in our cities. Yet navigating today's highly dynamic urban environments—with fluctuating traffic densities, unexpected obstacles, and unpredictable pedestrian behavior—remains a formidable challenge. Conventional decision-making frameworks, such as single-layer grid-based Markov Decision Processes (MDPs) or end-to-end deep learning pipelines, frequently struggle to scale, suffer from opaque reasoning, and cannot guarantee real-time performance in large, complex road networks.

To focus our efforts, we pose the primary research question: "How can we design and implement a decision-making framework for autonomous vehicles that balances scalability, robustness, and computational efficiency in dynamic urban environments?".

Published by Springer Nature Switzerland AG 2025
L. M. Camarinha-Matos and F. Ferrada (Eds.): DoCEIS 2025, IFIP AICT 759, pp. 238–249, 2025.
https://doi.org/10.1007/978-3-031-97051-1_17

We hypothesize that by partitioning environmental representation into multiple, weighted grid-layers, mg-MDP will achieve a reduction in policy computation time compared to single-layer MDPs, while maintaining equivalent collision rates and decision accuracy. To address this, we propose the Multi-Grid Markov Decision Process (mg-MDP): a hierarchical, multi-layer extension of traditional MDPs. By partitioning the environment into distinct grid layers, each encoding traffic flow, infrastructure constraints, safety considerations, and more: mg-MDP dynamically allocates computation where it matters most. This layered approach yields fine-grained policies in critical zones while lightening the load in simpler areas, accelerating policy updates and preserving decision accuracy. Moreover, mg-MDP supports on-the-fly adaptation to evolving conditions, delivering the scalability and resilience needed for real-world autonomous navigation and beyond.

1.1 Structure of This Paper

Following this introduction, Sect. 2 elaborates on the direct relevance of the research to the AI-powered Cyber-Physical systems (CPS). Section 3 provides a review of state-of-the-art techniques in autonomous vehicle decision-making, focusing on MDP-based methods, reinforcement learning, and open problems. Section 4 introduces the mg-MDP approach and outlines its core contributions and innovations. Section 5 discusses the initial results obtained in simulation and offers some insights into their implications. Section 6 presents conclusions and outlines further work in the doctoral research.

2 AI-Powered Cyber-Physical Systems

Our Multi-Grid Markov Decision Process (mg-MDP) framework advances the decision-making capabilities of autonomous vehicles by embedding a structured, multi-layered computational model that directly supports AI-powered Cyber-Physical Systems (CPS).

First, mg-MDP enhances CPS modularity by separating decision factors into distinct layers—traffic flow, infrastructure rules, safety constraints, environmental context, and user preferences. This separation enables each module to be developed, tested, and certified independently, while still contributing to a cohesive global policy. By dynamically adjusting grid resolution per layer, mg-MDP maintain real-time responsiveness without overloading onboard processors.

Second, mg-MDP fosters edge–cloud collaboration: critical layers requiring low-latency decisions (e.g., safety and infrastructure) are computed on-vehicle, while strategic layers (e.g., global route planning and environmental predictions) can be offloaded to edge servers or cloud-based digital twins over 5G + networks. This hybrid architecture optimizes resource utilization and supports fleet-wide coordination and shared learning. Third, the multi-layer structure inherently improves system explainability and auditability, which are essential for CPS regulation. Regulators and certification bodies can inspect individual layers, verifying traffic compliance, safety margins, and energy efficiency separately (before approving the overall policy).

3 State of the Art

3.1 Markov Decision Processes and Extensions

Markov Decision Processes (MDPs) are a foundational framework for sequential decision-making under uncertainty [1]. They provide a structured way to model decision-making by decomposing environments into states, actions, and transition probabilities. However, in autonomous driving, the complexity of real-world interactions, large state spaces, and uncertainty in sensor inputs pose significant challenges.

Traditional MDPs face two key limitations: They assume complete observability, which is unrealistic in real-world applications where occlusions and sensor noise exist; and as the number of states grows, solving MDPs using conventional methods becomes computationally infeasible. To address these challenges, various extensions to MDPs have been proposed, like.

Partially Observable MDPs (POMDPs) [2], that extend MDPs to handle uncertainty in state perception. While accurate, they introduce high computational demands [3].

Chance-Constrained MDPs incorporate probabilistic bounds on constraints for safety-critical applications [4, 5]. This approach ensures that constraints such as collision avoidance hold with high probability while maintaining an efficient policy.

Grid-Based MDPs spatially discretize the driving environment for path planning [6, 7]. However, uniform grid resolution can be inefficient, as different regions of the environment require varying levels of detail. Hierarchical extensions, such as multi-grid approaches, have been proposed to dynamically adjust granularity [8].

3.2 Reinforcement Learning and Machine Learning

Several research efforts integrate MDP frameworks with Deep Reinforcement Learning (DRL), where agents learn end-to-end driving policies from data. These approaches have demonstrated success in environments with well-defined reward structures but often require extensive training datasets and computational power [9, 10]. Deep recurrent Q-learning and hierarchical reinforcement learning have been explored to handle long-term dependencies in autonomous driving decision-making [3, 11]. These methods show promise in improving generalization across different traffic conditions, yet they remain susceptible to sample inefficiency and robustness concerns [12, 13]. Hierarchical reinforcement learning approaches, particularly under mixed observability settings, have been introduced to improve decision-making robustness [14].

These methods allow for structured policy learning where different levels of abstraction can address both high-level planning and low-level manoeuvring tasks. Multi-objective reinforcement learning has also gained attention, particularly in applications that require balancing competing objectives such as safety, efficiency, and passenger comfort [15].

Multi-objective policy gradient methods incorporating topological constraints have been proposed to improve exploration in complex driving environments [16].

3.3 Challenges and Open Problems

Despite significant advancements, existing techniques face several limitations. Efficient handling of large state spaces in dense environments remains a challenge, especially for traditional MDP and RL approaches [17], mostly during real-time applications.

The dynamic resolution adaptation is necessary to balance computational efficiency and precision, a problem that hierarchical multi model MDPs aim to address [8]. Moreover, combining modular decision layers (e.g. road topology, traffic flow, obstacle detection) while preserving real-time performance is an open research question [7] currently being explored by the CARLA Simulator community.

These gaps highlight the need for adaptive, multi-resolution decision frameworks like mg-MDP that integrate well with existing perception and decision-making modules.

4 Hierarchical Decision-Making for AVs

4.1 Introduction to Multi-grid Markov Decision Processes

Traditional Markov Decision Processes (MDPs) are widely used for decision-making in uncertain environments. However, their applicability to complex, dynamic settings, such as autonomous driving in urban environments, is limited by their inability to efficiently capture different aspects of the world simultaneously. Grid-based MDPs (GridMDPs) attempt to address some of these issues by discretizing the environment, but they still suffer from scalability challenges.

This research introduces **Multi-Grid Markov Decision Processes** (mg-MDP), which extend the Grid Markov Decision Processes (gMDP) by structuring the environment into multiple layers, each representing distinct aspects of the world. Instead of treating every environmental component as part of a single decision space, mg-MDPs model road topology, traffic flow, and dynamic obstacles as separate layers. This improves interpretability and allows faster policy updates through independent computations.

4.2 Foundations: MDPs and gMDPs

To understand mg-MDP, it is important to first review the fundamentals of Markov Decision Processes and their grid-based extensions. An MDP is formally defined as a tuple (S, A, P, R, γ), where:

- **S** is the state space.
- **A** is the set of available actions.
- **P(s' | s, a)** represents the transition probabilities.
- **R(s, a)** is the reward function.
- γ is the discount factor.

The discount factor balances the importance of the future rewards against immediate ones, ranges between 0 and 1, and is commonly fixed at 0.9. The transition function defines the probability of moving from one state to another, given a specific action. On a deterministic system, this probability is always one, but the same principles could be applied to a stochastic system.

The Grid Markov Decision Process extend the MDP framework by discretizing a continuous space into a finite grid, where each cell represents a state and actions dictate movement between adjacent cells. While this approach is effective for structured environments, it lacks adaptability in capturing different levels of abstraction across regions of varying complexity.

Figure 1 presents CARLA Simulation Town 02 and its conversion into a grid MDP with each cell roughly 3.3 m wide (lane width), which allows the environment to have basic properties, with the main road to be marked as a 0 (free flow), road margins and sidewalks as 1 (emergency flow with a penalty) and the gardens, buildings and other obstacles as 2 (not accessible).

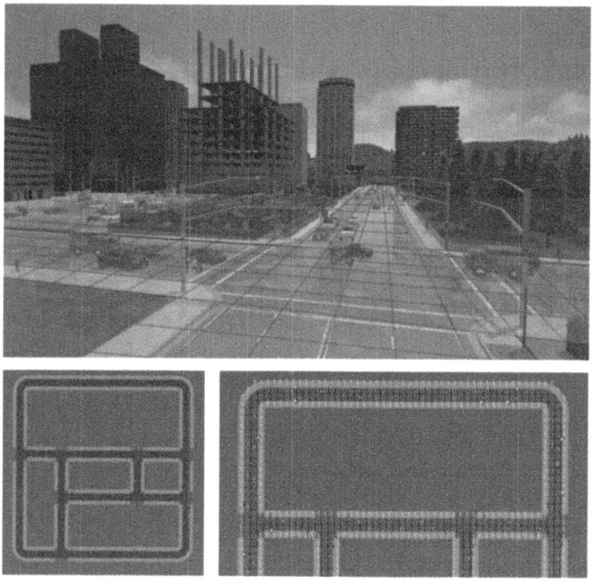

Fig. 1. Grid representation of a simulated urban environment as an MDP.

4.3 Extending to mg-MDP

This research extends GridMDPs by introducing the concept of **multi-layered decision processes**, where each environmental component is modelled separately. Instead of representing the entire world as a single MDP, mg-MDP decompose the decision process into multiple layers that interact dynamically.

Before describing specific applications, it is important to define the mg-MDP structure. A state s is influenced by multiple layers, each with its own reward function $R_l(s,a)$ and weight w_l, which together sum to one.

The overall reward function is computed as $R_w(s, a) = \sum_{i=1}^{n} w_i \cdot R_i(s, a)$, where each reward function $Ri(s, a)$ is bounded between 0 and 100. This formulation ensures that decisions integrate multiple sources of information efficiently while maintaining computational tractability. This decomposition reduces complexity in large-scale environments while providing structured prioritization based on different situational needs. The mg-MDP framework introduces fundamental properties that enhance its computational efficiency, adaptability, and scalability in decision-making tasks. By structuring decisions across multiple independent layers, mg-MDP provide mechanisms to optimize policies without recomputing them entirely for every environmental change.

A key advantage of mg-MDP is their ability to maintain the essential properties of Markov Decision Processes, ensuring **convergence** to an optimal policy. The Bellman optimality equation remains applicable as the mg-MDP structure upholds the Markov property across its layers. The aggregated reward function $R_w(s, a)$ ensures that conventional solution methods such as value iteration and policy iteration remain valid. Given that mg-MDP are designed to integrate multiple layers of information while preserving computational tractability, they converge reliably under typical discounting conditions.

One of the core optimizations in mg-MDP is the ability to **simplify** the model into a single-layer MDP when needed. This is achieved by collapsing all layers into a single aggregated reward function $R_{single}(s, a) = \sum_{i=1}^{n} w_i \cdot R_i(s, a)$, allowing compatibility with traditional MDP solvers. In many scenarios, not all layers contribute significantly to decision-making. The framework supports **compression** by identifying and removing non-impactful layers. If for any of the states or actions, the difference between a specific layer reward $R_I(s, a)$ and the aggregated reward $R_w(s, a)$ remains below a given threshold ε, then eliminating that layer will affect policy for that state. This allows for computational savings while maintaining optimal behavior.

The ability to **transform** mg-MDP dynamically is another important feature. Individual layers can be updated or replaced without recomputing the entire decision process. Given a modified layer l', the new reward function can be efficiently adjusted as $R'_w(s, a) = R_w(s, a) + w_l[R'_l(s, a) - R_l(s, a)]$. This capability enables real-time adaptation when external conditions change, such as new regulations, shifting user preferences, or environmental disturbances. Similarly, the weights can be **dynamically adjusted**, which allows the system to shift priorities between layers based on external conditions without a complete recalculation. The new reward $R'_w(s,a)$ is calculated as $R'_w(s, a) = \frac{R_w(s,a)+[\Delta w_x \cdot R_x(s,a)]}{1+\Delta w_x}$, where Δw_x is the change in weight for that layer, prior to overall weight normalization (weights must always satisfy a sum of 1). Adjustments in weights enable mg-MDP to (re)-prioritize factors such as congestion, safety, or user preferences.

Scalability is another key advantage, since each layer operates independently, mg-MDP allow parallel computation of state transitions and rewards, significantly reducing overall computation time. This parallelism makes mg-MDP particularly suited for large-scale environments.

Finally, the **Robustness** of mg-MDP is supported by a sensitivity analysis. Small perturbations in the reward values or weights do not significantly impact the optimal policy. If a minor perturbation δ is introduced to a layer reward, the impact on the value function remains bounded by $|V' * (s) - V * (s)| \leq \frac{\gamma\delta}{1-\gamma}$. This ensures that mg-MDP maintain stability even under minor environmental changes, making them highly reliable in real-world applications.

These properties collectively reinforce mg-MDPs as a structured, interpretable, and scalable framework for complex decision-making scenarios, particularly in autonomous driving applications.

4.4 Sample Application: Urban Navigation

Consider an autonomous vehicle navigating an urban intersection. In a traditional Grid-MDP, the vehicle must consider all environmental aspects simultaneously, leading to a high-dimensional decision space. In contrast, mg-MDP allow the problem to be decomposed into separate layers, ensuring that the **traffic layer** informs the agent of congestion levels, the **infrastructure layer** dictates legal traffic movements, and the **pedestrian layer** ensures safe interactions with non-vehicle agents. By structuring the problem in this way, mg-MDP enable more efficient policy computation and adaptation to real-time environmental changes.

To illustrate how the reward depends on the next state and remains independent across layers, consider a vehicle at an intersection deciding whether to move forward, turn left, or turn right. Different layers evaluate these actions based on distinct criteria. The traffic condition layer assigns low rewards for congested routes and high rewards for free-flowing lanes. The infrastructure layer ensures that the chosen action aligns with legal road regulations. A safety layer could incorporate the pedestrian presence or risk, discouraging movements that might lead to conflicts. The illustration and the table in Fig. 2 provide an example of how different layers contribute independent rewards based on the next state. By structuring decision-making in this manner, mg-MDP enable efficient updates where only relevant layers are recomputed when the environment shifts.

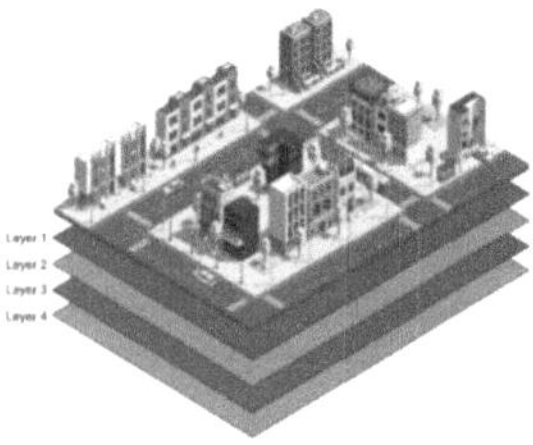

		Rewards per Action		
Layer	**Weight**	**Forward**	**Left**	**Right**
Traffic	0.3	15	50	25
Infrastructure	0.25	80	40	70
Safety	0.2	30	10	60
Environmental	0.15	50	20	40
User Preference	0.1	60	30	50
Weighted Reward		44	33	48

Fig. 2. Illustration of mg-MDP decision layers in an urban environment and the corresponding reward structure for different layers.

The Multi-Grid Markov Decision Process (mg-MDP) framework, although initially developed for autonomous vehicles, has a broad range of potential applications across multiple domains, such as Smart Cities, Healthcare, Supply Chain Management and Energy Grid optimization.

5 Validation in Urban Driving Scenarios

Building upon the theoretical foundation of mg-MDPs, we now validate the framework in an autonomous driving scenario within the CARLA simulator. The experiments evaluate how mg-MDPs efficiently compute optimal policies under dynamic urban conditions while leveraging their structural advantages.

5.1 Simulation Environment and Experimental Setup

CARLA provides a high-fidelity urban driving environment with structured road networks, realistic vehicle dynamics, and environmental perception sensors. The mg-MDP approach is tested on a simulated city grid where intersections, road segments, and traffic regulations define state transitions.

CARLA is selected due to its high-fidelity urban driving environment and the ability to extract precise waypoints, allowing controlled validation of mg-MDP decision layers. Waypoints extracted from CARLA's maps construct a grid-based representation of the city. Each lane segment and intersection correspond to an mg-MDP state. Available actions represent the next target cell, independent of vehicle maneuver limitations. Such limitations will impact only in the stochastic analysis (where the probability of going to the cell on the right at large speeds is nearly zero due to the vehicle inertia). While this implementation assumes a deterministic setting, future work should extend mg-MDPs to handle stochastic transitions, incorporating vehicle dynamics and motion uncertainty. Figure 3 illustrates the waypoint-based grid discretization used for decision-making, with the main waypoints being represented as red, and additional waypoints being generated by CARLA in-between.

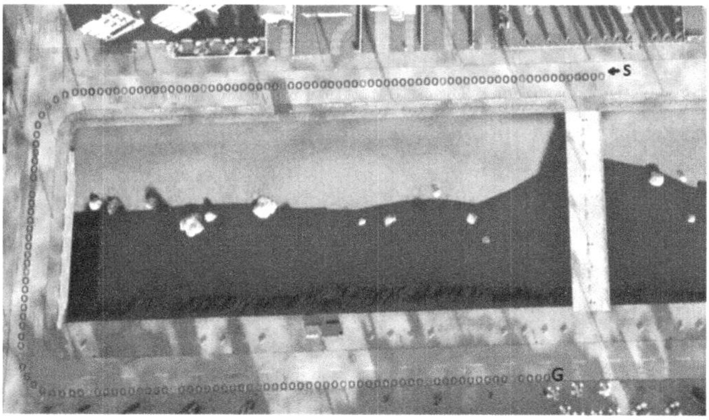

Fig. 3. Waypoint-based representation of the CARLA city grid (Color figure online).

The decision-making process incorporates multiple layers, each influencing the final policy. The traffic flow layer prioritizes uncongested routes, minimizing delays. The traffic rules layer ensures compliance with legal road usage, such as one-way streets and intersections. The safety layer accounts for safe driving behaviors, discouraging sharp turns and abrupt lane changes. Finally, the environmental layer optimizes energy efficiency by preferring smoother routes. To evaluate mg-MDP efficiency, a series of experiments were conducted.

5.2 Experimental Results and Analysis

Figure 4 presents a subset of the town's map and a comparison of policy calculations for different methods: open navigation and following traffic rules with a partial block (car breakdown). The system shows the adaptability of the MDP, with the overall analysis of the system and the generation of policies converging faster on the mg-MDP than the standard MDPs when handling dynamic road conditions. The ability to update only relevant layers significantly reduces computational overhead.

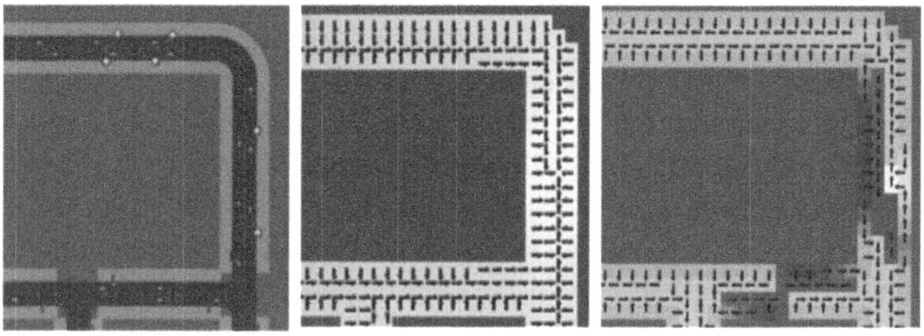

Fig. 4. Town 02 layout and two mg-MDP sample policies.

When simulating environmental changes such as road closures or traffic congestion, mg-MDP policies dynamically adjust to alternative paths without requiring a full recomputation of all state-action pairs. This supports the transformation property discussed in earlier sections. The scalability of mg-MDP computation is analyzed by evaluating the time complexity as the number of layers increases. Since layers operate independently, mg-MDPs allow for parallel computation of layer-specific rewards and state transitions.

5.3 Discussion on Real-World Applicability

The results validate that mg-MDPs provide a structured and efficient decision-making framework for autonomous vehicles in dynamic urban settings. By decomposing decision-making into multiple layers, mg-MDPs allow for targeted updates when local changes occur, significantly reducing computational overhead.

This modular approach ensures that modifications in one layer, such as traffic congestion updates or road closures, do not necessitate a full policy recomputation. Such adaptability is critical for real-time applications where quick responses to dynamic conditions are required. Beyond computational efficiency, the layered structure of mg-MDPs improves system interpretability, making it easier to analyze, debug, and refine policies. Each layer encapsulates distinct decision factors (e.g. traffic flow, infrastructure rules, safety constraints), allowing engineers and policymakers to isolate and adjust individual components without disrupting the entire framework. This structured approach aligns well with regulatory and deployment requirements for autonomous driving, providing a scalable and explainable decision-making methodology.

Looking ahead, we plan to deepen real-world applicability by systematically examining three edge-case domains. First, sensor uncertainty (including LiDAR occlusion, camera drop-out, and intermittent GPS loss) must be characterized so that mg-MDP layer weights can adapt to degraded perception. Second, kinematic constraints such as turning radius, braking latency, and actuator limits will be integrated into our transition model to ensure policies respect vehicle dynamics under all maneuvers. Finally, we will explore adversarial agents, from unpredictable pedestrians and cyclists to malfunctioning traffic lights, embedding scenario-based triggers that dynamically prioritize safety and compliance layers.

Addressing these challenges will guide the next phase of research, moving mg-MDP from high-fidelity simulation to robust, real-world deployment.

6 Conclusions and Future Work

This research presents Multi-Grid Markov Decision Processes (mg-MDPs) as an innovative decision-making framework designed to enhance scalability, adaptability, and computational efficiency in autonomous systems. By structuring decision processes into multiple layers, mg-MDPs enable more efficient policy updates while preserving interpretability and robustness in dynamic environments. This hierarchical decomposition allows for modular policy optimization, reducing the need for full recomputations and facilitating efficient decision-making in autonomous driving applications.

The mg-MDP framework was formulated to integrate multiple decision layers that model distinct aspects of dynamic environments. This research established formal propositions that enable simplification, compression, transformation, and scalability while ensuring policy convergence. The framework was validated in simulation using CARLA, demonstrating computational efficiency, adaptability to environmental changes, and improved decision-making over single-layer MDPs.

The system was implemented and tested in a real vehicle developed by the author, integrating the mg-MDP structure into an autonomous control system. The vehicle utilized onboard sensors and processing units to compute optimal policies in real-time while navigating structured environments. The results confirmed that mg-MDPs allow for efficient adaptation to environmental changes, reducing computational overhead while preserving optimality.

The experimental validation confirms that mg-MDPs outperform traditional MDPs by enabling modular updates to policies without requiring full recomputation. The framework provides a scalable solution applicable to real-world autonomous driving scenarios, demonstrating its potential to enhance decision-making in cyber-physical systems.

6.1 Future Work

Future research should focus on expanding mg-MDPs in the following areas. First, integrating mg-MDPs with **Deep Reinforcement Learning (DRL)** will allow dynamic adjustment of layer weights based on learned policies rather than predefined values.

Second, extending mg-MDPs to **multi-agent coordination** will facilitate real-time fleet-level optimization where multiple autonomous vehicles share environmental data. Finally, investigating **Partial Observability Handling** will improve mg-MDP decision-making in environments where sensor limitations introduce uncertainty.

As part of the doctoral program, we will also undertake a comprehensive real-vehicle validation of the mg-MDP framework on an experimental autonomous platform, measuring policy computation time, memory usage, and safety performance under real-world driving conditions.

These extensions will further enhance the applicability of mg-MDPs in real-world autonomous mobility networks while providing quantitative data about the overall improvements.

Acknowledgments. This work is supported by the Foundation for Science and Technology in Portugal under grant DOI: https://doi.org/10.54499/LA/P/0083/2020.

References

1. Bellman, R.: The theory of dynamic programming. In: Bulletin of the American Mathematical Society **60**(6), 503–515 (1954)
2. Lauri, M., Hsu, D., Pajarinen, J.: Partially observable markov decision processes in robotics: A survey. IEEE Trans. Rob. **39**(1), 21–40 (2022)
3. Matthew Hausknecht and Peter Stone. Deep recurrent q-learning for partially observable MDPs. In: 2015 AAAI fall symposium series (2015)
4. Yi, Z., et al.: A chance-constrained stochastic approach to intermodal container routing problems. PloS one **13**(2), e0192275 (2018)
5. Majid, K., et al.: Multi-agent chance-constrained stochastic shortest path with application to risk-aware intelligent intersection. In: arXiv cs.AI (2022)
6. Alexey, D., et al.: CARLA: An open urban driving simulator. In: Conference on robot learning. PMLR, pp. 1–16 (2017)
7. Sumbal, M., et al.: CARLA+: An Evolution of the CARLA Simulator for Complex Environment Using a Probabilistic Graphical Model. Drones **7**(2), 111 (2023)
8. Steimle, L.N., Kaufman, D.L., Denton, B.T.: Multi-model Markov decision processes. IISE Transactions **53**(10), 1124–1139 (2021)
9. Shuo, F., et al.: Dense reinforcement learning for safety validation of autonomous vehicles. Nature **615**(7953), 620–627 (2023)
10. Alex, K., et al.: Learning to drive in a day. In: 2019 International Conference on Robotics and Automation (ICRA), pp. 8248–8254. IEEE (2019)
11. Qiao, Z., et al.: Hierarchical reinforcement learning method for autonomous vehicle behavior planning. In: 2020 IEEE/RSJ International Conference on Intelligent Robots and Systems (IROS), pp. 6084–6089. IEEE (2020)
12. Wang, X., et al.: Traffic light optimization with low penetration rate vehicle trajectory data. Nature Communications **15**(1), 1306 (2024)
13. Najibi, M., et al.: Motion inspired unsupervised perception and prediction in autonomous driving. In: European Conference on Computer Vision, pp. 424–443. Springer (2022)
14. Hai, N., et al.: Hierarchical reinforcement learning under mixed observability. In: International Workshop on the Algorithmic Foundations of Robotics, pp. 188–204. Springer (2022)
15. Hayes, C.F., et al.: A practical guide to multi-objective reinforcement learning and planning. Autonomous Agents and Multi-Agent Systems **36**(1), 26 (2022)

16. Wray, K.H., et al.: Multi-objective policy gradients with topological constraints. In: 2022 IEEE/RSJ International Conference on Intelligent Robots and Systems (IROS), pp. 9034–9039. IEEE (2022)
17. Elia, K., et al.: Champion-level drone racing using deep reinforcement learning. Nature **620**(7976), 982–987 (2023)

High-Level Petri Nets for Modeling Cyber-Physical Multi-Agent Systems

Rui Guerreiro[1,2,4(✉)], João Paulo Barros[3,4], and Luís Gomes[1,4]

[1] Universidade Nova de Lisboa - Faculdade de Ciências e Tecnologia, Caparica, Portugal
lugo@fct.unl.pt
[2] ISEL, Instituto Superior de Engenharia de Lisboa, Lisbon, Portugal
rui.guerreiro@isel.pt
[3] Instituto Politécnico de Beja, Beja, Portugal
joao.barros@ipbeja.pt
[4] UNINOVA - CTS, Caparica, Portugal

Abstract. IOPT Petri nets are commonly used as a formalism for modeling digital control systems, and the existing tools are capable of verifying, simulating, and deploying the implementation of these systems. Low-level Petri nets are sufficient for simple use cases to express the system's behavior. However, using low-level nets quickly becomes challenging to manage for more complex cases, such as multi-agent systems. Furthermore, there is no easy formalism to express the interactions of these systems with Artificial Intelligence systems. To avoid node explosion and net complexity, characteristics of low-level approaches, and the use of high-level nets, with their capability to hold complex data in their tokens, contribute to reducing the net complexity and improving legibility. This leads to the need to develop tools for designing, validating, simulating, and deploying these high-level Petri nets across various target platforms, enabling the construction of cyber-physical multi-agent systems with AI capabilities. This paper outlines some challenges in modeling such systems, focusing on agents with decision-making processes that incorporate artificial intelligence, and proposes a high-level extension to the low-level IOPT net class, aiming for more compact models and more straightforward implementation of such systems.

Keywords: high · level Petri nets · nets · within · nets · IOPT Petri nets · multi · agent systems · AI · powered agents

1 Introduction

Implementing complex, mission-critical, or security-sensitive systems demands precision to ensure they perform as expected. Concurrent, distributed systems are extremely important to solve these types of problems, where Petri nets play a pivotal role [1] and have exact mathematical formalisms that guarantee desired behavior and adequate verification and analysis tools, A critical challenge lies in translating the model into software,

Published by Springer Nature Switzerland AG 2025
L. M. Camarinha-Matos and F. Ferrada (Eds.): DoCEIS 2025, IFIP AICT 759, pp. 250–260, 2025.
https://doi.org/10.1007/978-3-031-97051-1_18

hardware, or hybrid deployments without error. The IOPT Petri net class and its associated tools are designed to address these challenges [2]. However, a significant hurdle remains: modeling intricate concurrent and distributed cyber-physical systems (CPS), such as multi-agent systems (MAS), with low-level Petri nets. This task can quickly become overwhelming. The solution is to employ a high-level Petri net class that retains the automatic code generation capabilities of IOPT nets [3], offering advantages in model compactness and data handling.

A complete cyber-physical multi-agent system can be specified as a unified model, where agents interact with the environment via input/output signals and communicate with each other through messaging mechanisms. The integration of AI technologies into such systems can significantly improve their security, resilience, and efficiency. Multi-agent systems, where each agent is a cyber-physical system, pose challenges due to the real-time constraints typical of CPS [4], alongside the need for collaborative operation in a cooperative environment, where interaction with AI components is increasingly requested [5].

This work contributes to answer the question of which modeling formalism can be used in association with Petri Nets, using the nets-within-nets approach, to support the design of multi-agent, distributed cyber-physical systems.

In light of the previous considerations, this paper presents the relevance of this topic with AI-powered cyber-physical systems in Sect. 2; related work on multi-agent systems and Petri nets in Sect. 3; the proposed extension of IOPT class and an illustrative example in Sect. 4; finally, Sect. 5 presents some conclusions and directions for future work.

2 Relationship with AI-Powered Cyber-Physical Systems

This paper proposes an extension to the IOPT Petri net class, enabling complex multi-agent systems' design, validation, and implementation. The proposed high-level extension leverages the "nets-within-nets" semantics of high-level object-oriented Petri nets [6, 7], tailored for non-autonomous Petri nets. This modification paves the way for novel applications in IoT devices, whether stand-alone or interconnected, across flexible and fault-resilient networks.

Artificial intelligence plays a vital role in enhancing the capabilities of cyber-physical systems, particularly those structured as multi-agent systems. Complex interactions between agents and the environment create opportunities for AI to improve system security, resilience, and effectiveness. Integrating AI with awareness of the physical environment, makes AI-powered CPS systems more robust than traditional approaches. As the underlying technologies mature and their costs decrease, the adoption of such systems is expected to become more widespread.

With this new extension, we aim to model both the control mechanisms and AI-driven interactions in a single, compact model. This represents a significant step towards unifying the design and automatic verification of complex multi-agent cyber-physical systems with AI capabilities.

3 Related Work

3.1 Multi-Agent Systems

An agent is defined as an entity that operates in a specific environment, observes it, gathers knowledge, and makes decisions to affect that environment. These decisions are typically adaptive, evolving based on new observations and prior knowledge [8].

The hallmark of agent-based systems is their flexibility and adaptability. Requirements for such systems include standardization, interoperability, reconfigurability, and scalability [9]. At the system level, multi-agent configurations require support for distribution and reconfiguration [10].

Though agent-based systems have been studied for decades, their implementation in cyber-physical systems remains limited [4] with most research focusing on simulation rather than real-world applications. In a multi-agent system, communication between agents is crucial for system performance and adaptability. Various strategies are available to system designers, each balancing resilience, cost, computational overhead, and latency. Communication in complex MAS applications, especially those involving real-time, data-intensive tasks, is a significant challenge. Traditional communication protocols, being agnostic to the data being transmitted, often result in excessive resource consumption, leading to the development of task-oriented communication techniques that reduce data transmission between agents [5] and where message relevance is considered.

Security, both physical and cyber, is becoming a critical concern in MAS. A physical fault in a cyber-physical agent can lead to incorrect behavior or false information transmission, while a cyber-attack on a single agent could compromise the entire system. Thus, integrating mechanisms for fault detection and mitigation in MAS is essential [11].

Decentralized intelligence, a core feature of MAS, provides resilience to such attacks, as seen in critical systems like smart grids [12]. Techniques like Federated Learning offer promising avenues for securing and detecting intrusions in distributed MAS [13].

The integration of machine learning or deep reinforcement learning in multi-agent systems allows agents to continuously adapt based on their actions and interactions with other agents [14].

Although multi-agent systems have been accepted by computer science and software engineering fields for a long time [15, 16], this approach has gained popularity, particularly as cyber-physical systems have evolved to incorporate sensors and actuators, marking the transition from purely software-based systems to real-world CPS.

The rise of Industry 4.0 and 5.0 emphasized the importance of edge computing and sensor networks, which can be viewed as MAS. Applications such as smart grids and autonomous vehicles highlight the cooperative nature of modern multi-agent systems, optimizing traffic flow and enhancing safety [17–19].

3.2 Petri Nets

Petri Nets, introduced by Carl Adam Petri in his PhD thesis in 1962 [20], have become a powerful modeling tool for concurrent and distributed systems. Over time, Petri net theory has evolved to accommodate increasingly complex systems. In low-level Petri nets, tokens are undifferentiated, and only their count is significant.

Input-Output Place/Transition Petri nets (IOPT Petri nets) are an extension of the classic Place/Transition Petri net (P/T net) class. This class offers the ability to represent the interactions between the Petri net model and the surrounding environment, thus turning them into a non-autonomous Petri net class.

The interactions with the external world are modeled with the use of input and output signals and events:

- Input signals: used to read data from the external world that on a physical system may be associated with physical hardware pins. These signals may be used in guard conditions that inhibit transition firing.
- Output signals: used to manipulate actuators and control physical systems, are also associated with hardware pins. Signal values are controlled by output actions that are activated when specific places are marked, or transitions are fired.
- Input events: triggered by changes in input signal values, are also used to control transition firing.
- Output events: triggered by transition firing, causing changes in the value of output signals.

Each IOPT transition has a priority level, allowing deterministic evolution of the net marking in case several concurrent transitions get enabled simultaneously [21]. To prevent conflicts, IOPT nets also offer test arcs that enable the firing of transitions without removing tokens from the input places. Also, this Petri net class has a maximal step semantics [2], allowing its deterministic execution.

The design of critical mission cyber-physical systems should not be done using ad-hoc methodologies. Petri nets give the developer the tools to verify various properties including the computation of reachability graphs, and check net liveness and boundedness, among others [1, 22].

IOPT Petri nets are ideal for developing embedded systems, offering tools for modeling, analysis, and automatic generation of software or hardware (e.g., VHDL) that implements the system model. This eliminates the need for the designer to write a single line of code.

High-level Petri nets, such as Colored Petri Nets (CPN), extend the concept by allowing tokens to carry data [23]. Object Petri nets (OPNs) adopt an object-oriented approach, where tokens represent system objects with attributes and behaviors [24]. The building blocks of OPNs are of two kinds: System Net and Objects. The System Net is a regular Petri net that defines the overall system behavior and interactions between objects. It has the same structure and behavior as all other classes of Petri nets. Tokens are objects that are associated with individual objects within the system. They represent each object's internal state and behavior, including its attributes and methods, and can be modeled by a finite state machine.

The Object-oriented approach enables a modular representation of the system, while providing a clear separation between the overall system and the internal behaviors of individual objects, promoting better organization and understanding.

Due to the Object-oriented approach, object nets can be reused for different objects with similar functionalities, leading to a potentially more efficient model development.

Finally, the concept of encapsulation means that object-specific details are only known by the object itself, promoting better information hiding.

OPNs are used in various domains where object-oriented concepts are relevant, including modeling complex software systems [25], designing concurrent systems or specifying communication protocols based on the OO approach.

Nets-within-nets build on top of Object Petri nets and go a step further on the complexity of token Objects. The System Net has the same structure and properties as Object PNs, but tokens can be Petri nets [26] and are known as Token Nets.

Nets-within-nets have been mainly used to model autonomous intricate systems with nested behaviors, as a formalism and simulation tool of multi-agent systems, from cellular biology [27] to distributed software systems [28].

The two types of nets, system and tokens, operate together, where transitions in the System Net can trigger the firing of corresponding transitions in specific object nets. This behavior reflects how the system interacts with individual objects. Objects can also communicate with each other by sending and receiving messages, which are represented by tokens flowing through the System Net [6, 7].

Unlike all other high-level Petri net classes, nets-within-nets have additional complexity provided by the dynamic creation and destruction of Token Petri Nets. This behavior makes it more complicated to implement on tools, as we are not creating and destroying pure data (as in the case of all other high-level nets) but instead creating and destroying functionality provided by Token Nets.

However, some of these problems can be avoided by placing some restrictions on the hierarchy and/or semantics, as in the "unary elementary object systems", with its two-level hierarchy, where the System Net's tokens are instances of the same Token Net [29].

High-level Petri net classes such as CPN and nets-within-nets present convenient features and characteristics for modeling complex systems. However, these classes do not provide the capabilities needed to interact with the physical environment or require computational resources incompatible with most CPS-ready hardware (microcontrollers, FPGAs, etc.). Several authors have been working on modeling and analysis of CPS using high-level PNs, but this work has been limited to simulation purposes [30, 31].

Recent work has been done on IOPT Petri net class to extend it towards introducing high-level characteristics, namely some from CPN. This newly proposed extension allows a more compact design enabling implementing cyber-physical systems and their digital twins [3].

4 Modeling Cyber-Physical MAS with High Level PNs

The ongoing work focuses on the necessary formalism needed to express complex distributed cyber-physical systems in terms of a high-level expansion of the low-level IOPT net class, and to accommodate the nets-within-nets paradigm, so this formalism can be used on modeling, verifying and implementing these systems.

This approach also allows the integration of artificial intelligence (AI) techniques in the modeled processes. Object Petri nets, using the paradigm of nets-within-nets with the semantics of Reference nets have been touted as an excellent way of modeling and simulating multi-agent systems [24].

IOPT PNs and their accompanying tools are notable for their capability to model, analyze and automatically generate code and hardware to implement and deploy the models on physical hardware boards, with deterministic behavior. Thus, it is essential that the high-level, nets-within-nets extension of IOPT PNs maintain this characteristic.

Elementary object systems are of special interest, where tokens on the token nets are not nets themselves. This restriction finds much acceptance in the design of MAS-based software implementations, as it offers an intuitive representation for computational units, namely the token nets [32].

The new extension must consider the need for interaction between token nets and the system net, where the former must be able to influence transition firing on the marking or transition firing on the system net.

Another important aspect of research resides on whether to use reference semantics, where tokens on the system net are references to token nets or value semantics of token nets, where tokens on the system net are instances of token nets.

The Renew [6] tool, which implements the nets-within-nets paradigm with reference nets does not have maximal step semantics, therefore does not guarantee deterministic behavior. Also, this tool lacks an explicit non-autonomous component within its constructs, although that can be added though external Java code.

Independently of which semantics is chosen, process migration must be addressed to support distributed implementations. This leads to the need to employ a globally asynchronous locally synchronous (GALS) approach [33].

All these properties should be available to the designer if the developed tools for this approach build on already existing and well-tested low-level IOPT tools. These tools should support input and output signals, and events triggered by specific behaviors of these signals.

Summarizing, this development allows the modeling of multi-agent cyber-physical systems with non-autonomous, high-level Petri nets.

Consider the nets-within-nets classic fire and fireman agents Petri nets as an illustrative example. In Fig. 1 (adapted from [7]) we present an adaptation of that system to integrate input and output signals.

The model contains a System net, with the water source where robotic firefighters fill their buckets (place A), the fire location where firefighters dump water to extinguish the fire (place D), and two intermediary locations (places B and C). Each place with a star mark contains a Token net of type fireman, and its behavioral model is shown in Fig. 2.

The system models a fire that requires three buckets of water to be extinguished, a water source located at some distance from the fire, and three firemen, each carrying a bucket that must be filled at the water location and dumped on the fire. All locations have sensors to detect the arrival of firefighters from each neighboring location. Firefighters move and stop by the commands given by output signals. The system also features outputs to open and close the water tap for filling the bucket at location A, and outputs to discharge the water on the bucket into the fire at location D. Also located at these points 2 sensors indicate, respectively, that the bucket is full and the bucket is empty.

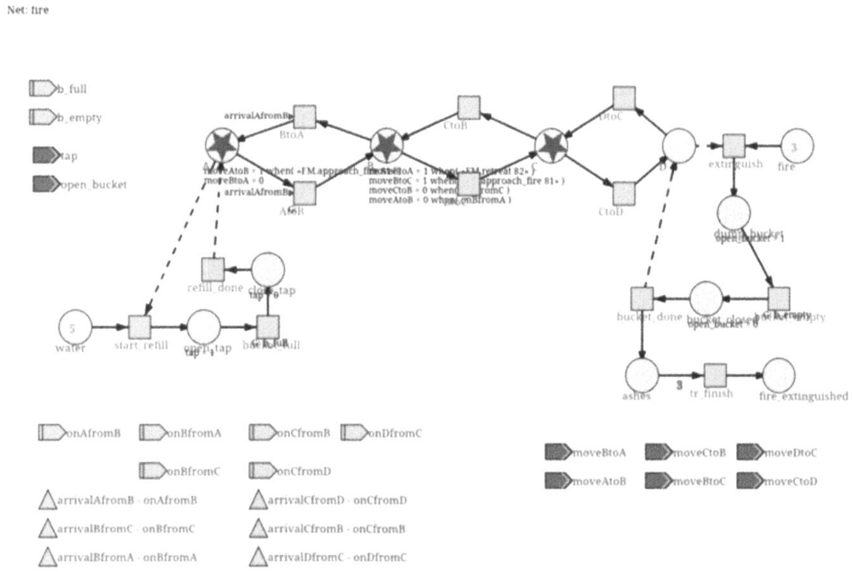

Fig. 1. System net "fire"

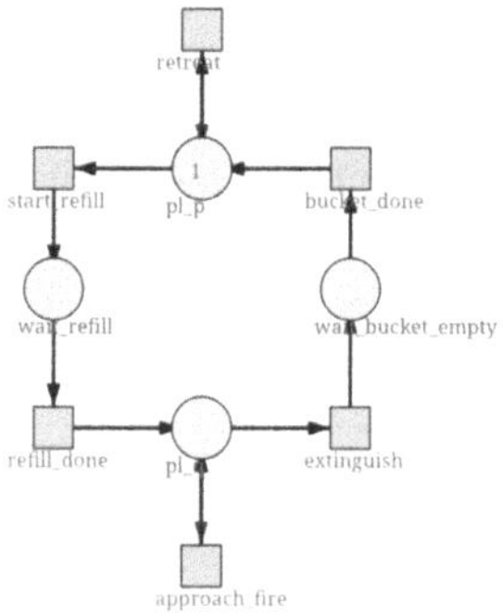

Fig. 2. Token net "fireman"

The system evolves through the interaction of transitions in the agents (fireman nets) and the respective transitions in the System net. Token nets are P/T nets, and their evolution depends on the firing of the homonymous System net's transitions. The relationship is represented on the System net, with the dashed arcs, a dynamic binding of channels between the agents and the system.

The marking of agents also affects their movement between locations. A set of input signals, events, and output signals governs this movement. Each area, from A to D, has specific conditions on the relevant output signals, and the occurrence of certain events governs the transitions of the System net. For clarity and ease of understanding, not all conditions, inputs, and outputs are shown in Fig. 1.

The actions of bucket refill and bucket discharge have their P/T-only parts of the System net. In these locations (A and D, respectively), the agents do not evolve on their internal net, yet the System net will have dot tokens evolving, controlled by inputs and controlling outputs. When a fireman arrives at location A to refill their bucket, transition start_refill fires and a token will be removed from the water to place it on open_tap. At this point, the output tap is activated, and the bucket refill starts. When the bucket is full, input b_full will cause transition bucket_full to fire, causing output tap to become disabled. At this point, transition refill_done on the System net is enabled, leading to the firing of transition refill_done on the Token net (agent).

Upon the arrival of an agent at location D, transition extinguish on the System net gets enabled, and fires, removing a token from the fire place. Output open_bucket is enabled and remains in that state until the bucket is empty (input b_empty). At that moment, System net's transition bucket_done is enabled, and that leads to the firing of the Token net's bucket_done and the agent can now retreat to locations C, B and A where it will refill the bucket. When all three initial tokens are removed from place fire and place ashes contains three tokens, System net tr_finished will fire, ending the fire condition, with a token on the fire_extinguished place.

It is clear that AI-powered cyber-physical systems will play an important role in future technologies. While the mission-critical system controllers and agents should be designed with an exact formalism that can be analyzed and proof-tested, the AI part of the decision-making does not fit well into this mathematical formulation. Therefore, one must consider a communication mechanism between the Petri net part and the AI sub-systems, whether it is run locally or remotely [34], allowing different parts of the model to exist at diverse time domains and exchange data.

The revised agent model, using these mechanisms to implement Federated Learning is presented in Fig. 3. The asynchronous communication channels, working at different time-domains from the agent, will serve the purpose of initially asking for the AI model, receiving it, applying data from the environment (fire intensity, temperature, wind, etc.), or possibly some specific to that particular agent (bucket capacity, speed, etc.), without transmitting it and finally sending the updated model to the AI module, represented on the right of the three asynchronous communication channels.

Recent work has been done on IOPT Petri net class to extend it towards introducing high-level characteristics, namely some from CPN. This newly proposed extension allows a more compact design enabling implementing cyber-physical systems and their digital twins [3].

The token game on this updated agent will be essentially the same. However, in this case, it will be more compact to use a higher-level Petri net class, such as CPN, to model the agent, and better portray acquired data and the required actions recommended by the AI. In this example, the agent will ask for an AI model to the ai_module, add collected information to it, run that model, and then calculate the optimal water flow. When finished, the updated model will be sent back to the AI module through the ai_model_upd channel.

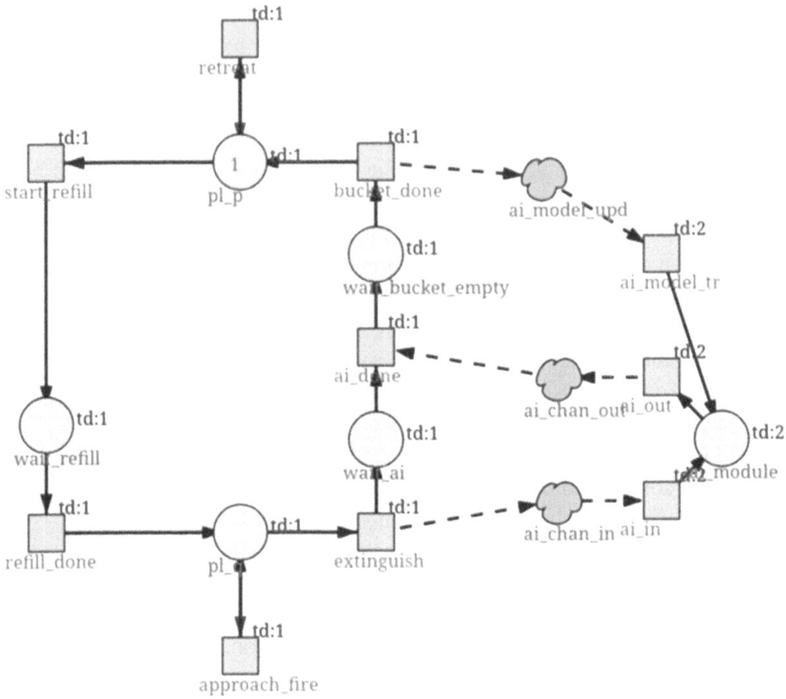

Fig. 3. Modified Token net "fireman" with AI

5 Conclusions and Further Work

Distributed cyber-physical systems can be quite complex to model. IOPT Petri nets provide a formal validation, verification, and analysis mechanism needed to specify concurrency, resource sharing, and interaction with the environment and between system components. The implementation and deployment phase must be made automatically using code generators without human intervention to avoid coding errors.

The proposed extension of the IOPT Petri net class will be designed to allow the modeling and effective deployment of multi-agent cyber-physical systems with the capability of interacting with AI systems to enhance the agents' behavior and ultimately the system's performance, and where coordination and orchestration of agents will be considered.

Even though the presented example does not produce direct evidence, AI-based methods will be modeled as modules with a defined interface, compatible with SaaS approaches, and interact with IOPT through input/output exchanges.

To achieve this goal, a set of extensions to the current IOPT Petri net class specification must be precisely defined and implemented. IOPT tools will also need to support these new extensions and allow the definition of nested high-level Petri nets in the modeling, analysis, verification, and code generation phases. Previous work on low-level IOPT Petri nets will be reused, as it consists of a considerable body of work, with mature and well-tested solutions. Finally, this work aims to diversify the applications range of IOPT beyond the digital controller area, with game design as one of the potential uses, while keeping in mind that simplicity and efficiency of the modeling process are essential.

References

1. Desel, J., Juhás, G.: "What Is a Petri Net?" Informal Answers for the Informed Reader. In: Ehrig, H., Padberg, J., Juhás, G., and Rozenberg, G. (eds.) Unifying Petri Nets: Advances in Petri Nets, pp. 1–25. Springer Berlin Heidelberg, Berlin, Heidelberg (2001). https://doi.org/10.1007/3-540-45541-8_1
2. Gomes, L., Barros, J.P., Costa, A., Nunes, R.: The input-output place-transition petri net class and associated tools. In: 2007 5th IEEE international conference on industrial informatics, pp. 509–514 (2007). https://doi.org/10.1109/INDIN.2007.4384809
3. Lagartinho-Oliveira, C., Moutinho, F., Gomes, L.: Extending IOPT-nets with high-level features: a power wheelchair digital twin case study. In: 2024 8th international young engineers forum on electrical and computer engineering (YEF-ECE), pp. 76–81 (2024). https://doi.org/10.1109/YEF-ECE62614.2024.10625607
4. Ribeiro, L., Gomes, L.: Describing structure and complex interactions in multiagent-based industrial cyber-physical systems. IEEE Access Pract. Innov. Open Solut. **9**, 153126–153141 (2021). https://doi.org/10.1109/ACCESS.2021.3127344
5. He, G., Feng, M., Zhang, Y., Liu, G., Dai, Y., Jiang, T.: Deep reinforcement learning based task-oriented communication in multi-agent systems. IEEE Wirel. Commun. **30**, 112–119 (2023). https://doi.org/10.1109/MWC.003.2200469
6. Kummer, O., et al.: Renew – The Reference Net Workshop, http://www.informatik.uni-hamburg.de/TGI/publikationen/public/data/2003/Kummer+03/Kummer+03.pdf
7. Valk, R.: Object Petri Nets -- Using the Nets-within-Nets Paradigm (2003). https://doi.org/10.1007/b98282
8. Dorri, A., Kanhere, S.S., Jurdak, R.: Multi-agent systems: a survey. IEEE Access Pract. Innov. Open Solut. **6**, 28573–28593 (2018). https://doi.org/10.1109/ACCESS.2018.2831228
9. Jammes, F., Smit, H.: Service-oriented paradigms in industrial automation. IEEE Trans. Ind. Inform. **1**, 62–70 (2005). https://doi.org/10.1109/TII.2005.844419
10. Olsen, S., Wang, J., Ramirez-Serrano, A., Brennan, R.W.: Contingencies-based reconfiguration of distributed factory automation. 14th Int. Conf. Flex. Autom. Intell. Manuf. **21**, 379–390 (2005). https://doi.org/10.1016/j.rcim.2004.11.011
11. Zhang, D., Feng, G., Shi, Y., Srinivasan, D.: Physical safety and cyber security analysis of multi-agent systems: a survey of recent advances. IEEECAA J. Autom. Sin. **8**, 319–333 (2021). https://doi.org/10.1109/JAS.2021.1003820
12. Izmirlioglu, Y., Pham, L., Son, T.C., Pontelli, E.: A survey of multi-agent systems for smartgrids. Energies. **17** (2024). https://doi.org/10.3390/en17153620
13. Ferrag, M.A., Friha, O., Hamouda, D., Maglaras, L., Janicke, H.: Edge-IIoTset: a new comprehensive realistic cyber security dataset of IoT and IIoT applications for centralized and federated learning. IEEE Access Pract. Innov. Open Solut. **10**, 40281–40306 (2022). https://doi.org/10.1109/ACCESS.2022.3165809
14. Oroojlooy, A., Hajinezhad, D.: A review of cooperative multi-agent deep reinforcement learning. Appl. Intell. **53**, 13677–13722 (2023). https://doi.org/10.1007/s10489-022-04105-y
15. Wooldridge, M.: Agent-based software engineering (1997). https://doi.org/10.1049/ip-sen:19971026
16. Zambonelli, F., Jennings, N.R., Wooldridge, M.: Developing multiagent systems: The Gaia methodology. ACM Trans Softw Eng Methodol. **12**, 317–370 (2003). https://doi.org/10.1145/958961.958963

17. Yu, X., Xue, Y.: Smart Grids: A Cyber-Physical Systems Perspective. Proc. IEEE **104**, 1058–1070 (2016). https://doi.org/10.1109/JPROC.2015.2503119
18. Palanisamy, P.: Multi-agent connected autonomous driving using deep reinforcement learning. In: 2020 international joint conference on neural networks (IJCNN), pp. 1–7 (2020). https://doi.org/10.1109/IJCNN48605.2020.9207663
19. Kumar, A., Dhatterwal, J.S., Kumar, S.: MAS for autonomous vehicle coordination in engineering. In: 2024 international conference on electrical electronics and computing technologies (ICEECT), pp. 1–6 (2024). https://doi.org/10.1109/ICEECT61758.2024.10739070
20. Brauer, W., Reisig, W.: Carl Adam Petri and "Petri Nets." In: Fundamental Concepts in Computer Science, pp. 129–139. https://doi.org/10.1142/9781848162914_0007
21. Gomes, L., et al.: Extending input-output place-transition Petri nets for distributed controller systems development. In: 2014 international conference on mechatronics and control (ICMC), pp. 1099–1104 (2014). https://doi.org/10.1109/ICMC.2014.7231723
22. Desel, J., Reisig, W.: The concepts of Petri nets. Softw. Syst. Model. **14**, 669–683 (2015). https://doi.org/10.1007/s10270-014-0423-3
23. Jensen, K., Kristensen, L.M., Wells, L.: Coloured Petri Nets and CPN Tools for modelling and validation of concurrent systems. Int. J. Softw. Tools Technol. Transf. **9**, 213–254 (2007). https://doi.org/10.1007/s10009-007-0038-x
24. Lakos, C.: The Object Orientation of Object Petri Nets. Univ, Tasman (1996)
25. Hong, J.-E., Bae, D.-H.: Software modeling and analysis using a hierarchical object-oriented Petri net. Inf. Sci. **130**, 133–164 (2000). https://doi.org/10.1016/S0020-0255(00)00090-6
26. Valk, R.: Petri Nets as Token Objects. In: Desel, J., Silva, M. (eds.) Application and Theory of Petri Nets 1998, pp. 1–24. Springer, Berlin Heidelberg, Berlin, Heidelberg (1998)
27. Bardini, R., Benso, A., Politano, G., Di Carlo, S.: Nets-within-nets for modeling emergent patterns in ontogenetic processes. Comput. Struct. Biotechnol. J. **19**, 5701–5721 (2021). https://doi.org/10.1016/j.csbj.2021.10.008
28. Köhler-Bussmeier, M., Capra, L.: Robustness: a natural definition based on nets-within-nets. In: PNSE@Petri nets (2023)
29. Köhler-Bußmeier, M., Rölke, H.: Properties of Object Petri Nets. In: Applications and Theory of Petri Nets 2004, p. 297. Springer, Berlin, Heidelberg (2004). https://doi.org/10.1007/978-3-540-27793-4_16
30. He, X.: Modeling and analyzing cyber physical systems using high level petri nets. In: 2018 IEEE international conference on software quality, reliability and security companion (QRS-c), pp. 469–476 (2018). https://doi.org/10.1109/QRS-C.2018.00086
31. Fernandes, N., Barros, J.P., Campos-Rebelo, R.: A graphical and executable model for production simulation in the context of industry 5.0. In: 2022 IEEE 31st international symposium on industrial electronics (ISIE), pp. 233–238 (2022). https://doi.org/10.1109/ISIE51582.2022.9831527
32. Köhler-Bussmeier, M., Capra, L.: Robustness: A natural Definition based on Nets-within-Nets. Presented at the CEUR Workshop Proceedings (2023)
33. Moutinho, F., Gomes, L.: Augmenting High-Level Petri Nets to Support GALS Distributed Embedded Systems Specification. In: Camarinha-Matos, L.M., Tomic, S., Graça, P. (eds.) Technological Innovation for the Internet of Things, pp. 221–228. Springer, Berlin Heidelberg, Berlin, Heidelberg (2013)
34. Moutinho, F., Gomes, L.: Asynchronous-Channels Within Petri Net-Based GALS Distributed Embedded Systems Modeling. IEEE Trans. Ind. Inform. **10**, 2024–2033 (2014). https://doi.org/10.1109/TII.2014.2341933

Intelligent Sensing and Communication Systems

Electronic Noses for Cyber-Physical Systems: Preliminary Results on TiO2 Thin Film as a Humidity Sensor

Tiago Reis[1,2](✉), Paulo A. Ribeiro[1], Susana Sério[1], Maria Helena Fino[2], and Maria Raposo[1]

[1] Laboratory of Instrumentation, Department of Physics, Biomedical Engineering and Radiation Physics (LIBPhys-UNL), LA-REAL, NOVA School of Science and Technology, NOVA University of Lisbon, 2829-516 Caparica, Portugal
tff.reis@campus.fct.unl.pt

[2] Department of Electrical and Computer Engineering, LASI, CTS—Centre for Technology and Systems, UNINOVA, NOVA School of Science and Technology, NOVA University of Lisbon, 2829-516 Caparica, Portugal

Abstract. Cyber-physical systems (CPS) use algorithms to interpret sensor's responses and model the physical environment they are connected to. Among the many application domains where CPS are used, the health-related field is one of the most promising areas that can benefit from CPS. This paper considers the development of sensors to be integrated into an electronic nose, e-nose, that will be responsible for collecting the information to be fed to the cyber component of a CPS. The work presented addresses the challenge of detecting Volatile Organic Compounds (VOCs) in the air at low concentrations with the main goal of diagnosing diseases through breath samples, using an electronic nose (e-nose) concept. Since the identification process of several VOCs can be highly sensitive to the level of humidity in the breath samples, the incorporation of a humidity sensor in the e-nose is proposed as a way of providing information that can be used to guarantee the accuracy of the results to be obtained. To this effect, a TiO_2-based sensor was tested as a solution, and preliminary results are presented. Results demonstrated clearly that it is necessary to maintain the e-nose at a controlled humidity to ensure that the responses from the different e-nose sensors are correct and reliable.

Keywords: e-nose · Cyber-physical systems · CPS · sensor · VOC · TiO2 · humidity

1 Introduction

Cyber-physical systems (CPS) are becoming a mature technology where the physical world is integrated with the cyber (computational) world [1]. As illustrated in Fig. 1, sensors play a fundamental role in CPS, being responsible for collecting data to be transmitted to the cyber system [2]. The collected data is then processed and analyzed in the cyberworld through the cloud and serve as a stimulus to control actuators.

The original version of the chapter has been revised. The Chapter 19 author's name has been corrected. A correction to this chapter can be found at https://doi.org/10.1007/978-3-031-97051-1_30

Published by Springer Nature Switzerland AG 2025
L. M. Camarinha-Matos and F. Ferrada (Eds.): DoCEIS 2025, IFIP AICT 759, pp. 263–274, 2025.
https://doi.org/10.1007/978-3-031-97051-1_19

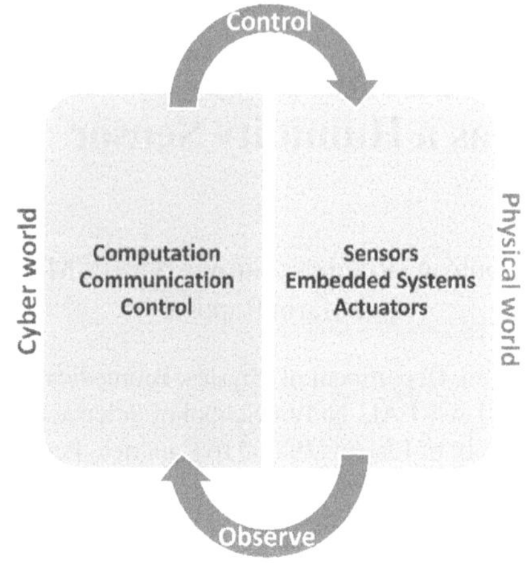

Fig. 1. Cyber-physical Systems overall structure. *Adapted from* [2]

CPSs have been proposed in the literature for a wide range of applications scenarios, such as smart manufacturing, emergency response, critical infrastructure (i.e. distribution of daily life supplies such as water or electricity), healthcare and medicine (i.e., monitoring heath conditions) or Intelligent Transportation (i.e. improving coordination in traffic management), among others [3]. In the particular case of healthcare, the patient's critical data may be collected by sensors and sent through either wired or wireless communication to the cloud, where it is processed, and relevant information regarding the patient's health status is evaluated. This information may be sent back to the CPS actuators to conduct the needed control measures. Given the specificity of the data to be collected healthcare CPS face specific challenges such as the need for granting the interoperability of the sub-systems that feed the patient health condition (e.g., simple/large image data *such as blood sugar level/ magnetic resonance imaging*, personal health history), as well as the accuracy of the evaluation results and the need for securing the protection of the data privacy.

In the process of collecting information regarding patient's health status, one major concern is the need to employ noninvasive techniques. A solution is the use of volatile organic compounds (VOCs) sensors. VOCs are compounds that have a high vapor pressure and low water solubility. In health-related applications, VOCs are usually organic substances that can be found in the air at small concentrations, i.e., parts per trillion (ppt) or parts per million (ppm) [4–7]. Because of this, our main goal is the develop an array of sensors for the detection of the existence of VOCs, associated with the presence of prostate cancer (PCa) through breath samples, as demonstrated in [7]. To collect samples, the patient could blow into a balloon with the sensor array. As such, my PhD work consists of preparing a system that can diagnose PCa by detecting those VOCs.

However, the breath samples are also composed of water vapor at different concentrations that influence the electrical response of the different sensors. So, this work focuses on a humidity sensor, based on TiO_2 thin films, to measure the relative humidity existing in the exhaled air to answer if affordable sensor arrays can be an alternative to powerful yet expensive sensors, the sensitivity to humidity of a metal oxide sensor will be studied.

Besides this introduction, the challenges associated with the use of e-noses, as well as the need for using machine learning techniques for subsequently identifying significant patterns and trends in the information to be used in CPS are addressed in Sect. 2. Section 3 is devoted to the literature review, and then the work developed is presented in Sect. 4. Finally, results are discussed in Sect. 5, whereas conclusions and future work are presented in Sect. 6.

2 VOC Identification with AI-Powered Medical CPSs

Cyber-Physical Systems consider the integration of physical processes with computation and communication. In the case of Medical Cyber-Physical Systems (MCPS), they may comprise robotics and sensor systems with data analysis to create feedback systems that may interact with patients, physicians, or other healthcare professionals. The physical component of CPS for healthcare considers the use of biomedical sensors that are responsible for collecting the relevant physiological data to be fed to the computation and communication system [8].

Over the last decade, systems comprising an array of electronic chemical sensors and an appropriate pattern-recognition module have been proposed as a way of providing an inexpensive way to analyse either gas or aqueous solutions. In the case where gas samples are analysed, these systems are usually referred to as electronic noses (e-noses) [9, 10]. In MCPS, e-noses can be used for diagnosis, monitoring, or phenotyping diseases, with the advantages of being non-invasive and inexpensive.

In diagnosis, e-nose sensors aim at identifying VOCs that can be detected in the exhaled breath. These volatiles may be produced either by cellular metabolic processes or inhaled/absorbed from exogenous sources [11] and the identification of an augmented concentration may lead to the identification of a specific disease. The PhD thesis encompassing this article considers the development of sensors to be integrated into an e-nose system for PCa detection through breath samples.

Another challenge associated with MCPS arises from the need to analyse very large datasets provided by the sensorial system. To overcome this problem, the Principal Component Analysis (PCA) [9] will be used in the pattern recognition module of the e-nose. This will enable the reduction of the dimensions of a dataset while preserving most of the variance in the first two components it generates [12–14]. However, the use of AI techniques for subsequently obtaining more relevant information is envisaged [15–21].

3 Literature Review

The evaluation of the concentration of VOCs has raised a relevant interest in the research community since it can serve to protect humans (e.g., in the detection of hazardous substances such as ammonia) [22–25] and to diagnose diseases, as their existence can correlate to some well-identified process within the body [26–33]. In the case of human protection, the Occupational Safety and Health Administration (OSHA) [34] as well as the European Agency for Safety and Health at Work have established the exposure limits to those VOCs. To diagnose diseases, sometimes just monitoring one VOC can serve as a good indicator [29]. This usually happens when high concentrations (in the ppm) can only be found when the patient is afflicted by a specific disease. However, the precision and range of diseases that VOCs can be used to diagnose can be increased and expanded, respectively, by detecting combinations of VOCs in such cases where the disease can be identified by a unique set of VOCs [6, 7, 35].

When identifying VOCs, the most common method used is Gas chromatography–mass spectrometry (GC–MS) [9, 36]. This method can accurately detect multiple VOCs [26, 36–38]. However, it is expensive, and the samples can suffer thermal degradation [39]. As such, other sensor technologies are being explored as alternatives. Among these, the most common are metal-oxide (MO/MOX) or metal-oxide semiconductor (MOS/SMO), field-effect transistor (FET), Conducting Polymers (CP), and other nanomaterials [9, 10, 40].

MO and FET are affordable while having high operation temperatures [40–43]. Conducting Polymers and nanomaterials have low limits of detection at room temperature, while lacking mechanical strength [44–46]. Electrochemical cells have low power consumption while suffering from poor selectivity [47, 48]. Currently, with these different strengths and weaknesses, no technology has been proven to be the most effective for VOC detection, and, as such, each one of them keeps being developed.

Another relevant approach for VOCs detection is the use of e-noses [9, 10, 49]. These consist of a sensor array that collects data and a pattern recognition unit that extracts relevant features from the multivariable analysis and extrapolates on them to make predictions [50]. This technology has been used for medical applications [14], and it is appropriate for VOC detection as it can enhance the sensors to reach low detection ranges in the presence of a complex matrix [10, 51].

Due to the large dimension of the data generated, methods for selecting the most relevant actors are usually needed. Over the last years, PCA has been the most popular algorithm since it can create areas associated with a class and correlate one or more components with the desired substance. The application of PCA in VOC detection has led to very promising results [26, 27, 37, 38].

As breath samples are practical to take, their study is of high interest. However, they have a high variance in relative humidity and temperature [52], both these factors affect the response of most MO and CP based sensors [53–55].

4 Work Developed

Over the last years, the analysis of exhaled breath has gained interest in the medical community. It yields the possibility for diagnosing different diseases by analysing the concentration, type, and other characteristics of different gases containing trace amounts of both VOCs and some non-volatile components, usually between one ppt and one ppm. The development of e-noses yields the possibility for identifying when one or more gas concentrations exceed a pre-defined range, indicating the presence of specific diseases.

The advantages of using e-noses for diagnosis concern their rapid identification capability, ease of use, portability, and avoidance of discomfort. However, the accuracy and reliability of the diagnosis may be hindered by the e-nose sensor's drift, which may be caused by the variance of the breath sample's relative humidity. To overcome this effect, the incorporation of a humidity sensor into the sensor array could be advantageous. In the literature, TiO_2 sensors have been demonstrated to produce good results in sensing humidity [56–59]. To explore their accuracy using the Impedance Spectra (IS) response, this sensor was chosen to experiment with.

4.1 Humidity Sensor Implementation and Results

TiO_2 is a notorious material for relative humidity (RH) sensors, as they are accurate and operate at room temperature [56–59]. Additionally, as a conducting polymer, it is a type of sensor commonly used in e-noses, making it easy to integrate into a sensor array. Due to these characteristics, a TiO_2 sensor was implemented to help the system monitor the RH and calibrate/correct the response from the other e-nose sensors. Each sensor integrates an interdigitated gold electrode on a ceramic support with a conducting polymer or metal oxide thin film, as demonstrated in [60]. The interdigitated electrodes used were IDEAU 200 from Metrohm DropSens, which have 200 microns lines and gaps.

For testing the sensor behaviour, a cylindrical vacuum chamber with a capacity of 58 dm^3 was used to produce different gas samples in a controlled manner. It consists of a glass and metal seal attached to a pulley system to raise and close the chamber itself. Additionally, it has as outputs for the vacuum pump and receiving air. The input is split and can take air from the room or from a connection to a dry air tank that includes a flask where mixtures can be inserted. Finally, it has BNC ports connected to the sensor(s) inside the chamber. This system is described in [60].

Each sensor can be sampled individually or have its own individual set of relevant features that need to be extracted. As such, measuring the Impedance Spectra response of a sensor is an appealing method when studying a sensor. There are many options for relevant features that can be used to test a sensor's performance, such as: absolute impedance, at a predetermined frequency; phase, at a predetermined frequency; poles and zeros.

As such, an experiment to test the correlation between the humidity in the chamber and the absolute impedance was conducted. The volume of ultrapure water inserted into the chamber was +0.3 ml than the last, starting at 0 ml. To measure each sample, the impedance spectra was considered, and five features were extracted. These were absolute impedance at 1 Hz, phase at 1 Hz, real and imaginary parts of the impedance at 1 Hz, and the Nyquist. In total, six samples were measured, and vacuum was made in the chamber between each sample. When sampling, three loops were measured, and the experiment was repeated twice at different room temperatures (RT). Sample 1 had a higher RT than sample 2. The Nyquist plots and the Impedance Spectra from the samples are illustrated in Figs. 2 and 3, respectively. The extracted features are illustrated in Fig. 4.

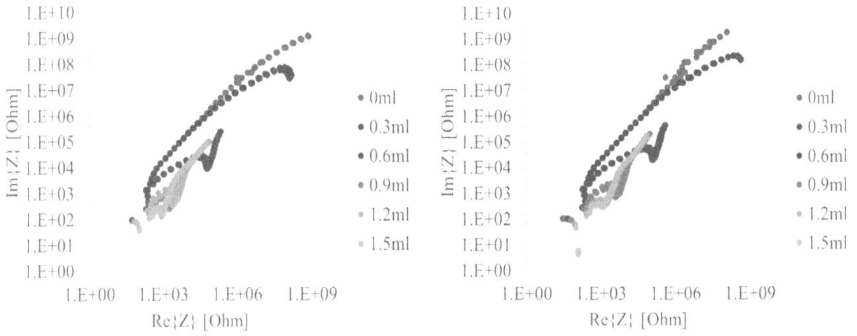

Fig. 2. Nyquist plot for samples 1 and 2 respectively.

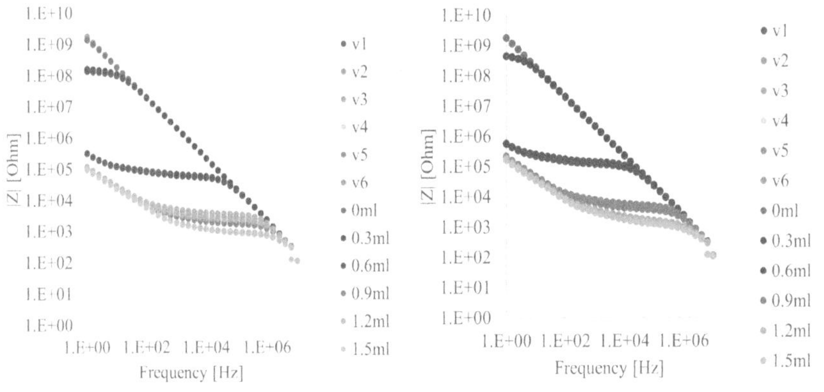

Fig. 3. Impedance Spectra, absolute impedance (|Z|) [Ohm] versus the frequency [Hz] for samples 1 and 2 respectively.

Based on these results, low-humidity samples only become conductive at low frequencies. As such the lower frequency measured was considered when studying the relation with humidity, i.e., 1 Hz.

To further appraise the quality of the absolute impedance and its imaginary part at low frequency, the fitting of both samples was carried out, and Fig. 5 illustrates the results.

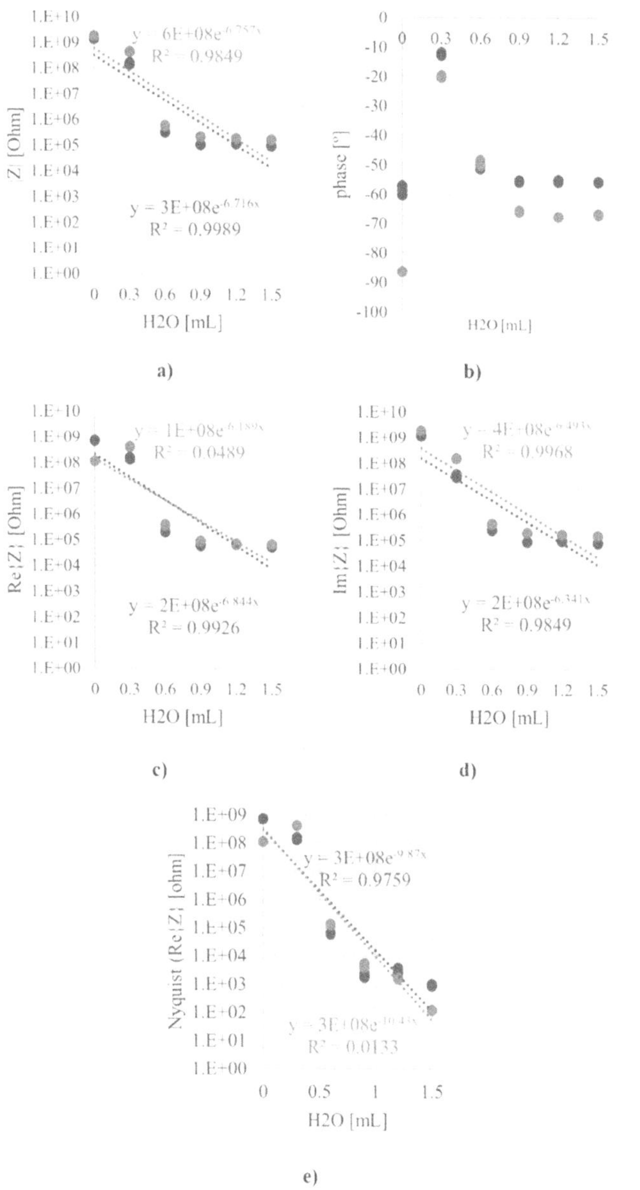

Fig. 4. Humidity response from TiO_2 film, as a function of ultrapure water inserted into the chamber [ml]. 1st sample: blue; 2nd sample: orange. a) |Z| [Ohm], b) Θ[°], c) Re{Z}[Ohm] d) Im{Z}[Ohm]. Each at 1 Hz. e) Nyquist (Re{Z}[Ohm]).

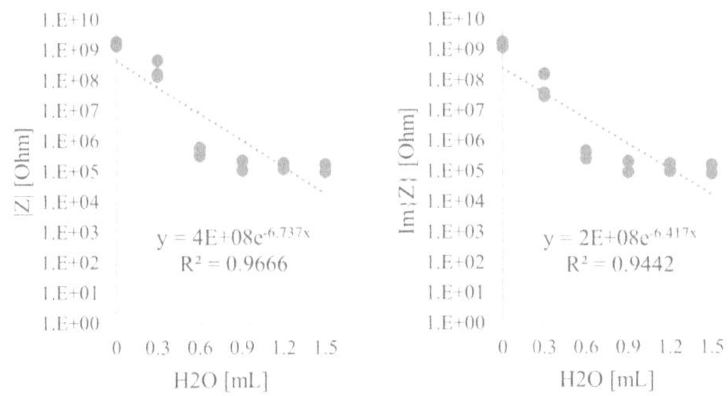

Fig. 5. |Z| and Im{Z} at, 1 Hz respectively, as function of volume of water introduced in the chamber.

5 Data Interpretation and Statistical Considerations

The absolute impedance and the imaginary part at 1 Hz showed the best results according to R^2. The current results also suggest that the phase was not related to the presence of water at 1 Hz. However, other frequencies could produce better results.

The results suggest that the presence of water increases conductivity. This is corroborated by the fact that the results with dry air and 0 ml of water are equivalent to those in the vacuum. However, the impedance plateaus at approximately 10^5 Ohms from 0.9 ml.

The results indicate a clear tendency. However, two factors still need to be controlled to achieve better results. First, the temperature inside the chamber was not monitored. Second, the samples were measured immediately after atmospheric pressure was reached inside the chamber, and as such, there was no time for the humidity to reach an equilibrium inside the chamber.

6 Conclusions and Future Work

This paper presented the preliminary experimental results for an RH sensor based on TiO_2 thin film to be used in the sensorial part of an e-nose system. In particular, the absolute impedance and its imaginary parts showed considerable sensitivity and reproducibility. Additionally, both absolute impedance and imaginary part had good fittings, with R^2 of 0.9666 and 0.9442, respectively. Although the obtained results show a good correlation between the presence of water and the conductivity of the device, the experimental conditions still need to be optimized so that more consistent results may be obtained. As such, future work will consist of repeating the experiments five times while monitoring the RH in the chamber in real-time until it reaches equilibrium. It is expected that under those conditions, enough data will be obtained to state definitively whether the TiO_2 thin film is appropriate to integrate into the sensor array.

Acknowledgments. This work was funded by Fundação para a Ciência e Tecnologia (FCT, Portugal) through national funds [UIDB/04559/2020 (LIBPhys)], [UIDP/04559/2020 (LIBPhys)],

[UI/BD/151321/2021], [LA/P/0117/2020], [PTDC/FIS-NAN/0909/2014], and Portuguese FCT program, Centre of Technology and Systems (CTS) CTS/00066.

References

1. García-Valls, M., Dubey, A., Botti, V.: Introducing the new paradigm of social dispersed computing: applications, technologies and challenges. J. Syst. Architect. **91**, 83–102 (2018). https://doi.org/10.1016/j.sysarc.2018.05.007
2. Khater, H.M., Sallabi, F., Serhani, M.A.: Empowering healthcare with cyber-physical system — a systematic literature review. IEEE Access. **12**, 83952–83993 (2024). https://doi.org/10.1109/ACCESS.2024.3407376
3. Gunes, V., Peter, S., Givargis, T., Vahid, F.: A survey on concepts, applications, and challenges in cyber-physical systems. KSII Trans. Internet Inf. Syst. **8**, 4242–4268 (2014). https://doi.org/10.3837/tiis.2014.12.001
4. Moura, P.C., Ribeiro, P.A., Raposo, M., Vassilenko, V.: The state of the art on graphene-based sensors for human health monitoring through breath biomarkers. Sensors **23**, (2023). https://doi.org/10.3390/s23229271
5. Vassilenko, V., Moura, P.C., Raposo, M.: Diagnosis of carcinogenic pathologies through breath biomarkers: present and future trends. Biomedicines **11** (2023). https://doi.org/10.3390/biomedicines11113029
6. Moura, P.C., Raposo, M., Vassilenko, V.: Breath biomarkers in Non-Carcinogenic diseases. Clinica Chimica Acta. **552**, 117692 (2024). https://doi.org/10.1016/j.cca.2023.117692
7. Moura, P.C., Raposo, M., Vassilenko, V.: Breath volatile organic compounds (VOCs) as biomarkers for the diagnosis of pathological conditions: A review. Biomed J. **46**, 100623 (2023). https://doi.org/10.1016/j.bj.2023.100623
8. Haque, S.A., Aziz, S.M., Rahman, M.: Review of Cyber-Physical System in Healthcare Review of Cyber-Physical System in Healthcare. (2014). https://doi.org/10.1155/2014/217415
9. Queralto, N., Berliner, A.N., Goldsmith, B., Martino, R., Rhodes, P., Lim, S.H.: Detecting cancer by breath volatile organic compound analysis: a review of array-based sensors. J. Breath Res. **8**, 027112 (2014). https://doi.org/10.1088/1752-7155/8/2/027112
10. Rabehi, A., Helal, H., Zappa, D., Comini, E.: Advancements and prospects of electronic nose in various applications: a comprehensive review. Applied Sciences. **14** (2024). https://doi.org/10.3390/app14114506
11. Mazzone, P.J.: Analysis of Volatile Organic Compounds in the Exhaled Breath for the Diagnosis of Lung Cancer. J. Thorac. Oncol. **3**, 774–780 (2008). https://doi.org/10.1097/JTO.0b013e31817c7439
12. Wold, S., Esbensen, K., Geladi, P.: Principal component analysis. Chemometrics and Intelligent Laboratory Systems **2**, 37–52 (1987). https://doi.org/10.1016/0169-7439(87)80084-9
13. Rasmus, B., Age, K.S.: Principal component analysis. Anal. Methods **6**, 2812–2831 (2014)
14. Jolliffe Ian, T., Jorge, C.: Principal component analysis: a review and recent developments. Royal Society **374** (2016)
15. Murthy, N.S., Bethala, C.: Review paper on research direction towards cancer prediction and prognosis using machine learning and deep learning models. J. Ambient. Intell. Humaniz. Comput. **14**, 5595–5613 (2023). https://doi.org/10.1007/s12652-021-03147-3
16. Ibrahim, A., Mohamed, H.K., Maher, A., Zhang, B.: A survey on human cancer categorization based on deep learning. Front Artif Intell. **5** (2022)

17. Kumar, Y., Gupta, S., Singla, R., Hu, Y.-C.: A systematic review of artificial intelligence techniques in cancer prediction and diagnosis. Archi. Computat. Methods in Eng. **29**, 2043–2070 (2022). https://doi.org/10.1007/s11831-021-09648-w
18. Mokoatle, M., et al.: A review and comparative study of cancer detection using machine learning: SBERT and SimCSE application. BMC Bioinformatics **24**, 112 (2023). https://doi.org/10.1186/s12859-023-05235-x
19. Shah, B., Alsadoon, A., Prasad, P.W.C., Al-Naymat, G., Beg, A.: DPV: a taxonomy for utilizing deep learning as a prediction technique for various types of cancers detection. Multimed Tools Appl. **80**, 21339–21361 (2021). https://doi.org/10.1007/s11042-021-10769-4
20. Huang, S., Yang, J., Fong, S., Zhao, Q.: Artificial intelligence in cancer diagnosis and prognosis: opportunities and challenges. Cancer Lett. **471**, 61–71 (2020). https://doi.org/10.1016/j.canlet.2019.12.007
21. Rai, H.M., Yoo, J., Atif Moqurrab, S., Dashkevych, S.: Advancements in traditional machine learning techniques for detection and diagnosis of fatal cancer types: Comprehensive review of biomedical imaging datasets. Measurement. **225**, 114059 (2024). https://doi.org/10.1016/j.measurement.2023.114059
22. Sun, C., et al.: Indoor exposure levels of ammonia in residences, schools, and offices in China from 1980 to 2019: A systematic review. Indoor Air. **31**, 1691–1706 (2021). https://doi.org/10.1111/ina.12864
23. Service, R.F.: New recipe produces ammonia from air, water, and sunlight. Science **345**(1979), 610 (2014). https://doi.org/10.1126/science.345.6197.610
24. Canter, L.W.: Nitrates in Groundwater. Routledge, New York (1997). https://doi.org/10.1201/9780203745793
25. Kinidi, L., et al.: Recent development in ammonia stripping process for industrial wastewater treatment. Int. J. Chem. Eng. **2018**, 3181087 (2018). https://doi.org/10.1155/2018/3181087
26. Peng, G., et al.: Detection of lung, breast, colorectal, and prostate cancers from exhaled breath using a single array of nanosensors. Br. J. Cancer **103**, 542–551 (2010). https://doi.org/10.1038/sj.bjc.6605810
27. Peng, G., Trock, E., Haick, H.: Detecting simulated patterns of lung cancer biomarkers by random network of single-walled carbon nanotubes coated with nonpolymeric organic materials. Nano Lett. **8**, 3631–3635 (2008). https://doi.org/10.1021/nl801577u
28. Bosso, N., et al.: Human urine biomarkers of renal cell carcinoma evaluated by ClinProt. Proteomics Clin. Appl. **2**, 1036–1046 (2008). https://doi.org/10.1002/prca.200780139
29. Ganti, S., et al.: Urinary acylcarnitines are altered in human kidney cancer. Int. J. Cancer. **130**, 2791–2800 (2012). https://doi.org/10.1002/ijc.26274
30. Eyben, F.E.V.: Biochemical markers in advanced testicular tumors. Serum lactate dehydrogenase, urinary chorionic gonadotropin and total urinary estrogens. Cancer. **41**, 648–652 (1978). https://doi.org/10.1002/1097-0142(197802)41:2<648::AID-CNCR2820410231>3.0.CO;2-M
31. Bax, C., Lotesoriere, B.J., Sironi, S., Capelli, L.: Review and comparison of cancer biomarker trends in urine as a basis for new diagnostic pathways. Cancers (Basel) **11**, (2019). https://doi.org/10.3390/cancers11091244
32. Zhou, J., Huang, Z.-A., Kumar, U., Chen, D.D.Y.: Review of recent developments in determining volatile organic compounds in exhaled breath as biomarkers for lung cancer diagnosis. Anal Chim. Acta. **996**, 1–9 (2017). https://doi.org/10.1016/j.aca.2017.09.021
33. Gallagher, M., Wysocki, C.J., Leyden, J.J., Spielman, A.I., Sun, X., Preti, G.: Analyses of volatile organic compounds from human skin. Br. J. Dermatol. **159**, 780–791 (2008). https://doi.org/10.1111/j.1365-2133.2008.08748.x
34. Occupational Safety and Health Administration (OSHA): Permissible Exposure Limits – Annotated Tables

35. Califf, R.M.: Biomarker definitions and their applications. Exp. Biol. Med. **243**, 213–221 (2018). https://doi.org/10.1177/1535370217750088
36. Sun, X., Shao, K., Wang, T.: Detection of volatile organic compounds (VOCs) from exhaled breath as noninvasive methods for cancer diagnosis. Anal. Bioanal. Chem. **408**, 2759–2780 (2016). https://doi.org/10.1007/s00216-015-9200-6
37. Hakim, M., et al.: Diagnosis of head-and-neck cancer from exhaled breath. Br. J. Cancer **104**, 1649–1655 (2011). https://doi.org/10.1038/bjc.2011.128
38. Peng, G., et al.: Diagnosing lung cancer in exhaled breath using gold nanoparticles. Nat. Nanotechnol. **4**, 669–673 (2009). https://doi.org/10.1038/nnano.2009.235
39. Lee, H.Z.S., Ong, M.C., Lim, J.L.W., Yap, T.W.A.: Challenges in GC–MS analysis: Case studies on phenibut and ethylphenidate. Forensic Sci. Int. **277**, 166–178 (2017). https://doi.org/10.1016/j.forsciint.2017.06.002
40. Kwak, D., Lei, Y., Maric, R.: Ammonia gas sensors: a comprehensive review. Talanta. **204**, 713–730 (2019). https://doi.org/10.1016/j.talanta.2019.06.034
41. Ostrick, B., Pohle, R., Fleischer, M., Meixner, H.: TiN in work function type sensors: a stable ammonia sensitive material for room temperature operation with low humidity cross sensitivity. Sens Actuators B Chem. **68**, 234–239 (2000). https://doi.org/10.1016/S0925-4005(00)00434-2
42. Korotcenkov, G.: Metal oxides for solid-state gas sensors: What determines our choice? Materials Science and Engineering: B. **139**, 1–23 (2007). https://doi.org/10.1016/j.mseb.2007.01.044
43. Huang, J., et al.: A novel highly sensitive gas ionization sensor for ammonia detection. Sens Actuators A Phys. **150**, 218–223 (2009). https://doi.org/10.1016/j.sna.2009.01.008
44. Verma, A., Gupta, R., Verma, A.S., Kumar, T.: A review of composite conducting polymer-based sensors for detection of industrial waste gases. Sensors and Actuators Reports. **5**, 100143 (2023). https://doi.org/10.1016/j.snr.2023.100143
45. Bai, H., Shi, G.: Gas sensors based on conducting polymers. Sensors. **7**, 267–307 (2007). https://doi.org/10.3390/s7030267
46. Liu, H., Kameoka, J., Czaplewski, D.A., Craighead, H.G.: Polymeric nanowire chemical sensor. Nano Lett. **4**, 671–675 (2004). https://doi.org/10.1021/nl049826f
47. Xiong, L., Compton, R.G.: Amperometric gas detection: a review. Int. J. Electrochem Sci. **9**, 7152–7181 (2014). https://doi.org/10.1016/S1452-3981(23)10957-6
48. Penza, M., Milella, E., Anisimkin, V.I.: Gas sensing properties of Langmuir-Blodgett polypyrrole film investigated by surface acoustic waves. IEEE Trans. Ultrason. Ferroelectr. Freq. Control **45**, 1125–1132 (1998). https://doi.org/10.1109/58.726434
49. Richards, E., Bessant, C., Saini, S.: Multivariate data analysis in electroanalytical chemistry. Electroanalysis. **14**, 1533–1542 (2002). https://doi.org/10.1002/1521-4109(200211)14:22<1533::AID-ELAN1533>3.0.CO;2-T
50. Paulovich, F.V., et al.: Information visualization techniques for sensing and biosensing. Analyst. **136**, 1344–1350 (2011). https://doi.org/10.1039/C0AN00822B
51. Oliveira, O.N., Pavinatto, F.J., Constantino, C.J.L., Paulovich, F.V., de Oliveira, M.C.F.: Information visualization to enhance sensitivity and selectivity in biosensing. Biointerphases **7**, 1–15 (2012). https://doi.org/10.1007/s13758-012-0053-7
52. Mansour, E., et al.: Measurement of temperature and relative humidity in exhaled breath. Sens Actuators B Chem. **304**, 127371 (2020). https://doi.org/10.1016/j.snb.2019.127371
53. Wang, C., Yin, L., Zhang, L., Xiang, D., Gao, R.: Metal oxide gas sensors: sensitivity and influencing factors. Sensors. **10**, 2088–2106 (2010). https://doi.org/10.3390/s100302088
54. Matsuguchi, M., Okamoto, A., Sakai, Y.: Effect of humidity on NH3 gas sensitivity of polyaniline blend films. Sens Actuators B Chem. **94**, 46–52 (2003). https://doi.org/10.1016/S0925-4005(03)00325-3

55. Nohria, R., et al.: Humidity sensor based on ultrathin polyaniline film deposited using layer-by-layer nano-assembly. Sens Actuators B Chem. **114**, 218–222 (2006). https://doi.org/10.1016/j.snb.2005.04.034
56. Li, P., Yang, F.: Preparation and performance of TiO2/ZnO humidity sensor based on TiO2. Materials Science and Engineering: B. **298**, 116902 (2023). https://doi.org/10.1016/j.mseb.2023.116902
57. Ghalamboran, M., Saedi, Y.: TiO2-TiO2 composite resistive humidity sensor: ethanol crosssensitivity. IOP Conf Ser Mater Sci Eng. **108**, 012039 (2016). https://doi.org/10.1088/1757-899X/108/1/012039
58. Yu, W., Chen, D., Li, J., Zhang, Z.: TiO2-SnS2 Nanoheterostructures for High-Performance Humidity Sensor. Crystals (Basel). **13** (2023). https://doi.org/10.3390/cryst13030482
59. Atalay, S., Izgi, T., Kolat, V.S., Erdemoglu, S., Inan, O.O.: Magnetoelastic Humidity Sensors with TiO2 Nanotube Sensing Layers. Sensors. **20** (2020). https://doi.org/10.3390/s20020425
60. Magro, C., et al.: Volatile organic compound monitoring during extreme wildfires: assessing the potential of sensors based on LbL and sputtering films. Sensors. **22** (2022). https://doi.org/10.3390/s22176677

AI for Plasmonic Nanoparticles: A Tool to Improve the Colorimetric Detection of PoC Devices

Caterina Serafinelli[1,2,3,4](✉), Alessandro Fantoni[1,3], Elisabete C. B. A. Alegria[1,2], and Manuela Vieira[1,3,4]

[1] Lisbon School of Engineering (ISEL)/Polytechnic University of Lisbon (IPL), Lisbon, Portugal
c.serafinelli@campus.fct.unl.pt

[2] Centro de Química Estrutural, Institute of Molecular Sciences, IST, Universidade de Lisboa, Lisbon, Portugal

[3] UNINOVA-CTS and LASI, Caparica, Portugal

[4] NOVA School of Science and Technology, Caparica, Portugal

Abstract. Colorimetric detection based on plasmonic nanoparticles is attracting a growing attention for the development of user-friendly devices. The *Color Picker System*, is a sensing device developed aiming to fast and reliable analysis of next generation, where the results are displayed on a smartphone and at the same time could be shared with the family doctor or an health center. A central part of the sensing mechanism is an array of plasmonic metal nanoparticles, which properties determine the sensing capability of the device. Herein, an Artificial Intelligence algorithm will be applied in order to classify spectra of different types of particles.

Keywords: AI algorithm · Plasmonic Nanoparticles · IoT · PoC devices

1 Introduction

In standard clinical practice, the diagnosis and the prognosis of diseases oncoming, progression or regression is performed on light of biomarkers present in human body fluids, and their early detection is a critical point to improve the chances of survival [1]. Within this contest, medical diagnostics is evolving towards portable sensing systems, the Point-of-Care (PoC) devices that allow a fast and reliable analysis of diagnostic biomarkers outside from the common clinics practice such as hospitals, emergency room or doctor office [2].

In colorimetric sensing the readout assessment of the color change is performed by naked eyes, without requiring the use of spectrometers, allowing a fast, simple and low-cost analysis. For its intrinsic properties colorimetric detection of molecules is attracting a growing attention during the last decades for the development of PoC devices [3].

In that scenario, noble metal nanoparticles stand out due to their remarkable optical properties arising from their Localized Surface Plasmon Resonance (LSPR), i.e. coherent

L. M. Camarinha-Matos and F. Ferrada (Eds.): DoCEIS 2025, IFIP AICT 759, pp. 275–290, 2025.
https://doi.org/10.1007/978-3-031-97051-1_20

and collective oscillations of free electrons of metallic nanoparticles upon excitation with an electromagnetic radiation [4]. The properties of the LSPR band such as width and resonance frequency rely on the NP size, shape and local dielectric surrounding [5].

Their LSPRs confer broad versatility for the development of sensing devices [6], and over the last two decades the use of nanostructures to generate plasmonic colors has produced a huge advancement in the implementation of innovative colorimetric approaches for molecule detection [7, 8].

While their optical properties have found applications for colorimetric detection, research is fueling on colloidal synthesis and assembly of plasmonic nanoparticles. During the last decades, the development of wet chemistry protocols for the synthesis of plasmonic metal nanoparticles evolved from spherical particles to anisotropic structures such as rods, stars, flowers, decahedra etc., obtaining a fine spectral LSPR tunability, from the Ultraviolet (UV) to far-infrared (IR) [9, 10].

Scaling up the optical properties of the plasmonic nanoparticles into real world applications requires a tight control on the particle characteristics, such as shape, size and dielectric environment. For example, it has been demonstrated that particles with large absorption cross section, and thus higher values for absorbance, improved the absorption of the light, enhancing the power conversion efficiency (PCE) of thin film polymer or organic solar cells (PSCs or OSCs) [11]. In this context, the manipulation of the AuNPs properties can lead to the development of new polymer solar cells for commercial use with the desired parameters and improved performances.

Motivated by the need for a fast and accurate analytical method suitable for home use, we are developing a sensing device—referred to as the *Color Picker System*—for the colorimetric detection of molecules based on the plasmonic colors of metal nanoparticles [12].

The *Color Picker Syste*m is an easy-to-use device for colorimetric quantification of the target analyte, eliminating the need for bulky instruments or trained personnel. It is designed to detect color changes resulting from biorecognition events occurring on the surface of particle arrays.

It is able to reproduce in the backlight of an I2C LCD 1602 RGB Display the color detected by the TCS34725 color sensor.

The DFRobot I2C LCD 1602 display and the TCS34725 Color sensor are controlled by Arduino Nano RP2040 provided with Wi-Fi® and Bluetooth® connectivity.

The Wi-Fi connectivity enables the synchronization between the Arduino Nano microcontroller and the Arduino Cloud Platform. The IoT Remote application enables the access to the data returned from the sensor with a common smartphone, so that the color changes in the plasmonic paper arising from the presence the analyte molecules will appear on the display.

The device through the connectivity can send data to the family doctor, medical center or hospital for a rapid response as well as to provide the possibility to perform a "home-made" approach for the analysis.

In Fig. 1 the *Color Picker System* is shown while measuring the color of the plasmonic paper. In the picture it is possible to observe the display of the smartphone visualizing the detected color as well as the TCS34725 color sensor at the bottom of the plasmonic paper, and the DFRobot 1602 display showing the measured RGB values, both controlled by Arduino Nano RP2040 microcontroller. Also, it is possible to note the power bank, inserted to introduce the portability into the system.

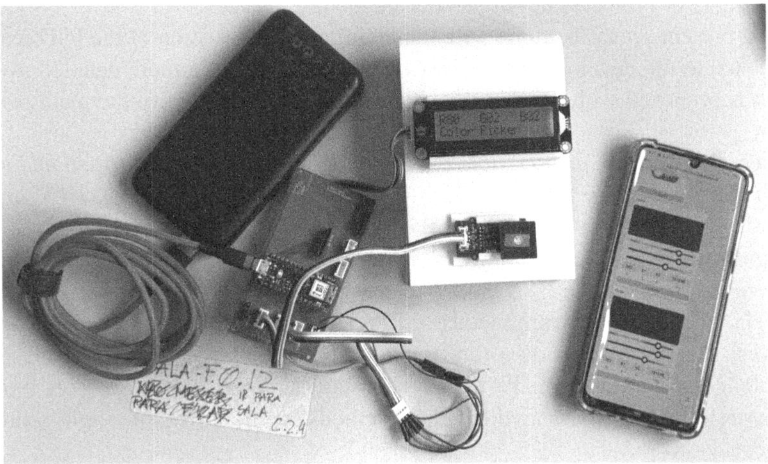

Fig. 1. *Color Picker System* measuring the color of the plasmonic paper.

The transducer of the *Color Picker System* is the plasmonic paper, arrays of plasmonic metal nanoparticles integrated into the three-dimensional fiber network of paper, and its properties are crucial for the performances of the device. Aiming to improve sensitivity and precision, in a previous work we found that arrays of particles with LSPR with high absorbance and localized at longer wavelengths produces the largest chromatic changes resulting in suitable candidates for the integration into the setup of the system [13]. In Fig. 2 a schematic illustrating the filtering properties of the plasmonic paper is reported.

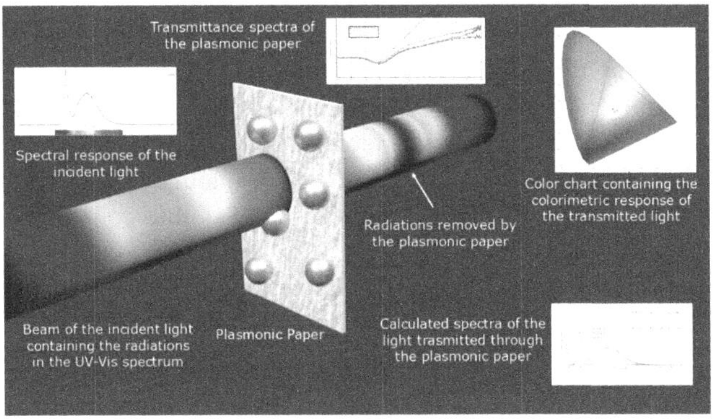

Fig. 2. Schematic of the filtering properties of the plasmonic paper from ref. [13]. Particles with higher absorbance and LSPR shifted at longer wavelengths result in higher chromatic changes increasing the sensitivity of colorimetric devices.

Although wet chemistry provides an exquisite control on the synthesis of plasmonic nanoparticles, identifying plasmonic particles with the desired optical properties for the implementation of advanced applications becomes a more and more difficult task in light of the plethora of protocols developed during the last decades.

In the present scenario, along with the main research question of the PhD research work related to the development of the *Color Picker System*, a more detailed research question is proposed with the aim to better understand and solidify the main research question.

Research question: *is it possible to develop a tool for the classification and recognition of metal plasmonic paper alternative to Dinamic Light Scattering (DLS) or TEM pictures?*

Hypothesis: "*Create a tool for the recognition and classification of plasmonic metal nanoparticles based on the CNN models*".

Herein, CNN models are presented to differentiate and classify the UV-visible spectra of AuNPs. We aim to provide a tool for the rational classification of the plasmonic nanoparticles properties to make their recognition simpler. It is a low-cost tool that can be considered an alternative to other methods, such as dynamic light scattering equipment.

Despite the benefits, some inaccuracies could arise when using the proposed CNN models. The dataset for the model training is composed of simulated spectra that take into account only the refractive index of the bulk medium, without considering the effect of the molecules functionalizing the particle surface. In practice, the position of the LSPR peak is affected also by the capping molecules: particles with same shape and size but functionalized with different ligands present LSPR peaks localized at different wavelengths.

2 Relationship of the Research Work with AI-Powered Cyber Physical Systems

The DoCeis 2025 has been organized to share research on AI powered Cyber Physical Systems (AI-powered CPS) so that in this section the proposed work will be inserted into the context of the conference. The first step to establish a relationship between the and the main topic of the conference is to identify the *Color Picker System* as a CPS.

Cyber Physical Systems (CPS) are a new type of intelligent systems that integrate communication, computing and control technologies [14], thus connecting the physical world and cyberspace.

In the work of Guzman [15] the critical features of the CPS have been defined as the combination of:

- Cooperative control through networked systems
- Real-time feedback control of physical processes through actuators and sensors.
- A threshold of automation level.

Different from CPS technology, Internet of Things (IoT) is a large network comprising web enabled smart devices employing incorporate systems such as sensors, processors and communication hardware to gather and send data [16].

Whereas IoT systems have just the perception of the physical world with simple or no control, CPSs are endowed with a strong controlling capability in addition to the perception [17]. Some of the main differences between IoT and CPS systems have been listed in Table 1 [15].

Table 1. Main differences between the IoT and CPS technologies.

	Internet of Things (IoT)	*Cyber Physical Systems (CPS)*
Final services	Mobile apps, cloud applications	Physical systems executing real-time control tasks in the physical world
Control actions	Limited to the awareness of information such as message display or sound notification for surveillance or monitoring	Control actions affect the new state of the sensor readings by actuator commands with effects in the physical world

Despite their distinct origin, most of the analysis recognizes an overlap between the CPS and IoT technologies and it has been possible to individuate four categories of overlapping [18], and in some cases, CPS are considered the grownup development of IoT [19].

In the *Color Picker System*, the color sensor TCS34725 and the microcontroller Arduino Nano RP2040 are connected through a wireless network, with the possibility of data monitoring by means of mobile app. The control is limited to the user awareness of the information, without affecting the physical space, so that can be classified as an IoT system. Considering IoT systems not isolated technologies, but an overlap with CPS technology, the Color Picker System can be regarded as a subset of CPS.

The second step to get a connection between the conference main theme and the proposed work is to identify the role of Artificial Intelligence in the Color Picker System.

Artificial Intelligence (AI) points out to emulate human-level intelligence in machines. Machine learning (ML) is focalized in the development of methods able to learn from dataset finding applications in different fields such as computer vision, medical science or speech recognition.

Deep Learning (DL) models are a subset of ML, take as model the functionality and structure of the human nervous system and brain, utilizing input, hidden and output layers to coordinate processing units. The nodes or the units of each layer are interconnected with those in the bottom layer [20].

Convolutional Neural Networks (CNN) are a class of DL models broadly applied in different fields, such as computer vision, image classification or object detection. A CNN is a type of neural network capable of extracting features from data with a convolution structure [21]. In Fig. 3 the relationship between AI, ML, DL and CNN is shown.

The transducer of the *Color Picker System* is the plasmonic paper, so that the synthesis of plasmonic metal nanoparticles plays a critical role for its development and performances. Herein we propose to develop a CNN model for the classification and

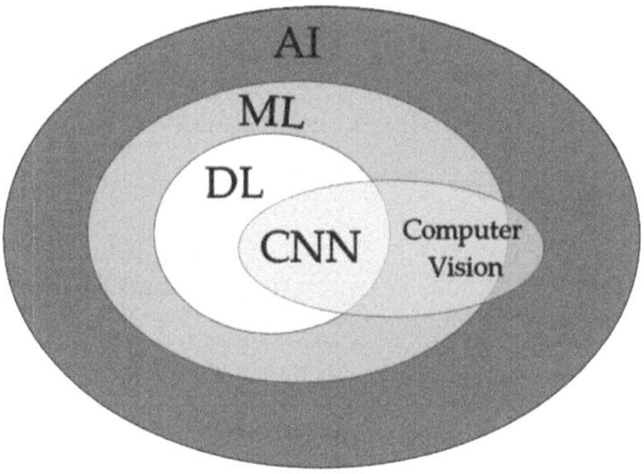

Fig. 3. Diagram of the relationship between AI and CNN

recognition of the metal plasmonic nanoparticles aiming to facilitate the preparation of the plasmonic paper that will be integrated into the device.

More appropriately, in the present work AI algorithms are not integrated into the system but rather have been developed as a tool for its implementation in real world applications. Anyway, the setup of the Color Picker Systems opens the way for the integration of AI. For example the Arduino Nano board could be replaced with a fpga board, that elaborates the data received from a multiplexed trasducer based on plasmonic structures, thus developing a fully AI powered-Cyber Physical System.

3 CNN for Plasmonic Metal Nanoparticles

In a previous work [22], a supervised learning model based on Convolutional Neural Network (CNN) has been developed to differentiate and classify Raman Spectra. The training and the design of the model has been performed using the spectra of methanol-ethanol mixtures with different compositions.

A supervised learning model with the same architecture will be designed and tested for the classification and the recognition of UV-Vis. Spectra of metal nanoparticles. The application of that model can facilitate the selection of a particular kind of metal nanoparticles on the basis of their optical properties. It allows to individuate particles with the specific optical properties required for the implementation of advanced systems and technologies.

The development of the supervised learning model is articulated in two main steps. Firstly, we create a population of UV-Vis. Spectra of different types of plasmonic nanoparticles by means of a simulation process based on the Discrete Dipole Approximation (DDA) which are the data set used to train the model. Upon training, the designed model will be used to make predictions and classify the spectra.

3.1 Data Acquisition

Several approaches have been used to describe the optical properties of plasmonic metal nanoparticles and between them the DDA is the most widely used for the reduced complexity of calculations.

In DDA the particle is discretized into an array of N cubic elements, referred to as voxel, in which each element is viewed as a dipole. The final optical response of each element results from the sum of the incident light electric field and its N-1 neighboring elements [23].

The key issue of DDA is to compute the polarization of each dipole (cubical voxel) to simulate the optical properties of a given particle.

It implies calculating 3N elements for the polarization vector, but it is computationally really expensive, requiring larger memory computing time when N increases.

Several procedures have been implemented to improve the DDA performances. One of the pioneering works has been realized by Drain and Flatau who developed an open source package in FORTRAN named Discrete Dipole Scattering (DDSCAT) [24]. The time and the memory required to calculate the polarizability of each element has been reduced with the application of 3D Fast Fourier Transform (3D FFT) combined with a number of iterative methods such as Biconjugate Gradient (BCG) and Complex Conjugate Gradient (CCG) techniques.

In a previous study [25], DDSCAT was used to simulate the optical properties of triangular gold nanoparticles. The particles were modeled as prisms with triangular bases, and the incident light was assumed to be perpendicular to the base.

To train the model, we have created a data set consisting of calculated spectra obtained by a simulation process based on DDA.

The optical properties of a population of plasmonic metal nanoparticles were calculated using the MPDDA package, as presented in the work of Shabaninezhad [26].

Taking inspiration from the work of Drain and Flatau, the authors reduced the computational time and memory by applying the BCG and FFT techniques to calculate the dipole moments of the elements.

Moreover, to further reduce the computational load, the MPDDA package offers the possibility to run through CPU as well as GPU platforms: using the parallel computing toolbox of MATLAB the package transfers the data from CPU to GPU, making the calculations process significantly faster.

To create the data set used to train the CNN model, the MATLAB package has been modified to calculate in a single run the full population of the spectra.

The dataset has been created considering the properties of the most commonly used particles for practical applications, i.e. gold spheres and rods as well as a range of dielectric environment representing most of the medium in which are immersed, so that for the synthesis of nanoparticles used in the actual practical implementation could be considered adequate, although for advanced and innovative applications based on different particles, the dataset needs to be increased with other particle shapes or materials.

The simulation of all the spectra has been realized considering the polarization direction of the incident light interacting with the electromagnetic field of the plasmonic metal nanoparticle perpendicular to the plane, whereas its direction of propagation is systematically changed.

Particles with three different morphologies, i.e. sphere, rod and ellipsoid, as well as with diverse sizes have been taken into account.

The effect of dielectric environment has been also considered by calculating the optical properties for various refractive indices of the bulk medium around the particle surface.

The actual size of the training dataset is 77454 spectra, whereas we are working on the testing set.

In Fig. 4 are reported the optical properties of a gold ellipsoid with an effective radius (radius of the sphere having the same volume of the ellipsoid) of 10 nm in a bulk medium with a refractive index with a value of 1,3617 (ethanol) calculated by the MPDDA package.

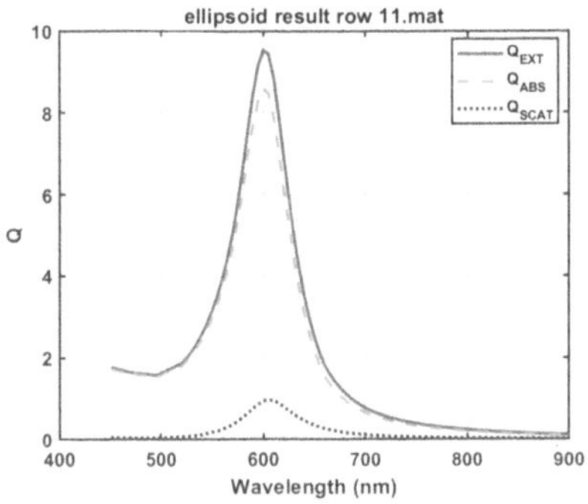

Fig. 4. Calculated optical properties of a gold ellipsoid with an effective radius of 10 nm embedded in a medium with RI = 1.3617 (ethanol).

3.2 Supervised Learning Model Architecture and Optimization

The architecture of the CNN model is reported in Fig. 5.

The input layer consists of 2D images of spectra obtained from simulations, each standardized to the same dimensions and represented using RGB channels. This layer is followed by two hidden layers, each comprising a convolutional layer, a batch normalization layer, a ReLU activation function, and a pooling layer. The classification of spectra is performed by the final component of the architecture—the output layer—which includes a fully connected layer followed by a SoftMax activation function and a classification layer.

The performances of a supervised learning model rely on the selection of the hyperparameters used for its training: they determine time, quality and more of the training process.

In Table 2 the hyperparameters that will be used to train the model are reported along with their description [27, 28].

The mentioned hyperparameters will be changed to optimize the model, and their effect will be evaluated in terms of model accuracy and precision and training time.

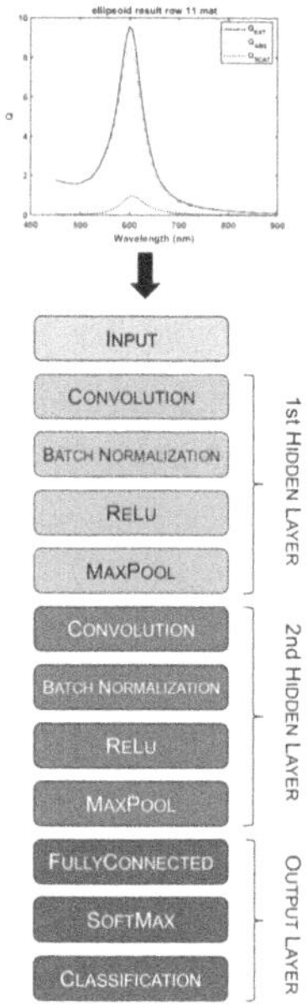

Fig. 5. Architecture of CNN model used to classify the UV-Spectra.

Table 2. Hyperparameters controlling the training of a CNN model.

HYPERPARAMETERS OF TRAINING	*DESCRIPTION*
INITIAL LEARN RATE	Controls the learning rate of the CNN model by defining the rate at which it adjusts its weight during the training
MINI- BATCH SIZE	Controls how many mini-batch observations are included on each iteration
MAXEPOCH	Indicate the maximum number of epochs that may occur during the training process

3.3 Performance Metrics of the Model

The effectiveness of the proposed CNN model will be calculated by using different performances metrics described as follows:

Confusion Matrix (CM): It is a square matrix that includes two categories "True Label" and "Predicted Label". The CM columns represent the predicted class labels, whereas the rows identify the instances of true class [29]. The diagonal elements of the confusion matrix represent the number of instances where the predicted label matches the true label. In binary classification terminology, the class of interest is referred to as the positive case, while the background is considered the negative case [30]. The four possible outcomes in a binary confusion matrix are: True Positive (TP), True Negative

(TN), False Positive (FP), and False Negative (FN), where 'true' or 'false' indicates whether the prediction is correct. Table 3 summarizes the meanings of these outcomes.

Table 3. Conceptualization of a binary classification confusion matrix

CM Indicator	*Indicator Full Name*	*Indicator Meaning*
TP	True Positive	Both the true and predicted values are positive. The model correctly predicts the positive class
TN	True Negative	The prediction is negative, and the true value is negative. The model correctly predicts the negative class
FP	False Positive	The true value is negative, although the prediction is positive. The model incorrectly predicts the positive class
FN	False Negative	Although the prediction is negative, the true value is positive. The model incorrectly predicts the negative class

From the outputs of the confusion matrix, it is possible to calculate a variety of indicators to assess the performance of the model [31–33].

Accuracy: It is defined as the fraction of the samples properly predicted to the total number of samples (Eq. 1)

$$\text{Accuracy} = (\text{TP} + \text{TN})/(\text{TP} + \text{TN} + \text{FP} + \text{FN}) \tag{1}$$

Precision: It is the fraction of the positive samples properly recognized to the number of samples identified as positive (Eq. 2)

$$\text{Precision} = \text{TP}/\text{TP} + \text{FP} \tag{2}$$

Recall (Sensitivity): It is defined as the fraction of the positive samples properly recognized to the total positive samples (Eq. 3)

$$\text{Recall} = \text{TP}/\text{TP} + \text{FN} \tag{3}$$

Specificity: It is defined as the fraction of the total number of true negatives to the total number of samples recognized as negatives (Eq. 4)

$$\text{Specificity} = \text{TN}/\text{TN} + \text{FP} \tag{4}$$

F1-score: It is calculated as the harmonic mean and precision (Eq. 5)

$$\text{F1 - score} = 2 * (\text{Recall} * \text{Precision})/(\text{Recall} + \text{Precision}) \tag{5}$$

ROC Curve Analysis: A way to explore the performances of a CNN model is the receiver operating characteristic **(ROC) curve**: it plots the True Positive Rate (TPR) against the False Positive Rate (FPR) at different discrimination thresholds [34].

The TPR and FPR are defined by Eqs. 6 and 7 [35]:

$$\text{TPR} = \text{TP}/\text{TP} + \text{FN} \tag{6}$$

$$\text{FPR} = \text{FP}/\text{FP} + \text{TN} \tag{7}$$

By comparison, it is possible to note that Eqs. 3 and 6 are equal, so TPR is also known as *sensitivity* or *recall*, i.e. proportion of the positive samples that were correctly classified. At the same time, considering Eq. 4, the FPR is related to the *specificity* from Eq. 8:

$$\text{FPR} = 1 - \text{Specificity} \tag{8}$$

so that it represents the ratio between the incorrectly classified negative samples to the total number of negative samples, i.e. the proportion of the negative samples that were incorrectly classified.

The analysis of the ROC curve provides a graphical representation of the test diagnostic performances, i.e. the test ability to distinguish between two classes such as positive and negative outcomes. More the apex of the curve is close to the upper left corner of the curve, and higher is the discriminatory ability of the test (i.e. the false positive rate is low, and true positive rate is high). A schematic representation of a ROC curve is depicted in Fig. 6.

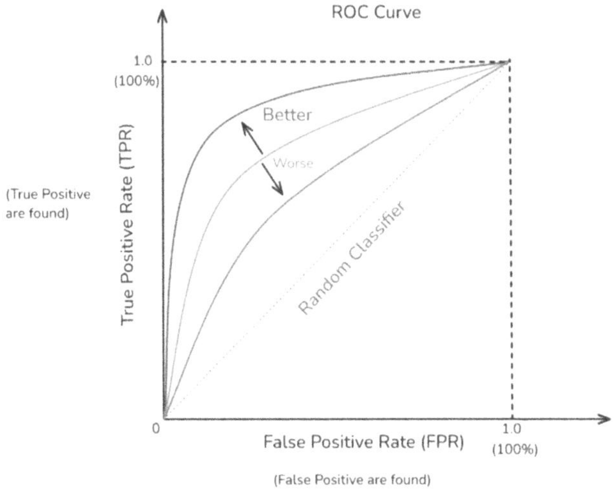

Fig. 6. Schematic representation of a ROC curve.

Although a ROC curve has a visual appeal, in order to straightly compare different classifiers, an aggregated scalar is introduced, so that it is often summarized by calculating the **Area Under the Curve (AUC)** [36]. The values of the area under the curve fall between 0 and 1. For an ideal classifier with perfect performances (i.e. 100% sensitive and 100% specific) the AUC value is equal to 1, whereas for a no discriminative classifier (i.e. 50% sensitive and 50% precise) the AUC value becomes 0.5 and it represented by the straight diagonal drawing out from the lower left to the upper right corner (random guessing) [37]. Models with an AUC value of 0.5 are defined as random classifiers. On this basis, higher values of AUC indicate a greater ability to distinguish between two classes, thus suggesting better model performances.

3.4 CNN Model Prediction

The primary objective of the CNN architecture is to predict the shape and size of a particle, as well as the dielectric environment surrounding its surface, for a given optical response.

For an accurate prediction, three models are firstly developed independently, with each of them providing predictions for a unique particle property. The main parameters affecting the optical properties have been selected for the different classifications. For each model, gold nanoparticles are considered, although other noble metals such as silver offer interesting optical properties. Silver nanoparticles for example are more sensitive to the changes in the dielectric environment [38, 39], thus resulting in more pronounced color changes and improving the sensitivity in a colorimetric analysis, but silver is really easy to oxidize, making its use difficult in practical applications. Differently from silver, gold is very stable so that is the most used for implementation in real-world applications. Also, gold is biocompatible, resulting attractive for innovative biomedical applications [40]. In light of their enhanced stability, we consider to simulate only the optical properties of gold nanoparticles, without considering other materials such as silver.

The first model is designed to make predictions on particle morphology. According to that model, the particles are classified into three classes: spherical and ellipsoidal particles as well as rods. According to their well-established synthetic protocols, especially for spheres and rods, these kinds of particles are the most used for practical applications, although other morphologies such as triangles or multispiked particles such as nanostars are attracting a growing attention [41]. The morphology is a feature affecting the optical properties of the particle resulting in LSPR peaks with different properties, such as position and shape for different particle shapes [42].

The particle size determines the position of its resonance peak: when the size is increasing the LSPR is shifted towards longer wavelengths affecting the optical response [43]. As an example, gold nanoparticles with resonances localized at longer wavelengths in the UV-Vis spectrum results in larger chromatic changes arising from variations in the refractive index of the medium around the surface [44]. So, when designing a system based on plasmonic nanoparticles, the size is a parameter to be considered. The second model predicts the optical properties of gold particles according to their effective radius, i.e. the radius of a sphere having the same volume as the particle. The first class of the model represents a value of 10 nm for the effective radius of the particles, whereas the remaining classes represent a value increased of 5 nm until to arrive a final value of 45 nm, for a total of eight classes.

The dielectric medium is a further parameter affecting the position of the LSPR of gold nanoparticles, with LSPR localized at longer wavelength for increasing values of the refractive index [45], so that the last model is designed to classify the optical properties of gold nanoparticles on the basis of the refractive index of the medium around the particle surface. The classes of the model represent the values of the refractive index of ethanol-glycerol mixtures containing different percentage of ethanol and where 1, 3617 is the refractive index of pure ethanol and 1.4722 is the one of absolute glycerol. The classes of the model includes also water, a common solvent for colloidal dispersions. They are representative of all solvents in which particles are dispersed and according to the model the particles are classified into eleven classes.

In Table 4 the classes for each one of the three models have been reported.

Upon their separate development, we evaluate the possibility of unifying all models into a single CNN model.

Table 4. Classes returned from each one of the three models designed.

Classes for each one of the three CNN models developed		
Shape	Size	Refractive index
Spherical	10	1.33
Rods	15	1.3617
Ellipsoid	20	1.372
	25	1.383
	30	1.3940
	35	1.4049
	40	1.41590
	45	1.4270
		1.4381
		1.4494
		1.4607
		1.4722

4 Applications and Future Trends

The input layer of the CNN model is based on the optical properties of particles with three different morphologies: spherical, rods and ellipsoid, but the synthesis protocols developed during last years produce also other structures, such as nanodecahedra, nanooctahedra, nanostars or nanotriangles.

For a more accurate prediction, the data set used to train the model can be further broadened by modifying the MATLAB package used for the simulations.

In fact, the package is generic and can be redesigned to calculate the optical properties of other plasmonic structures. It can include more plasmonic nanoparticles morphologies (triangles, decahedra or stars), but also nanoshells, multimers, embedded nanoparticles and periodic arrays.

5 Conclusions

Herein we have presented the application of Convolutional Neural Network (CNN) for the classification and recognition of the UV-Vis spectra of plasmonic metal nanoparticles. Firstly, we have created a data set by means of simulation study based on DDA for the training of CNN architecture. The data set is used for the implementation of three separate models to classify gold nanoparticles on the basis of the parameters affecting their optical properties. According to these models, gold nanostructures are classified on the basis of their shape, size and dielectric environment around the surface. The presented CNN architecture is developed with the aim to support the classification of plasmonic particles presenting well defined optical properties that can be used as a low-cost alternative to other tools such as equipment for dynamic light scattering measurements.

Acknowledgments. The authors would like to thank Oraib Almegdadi for her support with the Matlab script.

Funding. This research was supported by Portuguese national funds provided by FCT—Fundação para a Ciência e Tecnologia, through grant SFRH/BD/09347/2021, Center of Technology and Systems (CTS), UIDB/00066/2020/UIDP/00066/2020, UIDB/00100/2020, and UIDP/00100/2020 projects of Centro de Química Estrutural, LA/P/0056/2020 of the Institute of Molecular Sciences, and by project IPL/IDI&CA2024/OPAPIC2D_ISEL.

References

1. Mauriz, E., Dey, P., Lechuga, L.M.: Advances in nanoplasmonic biosensors for clinical applications. Analyst **144**(24), 7105–7129 (2019)
2. Adedokun, G., Alipanah, M., Fan, Z.H.: Sample preparation and detection methods in point-of-care devices towards future at-home testing. Lab on a Chip. (2024)
3. Jin, Z., et al.: Colorimetric sensing for translational applications: from colorants to mechanisms. Chemical Society Reviews (2024)
4. Zheng, G., et al.: Discrete metal nanoparticles with plasmonic chirality. Chem. Soc. Rev. **50**(6), 3738–3754 (2021)
5. Wu, Y., Ali, M.R., Chen, K., Fang, N., El-Sayed, M.A.: Gold nanoparticles in biological optical imaging. Nano Today **24**, 120–140 (2019)
6. Langer, J., Novikov, S.M., Liz-Marzán, L.M.: Sensing using plasmonic nanostructures and nanoparticles. Nanotechnology **26**(32), 322001 (2015)
7. Sun, J., Lu, Y., He, L., Pang, J., Yang, F., Liu, Y.: Colorimetric sensor array based on gold nanoparticles: Design principles and recent advances. TrAC, Trends Anal. Chem. **122**, 115754 (2020)

8. Chang, C.C., Chen, C.P., Wu, T.H., Yang, C.H., Lin, C.W., Chen, C.Y.: Gold nanoparticle-based colorimetric strategies for chemical and biological sensing applications. Nanomaterials **9**(6), 861 (2019)
9. Pearce, A.K., Wilks, T.R., Arno, M.C., O'Reilly, R.K.: Synthesis and applications of anisotropic nanoparticles with precisely defined dimensions. Nat. Rev. Chem. **5**(1), 21–45 (2021)
10. Fichthorn, K.A.: Theory of anisotropic metal nanostructures. Chem. Rev. **123**(7), 4146–4183 (2023)
11. Alkhalayfeh, M.A., Aziz, A.A., Pakhuruddin, M.Z.: An overview of enhanced polymer solar cells with embedded plasmonic nanoparticles. Renew. Sustain. Energy Rev. **141**, 110726 (2021)
12. Serafinelli, C., et al.: Design and Development of a Color Picker System to Integrate in POC Device Systems. In EPJ Web of Conferences, Vol. 305, p. 00007. EDP Sciences (2024)
13. Serafinelli, C., Fantoni, A., Alegria, E.C., Vieira, M.: Colorimetric Analysis of Transmitted Light Through Plasmonic Paper for Next-Generation Point-of-Care (PoC) Devices. Biosensors **15**(3), 144 (2025)
14. Yu, Z., Gao, H., Cong, X., Wu, N., Song, H.H.: A survey on cyber–physical systems security. IEEE Internet Things J. **10**(24), 21670–21686 (2023)
15. Carreras Guzman, N.H., Wied, M., Kozine, I., Lundteigen, M.A.: Conceptualizing the key features of cyber-physical systems in a multi-layered representation for safety and security analysis. Syst. Eng. **23**(2), 189–210 (2020)
16. Laghari, A.A., Wu, K., Laghari, R.A., Ali, M., Khan, A.A.: A review and state of art of Internet of Things (IoT). Archives of Computational Methods in Engineering, 1–19 (2021)
17. Liu, Y., Peng, Y., Wang, B., Yao, S., Liu, Z.: Review on cyber-physical systems. IEEE/CAA Journal of Automatica Sinica **4**(1), 27–40 (2017)
18. Greer, C., Burns, M., Wollman, D., Griffor, E.: Cyber-physical systems and internet of things (2019)
19. Nayyar, A., Pramanik, P.K.D., Mohana, R.: Introduction to the Special Issue on Evolving IoT and Cyber-Physical Systems: Advancements, Applications, and Solutions. Scalable Computing: Practice and Experience **21**(3), 347–348 (2020)
20. Mortezapour Shiri, F., Perumal, T., Mustapha, N., Mohamed, R.: A comprehensive overview and comparative analysis on deep learning models: CNN, RNN, LSTM, GRU. arXiv e-prints, arXiv-2305 (2023)
21. Li, Z., Liu, F., Yang, W., Peng, S., Zhou, J.: A survey of convolutional neural networks: analysis, applications, and prospects. IEEE Trans. Neural Netw. Learn. Sys. **33**(12), 6999–7019 (2021)
22. Domingos, C., Fantoni, A., Fernandes, M., Fidalgo, J., Pereira, S.A.: Low-cost raman spectroscopy setup combined with a machine learning model. Sensors **25**(3), 659 (2025)
23. Amirjani, A., Sadrnezhaad, S.K.: Computational electromagnetics in plasmonic nanostructures. J. Mat. Chem. C **9**(31), 9791–9819 (2021)
24. Draine, B.T., Flatau, P.J.: Discrete-dipole approximation for scattering calculations. J. Opt. Soc. Am. A **11**(4), 1491–1499 (1994)
25. Fantoni, A., et al.: Analysis of metallic nanoparticles embedded in thin film semiconductors for optoelectronic applications. Opt. Quant. Electron. **50**, 1–12 (2018)
26. MATLAB package for discrete dipole approximation by graphics processing unit: Fast Fourier Transform and Biconjugate Gradient
27. Akkuş, E., Bal, U., Koçoğlu, F.Ö., Beyhan, S.: Hyperparameter optimization of pre-trained convolutional neural networks using adolescent identity search algorithm. Neural Comput. Appl. **36**(4), 1523–1537 (2024)

28. Huang, W.T., Yang, S.C., Chou, F.I., Chou, J.H.: Automatic recognition of grinding quality of titanium alloy based on the convolutional neural network. The International Journal of Advanced Manufacturing Technology, 1–19 (2024)
29. Challa, S.K., Kumar, A., Semwal, V.B.: A multibranch CNN-BiLSTM model for human activity recognition using wearable sensor data. Vis. Comput. **38**(12), 4095–4109 (2022)
30. Maxwell, A.E., Warner, T.A., Guillén, L.A.: Accuracy assessment in convolutional neural network-based deep learning remote sensing studies—Part 1: Literature review. Remote Sensing **13**(13), 2450 (2021)
31. Junayed, M.S., et al.: AcneNet-a deep CNN based classification approach for acne classes. In: 2019 12th International Conference on Information & Communication Technology and System (ICTS), pp. 203–208 (2019)
32. Sathyanarayanan, S., Tantri, B.R.: Confusion matrix-based performance evaluation metrics. African Journal of Biomedical Research, 4023–4031 (2024)
33. El-Assy, A.M., Amer, H.M., Ibrahim, H.M., Mohamed, M.A.: A novel CNN architecture for accurate early detection and classification of Alzheimer's disease using MRI data. Sci. Rep. **14**(1), 3463 (2024)
34. Namdar, K., Haider, M.A., Khalvati, F.: A modified AUC for training convolutional neural networks: taking confidence into account. Frontiers in Artificial Intelligence **4**, 582928 (2021)
35. Tharwat, A.: Classification assessment methods. Applied Computing and Informatics **17**(1), 168–192 (2021)
36. Jaskowiak, P.A., Costa, I.G., Campello, R.J.: The area under the ROC curve as a measure of clustering quality. Data Min. Knowl. Disc. **36**(3), 1219–1245 (2022)
37. Fan, J., Upadhye, S., Worster, A.: Understanding receiver operating characteristic (ROC) curves. Canadian Journal of Emergency Medicine **8**(1), 19–20 (2006)
38. Firoozi, A., Khordad, R., Rastegar Sedehi, H.R.: Effects of geometry and size of noble metal nanoparticles on enhanced refractive index sensitivity. Appl. Phys. A **128**(12), 1074 (2022)
39. Alrahili, M.R., Algarni, M.: Optical properties and sensing characteristics of silver and gold nanoparticles: size-dependent extinction efficiencies. Sci. Adv. Mater. **16**(12), 1259–1266 (2024)
40. Anik, M.I., Mahmud, N., Al Masud, A., Hasan, M.: Gold nanoparticles (GNPs) in biomedical and clinical applications: a review. Nano Select **3**(4), 792–828 (2022)
41. Nguyen, Q.N., Wang, C., Shang, Y., Janssen, A., Xia, Y.: Colloidal synthesis of metal nanocrystals: from asymmetrical growth to symmetry breaking. Chem. Rev. **123**(7), 3693–3760 (2022)
42. Hegde, H.R., Chidangil, S., Sinha, R.K.: Refractive index sensitivity of Au nanostructures in solution and on the substrate. J. Mater. Sci.: Mater. Electron. **33**(7), 4011–4024 (2022)
43. Muldarisnur, M., et al.: Effect of nanoparticle geometry on sensitivity of metal nanoparticle based sensor. In IOP Conference Series: Materials Science and Engineering, Vol. 578, No. 1, p. 012036. IOP Publishing (2019)
44. Rabbani, A., Rudacille, R., Hasegawa, K.: Local refractive index sensitivity of localized surface plasmon resonance biosensors. The Journal of Physical Chemistry C **128**(45), 19210–19221 (2024)
45. Tuersun, P., Yusufu, T., Yimiti, A., Sidike, A.: Refractive index sensitivity analysis of gold nanoparticles. Optik **149**, 384–390 (2017)

Low Complexity and High Performance in Selective LIS

Ali Gashtasbi[1(✉)], Mario Marques da Silva[2], and Rui Dinis[1]

[1] School of Sciences and Technology, Universidade Nova de Lisboa, 2829-516 Caparica, Portugal
a.gashtasbi@campus.fct.unl.pt, rdinis@fct.pt
[2] Autonoma TechLab, 1169-023 Lisboa, Portugal
mmsilva@autonoma.pt

Abstract. The deployment of Large Intelligent Surfaces (LIS) has demonstrated considerable promise in improving the performance of wireless networks. However, the implementation of such systems is often complicated by their substantial architectural complexity. In this research, a refined strategy is presented wherein a limited array of antenna elements is selectively utilized to reduce the system's operational demands. Experimental evaluations demonstrate that progressively scaling the number of active units attenuates efficiency degradation, thereby facilitating an optimal trade-off between computational performance and resource utilization. When integrated with Low-Density Parity-Check (LDPC) error correction schemes, this selective approach offers a scalable and pragmatic alternative to full-scale LIS configurations, ideally suited for complex communication networks.

Keywords: Selective LIS · Full LIS · Low complexity · LDPC

1 Introduction

The ever-growing demand for higher data rates, energy efficiency, and reliable connectivity in next-generation technologies has motivated the exploration of novel technologies that are able to overcome the limitations of conventional communication systems. Among these emerging paradigms, Large Intelligent Surface (LIS) technology has gained considerable attention for its potential to reshape the wireless propagation environment, indirectly reduce traffic through fewer retransmissions and dramatically improve communication performance. LIS systems consist of large, programmable surfaces embedded with a massive number of antenna elements capable of dynamically manipulating electromagnetic waves. Such fine-grained control enables significant improvements in spectral efficiency, signal focusing, and energy usage, making LIS a promising candidate for 6G and beyond wireless architectures [1].

Despite these advantages, the practical implementation of full-scale LIS systems remains a formidable challenge. The dense deployment of antenna elements leads to increased hardware costs, higher energy consumption, and notably, an exponential rise in

Published by Springer Nature Switzerland AG 2025
L. M. Camarinha-Matos and F. Ferrada (Eds.): DoCEIS 2025, IFIP AICT 759, pp. 291–304, 2025.
https://doi.org/10.1007/978-3-031-97051-1_21

computational complexity associated with signal processing and data decoding tasks [2]. These challenges pose major obstacles to scalability and economic feasibility, especially in real-time or resource-constrained deployment scenarios.

To address these issues, the concept of selective LIS has emerged as a cost-effective and computationally efficient alternative. Rather than activating all antenna elements, this approach selectively engages only a subset of antennas that satisfy specific channel or system performance criteria. By doing so, it significantly reduces system complexity and energy expenditure while keeping appropriate performance standards [3]. However, the success of this technique depends heavily on the development of intelligent selection algorithms that can adapt to dynamic environments and maintain communication quality.

Furthermore, the inserting of Low-Density Parity-Check (LDPC) codes into the selective LIS framework introduces robust error correction capabilities that further enhance system reliability. While partial activation of antennas can introduce signal degradation or coverage gaps, the error resilience provided by LDPC codes helps to mitigate these effects, preserving data integrity and enabling reliable communication in scenarios with limited resources [4].

The main research question explored in this work is: Can a selective LIS system, integrated with advanced decoding techniques like LDPC, achieve a level of performance comparable to full LIS setups while significantly reducing complexity? The hypothesis is that Selective LIS, when combined with robust selection criteria and LDPC codes, provides a near-optimal trade-off between performance and resource efficiency.

The novelty of our work lies in combining various antenna selection strategies with LDPC coding and benchmarking their performance through comprehensive Monte Carlo simulations under different LIS configurations and receiver types. In this work, we investigate the synergy between selective LIS and LDPC coding as a comprehensive strategy for addressing the scalability and performance trade-offs in LIS-assisted wireless communication. Our contributions aim to provide insights into the design, optimization, and practical deployment of efficient LIS systems capable of meeting the demands of future wireless networks. This paper is structured as follows: Sect. 2 provides an overview of Selective and Full LIS systems; Sect. 3 details the proposed system model for LIS, including four decoding techniques; Sect. 4 introduces the Selective LIS Framework; Sect. 5 presents simulation results and analysis; and Sect. 6 offers the concluding remarks.

2 Relationship to AI-Powered Cyber-Physical Systems

The integration of LIS into wireless networks is a key enabler of future Cyber-Physical Systems (CPS), particularly in scenarios where smart environments require adaptive, scalable, and efficient communication infrastructures. AI-powered CPS benefit from context-aware connectivity, real-time data processing, and intelligent decision-making at the edge—all of which can be enhanced by low-complexity, high-performance communication subsystems like the one proposed in this work.

One of the main challenges in LIS-based systems is the presence of multi-user interference (MUI), which significantly limits performance in dense environments. Conventional receivers such as Maximum Ratio Combining (MRC) and Equal Gain Combining (EGC) do not inherently suppress interference during signal decoding. While advanced methods like Zero Forcing (ZF) and Minimum Mean Square Error (MMSE) can mitigate this issue, they require high computational effort due to matrix inversion.

Machine learning presents a promising solution to this trade-off. Instead of explicitly modeling the channel and performing complex operations, neural networks can learn representations directly from the received signals. Deep learning-based receivers have shown the ability to replace or augment traditional equalization and detection processes, even in challenging environments such as nonlinear or dispersive channels [5, 6]. These methods can be trained without detailed channel state information and may enable simplified, adaptive receiver architectures for LIS-based CPS.

While the current work focuses on Selective LIS systems and evaluates their performance using classic receivers (ZF, MMSE, MRC, EGC), it lays the foundation for future AI-driven enhancements. Specifically, we envision extending this framework with machine learning–based antenna selection and neural network receivers that dynamically adapt to environmental changes—essential traits for AI-powered CPS operating under real-world constraints.

3 Background

In recent years, LIS have been introduced as a disruptive paradigm in wireless communication, offering a flexible and controllable medium for electromagnetic wave manipulation. By deploying a dense array of programmable antennas over large surfaces, LIS can dynamically shape the wireless environment to boost communication efficiency, reduce latency, and enhance signal fidelity. The capability of LIS to manipulate signal reflection and refraction makes it a promising solution for challenging use cases like industrial automation, autonomous systems, and high-density user environments [7].

LIS technology, often referred to as a reconfigurable intelligent platform, enables the synthesis of virtual line-of-sight paths, even in obstructed or cluttered propagation scenarios. This feature is particularly beneficial in urban settings and complex indoor environments where traditional communication links are often compromised. Moreover, LIS systems have the potential to serve as low-profile infrastructure mounted on building facades or indoor walls, paving the way for seamless integration into future smart cities.

Despite its theoretical advantages, the deployment of a full LIS setup—where all antenna elements are continuously active—presents several operational bottlenecks. These include elevated power requirements, hardware scalability issues, and massive computational overhead stemming from the processing of high-dimensional channel information. Furthermore, full LIS systems demand continuous synchronization and calibration across potentially thousands of antenna elements, rendering their implementation expensive and energy-intensive [8].

To address these constraints, the concept of Selective LIS has gained traction. This approach advocates for the activation of only a subset of antenna elements, selected based on their effectiveness in contributing to the received signal quality. By leveraging environmental awareness and real-time channel state information (CSI), selective LIS can dynamically adapt its active configuration to current user distribution and communication demands. This not only alleviates the complexity and energy burden but also makes LIS more adaptable to scenarios with constrained resources.

An additional advantage of selective LIS is its adaptability in mobile scenarios, such as vehicle-to-infrastructure (V2I) or drone-based communication networks, where rapid reconfiguration of active panels is essential. In such use cases, the ability to quickly activate the most relevant antennas can significantly improve link stability and reduce handover interruptions.

Selection algorithms employed in selective LIS systems often consider multiple criteria: proximity to users, instantaneous channel quality, predicted signal strength, and even user priority levels. These smart selection schemes allow the system to retain most of the benefits of a full LIS while operating with significantly fewer active components. Furthermore, machine learning-based selection models are increasingly being adopted to forecast user behavior and channel variations, making antenna selection not only reactive but also predictive [6].

Moreover, the incorporation of forward error correction techniques, particularly LDPC codes, further enhances system robustness. LDPC coding compensates for the slight performance degradation introduced by the reduced diversity of active antennas, thus maintaining reliable communication. The synergy between LDPC codes and selective LIS proves particularly valuable in bandwidth-limited and power-constrained systems, such as IoT hubs or wearable communication modules [9].

The objective of the current study is to investigate the trade-offs between performance and complexity in selected LIS systems. Specifically, we explore how different antenna selection methods impact communication reliability, energy usage, and computational efficiency. Our work also investigates how the integration of LDPC coding into selective LIS frameworks can deliver near-optimal results in environments where full-scale LIS is impractical.

In summary, selective LIS represents a practical evolution of full LIS architecture, emphasizing flexibility, scalability, and efficiency without compromising core performance objectives. As future wireless networks continue to evolve toward more intelligent, user-centric, and sustainable infrastructures, selective LIS is expected to play a pivotal role.

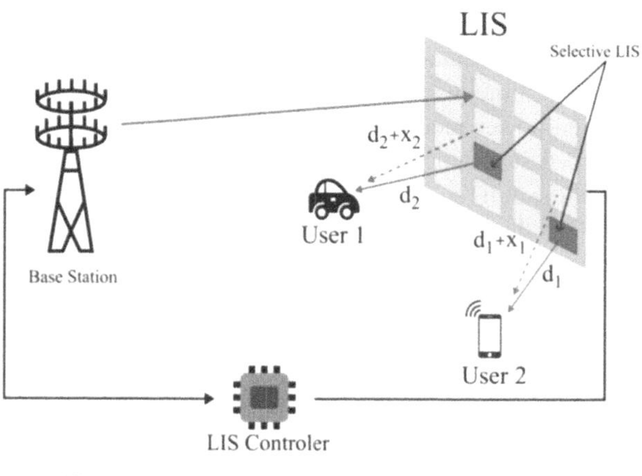

Fig. 1. A graphical schematic of the Selective LIS.

Figure 1 presents a conceptual diagram showing how users dynamically connect to the most optimal subset of the LIS surface based on their location and channel characteristics, thereby achieving efficient and reliable communication with minimal infrastructure overhead.

4 System Model

The transmission between the base station (BS) and the user equipment (UE) operates under a Single-Carrier Frequency Domain Equalization (SC-FDE) scheme, utilizing Quadrature Phase Shift Keying (QPSK) for modulation. Let $\boldsymbol{x}_n^{(t)}$ represent the n -th data block comprising N data symbols transmitted by the t-th UE. The corresponding signal received at the r-th antenna element of the LIS system is denoted by $\boldsymbol{y}_n^{(r)}$.

The transformation between the time-domain and frequency-domain representations for the k-th subcarrier—assumed to remain constant over the duration of a data block—is achieved via a Discrete Fourier Transform (DFT), denoted $DFT\left\{\boldsymbol{x}_n^{(t)} : n = 0, 1, \ldots, N-1\right\} = \left\{\boldsymbol{X}_k^{(t)} : k = 0, 1, \ldots, N-1\right\}$. This transformation framework also extends analogously to the received signal vector, the channel frequency response, and the additive noise.

The frequency-domain received signal can be expressed in matrix-vector notation as follows [10]:

$$\boldsymbol{Y}_k = \left[\boldsymbol{Y}_k^{(1)}, \ldots, \boldsymbol{Y}_k^{(R)}\right] = \boldsymbol{X}_k \boldsymbol{H}_k + \boldsymbol{N}_k \tag{1}$$

Here, $\boldsymbol{X}_k = \left[\boldsymbol{X}_k^{(1)}, \ldots, \boldsymbol{X}_k^{(T)}\right]^T$ denotes the transmitted data symbols in the frequency domain, $\boldsymbol{H}_k$ refers to the frequency response of the transmission channel for the k-th subcarrier, where the element in the (r, t)-th position is $\boldsymbol{H}_k^{(r,t)}$. The term $\boldsymbol{N}_k$ represents the corresponding noise vector in the frequency domain for the same subcarrier [10].

4.1 Receivers Equalization

In a non-iterative receiver setup, the estimation of frequency-domain data symbols $\tilde{\boldsymbol{X}}_k = \left[\tilde{\boldsymbol{X}}_k^{(1)}, \ldots, \tilde{\boldsymbol{X}}_k^{(R)}\right]^T$ is carried out as follows:

$$\tilde{\boldsymbol{x}}_k = \boldsymbol{E}_k \boldsymbol{Y}_k \tag{2}$$

Depending on type of receivers, the equalization vector E_k can be computed [11] as:

ZF approach seeks to cancel out inter-symbol interference by applying the inverse of the channel matrix, effectively aligning the received signal with the original transmitted signal.

$$\boldsymbol{E}_k = \left(\boldsymbol{H}_k^H \boldsymbol{H}_k\right)^{-1} \boldsymbol{H}_k^H \tag{3}$$

MMSE technique minimizes the expected value of the squared difference between the transmitted and detected signals, taking into account both the channel characteristics and the noise covariance.

$$\boldsymbol{E}_k = \left[\boldsymbol{H}_k^H \boldsymbol{H}_k + \beta \boldsymbol{I}\right]^{-1} \boldsymbol{H}_k^H \tag{4}$$

where $\beta = \sigma_N^2/\sigma_S^2 = \frac{E\left[|\boldsymbol{N}_k|^2\right]}{2} / \frac{E\left[|\boldsymbol{X}_k|^2\right]}{2}$ and $\boldsymbol{I}$ denotes an $R \times R$ identity matrix.

MRC enhances the received signal by coherently combining multiple antenna inputs, each weighted proportionally to their signal-to-noise ratio (SNR), thereby maximizing the overall SNR.

$$\boldsymbol{E}_k = \boldsymbol{H}_k^H \tag{5}$$

EGC improves signal strength by summing received signals from multiple branches with equal weighting, while maintaining their phase alignment to ensure constructive interference.

$$\boldsymbol{E}_k = \exp\left\{j \cdot \arg\left(\boldsymbol{H}_k^H\right)\right\} \tag{6}$$

5 Selected Strategies for LIS System

The Selected LIS structure aims to minimize system complexity while maintaining effective communication performance by activating only a subset of the most relevant antenna elements. Instead of relying on the full panel of LIS antennas, the system selects optimal elements based on a variety of strategic criteria. These criteria can be grouped into three main categories: Channel-Aware Selection**,** Position-Based Activation, and Performance-Enhancement Techniques [10]**.**

5.1 Channels-Aware Selection

1. **Channel State Information (CSI)-Based Selection**
   Antennas with the best instantaneous channel quality—such as those with the highest channel gain or SNR—are activated [11].
   Example: From a set of 400 antennas, only the top 100 with the highest SNR might be selected. It ensures only antennas with strong channel contribution are used, improving reliability and reducing unnecessary processing.
2. **Thresholding Approach**
   Antennas are only activated if their measured channel quality exceeds a predefined threshold [12].
   Example: Any antenna with SNR below 10 dB may be deactivated. It avoids activating elements that would add more noise than value, improving energy efficiency.

5.2 Position-Based Activation

1. **Proximity-Based Selection**
   Antennas situated nearest to the LoS path between the user and LIS panels are given precedence [13].
   Example: For a user directly in front of a rectangular LIS panel, central antennas might offer better performance due to their alignment with the shortest propagation path.
2. **Signal Strength-Based Selection**
   Selection is based on received signal power from each antenna, regardless of physical proximity [14].
   Example: Antennas near the user with the highest signal reception will be chosen, even if off-center.

5.3 Performance-Enhancement Techniques

1. **Integration with LDPC Coding**
   Selective LIS systems benefit from the incorporation LDPC codes, which improves error correction [15].
   Example: Systems can maintain low BER with only 25% of antennas active. LDPC codes balances reduced hardware usage with improved signal reliability.
2. **Advanced Beamforming Algorithms**
   Beamforming strategies such as ZF or MMSE are applied to shape signal paths more efficiently [16].
   Example: MMSE beamforming can direct energy toward active users while suppressing noise. It enhances communication quality and reduces interference without requiring full antenna deployment.

These criteria and techniques work together to ensure that Selective LIS systems can deliver high-quality wireless communication while staying energy-efficient, scalable, and computationally feasible for real-world applications, especially in dense or resource-limited environments (Fig. 2).

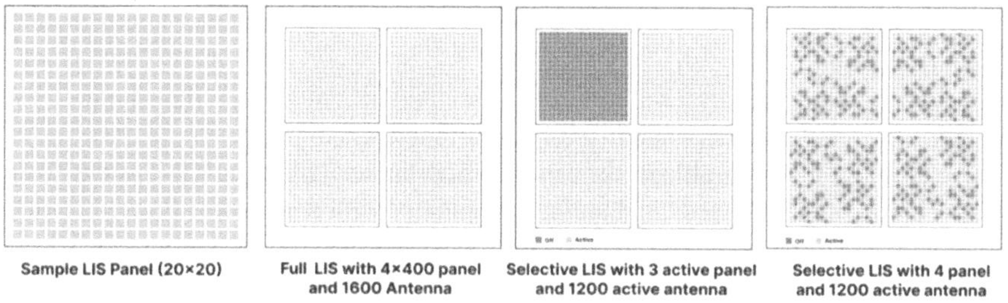

Fig. 2. Visual comparison between Selective and Full LIS implementations in the case study.

6 Simulations and Results

The current part provides a thorough investigation of BER performance conducted by Monte Carlo simulations, utilizing LIS technology with SC-FDE block transmission and LDPC error correction.. In the simulation model, E_b denotes the energy per bit, while N_0 indicates the one-sided noise power spectral density. The BER is assessed as a function of E_b/N_0. A transmission block consisting of $N = 256$ symbols under QPSK modulation was used, with consistent outcomes observed across larger block sizes, provided that N, as long as $N \gg 1$. LDPC codes of length 32,400 and a defined code rate ½ were employed, utilizing regular structures in which all variable and check nodes maintain uniform degrees.

To improve LIS system performance, a proximity-based antenna selection strategy is adopted. In this method, antenna elements located nearest to the direct LoS between the receiver and the transmitter are prioritized for activation due to their favourable channel characteristics. This selective activation boosts power efficiency and simplifies the system while preserving strong signal quality. The strategy is especially effective for users who are in the LIS panel's primary beam area. Figure 3 illustrates comparative BER performance for two LIS configurations. The full LIS model (4×400), featuring 400 antennas distributed across four panels, capitalizes on spatial diversity and array gain, delivering exceptional reliability—especially at elevated E_b/N_0 values. This architecture, however, demands significantly more hardware, energy, and computational resources to coordinate 400 antenna outputs, making it less suitable for resource-constrained settings.

Conversely, the Selective LIS design (1×400), which centralizes 400 antennas on a single panel, offers a cost-effective and less complex alternative. While this setup simplifies system design, it yields slightly inferior BER performance due to reduced spatial gain. The performance difference becomes more pronounced at higher E_b/N_0, levels. Quantitatively, the BER performance gap between the two systems is approximately 0.5 dB, yet the Selective LIS benefits from dramatically lower computational complexity.

When evaluating receiver techniques, ZF and MMSE outperform other methods in both LIS setups, closely approaching the theoretical Matched Filter Bound (MFB). In contrast, MRC and EGC offer lower computational overhead but fall short in performance, especially in the selective configuration. While ZF/MMSE helps mitigate the effects of reduced antenna count in the selective model, it does not completely close the performance gap.

The MFB curve serves as a reference benchmark, modeling the channel as a summation of delayed, independently Rayleigh-faded signal paths.

Overall, these results highlight the critical importance of aligning LIS system design with specific application needs, balancing complexity with communication robustness.

Figure 4 illustrates the BER behavior for detection methods including ZF, MMSE, MRC, and EGC, applied to LIS configurations comprising 400 antennas spread across 1 to 4 panels. The goal is to observe how panel distribution affects spatial diversity and interference suppression in multi-user environments. (The intention here is to examine how different panel distributions influence spatial diversity and the system's capacity to suppress interference in multi-user scenarios.) Detection schemes like ZF and MMSE

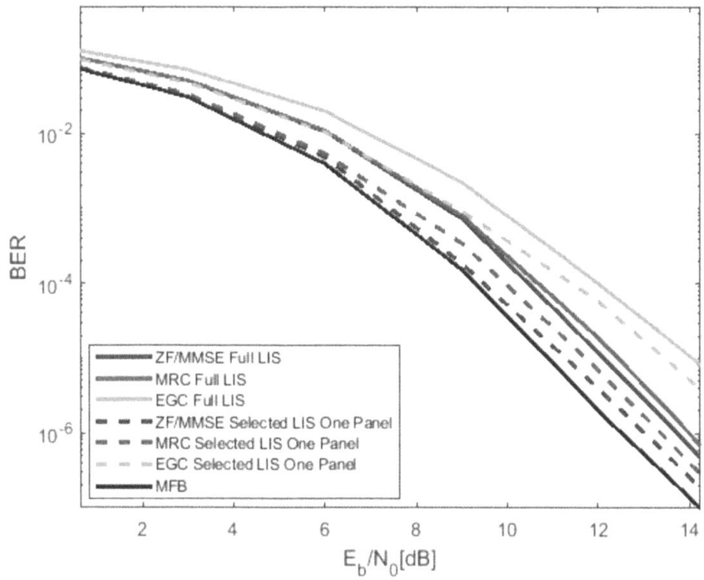

Fig. 3. BER performance of a 4 × 400 LIS system for four users, comparing configurations with and without selective LIS, in the absence of LDPC coding.

achieve superior interference mitigation, especially under higher values of E_b/N_0, outperforming MRC and EGC. Utilizing a greater number of panels—such as three or four—substantially enhances diversity and decreases signal correlation, thereby improving BER for all detection types. Conversely, configurations with only one panel experience a decline in performance due to reduced diversity and increased interference among users. Multi-panel layouts help ZF and MMSE techniques exploit spatial separation more effectively, improving user discrimination. While MRC and EGC offer computational simplicity, their error performance remains limited and shows marginal gains with additional panels. Notably, although increasing the number of panels boosts resilience against fading and interference, it also adds complexity to the system. Ultimately, configurations using 3 or 4 panels provide an efficient compromise between BER performance and system complexity, making them highly practical for LIS systems serving multiple users.

Figure 5 compares two different Full LIS configurations with the same total number of antennas (1200):

- 4 panels with 300 antennas each
- 3 panels with 400 antennas each

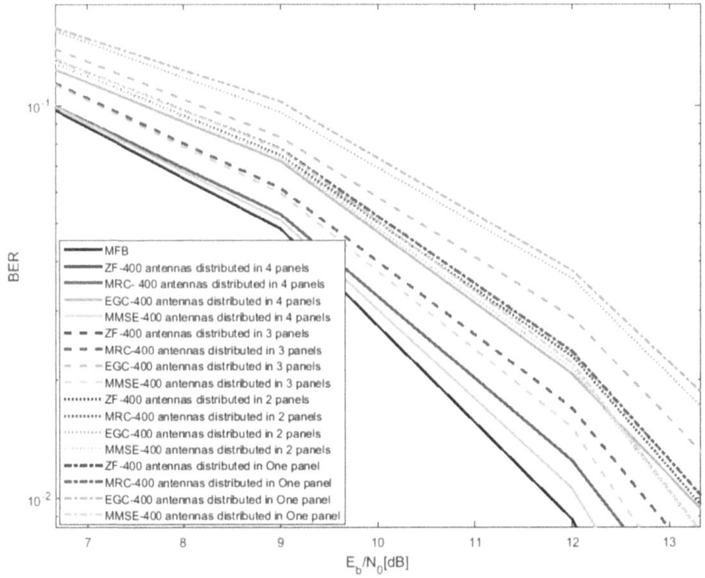

Fig. 4. Performance results for LIS System, with 4 users, without LDPC codes, with 400 Antennas Distributed across 1, 2, 3, or 4 Panels in Selective LIS.

This figure shows how antenna density per panel vs. spatial separation impacts BER performance under advanced receivers.

The configuration utilizing four-panels (exhibits enhanced performance, primarily attributed to its superior spatial diversity. This increased diversity facilitates more effective mitigation of noise and inter-user interference, particularly benefiting advanced detection schemes such as MMSE and ZF. In contrast, the three-panels arrangement, although offering higher antenna density per panel, suffers from elevated antenna correlation and reduced spatial separation, which negatively impacts interference suppression and BER outcomes. While the three-panels system may offer slight advantages in terms of deployment simplicity and energy efficiency, it does so at the cost of performance under demanding transmission conditions. Ultimately, the four-panels configuration provides a more favourable trade-off between system complexity and error performance, rendering it more suitable for applications requiring robust and high-diversity communication.

Figure 6 demonstrates the comparative performance of Selective LIS systems, both in the presence and absence of LDPC coding. Leveraging LDPC codes introduces strong forward error correction capabilities, which effectively counteract residual errors induced by noise and interference. The combination of these techniques enables dependable data transmission while minimizing hardware usage and computational overhead. Although Selective LIS inherently offers less spatial diversity than a full LIS configuration, the resulting SNR remains sufficient for LDPC decoders to correct errors effectively. This cooperative mechanism ensures solid BER outcomes, even in scenarios with constrained resources.

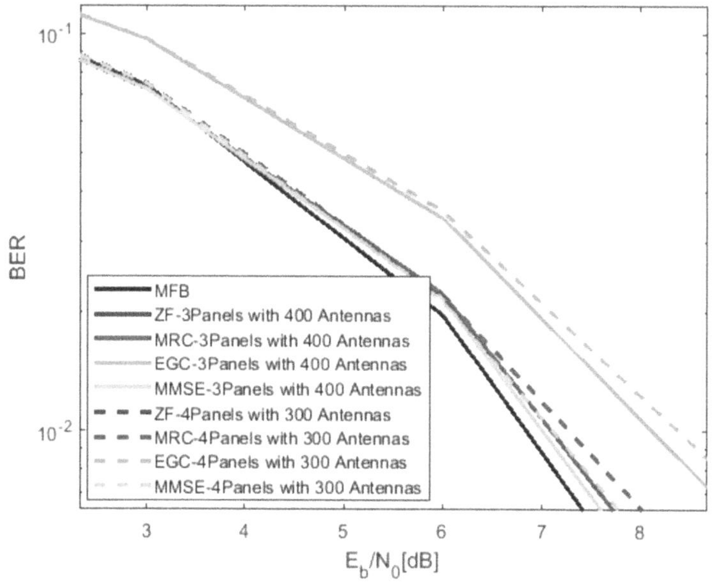

Fig. 5. BER Performance Comparison between Two Selective LIS Configurations: 3 Panels with 400 Antennas vs. 4 Panels with 300 Antennas (Total Antennas = 1200).

By selectively engaging a reduced number of antennas, the system significantly lowers structural and processing complexity. Simultaneously, LDPC integration enhances communication reliability, forming a well-balanced trade-off between system simplicity and performance. This architectural synergy proves especially advantageous in scenarios demanding low energy consumption and lightweight deployment, where activating a full set of antenna elements is not feasible. Simulation results further confirm that LDPC codes substantially improve BER performance across all receiver designs, particularly at lower E_b/N_0) rate values. While full LIS configurations outperform in terms of absolute BER due to richer diversity, their complexity remains a limiting factor. Conversely, the Selective LIS, supplemented by LDPC codes, provides a compelling alternative by achieving reliability with greater efficiency.

Balancing selective and full antenna configurations requires careful consideration of key factors, including system performance, architectural complexity, power consumption, and the potential for large-scale deployment. Table 1 summarizes these comparisons.

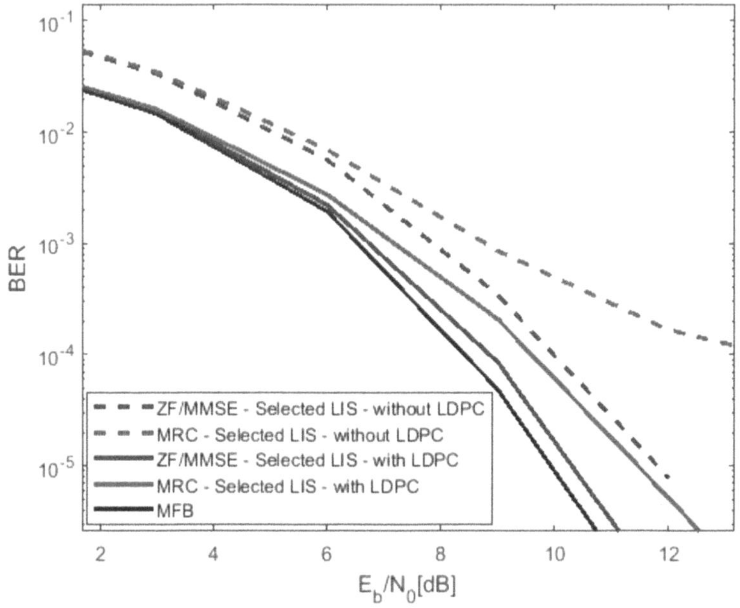

Fig. 6. BER performance of a 4 × 100 LIS configuration serving four users under Selective LIS, comparing scenarios with and without LDPC coding.

Table 1. Evaluation of Selective Antenna Approach Versus Full Deployment.

	Selective LIS	Full LIS
Number of Antennas	Only a selected portion of antennas are utilized	All antenna elements across all panels are active
Hardware Requirements	Operates on moderate hardware with lower processing demand	Requires advanced hardware and high processing capabilities
BER Performance	Slightly higher BER, but remains near optimal with efficient selection	Achieves the lowest BER due to full diversity
Scalability	Limited expansion potential, especially with single-panel setups	Highly scalable for large deployments with multiple panels
Energy Efficiency	Improved efficiency through reduced active components	High energy consumption due to full activation

7 Conclusions

In comparison to comprehensive LIS deployments, selective LIS systems provide an excellent approach for reducing complexity. This is accomplished through the implementation of advanced antenna selection and optimization techniques. The combination of modest complexity and exceptional performance makes Selective LIS a superb option for next-generation wireless networks, providing both scalability and energy economy. Selective LIS is particularly useful in resource-constrained CPS, such as IoT edge devices, where energy and hardware costs are critical.

Furthermore, integrating Selective LIS with LDPC codes enhances error correction, resulting in reliable communication that has the least performance impact. This approach is very useful for resource-constrained systems in current wireless infrastructures.

8 Future Work

The presented findings use proximity-based antenna selection, leaving various approaches for further research. Furthermore, future research should include a comparison of performance outcomes across different antenna selection criteria. LIS with advanced machine learning algorithms to optimize antenna selection based on real-time channel estimation, user distribution, and energy constraints. This framework aims to enhance system performance while minimizing complexity and power consumption, making it ideal for applications in 6G networks and IoT environments.

References

1. Huang, C., Zappone, A., Alexandropoulos, G.C., Debbah, M., Yuen, C.: Reconfigurable intelligent surfaces for energy efficiency in wireless communication. IEEE Trans. Wireless Commun. **18**(8), 4157–4170 (2020)
2. Sanchez, J.R., Edfors, O., Rusek, F., Liu, L.: Processing distribution and architecture tradeoff for large intelligent surface implementation. In: 2020 IEEE International Conference on Communications Workshops (ICC Workshops) (2020). https://doi.org/10.1109/ICCWorkshops49005.2020.9145210
3. Ma, T., Xiao, Y., Lie, X., Yang, P., Dobre, O.A.: Large Intelligent Surface Assisted Wireless Communications with Spatial Modulation and Antenna Selection. IEEE Journal on Selected Areas in Communications **38**(11) (2020)
4. Gashtasbi, A., Silva, M., Dinis, R., Guerreiro, J.: On the Performance of LDPC-Coded Large Intelligent Antenna System. In: MDPI, Appl. Sci. 2023, **13**(8), 4738 (2001). https://doi.org/10.3390/app13084738
5. Farsad, N., Goldsmith, A.: Detection algorithms for communication systems using deep learning. In: Proceedings of the 31st Conference on Neural Information Processing Systems (NeurIPS 2017). Long Beach, CA, USA (2017)
6. Xu, W., Zhong, Z., Be'ery, Y., You, X., Zhang, C.: Joint neural network equalizer and decoder. In: Proceedings of the 2018 International Symposium on Wireless Communication Systems (ISWCS), 28–31 August 2018, pp. 1–6. Lisbon, Portugal (2018). https://doi.org/10.1109/ISWCS.2018.8491177
7. Souto, P.V., Montejo-Sánchez, S., Rebelatto, J.L., Demo, R.: IRS-Aided Physical Layer Network Slicing for URLLC and eMBB. In IEEE Access **9**, 163086–163098 (2021). https://doi.org/10.1109/ACCESS.2021.3133139
8. Silva, M.M., Gashtasbi, A., Dinis, R., Pembele, G.: On the Performance of Partial LIS for 6G Systems. Electronics **13**(6), 1035 (2024). https://doi.org/10.3390/electronics13061035
9. Yen-Ming, Ch., Chi-Fu, L., Yeong-Luh, U.: An LDPC-coded generalized space shift keying scheme using a codebook-assisted low-complexity massive MIMO detector. IEEE Communications Letters **20**(3) (2016)
10. Borges, D., Carvalho, P., Dinis, R.: Low complexity MRC and EGC based receivers for SC-FDE modulations with massive MIMO schemes. IEEE Global Conference on Signal and Information Processing (GlobalSIP) (2017). https://doi.org/10.1109/GlobalSIP.2016.7905927

11. Pereira, A., Rusek, F., Gomes, M., Dinis, R.: On the Complexity Requirements of a Panel-Based Large Intelligent Surface. IEEE Global Communications Conference (2020)
12. Hu, Sh., Rusek, F., Edfore, O.: Beyond Massive MIMO: The Potential of Positioning with Large Intelligent Surfaces. IEEE Transactions on Signal Processing **66**(7) (2018)
13. Chen, Zh., et al.: Reconfigurable-Intelligent-Surface- Assisted B5G/6G Wireless Communications: Challenges, Solution, and Future Opportunities. IEEE Communications Magazine (2023)
14. Bithas, P.S., Rontogiannis, A.A., Karagiannidis G.K.: An improved threshold-based channel selection scheme for wireless communication systems. IEEE Transactions on Wireless Communications **15**(2) (2016)
15. Tsai, W.Ch., Chen, Ch.W., Teng, Ch.F., Wu, A.Y.: Low-Complexity Compressive Channel Estimation for IRS-Aided mmWave Systems With Hypernetwork-Assisted LAMP Network. IEEE Communications Letters **26**(8) (2022)
16. Tejas, K.S., Udaykumar, M., Varun, R., Suhailkhan, Dhruva Kumar, T.: Intelligent Reflecting Surface assisted wireless communication for coverage enhancement. International Conference on Smart Systems for applications in Electrical Sciences (ICSSES) (2023). https://doi.org/10.1109/ICSSES58299.2023.10200009
17. Silva, M.M., Dinis, R., Matins, G.: On the Performance of LDPC-Coded Massive MIMO Schemes with Power-Ordered NOMA Techniques. MDPI Applied Sciences **11**(18), 8684 (2021). https://doi.org/10.3390/app11188684
18. Donglin, J., Yi Zhong, Y. Zhou, X., Xu, A., Zhao, M.: Energy Efficiency in RIS-Assisted Wireless Networks: Impact of Phase Shift and Deployment. IEEE Wireless Communications and Networking Conference (WCNC) (2024). https://doi.org/10.1109/WCNC57260.2024.10571122

Improved Channel Estimation for LIS Systems Using Regularized RLS in SC-FDE Frameworks

Ali Gashtasbi[1](✉), Mario Marques da Silva[2], and Rui Dinis[1]

[1] School of Sciences and Technology, Universidade Nova de Lisboa, 2829-516 Caparica, Portugal
a.gashtasbi@campus.fct.unl.pt, rdinis@fct.pt
[2] Autonoma TechLab, 1169-023 Lisbon, Portugal
mmsilva@autonoma.pt

Abstract. Accurate channel estimation is a cornerstone for ensuring the performance of Large Intelligent Surface (LIS) systems, where the reliability of communication relies heavily on precise knowledge of the channel matrix. Conventional Least Squares (LS) estimation, while simple, suffers from high sensitivity to noise and poor performance in ill-conditioned scenarios, limiting its effectiveness in LIS environments. This paper proposes replacing LS with Regularized Recursive Least Squares (RLS) for channel estimation in LIS systems. The Regularized RLS method improves estimation accuracy by incorporating a regularization term to stabilize the solution in the presence of noise or poorly conditioned pilot matrices. Through theoretical analysis and simulation results, we demonstrate that Regularized RLS achieves better Bit Error Rate (BER) performance as a function of E_b/N_0 compared to LS, while maintaining computational efficiency. Unlike conventional RLS, the proposed method adds a regularization term that significantly improves robustness in low SNR and ill-conditioned environments, which are common in LIS systems. Furthermore, by integrating Low-density parity-check (LDPC) coding, the system achieves even lower BER, highlighting its effectiveness in mitigating errors and improving communication reliability. The proposed method is particularly well-suited for large-scale LIS systems, providing a robust and practical alternative to LS.

Keywords: Channel Estimation · Least Squares (LS) · Regularized RLS

1 Introduction

Large Intelligent Surface (LIS) systems mark a fundamental breakthrough in next-generation wireless communications, significantly enhancing spectral efficiency, network coverage, and energy management [1]. By utilizing extensive antenna arrays, LIS systems can intelligently interact with the environment, optimizing signal propagation and improving communication quality. A crucial factor in LIS performance is precise

Published by Springer Nature Switzerland AG 2025
L. M. Camarinha-Matos and F. Ferrada (Eds.): DoCEIS 2025, IFIP AICT 759, pp. 305–321, 2025.
https://doi.org/10.1007/978-3-031-97051-1_22

channel estimation, which plays a key role in signal detection and reliable data transmission. However, due to the large number of antennas, high-dimensional channel matrices, and dynamic environmental variations, channel estimation in LIS systems presents several challenges [2].

The Least Squares (LS) method is a popular choice for channel estimation due to its simplicity and low computational complexity. However, LS suffers from severe limitations, including high sensitivity to noise and poor performance in the presence of ill-conditioned pilot matrices [3]. These issues frequently arise in large-scale LIS systems, leading to degraded system performance, particularly under low signal-to-noise ratio (E_b/N_0) conditions. As a result, the inaccuracies in channel estimation significantly increase the Bit Error Rate (BER), impairing overall system efficiency.

To address these shortcomings, Recursive Least Squares (RLS) methods have been proposed, offering improved estimation accuracy by iteratively refining channel estimates based on incoming data. Standard RLS enhances BER performance over LS by assigning greater weight to recent observations, making it more effective in dynamic channel conditions [4]. Robust RLS further improves performance by employing robust weighting techniques to mitigate the impact of noise and outliers, achieving lower BER in noisy environments [5]. However, both Standard and Robust RLS struggle with numerical instability in systems with ill-conditioned pilot matrices, a common scenario in large-scale LIS deployments.

To overcome these challenges, this paper investigates the use of Regularized RLS as an effective replacement for LS, and Standard and Robust RLS, in LIS systems. By introducing a regularization parameter (μ), Regularized RLS stabilizes matrix inversion operations, significantly improving numerical robustness and accuracy in ill-conditioned scenarios [6]. Unlike Standard RLS, Regularized RLS remains stable and reliable even under low E_b/N_0 conditions. Furthermore, it provides a computationally efficient and practical alternative to Robust RLS, striking a better balance between robustness, complexity, and real-time adaptability [7].

This paper analyzes the impact of Regularized RLS on channel estimation and its ability to reduce BER across a range of E_b/N_0 values. Unlike Minimum Mean Square Error (MMSE), RLS-based methods do not require prior statistical knowledge of the channel, making them more suitable for real-time implementations in large-scale systems.

The main research question of this PhD work is: how to improve the accuracy and robustness of channel estimation in LIS systems without requiring prior knowledge of channel statistics or increasing complexity significantly.

The central hypothesis is that a regularized version of RLS can provide more stable and accurate estimation than conventional methods, especially in low SNR and under ill-conditioned pilot matrices, while keeping computational efficiency suitable for real-time implementations.

The contributions of this work are as follows:

1. **Proposal of an RLS-Based Channel Estimation Method:** An enhanced Regularized RLS algorithm is presented to address the limitations of conventional LS estimation in LIS systems [6].

2. **Simulation and Performance Analysis:** MATLAB simulations are conducted to evaluate the performance of Regularized RLS against LS and MMSE in terms of BER under various E_b/N_0 conditions.
3. **Insights on Regularization Parameter Selection:** The effect of the regularization parameter (μ) on balancing noise suppression and data fitting is analyzed, with optimized values identified for LIS environments [7].
4. **Demonstration of Computational Efficiency:** The computational complexity of Regularized RLS is shown to be comparable to LS, making it a viable alternative for large-scale and resource-constrained systems [8].

By addressing the limitations of traditional channel estimation methods, this work highlights the potential of Regularized RLS as a robust, scalable, and efficient solution for LIS systems. The findings presented in this paper contribute to advancing LIS technology, paving the way for its practical deployment in next-generation wireless networks.

The rest of the paper is organized as follows: Sect. 2 outlines the system model and channel estimation framework. Section 3 introduces the proposed RLS-based estimation method. Section 4 presents simulation results and performance analysis. Finally, Sect. 5 concludes the paper and discusses future work.

2 Relationship to AI-Powered Cyber-Physical Systems

The integration of LIS into wireless networks is a key enabler of future Cyber-Physical Systems (CPS), particularly in scenarios where smart environments require adaptive, scalable, and efficient communication infrastructures. AI-powered CPS benefit from context-aware connectivity, real-time data processing, and intelligent decision-making at the edge—all of which can be enhanced by low-complexity, high-performance communication subsystems like the one proposed in this work.

One of the main challenges in LIS-based systems is the presence of multi-user interference (MUI), which significantly limits performance in dense environments. Conventional receivers such as Maximum Ratio Combining (MRC) and Equal Gain Combining (EGC) do not inherently suppress interference during signal decoding. While advanced methods like Zero Forcing (ZF) and MMSE can mitigate this issue, they require high computational effort due to matrix inversion.

Machine learning presents a promising solution to this trade-off. Instead of explicitly modeling the channel and performing complex operations, neural networks can learn representations directly from the received signals. Deep learning-based receivers have shown the ability to replace or augment traditional equalization and detection processes, even in challenging environments such as nonlinear or dispersive channels [9, 10]. These methods can be trained without detailed channel state information and may enable simplified, adaptive receiver architectures for LIS-based CPS.

While the current work focuses on Selective LIS systems and evaluates their performance using classic receivers (ZF, MMSE, MRC, EGC), it lays the foundation for future AI-driven enhancements. Specifically, we envision extending this framework with machine learning–based antenna selection and neural network receivers that dynamically adapt to environmental changes—essential traits for AI-powered CPS operating under real-world constraints.

3 System Model

3.1 Channel Model

The block diagram outlines the signal flow in a LIS system using a SC-FDE framework. Data is modulated in QPSK and converted to parallel form, followed by the addition of a cyclic prefix (CP) to combat inter-symbol interference (ISI) [11] (Fig. 1).

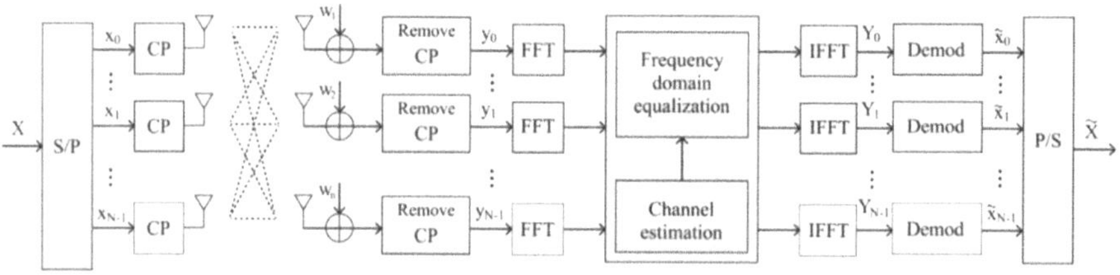

Fig. 1. Block diagram of LIS system with SC-FDE signals.

The n-th transmitted block, consisting of N data symbols sent by the t-th user equipment, is denoted as $\boldsymbol{x}_n^{(t)}$, while the corresponding block received by the r-th antenna of the LIS system is denoted as $\boldsymbol{y}_n^{(r)}$. The mapping between the time-domain signal and the frequency-domain signal for the k-th subcarrier (assumed that it remains invariant during the transmission of a given block) is represented by $DFT\left\{\boldsymbol{x}_n^{(t)} : n = 0, 1, ..., N-1\right\} = \left\{\boldsymbol{X}_k^{(t)} : k = 0, 1, ..., N-1\right\}$. This mapping applies similarly to the received signal block, the channel, and the noise, mutatis mutandis.

The received frequency-domain signal, represented in matrix-vector form, is given as follows [10]:

$$\boldsymbol{Y}_k = \left[\boldsymbol{Y}_k^{(1)}, \ldots, \boldsymbol{Y}_k^{(R)}\right]^T = \boldsymbol{H}_k \cdot \boldsymbol{X}_k + \boldsymbol{W}_k \tag{1}$$

where $\mathrm{X_k} = \left[\mathrm{X_k^{(1)}}, \ldots, \mathrm{X_k^{(T)}}\right]^\mathrm{T}$ represents the transmitted data symbols in the frequency domain, $\mathrm{H_k}$ denotes the $\mathrm{T} \times \mathrm{R}$ channel frequency-response for the k-th subcarrier, with (r, t)-th element $\mathrm{H_k^{(r,t)}}$. Moreover, $\mathrm{W_k}$ corresponds to the frequency-domain noise block for the subcarrier [12].

3.2 Equalization in SC-FDE

Assuming a non-iterative receiver, the estimated frequency domain data symbols $\tilde{\boldsymbol{X}}_k = \left[\tilde{X}_k^{(1)}, \ldots, \tilde{X}_k^{(R)}\right]^T$ are obtained as [13]:

$$\tilde{\boldsymbol{X}}_k = \boldsymbol{B}_k \cdot \boldsymbol{Y}_k \tag{2}$$

A. *ZF Equalization*

ZF equalization eliminates ISI by inverting the channel matrix (H^{-1}). In the case of frequency-selective channels with H being rectangular or near-singular, the Moore-Penrose pseudoinverse is used:

$$\boldsymbol{B}_k = \boldsymbol{H}_k^H \left(\boldsymbol{H}_k \boldsymbol{H}_k^H\right)^{-1} \tag{3}$$

B. *MMSE Equalization*

MMSE equalization balances noise suppression and ISI cancellation by minimizing the mean squared error between the transmitted and equalized signals. The equalization matrix is given by:

$$\boldsymbol{B}_k = \boldsymbol{H}_k^H \left(\boldsymbol{H}_k \boldsymbol{H}_k^H + \beta^2 \boldsymbol{I}\right)^{-1} \tag{4}$$

where $\beta = \sigma_W^2 / \sigma_X^2 = \frac{E\left[|\boldsymbol{W}_k|^2\right]}{2} / \frac{E\left[|\boldsymbol{X}_k|^2\right]}{2}$ and where $\boldsymbol{I}$ is an $R \times R$ identity matrix.

C. *MRC Equalization*

MRC is a diversity combining technique that maximizes the received signal-to-noise ratio (SNR) for each subcarrier. The equalization matrix is given by:

$$\boldsymbol{B}_k = \boldsymbol{H}_k^H \tag{5}$$

D. *EGC Equalization*

EGC is another diversity combining method, but it assigns equal weights to all the branches, preserving the phase of the received signals. The equalization matrix is given by:

$$\boldsymbol{B}_k = \exp\left\{j \cdot \arg\left(\boldsymbol{H}_k^H\right)\right\} \tag{6}$$

The Matched Filter Bound (MFB) represents the theoretical BER limit when the channel is perfectly known. It serves as a lower bound reference to evaluate the efficiency of practical channel estimation techniques. The MFB curve provides a benchmark for evaluating the performance of a channel, which is modeled as the sum of delayed and independently Rayleigh-fading rays.

3.3 Channel Estimation

The channel between the base station, employing a LIS system, and the user can be described as a beyond multiple-input multiple-output (MIMO) system, where the LIS elements act as a channel reflector. Accurate channel estimation is crucial for achieving reliable communication in LIS systems, as it directly impacts key performance metrics such as BER. The LS estimator is widely used due to its simplicity and low computational complexity. However, its performance deteriorates in low E_b/N_0 conditions due to noise amplification. The channel between the transmitter, LIS, and receiver can be modeled as a MIMO system, where the pilot symbols ($\boldsymbol{X}_p$) are used to estimate the channel matrix

($\boldsymbol{H}_p$). The relationship between the received pilot signals $\boldsymbol{Y}_p$ and the transmitted pilots $\boldsymbol{X}_p$ is given by [14]:

$$\boldsymbol{Y}_p = \boldsymbol{H}_p \boldsymbol{X}_p + \boldsymbol{W} \tag{7}$$

To estimate the channel matrix $\mathrm{H_p}$, conventional LS estimation solves the following optimization problem [12]:

$$\hat{\boldsymbol{H}}_{LS} = \arg\min_{H} \boldsymbol{Y}_p - \boldsymbol{H}_p \cdot \boldsymbol{X}_p^2 \tag{8}$$

The closed-form solution for LS estimation is [13]:

$$\hat{\boldsymbol{H}}_{LS} = \boldsymbol{Y}_p \cdot \tilde{\boldsymbol{X}}_p \tag{9}$$

where $\tilde{\mathrm{X}}_\mathrm{p} = \mathrm{X}_\mathrm{p}^\mathrm{H}\left(\mathrm{X}_\mathrm{p} \cdot \mathrm{X}_\mathrm{p}^\mathrm{H}\right)^{-1}$ is the Moore-Penrose pseudo inverse of $\mathrm{X_p}$.

While LS is computationally efficient, its performance is degraded in noisy environments due to its lack of robustness against noise. To address this, Regularized RLS introduces a regularization term to stabilize the solution [15].

The Regularized RLS algorithm introduces a regularization term to the cost function to address issues such as ill-conditioned data or overfitting. This improves the numerical stability of the estimation and ensures a more robust solution in scenarios with limited pilot symbols or high noise levels.

The cost function for Regularized RLS is [16]:

$$J(n) = \sum_{i=1}^{n} \lambda^{n-i}(\boldsymbol{y}(i) - \boldsymbol{H}^H \boldsymbol{x}(i)^2 + \mu \boldsymbol{H}_F^2) \tag{10}$$

where $\mu \succ 0$ shows regularization parameter, controlling the trade-off between minimizing the error and the penalty on the channel matrix H. $\mathrm{y(i)}$ is the received signal at time i, $\mathrm{x(i)}$ is the transmitted signal (input) at time i. $\lambda \in (0, 1]$ is the forgetting factor (compared to LS, which does not include a forgetting factor or regularization.). Also $\mathrm{H_F^2} = \mathrm{Tr}\left(\mathrm{H\,H^H}\right)$ is Frobenius Norm of the channel matrix.

Recursive Update at Time n: For each incoming signal:

Gain Vector [16]:

$$\boldsymbol{K}_{\mathrm{Reg}}(n) = \frac{\boldsymbol{P}_{n-1}\boldsymbol{x}(n)}{\lambda + \boldsymbol{x}^H(n)\boldsymbol{P}_{n-1}\boldsymbol{x}(n) + \mu} \tag{11}$$

Update the channel estimate [16]:

$$\boldsymbol{H}_n = \boldsymbol{H}_{n-1} + \boldsymbol{K}(n)\left[\boldsymbol{y}(n) - \boldsymbol{X}(n)\,\boldsymbol{H}_{n-1}^H\right] \tag{12}$$

Update the inverse correlation matrix [14]:

$$\boldsymbol{P}_n = \frac{1}{\lambda}\left[\boldsymbol{P}_{n-1} - \boldsymbol{K}(n)\boldsymbol{X}^H(n)\,\boldsymbol{P}_{n-1}\right] \tag{13}$$

RLS improves robustness without requiring prior knowledge of channel statistics, making it particularly suitable for LIS systems.

MMSE channel estimation is a popular alternative to LS and RLS methods, as it minimizes the mean squared error while leveraging statistical information about noise and channel characteristics. The MMSE estimator is given by [17]:

$$\hat{\boldsymbol{H}}_{MMSE} = \boldsymbol{Y}_p \cdot \boldsymbol{X}_p^H \left(\boldsymbol{X}_p \boldsymbol{X}_p^H + \sigma^2 \boldsymbol{I} \right)^{-1} \tag{14}$$

In this expression, σ^2 denotes the noise variance, while X_p represents the pilot matrix. While MMSE generally achieves lower BER compared to LS and RLS, it requires prior knowledge of the noise variance and channel statistics. This dependence can limit its applicability in dynamic or resource-constrained scenarios, where such information may not be readily available.

4 Proposed RLS-Based Channel Estimation Method

The design of pilot signals plays a significant role in LS-based channel estimation, particularly in LIS systems. The pilot should be carefully designed to provide enough information and channel state information (CSI) for a good estimation. This section explores the optimization of RLS channel estimation for improved accuracy and performance.

4.1 Motivation for Regularized RLS

Conventional LS channel estimation is widely used due to its simplicity and computational efficiency. However, LS suffers from two major drawbacks:

1. **Noise Sensitivity:** LS directly minimizes the squared error without considering noise characteristics, leading to significant degradation in performance under low SNR conditions [18].
2. **Ill-Conditioning:** In scenarios where the system matrix is ill-conditioned (e.g., due to closely spaced pilot symbols or weak channel paths); LS estimates become unstable, amplifying errors [18].
3. **Computational Efficiency:** The RLS method achieves significant performance gains without a notable increase in computational complexity compared to LS. This efficiency makes it viable for large-scale LIS systems, unlike more complex methods like MMSE, which require prior knowledge of channel statistics [20].
4. **Flexibility without Statistical Channel Knowledge:** Unlike MMSE or other advanced techniques, the RLS method does not rely on prior knowledge of channel statistics or noise variance. This feature enhances its adaptability to a wide range of deployment scenarios, including dynamic environments [21, 22].

To address these limitations, we propose using Regularized RLS estimation, which incorporates a regularization term to enhance robustness against noise and mitigate instability caused by ill-conditioning. The regularization effectively balances the trade-off between fitting the observed data and suppressing noise effects, leading to improved channel estimation accuracy in practical scenarios.

Although the proposed method is based on RLS, the inclusion of a regularization term brings notable improvements. In large-scale LIS systems, where the pilot matrix can be highly ill-conditioned and noise levels are high, standard RLS may become unstable. The regularized version stabilizes the solution and increases reliability, especially without needing prior channel statistics.

Sparse recovery methods are another group of techniques used for channel estimation in LIS systems. These methods assume that the wireless channel has only a few strong paths (sparse structure). Algorithms such as OMP (Orthogonal Matching Pursuit) or Least Absolute Shrinkage and Selection Operator (LASSO) are commonly used in this approach. While they can give good estimation results, they usually require many iterations and high computation. This makes them less suitable for real-time applications where speed and efficiency are important. In comparison, the Regularized RLS method is much faster and simpler, and it does not need any prior information about channel sparsity [23].

4.2 Regularization Parameter Selection

- μ Controls the strength of the penalty term added to the cost function in $J(n)$ RLS [16].
- Small μ: The regularization term $\mu \boldsymbol{H}_F^2$ has little effect, focusing primarily on minimizing the residual error [24].
- Large μ: The regularization term dominates, simplifying the solution but potentially introducing bias.

Effects of Different Values of μ [25]:

1. Small μ (e.g., $\mu(0, 1)$):
   - o Balances the trade-off between minimizing the residual error and controlling the model's complexity.
   - o Impact:
     - Improves robustness to noise.
     - Reduces overfitting without introducing significant bias in the solution.
   - o Typically works well in practical scenarios with some noise and moderate channel dynamics.
2. Large μ (e.g., $\mu = 1$):
   - o Strong regularization term, heavily penalizing large channel estimates.
   - o Impact:
     - Over-smooths or biases the channel estimate.
     - Reduces the model's ability to capture fine details of the channel.
   - o When the channel is nearly static, or the input-output relationship is simple.

In conventional systems, the value of μ is typically set within the range of 0.001 to 0.1. A smaller μ is preferred for channels with high SNR or rapid fluctuations, whereas a larger μ is more suitable for low SNR conditions or stable channels [26].

These results show that even a small regularization value (e.g., 0.001) can make a significant improvement in estimation stability and BER, especially under noise. This highlights the practical value of the regularization term.

An adaptive mechanism for tuning μ can be used. For instance, μ can be adjusted based on the estimated noise power or a feedback loop from the BER performance. Machine learning-based tuning may improve performance across changing conditions.

5 Impact of LDPC Coding on RLS Channel Estimation

Before QPSK modulation, the input bits are encoded using LDPC coding. After channel estimation and equalization, the received bits are decoded, and the BER is calculated. The integration of LDPC coding with RLS-based channel estimation significantly improves performance in LIS-assisted communication systems. The combination enhances error resilience, making the system more robust in noisy conditions. This highlights the potential of merging advanced channel estimation and error correction techniques for next-generation wireless networks [27].

6 Computational Complexity

Analyzing computational complexity is crucial in algorithm design and evaluation because it provides a theoretical framework to understand and compare the efficiency of different algorithms. Provide a brief overview of the LS, RLS, and MMSE algorithms, focusing on their mathematical operations [7, 8]:

- LS involve solving a matrix inversion problem.
- RLS updates the solution iteratively to avoid repeated matrix inversion.
- MMSE incorporates statistical prior information to minimize the error.

Compared to MMSE, which requires prior knowledge of noise and complex matrix operations, the proposed Regularized RLS keeps the complexity low, almost similar to LS. This makes it very suitable for real-time LIS systems.

Computational complexity helps identify how the execution time of an algorithm scales with input size (N, T). In Table 1, for matrix pilot $\boldsymbol{X} \in \mathbb{C}^{T \times N}$, comparing the $\mathrm{O}(N^3)$ complexity of the LS algorithm with the $\mathrm{O}(MN^2)$ complexity of RLS highlights the relative efficiency of the two methods for large inputs or streaming data. M Refers to the number of recursive updates, iterations, or data windows used in the RLS algorithm. It can depend on how the algorithm is structured for the given problem.

This confirms that Regularized RLS offers an excellent trade-off: much better performance than LS, and less complexity than MMSE (Table 2).

7 Simulation Results

The BER performance in LIS systems, using SC-FDE block transmission was evaluated through Monte Carlo simulations. The results are expressed as a function of the energy of the transmitted bits and the noise's one-sided power spectral density. A block size of N

Table 1. Computational Complexity Comparison of Channel Estimation Algorithms (LS, RLS, and MMSE)

Algorithm	Operation	Complexity
LS	Matrix inversion, multiplications	$O\left(TN^2 + N^3\right)$
RLS	Recursive updates	$O\left(MN^2\right)$
MMSE	Matrix inversion, multiplications	$O\left(TN^2 + N^3\right)$

Table 2. Comparison of Channel Estimation Methods (LS, RLS, and MMSE)

Method	Requires Prior Channel Statistics	Handles Ill-Conditioned Pilots	Robustness to Noise	Computational Complexity
Least Squares (LS)	No	No	Low	Low
Standard RLS	No	No	Medium	Medium
Regularized RLS (Proposed)	No	Yes	High	Medium
MMSE	Yes	Yes	High	High

= 256 symbols with QPSK modulation was used, and identical results were observed for different values of N (as long as $N > > 1$). The LIS system consists of multiple panels, each containing antenna elements spaced $\lambda/2$ apart. The channel correlation between antennas creates the beam described above, and the simulation included five statistically independent equal-power paths to model an extreme Rayleigh fading channel.

Figure 2 illustrates the BER performance versus E_b/N_0 for different values of, μ in the Regularized RLS algorithm across various estimation methods, including ZF/MMSE, MRC, and EGC.

The results indicate that a smaller, μ leads to improved BER performance, bringing the system closer to the MFB limit. Specifically, $\mu = 0.001$ achieves the best performance across all methods, with ZF/MMSE showing the closest resemblance to MFB. As μ increases, the BER degrades, demonstrating a loss of accuracy due to adaptation instability. Notably, when, $\mu = 1$, all methods exhibit the highest BER, highlighting the adverse effects of large step sizes.

Among the different estimation techniques, ZF/MMSE achieves the lowest BER, making it the most effective approach. MRC provides intermediate performance, while EGC consistently exhibits the highest BER across all μ values, making it the least favorable choice. The difference between step sizes is more pronounced in the low E_b/N_0 region, where noise significantly impacts system performance.

From these results, we conclude that selecting a small step size ($\mu = 0.001$) is optimal for achieving the best BER performance. However, if faster convergence is required, a moderate step size such as, $\mu = 0.01$ can be considered as a trade-off. In contrast, larger step sizes ($\mu \geq 0.1$) should be avoided due to their instability and performance degradation.

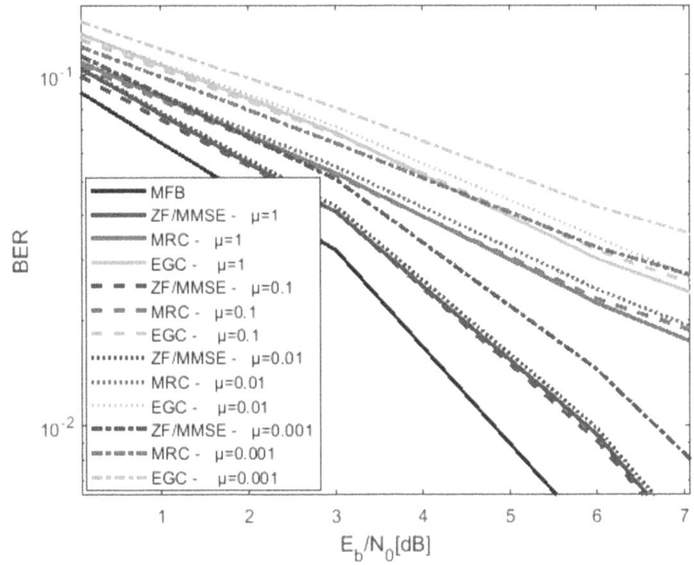

Fig. 2. BER results for Regularized RLS channel estimation for various regularization parameters in a LIS system.

Figure 3 compares the BER performance of LS, RLS, and MMSE channel estimation methods under varying E_b/N_0 conditions, along with the MFB. Despite its simplicity and computational efficiency, the LS method exhibits poor BER performance due to its high sensitivity to noise, particularly at low E_b/N_0 levels, limiting its applicability to low-noise, low-complexity systems.

In contrast, RLS outperforms LS by adaptively updating channel estimates, resulting in better noise suppression and improved BER across all E_b/N_0 values. Moreover, RLS is computationally more efficient than MMSE and does not require prior knowledge of noise variance or channel statistics, making it well-suited for dynamic and resource-constrained systems.

MMSE, on the other hand, delivers the best BER performance, approaching the MFB at higher E_b/N_0 levels. However, due to its high computational cost and reliance on precise knowledge of noise variance and channel statistics, it may not always be feasible in practical implementations.

Overall, the RLS method maintains an optimal balance between accuracy and computational complexity, making it a viable alternative to LS and MMSE. It is particularly well-suited for systems that require enhanced performance over LS while avoiding the high computational burden of MMSE.

Figure 4 presents a BER vs. E_b/N_0 comparison for different detection techniques, with and without LDPC coding. The results indicate that LDPC coding significantly

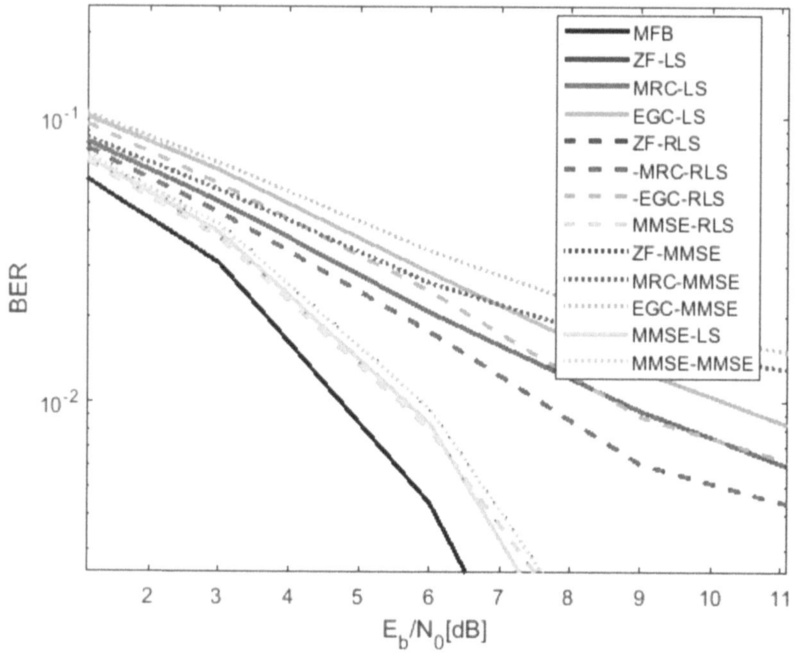

Fig. 3. BER Performance Comparison of LS, RLS, and MMSE Channel Estimation.

enhances performance by reducing BER across all detection schemes. Among the evaluated methods, the combination of MRC and LDPC achieves the lowest BER, closely approaching the MFB. Additionally, ZF/MMSE detectors benefit considerably from LDPC, demonstrating noticeable BER improvements compared to their non-LDPC counterparts.

Conversely, the EGC technique exhibits the weakest performance, with a relatively smaller gap between its LDPC and non-LDPC versions compared to other methods. At higher E_b/N_0 levels, the impact of LDPC coding becomes more pronounced, further emphasizing its effectiveness in mitigating noise. Across all scenarios, LDPC consistently outperforms the non-LDPC results, confirming the advantages of error correction in enhancing system reliability.

These findings suggest that MRC with LDPC is the most reliable choice for improving communication performance. Furthermore, the combination of ZF/MMSE with LDPC offers a well-balanced trade-off between computational complexity and error resilience. Overall, integrating LDPC coding with advanced detection techniques significantly enhances system robustness and efficiency.

Figure 5 evaluates the execution time of LS, RLS, and MMSE algorithms based on the number of antennas. LS achieve the lowest execution time with minimal growth due to its $O(MN^2)$ complexity, making it highly efficient for large systems but lacking adaptability. RLS improves LS by adding adaptability with its recursive updates, making it suitable for time-varying channels despite higher complexity $O(N^2)$. MMSE, with $O(TN^2 + N^3)$ complexity, provides the best accuracy but at a high computational cost,

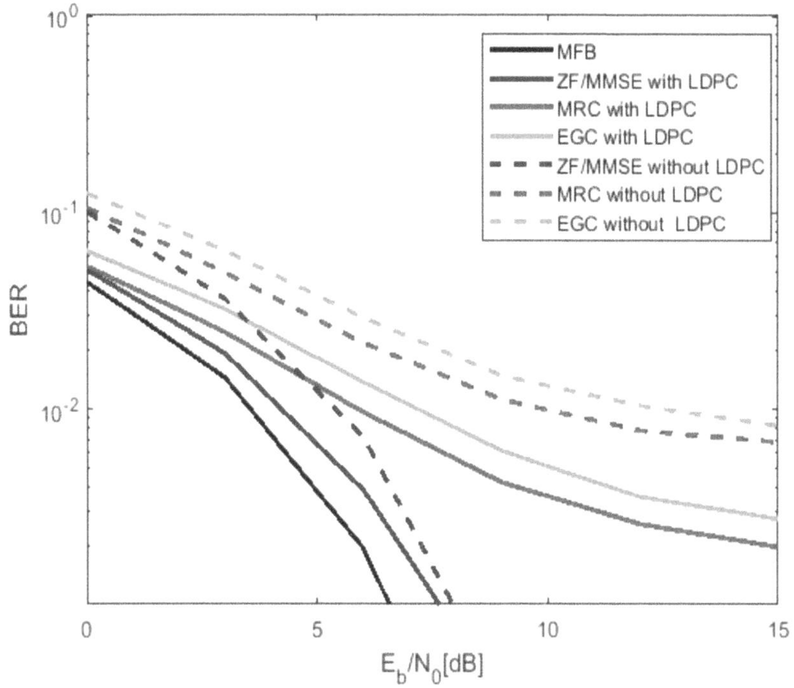

Fig. 4. BER Performance Comparison of RLS Channel Estimation with and without LDPC code.

limiting its practicality for large-scale or real-time systems. In comparison, RLS offers a good balance between accuracy and efficiency, making it a viable alternative to MMSE in many scenarios. Overall, LS can be enhanced with RLS, and RLS stands out as a practical and adaptive solution for scenarios where MMSE is too costly. The simulation results align closely with theoretical complexity analysis.

Table 3 demonstrates that Regularized RLS outperforms traditional LS in terms of channel estimation accuracy and approaches the performance of MMSE.

Recent studies have proposed deep learning-based channel estimation techniques. Although these methods often achieve high accuracy, they require extensive training, large datasets, and high computational resources, which may limit real-time deployment. In contrast, the proposed Regularized RLS offers a lightweight and adaptive solution without training overhead, making it suitable for real-world LIS systems.

In this study, noise variance is assumed to be known. However, in practical scenarios where the noise power is estimated and may be inaccurate, the performance of MMSE and other estimators can degrade. Since Regularized RLS does not rely on prior noise statistics, it remains more stable in such cases.

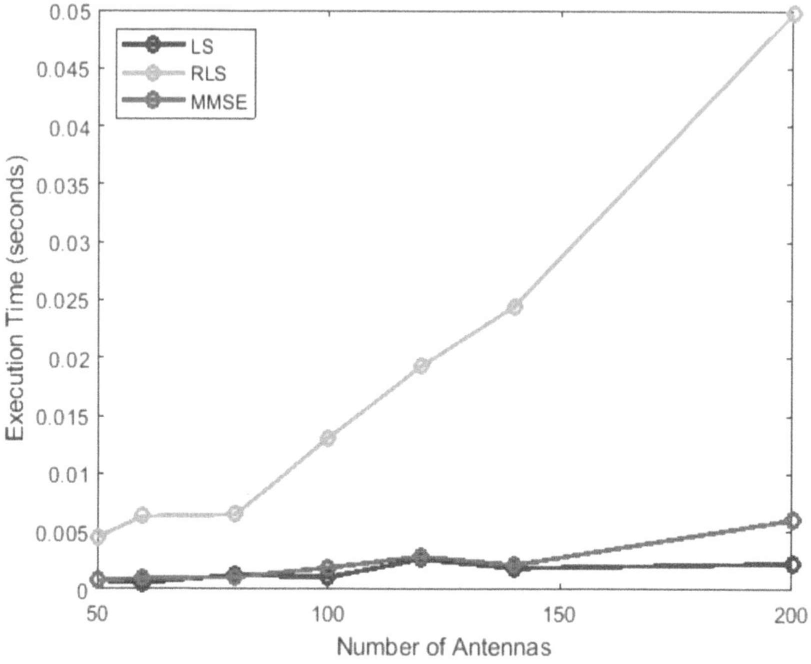

Fig. 5. Execution Time vs. Number of Antennas for LS, RLS, and MMSE Algorithm.

Table 3. Improved channel estimation with Regularized RLS compared to LS and MMSE.

Aspect	LS Channel Estimation	Regularized LS (RLS) Channel Estimation	MMSE Channel Estimation
Noise Suppression	Sensitive to noise, amplifies it in low SNR environments	Suppresses noise effectively with regularization	Balances noise suppression and inter-symbol interference (ISI) cancellation
Regularization Parameter (μ)	Not applicable	Optimal μ (e.g., 0.01) balances overfitting and underfitting	Not applicable
Bit Error Rate (BER)	Higher BER	Significantly reduced BER, especially at low-to-moderate E_b/N_0	Typically achieves the lowest BER but at higher computational cost

(continued)

Table 3. (*continued*)

Aspect	LS Channel Estimation	Regularized LS (RLS) Channel Estimation	MMSE Channel Estimation
Robustness to Noise	Low robustness in noisy scenarios	High robustness, particularly at $\mu = 0.01$	Strong robustness due to regularization
Adaptability	Poor adaptability to varying E_b/N_0	Adapts well to different signal-to-noise ratios	Highly dependent on accurate prior statistical information
Stability	Unstable with high pilot correlation or weak paths	Stabilized by regularization term (μI)	Stable due to statistical assumptions, but performance degrades with inaccurate priors
Computational Complexity	Low computational complexity	Comparable to LS, with slight overhead for regularization	Higher complexity due to statistical computations

8 Conclusions

This study presented an RLS method for channel estimation in LIS systems operating within the SC-FDE framework. By incorporating a regularization term, the proposed RLS approach demonstrated enhanced robustness against noise and improved channel estimation stability, particularly under challenging low SNR conditions. Simulation results highlighted significant improvements in BER performance, achieving a reduction in BER at moderate SNR levels compared to conventional LS estimation.

The computational simplicity and independence from prior channel statistics make Regularized RLS a viable solution for real-time implementations in large-scale LIS systems, particularly in dynamic or resource-constrained environments. Moreover, Regularized RLS provides a practical alternative to more complex methods like MMSE, striking a balance between performance improvement and computational efficiency. Furthermore, results showed that integrating LDPC coding further reduces BER, especially at higher E_b/N_0.

Overall, the method successfully balances performance and complexity, making it a practical and robust alternative to traditional LS and standard RLS for large LIS systems.

9 Future Work

Future research could focus on the adaptive selection of the regularization parameter to optimize performance under varying noise conditions and based on real-time SNR estimation. Additionally, extending this study to multi-user and multi-panel LIS scenarios, along with the implementation of higher-order modulation schemes such as 1024-QAM, would further expand the applicability of the RLS method in next-generation wireless networks. Lastly, while this work focused on LDPC coding, the integration of Polar Codes—which are known for their capacity-approaching performance—could be explored as an alternative error correction scheme. Comparative studies between LDPC and Polar codes may provide valuable insights for optimizing coding strategies in next-generation LIS communication systems.

References

1. Hu, Sh., Chitti, K., Rusek, F., Edfors, O.: User Assignment with Distributed Large Intelligent Surface (LIS) Systems. IEEE 29th Annual International Symposium on Personal, Indoor, and Mobile Radio Communications (PIMRC) (2018). https://doi.org/10.1109/PIMRC.2018.8580675
2. Hu, S., Rusek, F., Edfors, O.: The Potential of Using Large Antenna Arrays on Intelligent Surfaces. arXiv: 1702.03128v1 [cs.IT] 10 Feb 2017
3. Khan, A.M., Jeoti, V., Zakariya, M.A.: Improved Pilot–based LS and MMSE Channel Estimation using DFT for DVB-T OFDM Systems. IEEE, ISWTA (2013). https://doi.org/10.1109/ISWTA.2013.6688752
4. Yang, F., Albu, F., Yang, J.: An alternative solution to the dynamically regularized RLS algorithm. Proceedings of APSIPA Annual Summit and Conference (2019). https://doi.org/10.1109/APSIPAASC47483.2019.9023073
5. Paleologu, C., Benesty, J., Stanciu, C., Anghel, C., Stenta, M.: Robust Regularization of the Recursive Least-Squares Algorithm. IEEE, 8th International Conference on Electronics, Computers and Artificial Intelligence (ECAI) (2016). https://doi.org/10.1109/ECAI.2016.7861070
6. Ai, J., Yue, G., Cheng, X., Li, Sh.: Low Complexity RLS Channel Estimation for SC-FDE in 60 GHz Communications. IEEE 14th International Conference on Communication Technology (2012). https://doi.org/10.1109/ICCT.2012.6511212
7. Takano, Y., Hsuan-Jung, S.: A Low-Complexity LS turbo channel estimation technique for MU-MIMO Systems. IEEE Signal Processing Letters **25**(5) (2018). https://doi.org/10.1109/LSP.2018.2820811
8. Feng, Y., Chang, L., Hai, H., Chang-Hai, J., Kai-Yuan, C.: On the computational complexity of parameter estimation in adaptive testing strategies. 15th IEEE Pacific Rim International Symposium on Dependable Computing (2009). https://doi.org/10.1109/PRDC.2009.22
9. Farsad, N., Goldsmith, A.: Detection algorithms for communication systems using deep learning. In: Proceedings of the 31st Conference on Neural Information Processing Systems (NeurIPS 2017). Long Beach, CA, USA (2017)
10. Xu, W., Zhong, Z., Be'ery, Y., You, X., Zhang, C.: Joint neural network equalizer and decoder. In: Proceedings of the 2018 International Symposium on Wireless Communication Systems (ISWCS), pp. 1–6. Lisbon, Portugal (2018). https://doi.org/10.1109/ISWCS.2018.8491177(2018)11
11. Pereira, A., Rusek, F., Gomes, M., Dinis, R.: On the complexity requirements of a panel-based large intelligent surface. IEEE Global Communications Conference (2020)
12. Silva, M.M., Gashtasbi, A., Dinis, R., Pembele, G.: On the performance of partial LIS for 6G systems. Electronics **13**(6), 1035 (2024). https://doi.org/10.3390/electronics13061035
13. Silva, M.M, Dinis, R, Aleixo, J., Oliveira, M.L.: On the Performance of LDPC-Coded MIMO Schemes for Underwater Communications Using 5G-like Processing. MDPI, Appl. Sci. **12**(11), 5549 (2022). https://doi.org/10.3390/app12115549
14. Wang, H., Zhou, F., Yu, P.: An improved threshold wavelet denoising LS channel estimation algorithm based on IoT. IEEE, 2020 International Wireless Communications and Mobile Computing (IWCMC), pp. 326–330. Limassol, Cyprus (2020). https://doi.org/10.1109/IWCMC48107.2020.9148192

15. Elisei-Iliescu, C., et al.: Robust Variable-Regularized RLS Algorithms. IEEE, HSCMA (2017). https://doi.org/10.1109/HSCMA.2017.7895584
16. Elisei-Iliescu, C., Paleologu, C., Benesty, J., Stanciu, C., Anghel, C.: A Regularized RLS Algorithm for the Identification of Third-Order Tensors. IEEE, International Symposium on Electronics and Telecommunications (ISETC) (2020)
17. Kewen, L., Ke, X..: Research of MMSE and LS Channel Estimation in OFDM Systems. IEEE, 2nd International Conference on Information Science and Engineering (2010)
18. Zamiri-Jafarian, H., Pasupathy, S.: MIMO-OFDM Channel Estimation Using Improved LS Algorithm. IEEE Vehicular Technology Conference (2006). https://doi.org/10.1109/VTCF.2006.122
19. Kumar Mallik, S., Chakrabarti, S., Singh, S.N.: A Regularized Method for Solving Ill-Conditioned Hybrid State Estimation Problem. IEEE, 2012 2nd International Conference on Power, Control and Embedded Systems
20. Wang, H., Zhou, F., Yu, P., Liu, Sh.: An Improved Threshold Wavelet Denoising LS Channel Estimation Algorithm Based on IoT. IEEE 2020 International Wireless Communications and Mobile Computing (IWCMC)
21. Rana, M., Hosain, K.: Adaptive Channel Estimation Techniques for MIMO OFDM Systems. (IJACSA) Int. J. Adv. Comp. Sci. Appl. **1**(6) (2010)
22. Savaux, V., Louët, Y.: LMMSE channel estimation in OFDM context: A review. IET (2016). https://doi.org/10.1049/iet-spr.2016.0185
23. Crespo-Marques, E., Maciel, N., Naviner, L., Cai, H., Yang, J.: A review of sparse recovery algorithms. IEEE Access **7** (2018). https://doi.org/10.1109/ACCESS.2018.2886471
24. Babadi, B., Kalouptsidis, N., Tarokh, V.: SPARLS: The Sparse RLS Algorithm. IEEE, Transaction On Signal Processing **58**(8) (2010)
25. Suliman, M., Ballal, T., Al-Naffouri, T.Y.: Robust Regularized Least-Squares Beamforming Approach to Signal Estimation. IEEE, GlobalSIP (2016)
26. Hossain, M., Farhad, S.M., Riasat, T.: Performance analysis of RLS and VSS-LMS channel estimation techniques for 4G MIMO OFDM systems. IEEE, 15th International Conference on Computer and Information Technology (ICCIT) (2012)
27. Gashtasbi, A., Silva, M.M., Dinis, R., Guerreiro, J.: On the performance of LDPC-coded large intelligent antenna system. In: MDPI, Appl. Sci. 2023 **13**(8), 4738 (2024). https://doi.org/10.3390/app13084738

Smart Power Systems

Detection and Mitigation Using PCA – Adaptive Sliding Mode Controller

Seema Yadav[1](✉), Nand Kishor[2], and Shubhi Purwar[1]

[1] Department of Electrical Engineering, Motilal Nehru National Institute of Technology Allahabad, Teliarganj, India
seemayadaven1041@gmail.com, shubhi@mnnit.ac.in
[2] Østfold University College, Fredrikstad Campus, Oslo, Norway
nand.kishor@hiof.no

Abstract. This paper presents a novel integration of principal component analysis (PCA) for attack detection with adaptive sliding mode control (SMC) for mitigating cyber-physical attacks (CPAs) in power systems. Key contributions include: (1) an enhanced PCA framework with temporal correlations and adaptive thresholds achieving detection response times of $\pm$ 0.01 s; (2) an advanced SMC incorporating dynamic boundary layers and gain adaptation mechanisms that ensures robust performance under attack conditions; (3) a computationally efficient implementation suitable for real-time deployment. Simulations on an IEEE 3-machine 9-bus system demonstrate frequency deviations contained within $\pm$ 0.15 Hz and rotor angle stability maintained within $\pm 2.25°$. The integrated approach achieves 0.93 system resilience while reducing settling time and oscillation magnitude by approximately 30% compared to conventional control methods, demonstrating practical viability for enhancing power system security.

Keywords: Frequency Control · Principal Component Analysis · Power System Security · Sliding Mode Control

1 Introduction

Power system frequency stability has become increasingly critical with the growing complexity and interconnectedness of modern electrical grids. Load frequency deviations caused by disturbances and cyber physical attacks (CPAs) can severely impact system reliability, power quality, and overall grid stability [1]. While traditional frequency monitoring relies on threshold-based detection and conventional PID controllers, these approaches often lack sensitivity to detect subtle anomalies and may not respond quickly enough to prevent cascading failures [2].

Recent studies have explored detection approaches such as wavelet transforms [3], neural networks [4], and statistical methods [5]. Principal component analysis (PCA) has emerged as a promising detection method as it can capture complex relationships in multivariate data while being computationally efficient [6]. However, existing PCA

Published by Springer Nature Switzerland AG 2025
L. M. Camarinha-Matos and F. Ferrada (Eds.): DoCEIS 2025, IFIP AICT 759, pp. 325–336, 2025.
https://doi.org/10.1007/978-3-031-97051-1_23

implementations often treat detection as a static problem, despite the dynamic nature of load frequency variations [7], like fault detection and diagnosis systems [8].

For mitigation, strategies including model predictive control [9], H-infinity control [10], and sliding mode control (SMC) [11], have been proposed. Traditional SMC provides robustness against uncertainties but suffers from chattering that can stress system actuators. An adaptive SMC scheme proposed in [12] can reduce chattering, but slows the response times. Fault-tolerant control strategies [13] offer complementary perspectives but often lack the rapid response characteristics needed for CPAs.

1.1 Contribution to AI-Powered Cyber-Physical Systems

This research contributes to AI-powered cyber-physical systems via: (1) An enhanced PCA framework that intelligently separates measurement data into regular and irregular subspaces, detecting subtle attack patterns with response times of ± 0.01 s; (2) An SMC with adaptive gain mechanisms that autonomously adjusts control parameters based on system conditions, enabling intelligent response to varying attack intensities; (3) Integration of statistical anomaly detection with adaptive control theory, creating a closed-loop framework for autonomous threat detection and mitigation; (4) Resource efficient implementation suitable for compute-constrained environments, unlike compute-intensive deep learning methods. The framework achieves 0.93 system resilience across multiple simultaneous CPAs, showing practical applicability for next-generation power system security.

The rest of the paper is organized as follows: Sect. 2 presents problem formulation and system modeling. Section 3 details PCA-based detection framework. Section 4 describes adaptive SMC-based mitigation. Section 5 presents simulation result. Section 6 concludes the paper and provides future scope.

2 Problem Formulation and System Modelling

This section establishes mathematical foundation for an IEEE 3-machine 9-bus power system model shown in Fig. 1.

A standard continuous-time state-space representation of linearized model is built for each generator i. The state vector $x_i \in \mathbb{R}^4$ comprises four key variables, $x_i = [\,\Delta\delta_i\ \Delta\omega_i\ P_{mi}\ E_{fi}\,]^T$ where $\Delta\delta_i$ represents rotor angle deviation from reference (in radians), $\Delta\omega_i$ denotes the rotor speed deviation (in p.u.), P_{mi} indicates the mechanical power deviation (in p.u.), and E_{fi} represents the field voltage deviation (in p.u.). The continuous-time dynamics for generator i are described by:

$$\dot{\mathbf{x}}(t) = Ax_i(t) + B_i u_i(t) + E_i d_i(t), \tag{1}$$

where $u_i(t)$ represents the control input vector and $d_i(t)$ denotes the disturbance vector including load changes. The matrices A_i (4 ×4) captures dynamic relationships between state variables, $B_i(4 \times 1)$ maps control input to state changes, E_i (4 ×1) represents how

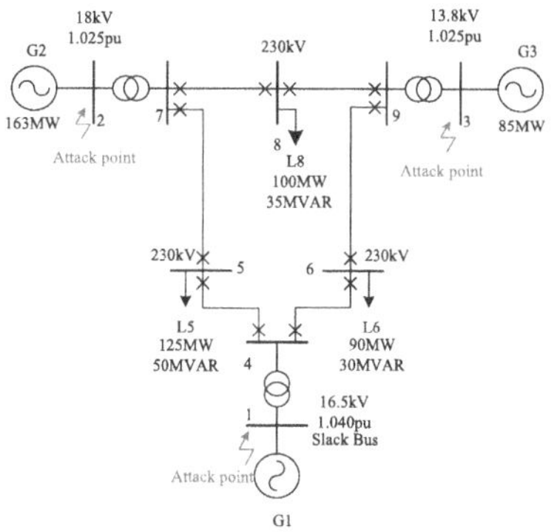

Fig. 1. IEEE 3-machine 9-bus system.

external disturbance impact the system states, structured as:

$$A_i = \begin{bmatrix} 0 & \omega_o & 0 & 0 \\ -K_{1i}/2H_i & -D_i/2H_i & 1/2H_i & K_{2i}/2H_i \\ 0 & 0 & -1/T_{vi} & 0 \\ -K_{3i}/T_{ai} & 0 & 0 & -1/T_{ai} \end{bmatrix} \tag{2}$$

$$B_i = [0\ 0\ 1/T_{vi}\ K_{4i}/T_{ai}]^T$$

$$E_i = \left[0\ -\frac{1}{2H_i}\ 0\ 0\right]^T.$$

The physical parameters in these matrices include the nominal system frequency ω_o (377 rad/s), inertia constant H_i, damping coefficient D_i, valve time constant T_{vi}, exciter time constant T_{ai}, and system gains K_{1i} through K_{4i}.

2.1 Measurement Model with Attack

The measurement equation for generator i for CPA is given by:

$$y_i(t) = C_i x_i(t) + w_i(t) + e_i(t), \tag{3}$$

where $w_i(t)$ represents measurement noise bounded by $|w_i(t)| \leq \delta_w$, $e_i(t)$ denotes false data injection (FDI), and C_i represents measurement matrix. The full system state vector $X \in \mathbb{R}^{12}$ is formed by concatenating the state vectors of all three generators: $X = \left[x_1^T\ x_2^T\ x_3^T\right]^T$. The attack vector $e_i(t)$ represents CPAs on sensors with support as:

$$\text{supp}(e_i(t)) = \{i \in P : e_i(t) \neq 0\}, \tag{4}$$

where $|\text{supp}(e_i(t))|$ denotes number of sensors under attack at time t.

2.2 Control Structure

For each generator i, the conventional control structure implements a proportional-integral (PI) controller:

$$u_i(t) = K_{Pi} y_i(t) + K_{Ii} \int_0^t y_i(\tau) d\tau, \tag{5}$$

where K_{P_i} and K_{I_i} represent the proportional and integral gains respectively. The control input depends on the area control error (ACE):

$$ACE_i = \beta_i \Delta f_i + \sum \Delta P_{tie^{ij}}, \tag{6}$$

where β_i is the frequency bias factor for generator i, Δf_i is frequency deviation, and $\Delta P_{tie^{ij}}$ is tie-line power deviation between generators i and j. The network coupling appears through the power flow equations:

$$\Delta Ptie_{ij} = T_{ij}(\delta_i - \delta_j), \tag{7}$$

where T_{ij} is the tie-line synchronizing coefficient between generators i and j. For practical implementation, the PI controller is discretized with a sampling period T:

$$xc[k+1] = x_c[k] + Ty[k] \tag{8}$$

$$u[k] = K_P y[k] + K_I x_c[k], \tag{9}$$

where x_c represents the controller state and k denotes the discrete time index.

3 PCA-Based Detection Framework

This section presents an enhanced PCA framework for detecting CPAs. Figure 2 illustrates a comprehensive protection framework for a power system with three generators (G_1, G_2, G_3) and associated remote terminal units (RTU_1, RTU_2, RTU_3).

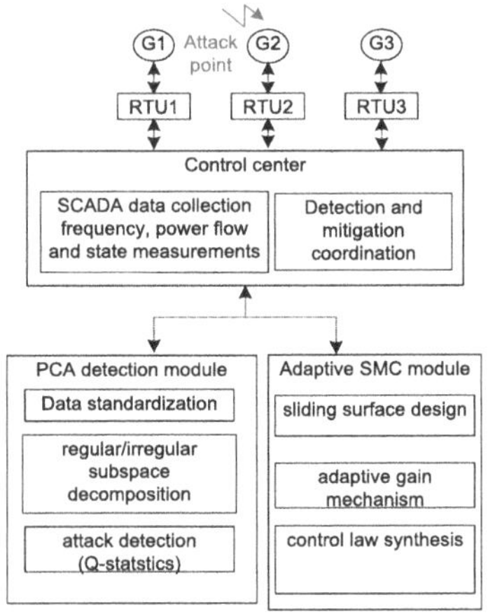

Fig. 2. Framework for CPA detection and mitigation with attack vector targeting RTU_2.

In this hierarchical architecture, RTUs interface directly with their respective generators and communicate with a centralized control centre, which serves as the primary coordination hub. It houses two essential components: the SCADA system and a detection and mitigation coordination unit. Below the control centre, the framework splits into two parallel modules. On the left, the PCA detection module [8] has three key functions: data standardization, subspace decomposition, and attack detection. On the right, the SMC module has three main components: sliding surface design, adaptive gain mechanism, and control law synthesis.

3.1 Principal Component Decomposition

Consider a power system with P transmission branches observed over T time intervals. Each element f_{ij} of the matrix $F \in \mathbb{R}^{PXT}$ represents the power flow through branch i at time j. These measurements undergo standardization according to:

$$Z_{ij} = \frac{f_{ij} - \mu_i}{\sigma_i}, \tag{10}$$

where μ_i and σ_i are the mean and standard deviation (S.D.) of power flows through branch i respectively. This standardized measurement matrix Z undergoes singular value decomposition:

$$Z = USV^T, \tag{11}$$

where $U \in \mathbb{R}^{PXP}$ contains the left singular vectors with orthonormal columns, $S \in \mathbb{R}^{PXT}$ represents the diagonal matrix of singular values arranged in descending order, and $V \in \mathbb{R}^{TXT}$ comprises the right singular vectors. The principal component coefficients matrix A is then defined as:

$$A = U. \tag{12}$$

The matrix A is partitioned into regular and irregular subspaces:

$$A = [A_r | A_i], \tag{13}$$

where $A_r \in \mathbb{R}^{PX(P-K)}$ represents the regular subspace containing the first (P – K) principal components and $A_i \in \mathbb{R}^{PXK}$ represents the irregular subspace. The partition parameter K is determined adaptively through:

$$\left(\sum_{i=1}^{P-K} \lambda_i\right) / \left(\sum_{i=1}^{P} \lambda_i\right) \geq \alpha, \tag{14}$$

where λ_i represents the ith singular value and α is typically set between 0.98 and 0.99 to capture the dominant system dynamics in the regular subspace.

3.2 Statistical Metrics and Detection

For each measurement vector z(t), the framework computes two primary statistics. The hotelling's T^2 statistic measures variations in the regular subspace:

$$T^2(t) = z(t)^T A_r A_r^T z(t). \tag{15}$$

The Q statistic quantifies deviations in the irregular subspace:

$$Q(t) = z(t)^T A_i A_i^T z(t). \tag{16}$$

The detection framework uses thresholds that evolve as per operating conditions:

$$\tau_a(t) = \mu_m(t) + k_\sigma \times MAD(t), \tag{17}$$

where $\mu_m(t)$ represents the median of a moving window of observations, MAD(t) denotes the median absolute deviation, and k_σ provides the scaling factor for detection sensitivity. The final attack detection signal d(t) incorporates multiple conditions to reduce false alarms while maintaining detection sensitivity:

$$\begin{aligned} &d(t) = \{\ 1, \text{if } Q(t) > \tau_q \text{ AND } p(t) > n_p \text{ AND } |\Delta Q(t)| > \Delta \\ &d(t) = 0, \text{otherwise } \}, \end{aligned} \tag{18}$$

where p(t) is the persistence counter that tracks consecutive threshold violations, n_p is the persistence threshold, and $\tau\Delta$ is the rate of change (RoC) threshold.

The implementation begins with standardization as per Eq. (10), ensuring comparability of measurements from different branches with varying magnitudes. These measurements are projected on pre-computed subspaces using (11)–(13), separating the data into regular and irregular subspace for capturing normal variations and highlighting potential anomalies, respectively. Post this, the Q-statistic and T^2-statistic are computed using (15) and (16). The adaptive thresholds are continuously updated as per Eq. (17), making them robust against outliers while maintaining sensitivity to attacks. The logic in Eq. (18) declares an attack if and only if Q-statistic, RoC, and the persistence counter exceed their respective thresholds. This reduces false alarms while ensuring high detection rates for attacks. The strategy creates a practical, deployable solution that achieves detection rates above 90% with false positive rates below 5% and detection delays under 0.5 s across varying attack scenarios.

4 Mitigation Using Adaptive Sliding Mode Controller

This section presents an adaptive SMC strategy for mitigating CPAs in power systems. The approach incorporates adaptive gains, boundary layer modulation, and disturbance estimation to ensure stable operation under varying attack conditions.

4.1 Sliding Surface Design

For each generator i, we define an enhanced sliding surface [12] that incorporates integral action to ensure both tracking performance and disturbance rejection. The sliding surface is formulated as:

$$s_i = \Delta\omega_i + \lambda_i \Delta\delta_i + \gamma_i \int \Delta\omega_i \, dt, \tag{19}$$

where, $\Delta\omega_i$, $\Delta\delta_i$ are the state variables defined in Sect. 2. λ_i is the proportional gain coefficient, and γ_i is the integral gain coefficient. This ensures both transient performance through the proportional term and steady-state accuracy through the integral term. The sliding surface directly connects to the system dynamics described in Sect. 2, creating a natural control pathway to stabilize the frequency during attacks.

To enhance robustness against varying attack conditions while ensuring smooth control response, we propose the following adaptation laws:

$$\lambda_i(t)=\lambda_{i,base}, \tag{20}$$

$$\eta_i(t) = \eta_{i,base} + k_{\eta i}\tanh(\alpha_{\eta i}|s_i|), \tag{21}$$

where $\tanh(\cdot)$ provides smooth, bounded adaptation. The parameters $k_{\lambda i}$, $k_{\eta i}$ control adaptation magnitude, while $\alpha_{\lambda i}$ and $\alpha_{\eta i}$ determine adaptation sensitivity.

4.2 Control Law Formulation

The control input for generator i is designed based on a simplified model of the governor-turbine dynamics:

$$u_i = u_{eq,i} + u_{sw,i} + u_{dist,i}. \tag{22}$$

The equivalent control $u_{eq,i}$ compensates for known system dynamics:

$$u_{eq,i} = \frac{1}{K_i}[K_{1i}\Delta\delta_i + D_i\Delta\omega_i - 2H_i(\lambda_i + \gamma_i)\Delta\omega_i - K_{2i}\Delta E_{fi}], \tag{22a}$$

where K_i is the effective gain from control input to mechanical power. The switching $u_{sw,i}$ provides robustness against uncertainties:

$$u_{sw,i} = -\frac{\eta_i(t)}{K_i}\text{sat}\left(\frac{s_i}{\phi_i(t)}\right), \tag{22b}$$

where $\text{sat}(\cdot)$ is the saturation function. The boundary layer thickness $\phi_i(t)$ adapts based on sliding surface magnitude:

$$\phi_i(t) = \phi_{i,min} + (\phi_{i,max} - \phi_{i,min}\exp(-\beta_i|s_i|^2). \tag{23}$$

This ensures ϕ_i remains bounded between $\phi_{i,min}$ and $\phi_{i,max}$, preventing numerical issues while maintaining adaptation capabilities. The disturbance compensation term $u_{dist,i}$ counteracts estimated attacks and uncertainties:

$$u_{dist,i} = \frac{\hat{d}_i}{K_i}, \tag{24}$$

where $\hat{d}_i$ is the estimated disturbance obtained via a dynamic observer:

$$\hat{d}_i(k) = \hat{d}_i(k-1) + L_i(\Delta\omega_i(k) - \Delta\hat{\omega}_i(k))dt, \tag{25}$$

where, L_i is the observer gain, and $\Delta\hat{\omega}_i(k)$ is the predicted frequency deviation. For stability analysis, please refer Appendix A.

Figure 3 presents the framework for deploying the PCA-based detection and enhanced SMC-based mitigation. Upon detecting an attack, the system activates mitigation by transitioning to the adaptive SMC strategy. The sliding surface $\sigma(t)$ is computed using measurements only from reliable sensors, incorporating the adaptive function $\psi(y_i)$ to provide improved damping characteristics compared to linear approaches. The control law in Eq. (22) combines equivalent control, switching control, and integral action components, with adaptive gains that adjust based on system conditions.

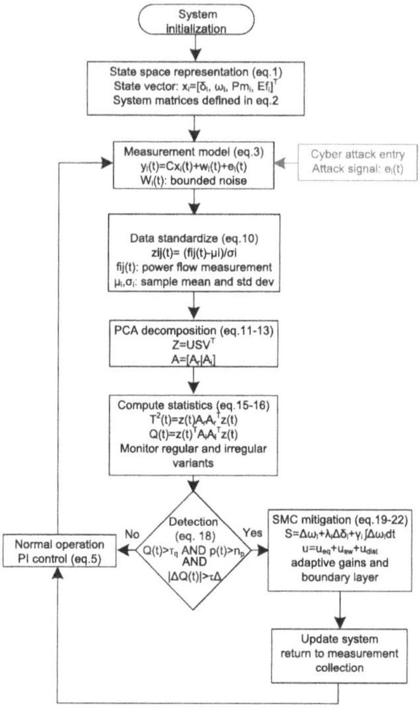

Fig. 3. Flowchart of implementation strategy.

5 Results and Discussion

The framework was evaluated through simulation studies. In Fig. 4(a), for FDI at t = 5 s, the controller maintains angle stability within ±2.25° compared to target of ±2°, validating the controller's ability to preserve system synchronism even under adversarial conditions. In Fig. 4(b) the S.D. remains contained, indicating effective mitigation of attack-induced oscillations. The residual variation analysis in Fig. 4(c) shows clear separation between normal conditions and FDI, and RoC measurements in Fig. 4(d) validate detection capabilities by tracking variations in system parameters during attacks. Detection scores in Fig. 4(e) achieve detection times of ±0.01 s. While this falls short of the ambitious target of ±0.0001 s, it remains within acceptable operational range of ±0.5 s.

Adaptive gains in Fig. 4(f) show adjustment to varying attack intensities, ensuring optimal control response. The control input profile in Fig. 4(g) reveals improvements over conventional sliding mode approaches, generating smooth control actions despite FDI attack. Frequency deviation is maintained within ±0.15 Hz, meeting system requirement of ±0.2 Hz.

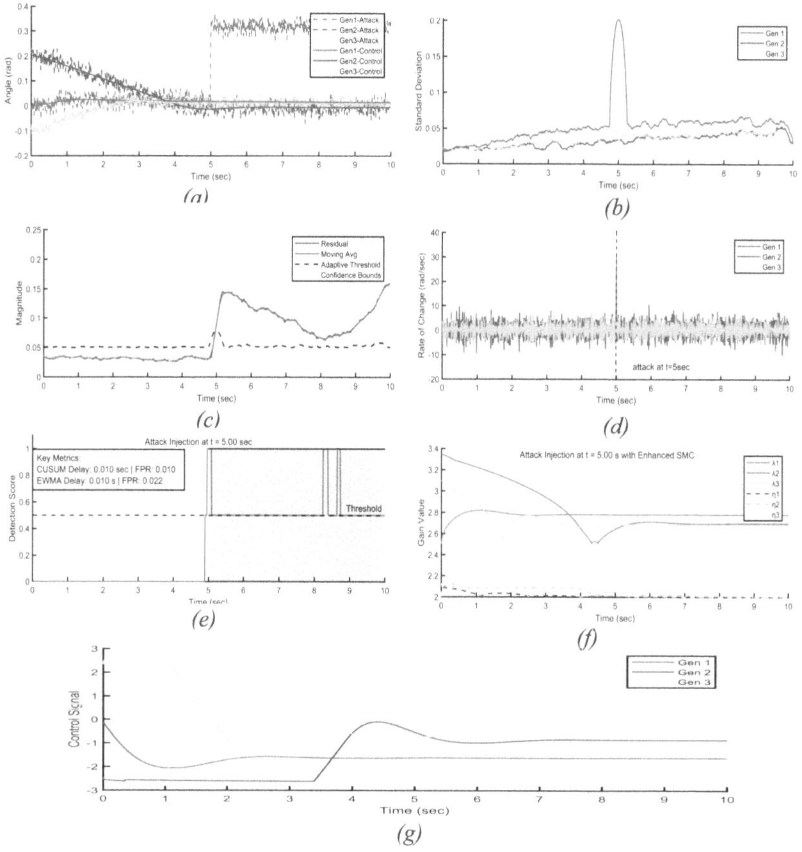

Fig. 4. Results w.r.t time (a) angle variation (b) rotor angle S.D. (c) residual variation (d) RoC (e) detection score using CUSUM and EWMA (f) adaptive gains (g) control input.

The metrics in Table 1 validate the framework's effectiveness. The achieved results consistently fall within acceptable operational ranges, though there remains room for improvement in meeting some of the more ambitious target values, particularly in detection speed.

The rotor angle variation under multiple attacks at t = 3.3, 5, 6.7 s in Fig. 5(a) shows stability with well-damped oscillations. The detection scores in Fig. 5(b) demonstrate reliable discrimination between normal operation and multiple attacks. The adaptive gains in Fig. 5(c) exhibit adjustment to varying attack intensities. The control input profile in Fig. 5(d) maintains smooth operation despite the complexity of CPAs.

Table 1. System Metrics.

Metric	Target value	Achieved value	Acceptable range
Detection rate	±0.0001 s	±0.01 s	±0.5s
Frequency deviation	±0.1 Hz	±0.15 Hz	±0.2 Hz
Rotor angle stability	±2°	±2.25°	±3°
System resilience	≥0.95	0.93	0.90–0.95

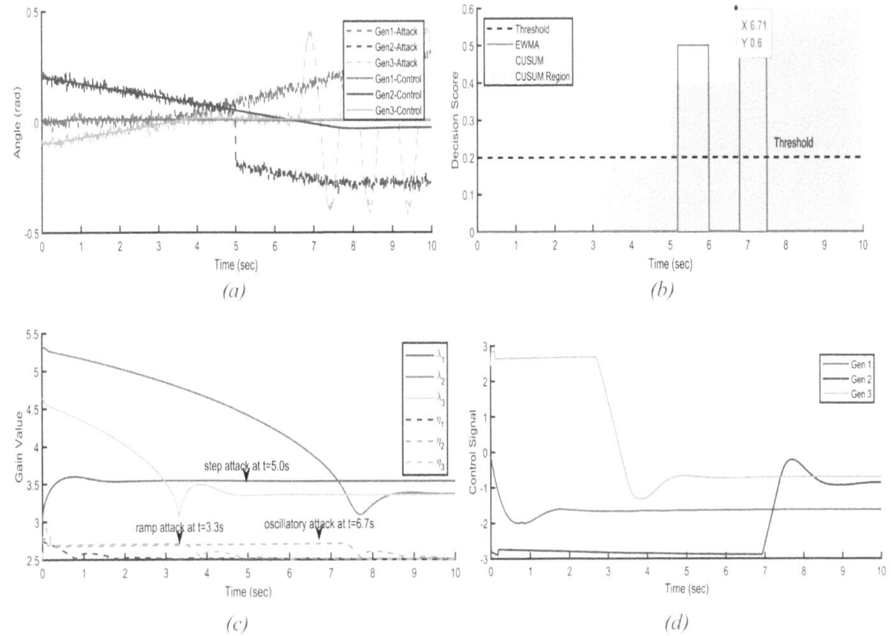

Fig. 5. Multiple attack scenario w.r.t time (a) rotor angle variation (b) detection score (c) adaptive gains (d) control input.

6 Conclusion

This research presents an integrated framework combining PCA-based detection with adaptive SMC for mitigating cyber-physical attacks. The approach achieves attack identification within ±0.01 s while maintaining frequency deviations within ±0.15 Hz and rotor angle stability within ±2.25°. The adaptive SMC reduces chattering while providing robust disturbance rejection, achieving 0.93 system resilience. Comprehensive performance across various realistic attack scenarios, modeled after documented threats, validates the framework's practical viability for power system security enhancement. Future work will focus on HIL experimental validation, and distributed architectures for improved scalability, enabling straightforward integration into existing power system control architectures of varying scales.

Appendix A: Stability Analysis for Adaptive SMC

For the model described in Sect. 2, following Lyapunov candidate function is taken:

$$V_i = \left(\frac{1}{2}\right) s_i^2 \tag{29}$$

As per Lyapunov stability theory [14], sliding mode exists if reaching condition is:

$$\dot{V}_i = s_i \dot{s}_i < 0, \forall s_i \neq 0 \tag{30}$$

Theorem 1: Under CPAs, the adaptive SMC with boundary layer adaptation mechanism in Eq. (23) and gain adaptation in Eq. (21) ensures boundedness of all closed-loop signals if the estimated disturbance from Eq. (25) converges such that $\left|\tilde{d}_i\right| \leq \rho_i$.

Proof: Under CPAs, the sensing vector may be corrupted. Hence, we must consider the modified sliding surface calculated with potentially corrupted measurements:

$$\hat{s}_i = \Delta\hat{\omega}_i + \lambda_i \Delta\hat{\delta}_i + \gamma_i \int \Delta\hat{\omega}_i dt \tag{31}$$

Where $\Delta\hat{\omega}_i = \Delta\omega_i + e_{\omega} i$ and $\Delta\hat{\delta}_i = \Delta\delta_i + e_{\delta i}$ represent measured values with attack components. The error between the true sliding surface and the calculated one is:

$$\tilde{s}_i = \hat{s}_i - s_i = e_{\omega i} + \lambda_i e_{\delta i} + \gamma_i \int e_{\omega i} dt \tag{32}$$

We can bound this error as $|\tilde{s}_i| \leq \mu_i$ for some positive μ_i. With the adaptive gain mechanism defined in Eq. (21):

$$\eta_{i(t)} = \eta_{\{i,base\}} + k_{\eta i} \tanh\left(\alpha_{\eta i} |s_i|\right) \tag{33}$$

The gain rises with larger sliding surface values, providing stronger robustness as deviations grow. Equation (23) ensures that boundary layer thickness reduces as sliding surface magnitude increases, providing tighter control during large deviations while avoiding chattering. Using Lyapunov analysis [14] we can show:

$$\dot{V}_i \leq \frac{(-\eta_i + \rho_i + \mu_i \lambda_{max}) |s_i|}{2H_i} \tag{34}$$

Where λ_{max} is the maximum possible value of λ_i. The bound inside boundary layer:

$$|s_i| \leq \frac{(\rho_i + \mu_i \lambda_{max}) \varphi_{i(t)}}{\eta_{i(t)}} \tag{35}$$

As $|s_i|$ increases, $\varphi_i(t)$ decreases and $\eta_i(t)$ increases, resulting in a tighter bound. $\tilde{d}_i$ remains bounded due to Eq. (25). As shown in Sect. 5, frequency deviation remains within $\pm$ 0.15 Hz and rotor angle stability within $\pm 2.25°$ even under severe attack.

Appendix B: Noise Robustness Analysis

Simulations show that acceptable performance is maintained even under significant additive white Gaussian noise at various SNR (20dB SNR) (Table 2).

Table 2. Performance Under Varying Noise Conditions

SNR (dB)	Detection rate (%)	Frequency deviation (Hz)	Rotor angle (°)	System resilience
40	95.3	± 0.15	± 2.3	0.93
30	92.8	± 0.16	± 2.4	0.91
20	88.6	± 0.18	± 2.5	0.89

References

1. Yadav, S., Kishor, N., Purwar, S., Raussi, P., Chakrabarti, S.: Switching attack modeling and vulnerability analysis of generator for dynamics study. Sustain. Energy, Grids Netw. **38**, 101297 (2024)
2. Yadav, S., Kishor, N., Purwar, S., Rajkumar, V.S., Ştefanov, A.: A state partition particle filter based approach for detection of switching attack. In: 2024 IEEE International Conference on Communications, Control, and Computing Technologies for Smart Grids (SmartGridComm), pp. 135–140. IEEE (2024)
3. Liu, H., Zhang, X., Dong, H., Liu, Z., Hu, X.: Magnetic anomaly detection based on energy-concentrated discrete cosine wavelet transform. IEEE Trans. Instrum. Meas. **72**, 1–10 (2023)
4. Siniosoglou, I., Radoglou-Grammatikis, P., Efstathopoulos, G., Fouliras, P., Sarigiannidis, P.: A unified deep learning anomaly detection and classification approach for smart grid environments. IEEE Trans. Netw. Serv. Manage. **18**(2), 1137–1151 (2021)
5. Fabio Ceschini, G., Gatta, N., Venturini, M., Hubauer, T., Murarasu, A.: Optimization of statistical methodologies for anomaly detection in gas turbine dynamic time series. J. Eng. Gas Turbines Power **140**(3), 032401 (2018)
6. Parizad, A., Hatziadoniu, C.J.: Cyber-attack detection using principal component analysis and noisy clustering algorithms: a collaborative machine learning-based framework. IEEE Trans. Smart Grid **13**(6), 4848–4861 (2022)
7. Khan, P.W., Byun, Y.-C.: Detecting anomaly classification using PCA-Kmeans and ensembled classifier for wind turbines. IEEE Open J. Power Energy **11**, 349–361 (2024). https://doi.org/10.1109/OAJPE.2024.3437414
8. Zhang, K., Wang, B.: Statistical learning approaches for fault detection and diagnosis in power systems: a comprehensive review. IEEE Trans. Neural Netw. Learn. Syst. **33**(7), 3082–3097 (2022)
9. Chen, P.Y., Yang, L.W., Lim, J.T.: Model predictive control for frequency regulation in power grids. IEEE Trans. Control Syst. Technol. **32**(4), 1430–1439 (2025)
10. Liao, K., Xu, Y.: A robust load frequency control scheme for power systems based on second-order sliding mode and extended disturbance observer. IEEE Trans. Industr. Inf. **14**(7), 3076–3086 (2017)
11. Aghababa, M.P.: Stabilization of canonical systems via adaptive chattering free sliding modes with no singularity problems. IEEE Trans. Syst., Man, Cybern.: Syst. **50**(5), 1696–1703 (2018)
12. Rodriguez, M., Martinez, J.L.: Hybrid fault-tolerant control strategies for power systems under sensor faults and cyber attacks: a resilience-oriented approach. IEEE Trans. Control Syst. Technol. **31**(5), 1987–2002 (2023)
13. Yang, Y., Li, J., Niu, Y.: Sliding mode quantized control of interval type-2 fuzzy systems under event-triggered scheme: stability analysis and performance optimization. IEEE Trans. Automat. Sci. Eng. **22**, 3295–3307 (2025)
14. H.K. Khalil.: Nonlinear Systems (3rd ed.), Upper Saddle River, NJ: Prentice Hall, 2002

Analytical Modeling and Simulation of a Superconducting Saturated Core Reactor

Leonardo Miúdo[1,2(✉)], João Murta-Pina[1], Nuno Amaro[1], and Nuno Vilhena[1]

[1] Center of Technology and Systems (UNINOVA-CTS) and Associated Lab of Intelligent Systems (LASI), NOVA School of Science and Technology, NOVA University Lisbon, 2829-516 Lisbon, Portugal

l.mudo@campus.fct.unl.pt

[2] Instituto Politécnico, Universidade Katyavala Bwila, 1725 Benguela, Angola

Abstract. A superconducting saturated core reactor is an electromagnetic device that plays a fundamental role in advanced electrical systems, providing increased efficiency and improved dynamic control over power flow in transmission lines, while also acting as a fault current limiter. In the context of AI-powered Cyber-Physical Systems (CPS), the development of precise analytical models is essential to optimize performance and reduce reliance on computationally intensive simulations. This paper proposes an analytical modeling approach that combines with numerical simulation for a three-phase superconducting saturated core reactor (SSCR) in a laboratory-scale prototype. Modeling a saturated core reactor relies on its magnetic characteristic, specifically the linked flux versus AC current. This characteristic can be obtained either through experimental measurements or using the finite element method (FEM). In this study, the reactor's magnetic characteristics are extracted using FEM from a 3D model of the laboratory-scale prototype developed in COMSOL Multiphysics employing A-formulation, where A represents the magnetic vector potential. The model is analyzed for different DC magnetization levels. An analytical equation is then fitted to the obtained data using MATLAB's Curve Fitting Toolbox (cftool) to determine four key parameters for each DC magnetization current. These parameters are subsequently used to compute flux, current, and voltage in the reactor through an analytical approach, enabling a quantitative comparison between the analytical model and FEM – based simulations. The error evaluation between the models confirms the accuracy and applicability of the proposed methodology. The results demonstrate that the analytical model provides an efficient solution for integration into AI-driven Cyber-Physical Systems, offering significant potential for its application in the analysis, optimization, and real-time control of electromagnetic devices within advanced electrical grids.

Keywords: Superconducting saturated core reactor · analytical modeling · COMSOL · MATLAB · curve fitting · finite element method · cyber-physical systems · artificial intelligence

Published by Springer Nature Switzerland AG 2025
L. M. Camarinha-Matos and F. Ferrada (Eds.): DoCEIS 2025, IFIP AICT 759, pp. 337–351, 2025.
https://doi.org/10.1007/978-3-031-97051-1_24

1 Introduction

The superconducting saturated core reactor (SSCR) is an electromagnetic device that functions as both a fault current limiter (FCL) and power flow controller in electrical systems [1]. It operates dynamically by adjusting its inductance in response to the applied current. The ability to model and simulate this inductance variation is essential for designing and optimizing the SSCR in its intended applications [2]. Despite the development of several modeling approaches, the challenge remains in balancing accuracy, complexity, and computational efficiency.

In recent years, the integration of intelligent control strategies and power electronics into electrical grids has increased the demand for advanced devices capable of dynamic adaptation to changing operating conditions [3]. Among these, superconducting devices stand out due to their ability to operate with minimal Joule losses and deliver fast response times [4, 5]. The SSCR, in particular, plays a dual role in enhancing grid reliability and flexibility by simultaneously limiting fault currents and regulating steady-state power flows [6–8]. However, its performance is strongly influenced by the nonlinear magnetic characteristics of the core, especially during transition to saturation under high-current conditions [9]. As a result, accurate modeling of the SSCR's inductive behaviour across a wide range of operating currents is critical.

Modeling approaches include both analytical and numerical techniques. Analytical models offer speed and ease of implementation but often oversimplify the nonlinear effects inherent in the device's operation [10]. In contrast, numerical approaches such as the finite element method (FEM) provide high-fidelity representations but are computationally expensive and not suitable for real-time applications or embedded systems [11]. This highlights the need for modeling strategies that can be easily implemented, accurate, and efficient in the simulation. Additionally, benchmarking these methods and validating them against realistic operating scenarios are essential steps to ensure reliability in practical applications such as cyber-physical power systems, where computational constraints and fast decision-making are key factors.

This paper presents a detailed approach for modeling the magnetic characteristics and dynamic behavior of the SSCR, using a simplified analytical model validated through finite element method (FEM). The proposed methodology enables real-time simulation of SSCR dynamics. The structure of the paper is as follows: Sect. 2 discusses the integration of SSCR into AI-powered cyber-physical systems. Section 3 presents the principles of operation and modeling of the SSCR, including a description of the 3D model, an analysis of existing modeling approaches, and a benchmarking comparison. In Sect. 4, the analytical modeling and simulation methodology are detailed, covering FEM simulation in COMSOL Multiphysics, curve fitting in MATLAB, and the analytical approach for transient simulation. Section 5 compares the results of the analytical model with FEM simulation and analyzes the model's accuracy and errors. Finally, Sect. 6 presents the conclusions and outlines directions for future work.

2 Integration with AI-Powered Cyber-Physical Systems

As power grids become more complex, they need smart systems to help manage them efficiently. AI-powered Cyber-Physical Systems (CPS) allow real-time grid operation monitoring, control, and optimization. An SSCR is an important device used to control power flow and fault current limiter, but its behavior makes it difficult to model accurately. Using AI-based simulations can help reduce the time and computing power needed to analyze SSCR while keeping the results accurate [12]. SSCR can be better integrated into CPS by developing precise analytical models, improving overall grid stability [8]. This integration helps power systems become more reliable, efficient, and adaptable to future energy demands.

3 Superconducting Saturated Core Reactor: Principles and Modeling

A saturated core reactor (SCR) is a magnetic device characterized by the nonlinear behavior of the iron core, which results from the variation of magnetic permeability (μ) as a function of the applied magnetic field intensity (H). This type of reactor is designed to have variable inductance, dynamically adjusting to the electric current or the applied magnetic field (B). Due to this property can be used in applications such as FCL and power flow control in power systems [1, 6, 7]. The SSCR typically consists of a superconducting DC coil, non-superconducting AC coils (usually copper coils), and an iron core, as shown in Fig. 1, the laboratory-scale prototype. The cryostat stores the liquid nitrogen and maintains the superconducting material at cryogenic temperatures. It is constructed with non-magnetic materials, such as stainless steel, to prevent interference with the magnetic field generated by the coil. The SSCR, when used as an FCL, operates with a single DC bias current, whereas power flow control operates across the entire range of DC currents. The SSCR's inductance varies with each DC current, making its operation more complex than when used as an FCL.

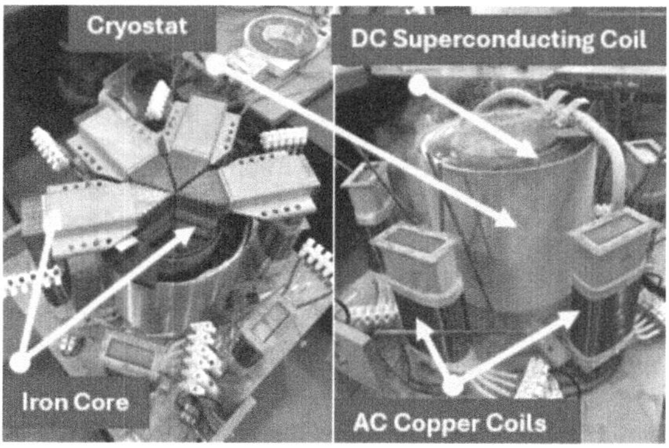

Fig. 1. Prototype of the SSCR at laboratory scale.

The use of high-temperature superconducting (HTS) materials in the DC coil is essential for significantly minimizing Joule losses, as superconductors exhibit near-zero electrical resistance when operating below their critical temperature. Additionally, superconducting coils can carry much higher current densities than conventional conductors such as copper, enabling the generation of intense magnetic fields. This is critical for driving the magnetic core into deep saturation, which optimizes the reactor's ability to modulate reactance via the AC coils. A strongly saturated core ensures precise control over power flow or fault current limiters.

3.1 3D Model of the SSCR

The 3D model of the SSCR, illustrated in Fig. 2 (on the left), represents the laboratory-scale prototype used for finite element simulations in COMSOL Multiphysics. This model was developed to accurately reflect the geometric configuration of the reactor, including the superconducting direct current (DC) coil, the AC copper, and the iron core. To ensure that the simulation results closely match real-world conditions, the iron core dimensions (in millimeters) were carefully defined, as shown in Fig. 2 (on the right). This 3D model serves as the basis for electromagnetic analysis using the FEM, allowing the extraction of the reactor's magnetic characteristics under different DC magnetization levels. The accuracy of this model is crucial to ensuring a reliable comparison between the FEM-based results and the proposed analytical model.

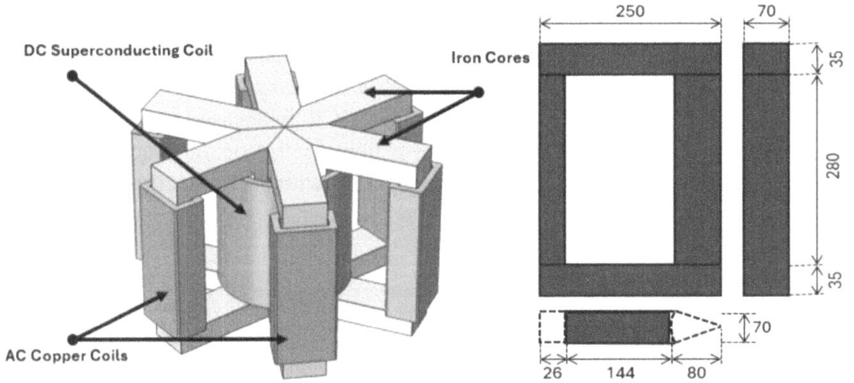

Fig. 2. 3D model of the SSCR (on the left) and dimensions in millimeters of the iron core (on the right).

3.2 Existing Modeling Approaches

The SSCR is designed to have a variable inductance [8]. To model this inductance, either an analytical model or a numerical model can be used. Table 1 provides comparative benchmarking of the modeling approaches for the SSCR. This comparison highlights the importance of selecting a model based on the specific goals of the study, whether for design, simulation, or real-time control. The analytical model, based on physical laws, is a simple way to represent the behavior of an SSCR. It helps explain the basic operating principles and is relatively easy to apply in simulations. This simplicity comes from assuming ideal core characteristics, which allow for a uniform distribution of B and H throughout the core. As a result, the inductance can be easily calculated [7]. However, these ideal assumptions are not always valid in practical applications such as power flow control and FCL [10]. An alternative analytical approach is the reluctance model, which represents magnetic circuits using resistors for flux paths and voltage sources for magnetomotive force (MMF) [13, 14]. This method effectively models magnetic behavior, but it is usually applied to cases where winding currents are known.

To simulate both magnetic and electric circuits together, the system must solve magnetic flux and electric current at the same time. Additionally, an energy transfer method is needed to facilitate the exchange of energy between the two circuits, making the model more complex. Thus, a numerical approach is required. Some researchers suggest that a reluctance model can be coupled with an electric circuit using electromagnetic induction. The numerical model, known as the gyrator-capacitor approach, which can be simulated in PSpice, addresses this coupling issue by using capacitors to maintain consistent flow variables and a gyrator as an interface between the magnetic and electric domains [15, 16]. However, the gyrator-capacitor approach is complex and difficult to use for modeling nonlinearities, which limits its practical use in SSCR. The main disadvantage of this model is the difficulty of applying it to commercial power system transient simulation tools. Another numerical modeling method is FEM-based models. Researchers often use FEM to design electromagnetic devices because it can analyze complex geometries with non-linear magnetic properties. FEM provides a variable inductance of the SSCR over a range of DC and instantaneous AC operating currents. The results from FEM create a two-dimensional data table (lookup table), which a transient circuit simulator uses to simulate the SSCR's operation in both stationary and transient conditions [11, 17]. Another approach is to co-simulating transient circuits with FEM [11]. However, a disadvantage of FEM for transient simulations is the time required to complete all mesh calculations for each time step, which can significantly increase simulation duration. Additionally, FEM does not directly apply to transient circuit simulations unless it is connected to a transient circuit simulator.

4 Analytical Model and Simulation Methodology

The proposed methodology is based on determining the magnetic characteristic of the SSCR, which relates to the AC current i to the linkage flux ψ. This characteristic describes the electromagnetic behavior of the SSCR. A similar methodology was previously used by [18, 19] but with a different mathematical equation. The first step is to determine the magnetic characteristic of the SSCR using 3D model and simulate it in COMSOL Multiphysics. The second step involves describing this characteristic using a mathematical equation (linkage flux equation, Eq. 1), and fitting a curve using MATLAB's Curve Fitting Toolbox (cftool), to identify four key parameters: $a^{I_{DC}}$, $b^{I_{DC}}$, $c^{I_{DC}}$ and $d^{I_{DC}}$. This simplified equation can predict the SSCR's behavior and be simulated in software such as MATLAB [20], as was done in [21], where the equation was applied to an FCL.

Table 1. Benchmarking of Modeling Approaches for SSCR

Criterion/Model	Analytical (Physical Laws)	Reluctance Model	Gyrator-Capacitor (GC)	FEM-Based Model	Circuit–FEM Co-simulation
Computational Complexity	Low	Low	High	Very High	Very High
Saturation Representation	Idealized	Approximate	Limited	Highly Accurate	Highly Accurate
Magnetic-Electric Coupling	Partial	Simple (if current is known)	Moderate (via GC interface)	Indirect (via LUT*)	Direct
Ability to Model Complex Geometry	No	Limited	Limited	High	High
Ease of Implementation	High	High	Low	Medium	Low
Real-Time/CPS Suitability	Moderate	High	Low	Very Low	Very Low
Transient Behavior Accuracy	Limited	Moderate	Moderate	High	Very High
Compatibility with Commercial Tools	High	High	Low	Medium (via LUT*)	Low

*LUT – Lookup Table.

This enables the SSCR's dynamic behavior to be simulated much faster than FEM software and can be applied to power flow control, as proposed in this paper. The third step involves computing the inductance. Inductance is the relationship between ψ and i, Eq. 2, and can be easily determined through Eq. 3 (the inductance equation) with the identified parameters.

$$\psi_{(i,I_{DC})} = a^{I_{DC}}\left[\tan^{-1}\left(b^{I_{DC}}\cdot i - c^{I_{DC}}\right) + \tan^{-1}\left(b^{I_{DC}}\cdot i + c^{I_{DC}}\right)\right] + d^{I_{DC}}\cdot i. \quad (1)$$

$$L(i, I_{DC}) = \frac{\partial\psi}{\partial i}. \quad (2)$$

$$L(i, I_{DC}) = a^{I_{DC}}\cdot b^{I_{DC}}\left[\frac{1}{1+\left(b^{I_{DC}}\cdot i - c^{I_{DC}}\right)^2} + \frac{1}{1+\left(b^{I_{DC}}\cdot i + c^{I_{DC}}\right)^2}\right] + d^{I_{DC}}. \quad (3)$$

4.1 FEM Simulation in COMSOL Multiphysics

The magnetic field simulations, coupled with the electrical circuit, were solved simultaneously in COMSOL based in Fig. 3, using the magnetic vector potential formulation, usually called A – formulation [22]. For the superconductor, copper was considered but with a high conductivity of $1 \cdot 10^{20}$ S/m. Although the model is three-phase, only one phase was simulated to reduce computation time. Two physics were used: the magnetic field and the electrical circuit.

The chosen simulation methodology consisted of two studies. First, a steady-state study was conducted, applying only the DC current. Then, with the DC current already applied, a transient study was performed by applying the AC source to the circuit, with a time range (0, 0.1, 100) in milliseconds. A fine mesh was used to achieve more accurate results, improve resolution due to the complex geometry, and reduce errors. The circuit data are presented in Table 2. The simulation was performed on a computer with an Intel Core i5 quad-core 2 GHz processor, 16 GB of RAM, and Windows 10 64-bit. The steady-state study took 45 min, while the transient study required 11 h to complete.

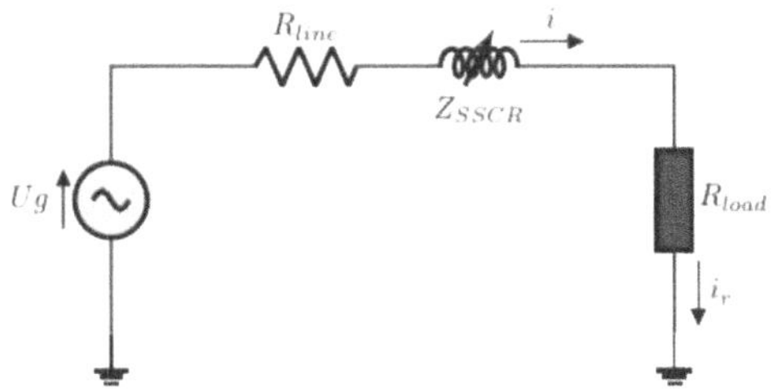

Fig. 3. Simplified power grid with SSCR in series with the transmission line.

Table 2. Voltage and powers of generation and specified load.

U_g (V)	R_{line} (Ω)	R_{load} (Ω)	N_{DC}	N_{AC}	U_{DC} (V)
311	0.001	1	45	60	0; 25; 50; 75 100;150

Figure 4 shows the uniform flux distribution, which results from the combination of the fluxes generated by the AC current (AC flux) and the DC current (DC flux). In each half-cycle of the AC current, the AC and DC fluxes subtract in one core and add in the other. In the subtraction of the flux, the operation causes the region of the B-H curve to be in the linear region, which increases the impedance of the line. On the other hand, in addition of the flux, it causes the core to operate in the saturation region. Working together throughout each half-cycle, the cores provide the magnetic characteristic, which is proportional to the B-H curve.

Figure 5 on the left shows the sum of the AC flux and the DC flux from the core on the right and the core on the left for a 50V DC current within the range of the instantaneous AC current. The sum of the flux linkage from the cores results in the total flux linkage, which is the magnetic characteristic of the SSCR. Figure 5 on the right shows the behavior of the flux linkage for different DC magnetization levels.

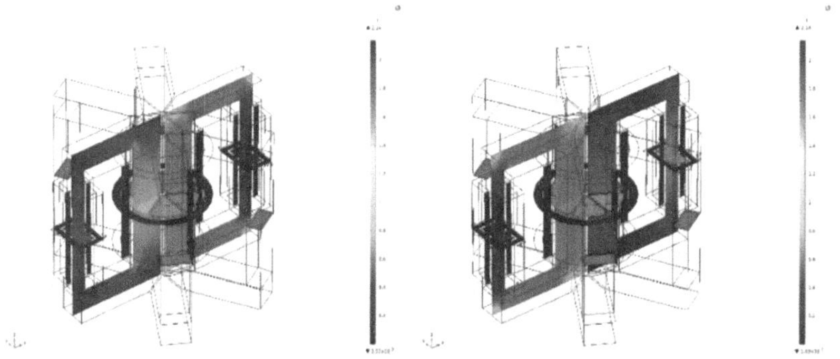

Fig. 4. Flux distribution in each half-cycle.

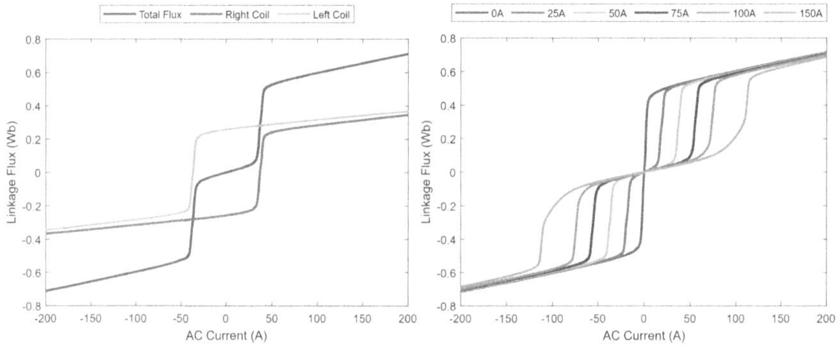

Fig. 5. Sum of the linkage flux from the core for the case of a 50V DC current (on the left); Flux linkage for different DC magnetization levels (on the right).

The differential inductance is the partial derivative of the flux linkage for the instantaneous AC current. The slope of the tangent line to the total flux linkage curve of the SSCR represents the differential inductance, and it was calculated numerically using Eq. 4. Figure 6 shows the differential inductance and the flux linkage for a 50V DC current and the resistance of the SSCR, $\boldsymbol{R_{SSCR}}$, remained the same, resulting in 0.1298 Ω.

$$L_{SSCR}(i, I_{DC}) = \frac{\partial \psi_{SSCR}}{\partial i_{line}} \quad L_{d_k} = \frac{\psi_k - \psi_{k-1}}{i_k - i_{k-1}} \tag{4}$$

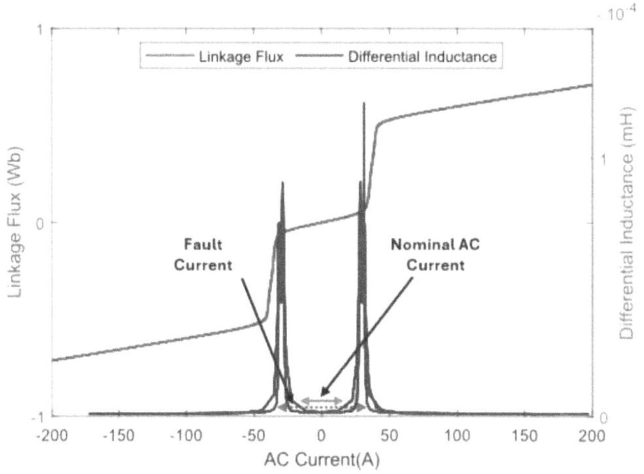

Fig. 6. Linkage Flux and differential inductance for 50V DC current.

4.2 Curve Fitting in MATLAB

The magnetic characteristic of the SSCR was modeled using Eq. 1, where the parameters $a^{I_{DC}}$, $b^{I_{DC}}$, $c^{I_{DC}}$ and $d^{I_{DC}}$ were determined through curve fitting. Figure 7, on the right, shows the curve extracted from COMSOL and the fitted curve for the case of a 50 V DC current, where good agreement can be observed. The fitted parameters were determined using MATLAB's *cftool* function for different DC current values and are presented in Table 3. Figure 7, on the right, shows, for the example of a 50V DC current, the differential inductance obtained from COMSOL and the differential inductance calculated using Eq. 3 with the fitted parameters, which also show good agreement. The differential inductance, calculated using Eq. 2 and the fitted parameters from Table 2 for different DC current values, is shown in Fig. 8.

The differential inductance, shown in Fig. 7 on the right, has two peaks separated by an instantaneous AC current range. This range, for each of the DC current curves, depends on the magnitude of the DC current. In other words, as the DC current increases, the separation between the peaks also increases, as shown in Fig. 8. For a DC current of zero, there is a single peak centered on the DC current, which is twice the magnitude of the peaks. The SSCR, as a power flow controller, operates across the entire DC current range. This operation differs from the FCL application, which operates at a single DC bias current.

4.3 Analytical Model Methodology for Transient Simulation of SSCR

The magnetic characteristic obtained from the analytical model for different DC current values, using a voltage u_g with an amplitude of 311 V, is used to simulate the behavior of the SSCR, but now considering a source amplitude u_g of 50 V. The voltage in the SSCR, u_{SSCR}, is given by the following Eq. 5:

$$u_{SSCR} = L_{SSCR}\frac{di_{line}}{dt} + R_{SSCR} \cdot i_{line}. \tag{5}$$

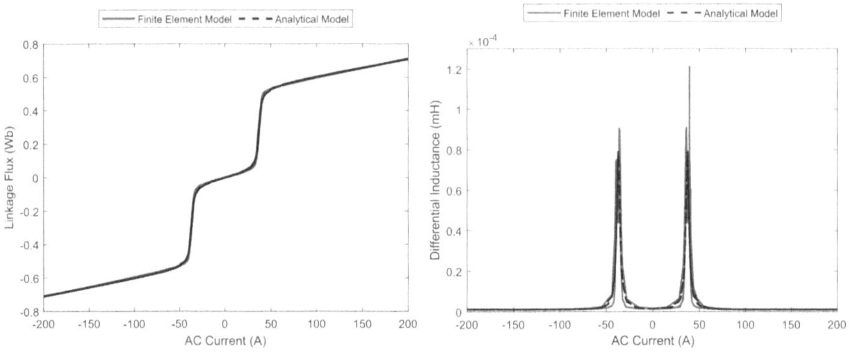

Fig. 7. Magnetic characteristic (on the left) and differential (on the right) curve from COMSOL with fitted curve for the case of a 50 V DC current.

Table 3. Fitted parameters.

DC Current (A)	Parameter *a*	Parameter *b*	Parameter *c*	Parameter *d*
0	0.1568	1.048	1.848	0.001121
50	-0.1611	-0.4862	-18.03	0.001036
100	0.1574	0.4632	-34.27	0.001052
150	0.1332	0.3291	-36.39	0.001424

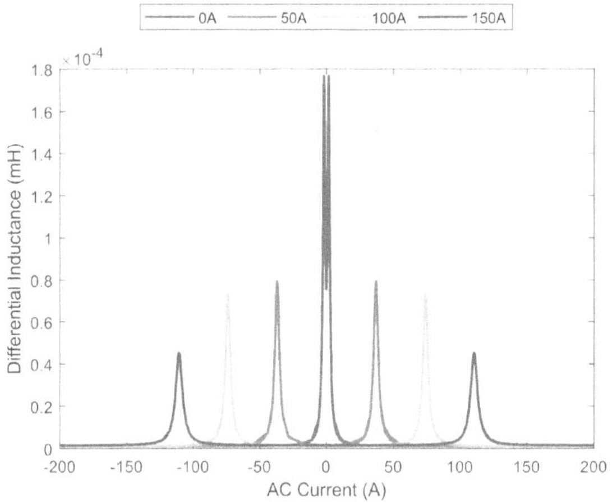

Fig. 8. Differential inductance for different DC magnetization levels using fitted parameters.

Since the inductance is equal to $L_{SSCR} = \frac{\partial \psi_{SSCR}}{\partial i_{line}}$, the voltage u_{SSCR} can be written as follows:

$$u_{SSCR} = \frac{d\psi_{SSCR}}{dt} + R_{SSCR} \cdot i_{line}. \tag{6}$$

The circuit equation of Fig. 3 is given by:

$$u_g = (R_{line} \cdot i_{line}) + \left(\frac{d\psi_{SSCR}}{dt} + R_{SSCR} \cdot i_{line} \right) + (R_{load} \cdot i_{line}). \tag{7}$$

Isolating the current in the line, i_{line}, and discretizing it using the Euler method, we will have:

$$i_{line}^{k+1} = i_{line}^{k} + \frac{u_g^k \cdot \Delta t}{\left.\frac{d\psi_{SSCR}}{di_{line}}\right|_k} - \frac{\left(R_{total} \cdot i_{line}^k\right) \cdot \Delta t}{\left.\frac{d\psi_{SSCR}}{di_{line}}\right|_k}. \tag{8}$$

$$i_{line}^{k+1} = i_{line}^{k} + \frac{u_g^k \cdot \Delta t}{L_{SSCR}|_k} - \frac{\left(R_{total} \cdot i_{line}^k\right) \cdot \Delta t}{L_{SSCR}|_k} \tag{9}$$

where R_{total} is $R_{total} = R_{line} + R_{SSCR} + R_{load}$. Equation 9 helps to find i_{line}, at time $t = (k+1)\Delta t$, where Δt is the sampling time and k is the previous iteration. The voltage in the SSCR is given by Eq. 10:

$$u_{SSCR}^k = \frac{\psi_k - \psi_{k-1}}{\Delta t} + R_{SSCR} \cdot i_{line}^k \tag{10}$$

5 Results and Discussion

Due to the experimental challenges involved in developing a laboratory-scale prototype, experimental validation is currently beyond the scope of this work. As an alternative, a high-resolution FEM model was used to validate the accuracy of the analytical predictions under various operating conditions.

5.1 Comparison Between COMSOL Simulation and Analytical Model

Figures 9 and 10 show the results of the FEM simulation and the analytical model for the flux linkage, line current, and voltage across the SSCR terminals at different DC currents. It can be observed that the curves obtained from both methods exhibit good agreement, indicating that the analytical model accurately represents the magnetic behavior of the SSCR and validates the accuracy of the adopted approach.

Figures 9 and 10 show that when the DC current increases, the reactor's inductance decreases due to core saturation, allowing more current to flow through the line. Similarly, when the DC current decreases, the inductance increases, restricting the current flow in the line. This behavior can be used to control the current power transmission systems efficiently.

These results provide confidence in the model's capacity to represent the essential dynamics of the SSCR for power system studies. One of the major motivations for developing an analytical model is its potential integration into CPS, where rapid computation and control decisions are required. The simplicity of the analytical model and its use of only four parameters make it particularly attractive for real-time simulation platforms such as Simulink.

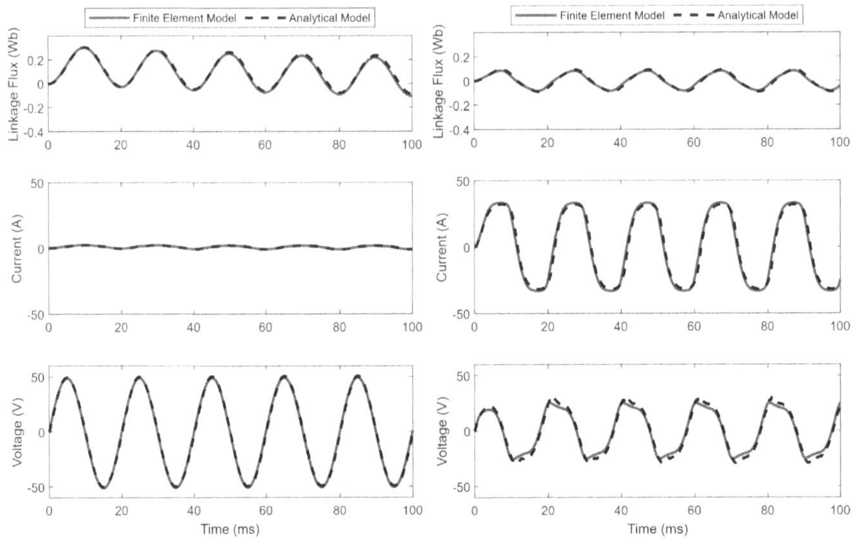

Fig. 9. Results of the linkage flux, current and voltage from FEM simulation and the analytical model, 0 V DC (on the left); 50 V DC (on the right).

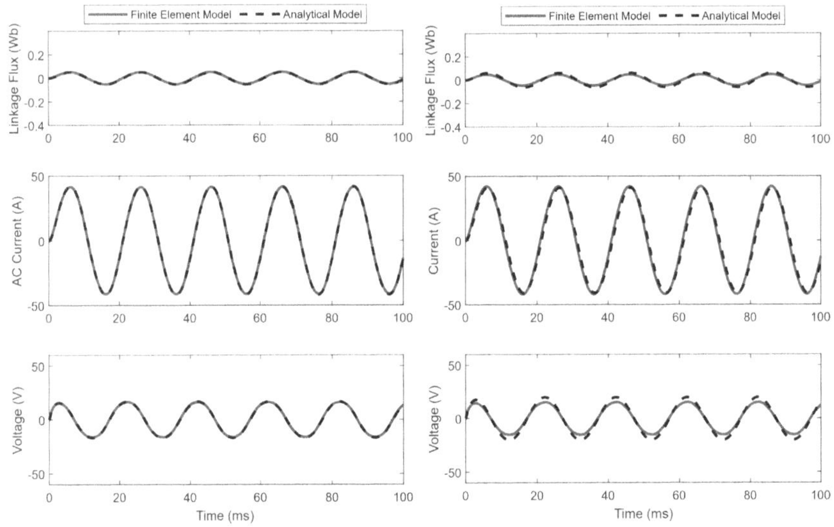

Fig. 10. Results of the linkage flux, current and voltage from FEM simulation and the analytical model, 100 V DC (on the left); 150 V DC (on the right)

Compared to the physical-law-based analytical model, this hybrid approach provides significantly improved accuracy in nonlinear and saturated regimes. Unlike full FEM or circuit–FEM co-simulation making it feasible for integration into real-time environments. Moreover, by condensing FEM results into a parametric form, the model remains compatible with conventional circuit simulators and CPS applications. This modelling strategy acts as a middle ground between detailed numerical analysis and real-time simulation requirements, preserving essential physical behaviour while enabling fast execution.

5.2 Error Analysis and Model Accuracy

The Normalized Root Mean Square Error (NRMSE) was used to analyze the model's accuracy, as it focuses on the correspondence between the predicted and actual values. Additionally, NRMSE significantly penalizes larger errors, being sensitive to large discrepancies between the measured and expected values, making it ideal for identifying modeling flaws and important deviations. Table 4 presents the NRMSE of the current in the line. The Table 4 shows that the NRMSE value is below 5%, indicating high accuracy in the current measurement, with minimal error compared to the expected value. This result demonstrates that the model used to calculate the current in the line performs efficiently and reliably.

Table 4. Normalized Root Mean Square Error – NRMSE of the current in the line.

DC Current (A)	NRMSE AC Current (%)
0	3.3948
50	4.2731
100	0.3255
150	3.4978

6 Conclusions and Future Work

The proposed analytical model provides an efficient and accurate method for simulating the behavior of the SSCR. Fitting the model to data obtained from COMSOL Multiphysics simulations successfully captures the dynamic inductance and voltage-current relationship across different operating conditions. The model's performance was validated through error analysis, which showed that the NRMSE values for the current were consistently below 5%. This demonstrates that the model can be used effectively for real-time simulations in power flow control applications. As future work, the goal is to use the fitted parameters in implementing a lookup table, simulate the transient regime in a power system in MATLAB/Simulink, and validate the results with experimental data.

Acknowledgments. This research was funded (in part) by the Portuguese FCT program, Center of Technology and Systems (CTS) CTS/00066, and we gratefully thank the Instituto Nacional de Gestão de Bolsas de Estudo (INAGBE – Angola) for financial support.

References

1. Dimitrovski, A., Member, S., Li, Z., Ozpineci, B., Member, S.: Applications of Saturable-core Reactors (SCR) in Power Systems. In: IEEE PES T&D Conference and Exposition, pp. 1–5. Chicago, IL, USA (2014). https://doi.org/10.1109/TDC.2014.6863404
2. Yuan, J., et al.: A compact saturated core fault current limiter magnetically integrated with decoupling windings. IEEE Trans. Power Delivery **38**, 2711–2723 (2023). https://doi.org/10.1109/TPWRD.2023.3255212
3. Dongyang, C., Jiewen, Z., Xiaolong, H.: Dynamic adaptation in power transmission: integrating robust optimization with online learning for renewable uncertainties. Front. Energ. Res. **12**, 1–12 (2024). https://doi.org/10.3389/fenrg.2024.1483170
4. Heidary, A., Yazdani-Asrami, M., Hesami, M., Sood, V.: The TRV improvement of fast circuit breakers using solid-state series superconducting reactor. IEEE Trans. Power Delivery **38**, 1259–1266 (2023). https://doi.org/10.1109/TPWRD.2022.3211778
5. Nikulshin, Y., Kafri, A., Yeshurun, Y., Wolfus, S.: Energy storing and fault current limiting in a unified superconducting magnetic device. IEEE Trans. Appl. Supercond. **33**, 1–5 (2023). https://doi.org/10.1109/TASC.2023.3273200
6. Hayakawa, N., et al.: Feasibility study of superconducting power flow controller and fault current limiter (SPFCL). IEEE Trans. Appl. Supercond. **23**, 3–6 (2013). https://doi.org/10.1109/TASC.2012.2230677
7. Heidary, A., Radmanesh, H., Rouzbehi, K., Moradi Cheshmehbeigi, H.: A multifunction high-temperature superconductive power flow controller and fault current limiter. IEEE Trans. Appl. Supercond. **30**(5), 1–8 (2020). https://doi.org/10.1109/TASC.2020.2966685
8. Miúdo, L., Pina, J.M., Amaro, N.: Superconducting saturable core reactor as variable inductance for controlling the power flow in a transmission line. In: Camarinha-Matos, L.M., Ferrada, F. (eds.) Technological Innovation for Connected Cyber Physical Spaces: 14th IFIP WG 5.5/SOCOLNET Doctoral Conference on Computing, Electrical and Industrial Systems, DoCEIS 2023, Caparica, Portugal, July 5–7, 2023, Proceedings, pp. 82–94. Springer Nature Switzerland, Cham (2023). https://doi.org/10.1007/978-3-031-36007-7_6
9. Yuan, J., Sun, Y., Zhang, W., Liu, Y., Zhou, H., Zhong, H.: A novel hybrid magnetic material based on three-phase saturated core fault current limiter. AIP Adv. (2024). https://doi.org/10.1063/9.0000829
10. Aaron, M., Ii, Y.: Saturable Reactor for Power Flow Control in Electric Transmission Systems: Modeling and System Impact Study
11. Young, M., Li, Z., Dimitrovski, A.: Modeling and simulation of continuously variable series reactor for power system transient analysis. IEEE Power and Energy Society General Meeting. IEEE Computer Society (2016). https://doi.org/10.1109/PESGM.2016.7741766
12. Hu, L., Zhang, F., Cheng, J., Wang, B., Huang, Y.: Application review of artificial intelligence in superconducting devices. In: Proceedings – 2024 International Conference on Artificial Intelligence and Digital Technology, ICAIDT, pp. 66–69 (2024). https://doi.org/10.1109/ICAIDT62617.2024.00022
13. Zheng, S., Wang, J., Wang, F., Tolbert, L.M.: DC-saturated continuously variable series reactors (CVSRs) for power flow control in power transmission systems. IEEE Trans. Power Delivery **37**, 268–278 (2022). https://doi.org/10.1109/TPWRD.2021.3057624
14. Pokharel, S., Dimitrovski, A.: Ferromagnetic core reactor modeling and design optimization. Adv. Sci. Technol. Eng. Syst. J. **6**(1), 810–818 (2021). https://doi.org/10.25046/aj060190
15. Hayerikhiyavi, M., Dimitrovski, A.: Gyrator-capacitor modeling of a continuously variable series reactor in different operating modes. In: 2021 IEEE Kansas Power and Energy Conference, KPEC 2021. Institute of Electrical and Electronics Engineers Inc. (2021). https://doi.org/10.1109/KPEC51835.2021.9446236

16. Young, M., Dimitrovski, A., Li, Z., Liu, Y.: Gyrator-capacitor approach to modeling a continuously variable series reactor. IEEE Trans. Power Delivery **31**, 1223–1232 (2016). https://doi.org/10.1109/TPWRD.2015.2510642
17. Vilhena, N., Arsénio, P., Murta-Pina, J., Pronto, A.G., Álvarez, A.: Development of a simulink model of a saturated cores superconducting fault current limiter. In: Camarinha-Matos, L., Baldissera, T., Di Orio, G., Marques, F. (eds.) Technological Innovation for Cloud-Based Engineering Systems. DoCEIS 2015. IFIP Advances in Information and Communication Technology, pp. I–II (2015). https://doi.org/10.1007/978-3-319-16766-4
18. Vilhena, N., Arsenio, P., Murta-Pina, J., Pronto, A., Alvarez, A.: A methodology for modeling and simulation of saturated cores fault current limiters. IEEE Trans. Appl. Supercond. **25**, 3–6 (2015). https://doi.org/10.1109/TASC.2014.2374179
19. Pina, J.M., Pereira, P., Pronto, A., Arsénio, P., Silva, T.: Modelling and simulation of inductive fault current limiters. Phys. Procedia **36**, 1248–1253 (2012). https://doi.org/10.1016/j.phpro.2012.06.284
20. Miúdo, L., et al.: Case-study of an HTS saturable core reactor for power flow control in a transmission grid. IEEE Trans. Appl. Superconductivity (2024). https://doi.org/10.1109/TASC.2024.3357050
21. Vilhena, N.M.G.: Contribution for the Study of the Integration of Inductive Superconducting Fault Current Limiters in Electrical Distribution Grids (2020)
22. Gameiro Carvalho, D.J., Ferreira, F., da Silva, J.F.P., da Fernandes, P.J., Branco, Costa: Finite-element recipes for HTS-coated conductors and HTS tape topologies. Supercond. Sci. Technol. **36**(10), 103001 (2023). https://doi.org/10.1088/1361-6668/acf4c3

Control of a Multiphase Superconducting Axial Machine Drive for Electric Aircraft

Fábio Encarnação-Gregório[1,2,3(✉)], João Murta-Pina[1,2,3], Mohammad Yazdani-Asrami[4], and Vitor Fernão Pires[5]

[1] Electrical and Computer Engineering Department, NOVA School of Science and Technology, 2829-516 Caparica, Portugal
f.gregorio@campus.fct.unl.pt, jmmp@fct.unl.pt
[2] Centre of Technology and Systems (CTS-UNINOVA and LASI), NOVA School of Science and Technology, 2829-516 Caparica, Portugal
[3] Intelligent Systems Associate Laboratory (LASI), 2829-516 Caparica, Portugal
[4] CryoElectric Research Lab, Propulsion, Electrification and Superconductivity Group, James Watt School of Engineering, University of Glasgow, Glasgow G12 8QQ, UK
mohammad.yazdani-asrami@glasgow.ac.uk
[5] Setúbal School of Technology, Polytechnic Institute of Setúbal, 2914-508 Setúbal, Portugal
vitor.pires@estsetubal.ips.pt

Abstract. In recent years, increasingly restrictive emissions regulations have driven the demand for sustainable aviation, leading to the development of electric propulsion systems – particularly high-power-density electrical machines – as one of the promising alternative solutions to traditional gas turbine engines, particularly high-power-density electrical machines. Applying High-Temperature Superconductors (HTS) to electrical machines is considered promising due to their high current density and negligible energy losses, enabling the creation of compact and power-dens machines that are viable for aviation applications. This work presents a preliminary study for the drive control of a multiphase axial-flux superconducting machine with an HTS disc rotor made of rare-earth barium copper oxide (REBCO) tapes, providing a presentation of the control architecture and simulation of the inverter. The double-stator is made of conventional windings, generating magnetic poles that can be changed electronically. Furthermore, multiphase machines are more fault-tolerant compared to traditional three-phase machines, making them more reliable for electric aviation.

Keywords: Electrical Aviation · Fault-Tolerant Motor Drive · High-Temperature Superconductors (HTS) · Superconducting Machine

1 Introduction

In recent years, many organizations have introduced stricter efficiency and emissions standards in aviation to make it more environmentally friendly. Although the contribution of aviation to the global CO_2 production is relatively small compared to other sources

Published by Springer Nature Switzerland AG 2025
L. M. Camarinha-Matos and F. Ferrada (Eds.): DoCEIS 2025, IFIP AICT 759, pp. 352–363, 2025.
https://doi.org/10.1007/978-3-031-97051-1_25

in other sectors (2% in 2022 [1], for example), it is expected a growing trend in the coming years due to the increasing jet fuel consumption caused by air traffic growth [1, 2]. The Advisory Council for Aviation Research and Innovation in Europe (ACARE) has set ambitious targets to reduce CO_2 emissions by 55% by 2030 and to eliminate them entirely by 2050 for domestic and European Union departing flights, relative to 1990 levels [3]. In Flightpath 2050 plan, the European Commission aims to reduce CO_2 emissions per passenger per kilometer by 75%, NOx emissions by 90%, and perceived aircraft noise from flying aircraft by 65% by 2050, compared with a baseline aircraft in 2000 [4].

In this context, the aviation industry is gradually transitioning toward electrification to promote a more sustainable sector. Several architectures have been proposed over the years, ranging from fully electric propulsion systems to hybrid configurations with varying degrees of electrification [5–8]. However, conventional electrical machines are not viable for larger aircraft due to their low Specific Power Density (SPD), i.e., power divided by weight, typically ranging from 4–8 kW/kg [9].

To address these limitations, cryo-electrification, i.e., the integration of cryogenics and superconductivity technologies, has emerged as a disruptive solution [9, 10]. Within this concept, High-Temperature Superconducting (HTS) machines are a promising technology for electric aviation. Superconductors have negligible losses below a given critical temperature, allowing 100 times more current density when compared with conventional materials, such as copper and aluminum [9, 11]. This leads to electrical machines with very low energy losses and, consequently, increased efficiency and high specific power density (SPD) in the order of 16–20 kW/kg, and potentially even larger, if cooling system weight and efficiency is addressed by employing liquid hydrogen on board aircraft, as both fuel for engines and coolant for superconducting propulsion and powertrain systems [10].

This work is part of a PhD research project focused on the design and optimization of a multiphase superconducting axial flux machine drive for electric aircraft. The research plan is divided into five parts: use case definition, HTS motor design, power electronics interface, control, and economic assessment. This paper concentrates on the power electronics and control aspects, presenting a preliminary study on the Fault-Tolerant Control (FTC) of the drive. It describes the considerations and aspects that should guide the development of the machine control. The development of fault-tolerant designs for future aircraft electrification is essential, as safety and reliability are crucial concepts in this sector.

The structure of the paper is as follows: Sect. 2 introduces the machine, namely the design and operation principle; Sect. 3 discusses the drive control of the machine with the control architecture, a multiphase inverter preliminary simulation with efficiency study considering different types of semiconductor devices, and the considerations that must be considered regarding the drive fault-tolerance; Sect. 4 presents the conclusion and future work.

2 Contribution to AI-Powered Cyber-Physical Systems

Safety and reliability are crucial in the aviation context. Therefore, in developing aircraft propulsion and powertrain systems, it is important to integrate real-time monitoring and anomaly detection to prevent operational issues to escalate to critical levels. Artificial Intelligence (AI)-Powered Cyber-Physical Models can play a key role in the design, manufacturing, monitoring, and maintenance of HTS machines improving their reliability and performance [10].

These AI-Powered Cyber-Physical systems have hardware and software tools for propulsion machine and power electronics which in general work as a digital twin for aircraft propulsion system [12, 13]. The distributed nature of AI-powered cyber–physical models with superior flexibility and scalability compared with conventional protection techniques, allows for seamless integration of additional motors or motor replacement without the requirement for extensive reconfiguration or infrastructure upgrades [12, 13]. In such systems, AI and ML, communication systems, cyber-physical models, digital control and networking play vital role. A vulnerability assessment is required for the propulsion motor and its drive system which arises from dramatic advancements in communication technologies and the increasing automation and intelligence of systems [14, 15]. This will become more crucial aspects of research as aviation sector is moving towards more electric aircraft with distributed propulsion motor systems.

Such AI-Powered Cyber-Physical systems can be coupled with mathematical frameworks as well as physical propulsion motors to find faults in the electric aircraft [16]. This fault detection system is integrated with the AI techniques and signal processing approaches, has ability to learn complex patterns and adapt to potentially changing motor conditions.

3 Machine Description

This section describes the design, i.e., the structure and components, and the operating principle of the machine. The machine features independently controlled windings and a superconducting disc rotor, allowing for flexible pole configurations.

3.1 Machine Design

The machine is composed of two conventional iron semi-stators, each equipped with independently controllable windings arranged in a double layer, as shown in Fig. 1.

Each semi-stator contains 24 slots and 24 windings, with a coil pitch of 4 slots. Consequently, the maximum number of phases is 24. Theoretically, this allows for six possible pole pair configurations: 1, 2, 3, 4, 6, and 12. However, the last two configurations (6 and 12 pole pairs) cause significant distortion in the airgap flux density, as each pole is covered by only one stator slot.

The rotor is a disc made of carbon fiber disc with 48 slices of rare-earth barium copper oxide (REBCO) HTS tapes radially arranged on both sides, as shown in Fig. 2 (a). The characteristics of these tapes, manufactured by SuperOx, are presented in Table 1. The robust and lightweight construction of the rotor ensures mechanical strength at low temperatures while allowing for a small airgap due to its reduced thickness.

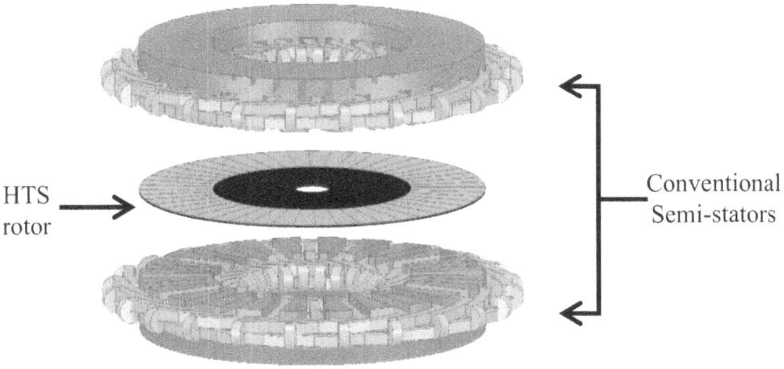

Fig. 1. Exploded view of the machine.

Table 1. Characteristics of the rotor REBCO HTS tape manufactured by SuperOx.

Parameter	Value
Thickness	60 μm
Width	12 mm
Critical Current (77 K, self-field)	620 A
Thickness of the copper layers	20 μm

This machine operates on the principle of a hysteresis machine. During startup, the stator windings generate a rotating magnetic field that axially penetrates the rotor. In this phase, the rotor experiences field slip, which generates losses. As the rotor accelerates, the magnetic flux becomes trapped in the REBCO tapes within the rotor, allowing it to reach synchronous speed, at which point the machine behaves like a permanent magnet machine. However, when the pole configuration changes or the torque demand is too high, slip occurs again, leading to additional losses.

A prototype was constructed to test and validate this concept, as depicted in Fig. 2 (a) and (b). Cooling is provided by a liquid nitrogen bath (LN2) at 77 K, as shown in Fig. 2 (c).

3.2 Operation Principle

The operating principle of this machine is based on a patent called "Polyphase Motor with Variable Number of Poles" [17] and is further described in [18, 19]. It operates based on varying the number of magnetic poles to prioritize either speed or torque. For example, increased torque is required at startup to overcome inertia, so the machine operates with more magnetic poles. Once the machine runs, a higher rotational speed becomes necessary, and the number of poles can be reduced to increase the speed. So, this machine can be described as an electronic gearbox, by adapting the performance of the machine to different operating conditions.

(a) (b) (c)

Fig. 2. Proof of concept of the machine. (a) Semi-stator with copper windings. (b) HTS REBCO superconducting disc rotor. (c) Test setup of the machine with LN_2 bath.

As described in Sect. 2.1, each semi-stator has 24 windings, each one independently controllable to enhance the flexibility of pole configurations. The phase shift, $\Delta\phi$, depends on the number of desired pole pairs, p, and the total number of slots, N_{slots}:

$$\Delta\phi = \frac{2\pi p}{N_{slots}}. \tag{1}$$

Since $N_{slots} = 24$, $\Delta\phi$ becomes $\frac{\pi}{12}p$, i.e., $15°p$. Figure 3 shows the phase voltage, ϕ, of each winding of the machine for four different pole configurations.

The synchronous speed N_s of the rotating magnetic field generated by the windings depends on the frequency of the applied voltage, f, and p, according to:

$$\mathrm{N_s}=\frac{60\,\mathrm{f}}{\mathrm{p}}. \tag{2}$$

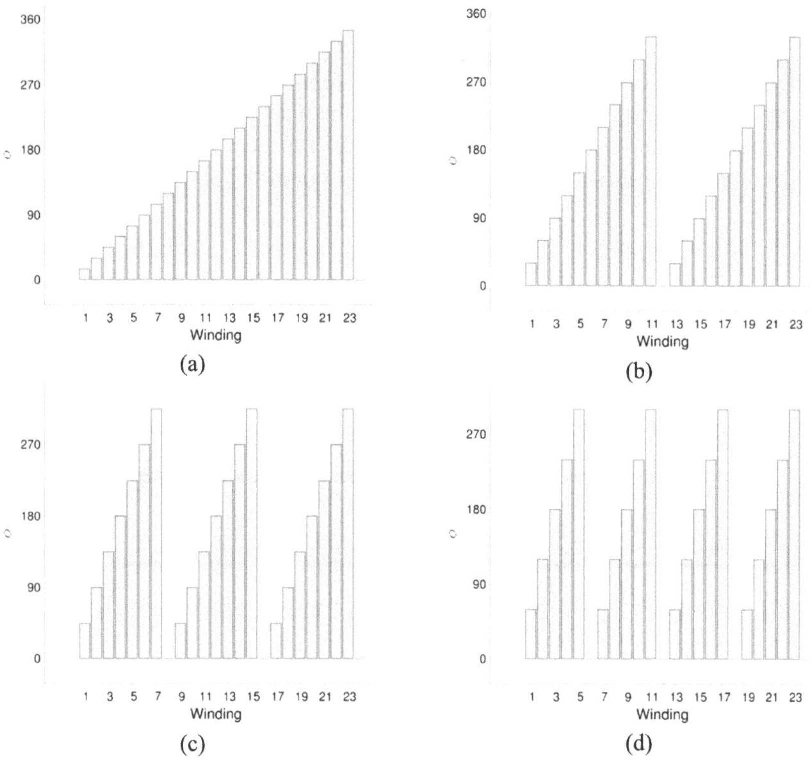

Fig. 3. Stator windings ϕ per winding for (a) $\Delta\phi = 15°; p = 1$, (b) $\Delta\phi = 30°; p = 2$, (c) $\Delta\phi = 45°; p = 3$ and (d) $\Delta\phi = 60°; p = 4$.

Table 2 resumes the phase shift values and synchronous speeds for four possible pole pair configurations of the machine, considering a 50 Hz input voltage frequency.

Table 2. Phase shift and synchronous speed for four possible pole-phase configurations of the machine considering a 50 Hz input voltage frequency.

No. of phases	p	$\Delta\phi$	N_s
24	1	15°	3000
12	2	30°	1500
8	3	45°	1000
6	4	60°	750

4 Drive Control

The proposed drive control system independently regulates the current in each stator winding to create different pole configurations for the machine, thereby controlling the speed, according to the operating principle described in Sect. 2.2. It is composed of two main components, as shown in Fig. 4: a cascade controller and a multiphase power inverter.

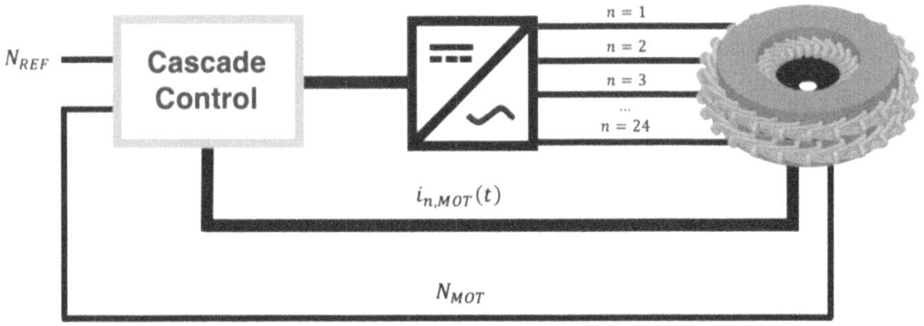

Fig. 4. Machine drive control schematic with its main elements.

4.1 Cascade Controller

The cascade controller compares the reference speed (N_{REF}) with the current machine speed (N_{MOT}) adjusting the amplitude of the machine current (i_{MOT}), by controlling the switches of the multiphase inverter, which generates current to machine windings ($n = 1, 2, \ldots, 24$). The current machine speed is continuously fed back into the control system, maintaining accurate regulation and ensuring that the machine operates at the reference speed.

The proposed cascade control is depicted in Fig. 5 and is composed of two stages. In the first stage, N_{REF} is compared with N_{MOT}. The difference is processed by a Proportional-Integral (PI) controller, which determines whether the machine current should increase or decrease. Next, the computed current value, I_{MAX}, is multiplied by a sinusoidal function corresponding to each machine winding. This sinusoidal function is retrieved from a look-up table, which defines the possible phase configurations based on the machine speed, as represented in Table 1.

The resulting phase current setpoint $i_n^*(t)$, $n = 1 \ldots 24$, then compared with the actual current in each winding. The difference is processed by a hysteresis controller, which regulates the switching signals for the single-sided multiphase inverter, S_{n1} and S_{n2}, as described in the next section.

4.2 Single-Sided Multiphase Inverter

The single-sided multiphase inverter consists of 24 phase legs, as shown in Fig. 6. Based on previous tests of the machine proof-of-concept and considering a safety margin, the

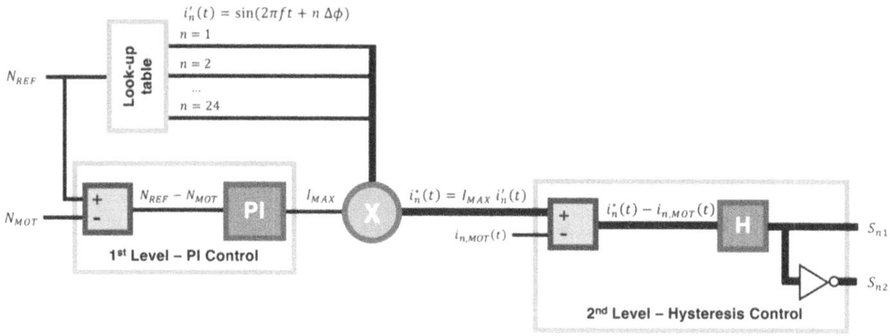

Fig. 5. MAFSM cascade speed control diagram.

rated voltage and current are 20 V and 20 A. Each phase leg controls one machine winding, L_n, with two semiconductor switches controlled by the previously described cascade control.

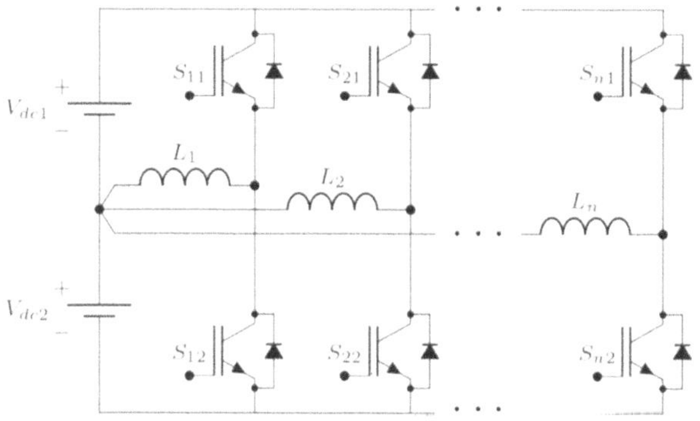

Fig. 6. Single-sided multiphase inverter schematic. The inverter is powered by two 20-V isolated DC voltage sources, U_{dc1} and U_{dc2}.

The hysteresis controller and multiphase inverter were simulated using MATLAB Simulink, considering a 1 mH inductance per winding. The $i_n^*(t)$ signal was considered as a perfect sinusoidal input, as the PI control is not included in this simulation. The results for two configurations are depicted in Fig. 7. The stator windings current amplitude is 20 A, following the inverter rated current.

Regarding the choice of semiconductors, three candidates were considered: MOSFET, SiC MOSFET, and GaN. In this work, its losses, efficiency and cost are calculated in the context of the proposed inverter at room temperature. However, considering further developments of the machine, the inverter must be scalable in terms of voltage, current, switching frequency, and number of legs. So, the choice of the most efficient device is important because losses are proportional to these parameters. Although in the first stage, the inverter can be designed for room-temperature operation, an evolution to cryogenic temperatures, i.e., 77–110 K, is considered for the future. Operate both the

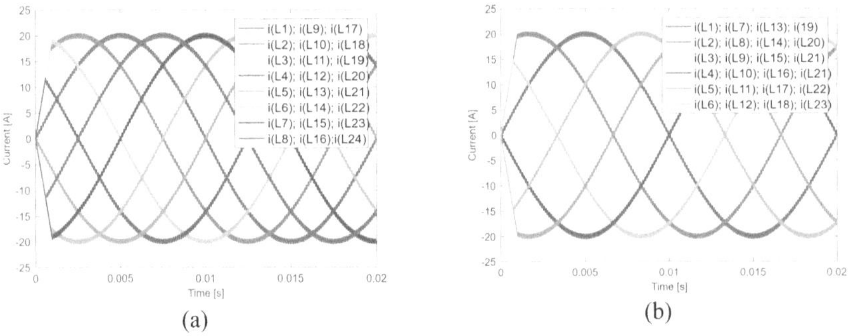

Fig. 7. Stator windings input current for (a) $\Delta\phi = 45°$; $p = 3$ and (b) $\Delta\phi = 60°$; $p = 4$.

machine and the power electronics in the same cryogenic environment reduces thermal leakage of the coolant [20].

For the efficiency calculation, η, conduction losses, P_{cond}, and switching losses, P_{sw}, were considered, as expressed in the following equation:

$$\eta[\%] = \frac{P_{out}}{P_{out} + P_{losses}} \times 100 = \frac{P_{out}}{P_{out} + P_{cond} + P_{sw}} \times 100, \quad (3)$$

where P_{out} is the inverter output power. A 0.9 power factor is assumed. The P_{cond} is obtained using:

$$P_{cond} = R_{ds(ON)} I_{rms}^2, \quad (4)$$

where $R_{ds(ON)}$ is the semiconductor on-resistance, and I_{rms} is the root-mean square of the inverter output current, which is 14.3 A, in this case. The P_{cond}, is calculated as follows:

$$P_{sw} = \frac{1}{2} U_{rms} I_{rms} \left(t_{on} + t_{off}\right) f_{sw}, \quad (5)$$

where U_{rms} is the root mean square of the inverter output voltage, which is 20 V, the t_{on} and t_{off} is the semiconductor turn-on and turn-off time, respectively, and f_{sw} is the switching frequency. A f_{sw} of 100 kHz is assumed.

The efficiency and cost results for each device are presented in Table 3.

As shown, GaN is the most efficient device, while MOSFET is the least efficient. The SiC MOSFET has an efficiency comparable to the MOSFET. However, it is not an ideal choice for future cryogenic power electronics development because its on-resistance, $R_{ds(ON)}$, increases by 70% at cryogenic temperatures (50–100K), leading to higher conduction losses, despite a 10% decrease in switching losses [20].

In contrast, GaN devices exhibit an 80% reduction in $R_{ds(ON)}$ and a 25% decrease in switching losses, making them strong candidates for cryogenic applications due to their superior scalability and efficiency in cryogenic temperatures [20]. While MOSFETs also experience a 60% $R_{ds(ON)}$ decrease and a 60% P_{sw}. Decrease at cryogenic temperatures, its losses are higher than in GaN [20].

Table 3. Candidate semiconductor devices comparison at room temperature. The cost is presented normalized to the MOSFET option.

	Type	Model	P_{cond}(W)	$P_{SW.}$ (W)	P_{losses}(W)	η(%)	Cost vs. (1)
(1)	MOSFET	IRLZ44N	211.20	67.20	278.40	95.64	1.00
(2)	SiC MOSFET	SCT040HU120G3AG	384.00	0.38	384.38	94.08	27.52
(3)	GaN	EPC2204	57.60	9.60	60.96	99.01	2.12

In conclusion, GaN devices should be strongly considered due to their superior performance in cryogenic environments and inverter scalability. However, for an initial version of the inverter operating at room temperature, MOSFETs may be a viable choice due to their greater market availability and affordability.

4.3 Machine Under Drive Fault

Aerospace applications, such as aviation, require highly reliable and fault-tolerant systems to prevent total shutdown or loss of thrust control [21]. The failure rate of aircraft systems must be extremely low, and in the event of a failure, the system must quickly detect the fault through fault detection and diagnosis (FDD) methods and respond to it using FTC strategies, preventing its propagation to healthy components and minimizing its impact [21, 22]. Therefore, in aircraft electrification, the development of drive systems with these characteristics is crucial.

In motor drive systems, the most vulnerable components are the power switching devices and the machine windings [21, 23]. A failure in power switching devices results in a partial short-circuit, while a failure in the machine windings can lead to an open-circuit or short-circuit fault [21]. In either case, effective FDD methods must be capable of rapidly identifying these fault types and isolating the affected components by disactivating the affected winding and the corresponding leg winding. However, this deactivation causes important spatial distortions in the Magnetomotive Force (MMF), which directly affects the generated flux density and consequently increases the torque oscillations. The development of FTC strategies of magnetic field reorganization is crucial to minimize the torque oscillation in case of failure. Figure 8 illustrates an example of a fault in winding number 5 of the presented machine for a 12-phase configuration. As shown, the magnetic field around the affected winding exhibits distortion.

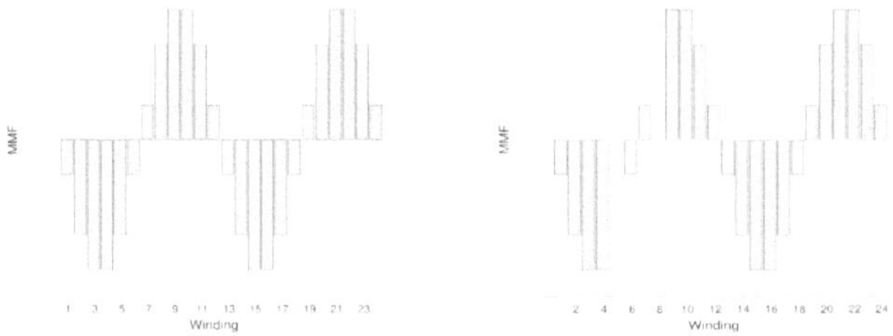

(a) (b)

Fig. 8. Qualitative representation of the MMF spatial distribution in a 24-phase machine stator at $\omega t = \pi/6$ for (a) a healthy stator and (b) a stator with a fault in winding 5.

5 Conclusion and Future Work

This work presents a preliminary study on the drive control of a multiphase axial flux superconducting machine. A more in-depth analysis is conducted on the multiphase inverter, including simulations and a preliminary evaluation of its efficiency. The drive control strategy must dynamically adjust the phase configuration and current to reorganize the pole arrangement, optimizing torque or speed based on the input.

Future work will focus on designing and validating fault-tolerance algorithms, which require an accurate model of the machine. This will be achieved through computational simulations, complemented by prototype testing. Moreover, a detailed analysis of the inverter performance and implementation is necessary to ensure optimal operation under varying conditions. Emphasizing scalability in the inverter design will support flexibility, including adaptation to cryogenic temperatures to enhance drive efficiency.

Acknowledgments. This research was supported by FCT under the framework of the research unit Center of Technology and Systems (CTS), with reference CTS/00066 and Fábio Encarnação-Gregório PhD grant from FCT, with reference 2023.04427.BD.

References

1. European Commission Reducing emissions from aviation. https://climate.ec.europa.eu/eu-action/transport/reducing-emissions-aviation_en. Accessed 4 Oct 2024
2. IEA: Reducing emissions from aviation. https://www.iea.org/reports/tracking-clean-energy-progress-2023 (2023). Accessed 24 Oct 2024
3. ACARE – Advisory Council for Aviation Research and Innovation in Europe – "ACARE Goals." https://www.acare4europe.org/acare-goals/. Accessed 3 Oct 2024
4. Flightpath 2050 Europe's Vision for Aviation. https://doi.org/10.2777/50266
5. Adu-Gyamfi, B.A., Good, C.: Electric aviation: a review of concepts and enabling technologies. Transport. Eng. **9**, 100134 (2022). https://doi.org/10.1016/j.treng.2022.100134
6. Xie, Y., Savvarisal, A., Tsourdos, A., Zhang, D., Gu, J.: Review of hybrid electric powered aircraft, its conceptual design and energy management methodologies. Chin. J. Aeronaut. **34**, 432–450 (2021)

7. Pornet, C., Isikveren, A.T.: Conceptual design of hybrid-electric transport aircraft. Prog. Aerosp. Sci. **79**, 114–135 (2015)
8. Brelje, B.J., Martins, J.R.R.A.: Electric, hybrid, and turboelectric fixed-wing aircraft: a review of concepts, models, and design approaches. Prog. Aerosp. Sci. **104**, 1–19 (2019)
9. Yazdani-Asrami, M., Seyyedbarzegar, S.M., Zhang, M., Yuan, W.: Insulation materials and systems for superconducting powertrain devices in future cryo-electrified aircraft: part i-material challenges and specifications, and device-level application. IEEE Electr. Insul. Mag. **38**, 23–36 (2022). https://doi.org/10.1109/MEI.2022.9716211
10. Yazdani-Asrami, M., et al.: Roadmap on artificial intelligence and big data techniques for superconductivity. Supercond. Sci. Technol. (2023). https://doi.org/10.1088/1361-6668/acbb34
11. Yazdani-Asrami, M., Zhang, M., Yuan, W.: Challenges for developing high temperature superconducting ring magnets for rotating electric machine applications in future electric aircrafts. J. Magn. Magn. Mater. (2021). https://doi.org/10.1016/j.jmmm.2020.167543
12. Altaf. S., Al-Anbuky, A., Gheitasi, A.: Enhancing Fault Detection in Distributed Motor Systems Using AI-Driven Cyber-Physical Sensor Networks. In: ECSA-11. MDPI, Basel Switzerland, p. 78 (2024)
13. Al-Anbuky, A., Altaf, S., Gheitasi, A.: Cyber-physical distributed intelligent motor fault detection. Sensors (2024). https://doi.org/10.3390/s24155012
14. Yang, B., Yang, H., Ye, J.: A four-layer cyber-physical security model for electric machine drives considering control information flow. IEEE J. Emerg. Sel. Top Power Electron. (2024). https://doi.org/10.1109/JESTPE.2024.3366089
15. Guo, L., Ye, J.: Cyber-Physical security of electric vehicles with four motor drives. IEEE Trans. Power Electron. **36**, 4463–4477 (2021). https://doi.org/10.1109/TPEL.2020.3025718
16. Hu, J.B., Li, F., Wu, J., Wang, J.H., Zhang, L.P.: Research on aviation electric power cyber physical systems. In: Advanced Materials Research, pp. 126–133 (2014)
17. Murta Pina, J.M.:Polyphase Motor with Variable Number of Poles, WIPO Patent WO2010013226 (2010)
18. Gregório-Encarnação, F., et al.: Preliminary assessment of a highly flexible HTS drive for electric aircraft. IEEE Trans. Appl. Supercond. (2025). https://doi.org/10.1109/TASC.2025.3548617
19. Pinto, J., Gregorio, F., Oliveira, R., Granados, X., Alvarez, A., Murta-Pina, J.: Preliminary Analysis of Core Losses and Performance of an Axial Flux Motor with High Temperature Superconducting Tapes on the Rotor. In: Proceedings – 2022 International Young Engineers Forum in Electrical and Computer Engineering, YEF-ECE 2022, pp. 25–32. Institute of Electrical and Electronics Engineers Inc. (2022)
20. Elwakeel, A., Liao, Y., Xiao, Y., Peña Alzola, R., Zhang, M., Yuan, W.: Review of cryogenic power electronics for all-electric aircraft. review of cryogenic power electronics for all-electric aircraft. IEEE Access (2025). https://doi.org/10.1109/ACCESS.2017
21. Cao, W., Mecrow, B.C., Atkinson, G.J., Bennett, J.W., Atkinson, D.J.: Overview of electric motor technologies used for more electric aircraft (MEA). IEEE Trans. Industr. Electron. **59**, 3523–3531 (2012). https://doi.org/10.1109/TIE.2011.2165453
22. Wang, Y., Zhang, C., Zhang, C., Li, L.: Review of high-power-density and fault-tolerant design of propulsion motors for electric aircraft. Energies **16**(19), 7015 (2023). https://doi.org/10.3390/en16197015
23. Liu, Z., Li, Y., Zheng, Z.: A review of drive techniques for multiphase machines. Trans. Electr. Mach. Syst. **2**(2), 243–251 (2018). https://doi.org/10.30941/CESTEMS.2018.00030

Investigation of the Impact of Geometrical and Operational Parameters on AC Transport Losses in HTS Pancake Coils Using Extensive FEM Simulations and Regression Analysis: Insights into Design Acceleration

Masoud Ardestani[1(✉)], João Murta-Pina[1], Simone Sparacio[2], Roberto A. H. de Oliveira[3], and Mohammad Yazdani-Asrami[4]

[1] NOVA School of Science and Technology, UNINOVA-CTS and LASI, NOVA University Lisbon, 2829-516 Caparica, Portugal
s.ardestani@campus.fct.unl.pt

[2] Department of Applied Science and Technology, Politecnico Di Torino, 10129 Turin, Italy

[3] Institute of Technical Physics (ITEP), Karlsruhe Institute of Technology, 76344 Eggenstein-Leopoldshafen, Germany

[4] Cryo-Electric Research Lab, Propulsion, Electrification and Superconductivity Group, James Watt School of Engineering, University of Glasgow, Glasgow, UK

Abstract. High-temperature superconducting (HTS) pancake coils play an essential role in numerous applications such as HTS transformers, Superconducting Magnetic Energy Storage (SMES) systems, and high-field magnets, among others. Recently, AI-powered cyber-physical systems (CPS) have made significant progress and are expected to enable rapid design, accelerated design optimization, and enhanced efficiency in HTS systems. This study employs the 2D axisymmetric T-A homogenization method to investigate the influence of geometrical and operational parameters on AC transport losses. A total of 2,700 Finite Element Method (FEM) simulations were generated. However, for readability and conciseness, only a specific fraction of these simulations, 270 cases, were analyzed in detail so that each parameter varied individually while keeping others constant. Regression analysis has been also performed to capture the relationship between AC transport losses versus geometrical and operational parameters. The results reveal distinct nonlinear dependencies. The turn number follows a nonlinear trend similar to the E-J power law, for which a fitting curve formula was derived. Inner radius and applied current amplitude also exhibit nonlinear behavior, though without a clear fitting curve due to interdependencies with other parameters. The effect of HTS tape width was also qualitatively analyzed for both 10 mm and 12 mm cases, while the influence of critical current was examined for $I_c = 300$ A, and $I_c = 400$ A, highlighting its impact on AC transport losses. This study establishes detailed correlations between AC transport losses and key parameters, offering valuable insights for optimizing HTS coil design. The findings provide a basis for AI-driven predictive modeling and optimization, contributing to the development of the next-generation of HTS devices within CPS frameworks.

Published by Springer Nature Switzerland AG 2025
L. M. Camarinha-Matos and F. Ferrada (Eds.): DoCEIS 2025, IFIP AICT 759, pp. 364–378, 2025.
https://doi.org/10.1007/978-3-031-97051-1_26

Keywords: Cyber-Physical System (CPS) · E-J Power Law · Finite Element Method · T-A Homogenization Formulation

1 Introduction

High-temperature superconducting (HTS) pancake coils are crucial components in a variety of applications, including superconducting magnetic energy storage (SMES) high-field magnets, electric machines, and advanced medical devices [1–7]. However, designing these coils for optimal performance is challenging due to the complex relationships between geometric parameters (e.g., coil turns, inner radius, tape width) and operational conditions (e.g., current amplitude, critical current limits).

Traditional design methods face significant limitations. For instance, Finite Element Methods (FEM), while it is accurate, is highly computationally intensive and unsuitable for highly iterative optimization analysis. Physical prototyping is also costly and time-consuming, while analytical models are limited to relatively simple scenarios and geometries and often rely on unrealistic simplifications.

To address these challenges, this study combines advanced computational modeling with regression analysis, creating a framework for future data-driven design of HTS pancake coils and windings. Leveraging the 2D axisymmetric T-A homogenization method [8–10]—which models the HTS layer as a 1D line rather than a rectangular shape and assumes the coil as a bulk—computational costs are significantly reduced while ensuring robustness and stability in convergence. This approach facilitates the rapid generation of extensive datasets for AC transport loss analysis. In this paper, only 270 cases from the total 2,700 FEM simulations have been used to analyze the AC transport loss dependencies on geometric and operational parameters. The datasets span a wide design space range, including inner radius (10–30 cm), turn numbers (50–1000), HTS tape widths (10 mm, 12 mm), and tape critical currents (300–500 A).

Regression analysis has also been performed, revealing distinct patterns corresponding to geometrical and operational parameters in relation to AC transport losses. A fitting curve formula has been obtained for the relationship between AC transport losses and turn number, similar to the E-J power law fitting curve. The goodness of fit is evaluated using the coefficient of determination (R^2), which has a value of 0.9998, confirming a good fit and strong variability across 18 datasets. Other parameters, such as inner radius and current amplitude, exhibited high non-linearity and interdependencies, preventing the capture of a fitting curve formula for them. However, they still provide useful qualitative insights. The HTS tape width and critical current correlations with AC transport losses are also described qualitatively [12, 13].

These findings directly support the development of Artificial Intelligence (AI)-based design tools for HTS coils and devices. The analyzed parameter correlations offer valuable insights for training machine learning models to optimize coil designs, which require highly iterative analyses to determine optimal parameters. This enables the refinement of optimization algorithms to ensure the feasibility of real-time performance in cyber-physical systems (CPS) [14, 15].

2 Contribution to AI-Powered Cyber-Physical Systems

This study contributes to AI-driven advancements in HTS technologies by developing a computational framework that bridges physics-based modeling and machine learning. The work establishes a comprehensive mapping of AC transport loss dependencies on coil geometry (e.g., turn number, inner diameter, HTS tape width) and operational parameters (e.g., applied current amplitude, critical current of tape). These analyses provide valuable insight into enabling HTS-based cyber physical systems (CPS) to optimize HTS pancake coil configurations, enhance energy efficiency, and mitigate operational risks. By accelerating the integration of HTS systems into AI-powered industrial applications, this work supports scalable, sustainable, and intelligent electrification aligned with next-generation technological demands.

3 2D Axisymmetric T-A Formulation

Various numerical techniques are available for modeling HTS components and devices, each with its own advantages and limitations. All these numerical approaches are fundamentally based on Maxwell's equations, which incorporate different formulations and employ specific dependent variables, such as A and T, to solve the equations. Among these, the T-A formulation stands out as one of the most effective techniques for HTS modeling, offering both speed and robustness, particularly when performing parametric sweeps across different scenarios. In this work, a 2D axisymmetric T-A formulation has been implemented using COMSOL Multiphysics® 6.2. Axisymmetry also significantly reduces the degrees of freedom (DOF) and computational time due to the symmetry of the physical model. The considered domain is half of the cross-section of the model geometry, and the solution is then rotated to generate the full 360° geometry of the model. Additionally, the T-A formulation assumes the HTS tape as a 1D line and accelerates the computations time significantly particularly when combined with the axisymmetric approach [8]. Figure 1 illustrates the 2D axisymmetric view of the HTS pancake coil. As can be seen in Fig. 1, the densely packed HTS tapes are considered homogenized bulk. This approach simplifies simulation modeling and considerably reduces computation time. Additionally, it can be applied in different formulations, such as H formulation, among others. In Fig. 1, δ is the thickness of HTS layer, d is the distance between HTS layers, and w is the width of the tape and bulk, which are equal. The R_{in} and R_{out} are also inner and outer radius of coil, respectively.

In addition, to implement the T-A homogenization for the 2D axisymmetric model, two modules namely, Magnetic fields (mf) and General Form PDE (g) have been applied in COMSOL. Magnetic fields module (mf) corresponds to calculate magnetic flux density (B) through the curl of magnetic vector potential (A) as shown in Eq. (1). Current density (J) also can be calculated by the curl of current vector potential (T) as given in Eq. (2). More precisely, the magnetic vector potential (A) is computed over the entire domain including HTS bulk, while the current vector potential (T) is computed only within the HTS bulk region. Both modules are also set to linear-linear, corresponding to the element order of the mesh used in the domain, which will be solved using the FEM technique.

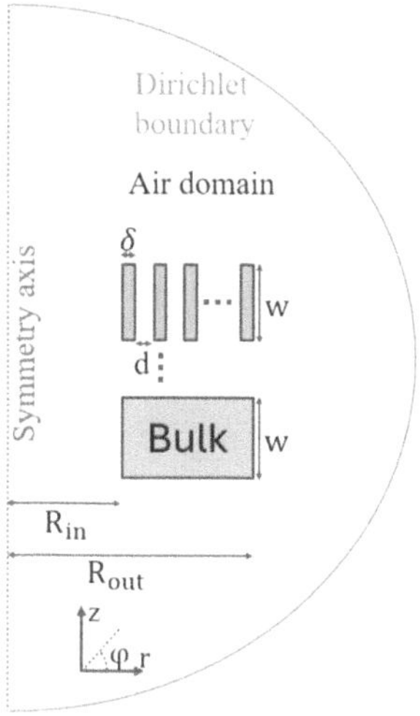

Fig. 1. 2D Axisymmetric T-A Homogenization layout.

It is also worth mentioning that the selection of linear-linear instead of quadratic for the mf module and linear for the g module was made to significantly reduce the computation time. Both scenarios, linear-linear and quadratic-linear, were also tested, and due to the negligible difference in the results, the linear-linear element order was selected. The mesh element size is also set to normal to balance computation time and acceptable accuracy. Time-dependent solvers were also used with a fully coupled implementation. To address the convergence issues also, the Automatic Newton Method was selected, even though it is more computationally expensive than the Constant Newton Method, but it offers superior robustness through a different algorithm with more iterations. The fully coupled solver solves the PDEs corresponding to Ampere law and Faraday law simultaneously (Eq. 5,11). All relevant equations are provided below:

$$B = \nabla \times A\,, \tag{1}$$

$$J = \nabla \times T. \tag{2}$$

By using Eq. (2), the current density in the coil can be obtained. Due to the symmetrical revolution of the current in the coil, only the φ-component is considered, with J_r and J_z being zero in the cylindrical coordinate system as shown in (3):

$$J_\varphi = \frac{\partial T_r}{\partial z} - \frac{\partial T_z}{\partial r} \cong \frac{\partial T_r}{\partial z}. \tag{3}$$

For simplicity and homogeneous current density distribution, only the term $\frac{\partial T_r}{\partial z}$ has been considered. This assumes the current density varies only along the r-axis (radial direction) and remains constant along the z-axis (axial direction). In addition to this, when the current starts to flow into the HTS coil, a magnetic field will be generated due to the current circulation, known as the self-field. Therefore, by defining A_φ as magnetic vector potential in (1) and substituting (1) and (2) in the Ampere's law given in (4), the (5) will be provided:

$$\nabla \times B = \mu_0 J . \tag{4}$$

The solution of (5) is also given in (6). The first derivative term with respect to r corresponds to the axial component of the magnetic flux density (B_z), while the second derivative term with respect to z corresponds to the radial component of magnetic flux density (B_r). COMSOL solves this equation numerically using the FEM technique and as a result, the magnetic vector potential A_φ, along with B_r and B_z will be computed simultaneously:

$$\nabla \times (\nabla \times A) = \mu_0(\nabla \times T). \tag{5}$$

Besides, as in the mf module, Ampere's law is used to relate the current density (J) to the magnetic flux density (B), which is resulting in the generation of current density:

$$\frac{\partial}{\partial r}\left(\frac{1}{r}\frac{\partial(rA_\varphi)}{\partial r}\right) + \frac{\partial}{\partial z}\left(\frac{1}{r}\frac{\partial(rA_\varphi)}{\partial z}\right) = -\mu_0 J_\varphi. \tag{6}$$

The g module, also, uses Faraday's law (10) to relate the time-varying magnetic flux density (B) to the induced electric field (E), which drives the current density.

In addition, to accurately model HTS materials, their nonlinear resistivity should be defined as given in (7), which has also been implemented in COMSOL:

$$\rho(J) = \frac{E_c}{J_c}\left(\frac{|J|}{J_C}\right)^{n-1}. \tag{7}$$

Then, by applying Ohm's law as shown in (8) and substituting (7) into it, relation (9) is obtained, from which the electric field can be derived. This relation is well known as E-J power law:

$$E = \rho(J)J , \tag{8}$$

$$E(J) = E_c\left(\frac{|J|}{J_c}\right)^n \frac{J}{|J|}. \tag{9}$$

In order to obtain electric field (E), the Faraday law (10) has also been implemented by COMSOL in g module. So, by substituting Ohm's law (8), and incorporating (1) and (2) relation into (10), the relation (11) will be obtained. Relation (11), computing induced electric field (E) which drives current density (J) and magnetic flux density (B) at the same time. In fact, the Ampere's and Faraday's laws are complementary components of Maxwell's equations and must both be satisfied with a self-consistent electromagnetic solution:

$$\nabla \times E = -\frac{\partial B}{\partial t}, \tag{10}$$

$$\nabla \times \rho_{HTS}(\nabla \times T) = -\frac{\partial(\nabla \times A)}{\partial t}. \quad (11)$$

Finally, by using E-J power law relation (9), and incorporating it into (12), instantaneous power loss in terms of watt was calculated by COMSOL. In COMSOL setting also, the volume is selected to compute current density inside volume. Then, by performing numerical integration method, namely trapezoidal approach as discussed below, the AC transport loss was calculated in joules per cycle [8–10]:

$$P_{inst\_loss} = \int_V E.J_{Bulk} dV. \quad (12)$$

J_{Bulk} in (12) is the current density within the bulk which can be defined as follows (13):

$$J_{Bulk} = J.\frac{\delta}{\Lambda}, \quad (13)$$

where δ is thickness of HTS layer and Λ is the axial pitch, defined as the sum of the HTS layer thickness (δ) and the gap between adjacent HTS layers. Concerning the trapezoidal integration method, the following relation expressed in (14) has been used, which numerically integrates the instantaneous power loss over time by approximating the area under the curve as discrete trapezoids and then summing these discretized trapezoids to calculate the total energy losses (J/cycle):

$$Q_{AC\_transport\_loss} = \int_{t_1}^{t_n} P(t).dt \cong \sum_{i=1}^{n-1} \frac{t_{i+1} - t_i}{2} \left[P(t_i) + P(t_{i+1})\right]. \quad (14)$$

Here, t_i and t_{i+1} are two-time steps one after another, so that, the interval between them is $\Delta t_i = t_{i+1} - t_i$. The terms of $P(t_i)$ and $P(t_{i+1})$ are the instantaneous power loss values at $t_i$and t_{i+1}, , respectively. The n also corresponds to the total number of data points and not the number of trapezoids. In other words, data points (n) produce $n - 1$ trapezoids. In this case, just for visualization, the number of trapezoids chosen is 10, which requires $n = 11$. The instantaneous power loss curve, obtained per watt in COMSOL by applying the trapezoidal integration method, is shown in Fig. 2.

The selected instantaneous power loss curve corresponds to a coil characterized by an applied current amplitude (I_m) of 90 A, a tape critical current (I_c) of 300 A, a tape width of 10 mm, an inner radius of 10 cm, and 500 turns. Besides, in this study, all computations were performed in MATLAB using 101 data points for the 20 ms-40 ms interval, which means that the trapezoidal integration used 100 trapezoids. As can be seen in Fig. 2, the transient part of the instantaneous power loss cannot be considered for calculating AC transport losses; only the steady state should be considered, which starts from 10 ms to 40 ms. In other words, since the frequency is 50 Hz, the time period is 20 ms, so, in this study period has been chosen from 20 ms to 40 ms. It is also worth mentioning that each instantaneous power loss curve, which is in watt, corresponds to one point in terms of joule per cycle. This is obtained by converting watts to joules using the trapezoidal integration method, as described above. Regarding the COMSOL simulation of the HTS pancake coils, a total of 2,700 FEM datasets (in watts) were first

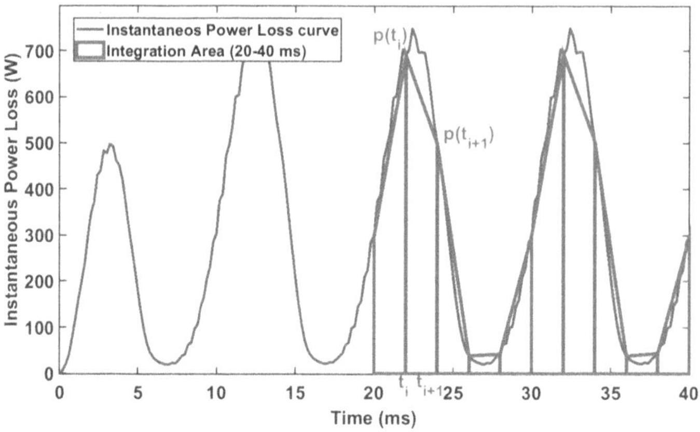

Fig. 2. Visualizing the trapezoidal integration method applied to instantaneous power loss curve.

generated by COMSOL and then converted to energy losses (J/cycle) using MATLAB, although only 270 of these datasets are presented for analysis. AC transport losses for the HTS pancake coils, across various configurations, were calculated in COMSOL using the fixed parameters outlined in Table 1. The analysis strategy in this study is also outlined in Table 2.

Table 1. Fixed parameters for HTS coil simulation.

Parameter	Value
Frequency	50 Hz
n-value	21
Distance Between HTS layers	0.4 mm
HTS Layer Thickness	1 μm
Electric Field Criterion (E_c)	10^{-4} V/m

As shown in Table 2, during the analysis, when one parameter varied, the others were kept constant to evaluate the impact of geometric and operational parameters on AC transport losses. The relationships between these parameters were analyzed, and the potential for deriving a fitting curve formula was also assessed. A fitting curve formula was successfully obtained for the number of turns. Further details and qualitative analyses of these relationships are provided in the following sections.

3.1 FEM Model Validation

The proposed T-A homogenization model was validated against results from [20, 21], which included both numerical and experimental measurements of AC transport losses in HTS pancake coils. The comparison results are presented in Table 3, showing AC

Table 2. Analysis strategy for AC transport losses dependency on geometrical and operational parameters.

Varied Parameters	Varied Parameters ranges	Fixed Parameters	Varied Turn Number Range
Turn Numbers	(50, 75, 100, 125, 150, 175, 200, 250, 300, 350,400, 450, 500, 600, 700, 800, 900, 1000)	$I_m = 90$ A, $I_C = 300$ A, $R_{in} = 10$ cm, w = 10 mm	-
Inner Radius (R_{in})	10 cm, 15 cm, 20 cm, 25 cm, 30 cm	$I_m = 90$ A, $I_C = 300$ A, w = 10 mm	50–1000
Width of Tapes (w)	10 mm, 12 mm	$I_m = 90$ A, $I_C = 300$ A, $R_{in} = 10$ cm	50–1000
Applied Current (I_m)	90 A, 120 A, 150 A, 180 A, 210 A	$I_C = 300$ A, $R_{in} =$ 10 cm, w = 10 mm	50–1000
Critical Current (I_C)	300 A, 400 A	$I_m = 120$ A, $R_{in} =$ 10 cm, w = 10 mm	50–1000

losses (in J/cycle and J/m/cycle) for three different coil configurations. The results for Coil 1 and Coil 2 are based on [Figs. 8 and 9, 20], where AC transport losses were calculated using COMSOL with the H-formulation and expressed in J/cycle. To validate the proposed T-A model against Fig. 8, a current with an amplitude of 90 A was applied in COMSOL. Since the critical current of the tape with 20 turns is 100 A, a current fraction ($f\_I_c = 0.9$) was used, and the current amplitude was calculated 90 A based on relation ($I_m = f\_I_c.I_c$).

For comparison, the line labeled const J_c, 0T was selected, since the condition includes only applied current without any external magnetic field to match the assumptions of the proposed T-A model. In Fig. 8, for a current of 90 A, the AC transport loss is located between 10^{-1} and 10^{-2} J/cycle. The approximate value shown in the figure is around 0.04 J/cycle, while the proposed T-A model produced a result of 0.038 J/cycle, indicating good agreement. Similarly, for Fig. 9, the same validation strategy has been followed. In this case, a current fraction 0.75 was used, to obtain current amplitude of 75 A (with the tape critical current of 100 A for a 50-turn coil). The same const J_c, 0T line shown in Fig. 9 was used for comparison. In Fig. 9, for 75 A, the AC transport loss is slightly below 0.1 J/cycle. The proposed T-A model obtained 0.096 J/cycle, further confirming the T-A model's consistency. The inner radius for both coils, namely 20,50 turns also mentioned in paper 30 mm (3 cm).

Regarding Coil 3 [21], the evaluation procedure differs, as AC transport losses are calculated in J/m/cycle rather than J/cycle. Therefore, at first the AC transport losses have already been calculated by proposed T-A model in COMSOL in J/cycle and divided into total length of coil to convert it to J/m/cycle. Total length of the coil has been obtained by using relation (15). Since the turn number of the coil is 10, the distance between HTS layers (d) is 0.4 mm, and HTS layer thickness (δ) is 1 μm, the total length of the HTS pancake coil has been obtained as 3.88 m. In relation (15) R_1 is an inner radius of coil, which is 6 cm, the factor of 1/2 is also included to average the turn-to-turn radial spacing, which increases linearly from zero at the first turn to a maximum at the tenth turn:

$$\mathrm{L_{Total}} = 2\pi R_1 \mathrm{N} + \frac{\mathrm{N}-1}{2}(\delta + \mathrm{d}). \tag{15}$$

For Coil 3, both the FEM technique using the A–φ–J formulation and an experimental approach with a lock-in amplifier were conducted. In Fig. 7 [21], the solid black line, titled, Calculation, $I_c = 260$ A, corresponds to the FEM results, while the green points represent the experimental measurements. The proposed T–A model was adjusted to the coil's specifications, including a frequency of 36 Hz, the tape's critical current of 260 A, among other factors. Based on the following relation ($I_m = f\_I_c.I_c$), and the fraction current (f_I_c) of 0.31, the current amplitude was obtained as 80.6 A.

Therefore, for validation, both the current amplitude and its corresponding AC transport loss (in J/m) has been considered in Fig. 7. In Fig. 7, the AC transport losses at 80.6 A is approximately 0.001 J/m. The experimental measurement point (green) at 80.6 A also has almost the same value of 0.001 J/m. Besides, the AC transport loss from the proposed T–A model was obtained 0.0044 J/cycle. By dividing this value to the total coil length (3.88 m), the AC transport losses were obtained as 0.0011 J/m. Thus, this result further confirms the accuracy of the proposed T–A model. The detailed validation comparison is also provided in Table 3 as follows.

4 AC Transport Losses Correlation Versus Geometrical Parameters

As already mentioned, AC transport losses [17–19] are dependent on both geometrical and operational parameters. In this part, the dependency of AC transport losses on turn number and inner radius has been evaluated. Regression analysis is also performed using FEM datasets, and the relationship between them is quantitatively and qualitatively have been discussed.

4.1 Turn Number

The FEM datasets showed that AC transport loss in HTS pancake coils follows a non-linear relationship, similar to the E-J power law. As the number of turns increases, AC transport losses also increase. The range of turn numbers is provided in Table 2. Each AC transport loss corresponds to a specific turn number. In total, 18 AC transport loss FEM datasets were used, and a fitted curve was generated for them using regression analysis, as shown in Fig. 3.

As shown in Fig. 3, regression analysis was performed on the FEM datasets, and the R-squared value was calculated. The high R-squared value is 0.9998, indicates that the fitting curve accurately captures the relationship between AC transport loss and the number of turns. The fitting curve formula is given in the following relation (16) [12, 13]:

$$\mathrm{Q_{predicted\_coil}} = \mathrm{a.(T)^b}, \tag{16}$$

Table 3. T-A model validation with three HTS pancake coils for AC transport losses: FEM and experimental comparison.

Parameter	Coil 1 (FEM) [Fig. 8, Ref. 20]	Coil 2 (FEM) [Fig. 9, Ref.20]	Coil 3 (FEM and Experiment) [Fig. 7, Ref. 21]
Inner Radius (cm)	3	3	6
Frequency (Hz)	50	50	36
Tape Width (mm)	4	4	12
Distance between HTS layers	0.2	0.2	0.4
(mm)	20	50	10
Turns	100	100	260
Tape critical current (A)	90	75	80.6
Applied Current Amplitude	0.9	0.75	0.31
(A)	0.038	0.096	0.0044
Fraction current	-	-	0.0011
AC Losses (J/cycle)- proposed model			
AC Losses (J/m)- proposed model			

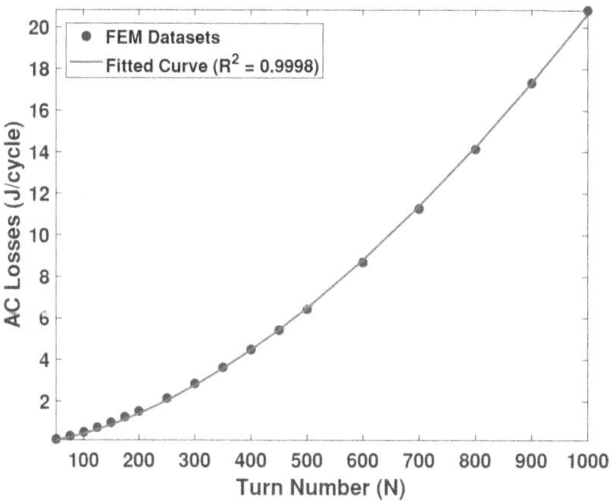

Fig. 3. AC transport loss FEM datasets and regression fitting curve.

where Q_(predicted_coil) is AC transport loss of HTS pancake coil obtained by regression analysis, T is turn number and a, b is coefficient corresponding to fitting curve. As much as b increases the curves will be sharper. R-Square and average (mean) have calculated through the relations 17 and 18 respectively [11, 16]:

$$R^2 = 1 - \frac{\sum_{n=1}^{N} (Q_{actual_{coil}} - Q_{predicted_{coil}})^2}{\sum_{n=1}^{N} (Q_{actual_{coil}} - Q_{mean})^2}, \tag{17}$$

$$Q_{mean} = \frac{1}{N}\sum_{n=1}^{N} Q_{actual\_coil}, \quad (18)$$

where Q_{actual_coil} is the actual AC transport loss points obtained by FEM and $Q_{predicted\_coil}$ is the AC transport loss of coil obtained based on the regression fitting curve model. Q_{mean} is the mean value of the actual AC transport losses. N is the total number of data points which is 18.

4.2 Inner Radius (R_{in})

Despite its linear appearance as shown in Fig. 4, the inner radius actually follows a nonlinear relationship with a very poor R-squared value. Various regression approaches were tested, but none could accurately capture the relationship. It is evident that the inner radius cannot be modeled using a simplified analytical regression model, as it depends on other geometric and operational factors. However, the dataset points offer valuable qualitative insights. Specifically, as the inner radius increases in each turn, AC transport losses also increase. Furthermore, as the number of turns increases, the slope of the curve changes significantly. This behavior is due to the nonlinear resistivity of the HTS tape. At low turn numbers, this nonlinearity is less significant, and the impact of resistance is relatively small. However, as the number of turns increases, this nonlinearity becomes much more tangible and disproportionate, making it clear that the relationship between the inner radius and AC transport loss cannot be captured by a simple analytical fitting curve formula.

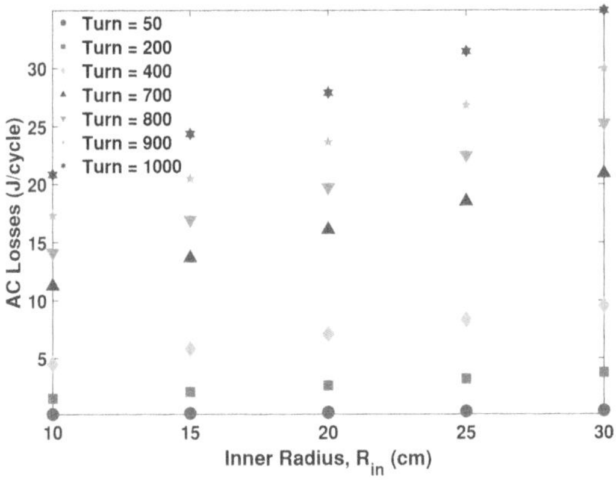

Fig. 4. AC transport losses datasets versus inner radius.

4.3 HTS Tape Width (W)

As expected, increasing the HTS tape width leads to an increase in AC transport loss, emphasizing that the impact of tape width in the design of HTS pancake coils can be significant, especially at high turn numbers. In Fig. 5, the dependency of AC transport loss on HTS tape width for different turn numbers is shown. The highest AC transport loss for a tape width of 10 mm is 20.81 J/cycle, while for 12 mm, it is 24.26 J/cycle. The lowest losses, 0.17 J/cycle, occur at a turn number of 50.

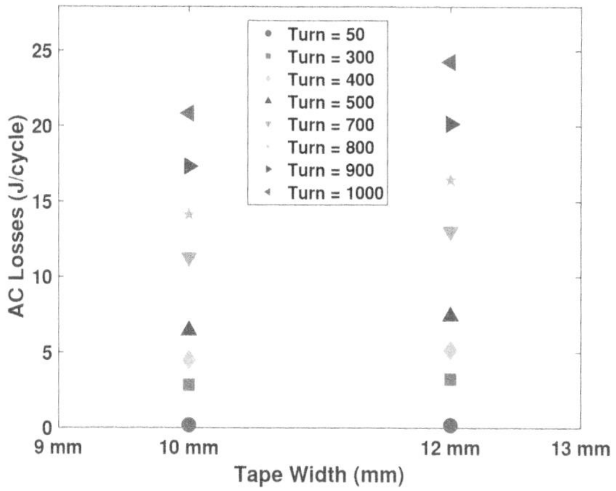

Fig. 5. AC transport loss datasets versus tape width.

5 AC Transport Losses Correlation with Operational Parameters

Operational parameters, similar to geometrical parameters, have a significant impact on the AC transport loss of an HTS coil, including current amplitude and critical current. The impact of each has been discussed as follows.

5.1 AC Transport Loss Behavior Versus Applied Current (I_m)

The current amplitude, similar inner diameter, exhibits a complex relationship with AC transport loss that cannot be fully captured by regression analysis. This is due to its dependence on several interrelated parameters that cannot be simplified into basic formulas. Different regression models, such as the E-J power law and logarithmic functions, among others were tested, but the low R-squared value (~0.2) indicates that while some datasets show similar trends, the models fail to explain the variability in the data. As shown in Fig. 6, the FEM datasets show a nonlinear exponential relationship, where AC transport losses increase with the current amplitude. However, this increase is not proportional, and for current amplitudes greater than 50% of the critical current (I_c = 300 A), the losses increase significantly. This nonlinearity is due to the resistivity of the HTS material, which follows a power-law relationship and becomes more significant at higher current amplitudes. Moreover, as the number of turns increases, both the nonlinearity and the current path distance increase, further amplifying the losses ($E = \rho(J)J$). For high turn numbers, such as 1000, the increase in losses becomes more noticeable. Current amplitude is a key factor with significant impact on AC transport losses in HTS pancake coils and should be considered effectively.

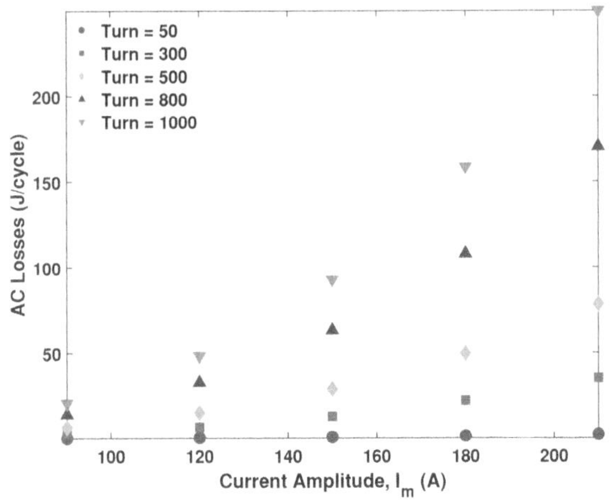

Fig. 6. AC transport loss datasets versus current amplitude.

5.2 AC Transport Loss Behavior Versus Critical Current (I_c)

In this analysis, the impact of the critical current (I_c) of the tape on AC losses was examined. Current with the same amplitude (120A) applied to the coils with two different HTS tapes with $I_c = 300$ A and $I_c = 400$ A. As shown in Fig. 7 it is evident that the coil with the $I_c = 400$ A exhibited lower AC losses. Despite a homogeneous current distribution across the coil, the differences in I_c between the two tapes played a critical role in determining the AC loss behavior. Since the current distribution was uniform, each tape experienced the same current, making the losses primarily dependent on the critical current (I_c) of the tapes. The tape with $I_c = 400$ A can carries higher current with lower current density J relative to J_c before approaching critical current conditions, leading to lower AC losses. In contrast, the tape with $I_c = 300$ A operates closer to its

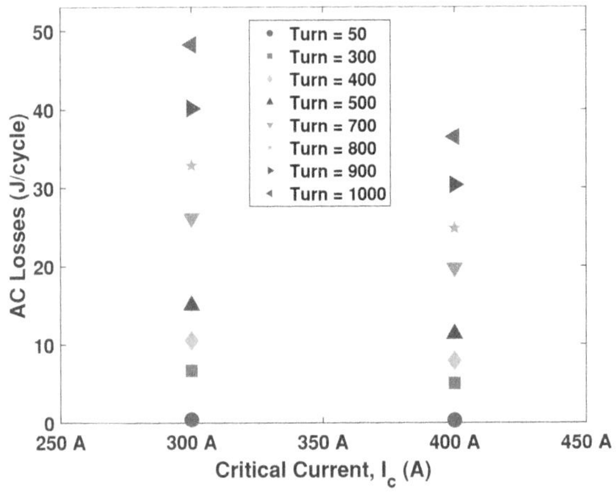

Fig. 7. AC transport loss datasets versus critical current.

critical current, and experienced higher current density J resulting in more AC losses at the same applied current. The difference in AC losses between the two tapes is due to their different effect in I_c values, even with a uniform current distribution across the coil.

6 Conclusions

This study systematically evaluated the influence of geometrical and operational parameters on AC transport losses in HTS pancake coils through extensive FEM simulations datasets and regression analysis. The findings highlight distinct nonlinear dependencies: turn numbers follow a power-law relationship, with a fitting curve formula obtained, while inner radius and applied current amplitude exhibit complex nonlinear trends due to interdependencies with other parameters and HTS material behavior. The analysis of HTS tape width for 10 mm and 12 mm cases provided qualitative insights into its impact on AC transport losses, revealing higher losses for wider tapes. Similarly, critical current variations ($I_c = 300$ A and $I_c = 400$ A) demonstrated that higher critical current reduces AC losses, emphasizing the role of material properties in optimizing coil performance.

By establishing precise correlations between AC transport losses and key design factors, this study provides valuable insights to accelerate design optimization of HTS coils. The gained insights support predictive modeling techniques for real-time feasibility in cyber-physical systems. Future research could also enhance this framework by integrating multi-physics simulations and advanced machine learning models to further refine non-linear parameter interactions, contributing to scalable, efficient, and high-performance of HTS technologies for next-generation energy systems.

References

1. Mohanty, A., Ramasamy, A.K., Verayiah, R., et al.: Intelligent event trigger based sliding mode control in a marine current turbine with superconducting magnetic energy storage. Sci. Rep. **15**, 12725 (2025)
2. Bang, J., et al.: Evidence that transverse variability of critical current density can greatly mitigate screening current stress in high field REBCO magnets. Sci. Rep. **14**(1), 31703 (2024)
3. Hahn, S., et al.: 45.5-tesla direct-current magnetic field generated with a high-temperature superconducting magnet. Nature **570**(7762), 496–499 (2019). https://doi.org/10.1038/s41586-019-1293-1
4. Pina, J.M., et al.: Research and development of alternative concepts in HTS machines. IEEE Trans. Appl. Supercond. **21**(3), 1141–1145 (2010)
5. Sekiguchi, D., et al.: Trial test of fully HTS induction/synchronous machine for next generation electric vehicle. IEEE Trans. Appl. Supercond. **22**(3), 5200904 (2011)
6. Ardestani, M., Izadfar, H.R.: Reduction of air-gap flux density distortion for a 20 kW HTS Induction Motor. In: Camarinha-Matos, L.M. (ed.) Technological Innovation for Digitalization and Virtualization: 13th IFIP WG 5.5/SOCOLNET Doctoral Conference on Computing, Electrical and Industrial Systems, DoCEIS 2022, Caparica, Portugal, June 29 – July 1, 2022, Proceedings, pp. 167–183. Springer International Publishing, Cham (2022). https://doi.org/10.1007/978-3-031-07520-9_16
7. Parkinson, B.: Design considerations and experimental results for MRI systems using HTS magnets. Supercond. Sci. Technol. **30**(1), 014009 (2016)

8. Sparacio, S., et al.: Analysis framework for nuclear heating effects on HTS-based conductors in fusion power plants. IEEE Trans. Appl. Supercond. **34**(3), 1–8 (2024). https://doi.org/10.1109/TASC.2024.3376490
9. Carvalho, D.G., da Silva, F.F., Fernandes, J.F.P., da Costa Branco, P.J.: Finite-element recipes for HTS-coated conductors and HTS tape topologies. Supercond. Sci. Technol. **36**(10), 103001 (2023)
10. Vargas-Llanos, C. R., Grilli, F.: 3D homogenized TA formulation for modeling HTS coils (2021)
11. Bonab, S.A., Russo, G., Morandi, A., Yazdani-Asrami, M.: A comprehensive machine learning-based investigation for the index-value prediction of 2G HTS coated conductor tapes. Machine Learn. Sci. Technol. **5**(2), 025040 (2024)
12. Alipour Bonab, S., Song, W., Yazdani-Asrami, M.: Enhancing the predictive modeling of n-value surfaces in various high temperature superconducting materials using a feed-forward deep neural network technique. Crystals **14**(7), 619 (2024)
13. Yazdani-Asrami, M., et al.: Roadmap on artificial intelligence and big data techniques for superconductivity. Supercond. Sci. Technol. **36**(4), 043501 (2023)
14. Yazdani-Asrami, M.: Artificial intelligence, machine learning, deep learning, and big data techniques for the advancements of superconducting technology: a road to smarter and intelligent superconductivity. Supercond. Sci. Technol. **36**(8), 084001 (2023)
15. Machura, P., Zhang, H., Kails, K., Li, Q.: Loss characteristics of superconducting pancakes, solenoid and spiral coils for wireless power transfer. Supercond. Sci. Technol. **33**(7), 074008 (2020)
16. Yazdani-Asrami, M., Song, W., Pei, X., Zhang, M., Yuan, W.: AC loss characterization of HTS pancake and solenoid coils carrying non- sinusoidal currents. IEEE Trans. Appl. Supercond. **30**(5), 1–9 (2020)
17. de Oliveira, R.A., et al.: Effects of non-characteristic harmonics on AC losses of high-temperature superconducting coils. IEEE Trans. Power Electron. **36**(12), 13697–13705 (2021)
18. Amaro, N., et al.: Ac losses in Bi-2223 single-pancake coils from 72 to 1152 Hz—Modeling and measurements. IEEE Trans. Appl. Supercond. **26**(8), 1–7 (2016)
19. Yazdani-Asrami, M., Song, W., Zhang, M., Yuan, W., Pei, X.: AC transport loss in superconductors carrying harmonic current with different phase angles for large-scale power components. IEEE Trans. Appl. Supercond. **31**(1), 1–5 (2020)
20. Ainslie, M.D., Hu, D., Zou, J., Cardwell, D.A.: Simulating the in-field AC and DC performance of high-temperature superconducting coils. IEEE Trans. Appl. Supercond. **25**(3), 1–5 (2014)
21. Gömöry, F., et al.: AC loss in pancake coil made from 12 mm wide REBCO tape. IEEE Trans. Appl. Supercond. **23**(3), 5900406 (2013)

Electronic Systems

A Comprehensive Study of the Reference Voltage Buffer Design for CR- and CS-Based SAR-ADCs

Hugo Viana[1,2(✉)], Pedro Barquinha[2], and João Goes[1]

[1] NOVA School of Science and Technology, UNINOVA-CTS and LASI, NOVA University Lisbon, 2829-516 Caparica, Portugal
hf.viana@campus.fct.unl.pt, goes@fct.unl.pt

[2] NOVA School of Science and Technology, I3N/CENIMAT, NOVA University Lisbon, 2829-516 Caparica, Portugal
pmcb@fct.unl.pt

Abstract. Analog-to-digital converters (ADCs) such as successive approximation register (SAR) rely on accurate reference voltage circuits (RVCs) to ensure precise signal conversion. This work examines how charge-redistribution (CR) and charge-sharing (CS) SAR-ADCs impact the design of the buffer, considering different RVC scheme and digital-to-analog converters architectures (DAC). CR-based SAR-ADCs require high-speed buffers due to continuous bit-dependent connections, leading to demanding power and bandwidth requirements. In contrast, CS-based SAR-ADCs, which operate passively during conversion, allow for relaxed buffer design with lower dominant pole frequency and improved power efficiency. Analytical expressions for the reference buffer behavior, including voltage accuracy and settling time, are derived for binary-weighted and C-2C CR- and CS-based SAR ADCs.

Keywords: Reference Voltage Circuit · SAR-ADC · CR SAR-ADC · CS SAR-ADC · Reference Buffer

1 Introduction

The analog-to-digital converter (ADC) is a crucial component in the transition from the analog input to digital processing. Its applications range from medical imaging to the Internet, including Cyber-Physical Systems (CPSs) and the Internet of Things (IoT). CPSs, in particular, integrate real-time interaction and control between computing and physical components [1, 2].

Reference circuits play a fundamental role in analog and data converter systems. There are many forms for generating a reference voltage, such as resistive or capacitive ladders and bandgap circuits. However, challenges arise when driving a large capacitor or an array of small capacitors (resulting in high capacitance), as seen in digital-to-analog converters (DACs), or when operating in high-speed or high-accuracy switched-capacitor (SC) applications. To address this, a reference buffer circuit (RVC) follows the reference

Published by Springer Nature Switzerland AG 2025
L. M. Camarinha-Matos and F. Ferrada (Eds.): DoCEIS 2025, IFIP AICT 759, pp. 381–394, 2025.
https://doi.org/10.1007/978-3-031-97051-1_27

voltage generator, ensuring that the reference voltage settles within the available time and maintains a specified error margin to avoid limiting the converter's accuracy and speed [1, 3].

This work studies different reference voltage generation schemes, analyzing their advantages and disadvantages. SAR-ADC architecture influences reference settling requirements, making it essential to compare charge-redistribution (CR) and charge-sharing (CS) schemes. Additionally, the digital-to-analog converter (DAC) architecture and capacitance (C_{DAC}) impact RVC performance. Therefore, two cases will be explored for each SAR-ADC architecture: the binary-weighted capacitor array (Bin-W) and the C-2C ladder. A comprehensive study will be conducted on reference voltage buffer design requirements, focusing on timing, accuracy, power, and energy considerations.

2 Connection Between ADCs and AI-Powered CPSs

The rapid advancement of cyber-physical systems (CPSs) is transforming various sectors of society. A CPS integrates a mechanical system with a computer system that monitors and controls it based on system states and external conditions. These systems are widely applied in fields such as automotive technology, energy management, and medical devices [2]. In parallel, artificial intelligence (AI) has seen significant progress in recent years, leading to its integration into CPSs. Specifically, AI-based controllers, such as deep neural networks, are being explored as alternatives to traditional CPS controllers to handle complex real-world scenarios [2].

A system capable of converting information from the external environment (physical), such as voltage, charge, current, or magnetic flux, into a format that can be processed by digital computing machinery (cyber) is essential. This is where analog-to-digital converters (ADCs) come into play. Different ADC topologies can be designed to meet specific application requirements, such as successive approximation register (SAR) and $\Delta\Sigma$-modulators. Regardless of the topology used, all ADCs require at least one reference quantity to compare and scale the analog input signal [1, 3, 4].

3 Successive Approximation Register ADC

Successive approximation register (SAR) analog-to-digital converters (ADCs) are ideal for low-to-medium resolution and moderate-speed applications due to their power efficiency and predominantly digital architecture, which makes them well-suited for advanced technology nodes [1, 5, 6]. As a result, SAR-based ADCs are increasingly used for moderate-to-high resolution and faster conversion speeds in deep-nanoscale technologies. This progress is enabled by innovations such as digital calibration, noise-shaping, time-interleaving, and pipelining, which extend the capabilities of SAR ADCs beyond their traditional limitations [6].

A generic structure of a SAR ADC is shown in Fig. 1a. It consists of a sample-and-hold (S&H) circuit, a DAC, a comparator, SAR logic, and the RVC.

3.1 Digital-To-Analog Converter for SAR-ADC

SAR-ADCs can be implemented using different types of DACs. One of the most commonly used DACs is the switched-capacitor (SC) DAC, due to its low power consumption [1]. The capacitive DAC is crucial to the energy efficiency of the SAR-ADC, as it consumes only dynamic energy and no static energy. Energy consumption largely depends on the capacitor switching scheme. One of the most efficient schemes is the common-mode voltage (V_{CM})-based scheme, where V_{CM} is typically set to $V_{REF}/2$. For instance, the V_{CM}-based charge-redistribution (CR) scheme can save over 85% of energy compared to conventional CR schemes. Although an additional buffer is required for the V_{CM}, the overall requirements are less stringent since the scheme is not bit-dependent, and its absolute value does not impact linearity as long as it remains stable during the conversion. Therefore, in this work, all schemes will be considered to be V_{CM}-based [5, 7].

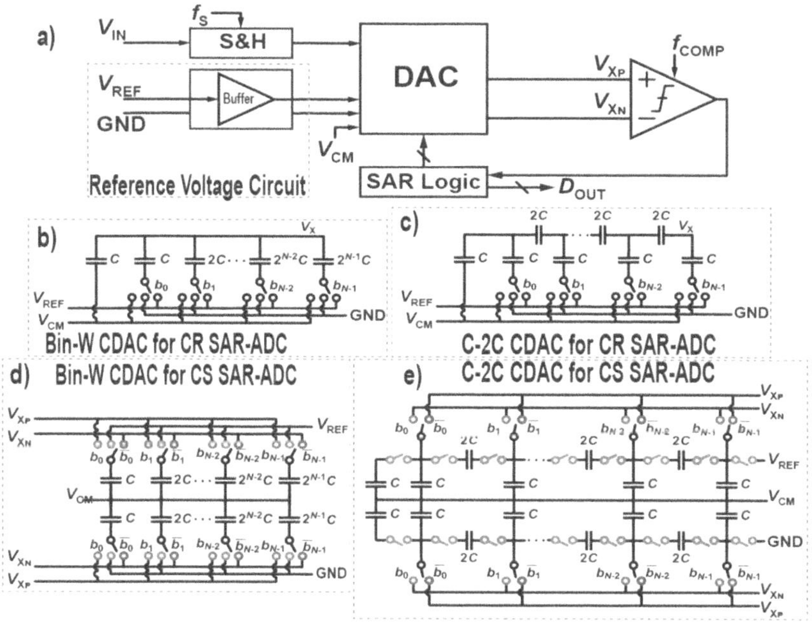

Fig. 1. a) Generic SAR- ADC architecture; b) Bin-W CDAC for CR SAR-ADC; c) C-2C CDAC for CR-ADC; d) Bin-W CDAC for CS SAR-ADC; e) C-2C CDAC for CS-ADC.

3.1.1 Binary-Weighted Capacitive DAC

The Bin-W capacitive DAC (CDAC) is one of the most commonly used switched-capacitor DACs. It consists of 2^{N-1}, 2^{N-2}, ..., 2^0, 2^1 unitary-capacitors (C) arranged in parallel. Each group of capacitors is controlled by the corresponding bit result (b_{N-1}, b_{N-2}, ..., b_1, b_0, respectively). This design helps reduce the relative mismatch between the base-2 weighted capacitors. A final unit capacitor, C, is added to complete the binary-weighted DAC that is always connected to V_{CM}. The single-ended representation is shown in Fig. 1b and d, with node V_X connected to the comparator's input [1, 7–9].

A major drawback of this scheme is the exponential increase in the total equivalent capacitance ($2^N C$) and area as the number of bits increases. Consequently, the RVC must drive exponentially more capacitance, and the die area required for DAC implementation also faces exponential growth [8, 9].

3.1.2 C-2C DAC

An alternative to the binary-weighted capacitive array is the segmented capacitor array, implemented through a bridge capacitor. The most extreme case of this configuration is the C-2C DAC, as shown in Fig. 1c and e. This DAC uses two capacitor sizes: C and $2C$, where two C units are grouped to minimize the relative capacitor mismatch. The C capacitor functions as the branch capacitor, influenced by bit resolution, while the 2C capacitor serves as the bridge capacitor. The primary advantage of this configuration is its constant input capacitance to the comparator, always equal to 2C, regardless of bit resolution. This stability helps reduce area and power consumption, making it a favorable choice for certain applications [8, 10–12].

Nevertheless, the architecture is highly sensitive to parasitic capacitances, primarily from the bottom plates of the $2C$ capacitors. These exhibit higher parasitic capacitance to ground compared to the top plates of C and $2C$, leading to non-linear errors and limiting the applicability of the C-2C DAC to low- and medium-resolution designs [8, 11, 12]. To mitigate these effects, various techniques have been proposed, such as [10] and [11]. Additionally, digital calibration can further compensate for parasitic capacitance, although it introduces extra power consumption and increased timing complexity [1].

3.2 Charge-Redistribution-Based SAR-ADC

The majority of SAR ADCs rely on CR to perform the successive approximation algorithm. In this approach, the sample-and-hold (S&H) and capacitive DAC functions are combined, allowing the input signal (V_{IN}) to be sampled onto the top plate of the DAC, while its bottom plate is connected to V_{CM}. Figure 1b and c present a single-ended configuration CR SAR-ADC with Bin-W and C-2C CDAC, respectively. Alternatively, sampling onto the DAC's bottom plate is possible, but it requires an additional step to transfer the equivalent charge to the top plate, where the comparator is connected. V_{IN} is then compared with V_{CM}, resulting in a logic "1" if V_{IN} is greater than V_{CM}; otherwise, the comparator outputs a logic "0." Based on this decision, the bottom plate of the most significant bit (MSB) capacitor (C_{MSB}) is switched to either ground (GND) or V_{REF} for a "1" or "0," respectively. This process continues bit by bit until the remaining voltage difference is less than one least significant bit (LSB) – 1 $A_{LSB} = A_{REF}/2^N$, where A is physical quantity and N is the number of bits. Ideally, the DAC output voltage is determined by (1), where i represents the step. The final digital output is an N-bit word obtained from the combined comparator results [1, 5, 7].

$$V_{DAC,CR\ SAR\text{-}ADC}(i) = V_{IN} - \frac{(2 \cdot b_{N-i} - 1)(V_{REF} - V_{CM})}{2^i} \quad (1)$$

The timing diagram is presented in Fig. 2a. Each bit decision consists of three time components: comparison time (T_{COMP}), SAR logic processing time (T_{LOGIC}), and DAC settling time (T_{DAC}). In high-speed and high-resolution applications, the time allocated for each is limited. Insufficient T_{COMP} and T_{LOGIC} can lead to metastability errors, while inadequate T_{DAC} may introduce non-linear conversion errors [7].

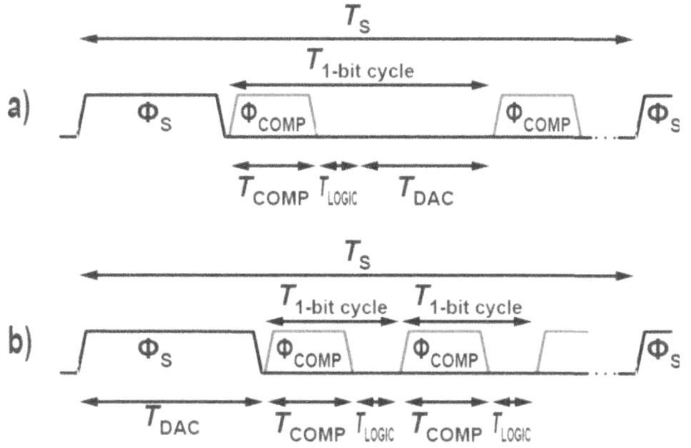

Fig. 2. a) CR-based SAR-ADC timing diagram; b) CR-based SAR-ADC timing diagram.

3.3 Charge-Sharing-Based SAR-ADC

The successive approximation algorithm can also be implemented using a charge-sharing (CS) architecture. While CR-SAR ADCs perform quantization in the voltage domain, CS-SAR ADCs operate in the charge domain [5, 9].

The conversion starts by sampling the input signal into a couple of explicit S&H capacitors ($C_{S\&H}$). The stored charges are proportional to the input signal and $C_{S\&H}$ ($Q_{S\&H} = C_{S\&H} \cdot \Delta V_{IN}$). Simultaneously, the DAC capacitor array is pre-charged to V_{REF} (as presented in Fig. 1d and e. At the start of the conversion phase, the comparator is latched, and the most significant bit (MSB) is determined directly from $C_{S\&H}$, without requiring any charge processing – similar to top-plate sampling in CR-SAR ADCs. Once the MSB decision is made, the largest DAC capacitor is connected either in parallel ($b_{MSB} = 0$) or anti-parallel ($b_{MSB} = 1$) with $C_{S\&H}$. The total charge across both capacitors is $Q_1 = C_{S\&H} \cdot \Delta V_{IN} - (2 \cdot b_{MSB} - 1) C_{MSB} \cdot V_{REF}$. The resulting charge variation translates into a voltage shift, which the comparator uses to determine the next bit, as expressed in (2). The remaining least significant bits (LSBs) are determined in the same manner, with DAC capacitors connected sequentially until the accumulated charge approaches zero. The comparator derives each bit based on the sign of the differential charge at its inputs, effectively converting charge-domain information into a digital output. In summary, the switches in Fig. 1d and e connect to the blue segment during sampling. During conversion phase and, based on bit order and comparator's decision, switch to the red segment if $b_{N-i} = 0$ or the green segment if $b_{N-i} =$

1 [5, 6, 9, 13].

$$V_{\mathrm{DAC,CS}}(i) = \frac{C_{\mathrm{S\&H}} \cdot \Delta V_{\mathrm{IN}} - \sum_{i=1}^{N}(2b_{N-i} - 1) \cdot 2^{N-i-1} \cdot C \cdot 2V_{\mathrm{REF}}}{C_{\mathrm{S\&H}} + 2 \cdot \sum_{i=1}^{N} 2^{N-i-1} \cdot C} \tag{2}$$

However, this architecture presents some drawbacks. The total DAC capacitance increases due to the connection of the capacitor array to the $C_{\mathrm{S\&H}}$, leading to voltage signal attenuation. While this attenuation is not critical for the comparator – since it only evaluates the sign of the charge – it does reduce the signal-to-noise ratio (SNR) at the comparator inputs. As a result, the comparator must be designed to handle more stringent noise requirements [5, 13].

Another key concern is the comparator offset. In voltage-domain SAR ADCs, offset merely shifts the ADC transfer curve. However, in charge-domain ADCs, comparator offset introduces additional nonlinearities due to the non-linear charge-to-voltage relationship during conversion. If the comparator has an offset of V_{OFFSET}, the initial charge offset is $Q_{\mathrm{OFFSET}} = V_{\mathrm{OFFSET}} \cdot C_{\mathrm{S\&H}}$, at the end of the conversion will have $Q_{\mathrm{OFFSET}} = V_{\mathrm{OFFSET}} \cdot (C_{\mathrm{S\&H}} + C_{\mathrm{DAC,COMP}})$, where $C_{\mathrm{DAC,COMP}}$ is the DAC capacitance from the comparator's inputs perspective [5, 13].

4 Reference Voltage Circuit

Reference circuits play a critical role in analog and data converter systems. They are used for circuit biasing, signal comparison, and arithmetic operations such as addition and subtraction. The most common reference quantities include voltage, current, charge, and time. For example, a bandgap circuit generates a stable voltage reference, while a resistor-based voltage or a capacitor's voltage can serve as a current or charge reference, respectively. A time-period reference can be established using a crystal clock [1, 3].

In data converters, reference signals define the analog signal range. The ratio between the analog input and the reference value corresponds to the ratio between the digital output and the digital code range. In an N-bit converter, both the input signal and reference are divided into 2^N discrete levels, where each division represents one LSB, therefore one A_{LSB}. In this work, voltage (V_{LSB}) will be the primary reference quantity [1].

During operation, the reference voltage may need to drive a large capacitor or multiple small capacitors, as seen in certain DAC architectures, leading to an equivalent large capacitance. Additionally, in high-speed or high-accuracy SC circuits, such as SAR-ADCs, the reference voltage must settle within a precise time frame. Any voltage or timing errors in reference settling can degrade overall system performance, [1, 3, 4, 7, 14, 15].

To ensure adequate driving capability and minimize inaccuracies, a buffer is typically placed after the reference voltage generator. The voltage settling accuracy should be at least within 1 V_{LSB} [14]. In this work, a stricter accuracy of $V_{\mathrm{LSB}}/2$ will be considered, as in, although some studies propose an even tighter requirement of $V_{\mathrm{LSB}}/4$ [4].

Several reference buffer schemes have been reported in the literature, as shown in Fig. 3. One approach is an on-chip buffer without a decoupling capacitor (C_{DEC}), as illustrated in Fig. 3a and Fig. 3b. This design requires a high-speed buffer with a wide bandwidth, which results in significant power consumption. Additionally, as frequency increases, the output impedance also rises, leading to demanding noise requirements [3, 14].

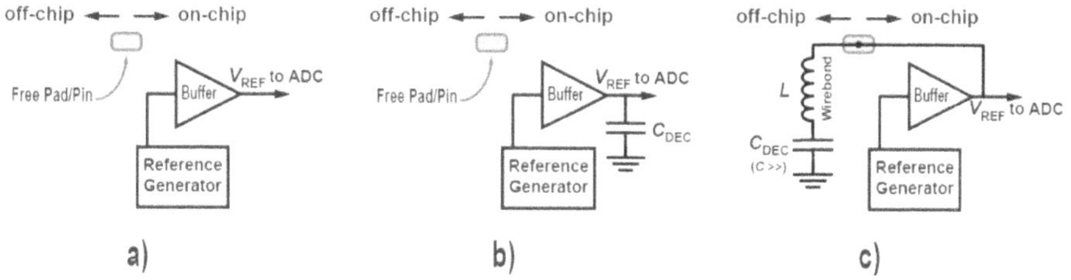

Fig. 3. Different RVCs: a) buffer without C_{DEC}; b) buffer with internal C_{DEC}; c) buffer with external C_{DEC}.

Another common design is an on-chip buffer with an internal decoupling capacitor, as shown in Fig. 3a and Fig. 3b. This scheme integrates a large on-chip capacitor, forming an RC filter. The added capacitance helps relax the buffer's bandwidth requirements, reducing the demand for a high-speed design. However, it still necessitates a relatively wideband reference buffer, which remains a considerable contributor to overall power consumption [3, 4, 14].

A third alternative is a buffer with an external decoupling capacitor, represented in Fig. 3c. This configuration allows for a larger discrete capacitor, which requires an additional pin and wirebond connection. The external capacitor significantly relaxes the buffer's bandwidth requirements, resulting in lower power consumption. Additionally, it forms an RC filter, improving both stability and noise performance.

The noise performance and output impedance of this configuration depend on the quality of the capacitor, particularly its equivalent series resistance (ESR) and equivalent series inductance (ESL). The primary issue with this design is the ringing of the reference voltage, which is caused by the inductance of the wirebond. This ringing leads to oscillations at the natural frequency of the LC tank. To mitigate these oscillations, a damping resistor – either on-chip or off-chip – can be used [3, 14, 15]. However, due to the ringing issue and the additional pin required for implementation, this configuration will not be considered in the following sections. Nonetheless, the analysis is very similar with the on-chip decoupling capacitor.

The overall performance of the reference voltage buffer across different configurations is summarized in Table 1. This includes without a decoupling capacitor, with an on-chip decoupling capacitor, and with an off-chip decoupling capacitor [3].

5 Buffer Design Requirements

The settling timing and accuracy requirements for the reference buffer design depend on the SAR-ADC scheme, DAC architecture, and buffer structure, as shown in Fig. 4. These requirements will be derived by analyzing four configurations: Bin-W CR-based [1], C-2C CR-based [11], Bin-W CS-based [9], and C-2C CS-based SAR-ADC [12].

Table 1. Comparison between the different RVC schemes (▲–Strong; ■ –Moderate; ▼–Weak.)

	Accuracy	Power	Speed	On-chip Area	Off-chip area
Buffer w/o decoupling capacitor	▲	▼	▲	■	▲
Buffer w/ on-chip decoupling capacitor	▲	■	■	▼	▲
Buffer w/ off-chip decoupling capacitor	■	▲	▼	■	▼

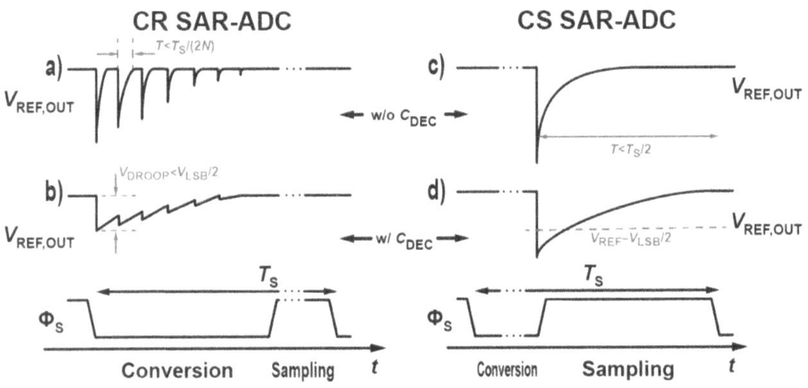

Fig. 4. Settling timing and accuracy diagram of the buffer: a) for CR SAR-ADC without C_{DEC}; b) CR SAR-ADC with C_{DEC}; c) for CS SAR-ADC without C_{DEC}; d) CS SAR-ADC with C_{DEC}.

The CR-based SAR-ADC interacts with the reference buffer in every bit cycle, continuously drawing current throughout the entire conversion phase for both binary-weighted capacitive and C-2C DAC architectures, as represented in Fig. 5a. This results in a switching energy dependency on the digital code, which can introduce nonlinearities due to reference voltage instability. Minimizing these fluctuations is essential to maintaining accuracy. Additionally, high-speed CR-based SAR-ADCs require an on-chip reference that is both stable and capable of operating with high accuracy while driving large capacitive loads. These stringent requirements make reference buffers particularly power-intensive [5, 9, 13].

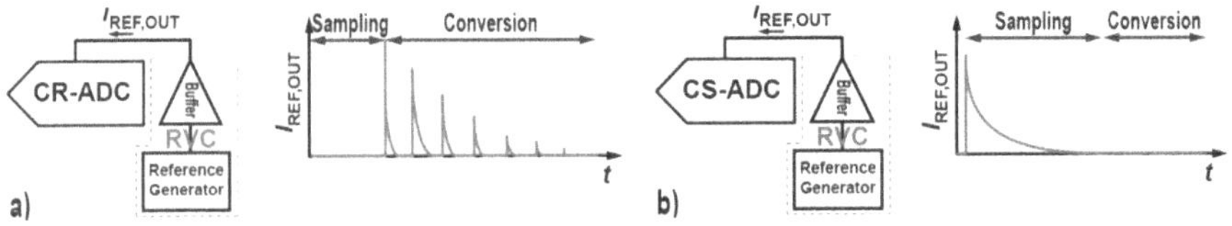

Fig. 5. Current drawn from reference source V_{REF}: a) CR ADC; b) CS ADC; adapted from [5].

Contrarily, in CS-based SAR-ADCs, the capacitor array is pre-charged to V_{REF} during the sampling phase, using either a binary-scaled capacitive or C-2C ladder DAC configuration. During the conversion phase, these capacitors are connected in parallel or anti-parallel, depending on the bit being resolved. Since this configuration operates passively, it does not draw current from the reference buffer during the conversion process, as depicted in Fig. 5b. This eliminates inaccuracies associated with reference voltage fluctuations, allowing the reference buffer to function as a duty-cycled block, significantly improving power efficiency. Additionally, the relatively long sampling phase relaxes the settling time requirements. As a result, the reference buffer can be designed with a higher output impedance, reducing circuit area and further enhancing overall power efficiency [5, 9, 13].

5.1 DAC Capacitance

The maximum input DAC capacitance from the perspective of the RVC for the Bin-W CR-based, C-2C CR-based, Bin-W CS-based, and C-2C CS-based SAR-ADCs is defined by (3), (4), (5), and (6). For the Bin-W CR-based SAR-ADC, the maximum input capacitance occurs when the most significant bit (MSB) capacitor is switched from V_{CM} to V_{REF}. In contrast, for the C-2C CR-based SAR-ADC, the highest capacitance demand occurs at the final bit transition. As previously mentioned, CS-based SAR-ADCs only draw current from the reference buffer during the sampling phase, at which point the entire DAC is connected. Consequently, in CS-based architectures, the capacitance is independent of the bit-by-bit conversion steps.

$$C_{DAC_{\text{Bin-W CR SAR-ADC}}} = 2^{N-2}C \tag{3}$$

$$C_{DAC_{\text{C-2C CR SAR-ADC}}} = \frac{\left(\sum_{i=1}^{N} 2^{2N-1}\right) \cdot C}{2^{2N-1}} \tag{4}$$

$$C_{DAC_{\text{Bin-W CS SAR-ADC}}} = 2^{N-1}C \tag{5}$$

$$C_{DAC_{\text{C-2C CS SAR-ADC}}} = 2C \tag{6}$$

The buffer supplies the total charge when no decoupling capacitor is used. However, when a decoupling capacitor is present, it primarily provides the charge, with the buffer replenishing it. Regardless of the buffer configuration, when the RVC is connected to the DAC, a charge transfer occurs, leading to a voltage droop (V_{DROOP}) at the RVC output due to its finite output impedance.

To maintain accuracy, the buffer must recover this V_{DROOP} before the next conversion step begins [3, 4, 7, 14]. The maximum allowable voltage error is set at $V_{LSB}/2$, or equivalently $V_{REF}/2^{N+1}$, as considered in this work. This ensures that by the end of each conversion step, the voltage at the bottom plate of the capacitor reaches at least $V_{REF}(1 - 1/2^{N+1})$.

5.2 Accuracy Requirements

The buffer can be modeled as an output resistance (R_{OUT}) and an output capacitance (C_{OUT}). If a C_{DEC} is present, it is added in parallel to C_{OUT}, as illustrated in Fig. 6.

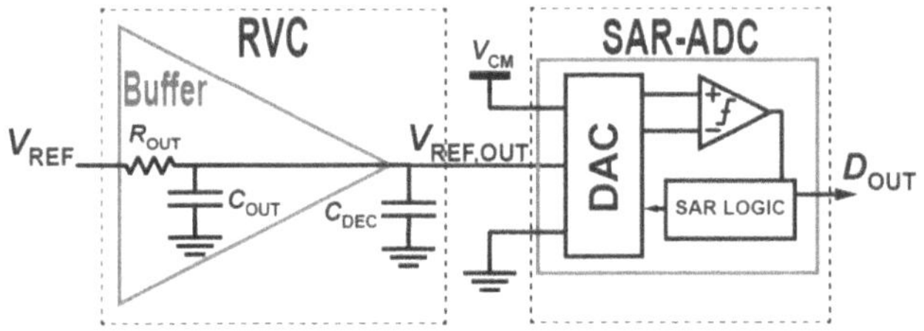

Fig. 6. Buffer modeled as R_{OUT} and C_{OUT}. RVC provides the charges for DAC; adapted from [7].

Consequently, RVC can be approximated as a single-pole closed-loop system, since the on-resistance is negligible. The charging process follows (7), where $V_{REF,OUT}(i,t)$ represents the buffer output voltage at time instant t during step i. At the same time, V_{REF} denotes the voltage from the reference source generator. The time constant τ is given by $R_{OUT}{\cdot}(C_{OUT} + C_{DEC})$, determining the system's settling behavior. The parameter i represents the interaction points between the RVC and the DAC. In a CR-based SAR-ADC, i ranges from 0 to N–1, corresponding to each bit decision. In contrast, for a CS-based SAR-ADC, $i = 1$, as the interaction occurs only once during the sampling phase. In both cases, t resets whenever i changes.

$$V_{REF,OUT}(i,t) = V_{REF,OUT}(i,0) + \left(V_{REF} - V_{REF,OUT}(i,0)\right) \cdot \left(1 - e^{-t(i)/\tau}\right) \quad (7)$$

Charge conservation is applied to determine $V_{REF,OUT}(i,0)$, even though it is not fully valid throughout the conversion step due to the continuous connection of the RVC to C_{DEC}. However, this principle holds at $t = 0$. The initial voltage $V_{REF,OUT}(i,0)$ depends on the SAR-ADC scheme and DAC architecture, with the most critical step being analyzed – corresponding to the largest voltage step the RVC must recover, thus defining the buffer's dynamic limitations.

For a Bin-W CR-based SAR-ADC, the critical step occurs when the MSB capacitor ($C_{MSB} = 2^{N-1}C$) is switched, at step $i = 1$, resulting in $V_{REF,OUT}(1,0)$ as given by (8). Similarly, in a C-2C CR-based SAR-ADC, the first step also corresponds to the largest $V_{REF,OUT}(i,0)$, despite the maximum capacitance being in the last step – as presented in (4). This occurs because the largest capacitance variation happens when the MSB is switched, and $V_{REF,OUT}(1,0)$ follows (9). For cases where the RVC is designed without C_{DEC}, (8) and (9) remain valid, assuming $C_{DEC} = 0$. Notably, in CR-based SAR ADCs, (7) is bit-dependent. To generalize, the term $(-b_{N-i} + 1)$ can be introduced, where b_{N-i} represents the bit decision at that step i. The larger $V_{REF,OUT}(i,0)$ is determined based on the first $b_{N-i} = 0$ response, which could not happen in the MSB (b_{N-1}). Since it is only in these scenarios that RVC must supply charge to compensate for the capacitor switching.

If $b_{N\text{-}i} = 1$, the bottom-plate is connected to GND instead, meaning no charge transfer occurs between the RVC and the DAC, and consequently, there is no interaction affecting $V_{\text{REF,OUT}}(i,0)$. The RVC must be designed to meet these worst-case requirements, which means that the MSB, $b_{N\text{-}1} = b_{MSB} = 0$. For the CS-based SAR-ADC, the entire DAC is connected to the RVC during the sampling phase, meaning that the buffer must supply charge to the full capacitance of the DAC at once, which implies that the only value for i is 1. The equivalent capacitance Bin-W DAC and a C-2C DAC is given by (5) and (6), respectively. Consequently, the corresponding $V_{\text{REF,OUT}}(1,0)$ values, which describe the reference voltage behavior under these conditions, are provided in (10) and (11).

$$V_{\text{REF,OUT-CR Bin-W SAR-ADC}}(1,0) = \frac{2^{N-1}C \cdot (V_{\text{REF}} - V_{\text{CM}})}{2^{N-1}C+(2C_{\text{DEC}} + C_{\text{OUT}})} \tag{8}$$

$$V_{\text{REF,OUT-CR C-2C SAR-ADC}}(1,0) = \frac{C \cdot (V_{\text{REF}} - V_{\text{CM}})}{C+(2C_{\text{DEC}} + C_{\text{OUT}})} \tag{9}$$

$$V_{\text{REF,OUT-CS Bin-W SAR-ADC}}(1,0) = \frac{C_{\text{DEC}} \cdot V_{\text{REF}} + 2^{N-1}C \cdot V_{\text{CM}}}{2^{N-1}C + C_{\text{DEC}}} \tag{10}$$

$$V_{\text{REF,OUT-CS C-2C SAR-ADC}}(1,0) = \frac{C_{\text{DEC}} \cdot V_{\text{REF}} + 2C \cdot V_{\text{CM}}}{2C + C_{\text{DEC}}} \tag{11}$$

The current drawn from the RVC, denoted as $I_{\text{REF}}(i,t)$, is determined based on the interaction between the DAC and the reference buffer provided in (12). By evaluating the root-mean-square (RMS)[1] of (12) for all i values, an estimation of the power dissipation of the RVC can be obtained. The power dissipation estimation is given by (13), where the summation upper bond n is N–1 or 1 for CR- or CS-based SAR-ADC, respectively. Similarly, the energy consumed is possible to calculate considering (14). These two metrics provide insight into the power- and energy-efficiency of the system.

$$I_{\text{REF}}(i,t) = \frac{V_{\text{REF,OUT}}(i,0)}{R_{\text{OUT}}} \, e^{-t(i)/\tau} \tag{12}$$

$$P_{\text{REF}} = V_{\text{REF}} \cdot \sqrt{\sum_{i=1}^{n} \text{RMS}(I_{\text{REF}}(i))^2} \tag{13}$$

$$E_{\text{REF}}(i) = \int_0^t I_{\text{REF}}(i,t) \cdot V_{\text{REF}}(i,t) \tag{14}$$

5.3 Timing Requirements

The sampling frequency (f_S) determines the total available time for conversion, given by $T_S = 1/f_S$. Since the SAR-ADC operates in two phases – sampling and conversion – the maximum available time for conversion is $T_S/2$. For CR-based SAR-ADCs, the time

[1] The RMS is obtained by calculating $\text{RMS(IREF(i))} = \sqrt{\frac{1}{T}\int_{t=0}^{T} I_{\text{REF}}^2(i,t)dt}$ [1].

allocated per bit decision is the sum of T_{COMP}, T_{LOGIC}, T_{DAC}. As a result, the time per bit decision must be lower than the threshold defined by (15). Given that T_{DAC} significantly impacts the converter's performance, it is often assumed to be approximately equal to the sum of T_{COMP} and T_{LOGIC}, as expressed by (16). By combining (15) and (16), the required T_{DAC} for CR-based SAR-ADCs is derived in (17). In SC circuits, the voltage at the exact moment a capacitor switches off is the relevant one. Consequently, RVC must settle within a time frame shorter than that specified in (17) to ensure accurate charge transfer and minimize conversion errors.

$$T_{\mathrm{COMP,\,CR\,SAR\text{-}ADC}} + T_{\mathrm{LOGIC}} + T_{\mathrm{DAC}} < \frac{T_{\mathrm{S}}}{2 \cdot N} \tag{15}$$

$$T_{\mathrm{DAC,CR\,SAR\text{-}ADC}} = T_{\mathrm{LOGIC}} + T_{\mathrm{COMP}} \tag{16}$$

$$T_{\mathrm{DAC,\,CR\,SAR\text{-}ADC}} < \frac{T_{\mathrm{S}}}{4 \cdot N} \tag{17}$$

During the conversion phase of a CS-based SAR-ADC, only T_{COMP} and T_{LOGIC} play a role, but these aspects are beyond the scope of this work. Focusing on T_{DAC} for CS-based converters, its maximum allowable time is dictated solely by f_{S}. Since DAC pre-charging occurs during the sampling phase rather than the conversion phase, the settling time requirement is relaxed compared to CR-based SAR-ADCs. The maximum T_{DAC} for CS-based converters is therefore defined by (18).

$$T_{\mathrm{DAC,\,CS\,SAR\text{-}ADC}} < \frac{T_{\mathrm{S}}}{2} \tag{18}$$

The worst-case T_{DAC} scenario occurs when $V_{\mathrm{RFEF,OUT}}(1{,}0)$ is at V_{CM}, and the output must settle to at least $V_{\mathrm{REF}}(1{-}1/2^{N+1})$ within the settling time. This requirement is expressed in (19). A single-pole closed-loop configuration is considered, given the negligible on-resistance of the switch. Therefore, the time constant, τ, is given by (20), where $\omega_{-3\mathrm{dB}}$ is the –3dB frequency, β is the feedback factor, and ω_{ug} is the unity-gain frequency. In the case of a buffer configuration, β equals 1, so τ simplifies to $1/\omega_{\mathrm{ug}}$ (or $1/\omega_{-3\mathrm{dB}}$). By combining (19) and (20), we can determine the buffer's dominant pole, which is represented by (21).

$$V_{\mathrm{REF,OUT}}(T_{\mathrm{DAC}}) > V_{\mathrm{REF}}/2^{N+1} \Leftrightarrow T_{\mathrm{DAC}} < -\ln(1/2^{N}) \cdot \tau \tag{19}$$

$$\tau = R_{\mathrm{OUT}} \cdot C_{\mathrm{OUT}} = 1/\omega_{-3\mathrm{dB}} = 1/(\beta \cdot \omega_{\mathrm{ug}}) \tag{20}$$

$$f_{-3\mathrm{dB}} = f_{\mathrm{ug}} > \frac{-\ln(1/2^{N})}{2\pi \cdot T_{\mathrm{DAC}}} \tag{21}$$

The relationship between the sampling frequency and the required buffer's dominant pole (f_{P}) can be derived for both CR- and CS-based SAR ADCs. For the CR-based SAR ADC, this is achieved by combining (17) with (21), while for the CS-based SAR ADC, it is obtained by combining (18) with (21). The resulting expressions are (22) and

(23), respectively. In this way, the necessary dominant pole for the buffer in both CR- and CS-based SAR ADCs can be determined based on the sampling frequency and the specific characteristics of the converter's architecture.

$$f_{\mathrm{P,\,CR\;SAR\text{-}ADC}} > \frac{-\ln\left(1/2^{N}\right)}{\pi} \cdot 2N \cdot f_{\mathrm{S,\,CR\;SAR\text{-}ADC}} \tag{22}$$

$$f_{\mathrm{P,\,CS\;SAR\text{-}ADC}} > \frac{-\ln(1/2^{N})}{\pi} \cdot f_{\mathrm{S,\,CS\;SAR\text{-}ADC}} \tag{23}$$

For instance, for a 10-bit resolution ($N = 10$) and a sampling rate of 100 MS/s, the required dominant pole frequency for the CR-based SAR ADC ($f_{\mathrm{P,CR\;SAR\text{-}ADC}}$) is calculated to be 4.41 GHz, while for the CS-based SAR ADC ($f_{\mathrm{P,\,CS\;SAR\text{-}ADC}}$), it is 221 MHz. This significant difference in the required pole frequency illustrates that the buffer design for the CS-based SAR ADC is much less demanding. As a result, the buffer design can be simplified, allowing for a lower current requirement and a more power-efficient RVC. This reduction in the required pole frequency for the CS-based SAR ADC contributes to improved overall power efficiency, making it a more attractive option for high-performance, low-power applications.

6 Conclusion

This work derives analytical expressions for reference buffer behavior in SAR ADCs, focusing on voltage accuracy and settling time for binary-weighted and C-2C CR- and CS-based architectures. The analysis highlights the challenging requirements imposed on the reference buffer in CR-based SAR ADCs due to continuous DAC, demanding high-speed and power-intensive designs. Contrarily, CS-based SAR ADCs exhibit a more relaxed reference buffer design, as the DAC settles during the sampling phase, enabling lower power consumption and reduced bandwidth requirements. The derived expressions provide insights into buffer design trade-offs, including output impedance, capacitance, and dominant pole frequency. A comparison between CR- and CS-based SAR ADCs indicates that CS architectures generally offer improved power efficiency and place less stringent requirements on buffer design. However, other critical blocks—such as the comparator—may benefit from the more relaxed constraints typically associated with CR-based topologies.

Acknowledgments. This work was supported by the Portuguese National Foundation for Science and Technology (FCT) through the grant 2023.00298.BD, and funded through CTS/00066, LISBOA2030-FEDER-00917900 project no. 14680, LA/P/0037/2020, UIDP/50025/2020 and UIDB/50025/2020.

References

1. Pelgrom, M.J.M.: Analog-to-Digital Conversion. Springer International Publishing, Cham (2022). https://doi.org/10.1007/978-3-030-90808-9

2. Song, J., Lyu, D., Zhang, Z., Wang, Z., Zhang, T., Ma, L.: When cyber-physical systems meet AI. In: Proceedings of the 44th International Conference on Software Engineering: Software Engineering in Practice. pp. 343–352. ACM, New York, NY, USA (2022). https://doi.org/10.1145/3510457.3513049
3. Figueiredo, M., Goes, J., Evans, G.: Reference-Free CMOS Pipeline Analog-to-Digital Converters. Springer New York, New York, NY (2013). https://doi.org/10.1007/978-1-4614-3467-2
4. Li, W., Li, F., Wang, Z.: Reference voltage buffer. In: High-Resolution and High-Speed Integrated CMOS AD Converters for Low-Power Applications, pp. 47–74. Springer International Publishing, Cham (2018). https://doi.org/10.1007/978-3-319-62012-1_3
5. Rabuske, T., Fernandes, J.: Charge-Sharing SAR ADCs for Low-Voltage Low-Power Applications. Springer International Publishing, Cham (2017)
6. Rabuske, T., Fernandes, J.: A SAR ADC With a MOSCAP-DAC. IEEE J. Solid-State Circuits **51**, 1410–1422 (2016). https://doi.org/10.1109/JSSC.2016.2548486
7. Li, C., Chan, C.-H., Zhu, Y., Martins, R.P.: Analysis of reference error in high-speed SAR ADCs with capacitive DAC. IEEE Trans. Circuits Syst. I Regul. Pap. **66**, 82–93 (2019). https://doi.org/10.1109/TCSI.2018.2861835
8. Rodriguez-Perez, A., Rodriguez-Rodriguez, J.A., Medeiro, F., Delgado-Restituto, M.: Impact of parasitic capacitances on the performance of SAR ADCs based on capacitive arrays. In: 2010 First IEEE Latin American Symposium on Circuits and Systems (LASCAS). pp. 124–127. IEEE (2010). https://doi.org/10.1109/LASCAS.2010.7410236
9. Craninckx, J., van der Plas, G.: A 65fJ/conversion-step 0-to-50MS/s 0-to-0.7mW 9b charge-sharing SAR ADC in 90 nm digital CMOS. In: 2007 IEEE International Solid-State Circuits Conference. Digest of Technical Papers. pp. 246–600. IEEE (2007). https://doi.org/10.1109/ISSCC.2007.373386
10. Cong, L.: Pseudo C-2C ladder-based data converter technique. IEEE Trans. Circuits Syst. II Analog Digital Signal Proc. **48**, 927–929 (2001). https://doi.org/10.1109/82.974780
11. Razavi, B.: The R-2R and C-2C ladders. IEEE Solid-State Circuits Mag. **11**, 10–15 (2019). https://doi.org/10.1109/MSSC.2019.2922886
12. Viana, H., Xavier, J., Barquinha, P., Goes, J.: An energy-efficient C-2αC charge-sharing SAR ADC. (2024). https://doi.org/10.22541/au.173329231.17835955/v1
13. Malki, B., Yamamoto, T., Verbruggen, B., Wambacq, P., Craninckx, J.: A 70 dB DR 10 b 0-to-80 MS/s current-integrating SAR ADC with adaptive dynamic range. IEEE J. Solid-State Circuits **49**, 1173–1183 (2014). https://doi.org/10.1109/JSSC.2014.2309086
14. Liu, M., van Roermund, A., Harpe, P.: A 10b 20MS/s SAR ADC with a low-power and area-efficient DAC-compensated reference. In: ESSCIRC 2017 - 43rd IEEE European Solid State Circuits Conference. pp. 231–234. IEEE (2017). https://doi.org/10.11s09/ESSCIRC.2017.8094568
15. Harikumar, P., Wikner, J.J.: Design of a reference voltage buffer for a 10-bit 50 MS/s SAR ADC in 65 nm CMOS. In: 2015 IEEE International Symposium on Circuits and Systems (ISCAS). pp. 249–252. IEEE (2015). https://doi.org/10.1109/ISCAS.2015.7168617

A Physically Unclonable Function Systematic Performance Analysis Methodology

João Cabacinho[1,2](✉), João Casaleiro[2,3], and Luis B. Oliveira[1,2]

[1] Department of Electrical and Computer Engineering, NOVA School of Science and Technology, Caparica, Portugal
j.cabacinho@campus.fct.unl.pt

[2] Centre of Technology and Systems (CTS) – UNINOVA and LASI, Lisbon, Portugal

[3] Department Electrical, Telecommunications and Computers Engineering, Instituto Superior de Engenharia de Lisboa (ISEL), Lisbon, Portugal

Abstract. Physically Unclonable Functions (PUFs) are a promising hardware security primitive for AI-powered Cyber-Physical Systems (AI-CPS), offering low-cost, low-area, tamper-resistant, and unique key generation. However, the lack of a standardized methodology and lack of consensus in PUF performance metric definition does not allow for fair comparisons across designs which can impact their confidence in use for security. This paper presents a systematic analysis methodology for evaluating PUFs at the circuit simulation level. The methodology establishes transient Monte Carlo simulation strategies, structured data extraction and processing, and metric computation. It addresses the nuanced simulation requirements for each performance metric—uniqueness, repeatability, identifiability, reliability, and randomness—ensuring that each is accurately and fairly assessed. A practical explanation using an Arbiter PUF in Cadence® is provided, along with data handling and metric calculation examples in Python. The proposed methodology facilitates reproducibility and comparability across PUF designs.

Keywords: Physically Unclonable Functions (PUF) · Hardware Security · AI · Cyber Physical Systems (CPS)

1 Introduction

Physically Unclonable Functions (PUFs) are emerging as a promising hardware-based security solution. However, the academic community currently lacks consensus regarding the definition and evaluation of the definition and evaluation of commonly used PUF performance metrics. Many of these metrics, mathematical definitions and interpretations vary significantly. This work aims to establish a systematic methodology for PUF evaluation.

Cyber-Physical Systems (CPS) integrate hardware and software components, and the incorporation of Artificial Intelligence (AI) transforms these systems into intelligent, autonomous platforms. AI powered CPS (AI-CPS) can achieve real-time decision-making and autonomous behavior, allowing systems not only to reason and plan but also to interact with and manipulate the physical world.

Published by Springer Nature Switzerland AG 2025
L. M. Camarinha-Matos and F. Ferrada (Eds.): DoCEIS 2025, IFIP AICT 759, pp. 395–409, 2025.
https://doi.org/10.1007/978-3-031-97051-1_28

However, the interconnected nature of these systems introduces major security concerns. AI-CPS components must exchange data, coordinate actions and even learn from each other, often in distributed networks. Without strong security, cyberattacks can propagate through the system, jeopardizing safety, data integrity and functionality. These challenges are specially critical in resource constrained environments such as battery-operated machines, where power, area, and costs are limited [1].

PUFs are well suited for such applications. They can be implemented in deep-nanoscale CMOS technology, offering low-power and low-area overhead. By leveraging intrinsic manufacturing variations, PUFs generate a unique and unclonable hardware fingerprint tied to each device. This attribute gives it an advantage over other software-based security primitives because, even with physical access, it is impossible to replicate the intrinsic characteristics of the device even by the manufacturer, using the same photolithography masks. Additionally, the keys are only generated and accessed when the PUF is powered on, adding another layer of security [2].

2 AI-Powered Cyber-Physical Systems

As AI-CPS grow increasingly interconnected and autonomous, ensuring secure authentication and protection against adversarial threats is crucial.

PUFs offer hardware-level cryptographic primitive that is particularly well suited for AI-CPS, enabling secure key generation for secure authentication, data encryption, and integrity verification.

Establishing a robust methodology for simulating and evaluating PUFs is therefore a foundational step toward integrating them into AI-CPS security architectures. The work presented in this paper contributes to that goal by systematically addressing how PUF performance metrics can be analyzed to ensure they meet the stringent reliability and security demands of AI-CPS.

3 Physically Unclonable Functions

PUFs were first introduced by Lofstrom et al. [3] as a hardware-based security primitive for integrated circuit (IC) identification. PUFs exploit the inherent variations introduced during the semiconductor manufacturing process (known as mismatches) to produce a reproducible (Fig. 1a) and unique (Fig. 1b) response that serves as a hardware fingerprint.

This characteristic offers a significant advantage over software-based security primitives, as replicating the intrinsic physical properties of the device is infeasible even with physical access and using the same photolithography masks. Additionally, PUFs generate keys only when powered on, enhancing security by avoiding storage of secret keys [2]. Furthermore, since PUFs can be implemented in deep-nanoscale CMOS technology, they provide a low-power, and low-area solution for secure device authentication and key generation.

PUFs have been defined by Chang et al. [2] as a physical system that probabilistically maps an input stimulus known as challenge c, to a corresponding response r, called challenge-response pair (CRP). Due to its intrinsic stochastic properties, each PUF device

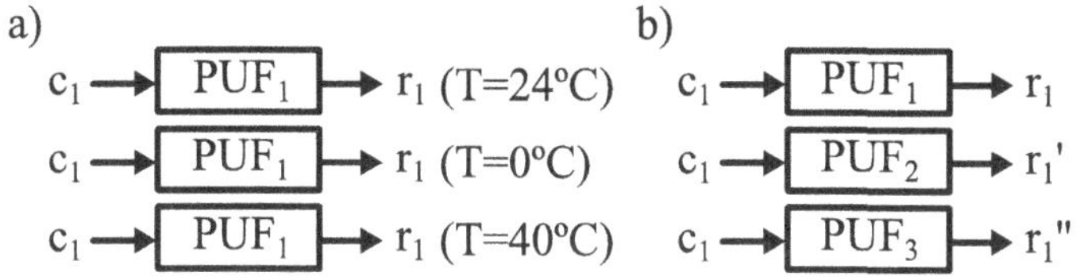

Fig. 1. PUF work principal a) Reproducible responses b) Unique responses.

d is unique, meaning that a given challenge *c* will produce a device-specific response *r*, as described mathematically in Eq. (1).

$$r \leftarrow PUF_d(c) \tag{1}$$

Equation (1) models the fundamental challenge-response behavior of a PUF. Its mathematical definition can be further extended to reflect the behavior between PUF devices. Given the uniqueness property, a specific PUF device *d*, when presented with a challenge *c*, is expected to produce the same response regardless of the access instance *a* or the operating condition *e*. This behavior is formally represented in Eq. (2), *a'* and *e'* are a different access and operating condition respectively.

$$PUF_{a,d,e}(c) = PUF_{a',d,e'}(c) \forall a, a', d, e, e', c. \tag{2}$$

4 PUF Analysis Metrics

Since the early development of PUFs, several metrics have been proposed and widely adopted to evaluate their security and performance. Among the most relevant are Uniqueness, Repeatability, Identifiability, Stability, and Randomness. Given the diversity of PUF designs, standardized definitions of these metrics are crucial for fair evaluation and comparison. However, in practice, inconsistencies in the mathematical definitions and computation methods of these metrics often hinder accurate benchmarking reproducibility.

4.1 Uniqueness (Inter-HD)

Uniqueness quantifies how distinguishable the responses of different PUF instances are when subjected to the same challenge. Ideally, these responses should be statistically independent and uniformly distributed. Given that PUFs responses are binary, this implies an expected hamming distance (HD) of n/2 between any two n-bit responses. HD close to this ideal value indicates higher tolerance to bit errors without leading to misidentification [4].

Uniqueness is typically computed through the mean Inter-Hamming Distance (Inter-HD), calculated across response pairs from distinct PUF instances. However, the literature presents several variations in how this pairing is formed. For instance, some studies only compare golden responses (nominal operating conditions) [5, 6], while others include responses under multiple operating conditions [7]. Additionally, some only compare responses generated by the same challenge [6], whereas others aggregate all responses data disregarding if responses are generated by the same challenge [5]. These methodological inconsistencies pose challenges for the definition and practical use of Inter-HD as standardized metric.

4.2 Repeatability (Intra-HD)

Repeatability assesses the consistency of a single PUF instance in producing the same response when exposed to varying environmental conditions, such as temperature, voltage, and noise. Ideally, given a fixed challenge, a PUF device should consistently generate an identical response regardless of external factors.

This metric is typically quantified by the mean Intra-Hamming Distance (Intra-HD), computed between a reference 'golden' response and the responses obtained under varying conditions. An ideal Intra-HD of 0 implies perfect reproducibility, meaning all bits in the response remain unchanged.

However, there is no universal definition of the golden response. It is often chosen as the first response under nominal conditions [5, 6], though other definitions exist. Additionally, inconsistencies also arise in how Intra-HD is calculated, some studies restrict evaluation to only nominal results, while others incorporate responses from a range of environmental variations [7].

4.3 Identifiability (Inter-HD/Intra-HD)

Identifiability is defined as ratio between Uniqueness and the Repeatability [8]. Uniqueness captures how distinguishable responses are across devices, while Repeatability measures internal consistency of a single PUF device across multiple measurements and varying operating conditions. Identifiability, therefore, reflects how responses are both distinct across devices and robust within each device.

4.4 Reliability (BER)

Reliability reflects a PUF's ability to consistently produce the same responses under varying environmental conditions. It is commonly computed by the Bit Error Rate (BER), which quantifies the proportion of response bits incorrectly generated under varying environmental conditions.

BER is derived from the Intra-HD distribution and can be computed using the mean or maximum values at each environmental condition. It is often visualized through line plots [6, 7] or heatmaps [5], which illustrate the extent to which a response consistency is maintained or degraded. These visual tools provide insight into the PUF's robustness for a specific environmental scenario.

4.5 Randomness

Randomness assesses the unpredictability of bits generated by a PUF. Although PUFs are deterministic by design, their responses are expected to exhibit statistical randomness.

To evaluate randomness, the National Institute of Standards and Technology (NIST) Pub SP800–22 test suites are commonly used [9]. This standardized suite consists of 15 statistical tests, each designed to assess different statistical properties associated with randomness in binary sequences. The NIST Test Suite's standardization and widespread recognition offer a robust evaluation framework, contrasting with other metrics that may lack standardization and transparency.

A PUF is said to exhibit strong randomness if the generated bitstream passes all applicable NIST tests. Importantly, sufficient sequence length is required for meaningful results.

5 PUF Analysis Methodology

The proposed methodology for evaluation of PUFs is structured in four main steps: (1) PUF design, (2) circuit-level simulation, (3) data processing, and (4) evaluation. These steps illustrated in Fig. 2.

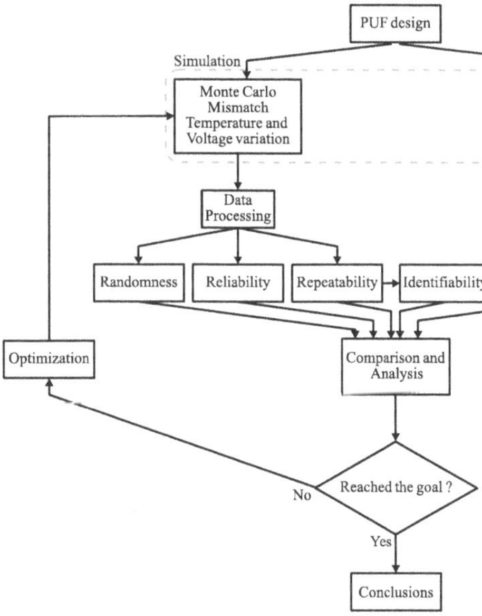

Fig. 2. PUF analysis methodology diagram.

The methodology starts with selecting the PUF design, first it is essential to clearly define the performance and security goals. These goals guide the selection of the appropriate architecture aligned with the target application. Next the PUF is implemented at the circuit level.

The second step involves simulation. Since PUFs rely on intrinsic transistor mismatches to generate unique responses, Monte Carlo (MC) simulations are required to accurately model these variations. Transient MC simulations enable the extraction of responses across several mismatch configurations for each different challenge. From these results, the CRPs are captured and used for metric evaluation.

The third step is data processing, where the extracted simulation outputs such as responses, challenges, and operating conditions are prepared for analysis. Each performance metric may require specific simulation conditions. For instance, reliability must be assessed under temperature and voltage variations, while uniqueness is evaluated under nominal conditions.

The final step is the analysis and comparison of the PUF. By computing the performance metrics and comparing them into existing works in literature, one can assess whether the design objectives were met. If not, the insight gained can guide further iterations of the design.

5.1 PUF Design

In this work, an Arbiter PUF is used as a case study to demonstrate the simulation and evaluation methodology. The Arbiter PUF is one of the most widely recognized PUF architectures, originally proposed by Lee et al. [10], a typical design is illustrated in Fig. 3a). It operates by simultaneously exciting two delay paths with a rising edge, creating a race between them. An arbiter at the output determines which edge arrives first, outputting either a logical 0 or 1 as the final response as shown in Fig. 3b).

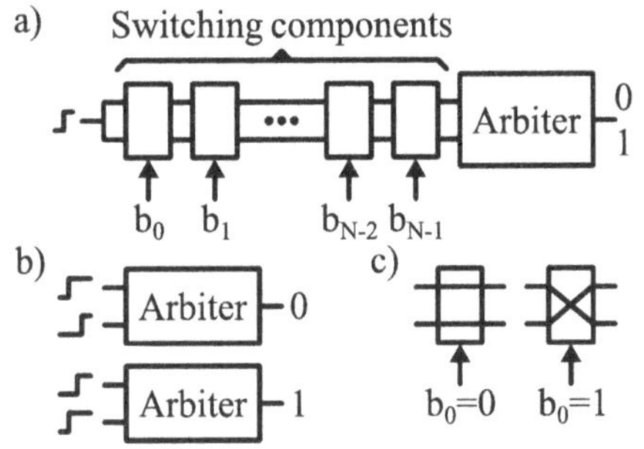

Fig. 3. Arbiter PUF a) Design b) Arbiter block operation c) Switching component operation.

The N delay paths are controlled by an N-bit challenge, with each bit (b_i) configuring a switching element. These switching elements determine whether the two paths are straight-through ($b_i = 0$) or crossed ($b_i = 1$) as illustrated in Fig. 3b. Due to inevitable manufacturing mismatches in the delay elements. The relative timing of the paths will vary across PUF instances, producing a unique repeatable response.

For simulation purposes, challenges are applied using an N-bit random number generator (RNG) initialized by a seed. This allows for the reproduction of the same set of challenges across multiple simulations. To operate this PUF, an initial impulse signal applied to the input, triggering a race through the delay paths. The output of this race is then captured by an arbiter block to produce a single-bit response based on the relative delays.

To simulate this behavior at circuit level, the design is implemented in schematic form and integrated into a testbench, as shown in Fig. 4.

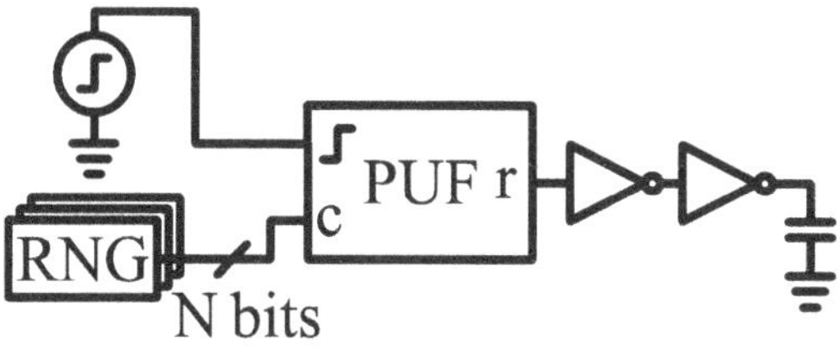

Fig. 4. PUF test bench.

The testbench includes a load capacitor at the output to emulate the input capacitance of the subsequent circuitry that the PUF would typically drive. Additionally, an output buffer is used to isolate the PUF from the effects of capacitive loading and to ensure clean signal transitions.

5.2 Simulation

In this work, all simulations results were obtained through transient analysis with the Cadence® ADE Assembler tool. Since PUF behavior depends on intrinsic transistor-level mismatches introduced during fabrication, replicating these variations is essential for accurate simulations. Without them, the PUF would not exhibit its expected behavior. To model these random mismatches, MC simulations are used.

Depending on the performance metric being evaluated, different MC simulations strategies are adopted. Two main simulations strategies are considered: (1) Monte Carlo simulation with mismatch-only variation, and (2) Monte Carlo simulation with both mismatch and process variation. Each approach is chosen to align with the nature of the target metric.

During simulation, key data must be captured for each MC iteration: the output response r, the applied challenge c and respective RNG seed, and, when applicable, noise seed a, temperature, and supply voltage e.

All data was exported from Cadence® into separate CSV files. This involves selecting the desired data, plotting all data points, and exporting the resulting table to CSV format.

a)

MC Iteration	Response				
	R1	R2	R3	...	RN
1	0	0	0		0
2	0	0	0		0
3	1	1	0	...	0
4	1	1	0		0
5	1	1	0		0

R1= Response; Noise seed 1; RNG seed 100; Vdd 0.9; Temperature 27;
R2= Response; Noise seed 1; RNG seed 100; Vdd 0.9; Temperature 40;
R3= Response; Noise seed 1; RNG seed 100; Vdd 1; Temperature 27;
RN= Response; Noise seed 2; RNG seed 105; Vdd 1; temperature 40;

b)

c bit	Challenge				
	C1	C2	C3	...	CN
/bi<0>	0.0	0.0	0.0		0.0
/bi<1>	0.0	0.0	0.0		0.9
/bi<2>	0.0	0.0	0.0		0.9
/bi<3>	0.0	0.0	0.0	...	0.9
/bi<...>		⋮			
/bi<N-2>	0.9	0.9	0.9		0.9
/bi<N-1>	0.9	0.9	0.9		0.0

C1= Challenge; MC Iteration 1; Noise_seed 1; RNG_seed 100; Vdd 0.9; Temperature 27;
C2= Challenge; MC Iteration 1; Noise seed 1; RNG seed 100; Vdd 0.9 Temperature 40;
C3= Challenge; MC Iteration 1; Noise seed 1; RNG seed 100; Vdd 1; Temperature 27;
CN= Challenge; MC Iteration 5; Noise seed 2; RNG seed 105; Vdd 1; Temperature 40;

Fig. 5. Extracted data from simulation examples a) Responses b) Challenges.

All extracted data, except for challenges, is indexed by MC iteration number Fig. 5a. Challenge data is organized differently: by changing the plot's x-axis from Mc iteration to challenge bit position (b_i), each column corresponds to a bit, allowing for easier reconstruction of binary challenge strings and alignment with other datasets Fig. 5b.

Transient Analysis with Monte Carlos Mismatch-Only Simulation
This type of simulation introduces only local mismatch between transistors, keeping global process parameters constant. It is ideal when analyzing the behavior of a single PUF instance under various conditions allowing for aggregation of bits across MC runs to form a multi-bit response.

This simulation strategy is suited to:

- **Repeatability (Intra-HD):** simulating the same PUF instance under multiple challenges, operating conditions (e.g., temperature, voltage and noise).
- **Reliability:** evaluations bit stability across varying operating conditions.
- **Randomness:** assessing entropy from responses collected under nominal conditions.

To support these metrics, the simulation must sweep across different RNG seeds (to test several challenges, c) and vary operation conditions (e), such as temperature, supply voltage and noise seed. For each MC iteration, the following data: MC iteration number, the noise seed, RNG seed, challenge, supply voltage, the temperature and the responses.

Transient Analysis Monte Carlo Mismatch and Process Simulation
In this simulation, both local transistor mismatch and global process variation are introduced. Each MC iteration emulates a different PUF instance fabricated under slightly different conditions, capturing both die-to-die and withing-die variability.

This simulation strategy is required for metrics that depend on comparing responses from multiple PUF devices, such as:

- **Uniqueness (Inter-HD):** comparing responses from different PUF instances to the same challenge, under nominal conditions.

For this metric, simulations should sweep across multiple RNG seeds at nominal operating conditions. The following data must be recorded: MC iteration number, the RNG seed, the challenges and the responses.

5.3 Data Processing

In this work, all data processing was performed using the Python programming environment, which provides powerful libraries such as pandas for efficient data handling.

After each simulation, the extracted data must be organized into structured, column-based formats. This step is essential not only for improving readability but also for ensuring consistency and enabling easy reuse or further analysis.

The attributes included in the data depend on the type of simulation. For transient analysis mismatch-only MC simulation, the data includes: Noise seed, RNG seed, Challenge, Response, Temperature and Supply Voltage. For transient analysis mismatch and process MC simulation, data include: RNG seed, Challenge, Response. Each data type is exported separately from Cadence® in individual CSV files.

To prepare the data for analysis, these separate CSV files are merged into a single unified dataset. First, each CSV file is loaded using `pandas.read_csv("path")`, which creates a DataFrame, a flexible tabular structure in Python. Then, Code 1 below demonstrates how to use `pandas.melt()` function to reshape wide-format tables (where each column represents a different simulation parameter) into a long format. This transformation groups all response values into a single column while retaining the associated MC iteration as illustrated in Fig. 6. After reshaping, the "Variable" column, automatically created during the `pandas.melt()` operation is removed using `drop()`.

Code 1 example of *pandas.melt()* to create the response DataFrame

```
#reshape columns
response_df = pandas.melt("csv path", id_vars=["MC
iteration"], value_name="Response")
#drop undesirable column
response_df= response_df.drop(columns=["Variable"])
```

MC Iteration	R1	R2	R3	R4
1	0	1	1	0
2	0	0	1	1
3	1	1	0	0

R1= Response; Noise seed 1; RNG seed 100; Vdd 0.9; Temperature 27;
R2= Response; Noise seed 1; RNG seed 100; Vdd 0.9; Temperature 40;
R3= Response; Noise seed 1; RNG seed 100; Vdd 1; Temperature 27;
R4= Response; Noise seed 1; RNG seed 100; Vdd 1; Temperature 40;

MC Iteration	Variable	Response
1	Response	0
2	Response	0
3	Response	1
1	Response	1
2	Response	0
3	Response	1
1	Response	1
2	Response	1
3	Response	0
1	Response	0
2	Response	1
3	Response	0

Fig. 6. Example of *pandas.melt()* reshape.

To process challenge, which are initially stored as analog voltages (each row representing bit position), thresholding is applied. Voltages are converted into binary, voltages $\geq (V_{DD}/2)$ become 1, and values $< (V_{DD}/2)$ are converted to 0. These individual bits are then concatenated to reconstruct the full binary challenge string.

Code 2 demonstrate how this process is implemented in Python by iterating through each column of challenge bits, converting the analog values to binary, and using `join()` to create the bitstrings. These are then collected using `extend()`, aligned with the indexing of the response DataFrame, as illustrated in Fig. 7.

Once all data types are structured and aligned, they are concatenated into a single DataFrame. The resulting dataset, illustrated in Fig. 8, is then exported into a new CSV file for subsequent metric evaluation.

Code 2 Converting challenges extracted data to desired format

```
#convert analog voltages to binary
challenge_columns = (
      (challenge_columns*0).where(challenge_columns<0.45,
      1).astype(in))
#converting challenge_columns into the right format
challenge_values = []
for col in challenge_columns.columns:
   col_string="".join(challenge_columns[col].astype(str))
   challenge_values.extend([col_string] * montecarlo_num)
#Naming the table header
challenge_df=pd.DataFrame({"Challenge":challenge_values})
```

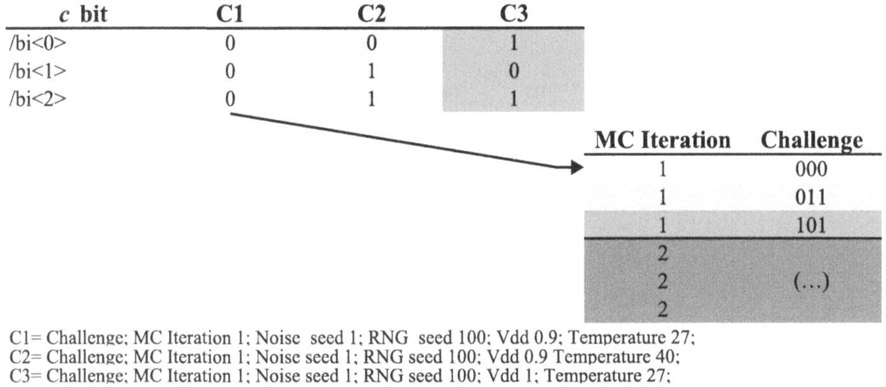

Fig. 7. Conversion of challenge bit columns into binary string.

5.4 Performance Metrics Calculation

To determine whether a PUF is suitable for cryptographic applications, it must be evaluated through several performance metrics. These metrics quantify properties such as uniqueness, repeatability, identifiability, reliability, and randomness, each contributing to the overall security and robustness of the PUF. This section presents the mathematical definitions of each metric, along with guidance on how they can be computed.

Uniqueness and Inter-HD

Uniqueness is evaluated by computing the mean inter-hamming distance (Inter-HD) between the responses from different PUF instances, under nominal conditions.

To accurately simulate this metric, transient MC simulations include both mismatch and process variations. Ensuring that each MC iteration emulates a distinct PUF device.

MC Iteration	Noise seed	RNG seed	Challenge	Supply Voltage	Temperature	Response
1	1	100	0000011000010010	0.9	27	0
1	1	100	0000011000010010	0.9	40	0
1	1	100	0000011000010010	1.0	27	0
1	1	100	0000011000010010	1.0	40	0
1	1	101	0011010011101011	0.9	27	1
1	1	101	0011010011101011	0.9	40	1
1	1	101	0011010011101011	1.0	27	0
1	1	101	0011010011101011	1.0	40	0
1	2	100	0000011000010010	0.9	27	0
1	2	100	0000011000010010	0.9	40	0
1	2	100	0000011000010010	1.0	27	0
1	2	100	0000011000010010	1.0	40	0
1	2	101	0011010011101011	0.9	27	1
1	2	101	0011010011101011	0.9	40	1
1	2	101	0011010011101011	1.0	27	0
1	2	101	0011010011101011	1.0	40	0
2	1	100	0000011000010010	0.9	27	0
2	1	100	0000011000010010	0.9	40	0
2	1	100	0000011000010010	1.0	27	0
2	1	100	0000011000010010	1.0	40	0
2	1	101	0011010011101011	0.9	27	0
2	1	101	0011010011101011	0.9	40	0
2	1	101	0011010011101011	1.0	27	0
2	1	101	0011010011101011	1.0	40	0
2	2	100	0000011000010010	0.9	27	0
2	2	100	0000011000010010	0.9	40	0
2	2	100	0000011000010010	1.0	27	0
2	2	100	0000011000010010	1.0	40	0
2	2	101	0011010011101011	0.9	27	0
2	2	101	0011010011101011	0.9	40	0

Fig. 8. Merged dataset from transient analysis mismatch-only MC.

Uniqueness should only compare golden responses, as being distinct is independent of their repeatability/reliability. Also, response pairs should be formed between responses generated by the same challenge, since PUFs are unique by their CRPs and not by their individual responses. Mathematically, the Inter- HD for a specific challenge *c* and device pair (*d,d'*) is defined as:

$$h_{c,d''} = 1/B \cdot \sum\nolimits_{b=1}^{B} (\bar{x}_{b,c,d} \circledast \bar{x}_{b,c,d'}) \quad (3)$$

where B is the number of bits in the response. In Eq. (3), $h_{c,d''}$ is computed for each challenge and all pairs of responses which contributes to Inter-HD histogram which is a widely used way of representing Inter-HD. Uniqueness is then calculated as the mean Inter-HD across all possible points as in Eq. (4).

$$Uniqueness = 2/(CD(D-1)) \cdot \sum\nolimits_{c=1}^{C} \sum\nolimits_{d''=1}^{D(D-1)/2} h_{c,d''} \cdot 100\% \quad (4)$$

where C is the total number of challenges and D the total number of devices. To compute the Inter-HD, a Python script (Code 3) groups the responses by challenges, reshapes them to a desired response format, and performs pairwise comparison to calculate HDs. These HDs are stored to compute the mean and standard deviation.

Code 3 Uniqueness and Inter-HD calculation

```
# Group response bits into fixed-size groups (num_bits
and bit_group defined by the user)
num_bit_group = int(num_bits / bit_group)
crp_response = np.zeros([crp_num, num_bit_group,
bit_group])
# Organize data into a 3D matrix [challenges x response
groups x bits per group]
for idx, seed in enumerate(rng_seed_list):
    crp_response_values = data_csv.loc[ data_csv["RNG
    seed"] == seed,["Response (bit)"]]
     crp_response[idx, :, :] = np.reshape(
         crp_response_values.values.astype(int),
 (num_bit_group,bit_group)
        )
# Calculate number of response pairs
num_hd = int((num_bit_group * (num_bit_group - 1)) / 2)
hamming_distance = np.zeros([len(rng_seed_list), num_hd])
# Compute Hamming Distance for each response pair
for idx, seed in enumerate(rng_seed_list):
    iteration = 0
    for idy in range(num_bit_group - 1):
        for idz in range(idy + 1, num_bit_group):
            hamming_distance[idx, iteration] = float(
              hamming(crp_response[idx,idy,:],crp_response[
              idx,idz,:])
              )
            iteration += 1
# Calculate Uniqueness and standard deviation of Inter-HD
hd_mean = np.mean(hamming_distance)
hd_std = np.std(hamming_distance)
```

Repeatability and Intra-HD

Repeatability is quantified using the Intra-HD, which reflects how consistent a PUF responds to the same challenge under varying operating conditions such varying temperature, supply voltage, and noise conditions.

Ideally, a PUF should generate identical responses to a given challenge regardless of such operating conditions. To simulate this behaviour, transient mismatch-only variation MC simulation is used. These preserve the identity of the PUF instance across iterations, allowing for analysis of its behaviour under varying conditions.

During simulation, the responses are aggregated into multi-bit responses by grouping bits from multiple MC iterations. These are groupped by challenge and noise seed.

The Intra-HD is mathematically defined by Eq. (5).

$$h_{a,c,d,e} = 1/B \sum_{b=1}^{B} (\overline{x}_{a,b,c,d,e} \circledast \overline{x}_{b,c,d}) \tag{5}$$

where B is the number of bits in the response, $\overline{x}_{a,b,c,d,e}$ is the response bit b, to access a, challenge c, by device d, under condition e, and $\overline{x}_{b,c,d}$ is the corresponding golden response bit for the same challenge and device.

Repeatability is calculated as the mean of all Intra-HD values across all challenges C, devices D, and operating conditions E, as defined in Eq. (6):

$$Repeatability = 1/(CDE) \cdot \sum_{c=1}^{C}\sum_{d=1}^{D}\sum_{e=1}^{E} h_{a,c,d,e} \cdot 100\% \tag{6}$$

To compute this metric, the Python script Code 4 was used. This requires storing of golden responses (stored as `intraNOM_crp_responses`) and variable-condition responses (stored as `intra_crp_responses`). These are preprocessed using the same data structure as described in the data perparation section. CRPs are grouped by challenge, and indexed across combinations of supply voltage, temperature, and noise seed.

Code 4 Repeatability and Intra-HD calculation.

```
# Initialize Intra-HD array
intra_hamming_distance =
np.zeros([len(intra_rng_seed_list), intra_iteration_num *
intra_num_bit_group])
# Coompute Hamming Distance for each challenge and
condition
for idx, seed in enumerate(intra_rng_seed_list):
    for idy in range(intra_iteration_num):
        for idz in range(intra_num_bit_group):
            intra_hamming_distance[idx, idy]=float(
              hamming(intraNOM_crp_response[idx,idz,:],intr
              a_crp_response[idx, idy, idz, :]))
# Calculate Repeatability and standard deviation of
Intra-HD
intra_hd_mean = np.mean(intra_hamming_distance)
intra_hd_std = np.std(intra_hamming_distance)
```

Identifiability

Identifiability reflects the overall distinguishability between devices, by combining inter- and intra- device variation. It is calculated as the ration in Eq. (7).

$$Identifiability = Uniqueness/Repeatability \tag{7}$$

A high identifiability indicates a highly distinguishable PUF device (high uniqueness) that also exhibit stable behaviour (low repeatability).

Reliability and BER

Reliability reflects how well a PUF maintains consistent output under different operating conditions and is typically expressed in terms of BER. Unlike repeatability, which focuses on average consistency across all conditions, reliability emphasizes worst-case behavior, giving insight into most error-prone scenarios.

Traditionally, BER is calculated as the mean Inter-HD for each environmental condition. However, this method overlaps conceptually with repeatability, which already evaluates the average consistency of a single PUF instance.

Instead, this methodology evaluates BER by computing the maximum error at each operating condition which better highlights the limits of the PUF, thus, providing a clear measure of whether the PUF is sufficiently stable under various conditions.

From the previously calculated Intra-HD $h_{a,c,d,e}$, the maximum BER for each operating condition e, is defined as in Eq. (8):

$$BER_{max}(e) = max_{a,c,d}\left(h_{a,c,d,e}\right) \tag{8}$$

This represents the highest error rate observed among all CRPs for a given condition. Then, reliability is defined as the complement of BER as in Eq. (9):

$$Reliability(e) = 1 - BER_{max}(e) \tag{9}$$

As previously discussed in Chapter 4, reliability is often represented using line plots or heatmaps for each operating condition. Reliability = 1, indicates a perfectly stable response.

Randomness

Randomness is computed by transient mismatch-only MC simulations, filtered to retain only nominal operating conditions results.

To perform this analysis, all simulated response bits are concatenated into a single bitstream. Since many NIST SP 800–22 tests require a minimum number of bits (some in the order of 10^6), the reliability and validity of the results improves as the number of simulated bits increases. If a sufficiently large stream is obtained, it is divided into smaller segments. Each segment is tested individually.

This approach allows the test suite to be repeated multiple times, strengthening statistical confidence in the results. Finally, there is an open-source Python implementation of the test suite implemented by Ang [11].

6 Conclusions

This work presents a systematic methodology for evaluating the performance of PUFs. By clearly specifying the simulation configurations required for each performance metric and standardizing the data processing and analysis steps, the proposed methodology ensures that PUF analysis becomes a straightforward process, facilitating PUF evaluation which can benefit the overall perception of PUF.

It addresses inconsistencies commonly found in the literature such as mathematical definitions, computation interpretations, interpretation of golden responses, Inter- and Intra-HD, and the distinction between process and mismatch-only variation.

As AI-CPS increasingly relies on robust hardware-based security primitives, having a consistent and replicate methodology for PUF evaluation is crucial. This methodology allows designers to quantify key properties such as uniqueness, repeatability, and reliability in a practical manner for PUFs in AI-CPS platforms.

Acknowledgments. This work was supported by FCT under PhD grant 2023.00267.BD, and CTS multi-annual funding program fund CTS/00066.

References

1. Cittadini, E., Marinoni, M., Biondi, A., Cicero, G., Buttazzo, G.: Supporting AI-powered real-time cyber-physical systems on heterogeneous platforms via hypervisor technology. Real-Time Syst. **59**(4), 609–635 (2023). https://doi.org/10.1007/s11241-023-09402-4
2. Chang, C.-H., Zheng, Y., Zhang, L.: A Retrospective and a look forward: fifteen years of physical unclonable function advancement. IEEE Circuits Syst. Mag. **17**(3), 32–62 (2017). https://doi.org/10.1109/MCAS.2017.2713305
3. Lofstrom, K., Daasch, W.R., Taylor, D.: IC identification circuit using device mismatch. In: 2000 IEEE International Solid-State Circuits Conference. Digest of Technical Papers (Cat. No.00CH37056), San Francisco, CA, USA: IEEE, pp. 372–373 (2000). https://doi.org/10.1109/ISSCC.2000.839821
4. Wilde, F.K.A.: Metrics for physical unclonable functions. PhD Thesis, Fakultät für Elektrotechnik und Informationstechnik (2021). https://mediatum.ub.tum.de/doc/1612868/1612868.pdf
5. Zhang, J., et al.: A 4T/cell amplifier-chain-based XOR PUF with strong machine learning attack resilience. IEEE Trans. Circuits Syst. Regul. Pap. **69**(1), 366–377 (2022). https://doi.org/10.1109/TCSI.2021.3114084
6. Cao, Y., Liu, C.Q., Chang, C.H.: A low power diode-clamped inverter-based strong physical unclonable function for robust and lightweight authentication. IEEE Trans. Circuits Syst. Regul. Pap. **65**(11), 3864–3873 (2018). https://doi.org/10.1109/TCSI.2018.2855061
7. Zhuang, H., Xi, X., Sun, N., Orshansky, M.: A strong subthreshold current array puf resilient to machine learning attacks. IEEE Trans. Circuits Syst. Regul. Pap. **67**(1), 135–144 (2020). https://doi.org/10.1109/TCSI.2019.2945247
8. Alioto, M.: Trends in hardware security: from basics to ASICs. IEEE Solid-State Circuits Mag. **11**(3), 56–74 (2019). https://doi.org/10.1109/MSSC.2019.2923503
9. Bassham, L., et al.: Banks D: A Statistical Test Suite for Random and Pseudorandom Number Generators for Cryptographic Applications. Spec. Publ, NIST SP (2010)
10. Lee, J.W., Daihyun, L., Gassend, B., Suh, G.E., Van Dijk, M., Devadas, S.: A technique to build a secret key in integrated circuits for identification and authentication applications. In: 2004 Symposium on VLSI Circuits. Digest of Technical Papers (IEEE Cat. No.04CH37525), Honolulu, HI, USA: Widerkehr and Associates, pp. 176–179 (2004). https://doi.org/10.1109/VLSIC.2004.1346548
11. Ang, S.K.: stevenang/randomness_testsuite. (Feb. 20, 2025). E. Accessed: 14 Mar. 2025. https://github.com/stevenang/randomness_testsuite

Recent Trends in Audio Power Amplifiers for Battery-Powered Applications

José Francisco Luís[1,2](✉) and Nuno Paulino[1]

[1] NOVA School of Science and Technology, UNINOVA-CTS and LASI, NOVA University Lisbon, 2829-516 Caparica, Portugal
jfr.luis@campus.fct.unl.pt, nuno.f.paulino@fct.unl.pt

[2] Faculty of Engineering and Technologies, University of Namibe, Namibe, Moçâmedes, Angola

Abstract. AI cyber-physical systems often rely on voice interfaces that require audio power amplifiers. Designing amplifiers that balance high efficiency with dynamic response is challenging due to the complexity of their design and the influence of integrated components on performance. Energy efficiency is crucial for audio amplifiers in mobile devices, as it directly affects battery life. Recent research has concentrated on enhancing audio quality and efficiency, particularly in Class G and Class H audio amplifiers. This article reviews the latest advancements and trends in mobile amplifier design, focusing on improvements in efficiency, power supply noise rejection (PSRR), and total harmonic distortion plus noise (THD+N).

Keywords: Audio amplifiers · technological advancements · battery-powered devices · Audio quality

1 Introduction

Audio amplifiers are devices that are widely used in numerous applications, and their design is a demanding and labor-intensive task, given the complexity of the various variables that influence the performance of these devices [1]. Nowadays, mobile and battery-powered devices with built-in audio amplifiers are abundant. Given that these devices have a limited battery capacity, the efficiency of the audio amplifier becomes crucial to extend the battery life [2–5]. Advanced semiconductors, such as CMOS, GaN, and GaN-SiC drive the technological evolution in power amplifiers [6–8]. Which offer high efficiency, thermal conductivity, and burst voltage. Initially restricted to academia, these technologies are quickly becoming commercialized in mobile devices, sectors such as automotive and aerospace.

Audio amplifier design has matured over the past few decades [9, 10]. However, despite this maturation, integrating these amplifiers into portable and battery-powered devices is still a challenge. This task poses difficulties, such as immunity to battery disturbances, ground-referenced outputs, and extended music playback time. This is in

Published by Springer Nature Switzerland AG 2025
L. M. Camarinha-Matos and F. Ferrada (Eds.): DoCEIS 2025, IFIP AICT 759, pp. 410–422, 2025.
https://doi.org/10.1007/978-3-031-97051-1_29

addition to meeting other performance requirements such as output power and audio fidelity [11]. Considering that the battery is the main energy source in battery-powered portable devices, the amplifier should have the lowest possible power dissipation for the best possible performance. Achieving these goals may require efforts in the design of amplifiers to optimize their usefulness in devices of this type, so this becomes an interest for both engineers and users of these devices.

This article reviews recent trends in applications and techniques for improving audio amplifier architectures for battery-powered mobile devices. Articles published over several years on the design of power amplifiers were analyzed, as well as the techniques used to make them more efficient. In this context, the importance of DC-DC converters to ensure the good performance and efficient operation of these classes of audio amplifiers was highlighted, with a focus on Class AB, D, G, and H amplifiers and efficient DC-DC converters. The selection was based on relevance to mobile applications, energy efficiency, THD, and dynamic energy strategies.

Additionally, this paper examines the techniques applied to low-power and high-performance audio amplifier architectures, exploring how these solutions meet the demanding requirements for efficient operation. This article is organized as follows: Sect. 2 presents the framework of audio power amplifiers for AI-driven energy-efficient cyber-physical systems; Sect. 3 compares the various classes of amplifiers, with emphasis on classes G and H, as well as analyzing the integration of DC-DC converters for their supply; Sect. 4 explores the innovation and applications of power amplifiers in modern technologies; Sect. 5 analyzes, discusses, and presents simulation results; and, finally, in Sect. 6, the conclusions are presented.

2 Audio Power Amplifiers for Energy-Efficient AI-Driven Cyber-Physical Systems

Many AI applications are shifting towards edge computing, where data processing occurs closer to the source rather than relying on a centralized cloud [12, 13], his approach is particularly important for battery-powered devices, which operate with limited energy capacity. Efficient audio processing is crucial in voice control, environmental monitoring, and human-machine interaction applications.

Audio power amplifiers have evolved significantly to meet the increasing demands for energy efficiency and sound quality in battery-powered devices [2–5, 11]. These improvements are essential for AI-powered cyber-physical systems requiring real-time signal processing and optimized energy management. Efficient amplifiers enhance performance in mobile and autonomous applications, such as IoT devices, drones, and communication systems. Its integration into compact designers drives the development of efficient, high-performance cyber-physical systems.

3 Comparison of Class Audio Amplifiers: AB, D, G, and H

Currently, there are several classes of audio amplifiers, each based on different architectures and specific operating principles. This section compares classes AB, D, G, and H, highlighting their main characteristics, advantages, and limitations.

3.1 Architectural Characteristics of Class AB and D Amplifiers

At present, two classes of audio amplifiers dominate the market for battery-powered devices: the Class AB audio amplifier (linear amplifier) and the Class D audio amplifier (switching amplifier) [2, 3]. The Class AB audio amplifier, due to its configuration, typically exhibits high linearity, a low total harmonic distortion to noise ratio (THD + N), and a high-power supply rejection ratio (PSRR) [14, 15]. When used with a sinewave signal at full power, these amplifiers exhibit a maximum efficiency of around 78%. However, this efficiency tends to be much lower for typical audio signals at normal audio power levels [16]. Although work is still being conducted on these types of amplifiers [17].

Unlike the previous Class, the Class D audio amplifier, due to its configuration, typically exhibits high efficiency but lower linearity performance and produces EMI. This results from multiple sources of nonlinearity introduced by the non-ideal PWM modulator, the quiet time, and the filter output [18]. These amplifiers tend to achieve an efficiency of over 90% for various power levels, resulting in low heat dissipation [16]. A concern in this class of amplifiers is the issue of power supply rejection rate (PSRR), which becomes even more acute since the supply noise can demodulate with the pulse-width modulation (PWM) signal, generating power supply-induced intermodulation distortion (PS-IMD), which can sometimes be greater than the output distortion component at the power noise frequency [19]. A Class D amplifier's output power transistors operate as switches, meaning either the current will be zero (when OFF) or the voltage across them will be close to zero (when ON). In both modes, the power dissipation is very low. This approach results in a very highly efficient amplifier. Requiring less power from the power supply allows for the use of smaller heat sinks for the amplifier [16].

3.2 Advances in Efficiency: Class G and Class H Amplifiers

To achieve an optimal balance between linearity, efficiency, power supply rejection ratio (PSRR), and electromagnetic interference (EMI), a Class AB amplifier with adaptive supply voltage can be used, by reducing the output power voltage when the output signal is low the power dissipation of the output power transistors is reduced resulting in an increase of efficiency for lower power levels [20]. Two classes of audio amplifiers stand out: Class G and Class H. The Class G audio amplifier uses multiple supply voltage levels, dynamically switching between them according to the audio signal's amplitude. In low amplitude conditions, it operates at reduced voltages, raising to higher levels only when necessary [21, 22]. Class H continuously adjusts the output power supply voltage by following the output signal amplitude. They can offer higher efficiency at reduced output power levels, making them particularly suitable for audio applications with a high crest factor. Class G and Class H amplifiers stand out in battery-powered audio devices, significantly increasing music playback time, with Class G gaining popularity for its higher efficiency over Class AB [11, 21]. To meet the demands of high-quality audio, they must prioritize low-power reproduction with high fidelity, low Total Harmonic Distortion (THD), wide dynamic range (DR), and high efficiency. In addition, a high-power supply rejection rate (PSRR) is essential throughout the audio band to minimize switching noise and maintain sound quality [23]. They outperform Class D amplifiers by minimizing EMI issues, making integrating with RF systems such as cellular, Wi-Fi, Bluetooth, GPS, and FM radio easier, however, the efficiency of Class G amplifiers is still lower than that of Class D amplifiers. The Class G amplifier topology offers relatively higher energy efficiency compared to Class AB amplifiers and better linearity than Class D amplifiers, providing an ideal solution for portable audio applications [24]. Class H audio amplifiers are designed to solve some limitations of Class G amplifiers, such as efficiency at varying loads and abrupt voltage transitions. These amplifiers are good candidates for improving energy efficiency in mobile devices, providing longer battery life, and minimizing EMI issues [11, 21, 23]. In a Class H amplifier, the power supply of the Class AB amplifier is continuously modulated to keep up with the output voltage, improving efficiency concerning Class G and approaching Class D. To optimize this efficiency, the power supply must follow the output voltage at all levels, which requires advanced circuitry control [3, 21, 22].

The progress of power amplifiers in Class G topologies has considerably reduced power consumption compared to other traditional architectures, such as Class A and Class AB. Although some technologies are relatively recent, their combination has proven to be an asset to amplifier technology trends, such as the construction of a highly efficient transmitter based on a Class G SCPA [25], implemented in 65 nm CMOS technology, although no longer so recent, demonstrates that combining this architecture with this technology represents an efficient integration into a system that improves performance and practical feasibility.

[26] compared the efficiency of Class H, Class AB, and Class G amplifiers, demonstrating that Class H achieves higher efficiency through dynamic supply voltage tracking. This reduces voltage drops in power transistors and increases efficiency as power output rises. The Class H topology also avoids abrupt power level changes seen in Class AB amplifiers, preventing unwanted spikes or faults at all output voltage levels. Although the ideal efficiency of Class H can be achieved, it may not always be possible, as shown in previous works [2, 14].

Table 1 Presents a technical comparison of Class AB, D, G, and H audio amplifiers under the aspects of efficiency, linearity, complexity, and application. Class AB architecture has moderate efficiency and is used in mid-range audio systems. Of note are the G and H Classes, which combine high energy efficiency with excellent linearity, making them particularly attractive for mobile and battery-powered devices. In addition, they are widely used in applications that require high-fidelity sound, such as Bluetooth speakers, headphones, earbuds, and high-performance speakers.

Table 1. Technical Comparison of Audio Amplifier Architectures.

Architecture	Efficiency	Linearity	Complexity	Typical Applications
Class AB	Moderate	High	Low	Mid-range audio systems
Class D	Very High	Moderate	Moderate	Smartphones, wearables
Class G	High	High	High	Portable speakers
Class H	High	High	Very High	High-fidelity devices

3.3 Integration of DC-DC Converters in Audio Amplifiers: Strategies to Maximize Energy Efficiency in Portable Systems

Improving the efficiency of Class G/H amplifiers has, in recent years, been the focus of many studies. Techniques such as embedding audio input signal amplitude information into the Class AB amplifier's output common-mode voltage level allow the amplifier to operate with only a single-rail power supply. This leads to smoother transitions between light load and heavy load modes, achieving lower total harmonic distortion (THD) across a wide load range [2]. The use of a buck converter dynamically adjusts the amplifier's supply voltage, improving energy efficiency while maintaining sound quality and reducing power consumption [27].

To address issues like inaccurate envelope tracking limiting full-path efficiency, THD + N degradation due to limited PSRR in output drivers, and high-temperature distortions from DAC reference bias drift caused by gate leakage in advanced processes, design challenges must be considered for high-fidelity Class G/H amplifiers [21] implemented several solutions: (1) an inductor-based supply modulator for efficient envelope tracking above 1 kHz, improving efficiency to 34.8% at 10 mW output; (2) a gain-boosting CMFB circuit with enhanced frequency compensation to increase loop gain without compromising stability; (3) a ROFF-controlled technique to mitigate DAC reference bias drift, maintaining THD + N up to 85 °C. These techniques enable the Class H amplifier to achieve −108 dBc THD + N, 126 dB DR, and 2.3 mW quiescent power, implementing a SIMO (Single-Inductor Multiple-Output) converter to power the Class H amplifier, providing a fixed negative supply (VSS) for analog DAC circuits and two envelope-tracking supplies (PVDD and PVSS) for stereo headphone amplifiers. The converter charges the output whenever any supply voltage drops below its target, prioritizing VSS to ensure proper operation.

To improve the CMFB loop gain against supply ripples, a 3-stage CMFB amplifier is used. In conventional designs, the transconductance of the CM-sense amplifier (Gm, CM) is underutilized, as only one output (M1,2) is coupled to the main amplifier's first-stage output (Gm1) via a current mirror (M5–7), while the other output (M3,4) is connected to a dummy diode load [21].

Class G amplification with an integrated charge converter and adaptive voltage regulation enhances efficiency by optimizing the relationship between the audio amplifier and the DC-DC converter [14]. Achieving high efficiency requires minimizing energy conversion losses, making low-loss DC-DC converters essential alongside amplifiers.

Techniques for integrating DC-DC converters with audio amplifiers improve energy efficiency, especially in systems powering amplifiers or loudspeakers. A multi-mode dual-voltage charge pump (MMDV-CP) with an impedance detector dynamically adjusts supply voltages, minimizing energy losses. This can theoretically boost Class G amplifier efficiency by up to 27% with 16Ω loads. However, if charge pump losses exceed current savings, frequent switching in Class G should be avoided to optimize system efficiency [23, 28].

The technique in [29] improves full-path efficiency from 31% to 37% compared to a conventional 2-level fixed Class G amplifier, saving 1.45 mA from a 1.8 V source while delivering 5 mW to a 16 Ω load. The amplifier achieves a PSRR of 130 dB at 217 Hz, remaining above 100 dB up to 20 kHz. Additionally, the decoder and amplifier reach 108 dB DR and 95 dB SNDR with a 16Ω headphone load.

Techniques to reduce losses in Class G amplifiers are useful because of the growing demand for battery-powered devices. This topology's main advantage is excellent performance in low-power applications, such as mobile devices.

4 Innovation and Applications of Power Amplifiers in Modern Technologies

Technological evolution in power amplifiers is driven by advanced semiconductors like CMOS, GaN, and GaN-SiC [6–8]. These materials provide high efficiency, thermal conductivity, and burst voltage, making them ideal for modern applications. GaN-based technologies stand out for their high voltage tolerance, power density, and wide bandwidth operation [30].

To enhance high-fidelity audio, various amplifier architectures have been developed. The Class G amplifier in [14], implemented in 0.18 μm CMOS, achieves a 130 dB PSRR at 217 Hz, 108 dB DR, and 95 dB SNDR. Its optimized efficiency and noise resistance make it ideal for mobile devices requiring sound fidelity and electrical robustness.

The proposal in [24] eliminates inductors in Class G amplifiers for portable applications. Built on 0.35 μm double-well CMOS technology, it reduces cost and EMI, delivering 1.45 W with only 5 mA of quiescent current. With an SNR of 97.3 dB and THD under 0.05%, this solution is ideal for portable devices requiring energy efficiency and interference resistance.

Class G and H amplifiers have significantly contributed to the evolution of mobile devices by combining energy efficiency and high sound performance. For instance, the Class G stereo headphone driver in [11], built with 0.18 μm CMOS, achieves 111 dB DR and 120 dB PSRR, offering high efficiency for low-amplitude signals. This Class AB/B architecture with a dual-voltage charge pump extends playback time, making it ideal for mobile devices that require longer battery life and resistance to wireless interference.

Class G amplifiers are ideal for applications requiring simplicity, low cost, and extended battery life, making them well-suited for modern portable devices. Their combination of high-fidelity sound, noise immunity, and energy efficiency makes them essential for EMI-sensitive technologies.

Two recent Class H amplifier designs stand out in efficiency and power. In [3], a design based on the GF 55 nm BCDlite process achieves 85.1% efficiency and delivers up to 186.8 mW at 16 Ω loads. It also features low total harmonic distortion and noise (THD + N) of −82 dB at 1 kHz and -81.5 dB at 20 kHz, making it ideal for low-power mobile devices.

Another proposal in [27], uses GaN transistors to achieve 87% efficiency, delivering 37% power for 32 Ω loads with THD + N of −70.17 dB. This design is well-suited for higher-power audio systems, offering significant advantages for both mobile and high-performance applications.

Table 2 shows Class AB, D, G, and H audio amplifiers, highlighting parameters such as manufacturing technology, input voltage, efficiency, SNR, DR, PSRR, maximum output power, and quiescent power. It allows you to evaluate amplifiers' performance in terms of energy efficiency, sound quality, and suitability for mobile devices, making it easier to identify the best options for high-performance portable applications.

Table 2. Comparison of Audio Amplifier Architectures and Their Applications.

Publication	[20]	[17]	[23]	[11]	[14]	[27]	[3]	[21]
Year	2012	2018	2010	2012	2015	2018	2023	2024
Class	AB/D	AB	G	G	G	H	H	H
Technology (nm)	153 CMOS	180 CMOS	65 CMOS	180 CMOS	180 CMOS	180 BCD	GF55 BCDLite	28 CMOS
Supply Voltage (VDD)	3.3-3.7–5	1.2	0.35–1.4	2.65–4.5	1.8	48–5	1.2–2.5	--
Max. Pout (mW)@THD + N = 1%	1230	- -	0.5	60	62	37	186.8	--
Quiescent Current (mA)	1.9	0.18	0.4	1.15	1.35	--	--	--
Quiescent Power (mW)	7.03	0.216	0.71	0.41	1.56	706.3	4.9	2.3
Load (Ω)	8	- -	16–32	16–60	16	37	16	16
Peak Power Efficiency (%)	90%	- -	30%	30%	46.8%	87%	85.08%	85%
THD + N (dB)	74 (AB), 76 (D)	- -	−80	−95	−95	-70.17	--	−108
SNR (dB)	100	- -	101	101	95	--	--	126
PSRR	106 and 100	92	--	120	130	--	--	--

5 Comparative Analysis of Ideal and Real Conditions

Figure 1 shows a simplified diagram of a differential amplifier powered by a DC-DC converter. The converter creates a variable voltage VDDV to the amplifier from VDD, which receives an input signal VIN and generates an amplified output signal for the load. The diagram also shows the power supply current IL. This diagram will be used to analyze the efficiency of the amplifier working in Class AB and Class G.

The differential output voltage (VOUT) varies between - VDDV and + VDDV (assuming that VSS = 0V), in the case of Class AB VDDV is equal to VDD, in the

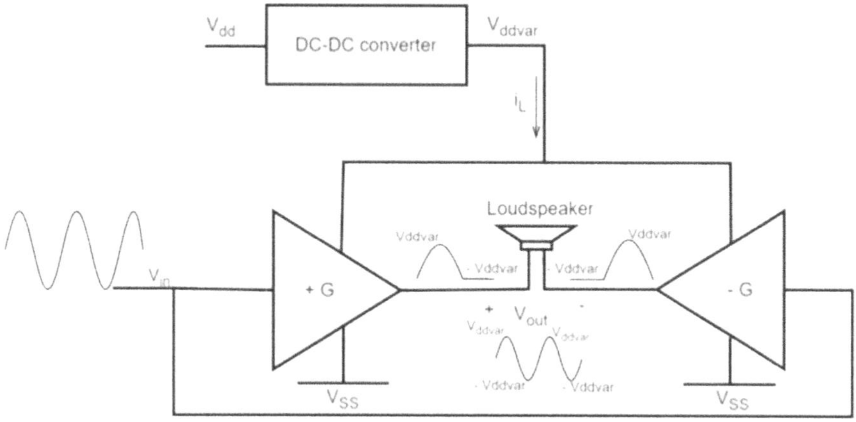

Fig. 1. Class G differential amplifier with DC-DC power supply diagram.

case of Class G the value of VDDV will be adjusted, by selecting between a set predetermined value, depending on the value of VOUT. The value of VDDV should be selected to guarantee that VDDV > VOUT to avoid clipping, noting that the maximum possible value is VDD. The efficiency of the amplifier for a given output signal (VOUT(t)) is obtained by first calculating the instantaneous load power (pload(t)):

$$i_{load}(t) = \frac{v_{out}(t)}{R_{load}}; \quad p_{load}(t) = v_{load}(t) \times i_{load}(t) \tag{1}$$

Assuming that the amplifiers bias current is 0 (ideal case), the instantaneous supply power (p_{VDDV}(t)) can then be obtained:

$$p_{VDDV}(t) = |i_{load}(t)| \times v_{DDV}(t) \tag{2}$$

The efficiency of the amplifier during a given time interval is given by:

$$\eta = 100 \times \frac{AVG(p_{load}(t))}{AVG(p_{VDDV}(t))} \tag{3}$$

The value of VVDDV(t) depends on the value of VOUT(t), in the ideal case, it is instantaneously selected from the set {1.8 V, 1.2 V, 0.6 V} to guarantee that VDDV > VOUT. In a real application, the DC-DC converter cannot instantly adjust VDDV and therefore there is a minimum adjust time (Tadj) that must be considered. This is shown in Fig. 2a where VDDV is instantly adjusted to closely follow the amplitude of a sinewave signal and in Fig. 2b where VDDV is adjusted every Tadj = 0.1 s to follow a real-world signal. This requires that the signal is monitored to determine its maximum value within the Tadj. Capability of the DC-DC converter.

In this context, let's compare the two operating classes in real conditions. Here, we assume that both classes are powered by a buck converter presented in [31], and that it presents a behavior in terms of efficiency as shown in Fig. 3, looking at the same conditions considering a load of 16 Ω, the DC-DC Converter, allows to generate three output

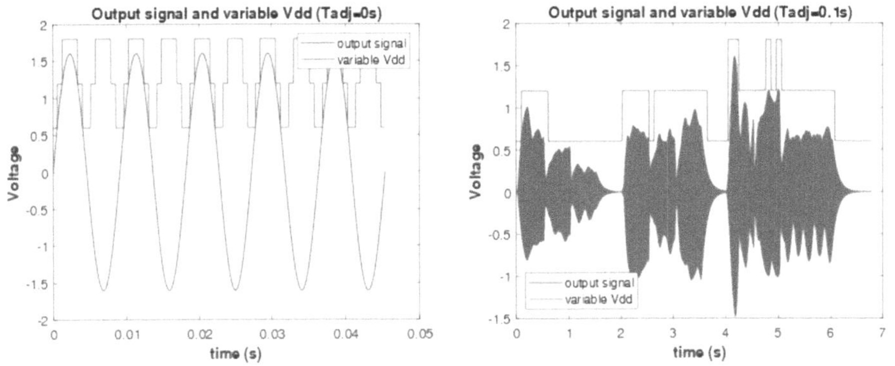

Fig. 2. Output signal as a function of Vdd variation: a) Vdd variable (Tadj = 0 s), b) Vdd variable (Tadj = 0.1 s).

voltages of 0.6 V, 1.2 V, and 1.8 V respectively, the analysis is made considering these conditions of supply of the DC-DC converter. The amplifier's efficiency is calculated for different volume levels by linearly scaling the maximum signal value from −1 dB to −20 dB of VDD. For each volume level, the efficiency of the amplifier was computed for the case of VDDV = VDD (Class AB), with VDDV adjusted with Tadj = 0 s (Class G ideal) and with VDDV adjusted with Tadj = 0.1 s (Class G real). To introduce the efficiency of the DC-DC converter, the supply power (pVDDV(t)) is calculated using:

$$p_{VDD}(t) = \frac{p_{VDDV}(t)}{\eta_{conv}(V_{VDDV})} \tag{4}$$

Figure 3 shows the efficiency curves for different output voltages (VOUT) as a function of the output current (IOUT). It can be observed that the efficiency increases with IOUT at low currents, reaches a peak, and then stabilizes. Higher voltages, such as VOUT = 1.8 V, exhibit higher efficiency, while VOUT = 0.6 V experiences higher losses. This highlights the importance of selecting the proper operating conditions to maximize efficiency, especially in Class G amplifiers. These results are shown in Fig. 4a for a sinewave signal and in Fig. 4b for a real signal. It is possible to conclude that the efficiency of Class G is significantly better than the efficiency of Class AB, especially in the case of real-world signals. In the case of a sinewave signal, there is no difference in the efficiency of amplitudes larger than 1.2 V, but this is not a realistic scenario. It is also possible to conclude that by decreasing Tadj, the efficiency increases, with the best case corresponding to the ideal case (Tadj = 0 s).

The results presented in Fig. 4 clearly show the differences between these two classes when powered by low voltages, highlighting the importance of a highly efficient DC-DC converter in power transfer. This reinforces that the performance of audio amplifiers depends significantly on the efficiency of the DC-DC converter. Therefore, the choice of converter must ensure that the amplifier is supplied as efficiently as possible. For this, its merit figure must be sufficiently high, as efficient energy conversion results in better amplification capacity in power amplifiers.

The efficiency shown in Fig. 4 was computed assuming that the VDDvar voltage is instantly adjusted to follow the output signal (as shown in Fig. 2). However, in practice,

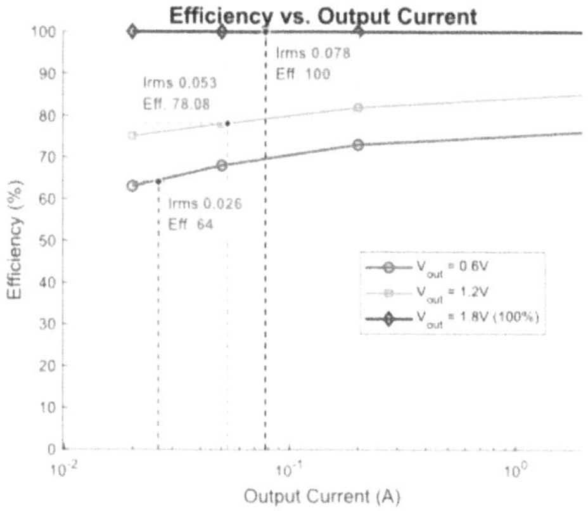

Fig. 3. Current and voltage (η(VDDC)).

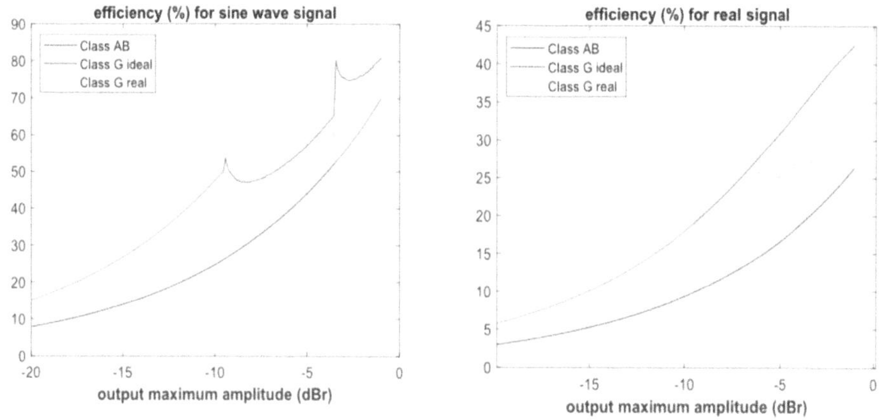

Fig. 4. Efficiency of Class AB and Class G amplifiers under real conditions: (a) sine signal, and (b) real signal.

this behavior is unfeasible, as real converters have finite response time, oscillations, switching losses, noise, and difficulties in following rapid signal variations without distortions. Thus, it is essential to design a converter that comes as close as possible to optimal behavior.

6 Conclusions

Recent trends in audio amplifiers for battery-powered applications demonstrate significant advancements in efficiency, size, and performance. The increased demand for mobile devices, combined with the need for longer battery life, drives the development of amplifiers that balance high sound quality and low power consumption. Technologies such as classes G and H, highly efficient but complex in their implementation, have been fundamental to extending battery life.

If it is possible to design a highly efficient converter with a figure of merit that provides the desired efficiency, it will be feasible to achieve high and optimized performance of audio amplifiers. In addition, an essential factor in the search for good functioning of the converters is the dynamic control of the supply voltage. This approach can contribute significantly to the development of highly efficient DC-DC converters, ensuring good conditions to adapt amplifiers to load variations and providing maximum performance with minimum power losses. As a future work, it is intended to develop a hybrid DC-DC converter to power a class G/H amplifier, considering that the efficiency and good performance of these amplifiers depend strongly on the quality of the DC-DC converters used.

References

1. Bortoni, R., Filho, S.N., Seara, R.: Dimensionamento e avaliação de estágios de potência de amplificadores de áudio classes A, B, AB, G E H, assistido por análise computacional
2. Zhang, X., Siek, L.: An 80.4% peak power efficiency adaptive supply class h power amplifier for audio applications. IEEE Trans. Very Large Scale Integr. VLSI Syst. **25**(6), 1954–1965 (2017). https://doi.org/10.1109/TVLSI.2017.2666268
3. Utomo, N., et al.: An 85.1% peak efficiency, low power class H audio amplifier with full class H operation. IEEE Trans. Circuits Syst. I Regul. Pap. **70**(12), 4692–4704 (2023). https://doi.org/10.1109/TCSI.2023.3305622
4. Abdelfattah, K., et al.: A 40 nm fully integrated 82 mW stereo headphone module for mobile applications. IEEE J. Solid-State Circuits **49**, 1702–1714 (2014). https://doi.org/10.1109/JSSC.2014.2314449
5. Russo, P., Yengui, F., Pillonnet, G., Taupin, S., Abouchi, N.: Dynamic voltage scaling for series hybrid amplifiers. Microelectronics J. **44**, 753–763 (2013). https://doi.org/10.1016/j.mejo.2013.03.016
6. Radamson, H.H., et al.: State of the art and future perspectives in advanced CMOS technology. (2020). https://doi.org/10.3390/nano10081555
7. Venkatesh Murthy, B.T., Manjushree, T.M., Meghana, N., Ramya, H.G., Vaishnavi, V.: A millimeter wave MMIC power amplifier using 0.15 um GaN for space communication systems. In: International Conference on Smart Systems for Applications in Electrical Sciences, ICSSES 2024. Institute of Electrical and Electronics Engineers Inc. (2024). https://doi.org/10.1109/ICSSES62373.2024.10561334
8. Neininger, P., et al.: Advances in GaN devices and circuits at higher mm-wave frequencies. e-Prime Adv. Electr. Eng. Electron. Energy **4**, 100177 (2023). https://doi.org/10.1016/j.prime.2023.100177
9. Bonnaud, P., Hammes, M., Hanke, A., Kissing, J., Koch, R., Labarre, E., Schwoerer, C.: A Fully integrated SoC for GSM/GPRS in 0.13/spl mu/m CMOS. In: 2006 IEEE International Solid State Circuits Conference - Digest of Technical Papers. pp. 1942–1951. IEEE (2006). https://doi.org/10.1109/ISSCC.2006.1696252
10. Hammes, M., Kranz, C., Kissing, J., Seippel, D., Bonnaud, P.-H., Pelos, E.: A GSM baseband radio in 0.13μm CMOS with fully integrated power-management. In: 2007 IEEE International Solid-State Circuits Conference. Digest of Technical Papers. pp. 264–602. IEEE (2007). https://doi.org/10.1109/ISSCC.2007.373395
11. Galal, S., et al.: A 60 mW class-G stereo headphone driver for portable battery-powered devices. IEEE J. Solid-State Circuits **47**, 1921–1934 (2012). https://doi.org/10.1109/JSSC.2012.2197155

12. Edge AI, benefícios da Inteligência Artificial local - Mecalux.com.br. https://www.mecalux.com.br/blog/edge-ai. Last accessed 31 Jan 2025
13. Computação na Borda: Processamento de Dados Distribuídos. https://embarcados.com.br/computacao-na-borda-edge-computing-o-futuro-do-processamento-de-dados-distribuidos/. Last accessed 31 Jan 2025
14. Wen, S.-H., et al.: A 130dB PSRR, 108dB DR and 95dB SNDR, ground-referenced audio decoder with PSRR-enhanced load-adaptive Class-G 16Ohm headphone amplifiers. In: 2015 IEEE Asian Solid-State Circuits Conference (A-SSCC). pp. 1–4. IEEE (2015). https://doi.org/10.1109/ASSCC.2015.7387442
15. Jiang, X.: Fundamentals of audio class D amplifier design: a review of schemes and architectures. IEEE Solid-State Circuits Mag. **9**, 14–25 (2017). https://doi.org/10.1109/MSSC.2017.2712368
16. Malvino, A.P.B.D.J.: Eletrônica. AMGH Editora, Porto Alegre (2016)
17. Far, A.: Class AB amplifier with noise reduction, speed boost, gain enhancement, and ultra low power. In: 2018 IEEE 9th Latin American Symposium on Circuits & Systems (LASCAS). pp. 1–4. IEEE (2018). https://doi.org/10.1109/LASCAS.2018.8399961
18. Tan, M.T., Chang, J.S., Chua, H.C., Gwee, B.H.: An investigation into the parameters affecting total harmonic distortion in low-voltage low-power Class-D amplifiers. IEEE Trans. Circuits Syst. I Fundam. Theor. Appl. **50**(10), 1304–1315 (2003). https://doi.org/10.1109/TCSI.2003.817770
19. Ge, T., Chang, J.S.: Modeling and technique to improve PSRR and PS-IMD in analog PWM Class-D amplifiers. IEEE Trans. Circuits Syst. II Express Briefs **55**(6), 512–516 (2008). https://doi.org/10.1109/TCSII.2007.914900
20. Chen, K.H., Hsu, Y.S.: A high-PSRR reconfigurable class-AB/D audio amplifier driving a hands-free/receiver 2-in-1 loudspeaker. IEEE J. Solid-State Circuits **47**, 2586–2603 (2012). https://doi.org/10.1109/JSSC.2012.2211657
21. Wen, S.H., et al.: 21.4 A -108dBc THD+N, 2.3 mW Class-H headphone amplifier with power-aware SIMO supply modulator. In: Digest of Technical Papers - IEEE International Solid-State Circuits Conference. pp. 384–386. Institute of Electrical and Electronics Engineers Inc. (2024). https://doi.org/10.1109/ISSCC49657.2024.10454450
22. Gong, G., Ertl, H., Kolar, J.W.: Novel tracking power supply for linear power amplifiers. IEEE Trans. Industr. Electron. **55**, 684–698 (2008). https://doi.org/10.1109/TIE.2007.896152
23. Lollio, A., Bollati, G., Castello, R.: Class-G headphone driver in 65 nm CMOS technology. In: 2010 IEEE International Solid-State Circuits Conference - (ISSCC). pp. 84–85. IEEE (2010). https://doi.org/10.1109/ISSCC.2010.5434039
24. Zhang, H., Tan, M.T., Chan, P.K.: A single-supply inductorless CMOS class G speaker amplifier. In: 2011 IEEE 54th International Midwest Symposium on Circuits and Systems (MWSCAS). pp. 1–4. IEEE (2011). https://doi.org/10.1109/MWSCAS.2011.6026683
25. Yoo, S.M., et al.: A class-G switched-capacitor RF power amplifier. IEEE J. Solid-State Circuits **48**, 1212–1224 (2013). https://doi.org/10.1109/JSSC.2013.2252754
26. Analysis and design of an adaptive-supply class H audio power amplifier for mobile devices, http://hdl.handle.net/10356/72875. (2017). https://doi.org/10.32657/10356/72875
27. Utomo, N., Siek, L., Yap, H.G., Disney, D., Selvaraj, L., Peng, L.: An 87% peak efficiency, 37 W, Class H audio amplifier with GaN output stage. In: 2018 IEEE Nordic Circuits and Systems Conference (NORCAS): NORCHIP and International Symposium of System-on-Chip (SoC). pp. 1–6. IEEE (2018). https://doi.org/10.1109/NORCHIP.2018.8573508
28. TC1225 TC1226 TC1227 Inverting Dual (-V IN ,-2V IN) Charge Pump Voltage Converters FEATURES. (2001)
29. Wen, S.H., et al.: A load-adaptive Class-G headphone amplifier with supply-rejection bandwidth enhancement technique. IEEE J. Solid-State Circuits **51**, 2241–2251 (2016). https://doi.org/10.1109/JSSC.2016.2581802

30. Monprasert, G., Suebsombut, P., Pongthavornkamol, T., Chalermwisutkul, S.: 2.45 GHz GaN HEMT Class-AB RF power amplifier design for wireless communication systems
31. ETA3458 – ETA Semiconductor Limited. https://www.eta-semi.com/product/1085.html. Last accessed 19 April 2025

Correction to: Electronic Noses for Cyber-Physical Systems: Preliminary Results on TiO2 Thin Film as a Humidity Sensor

Tiago Reis, Paulo A. Ribeiro, Susana Sério, Maria Helena Fino, and Maria Raposo

Correction to:
Chapter 19 in: L. M. Camarinha-Matos and F. Ferrada (Eds.): ***Technological Innovation for AI-Powered Cyber-Physical Systems*****,**
IFIP AICT 759, https://doi.org/10.1007/978-3-031-97051-1_19

The Co- Author's name in the chapter "Electronic Noses for Cyber-Physical Systems: Preliminary Results on TiO_2 Thin Film as a Humidity Sensor" was updated from "Susana Ribeiro" to "Susana Sério".

The updated version of this chapter can be found at
https://doi.org/10.1007/978-3-031-97051-1_19

Published by Springer Nature Switzerland AG 2025
L. M. Camarinha-Matos and F. Ferrada (Eds.): DoCEIS 2025, IFIP AICT 759, p. C1, 2025.
https://doi.org/10.1007/978-3-031-97051-1_30

Author Index

Published by Springer Nature Switzerland AG 2025
L. M. Camarinha-Matos and F. Ferrada (Eds.): DoCEIS 2025, IFIP AICT 759, pp. 423–424, 2025.
https://doi.org/10.1007/978-3-031-97051-1

The manufacturer's authorised representative in the EU is Springer Nature Customer Service Centre GmbH, Europaplatz 3, 69115 Heidelberg, Germany. If you have any concerns regarding our products, please contact ProductSafety@springernature.com

Printed and bound by CPI Group (UK) Ltd, Croydon, CR0 4YY
01/10/2026
02225968-0015